RELEASE

MORAL ISSUES IN BUSINESS

Vincent Barry
Bakersfield College

Wadsworth Publishing Company, Belmont, California
A Division of Wadsworth, Inc.

197791

Philosophy Editor: Kenneth King
Production Editor: Anne Kelly
Designer: Kate Michels

Printed in the United States of America

2 3 4 5 6 7 8 9 10—83 82 81 80

Library of Congress Cataloging in Publication Data

Barry, Vincent E
  Moral issues in business.

  Includes bibliographies and index.
  1. Business ethics. 2. Business ethics—Addresses,
essays, lectures. I. Title.
HF5387.B35   174'.4   79-14553
ISBN 0-534-00709-0

For Jeannine

CONTENTS

PART II: BUSINESS AND THE PEOPLE IN IT   83

3. HIRING, PROMOTIONS, DISCIPLINE, AND DISCHARGE   84

4. JOB ATMOSPHERE   112

5. ORGANIZATIONAL INFLUENCE IN PRIVATE LIVES 149

6. EMPLOYEE RESPONSIBILITIES 192

PART III: BUSINESS AND SOCIETY

7. BUSINESS AND THE CONSUMER

8. WOMEN AND OTHER DISADVANTAGED GROUPS

PREFACE

I have found a curiously common reaction among those who discover that I teach a course in business ethics. This reaction takes various forms from the baffled, "Business ethics?" or "Isn't that a contradiction?" to the sceptical, "You've got to be kidding," to the decisive, "There are no ethics in business." If one person's experience can indicate contemporary feeling, then mine suggests that many people believe that ethics and business are fundamentally opposed. In part, this book attempts to dispel that notion and to suggest vigorously that business must incorporate some clearly conceived and seriously implemented moral principles into its enabling assumptions and institutions. If business does not do so, it invites its own dismantling.

While such a lofty intention did somewhat inspire the writing of this text, *Moral Issues in Business* tries, in essence, to meet three challenges that I've faced in teaching business ethics. The first challenge is to raise the moral recognition level of students. Many students, whether preparing for business or nonbusiness careers, simply don't perceive in business decisions the moral dimensions that exist on the personal and organizational levels. As a result, students need to develop and refine their understanding of what is morally at stake in the issues of hiring and firing people, maintaining a healthy job atmosphere, relating consumerism and ecology, and so on.

The second recurring challenge is to provide students with the apparatus to make moral decisions in a business context. Even when students recognize the moral aspect of a business decision, they often don't know what to do about it—how to initiate and conduct an inquiry into the problem in order to reach an acceptable moral resolution.

The third challenge I've found in teaching business ethics is to blend theory with practice. This problem seems especially difficult in business ethics courses because they are generally taught by either a professor of philosophy or a professor of business, but rarely by one grounded in both disciplines. In the first case, the philosophy teacher may supply students with ample ethical theory but fail to concretize the theory in the real world of tough business situations. On the other hand, the business specialist may sacrifice ethical theory entirely and focus instead on interpersonal or intergroup relations. In short, the challenge of providing business ethics students with both traditional moral theory and its practical applications can require much time and energy in teaching.

Unfortunately, most textbooks currently available offer little assistance toward meeting these three challenges—raising the moral recognition level of students, providing theoretical bases for moral business decisions, and blending theory with practice. *Moral Issues in Business* meets these challenges head-on. To understand how this is done, let's consider the text's structure, style, organization, and coverage.

The structure of *Moral Issues in Business* combines textbook and reader. In general, the text of each chapter considers a particular related cluster of business issues (for example, job atmosphere or women and other disadvantaged groups in the work place) and demonstrates how some ethical theories may be applied to it. More specifically, each chapter opens with a case story that functions as a springboard to the chapter's content. To maintain practicality, each chapter includes examples and illustrations. In effect, then, the text mixes practical business issues with ethical theory.

The text of each chapter is usually followed by a section of "Case Presentations"—situations involving individuals who must make business decisions that carry moral overtones. Following each case is a series of questions to direct analysis and discussion. These case presentations will not only personalize many of the issues raised in the text but will also help the instructor open class discussions and guide further research.

The reading selections that conclude each chapter should be particularly useful. In selecting these, I applied three primary criteria: appropriateness, readability, and respectability. First, each reading is appropriately related to a main business concern of the chapter's text. Most of the selections will enhance students' understanding of a pertinent topic; many go beyond the content of the text and introduce additional dimensions to the issues. Second, each reading is understandable to a student who is new to ethics, and each is especially meaningful to one who intends to enter business. I have purposely avoided readings that are purely philosophical or highly abstract. Finally, each reading is recent and has been written by an acknowledged scholar in the field of business or in an area of immediate interest to business, such as the behavioral sciences. Most of the selections have also appeared in business journals of generally high quality—*Harvard Business Review, Business Horizons*, and so on. Following the selections in each chapter are suggestions for further reading.

The style of *Moral Issues in Business* is informal and as free from jargon as is practical. I hope that this approach facilitates a general grasp of ethical thought in the business context.

In organizing *Moral Issues in Business*, I have tried to provide some logical order of the material and still allow enough flexibility for personal tastes and emphasis. The result is that, after studying Chapters 1 and 2 first, readers may consider the other eight chapters in whatever order they choose. Those who prefer a linear development, however, can read each chapter in the order it is presented.

Part I consists of two chapters. The first is largely an overview of the contemporary moral climate of business. Useful terms, including *ethics* and *business ethics,* are defined, and the need to study business ethics is discussed. Chapter 1 shows why business codes of conduct, as currently conceived and practiced, are inadequate guides for moral behavior. The first chapter also makes important distinctions between law and morality. Chapter 2 surveys eight ethical theories relevant in the business context. The text describes these theories, discusses their strengths and weaknesses, and gives particular attention to how these theories can be applied to business. The coverage of Chapter 2 is very thorough; anything less would leave the theories insufficiently explained and the students ignorant of the wide variety of ethical positions possible on both personal and organizational levels.

Following these basically introductory chapters, the text launches into specific business concerns. Part II deals with topics that relate essentially to the in-house concerns of business and the people in it—the problems stemming from the relationship between a business organization and its employees. Thus, Chapter 3 investigates hiring, promotions, discipline, and discharge. Chapter 4 discusses job atmosphere. Chapter 5 considers the intrusion of the business organization into the private lives of employees. Chapter 6 deals with employee responsibilities to the organization.

Having touched on some significant intraorganizational issues with moral overtones, the text in Part III turns to concerns outside the organization that arise from the relationship between business and society. Although many issues could have been included in this part, I have focused on three that seem most significant: consumerism (Chapter 7), the treatment of women and other disadvantaged groups (Chapter 8), and the environment (Chapter 9).

Finally, Part IV consists of just one chapter, Chapter 10. This chapter introduces some of the basic assumptions and operating procedures evident in the practice of contemporary capitalism and examines their impact on morality in business. Some instructors may want to consider this topic earlier, perhaps in conjunction with Part I. This can be done because Chapter 10 requires no textual background, although I feel it functions more effectively as a capstone to the book. In short, then, *Moral Issues in Business* unfolds in a logical way but at the same time allows readers the option of considering the topics in whatever order they prefer.

In discussing the coverage of *Moral Issues in Business,* I would like to point out that no book will cover precisely what every reader would like. What's more, preparing a business ethics text presents unique problems because so few have been written. As a result, there is little consensus about what topics, issues, and concerns must be covered or about the proper balance between ethical theory and business applications. In fact, most of the textbooks that would qualify under even the most generous extension of the category "business ethics" deal primarily with the relationship between business and society. While such approaches are needed and many have been rendered artfully, these texts often have the effect of depersonalizing the subject. Readers may become aware of the broad range of social issues that involve business, but they remain ignorant of their own personal responsibilities in dealing with the issues. In *Moral Issues in Business*, I have tried to stimulate this sense of personal responsibility by considering first the in-house issues and then the issues of business as a social institution (although the two are not so neatly divided). Thus, the coverage reflects a concern with the relationships both between business and its employees and between business and society. In both instances, I've included topics of recurring concern and of immediate interest.

The ethical theories covered include those of traditionally high philosophical repute and those that are relevant to business: egoism, utilitarianism, situational ethics, Golden Rule, categorical imperative, prima facie duties, maximin principle of justice, and the principle of proportionality. Also, Chapter 1 includes a discussion of ethical relativism.

In conclusion, all authors are heavily indebted to the scholarly work that has preceded their own attempts to add to the knowledge and understanding of a subject. This is especially true in my case. I have not only capitalized on the thoughts of renowned philosophers but also on that of scholars in business and related fields. In particular, I would like to acknowledge Ron Munson, whose text in medical ethics provided a paradigm for my own excursion into business ethics. In addition, Max Oelschlaeger of North Texas State University offered invaluable suggestions for improving the quality of this text. Also providing welcome assistance were the reviewers: Eva H. Cadwallader, Westminster College; Louis I. Katzner, Bowling Green State University; William E. Mann, The University of Vermont; Jack F. Padgett, Albion College; Donald L. Provence, San Francisco State University; and Jerome A. Stone, Kendall College. Their encouragement and advice at the planning stage were most helpful. A word of thanks is also due to the many students whose ideas and insights have constantly reminded me how much of teaching is learning. A special note of gratitude must go to Wadsworth philosophy editor Ken King, whose many talents include his ability to instill in an author what a giant of American literature once termed the capacity to endure and to prevail. Finally, I would also like to acknowledge the work of production editor Anne Kelly and designer Kate Michels. Despite the contributions of so many, any errors of fact or omission are my own responsibility.

Vincent Barry

MORAL ISSUES IN BUSINESS

Part I
BUSINESS DECISIONS AND ETHICAL THEORY

1
THE MORAL CLIMATE OF BUSINESS

Fred Turner, chief operating officer with an aircraft corporation, is in Tokyo trying to sell $200 million worth of jets. Japanese business and political leaders seem willing to make a deal if the corporation produces about $10 million in bribes.

Across the Pacific in Santa Monica, California, Carl Phillips is selling used cars. He feels compelled to meet his competitors' extravagant claims and their questionable tactics, such as turning back odometers, concealing defects, and pressuring shoppers. Phillips is repelled by such behavior, but what can he do? If he acts any other way, he won't survive.

Halfway across the country Sally Richmann, working out of Kansas City for a stockbrokerage, has just been ordered to recommend some bonds to her clients. She doesn't think that the bonds are a good investment at this time. In fact, she feels they are being pushed in order to reduce her company's heavy inventory. Ordinarily Richmann wouldn't recommend the bonds, but orders are orders.

These imaginary people in hypothetical situations face very real moral decisions. Turner must decide whether to bribe Japanese officials and ensure a sale or not to and risk losing it. Phillips must decide whether to employ questionable selling tactics and stay in business or not to and risk business failure. And Richmann must decide whether to follow orders and recommend bonds which she feels are inferior or buck her orders and suffer the consequences. In short, each person must decide the right thing to do.

These situations represent only a smattering of the multitude of moral dilemmas that arise daily in business. One need only skim the pages of a daily newspaper to find examples. Some situations such as those involving high level, international bribery are quite dramatic. Others by contrast seem mundane. The cases are far too many to compile, but consider these questions that typify the issues: Is it ever right to use privileged information to advance one's self-interests? Is it always wrong to pad an expense account? Does a company have any obligation to help remedy social problems, such as poverty, pollution, and urban decay? Does a firm have the right to subject its employees to lie-detector tests as a condition of employment? What, if anything, must business do to improve the work atmosphere? Is a personnel director ever justified in hiring or promoting someone on grounds other than competence? Is a manufacturer obliged to reveal product defects? Must business help fight racial and sexual discrimination in the work place? What, if anything, does business owe the consumer?

These questions not only typify business issues that have moral overtones, they also suggest the central concern of this opening chapter: the need to study business ethics. We raise this need at the outset because the study of business ethics is new to most college curricula and requires a more elaborate justification than more established courses. This chapter will demonstrate that there is a need for business ethics and that the need is urgent.

One reason for studying business ethics has already been suggested: the increasing ethical content of business decisions. More and more people must decide not only what is the most profitable thing to do but what is the right thing to do. We'll find out why business decisions have assumed moral overtones and how this is creating a pressing need for the study of business ethics.

Another justification for studying business ethics is to understand the double bind that business people frequently experience when they try to separate their personal values from their business responsibilities. This feat seldom works and can cause more problems than it solves.

Finally, a good rationale for studying business ethics relates to the multifaceted quandary of moral decision making in a business context: (1) business people must make moral decisions without clear-cut standards to guide them; (2) although moral behavior in business is rooted in the concepts of rights and responsibilities, business is woefully deficient in defining these concepts and assigning them to the proper parties; (3) individuals in business seldom have well-formed ideas about moral accountability for policies, decisions, or actions. Lacking such concepts they frequently relinquish any responsibility and, in effect, invite immorality into the working place. We'll see how this three-pronged quandary further intensifies the need to investigate business ethics.

Before launching our discussion, however, it's important to clarify some basic terms such as *ethics, business ethics,* and *morality*. With mutual understanding behind us, we'll be better able to react to and converse about the issues that await us in the chapters ahead.

Ethics and Business Ethics

In the chapters ahead we'll consider problems and issues that raise questions about good and bad human conduct. *The study of what constitutes good and bad human conduct, including related actions and values, is called ethics.*

Occasionally the term *ethics* is used interchangeably with *morals.* Although this usage is acceptable, it is more accurate to restrict the terms *morals* and *morality* to the conduct itself. The terms *ethics* and *ethical* refer to the study of moral conduct or to the code one follows. When we use *moral*, we refer to an action or a person insofar as either is considered right or good. When we use *immoral*, we refer to an action or person insofar as either one is considered wrong or bad. *Morality, then, refers to the property of an action by which it conforms to a standard or norm of human conduct.*

Sometimes in the study of ethics the term *nonmoral* arises. This word refers to something outside the sphere of moral concern. For example, whether manufacturers package products in vertical or horizontal containers is a nonmoral question; it simply isn't a moral issue. But whether the shape of the container misrepresents the quantity of its contents could be a moral question.

In ethics we're concerned with questions of right and wrong, duty and obligation, and moral responsibility. When moralists use words like *good* or *right* to describe a person or action, they generally mean that the person or action conforms with some moral standards. A good person or action has desirable qualities. While moralists often disagree about the nature of these qualities, they all agree that having determined the right thing to do, one must do it and avoid wrong.

In this text, we'll be concerned with ethics as it applies to the sphere of business. *Business ethics is the study of what constitutes good and bad human conduct, including related actions and values, in a business context.* One difficulty that arises in talking about business ethics is that various meanings are attached to the words *business* and *business person*. *Business* may be applied with equal propriety to a corner burger stand or to a corporation with multimillion-dollar assets. Similarly, a business person may be the neighborhood grocer engaged in a one-person operation or a corporation president responsible for thousands of employees and huge corporate investments. For simplicity, we will use the word *business* in the sense of any organization whose objective is to provide goods or services for profit. Thus business people are those who take part in planning, organizing, or directing the work of a business.[1]

Moral Issues in Business, then, is concerned with what constitutes good and bad human conduct in the context of business practice, policy, and relationships. It deals with the behavior of people in business situations, the effects of their actions on persons within and without the firm, taken as individuals or as members of a group. However, since the study of business ethics is part of the general study of ethics, this book will frequently discuss general ethical concepts. For example, if we are to discover whether there are any guidelines to help Fred Turner, Carl Phillips, and Sally Richmann make moral decisions in a business context, we must first explore whether there are any guidelines for making moral decisions. In other words, we must turn to general ethical theories. The intimacy between general ethical theory and business ethics underscores a most important point that should be grasped at the outset. One's personal ethics cannot be separated from one's business ethics. In fact, it's safe to say that those who have studied and thought seriously about ethics in general have a more useful basis for making moral decisions in a business context than

---

1. *Raymond Baumhart,* Ethics in Business *(New York: Holt, Rinehart and Winston, 1968), p. 10.*

those who have not. We might even say that business will never be any more moral than the individuals who are in it.

The Need for Business Ethics

Although numerous contemporary realities point to the need to investigate business ethics, for simplicity we will concentrate on three: the ethical content of business decisions, the human dimension in business, and the current moral quandary that business faces.

The Ethical Content of Business

We can obtain a good understanding of the profuse ethical content of business in the United States today by organizing our discussion around two factors. One factor is that the part business plays in influencing the social system has recently become more apparent. The second factor is related. In the last fifteen years society's expectations of what business can and should do to help solve social problems have increased proportionately with society's understanding of those problems.

BUSINESS'S ROLE IN THE SOCIAL SYSTEM.   If Fred Turner, Carl Phillips, and Sally Richmann viewed their decisions strictly in terms of sound business, they'd probably have little trouble deciding what to do. They would simply decide what would be best for their business interests. This doesn't mean that they'd necessarily offer the bribe, set back the odometer, or counsel the bad investment. It means, rather, that they could reduce their considerations to essentially one: the welfare of the business. What troubles them, however, is an elementary but crucial fact that's becoming widely acknowledged: business does not operate in a vacuum.

Business is not an independent, self-sustaining mechanism. On the contrary, it's related to the world around it, and what's around it relates to business. We call this interdependent network of relationships observable in society the social system. *Specifically, a social system is a combination of interrelated people and their institutions which operate as a whole.*

Because business functions within the social system, it is affected by concerns and values outside narrow self-interests. Social interests and assessments of worth inevitably enter the work place, often introducing ethical content into business decisions.

For example, in recent years the public has become increasingly impatient with the extent of economic hardship, such as hard-core poverty and unemployment, especially when it applies to traditionally disadvantaged groups. Similarly, average Americans are less tolerant of continued racial and sexual discrimination in the work place. Society has become concerned that everyone be treated fairly. In a word, justice and equality have become important social values and have infiltrated the business world perhaps as never before. This moral awareness has heightened public concern about the *right* thing to do about providing equal job opportunities, distributing wealth, restoring ravaged cities, and so on.

Again, consider the growing public resentment with being duped and deceived in the marketplace. People are tired of being ripped off. They expect a fair shake. Society seems to have rediscovered the values of truth and honesty. As a result, whether it wants to or not, business must now consider questions about the right way to manufacture, market, and retail goods and services.

In addition, society is growing more sensitive about environmental matters. People are concerned with cleaning up existing pollution, designing processes to prevent further pollution, making aesthetic improvements, controlling noise and land use, and recycling materials. Conservation and preservation are important values in our society. They reflect a fundamental respect for life and for the intricate network of interrelationships needed to sustain it. What's more these values have had an impact on business. Thus Kodak wants to cut water pollution in the Genesee River in Rochester, New York; Mobil Oil Corporation announces that responsible enterprise shouldn't merely lament the sparrow's fall, but try to prevent it.

As part of the social system, business inevitably feels the press of society's concerns and values: justice, equality, truth, honesty, respect for life. Frequently values clash with one another. Thus we want everyone to have an equal employment opportunity, but we don't want to give anyone preferred and unfair consideration. We want to be protected from the hazards of a product, but we want the freedom to use it if we wish. We want our air cleaned up, but we brook no restrictions on the size of the car we will drive. Predictably, these clashes show up in business. They demand choices, often moral decisions. The result? Business decisions are taking on moral overtones. This phenomenon is being intensified by a second factor: society's expectations of business.

SOCIAL EXPECTATIONS.   There's no question that for the better part of United States history business has had one primary objective: the maximization of profit. In the past, business viewed its social charge as little more than providing goods and services as efficiently as possible. This left it free to focus on the economic realities of costs and prices. Its main responsibility was to produce products for a profit and at a fair price. True, business did have other social responsibilities, such as to provide jobs or to refrain from restraint of trade, but these were more economic than social. In brief, according to this classical view, business acted responsibly when it made efficient use of its resources in producing goods and services at prices consumers were willing to pay.

While some economists, like Milton Friedman, still maintain this classical view, most economists have a greatly expanded concept of business's social responsibility. As a result, while there exists no consensus on either the precise meaning or extent of business's social responsibilities, there is an increasing demand that business pursue actions which reflect society's values. Those exhorting business to conduct its operations in socially responsible ways seem to expect business people to show intelligent and objective concern for the good of society, variously as that may be defined. In a classic discussion of the topic,

Howard R. Bowen enjoined business to "pursue those policies, to make those decisions, or to follow those lines of action which are desirable in terms of the objectives and values of our society."[2] Other economists, like Keith Davis, have addressed the need for business to broaden its classical self-conception. Social responsibilities must be viewed in terms of business "decisions and actions taken for reasons at least partially beyond the firm's direct economic or technical interest."[3] Likewise, other advocates of a broadening of the classical view, such as Kenneth Andrews, expect business to avoid socially destructive behavior, regardless of the economics involved. In Andrews's words: "By 'social responsibility' we mean the intelligent and objective concern for the welfare of society that restrains individual and corporate behavior from ultimately destructive activities, no matter how immediately profitable, and leads in the direction of positive contributions to human betterment. . . ."[4] Whatever their emphasis, it's clear that those who are calling for social responsibility today expect business to think not only of narrow organizational or individual interests but of the entire social system of which business is a part.

Clearly the basis for social responsibility is concern for how one's actions affect the lives and interests of others. When business people act in a socially responsible way, then, they're concerned with the impact of their actions on others, both in and out of business. This concern may be quite personal, as in the cases of Turner, Phillips, or Richmann. Or it may be institutional, as in the case of firms which are trying to create equal employment opportunities or to prevent environmental pollution. Society's expectations of business, therefore, are heightening the ethical content of business decisions on both individual and organizational levels.

Furthermore, the range of societal expectations seems to be ever widening. Society is quickly coming to expect business to help solve problems which it is only indirectly involved with. Thus, at various times, business has been called on to employ its resources and expertise to solve community problems, to set up and maintain health-care facilities, to underwrite artistic endeavors, to subsidize educational enterprises, and to provide day-care centers for children of working mothers.

In short, numerous interests are pressuring business to address itself to a wide range of social problems and needs. Whether or not this is advisable, justifiable, or even possible doesn't concern us here. What does is the fact that society's expectation that business behave "morally"—that is, in a socially responsible way—has never been greater. As a result, business decisions which once raised only economic concerns now ignite moral debate. Lacking a firm grounding in business ethics, many business people find it difficult to participate meaningfully in such an exchange. In fact, they frequently view it as a preamble to the dismantling of the free enterprise system.

2.   *Howard R. Bowen,* Social Responsibilities of the Businessman *(New York: Harper & Row, 1953), p. 6.*

3.   *Keith Davis, "Can Business Afford to Ignore Social Responsibilities?"* California Management Review, *Spring, 1960, p. 70.*

4.   *Kenneth Andrews,* The Concept of Corporate Strategy *(Homewood, Illinois: Dow Jones-Irwin, Inc., 1971), p. 120.*

Undoubtedly the implications of business's influential role in the social system and society's rising expectations of social responsibility have put tremendous pressure on business people to determine their ethical whereabouts. This pressure increases the burden on an already morally troubled and unsettled group who long have silently suffered from the war between their private values and their business lives. Their plight deserves attention; it alone seems enough to justify the study of business ethics.

The Individual in Business

One needn't observe the business scene very long before noting the double bind business people frequently experience because of the dual roles they sometimes must play. The first role is that of the private individual: a decent and ethical human being who readily admits the need for moral principles on a personal and social level. The second role is that of a business person: a human being who rarely exhibits any of the marked moral sensitivity of the private individual. Not only do these roles or "personalities" share little moral ground, the second one can often brutalize the first when value conflicts arise in a business context.

As a dramatic example of this, consider the sentiments of Dan Drew, church builder and founder of Drew Theological Seminary, who shared these thoughts with business people of the nineteenth century.

> Sentiment is all right up in the part of the city where your home is. But downtown, no. Down there the dog that snaps the quickest gets the bone. Friendship is very nice for a Sunday afternoon when you're sitting around the dinner table with your relations, talking about the sermon that morning. But nine o'clock Monday morning, notions should be brushed aside like cobwebs from a machine. I never took any stock in a man who mixed up business with anything else. He can go into other things outside of business hours but when he's in the office, he ought not to have a relation in the world—and least of all a poor relation.[5]

It seems that many business people live by this code. "Downtown" the dominant business-person personality represses the values that the private-individual personality lives by at home. When conflicts arise, the "decent" personality is sacrificed on the altar of expedience with a prayerful "That's business."

But don't assume that business people wouldn't prefer things to be different. On the contrary, a basic assumption of this author is that they would prefer to do what is right rather than what's wrong. But how? Personal codes of ethics don't seem to apply to specific business decisions, or at least business people can't see the application. They need specific direction on making moral decisions in a business context.

True, some people would probably disagree. Rather than an immersion in business ethics, they'd suggest that business people realize the wisdom of Dan Drew's observations. Personal values are and must be kept separate and distinct

5. *Quoted in Robert Bartels, ed.,* Ethics in Business *(Columbus: Ohio State University Press, 1963), p. 35.*

from business lives. If business people could just accept and practice this, the dissenters claim, they would eliminate much internal conflict in trying to reconcile personal values and business demands. Because many business people seemingly practice this view—though rarely expressing it as forcefully as Drew did—it bears examination. If the view is sound, then there would be little need to study business ethics. But if the view is unsound, then we should investigate business ethics, if only to facilitate moral decision making for the people in it. There are a number of objectionable points about the view as described. First, to argue that morality has no place in business is to take a constricted and narrow view of business. It's to think of business only as an economic enterprise. But we've already seen that business functions as part of a social system. As such it is characterized by a network of human relationships that are secured and preserved by rules, standards, and principles that regulate conduct between individuals. To deny this, as the aforementioned view does, is to deny the nature of business.

A second point addresses the proposition that personal values and ethics don't or can't play any part in a business context. Such a thesis poses a grossly distorted view of human nature and of individual persons, one characterized by an inscrutable ability to leave at home what most people consider a fundamental element in individual identity: one's value system. The fact is that business involves individuals who have a collection of beliefs, attitudes, outlooks, assumptions, hopes, fears, and *moral values.* To expect less is to fly in the face of human nature and experience.

A third, related psychological point needs mentioning. The question of values involves an inquiry into what human existence is all about, that is, what it means to be human. This concern with meaning is unique and essential to the human animal. As far as we know no other animal is concerned with questions like who am I? Why am I here? Where am I going? Psychoanalyst Eric Fromm has put it this way: "Man is the only animal who finds his own existence a problem which he has to solve and from which he cannot escape."[6]

Clearly, then, the question of values is crucial to personal meaning and to individual well-being. Moral values describe individual assessments of worth at a foundational level. They largely define how we'll interact with others, what goals we'll seek, how we'll adapt to new demands. If we choose values dissonant either with our needs or with reality, we inexorably move toward our own undoing. We court anxiety, misery, ultimate destruction. Therefore, the proposition that moral values have no place "downtown" is, apart from any social considerations, psychologically dangerous. Divorcing values from activities that consume almost half individuals' waking lives invites profound psychological dislocation.

All of this commentary makes a simple but important point. Because business involves people, the need to make moral decisions must be present. Indeed, the double-bind situation we've been discussing underscores this, because it's an attempt to reconcile conflicting realities. The challenge for business

---

6. *Eric Fromm,* The Sane Society *(New York: Holt, Rinehart and Winston, 1955), pp. 23–24.*

in the years ahead is whether it will persist in fostering this kind of schizo-phrenic pattern of maladjustment, or whether it will devise an ideology whereby individuals can keep their integrity and their ability to relate to people on a human, feeling level while at the same time looking out for business concerns. Without an ideology within which they can function, business people run the risk of rising to the top of the corporate ladder at the cost of losing their personhood.

By now it should be clear that personal lives cannot be separated from business lives. How, then, can they be reconciled? Business ethics provides a substantial part of the answer because, though confined to a single profession, it uses the general ethical theory which is the basis of personal moral codes. Business ethics can build a bridge between the personal and the professional, although it cannot promise to eliminate or to resolve every instance of a value conflict. In a word, there's an internal need for business ethics, apart from the external factors—previously mentioned—that are increasing the ethical content of business decisions.

Taken together, the increased ethical content of business decisions and the struggle to reconcile personal values with business demands have thrown business people into a quandary. They must make decisions, but on what basis? How can Fred Turner, Carl Phillips, and Sally Richmann decide what to do? The nature of this quandary serves further to increase the need for business ethics.

Business's Moral Quandary

Although many facts characterize what we're terming "business's moral quandary" today, we'll focus on three of major ethical importance: the absence of a clear moral standard, the uncertainty in defining and assigning rights and responsibilities, the ill-defined concept of moral accountability.

THE ABSENCE OF A CLEAR MORAL STANDARD. At a time when the moral content of business decisions is increasing, agreement on an ethical standard or norm is declining. In other words, there seems to be no measuring rod against which business people can judge their actions as morally right or wrong. Thus some people make decisions strictly on the basis of self-interest. Others look to the interests of all concerned or to what the law proscribes. Still others attempt to employ some maxim of moral behavior such as the Golden Rule. And then there are people who operate strictly on whim, for example, lying in one situation while not lying in an identical situation. Of course, business has never been in universal agreement about how to determine moral behavior. But the proliferation of social concerns and their subsequent entry into the work place seem to have divided business people more than ever over the question of just how moral behavior is to be decided.

Two popular sources of business's ethical norms are professional codes and the law. As useful as these may be, they are not enough.

The professional code generally dedicates the firm to such goals as the maintenance of human dignity and self-respect, the earning of a fair profit in order to make possible the economic stability and growth of the company, the furtherance of worthwhile community objectives and programs, and so on. Professional codes establish a general ideal which the firm aspires to. They also indicate how to attain this goal within a context of obligations to each of the major claimants on business: owners, employees, customers, and society. One problem with these codes as standards of moral behavior is that they're as numerous as there are firms that devise them (and, of course, not all firms do). What's more, they're by no means equivalent to each other; some firms may eloquently address conflicts of interest, others may give it little attention. The point is that there is neither a uniform code nor format for governing ethical business behavior. Furthermore, the rules expressed in codes of conduct can conflict with moral beliefs. For example, during the Vietnam conflict Dow Chemical was producing napalm for military use. Suppose a Dow scientist had thought the war immoral or the use of napalm wrong. What should the scientist have done? Adhere to Dow's commitment to good citizenship, which in this case it viewed as supplying goods to the Defense Department? Or honor personal moral sentiments, which in this case would have been incompatible with Dow's position? The only way to resolve such conflicts is by going beyond the codes themselves to more general ethical principles.

Another fact about codes is that ordinarily they strictly echo the law. There's nothing necessarily wrong with this, but it does lead to certain assumptions: what's legal is therefore moral; what's not prohibited by law is ethical; what minimally meets the law is proper. These three assumptions are erroneous.

In theory and practice, the law functions to codify the customs, ideals, beliefs, and moral values of a society. As such it undoubtedly reflects changes in a society's way of thinking, in what it views as right and wrong. It's a mistake, however, to look on the law as establishing a society's standard of morality. The law simply can't cover the wide variety of human conduct that any society exhibits. True, the law prohibits the most outrageous violations of what a society considers ethical standards. But what about the countless cases that don't involve a wanton breach of ethical standards? Thus it's altogether legal to appeal to sex, status, prestige, romance, and adventure to sell anything from plastic surgery to toothpaste. Is it moral? Again, a firm may legally do nothing to improve the cultural climate of the community where it is located. Is that moral? In a word, the law itself, professional codes of conduct, or codes based on the law cannot be taken in and of themselves as acceptable guides to moral conduct.

Because business people do not have a clear-cut standard of approved ethical action to rely on for making specific operational decisions, they usually turn to their own moral devices. This point was amply demonstrated about fifteen years ago in an exhaustive study of business ethics. When asked what the term *ethical* meant to them, 50 percent of the business people responding indicated that it was "what my feelings tell me is right."[7] There's no reason to believe that a significant number of today's business people would respond differently. Where "feeling" is grounded in a thorough exposure to and understanding of ethical thought, then it can function as a kind of energizing impulse to moral behavior. But when "feeling" is tantamount to caprice or inclination, then serious questions arise regarding the merit of its foundation.

7. *Baumhart, p. 10.*

Is appeal to one's feelings a sound standard for moral decisions in business? If it is, then there's little reason to concern ourselves about such subjectivity. If it isn't, we must discover a firmer foundation for moral decision making in business.

To answer the question of whether personal feelings are a sound standard for moral decision making, we must examine the doctrine of ethical relativism that underlies it. *Ethical relativism is the view that rejects the existence of an absolute or universal moral principle.* In other words, relativism denies the existence of a moral standard that applies to everyone at all times everywhere. Stated positively, ethical relativism asserts that standards of right and wrong depend exclusively on temporal and environmental considerations, that what's right or wrong coincides with what a group of people in a particular place and a specific time think is right or wrong. Consequently, for relativists no objective basis exists for asserting that an action is right or wrong independent of group feeling.

No doubt ethical relativism has an enormous following among persons both in and out of business. Part of this is probably explained by the general confusion felt in trying to find ethical principles to endorse. Faced with the apparently insoluble problem of finding true ethical principles, we seriously question whether they exist. Thus we go with our feelings, which, in effect, is a form of relativism. It translates into "What I feel is right, is right or ethical." Another important reason for the popularity of ethical relativism is that, through the efforts of the social sciences, our society has become educated to the diversity of cultures and societies in the world, together with their dizzying tapestry of moral values and codes of conduct. We learn that Eskimos abandon their elderly on the ice and allow them to die of starvation and exposure. We hear of African tribes who kill twins at birth or require a man to marry his brother's widow. With respect to business, we read in the daily newspapers of some cultures that permit, even approve of, bribery, "greasing," and other forms of business conduct we'd probably look at askance. Awareness of different—and often conflicting—value systems and codes of conduct has caused us to question the proposition that absolute moral standards exist. We have taken the existence of diverse social standards to indicate that no moral standard exists, that moral principles are always relative.

Undoubtedly ethical relativism has its strengths. For one, it is tolerant of divergent views. For another, it makes use of familiar facts to develop its doctrine. At the same time, however, relativism has distinct weaknesses that bear on business's moral quandary.

First, that societies often differ in what they judge to be right does not sufficiently demonstrate that they hold different or conflicting ethical principles. Indeed, some anthropologists claim that all cultures and societies endorse such basic principles as "Senseless killing is wrong," "You should not lie or steal," and "Treat people fairly." Where differences exist, they're better explained by application, not principle. For example, in our society we consider it wrong to make demands and ask payment for what is supposed to be done under the terms of one's work. In other words, we disapprove of extortion. But in some other societies extortion is acceptable. Consider the millions of dollars in extortion demands and bribes that companies such as Lockheed, Exxon, Gulf, and Phillips Petroleum have admitted to paying abroad. The fact that some societies tolerate these practices doesn't mean that they have no principles about fairness and honesty. It just means that they don't apply the principles in these cases the way we might. What's considered fair in one society is not necessarily considered fair in another.

But even if societies do hold different ethical principles, this does not mean that there aren't any correct or true principles. Cultures, societies, and individuals exhibit a vast array of beliefs about a wide range of subjects. But obviously this does not mean that all beliefs on a subject are correct, that they are equally worthwhile, or that the final choice is ultimately arbitrary. The final determinant of the worth of any belief is the justification that supports it. This is as true of moral beliefs as it is of scientific ones.

If we've ever thought seriously about ethics, we don't espouse moral principles simply because that's the way we've been brought up, because the people around us espouse them, or because we *feel* that they're right. Undoubtedly, each of these factors influences our inquiry and judgment, but in the last analysis thoughtful persons endorse or reject principles because they have solid grounds for doing so. Of course, we should not become overbearing or intolerant in our views. On the contrary, we should acknowledge that beliefs differ but also that not all beliefs are equally worth our pursuit and endorsement. In a word, we don't suspend rational analysis and surrender to feeling simply because we have entered the world of morality.

Finally, ethical relativism seems to fly in the face of everyday experience and beliefs in a number of ways. First, in facing their moral decisions, Fred Turner, Carl Phillips, Sally Richmann, and all of us deliberate in an attempt to decide the right thing to do. If someone suggested that they and we should base our decisions strictly on what the most frequent decision in society would be or exclusively on the way we feel, we'd likely consider the suggestion less than thoughtful. After all, we're interested in determining the *right* thing to do, not what popular feeling or even our own unsupported feelings incline us to do. True, the right thing may coincide with both of these, but this would mean only that in this particular case society and ourselves agree about the right thing.

Furthermore, when we make statements like "It's wrong for an investment counselor willfully to counsel someone into a bad investment" or "It's wrong to misrepresent the condition of a used car," we're hardly asserting these as moral principles only for our society. While it's true that acculturation may predispose us toward a specific moral view, or sensitize us to one, in the last analysis we offer a moral judgment as one binding on all people at all times everywhere. Thus, if we condemn the wanton sale of unsafe products or the reliance on deliberate deception in advertising, we do so whether it occurs in the streets of New York or in the markets of Mombasa, whether a business person with one firm or with another does it.

The point is that although moral relativism may sound attractive, on close inspection it actually offends our basic concept of morality. We cannot be guided by its doctrine. On the contrary, our attempts to resolve moral problems betray a commitment to the proposition that ethical principles can be binding on all people. At the same time we must admit the possibility that we could be wrong in our assessment. Nevertheless, such an assumption seems a more fruitful approach to making moral decisions in a business context than it's contrary.

In sum, one thing that makes it difficult for business people to deal with the moral problems that confront them is the absence of a clear moral standard. But the absence of a standard doesn't prove the relativistic claim that no standard exists or can be discovered. Furthermore, since relativism itself is a highly questionable doctrine, those who believe in it have a weak philosophical basis for abandoning the search for some basic moral principles to direct business conduct. On the contrary, the issues that face business people, the decisions they must make, the conflicts they must resolve, all point to the urgent need for the moral principles that a study of business ethics is designed to explore. What's more, even if after thoroughly examining various ethical systems, business people cannot agree on one, they're in an advantageous position to apply an accepted principle in a specific situation. Having knowledge of the options open to them, in fact, not only facilitates moral decision making but serves as the basis for moral responsibility. As one author expressed it: "A morally responsible executive is one who knows the various kinds of value systems that may be employed in a particular situation and has a rather clear idea of what values hold ascendancy over others in a conflict."[8]

Moral responsibility suggests the second of the three facts that we are focusing on to understand business's moral quandary. Let's now look at it.

RIGHTS AND RESPONSIBILITIES. *When we use the term* responsibility *in business affairs, we refer to a sphere of duty or obligation assigned to a person by the nature of that person's position, function, or work.* Business and the people in it clearly have responsibilities to stockholders, employees, consumers, and society at large. Thus a corporate executive has responsibilities to owners to maximize the profitability of their investments; manufacturers have responsibilities to consumers to ensure that products live up to their billings. Conversely, owners have the *right* to expect corporate executives to maximize the profitability of owner investments; consumers have the *right* to expect manufacturers to ensure that products live up to their billings. Responsibilities and rights, then, are inextricably joined. Responsibilities imply rights, rights imply responsibilities. *While there are various definitions of a right, we view a right as a claim or a sphere of decision that is, or ought to be, respected by other individuals and protected by society.*[9] While this definition is not entirely satisfactory, it is useful in business matters.

Although we can safely indicate the parties who have rights and responsibilities, it's very difficult to sort out the rights and responsibilities themselves and to resolve conflicts when they arise. Thus stockholders may have the right to a maximum profit on their investments, but consumers also have the right to a fair price. What happens when these rights conflict? Where does business's responsibility lie? To get some idea of how complex this question can become, consider this simple illustration.

The Sweet Treat Candy Company manufactures chocolates. On the box of

8.   *Clarence C. Walton, ed.,* Ethos and the Executive *(Englewood Cliffs, N.J.: Prentice-Hall, 1969), p. 64.*

9.   *Carl Wellman,* Morals and Ethics *(Glenview, Ill.: Scott, Foresman and Company, 1975), p. 252.*

one of its items, a picture shows roughly an even distribution of a half-dozen candies. But the contents, while including each variety, clearly favors the cheaper varieties. Some would say that the candy packer has acted wrongly in misrepresenting the contents of the package.

The candy packer may very well have acted immorally. But before passing judgment, it's at least provocative to consider the responsibilities involved here. What's the extent of the packer's responsibility toward consumers, on the one hand, and toward owners on the other? Let's assume that a more accurate representation would reduce the number of boxes sold. In that event, Sweet Treat would neither require nor could it maintain as large a work force as it currently employs. Workers would be laid off. What's the extent of the candy packer's responsibility to employees? We might further wonder whether we're correct in assigning the responsibility to the candy packer in the first place. In other words, in addition to defining the extent of the rights and responsibilities here, we also face the problem of assigning them to the proper parties. Maybe the designers of the box bear the responsibility for the misrepresentation. Perhaps it's the retailer who fails to indicate to customers the misrepresentation. Could the consumer bear the brunt of the responsibility for continuing to buy the product? Or possibly they all share in the responsibility.

The point is that defining and assigning rights and responsibilities often poses a difficult problem, especially in complex social issues such as pollution control, urban renewal, and equal opportunity. The moral dilemma that business people face is twofold. First, they must acknowledge and discharge duties and obligations to their four primary claimants: stockholders, employees, consumers, and society. Second, and more pivotal, they must define and assign these to the proper claimants in the proper degree. This latter task can be especially troublesome for people who find themselves operating within a corporate structure.

Although corporations are established, owned, and run by individual persons, their structures can be so complex that it's nearly impossible to assign responsibilities to specific individuals. This is the case at Sweet Treat. Precisely who bears the responsibility for the misrepresentation? Who is responsible for ensuring that such misrepresentation does not occur? Faced with what appears to be an insoluble task, business people often refrain from making moral judgments in discharging their work duties or they ascribe these responsibilities to the corporation. The danger of not making the moral judgment, of course, is that it becomes an open invitation to immorality. On the other hand, ascribing all responsibilities to the corporation is an evasion of personal responsibility.

An alternative to either of these approaches is to scrutinize individual cases involving rights and responsibilities and identify specific persons to whom these can be properly assigned. The fact is that even when dealing with large corporations, rights and responsibilities can be assigned to specific individuals. For example, a company's right not to be embezzled can be viewed as a collection of rights assignable to individual owners, employees, perhaps even to customers. Likewise, a corporation's responsibility to avoid price fixing can be sorted out into the components of a collection of responsibilities that owners, upper managers, and competitors bear to avoid injuring consumers and other competitors by artificially managing the free market system. Clearly, in these and numerous cases of corporate decisions and actions, not one but many individuals share the responsibility. True, one person may merit responsibility more than another, but that doesn't justify placing all the blame or praise on that individual person.[10]

In sum, in dealing with the problems of decision making, business people must grapple with the question of rights and responsibilities. While determining the areas where these rights and responsibilities lie isn't difficult, defining and assigning them often pose a monumental undertaking. What businesses and business people need is some appropriate direction in these matters. Business ethics, which is designed to sort out rights and responsibilities, can fill this need.

But even if the responsibility has been properly assigned, we can still ask: is the individual blameworthy (or praiseworthy) in this instance? Can we rightly hold this person morally accountable? Suppose we decide that the candy packer does, indeed, bear the responsibility of ensuring that no misrepresentation occurs in advertising the contents of the package. We can still ask: is the candy packer at fault for the misrepresentation? Perhaps that person couldn't avoid doing what he or she did. Maybe the person's choices were so constrained that no other alternative was genuinely available.

Rather than asking what the responsibilities are and who has them, this latter inquiry asks: under what conditions do we hold people morally responsible for their actions? Not only is this question foundational to any study of ethics, it is of uppermost concern in corporate organizations where individuals defend or justify questionable actions and transactions by appealing to severe restrictions on their personal freedom and choice. This problem looms large in the business context precisely because rights and responsibilities aren't always easy to define and assign. In short, moral accountability is a third issue we should consider in examining business's moral quandary and in explaining the need to study business ethics.

MORAL ACCOUNTABILITY.   We've seen that an increasing dilemma for business consists in defining and assigning rights and responsibilities. But even after this challenge is met, another looms. It centers on blame and praise—on what is called moral accountability or responsibility. Since we've already used the term *responsibility* to refer to duty or obligation, we will confine ourselves to the term *moral accountability. Moral accountability refers to blaming or praising someone for an action.* When we hold someone morally accountable for an action, we mean that the person should be blamed (or praised) for it.

The nature and structure of contemporary business allows virtually everyone to share the accountability for an action. In theory, this means everyone's to blame (or to praise). But, in practice, this often means that no one is held morally accountable. As indicated earlier, nothing threatens morality in the work place more than a doctrine of nonaccountability.

Just as it's important to sort out cases of rights and responsibilities in order

10.   *See Robert Baum, ed.,* Ethical Arguments for Analysis *(New York: Holt, Rinehart and Winston, 1975),* p. 202.

to assign them to specific individuals, it's equally important to stress the conditions under which we hold people morally accountable for their actions. Otherwise we invite business people to founder on the shoals of the "Bormann defense." The Bormann defense takes its name from Martin Bormann, third deputy under the German Nazi regime, whose defense for wartime atrocities was that he was following orders. Similarly, Adolf Eichmann, who was hanged for his role in those outrages, pleaded that he could not have acted other than he did, that he was following orders of superiors. In the 1970s the American Lt. William Calley, convicted of the deliberate and unprovoked slaying of civilians at My Lai, Vietnam, claimed he, too, was following orders. And many of the White House officials who were caught in the web of the Watergate scandal lodged similar defenses, as did numerous of their cohorts.

There are standard features in the structure of modern business which encourage similar moral rationalizations. One feature is the autocratic nature of most businesses. When confronted by a tight chain of command in which decisions are made "at the top" and then passed down, most business people probably survive by not questioning the orders of their superiors. Moreover, the complex structure of many business organizations almost encourages a dilution of personal accountability. So many people are involved at so many levels that moral buck passing can easily become the order of the day. There is also the blind pursuit of profitability which blurs moral accountability. And finally the intense pressure related to keeping one's job and securing promotions can be used to justify virtually anything. The point is that it can be a simple matter to abdicate personal moral accountability for decisions and actions in business.

The above examples should be reason enough for being aware of the conditions under which we hold people morally accountable. A convenient way of approaching these conditions is to isolate the circumstances under which we ordinarily excuse people, that is, hold them blameless or not morally accountable. Professor of Philosophy Paul Taylor suggests four of these circumstances.[11]

1. *Excusable ignorance of consequences.* We excuse people when we don't believe they were aware of the unfavorable consequences their actions would produce or because they couldn't reasonably be expected to have known how to prevent the consequences. For example, between 1976 and 1978 Los Angeles women were terrorized by numerous rapes and strangulations attributed to the so-called Hillside Strangler. During this period a hairdresser, as part of a promotional campaign, displayed the photo of a well-coiffed female model with male companion's hand resting provocatively around her neck. The ad was rather typical of the promotional material that the hairdresser had previously used, and at any other time undoubtedly would have gone unnoticed. But not this time. Picketers deploring crass sensationalism and vicious male chauvinism paraded in front of the shop and threatened to remain until the owner withdrew the ad. The owner did, expressing bewilderment over the furor.

11. *Paul Taylor,* Problems of Moral Philosophy *(Belmont, Calif.: Dickenson Publishing Company, 1972), p. 277.*

Given the temper of the times, perhaps the hairdresser should have been more discreet in his advertisements. At the same time it would be difficult to hold him morally accountable for what he did since, in all likelihood, he wasn't aware of the unfavorable consequences his action would elicit.

In other cases we excuse people because, in our estimation, they couldn't reasonably be expected to have known how to prevent the consequences from happening. If, for example, a child grows deathly ill after ingesting some D-Con mouse poison that the child's parents have placed in the corner of the kitchen, we'd not be likely to hold the manufacturer responsible. The manufacturer couldn't be expected reasonably to have known how to prevent the accident. It's true that in recent years we've seen an increase in safety awareness, especially in the area of child-proof caps. But D-Con is a mouse poison, not a bottle of aspirin. The mouse must be able to get at it easily. Also the poison must be in a place where mice can reach it. Unfortunately, both conditions can pose threats to the curious child, over whom the manufacturer has little control except to warn the adult consumer of the danger. Clearly the moral accountability here lies not with the manufacturer but with the parents who chose D-Con, rather than some kind of trap, and who could have known how to prevent the child from eating the poison.

2. *Constraints.* We usually excuse people when we think that they couldn't help what they did. In other words, they had little or no choice in a matter. They labored under some external constraint or inner compulsion which made them do something and left them powerless to do anything else.

In the case of external constraints, that is, outside factors or forces, we speak of people acting against their wills. Employees who turn over their employers' receipts at gunpoint are acting against their will. They are not morally accountable for their actions.

In the second form of constraint, the compelling element comes from within, not without. Thus we speak of people who act in certain ways because they feel an overwhelming inner urge, desire, craving, or impulse to do so. We'd hardly hold a kleptomaniac morally accountable for shoplifting a watch from a jewelry shop.

3. *Uncontrollable circumstances.* When, in our estimation, the circumstances of an act were beyond the person's control, we generally excuse the behavior. There are numerous circumstantial excuses that we readily accept as legitimate excuses. In each instance the circumstances must truly be beyond the person's control and not have resulted from past voluntary actions of the person. We probably would not hold George Greg morally accountable for being late for work if, through no fault of his own, he had been involved in an automobile accident. But we would hold him accountable if the accident resulted from his reckless driving.

4. *Lack of alternatives.* Ordinarily we excuse actions when we think that people lacked either the ability or the opportunity to do the right act. For example, effective January 1, 1978, eighty-five decibels became the maximum noise

level which a worker can be subjected to during an eight-hour work day. A number of companies have not been able to comply with this standard. For example, at present there is no way to quiet the impact of forging hammers and the combustion noise from industry furnaces. Similarly, there doesn't seem to be an economical way of coping with "snap-through," the noise metal makes when it leaves a stamping die. If there's no way to comply with the standard except to shut down and let the country bear the consequences, then we don't hold violators of this regulation morally accountable. Similarly, if they weren't given reasonably sufficient notice to comply with the standard, then they couldn't be held accountable for not meeting it. In the first case, they wouldn't have had the ability to meet the standard; in the second, they wouldn't have had the opportunity.

In everyday situations, then, there are occasions when we excuse people and occasions when we hold them responsible. When any of the above conditions accompanies a person's action, whether in or out of business, we don't hold the person responsible. On the other hand, when none of these conditions is present, we do not excuse the person. On the contrary, we hold the person morally accountable. Keeping these conditions in mind can help business people deal with this one aspect of the moral quandary they face.

Summary

The need to study business ethics arises from a consideration of several factors. The first factor is the ethical content of business decisions. Both business's role in and influence on the social system, as well as society's expectations that business behave in socially responsible ways, have dramatically increased the moral dimension of business decisions. As a result, business people need the moral grounding that business ethics provides.

A second contributing factor is the continued plight of individual business persons who too often find themselves morally divided between personal values and business responsibilities. These people need the on-the-job moral direction that business ethics provides.

A third factor related to the need for business ethics is what we have termed business's moral quandary. Although business people are asked to make moral decisions in a business context, they lack the wherewithal to decide. They have no clear-cut moral standard to guide them. What's more, their decisions must turn on clearly defined and specifically assigned rights and responsibilities, which they rarely have. This quandary is further intensified by the erosion of moral accountability, stemming in part from the complex nature and structure of big business, which invites a vague and distorted view of the circumstances under which we either excuse people or hold them morally accountable. The study of business ethics is helpful in dealing with this quandary because it airs standards of moral conduct, investigates rights and responsibilities, and refines one's ability to recognize and act with moral accountability.

Ethics and the New Ideology: Can Business Adjust?

George Cabot Lodge

It's helpful to view all that we have said in this opening chapter about the increasing ethical content of business decisions and business's moral quandary against a backdrop of profound social and cultural change. In a word, the America we know today vastly differs from what it was a half-century, or even two decades ago. And yet, our conceptual framework—our basic assumptions, how we see things, what values we hold—has not kept pace with this changing reality. The result: we often find ourselves having to resolve today's problems within the context of yesterday's ideology. Many ethical dilemmas business faces result from this gap, or so argues Harvard Professor of Business Administration George Cabot Lodge in the following essay, adapted from a paper he presented at Bentley College's First Annual Conference on Business Ethics, held on March 11, 1977. In reading Professor Lodge's essay, note the five great ideas that characterized America's traditional ideology, how these are changing, and how many ethical problems confronting business can be viewed in the light of this ideological transition.

Standards of right and wrong depend upon time, place, and situation. The Christian admonition to love thy neighbor as thyself and its Judaic counterpart to do justly, love mercy, and walk humbly with thy God are universally noncontroversial. But their application, definition, and institutionalization provoke disagreement and vary according to when, where, and under what circumstances.

Today there is much concern on all sides about the ethics of business, especially about what is considered to be the wrong conduct of managers of large corporations. (It is significant that the corner grocer is nowhere near as suspect.) Is this because the number of sinners in executive suites has suddenly increased? I think not. Rather it is because the definition of sin, of right and wrong, has been changing radically and, in changing, is both unclear and controversial.

Business's critics say it lacks a sense of social responsibility. But just what is "responsibility"? At the least, as philosopher Charles Frankel says, it is "the product of definite social arrangements," from which flow the dos and don'ts that constitute a more or less coercive framework by which the community assesses and controls behavior.

Today, however, the framework is in disarray. Sufficient though it may be to help identify clear-cut villainies and punish the perpetrators, it is less helpful in appraising the actions of managers who, in their own judgment and that of many of

their peers, consider their conduct justifiable and well meaning, even though large segments of public opinion consider it inhuman, irresponsible, and corrupt.

In examining these differing opinions, it is useful to bear in mind Frankel's "definite social arrangements"—defined here as ideology, or framework of ideas, which a community uses to define values and to make them explicit. Ideology is the source of legitimacy of institutions and the justification for the authority of those who manage them. Ideology also can be seen as a bridge, which a community uses to get from timeless, universal, noncontroversial notions such as justice, economy, self-fulfillment, and self-respect to the application of such notions in the real world.

As the real world changes, so does its definition of values and its ideology. Frequently, however, there is a lag; society tends to linger with an old ideology even after its institutions have perforce departed from it. The status quo tends to use the old ideas to justify itself.

The real world of America is obviously vastly different today from what it was 100, 50, or even 20 years ago. Consequently, the traditional ideology of America has also changed. Living with a new reality, we are in transit from one ideology to another, and many of the ethical dilemmas we now face are the result of this transition.

Two things have happened: First, the "traditional ideology" of this country has become in-consistent with the real world. Second, great institutions have departed from the traditional ideology, thereby contributing to its subversion and replacement.

Corporate America (not the corner grocery) has outgrown the ideology to which it and the community generally have traditionally looked for its legitimacy. In structure and practice it reflects a new ideology, one that has not yet been fully ar-ticulated and is vague, confusing, and somewhat fearful.

Other institutions, especially government, have also left the old ideology behind, even though their leaders as well as society in general tend to sing the old hymns. Indeed, it almost seems that the farther the departure from the old framework of values the greater becomes our de-votion to it. We are thus looking for legitimacy and authority in ideas that are becoming increasingly inconsistent with practice and reality.

The Lockean Five

The traditional ideology of this country is not difficult to identify. It is composed of five great ideas that were first brought to America in the eighteenth century, having been set down in seventeenth-century England by John Locke, among others, as "natural" laws. These ideas found fertile soil in the wilderness of a developing America and served well for a hundred years or more.

The Lockean Five are:

1. *Individualism.* This is the atomistic notion that the community is no more than the sum of the individuals in it. It is the idea that fulfillment lies in an essentially lonely struggle in what amounts to a wilderness where the fit survive—and where, if you do not survive, you are somehow unfit. Closely tied to indi-vidualism is the idea of *equality*, in the sense implied in the phrase "equal opportunity," and the idea of *contract*, the inviolate device by which individuals are tied together as buyers and sellers.

2. *Property rights.* Traditionally, the best guaran-tee of individual rights was held to be the sanctity of property rights. By virtue of this concept, the individual was assured freedom from the predatory powers of the sovereign.

3. *Competition → consumer desire.* Adam Smith most eloquently articulated the idea that the uses of property are best controlled by each individual proprietor competing in an open market to satisfy individual desires. This idea is explicit in U.S. antitrust law and practice.

4. *The limited state.* In reaction to the powerful hierarchies of medievalism, the conviction grew that the least government is the best government.

5. *Scientific specialization and fragmentation.* This is the corruption of Newtonian mechanics which states that, if we attend to the parts, as experts and specialists, the whole will take care of itself.

While it can be argued that the Lockean Five may be valid as ideals, in practice we have often departed from them. For example, history is re-plete with examples of business going to "the limited state" and seeking protection or favor. While this might be justified in the name of prop-erty rights, it has had the effect of forcing govern-ment into an active planning mode.

Or one might cite the many examples in America of ethnic communities with a high sense of interdependency—organic social constructs in-stead of the atomistic conglomerations of Locke. Immigrants did indeed bring a strong sense of community with them, but over time this sense weakened for lack of nourishment from the sur-rounding social system. Whatever may have been our historic inconsistencies with the traditional ideology, for most of our history it served as the principal justification for our institutional life and behavior. Departures from it were excep-tional, and every effort was made to minimize their significance.

Today, however, the exceptions are over-whelming. Although many small enterprises re-main comfortably and acceptably consistent with the Lockean Five and hopefully can continue so, the managers of large institutions in both the so-called private and public sectors are forced not to practice what they preach. It is this gap between the behavior of institutions and what they some-times thoughtlessly claim as a source of authority that causes trauma.

What then is the ideology that would legitimize the behavior of these institutions? The answer may be five counterparts to the Lockean Five.

The New Ideology

1. Communitarianism. The community—New York City, for example—is more than the sum of the individuals in it. It has special and urgent needs as a community, and the survival and self-respect of the individuals in it depend on the recognition of these needs. Few can get their kicks à la John Wayne, although many try. Individual fulfillment depends mostly on a place in a community, an identity with a whole, participation in an organic social process. Furthermore, if the group—the community, factory, or neighborhood—is well designed, its members will have a sense of identity with it. If, on the other hand, it is poorly designed, the individuals within it will be correspondingly alienated and frustrated. In the complex and highly organized America of today, few can live according to the principles John Locke had in mind.

Both corporations and unions have played leading roles in creating the circumstances that led to the erosion of the old idea of individualism and created the new framework of values. But invariably they have been ideologically unmindful of what they have done and have, therefore, tended to linger with the old forms and assumptions, even after those have been critically altered.

A central component of the old notion of individualism is the so-called Protestant ethic: hard work, thrift, delayed gratification, and obedience to authority. Business has extolled these virtues on the production side while systematically undercutting them on the marketing side. Advertising departments spend millions reminding us that the good life entails immediate gratification of our most lurid desires—gratification that we can buy now and pay for later.

Similarly, the assembly worker has been led to believe by management, early parental training, and TV that the old idea of individual fulfillment is valid. But finding himself constrained by an inescapable work setting dramatically unlike anything that he has been led to expect, he is one day liable to strike out—perhaps violently. Or he may join the absentee lists, taking Fridays and Mondays off to eke out some spurious individualism via drugs, drink, old movies, or—if he is lucky—a walk in the hills.

Paradoxically, such behavior puzzles both management and unions. They cling to the traditional, individualistic idea of the contract, long after the contract has ceased being individualistic and has become "collective," unmindful of the inevitable dissonance between the idea of contract and the new forms of consensus toward which communitarianism is leaning.

Our traditional social policy attempted to guarantee that each worker had equal opportunity. The lawyers enforcing today's equal employment legislation have taken a different tack. In the case of American Telephone & Telegraph, for example, they argued that discrimination had become institutionalized, that it, in fact, had become endemic to the AT&T community, and that women, in particular, were being slotted into certain tasks.

When this kind of argument receives acceptance, it is no longer necessary to prove individual discrimination to get redress.

Subsequently, the government moved to change the makeup of the company's workforce to provide, in effect, for equality of representation at all levels. The issue became one of *equality of result*, not of opportunity; and with that, a communitarian idea had superseded an individualistic one.

2. Rights and duties of membership. A curious thing has happened to private property—it has stopped being very important. What difference does it really make today whether a person owns or just enjoys property? He may get certain psychic kicks out of owning a jewel, a car, a TV set, or a house—but does it really make a difference whether he owns or rents?

Even land—that most basic element of property—has gone beyond the bounds of the traditional ideology. The United Nations Commission on Human Settlements (as quoted in the *New York Times,* June 7, 1976) said that because of the crucial role land plays in human settlements, it "cannot be treated as an ordinary asset controlled by individuals and subject to the pressures and inefficiencies of the market."

Today, a new right, which clearly supersedes property rights in political and social importance, is the right to survive—to enjoy income, health, and other rights associated with membership in the American community or in some component of that community, including a corporation.

Such rights derive not from any individualistic action or need; they do not emanate from a contract. Rather, they are communitarian rights, which public opinion holds to be consistent with a good community. This is a revolutionary departure from the old Lockean concept under which only the fit survive.

Escalating rights of membership, however, have strained the ability of governments to pay the bill. Transfer payments to pay for these rights have risen from 33 percent of the federal budget in 1972 to 42 percent in 1975. New York City hovers on the brink of bankruptcy. Inevitably, therefore, the necessity of membership *duties* emerges, and a question follows: Who decides the duties? The individual or the state? If government is to be the employer of last resort, does that impose an ultimate obligation to work at a job prescribed by government? And what do we do with the increasing numbers of persons in the workforce who are simply not needed?

The new ideology presents us with rather ominous choices.

The utility of property as a legitimizing idea has eroded as well. It is now quite obvious that our large public corporations are not private property at all. The 1.5 million shareholders of General Motors, for example, do not and cannot control, direct, or in any real sense be responsible for "their" company. The vast majority are investors pure and simple, and if they do not get a good return on their investment, they will put their money elsewhere.

"Campaign GM" and other similar attempts at stockholder agitation represent heroic but naively conservative strategies to force shareholders to behave like owners and thus to legitimize corporations as property. It is a peculiar irony that James Roche, as GM chairman, branded such agitation as radical, as the machinations of an "adversary culture . . . antagonistic to our American ideas of private property and individual responsibility." In truth, of course, GM was the radical; Nader et al. were acting as conservatives, trying to bring the corporation back into ideological line.

But if GM and the hundreds of other large corporations like it are not property, then what are they? The best we can say is that they are some sort of collective, floating in philosophic limbo, dangerously vulnerable to the charge of illegitimacy and to the charge that they are not amenable to community control. Consider how the management of this nonproprietary institution is selected. The myth is that the stockholders select the board of directors, which in turn selects the management. This is not true, however; in reality, the management selects the board, and the board, generally speaking, blesses management.

Managers thus get to be managers according to some mystical, circular process of questionable legitimacy. Under such circumstances, it is not surprising that "management's rights" are fragile and its authority waning.

3. Community need. It was to the notion of community need that ITT appealed in 1971 when it sought to prevent the Justice Department from divesting it of Hartford Fire Insurance. The company lawyers said, in effect: "Don't visit that old idea of competition on us. The public interest requires ITT to be big and strong at home so it can withstand the blows of Allende in Chile, Castro in Cuba, and the Japanese in general. Before you apply the antitrust laws to us, the secretary of the treasury, the secretary of commerce, and the Council of Economic Advisers should meet to decide what, in the light of our balance-of-payments problems and domestic economic difficulties, the national interest is."

Here again it was the company arguing the ideologically radical case. The suggestion was obvious: ITT was a partner with the government—indeed with the Cabinet—in defining and fulfilling the community needs of the United States. This concept is radically different from the traditional idea underlying the antitrust laws—namely that the public interest emerges naturally from free and vigorous competition among numerous aggressive, individualistic, and preferably small companies attempting to satisfy consumer desires.

In the face of serious pressures from Japanese and European business organizations, which emanate from ideological settings quite different from our own, there will be more reason to set aside the old idea of domestic competition to organize U.S. business effectively for meeting world competition. Managers will probably welcome, if not urge, such a step; they may, however, be less willing to accept the necessary concomitant: if, in the name of efficiency, of economies of scale, and of the demands of world markets, we allow restraints on the free play of domestic market forces, then other forces will have to be used to define and preserve the public interest. These "other forces" will amount to clearer control by the political order in some form or other.

This leads to other questions, as, for example, the matter of corporate size and concentration. The confusion between consumer desire and community need is also the source of considerable criticism of business. Is the automobile industry supposed to satisfy consumer desire for large cars or serve community need for smaller ones? Can the industry decide this question, or is it up to the community acting through its government?

4. Active, planning state. The role of the state is changing radically; it is becoming the setter of our sights and the arbiter of community needs. Inevitably, it will take on unprecedented tasks of coordination, priority setting, and planning in the largest sense. It will need to become far more efficient and authoritative, capable of making the difficult and subtle tradeoffs that now confront us—as, for example, those of environmental purity and energy supply.

Government is already big in the United States, probably bigger in proportion to the population than in countries we call "socialist." Some 16 percent of the labor force now works for one or another governmental agency, and the total tends to keep increasing. U.S. institutions more and more are living on government largess—subsidies, allowances, and contracts to farmers, corporations, and universities—and individuals benefit from social insurance, medical care, and housing allowances. The pretense of the "limited state," however, means that these huge allocations are relatively haphazard, reflecting the crisis of the moment and the power of interest groups rather than any sort of coherent and objective plan.

If the role of government were more precisely and consciously defined, the government could be smaller in size. To a great extent, the plethora of bureaucracies today is the result of a lack of focus and comprehension, an ironic bit of fallout from the old notion of the limited state. With more awareness we could also consider more fruitfully which issues are best left to local or regional planning and which, in fact, transcend the nation state and require a more global approach.

5. Holism—interdependence. Finally, and perhaps most fundamentally, the old idea of scientific specialization has given way to a new consciousness of the interrelatedness of all things. Spaceship earth, the limits of growth, and the fragility of our life-supporting biosphere have dramatized the ecological and philosophical truth that everything is related to everything else. Harmony between the works of man and the demands of nature is no longer the romantic plea of conservationists. It is an absolute rule of survival and thus is of profound ideological significance, subverting in many ways all of the Lockean ideas.

Ethical Applications

Many of the ethical issues of our time can be better understood if we view them in the light of this ideological transition.

In the aftermath of Watergate came the disclosure that scores of America's most important corporations had violated the Corrupt Practices Act, making illegal contributions to political campaigns and payoffs to many politicians for presumed favors. While, in general, it is wrong to violate the law, there are plainly exceptions to the rule as the experience of prohibition demonstrates. There are also degrees of wrongness. Political payoffs are in a sense a perfectly natural result of the traditional ideology. If the institution of government is held in low repute, if it is indeed regarded essentially as a necessary evil, and if its direction is supposed to arise from the pulling and hauling of innumerable interest groups, then it is natural that those groups will tend to use every means, fair or foul, to work their will. It is the way the system works.

How do we change the system?

We provide government with a more revered status; we acknowledge that it has a central role in the definition of the needs of the community and in the determination of priorities and that this role requires a certain objective distance from special interests. We then restrict the practice of lobbying, insulate government from pressure groups, and charge it with the responsibility of acting coherently in the national interest.

But even as we do this we can sense the predictable threats that the communitarian state breeds: elitism, unresponsiveness, and perhaps an increasing partnership between government and large corporations, replacing the adversary relationship in the traditional ideology and evolving possibly into a form of corporate statism, which could erode the essential elements of democracy.

So without excusing the illegality of those making and receiving the payoffs or in any sense minimizing their ethical flabbiness, we must acknowledge that perhaps more important is the systemic weakness that their behavior exposed. Of equal importance is an awareness of the consequences of correcting that weakness and a precise recognition of our choices.

One of the most important uses of ideological analysis is that it helps make explicit the full range of possibilities flowing from a change in practice. There is a propensity in any society for these possibilities to be obscured or muted by those who are seeking the change, and it is perfectly possible for the United States to get the worst of communitarianism unless we are fully alert to the choices that the transition requires.

The unethical fallout of Watergate also disclosed large and questionable payments to foreign governments by many corporations. Bob R. Dorsey, Gulf's chairman, defended a payment of $3 million to Korea's ruling party in 1970 as necessary to secure the continued favor of the regime. Senators questioning him pointed out that the company's investments in Korea were fully insured by the U.S. government against expropriation and that U.S. assistance to and influence in South Korea were substantial. In view of this, Dorsey was asked why he had not told the U.S. embassy about the problems he was having with the government. His answer is hard to take seriously, but at the same time is symptomatic of a larger problem. He said:

"Well, I suppose it goes back to a sort of lifetime habit, a lifetime experience of having received little help from the State Department and the American government in foreign endeavors and very often finding they had little interest and would just as soon not talk to us." Noting that he was not talking about the embassy staff in Korea, who had always been "extremely helpful," he went on: "Maybe I was basically ashamed of what was going on, I do not know. . . ." Further on in his testimony, in speaking of American companies abroad and their relationship to the American government, he said, "They were sort of like motherless children, they had to make their way in the world. . . ."

What is at stake here? First we must remember the time and place: South Korea, 1970—a government strongly supported by the United States and threatened by North Korea. The politicians from whom Gulf had received good treatment and who were friends of the United States had asked for money. It was a price of doing business, and it is understandable that he did not turn them down flat. What is not so clear is why Dorsey did not go to the embassy and report the matter; the national interest of the United States was clearly involved as was that of a U.S. corporation. Why then did he not? Some old assumptions, he said, about the relationship between government and business—vestigial remains of the limited state and property rights.

Dorsey may, in fact, be something of a hero. It seems altogether possible that throughout the 1960s the embassy, probably through the CIA, was assisting the ruling party and that Dorsey was the conduit for U.S. government funds. If this were the case, is Dorsey then perhaps to be praised for protecting his CIA connection? Or, if that is what he was doing, was he being unethical? That depends upon one's definition of the national interest and the confidence with which one leaves that definition to the institutions of government.

In either case the issue becomes one of the relationship over time between large U.S. corporations and the U.S. government. This brings us to Dorsey's contention that, in his experience, U.S. oil companies got little help from the State Department. The record, however, seems to indicate that, quite to the contrary, the U.S. government in the Middle East, Peru, and elsewhere has been more than solicitous of oil company interests. Indeed, the record shows a clear, if covert, partnership between the companies and the departments of State and Defense, although there is considerable doubt about who the senior partner was.

Looking to the future and to the enormous importance of the oil companies to the community need of the United States, there will be increasing ethical difficulties as long as the terms of the partnership are not made explicit and public. Take the natural gas crisis that paralyzed the country in the winter of 1977. Who and what are to blame? Some say it is regulation; others argue that it is greedy companies seeking to maximize short-term profits. But it is pointless and superfluous to look for villains in this matter. Again, the problem is systemic. Sooner or later government will perceive the energy problem as the holistic problem it is and begin to offer some coherent leadership. Until it does, catastrophe will mount, as will unethical behavior.

Ideally, it seems that the ethical corporate executive would address reality, urge government to do the coherent planning required, offer to assist—careful not to dominate or dictate—and then proceed to implement the plan with the efficiency for which U.S. corporations are justly respected. Only in this way can the investment decisions of, for example, the oil companies be both intelligent and just.

What stands in the way of such a course of action is principally a good deal of irrelevant ideology on the part of government, business, and the public in general.

The Lockheed case raises other issues of government-business relationships. In August 1975, Lockheed, a major defense contractor, admitted it had made under-the-table payments totaling some $22 million since 1970. Part of the payments, particularly those made in Japan, were used to promote overseas sales of the L-1011 Tri-Star jet liner. Difficulties with both producing and selling the L-1011 had placed the company on the brink of bankruptcy in 1971, when Congress bailed it out by agreeing to guarantee a $250 million loan. Management defended its questionable foreign payments, arguing that they were necessary to consummate foreign sales. The company also believed that such practices were "consistent with practices engaged in by numerous other companies abroad, including many of its competitors, and are in keeping with business practices in many foreign countries."

A central issue in this case is certainly the relationship between Lockheed and the U.S. government. Lockheed is a major defense contractor. It is answerable to a Loan Guarantee Board, of which the secretary of the treasury is chairman. It is a major exporter of military aircraft. However, the evidence suggests that these relationships with government were and still are vague and unclear.

Was Lockheed acting in the national interest or its shareholders' interest? Daniel J. Haughton, then chairman of Lockheed's board, in Senate subcommittee testimony claimed the latter, but, by inference, his mention of the French as serious competition in sales of wide-bodied aircraft, suggests he was thinking of the former.

Here, again, clarity and explicitness are essential. The question of what U.S. business sells in the way of military equipment around the world is surely infused with the national interest. It relates to our defense posture, our diplomatic alliances, and our balance of payments. Haughton's problem, like Dorsey's, may well have been as much a matter of the definition of the terms of his company's partnership with government as it was a matter of ethics.

The plight of New York City suggests a host of intriguing ethical issues for business. In 1976 the Episcopal bishop of New York chastised companies that were leaving New York for pleasanter and more secure suburban settings. Indeed, one cannot but have sympathy with such a stand—New York's principal difficulty is the erosion of its economic base.

What does the ethical business executive do? First, it would seem that ad hoc contributions to charitable causes, although worthy, are irrelevant to the problem. No amount of charity will do any good. Second, the problem must be seen as one involving all components of the New York community; it is an organic problem. Indeed, the problem extends to the suburbs of New Jersey and Connecticut and beyond. Much as some may object, New York is in many important ways a creature of the nation and of national demographic flows and pressures. What is the relevant community in this case? And what are its needs? Surely in answering these questions, the political order of the city, New York State, the several neighboring states, and the federal government will have to take leadership. Also, the city's bankers as well as the general public will have to realize that the banks are as important politically as they are economically. They are, in fact, inextricably connected to the political order. Their distance from it has been part of the problem.

The point is that there is little that business can do alone. The solution requires a partnership with the political order, and before that can occur, the political order must become more coherent and more alert to its planning function. Until business recognizes this, it will be blamed—unfairly perhaps—but blamed nevertheless for the systemic breakdown that New York represents.

Inside the corporation, ethical questions abound concerning the proper relationship between employers and employees. Work, it is said, is dehumanizing, alienating, and boring. The old notions of managerial authority rooted in property rights and contract no longer seem to be acceptable. Consequently, many firms are moving away from the old notions to new ones of consensus and rights and duties of membership in which the right to manage actually comes from the managed. Consensual arrangements naturally threaten the old institutions attached to the contract both in management and labor. Trade unions are particularly anxious about the new development.

The new approaches will come easier—and more ethically—if we are mindful of the radical implications of what we are doing. The old institutions need to be treated gently so that their resistance will be minimized. There may after all be an important role for unions in the new consensual arrangements. Workers' participation in management can be made more effective by a properly functioning union. Both management and labor need to learn new techniques. Also, the new way is not without its own threats and dangers. The idea of the contract emerged to protect the individual from the worst abuses of ancient and medieval communitarianism. Unless we are careful, hideous injustice can be perpetrated in the name of consensus; all sorts can be excluded, for example, the weak, the black, the white, women, men, or those we merely do not like.

It is worth emphasizing that perhaps the most appalling ethical problems we may face are those associated with the new ideology. How can we preserve and protect some of the most cherished attributes of the old as we move inexorably toward the new? How can we safeguard individual rights in the face of communitarianism and the rights of privacy, choice, and liberty? How can we avoid the grim excesses of centralized, authoritarian, impersonal bureaucracy? How can we ensure democracy at all levels of our political system? How can we enliven efficiency as the definition of what is a cost and what is a benefit becomes increasingly obscure?

The general answer to these questions is alertness—consciousness of what is happening. This is no time to sing the old hymns. It is essential to compose new ones. It is, after all, not beyond the realm of possibility that we could find ourselves marching stolidly into a communitarian prison lustily singing Lockean hymns.

The specific answers must flow from specific situations. The ethical manager will be realistic about both the situation and the roles and functions of business, government, and other institutions in dealing with it. He will also bear in mind the long-term interests of the persons and communities that he affects, having the courage to place those interests above his own short-term preoccupations. He will see his problems in the context of all their relationships, employing his skills as a generalist to help produce appropriately systemic solutions.

Can an Executive Afford a Conscience?

Albert Z. Carr

Our opening chapter devoted much discussion to the personal agony business people face when attempting to reconcile their own ethics with those of their employers' "anything for earnings" attitudes. In the following essay, Albert Carr addresses this dilemma with vigorous concern. Specifically, he attempts to answer some knotty questions. What should corporate executives who find themselves faced with implementing, or at least condoning, unethical corporate practices do? Should they blink at it? If so, what impact will this approach have on them? If not, what can executives do about it? Mr. Carr has personally experienced the bind he speaks of and has long been concerned with corporate ethics as a consultant, an entrepreneur, a government official, and a writer. This article has been adapted from a chapter of his book The Executive Conscience.

Ask a business executive whether his company employs child labor, and he will either think you are joking or be angered by the implied slur on his ethical standards. In the 1970's the employment of children in factories is clearly considered morally wrong as well as illegal.

Yet it was not until comparatively recently (1941) that the U.S. Supreme Court finally sustained the constitutionality of the long-contested Child Labor Act, which Congress had passed four years earlier. During most of the previous eight decades, the fact that children 10 years old worked at manual jobs for an average of 11 hours a day under conditions of virtual slavery had aroused little indignation in business circles.

To be sure, only a few industries found the practice profitable, and the majority of businessmen would doubtless have been glad to see it stopped. But in order to stop it the government had to act, and any interference with business by government was regarded as a crime against God, Nature, and Respectability. If a company sought to hold down production costs by employing children in factories where the work did not demand adult skills or muscle, that was surely a matter to be settled between the employer and the child's parents or the orphanage.

To permit legitimate private enterprise to be balked by unrealistic do-gooders was to open the gate to socialism and anarchy—such was the prevailing sentiment of businessmen, as shown in the business press, from the 1860's to the 1930's.

Every important advance in business ethics has been achieved through a long history of pain and protest.[1] The process of change begins when a previously accepted practice arouses misgivings among sensitive observers. Their efforts at moral suasion are usually ignored, however, until changes in economic conditions or new technology make the practice seem increasingly undesirable.

Businessmen who profit by the practice defend it heatedly, and a long period of public controversy ensues, climaxed at last by the adoption of laws forbidding it. After another 20 or 30 years, the new generation of businessmen regard the practice with retrospective moral indignation and wonder why it was ever tolerated.

A century of increasingly violent debate culminating in civil war had to be lived through before black slavery, long regarded as an excellent business proposition, was declared unlawful in the United States. To achieve laws forbidding racial discrimination in hiring practices required another century. It took 80 years of often bloody labor disputes to win acceptance of the principle of collective bargaining, and the country endured about 110 years of flagrant financial abuses before enactment of effective measures regulating banks and stock exchanges.

In time, all of these forward steps, once bitterly opposed by most businessmen, came to be accepted as part of the ethical foundation of the American private enterprise economy.

Jesse James vs. Nero

In the second half of the twentieth century, with the population, money supply, military power, and industrial technology of the United States expanding rapidly at the same time, serious new ethical issues have arisen for businessmen—notably the pollution of the biosphere, the concentration of economic power in a relatively few vast corporations, increasing military domination of the economy, and the complex interrelationship between business interests and the threat of war. These issues are the more formidable because they demand swift response; they will not wait a century or even a generation for a change in corporate ethics that will stimulate businessmen to act.

The problems they present to business and our society as a whole are immediate, critical, and worsening. If they are not promptly dealt with by farsighted and effective measures, they could even bring down political democracy and the entrepreneurial system together.

In fact, given the close relationship between our domestic economic situation and our military commitments abroad, and the perils implicit in the worldwide armaments buildup, it is not extreme to say that the extent to which businessmen are able to open their minds to new ethical imperatives in the decade ahead may have decisive influence in this century on the future of the human species.

Considering the magnitude of these rapidly

developing issues, old standards of ethical judgment seem almost irrelevant. It is of course desirable that a businessman be honest in his accountings and faithful to his contracts—that he should not advertise misleadingly, rig prices, deceive stockholders, deny workers their due, cheat customers, spread false rumors about competitors, or stab associates in the back. Such a person has in the past qualified as "highly ethical," and he could feel morally superior to many of those he saw around him—the chiselers, the connivers, the betrayers of trust.

But standards of personal conduct in themselves are no longer an adequate index of business ethics. Everyone knows that a minority of businessmen commit commercial mayhem on each other and on the public with practices ranging from subtle conflicts of interest to the sale of injurious drugs and unsafe automobiles, but in the moral crisis through which we are living such tales of executive wrongdoing, like nudity in motion pictures, have lost their power to shock.

The public shrugs at the company president who conspires with his peers to fix prices. It grins at the vice president in charge of sales who provides call girls for a customer. After we have heard a few such stories, they become monotonous.

We cannot shrug or grin, however, at the refusal of powerful corporations to take vigorous action against great dangers threatening the society, and to which they contribute. Compared with such a corporation or with the executive who is willing to jeopardize the health and well-being of an entire people in order to add something to current earnings, the man who merely embezzles company funds is as insignificant in the annals of morality as Jesse James is compared with Nero.

The moral position of the executive who works for a company that fails in the ethics of social responsibility is ambiguous. The fact that he does not control company policy cannot entirely exonerate him from blame. He is guilty, so to speak, by employment.

If he is aware that the company's factories pollute the environment or its products injure the consumer and he does not exert himself to change the related company policies, he becomes morally suspect. If he lends himself to devious evasions of laws against racial discrimination in hiring practices, he adds to the probability of destructive racial confrontations and is in some degree an agent of social disruption. If he knows that his company is involved in the bribery of legislators or government officials, or makes under-the-table deals with labor union officials, or uses the services of companies known to be controlled by criminal syndicates, he contributes through his work to disrespect for law and the spread of crime.

If his company, in its desire for military contracts, lobbies to oppose justifiable cuts in the government's enormous military budget, he bears some share of responsibility for the constriction of the civilian economy; for price inflation, urban decay, and shortages of housing, transportation, and schools; and for failure to mitigate the hardships of the poor.

From this standpoint, the carefully correct executive who never violates a law or fails to observe the canons of gentlemanly behavior may be as open to ethical challenge as the crooks and the cheaters.

"Toxins of Suppressed Guilt"

The practical question arises: If a man in a responsible corporate position finds that certain policies of his company are socially injurious, what can he do about it without jeopardizing his job?

Contrary to common opinion, he is not necessarily without recourse. The nature of that recourse I shall discuss in the final section of this article. Here, I want to point out that unless the executive's sense of social responsibility is accompanied by a high degree of realism about tactics, then he is likely to end in frustration or cynicism.

One executive of my acquaintance who wrote several memoranda to his chief, detailing instances of serious environmental contamination for which the company was responsible and which called for early remedy, was sharply rebuked for a "negative attitude."

Another, a successful executive of a large corporation, said to me quite seriously in a confidential moment that he did not think a man in a job like his could afford the luxury of a conscience in the office. He was frank to say that he had become unhappy about certain policies of his company. He could no longer deny to himself that the company was not living up to its social responsibilities and was engaged in some political practices that smacked of corruption.

But what were his options? He had only three

that he could see, and he told me he disliked them all:

If he argued for a change in policies that were helping to keep net earnings high, he might be branded by his superiors as "unrealistic" or "idealistic"—adjectives that could check his career and might, if he pushed too hard, compel his resignation.

Continued silence not only would spoil his enjoyment of his work, but might cause him to lose respect for himself.

If he moved to one of the other companies in his industry, he would merely be exchanging one set of moral misgivings for another.

He added with a sigh that he envied his associates whose consciences had never developed beyond the Neanderthal stage and who had no difficulty in accepting things as they were. He said he wondered whether he ought not to try to discipline himself to be as indifferent as they to the social implications of policies which, after all, were common in business.

Perhaps he made this effort and succeeded in it, for he remained with the company and forged ahead. He may even have fancied that he had killed his conscience—as the narrator in Mark Twain's symbolic story did when he gradually reached the point where he could blithely murder the tramps who came to his door asking for handouts.

But conscience is never killed; when ignored, it merely goes underground, where it manufactures the toxins of suppressed guilt, often with serious psychological and physical consequences. The hard fact is that the executive who has a well-developed contemporary conscience is at an increasing disadvantage in business unless he is able to find some personal policy by which he can maintain his drive for success without serious moral reservations.

Distrustful Public

The problem faced by the ethically motivated man in corporate life is compounded by growing public distrust of business morality.

The corporation executive is popularly envied for his relative affluence and respected for his powers of achievement, but many people deeply suspect his ethics—as not a few successful businessmen have been informed by their children. Surveys made in a number of universities across the country indicate that a large majority of students aiming at college degrees are convinced that business is a dog-eat-dog proposition, with which most of them do not want to be connected.

This low opinion is by no means confined to youngsters; a poll of 2,000 representative Americans brought to light the belief of nearly half of them that "most businessmen would try anything, honest or not, for a buck."[2] The unfairness of the notion does not make it less significant as a clue to public opinion. (This poll also showed that most Americans are aware of the notable contributions of business to the material satisfactions of their lives; the two opinions are not inconsistent.)

Many businessmen, too, are deeply disturbed by the level of executive morality in their sphere of observation. Although about 90% of executives in another survey stated that they regarded themselves as "ethical," 80% affirmed "the presence of numerous generally accepted practices in their industry which they consider unethical," such as bribery of government officials, rigging of prices, and collusion in contract bidding.[3]

The public is by no means unaware of such practices. In conversations about business ethics with a cross-section sampling of citizens in a New England town, I found that they mentioned kickbacks and industrial espionage as often as embezzlement and fraud. One man pointed out that the kickback is now taken so much for granted in corporations that the Internal Revenue Service provides detailed instructions for businessmen on how to report income from this source on their tax returns.

The indifference of many companies to consumers' health and safety was a major source of criticism. Several of the persons interviewed spoke of conflicts of interest among corporation heads, accounts of which had been featured not long before in the press. Others had learned from television dramas about the ruthlessness of the struggle for survival and the hail-fellow hypocrisy that is common in executive offices.

Housewives drew on their shopping experience to denounce the decline in the quality of necessities for which they had to pay ever-higher prices. Two or three had read in *Consumer Reports* about "planned obsolescence."

I came to the conclusion that if my sample is at

all representative—and I think it is—the public has learned more about the ways of men in corporate life than most boards of directors yet realize.

These opinions were voiced by people who for the most part had not yet given much thought to the part played by industrial wastes in the condition of the environment, or to the inroads made on their economic well-being by the influence of corporation lobbyists on military decision makers. It is to be expected that if, as a result of deteriorating social and economic conditions, these and other major concerns take on more meaning for the public, criticism of business ethics will widen and become sharper.

If the threats of widespread water shortage in the 1970's and of regional clean air shortages in the 1980's are allowed to materialize, and military expenditures continue to constrict civilian life, popular resentment may well be translated into active protest directed against many corporations as well as against the government. In that event, the moral pressure on individual executives will become increasingly acute.

Regard for public opinion certainly helped to influence many companies in the 1950's and 1960's to pledge to reduce their waste discharges into the air and water and to hire more people with dark skins. Such declarations were balm for the sore business conscience.

The vogue for "social responsibility" has now grown until, as one commentator put it, "pronouncements about social responsibility issue forth so abundantly from the corporations that it is hard for one to get a decent play in the press. Everybody is in on the act, and nearly all of them actually mean what they say!"[4] More than a few companies have spent considerable sums to advertise their efforts to protect a stream, clean up smokestack emissions, or train "hard-core unemployables."

These are worthy undertakings, as far as they have gone, but for the most part they have not gone very far. In 1970 it has become obvious that the performance of U.S. corporations in the area of social responsibility has generally been trivial, considering the scope of their operations.

Behind the Boardroom Door

No company that I have ever heard of employs a vice president in charge of ethical stan-

dards; and sooner or later the conscientious executive is likely to come up against a stone wall of corporate indifference to private moral values.

When the men who hold the real power in the company come together to decide policy, they may give lip service to the moral element in the issue, but not much more. The decision-making process at top-management levels has little room for social responsibilities not definitely required by law or public opinion.

Proposals that fail to promise an early payoff for the company and that involve substantial expense are accepted only if they represent a means of escaping drastic penalties, such as might be inflicted by a government suit, a labor strike, or a consumer boycott. To invest heavily in antipollution equipment or in programs for hiring and training workers on the fringe of employability, or to accept higher taxation in the interest of better education for the children of a community—for some distant, intangible return in a cloudy future—normally goes against the grain of every profit-minded management.

It could hardly be otherwise. In the prevailing concept of corporate efficiency, a continual lowering of costs relative to sales is cardinal. For low costs are a key not only to higher profits but to corporate maneuverability, to advantage in recruiting the best men, and to the ability to at least hold a share of a competitive market.

Of the savings accruing to a company from lowered costs, the fraction that finds its way into the area of social responsibility is usually miniscule. To expend such savings on nonremunerative activities is regarded as weakening the corporate structure.

The late Chester A. Barnard, one of the more enlightened business leaders of the previous generation and a man deeply concerned with ethics, voiced the position of management in the form of a question: "To what extent is one morally justified in loading a productive undertaking with heavy charges in the attempt to protect against a remote possibility, or even one not so remote?"[5] Speaking of accident prevention in plants, which he favored in principle, he warned that if the outlay for such a purpose weakened the company's finances, "the community might lose a service and the entrepreneur an opportunity."

Corporate managers apply the same line of reasoning to proposals for expenditure in the area of social responsibility. "We can't afford to sink that amount of money in nonproductive uses," they say, and, "We need all our cash for expansion."

The entrepreneur who is willing to accept some reduction of his income—the type is not unknown—may be able to operate his enterprise in a way that satisfies an active conscience; but a company with a competitive team of managers, a board of directors, and a pride of stockholders cannot harbor such an unbusinesslike intention.

Occasionally, statesmen, writers, and even some high-minded executives, such as the late Clarence B. Randall, have made the appeal of conscience to corporations. They have argued that, since the managers and directors of companies are for the most part men of goodwill in their private lives, their corporate decisions also should be guided by conscience.

Even the distinguished economist A. A. Berle, Jr. has expressed the view that the healthy development of our society requires "the growth of conscience" in the corporation of our time.[6] But if by "conscience" he meant a sense of right and wrong transcending the economic, he was asking the impossible.

A business that defined "right" and "wrong" in terms that would satisfy a well-developed contemporary conscience could not survive. No company can be expected to serve the social interest unless its self-interest is also served, either by the expectation of profit or by the avoidance of punishment.

"Gresham's Law" of Ethics

Before responsibility to the public can properly be brought into the framework of a top-management decision, it must have an economic justification. For instance, executives might say:

"We'd better install the new safety feature because, if we don't, we'll have the government on our necks, and the bad publicity will cost us more than we are now saving in production."

"We should spend the money for equipment to take the sulfides out of our smokestacks at the plant. Otherwise we'll have trouble recruiting labor and have a costly PR problem in the community."

It is worth noting that Henry Ford II felt constrained to explain to stockholders of the Ford Motor Company that his earnest and socially aware effort to recruit workers from Detroit's "hard-core unemployed" was a preventive measure against the recurrence of ghetto riots carrying a threat to the company.

In another situation, when a number of life insurance companies agreed to invest money in slum reconstruction at interest rates somewhat below the market, their executives were quick to forestall possible complaints from stockholders by pointing out that they were opening up future markets for life insurance. Rationally, the successful corporate manager can contemplate expense for the benefit of society only if failure to spend points to an eventual loss of security or opportunity that exceeds the cost.

There can be no conscience without a sense of personal responsibility, and the corporation, as Ambrose Bierce remarked, is "an ingenious device for obtaining individual profit without individual responsibility." When the directors and managers of a corporation enter the boardroom to debate policy, they park their private consciences outside.

If they did not subordinate their inner scruples to considerations of profitability and growth, they would fail in their responsibility to the company that pays them. A kind of Gresham's Law of ethics operates here; the ethic of corporate advantage invariably silences and drives out the ethic of individual self-restraint.

(This, incidentally, is true at every level of the corporate structure. An executive who adheres to ethical standards disregarded by his associates is asking for trouble. No one, for example, is so much hated in a purchasing department where graft is rife as the man who refuses to take kickbacks from suppliers, for he threatens the security of the others. Unless he conforms, they are all too likely to "get him.")

The crucial question in boardroom meetings where social responsibility is discussed is not, "Are we morally obligated to do it?" but, rather, "What will happen if we don't do it?" or, perhaps, "How will this affect the rate of return on investment?"

If the house counsel assures management that there will be no serious punishment under the law if the company does not take on the added expense, and the marketing man sees no danger to sales, and the public relations man is confident he can avoid injury to the corporate image, then the money, if it amounts to any considerable sum, will not be spent—social responsibility or no social responsibility.

Even the compulsion of law is often regarded in corporate thinking as an element in a contest between government and the corporation, rather than as a description of "right" and "wrong." The files of the Federal Trade Commission, the Food and Drug Administration, and other government agencies are filled with records of respectable companies that have not hesitated to break or stretch the law when they believed they could get away with it.

It is not unusual for company managements to break a law, even when they expect to be caught, if they calculate that the fine they eventually must pay represents only a fraction of the profits that the violation will enable them to collect in the meantime. More than one corporate merger has been announced to permit insiders to make stock-market killings even though the companies concerned recognized that the antitrust laws would probably compel their eventual separation.

What Can the Executive Do?

One can dream of a big-business community that considers it sound economics to sacrifice a portion of short-term profits in order to protect the environment and reduce social tensions.

It is theoretically conceivable that top managers as a class may come to perceive the profound dangers, for the free-enterprise system and for themselves, in the trend toward the militarization of our society, and will press the government to resist the demand for nonessential military orders and overpermissive contracts from sections of industry and elements in the Armed Services. At the same level of wishfulness, we can imagine the federal government making it clear to U.S. companies investing abroad that protection of their investments is not the government's responsibility.

We can even envisage a time when the bonds of a corporation that is responsive to social needs will command a higher rating by Moody's than those of a company that neglects such values, since the latter is more vulnerable to public condemnation; and a time when a powerful Executive League for Social Responsibility will come into being to stimulate and assist top managements in formulating long-range economic policies that

embrace social issues. In such a private-enterprise utopia the executive with a social conscience would be able to work without weakening qualms.

In the real world of today's business, however, he is almost sure to be a troubled man. Perhaps there are some executives who are so strongly positioned that they can afford to urge their managements to accept a reduced rate of return on investment for the sake of the society of which they are a part. But for the large majority of corporate employees who want to keep their jobs and win their superiors' approbation, to propose such a thing would be inviting oneself to the corporate guillotine.

He Is Not Powerless

But this does not necessarily mean that the ethically motivated executive can do nothing. In fact, if he does nothing, he may so bleach his conception of himself as a man of conviction as to reduce his personal force and value to the company. His situation calls for sagacity as well as courage. Whatever ideas he advocates to express his sense of social responsibility must be shaped to the company's interests.

Asking management flatly to place social values ahead of profits would be foolhardy, but if he can demonstrate that, on the basis of long-range profitability, the concept of corporate efficiency needs to be broadened to include social values, he may be able to make his point without injury—indeed, with benefit—to his status in the company. A man respected for competence in his job, who knows how to justify ethically based programs in economic terms and to overcome elements of resistance in the psychology of top management, may well be demonstrating his own qualifications for top management.

In essence, any ethically oriented proposal made to a manager is a proposal to take a longer-range view of his problems—to lift his sights. Nonethical practice is shortsighted almost by definition, if for no other reason than that it exposes the company to eventual reprisals.

The longer range a realistic business projection is, the more likely it is to find a sound ethical footing. I would go so far as to say that almost anything an executive does, on whatever level, to extend the range of thinking of his superiors tends to effect an ethical advance.

The hope and the opportunity of the individual executive with a contemporary conscience lies in the constructive connection of the long economic view with the socially aware outlook. He must show convincingly a net advantage for the corporation in accelerating expenditures or accepting other costs in the sphere of social responsibility.

I was recently able to observe an instance in which an executive persuaded his company's management to make a major advance in its antipollution policy. His presentation of the alternatives, on which he had spent weeks of careful preparation, showed in essence that, under his plan, costs which would have to be absorbed over a three-year period would within six years prove to be substantially less than the potential costs of less vigorous action.

When he finished his statement, no man among his listeners, not even his most active rivals, chose to resist him. He had done more than serve his company and satisfy his own ethical urge; he had shown that the gap between the corporate decision and the private conscience is not unbridgeable if a person is strong enough, able enough, and brave enough to do what needs to be done.

It may be that the future of our enterprise system will depend on the emergence of a sufficient number of men of this breed who believe that in order to save itself business will be impelled to help save the society.

Notes

1. For amplifications of this view, see Robert W. Austin, "Responsibility for Social Change," HBR July–August 1965, p. 45; and Theodore Levitt, "Why Business Always Loses," HBR March–April 1968, p. 81.

2. Louis B. Harris and Associates, in a survey reported at a National Industrial Conference Board meeting, April 21, 1966.

3. Raymond C. Baumhart, S.J., "How Ethical Are Businessmen?" HBR July–August 1961, p. 6.

4. Theodore Levitt, "The Dangers of Social Responsibility," HBR September–October 1958, p. 41.

5. Elementary Conditions of Business Morals (Berkeley, Committee on the Barbara Weinstock Lectures, University of California, 1958).

6. The Twentieth Century Capitalist Revolution (New York, Harcourt, Brace & Company, 1954), pp. 113–114.

Business Ethics: Age-Old Ideal, Now Real

James Owens

In discussing the increased ethical content of business, we confined our observations to business's role in and influence on the social system, to society's expectations of business, and to individuals' conflicts between personal values and business responsibilities. While these factors go a long way toward explaining both the increased moral content of business decisions and the need for business ethics, they don't exhaust the issue. In fact, the Lodge essay explained the role ideological transition plays in today's business scene. In the following essay we will learn about the impact scientific and technological advances in communications have had on business ethics. The author, James Owens, Director of the Division of Management Sciences at the American University School of Business, argues that the age of "information technology" and public insistence on ethical behavior has made a written, enforceable code of ethics a practical necessity for the survival of business organizations. Owens provides some timely observations about the nature of ethics which not only tie in with our present discussion but also anticipate the next chapter of this book, which deals with standards of morality.

Scientific and technological advances in the communications field, now operating in our daily lives, have catapulted the American people, its businesses, and its other institutions into the strange new age of "real-time" information. Computers, interesting toys just a few years ago, now

James Owens, "Business Ethics: Age-Old Ideal, Now Real," Business Horizons, February, 1978. Copyright, 1978, by the Foundation for the School of Business at Indiana University. Reprinted by permission.

make possible databanks capable of retrieving, sorting, storing, and providing anyone instantly with all known information about any person or organization. The development of telephone and similar communication has reached mature sophistication. Newspapers, magazines, radio, and television can, in today's world of "freedom of information," "full-disclosure," and similar laws or public policies, dig out and publicize critical information about any person or organization. In any twenty-four-hour period, any person or organization can easily be "made ready," and the information fully developed (usually with entertaining and dramatic impact), for the 6:00 o'clock news. It happens every night on television, every day in the newspapers, and every week or month in magazines.

This age of "real-time" information creates some radical advantages for human beings (as in medicine, education, and daily conveniences) and some major problems as well. For example, today's managers now operate, whether they realize it or not, as though they were in a well-illuminated fish bowl, instantly under the public's scrutiny. With the advent of the late 1970s, business managers and their daily decisions are suddenly "on stage," carefully monitored, reported on and evaluated, and kept on "continuing file."

The full implications of databank capability and instant availability of information in general require many theoretical and practical reassessments by managers and management educators alike. These considerations, however, are beyond the scope of this article. Here we will consider only the impact of the new age of instant information upon business ethics.

For centuries, and especially over the past two decades, "business ethics" has been a popular research and conversational topic, but it was always dealt with as an "ideal" and certainly not something to practice in the tough, real world of business decision-making. Today, all of a sudden, business ethics has become a practical necessity for all organizations and their managers.

The new age of instant information availability puts the operations and decisions of today's managers under constant public scrutiny, a condition of business life no previous American managers had to cope with or live with daily. Managers and entrepreneurs of the past in America, including U.S. presidents, operated routinely in

private and secrecy, an option modern American managers understandably would relish. But the luxury of privacy, secrecy, and confidential executive decision-making no longer exists in the world of the 1970s. The issue of business ethics cannot be approached with mere sentimental "moralizing"; integrity and sound professional ethics are now essential conditions for practical effectiveness—even survival.

Thus, in addition to exploring other requirements of effective management, managers and their organizations must maintain an operational and continuing concern for the ethical integrity increasingly demanded by the public. Consider, for example, recent outcries in the newspapers and on television concerning misuse of funds, kickbacks, collusion, corruption in public office, fraudulent use of welfare and other public funds by doctors and corporations, deceptive advertising, and so forth.

Achieving a reputation for ethical integrity, both internal and external to the organization, implies a continuing development and refinement of clear, specific, and well-publicized codes of professional ethics and persistent reference to the fundamental concepts embodied in the historical literature of philosophical ethics. It is the concepts of ethics that provide the theoretical framework and solid foundation for specific codes of ethics; without such a foundation, ethical "codes" usually degenerate into either blind reactions to current crises or flabby and meaningless generalities. This article addresses primarily these underlying concepts. I have attempted to spare the reader, as far as is possible, unnecessary jargon and theoretical trivia in order to provide a clear basis for the ongoing and much-needed development of ethical codes for managers and their organizations.

The trend toward a "profession" of management is well under way. Managers of the future, if they are to become or remain such, will be professional in the best sense of the term, including the ethical. By a kind of natural evolution, one mark of the future manager will become his unerring ability to comprehend and evaluate the ethical dimensions of his decisions; lacking this ability and sensitivity to ethical issues, he will be a net liability—and often a latent menace—to his organization.

Integrity and consequent credibility have become a practical necessity for businesses and executives. In the current age of instant communication through telephone, computer, and television, and of super-sensitivity on the part of aggressive public pressure groups, consumer advocates, and government regulators, the "new realism" dictates in fact that from a fully *practical* point of view "good ethics is good business."

"Good" Doctors and "Bad" Humans

Few words suffer semantic butchery as does the word "ethical." Some regard themselves ethical if their legal staff can keep them safely within the law. Others feel ethical if they have a generally good "feeling" toward others—at least on the Sabbath. Still others construe themselves as ethical, even within the turmoil of hard, ambiguous "business" situations, if they execute exactly the boss's (or a client's) orders (although they might concede that the boss is unethical in some of those orders).

Operationally, "ethics" can be defined as a "set of standards, or code, developed by human reason and experience, by which free, human actions are determined as humanly right or wrong, good or evil." If an action conforms to such standards, it is deemed ethical; if it does not, it is deemed unethical.

The term "humanly" in the above definition carries a special meaning and is critical. It implies and urges important distinctions among the various senses of the "good." What is "good" ethically, in the ultimate human sense of the term, transcends such common uses of the word as in "good looks," "a good steak," "feeling good," or a "good automobile mechanic." Such uses indicate what is *desirable* in terms of appearance, food tastes, personal feeling, and job performance. Ethical "good" (the "good" humanly interpreted) raises the question: what is a good human being? A doctor who demonstrates remarkable skill in experimental surgery upon healthy, unwilling prisoners is clearly a good surgeon but an evil and unethical person. Similarly, a good salesperson, manager, or lawyer might employ tactics that are *ethically* wrong.

Ethics and Law

The law is a set of imperative statements promulgated by the state and enforced by the power of the state. Thus, laws and ethics are not equatable, even though many laws tend to coincide with a particular society's ethics (as in the case of the common prohibition against lying by both law and ethics in America). But law and ethics often conflict, as in the case of the Nazi regime's laws, which violated all sense of human ethics, or the many "blue laws" in the United States that no longer represent current ethical attitudes. When a law conflicts with a person's ethics to the extent that, in good conscience, he must openly violate that law, the person is engaging in "civil disobedience." Thus, the "legal" and the "ethical" are not the same thing; but in general the formulation of law follows a society's ethical attitudes and results in a gradual merging of the two.

Positive and Negative Ethics

Most discussions of organizational and public ethics track the more sensational and newsworthy instances of wrongdoing. The news business zeroes in upon the *un*ethical, thereby optimizing newspaper readership and subscriptions. But it is important to note that such preoccupation with wrongdoing is only one part of ethics, the *negative* part. Negative ethics centers on the analysis of what human beings do that is wrong ethically and by what standards it is judged as wrong.

The other side of ethics is *positive* ethics: the analysis of what people do that is ethically "good" and by what standards it is so judged. For example, top executives of a large firm decide to use corporate money to hire, train, and employ a number of hard-core "unemployables" in order to better the lives of such people suffering from joblessness and little opportunity. In the development of specific ethical codes for an entire industry, the positive approach to ethics is as important as a narrow, negative approach, although both are necessary.

Ethical Sanctions

A key concept in the literature of ethics is sanctions, the rewards that prompt people toward ethical actions and the penalties that prompt them to avoid unethical actions. What prompts an executive to contribute his services one night a week to help train hard-core unemployables (positive ethics) or to avoid padding his expense account (negative ethics)? The following sanctions are common throughout the literature of philosophical ethics: personal value-systems and "conscience"; pressures of public opinion expressed in the public media; common and statute laws; religious belief and commitment; personal peace of mind; fear of retaliation—or exposure—regarding wrongdoing; fear of government intervention and regulation in the absence of ethical codes initiated (generally more sensibly and realistically) by industry people themselves; and an organization's rules, policies, and codes that are realistically enforced upon members. Any organizational code of ethics must incorporate the above sanction considerations into its code or rightly anticipate failure or, at best, superficial compliance.

Ethical Principles and Standards

"Principles of ethics" involve the most theoretical—and controversial—aspects of philosophical ethics. Fortunately, they are unnecessary in a practical treatment of ethics, as space does not permit us to discuss them here. The standards of ethics, derived from most "principle-oriented" and "ethical-system" approaches, happen to coincide with the most common historical standards of ethics. Several major ethical standards that are viable and have survived many hundreds of years of human experience are listed below, not necessarily in order of importance or validity.

Treat all human beings with fairness. This is the rule of justice and an inspiring maxim. However, it requires careful analysis of the rights of all parties in situations involving conflicting interests. "Fairness" to stockholders is perceived differently than fairness to employees, customers, or suppliers.

Do unto others as you would have them do unto you. The golden rule is among the most enduring of ethical standards. With slight variations in phrasing (for example, the Chinese version by Confucius in the sixth century B.C.: "What you do not want done to yourself, do not do to others"), the golden rule has been a prominent ethical force in Buddhism, ancient Greek philosophy, Hinduism, Judaism, Christianity, and many other systems of thought.

The long-range utility standard states: "So act that your act will produce, over the long range, maximum personal happiness." In explicitly stated form, this standard can be found throughout history from the ancient Greek philosophers up to American pragmatists William James and John Dewey. William James, reacting against what he interpreted as the noble-sounding but literally useless generalities of idealists, attempted to popularize the long-range utility standard as "solid ethics" and as the clear and realistic approach. This standard requires that actions be judged as ethical or unethical according to their ultimate long-range consequences for the individual. Thus, breaking a promise might be expedient in a present situation but greatly risks bad reputation—and consequent failure—for the long-term future, and is therefore judged to be unethical.

A consultant, accepting an assignment that he knows is beyond his capability, may ease immediate financial pressures; but when his mediocre performance becomes known, his reputation and success for the long term are jeopardized. Also unethical by the long-range utility standard are practices that, although currently convenient and profitable for an organization, lead to stiff and excessive government regulation. In essence, this standard builds ethics upon a realistic foundation of enlightened self-interest, intelligent self-interest, mutual self-interest, and similar expressions to be found in the literature of pragmatism.

The general law standard states: So act that your act could be made a general law which could be proved, from human experience, to work toward general human and social success. We have the German philosopher Immanuel Kant and, later, the American pragmatists to thank for the general law standard; it serves as a most interesting—and usually quite revealing—test of the basic ethicalness of any contemplated action or decision. The general law standard requires that we judge action as ethical or unethical by asking, "Suppose *everybody* did this." For example, suppose a securities broker is sorely tempted to misrepresent certain stocks and has, in his mind, just about "justified" it for reasons of personal problems and pressures; then he calls upon the general law standard and puts his contemplated action to the test by saying, "Suppose *everybody* did this." Assuming any degree of objectivity, reasonableness, and realism on his part, he would have to conclude that if everybody misrepresented securities, obviously a vital social structure would simply collapse. Hence, the act is clearly unethical. The act of a consultant accepting an assignment for which he is not really qualified also fails to pass the test of the general law standard.

Ethical Codes

Using the two terms in the strict sense, as conventionally employed in the literature of ethics, ethical *standards* are general maxims and ethical *codes* are very specific statements of what is regarded as right or wrong within a particular situation in the here and now. Of course, whether or not such a code is enforced is another question, which was discussed in the section on ethical sanctions. The concept of a code of ethics is precise; it is a set of specific statements indicating actions considered ethical (positive) and actions considered unethical (negative). Such statements are developed by the realistic application of general ethical standards to current situations and environment. For example, a consulting organization might adopt, as part of its ethical code, the statement that "no member consultant shall accept an assignment when there is any doubt about his qualifications to attempt the assignment," such statements representing a clear application of the golden rule, long-range utility, and general law standards.

A written code of ethics provides quick and clear-cut ethical criteria for day-to-day actions, as well as the determination of the ethicalness of such actions. A clear, specific code of ethics (or the lack thereof) patently demonstrates any organization's serious interest (or lack thereof) in a professional ethical posture.

The most critical, and difficult, part of ethical analysis is this *application* of general ethical standards in an attempt to develop specific norms for ethical action within an organization and to determine the true ethical quality of a particular action in a concrete situation. The most common errors in ethical analysis occur in this area of application:

> An organizational code of ethics is developed that is carelessly or deliberately vague and too general to apply.

> Ethical standards are applied to a specific issue or concrete case in which the factual situation is inadequately or inaccurately understood. For example, is it unethical for the consultant to accept a job when he has informed the client of some limitation in qualification and, despite this, the client asks him to "at least try"?

> In attempting to conduct intelligent ethical analysis, vague or no reference is made to any theoretical and systematic framework—most importantly to the broad ethical standards.

> No sanctions, or vague or unrealistic sanctions, are adopted for an ethical code. Sanctions, such as rules, policies, managerial control systems, and appropriate rewards for compliance and penalties for noncompliance, are essential to the enforcement of an ethical code.

In summary, a new age of instant information and public insistence on ethical behavior has transformed business ethics from an ideal condition to a reality, from a luxury to a practical necessity for the survival and success of organizations. The central instrument for making ethics operational and real in an organization is a written code of ethics which is specific, is both positive and negative in its ethical content, is based upon general ethical standards, and is enforceable by appropriate sanctions.

For Further Reading

Drucker, P. *The age of discontinuity: Guidelines to our changing society.* New York: Harper & Row, 1969.

Elbing, A. O., Jr., & Elbing, C. J. *The value issue of business.* New York: McGraw-Hill, 1967.

Ginzberg, E., Hiestad, D. L., & Reubens, B. G. *The pluralistic economy.* New York: McGraw-Hill, 1965.

Gorney, R. *The human agenda.* New York: Simon & Schuster, 1972.

Leys, J. A. *Ethics for policy decisions.* Englewood Cliffs, N.J.: Prentice-Hall, 1952.

Moore, W. E. *The conduct of the corporation.* New York: Random House, 1962.

Olafson, F. A. *Society, law, and morality.* Englewood Cliffs, N.J.: Prentice-Hall, 1961.

Reich, C. *The greening of America.* New York: Random House, 1970.

Segal, R. *The Americans: A conflict of creed and reality.* New York: Viking Press, 1969.

Steiner, G. A. (Ed.). *The changing business role in modern society.* Los Angeles: Graduate School of Management, U.C.L.A. Press, 1972.

Sutton, F. X., et al. *The American business creed.* Cambridge, Mass.: Harvard University Press, 1956.

Thompson, S. *Management creeds and philosophies.* New York: American Management Association, 1958.

Walton, S. D. *American business and its environment.* New York: Macmillan, 1966.

2
ETHICAL THEORIES IN BUSINESS

Frank Grogan wished he'd never heard of Icarus Aircraft, let alone JLP-23. Why had he been assigned to that project? After all, Icarus manufactured a whole fleet of executive aircraft that could keep a young engineer busy for years to come. Why JLP-23?

The irony, of course, was that Grogan first saw it as a rare opportunity to practice his specialty: aircraft fuselage and airfoil design. But ever since he'd become aware of some potentially dangerous wing-design specifications, the project had become a nightmare.

The whole thing was getting too sticky. Sometimes he wished he hadn't said anything, that he'd kept his mouth shut. But oh no, not him! Not getting any satisfaction below, he had to go right to the top, to President Wendell Kravits himself. Kravits's reaction baffled Grogan. What did Kravits think? Did he believe that one of his engineers knew no more about wing design than a kid assembling a model plane?

"Precipitate," that's what Kravits had termed his alarm, "precipitate." "Not that I don't commend your vigilant concern, Frank," Kravits had added, "but the danger you speak of could materialize under only the most extreme and unrealistic of conditions, conditions, in fact, more proper to military flying than to civilian."

"Maybe the old man was right," Grogan thought. Kravits certainly had a lot more experience than he had. Still, that didn't make Kravits an authority on wing specifications. No, Kravits was wrong. That was all there was to it. Maybe Kravits didn't believe it, but it was so. Given just the right conditions, the wing sections of the JLP-23 could separate from the fuselage.

Now Grogan had to decide whether to drop the whole thing or go beyond Kravits to the stockholders or perhaps to the press. More than anything else, Grogan wanted to do the right thing. But what was that?

In our opening chapter we said that one fact contributing to business's moral quandary is the absence of a decisive moral standard which could enable business people to make moral decisions. Grogan's problem illustrates this point. How will Grogan decide what to do? Where can he turn for help in charting a moral course, in deciding the right thing? In order to answer the question of whether there are any guidelines for making moral decisions in a business context, we must first determine whether there are any guidelines for making moral decisions generally. We must examine general ethical theories.

In this chapter, we'll discuss those ethical theories that have been most influential in the history of moral thought. We'll see that each theory sets forth principles that are useful in making moral decisions. We'll examine the strengths and weaknesses of these principles. Most important, we'll learn how the principles can be applied in the business context. In subsequent chapters we'll suggest how these moral theories might be used in specific business issues. We should point out, however, that it's unwise and incorrect to approach the use of these theories as a static process in which we crank in data and mechanically get an ethical answer. Rather, these theories are aids in the processes of inquiry prior to making a moral decision.

The moral theories we will consider can be divided into three groups: those that appeal exclusively to the consequences of an action in determining its morality; those that appeal to a single rule; and those that appeal to multiple rules. In moral philosophy, the theories that rely on a consideration of consequences are generally termed *teleological;* those relying on factors other than consequences (a single rule or multiple rules) *deontological.* But since the terms *consequential* and *nonconsequential* pinpoint the differences between these two broad classifications of moral theories, we'll use them.[1] Thus we have three groups of ethical theories to consider: (1) consequential, (2) single-rule nonconsequential, and (3) multiple-rule nonconsequential. Because of space limitations, we'll only outline each theory, hoping that this will be enough to facilitate its usage in subsequent chapters and in business.[2]

Consequential Theories

Traditionally, many theorists contend that the moral rightness of an action can be determined by looking at its consequences. If the consequences are good, the act is right; if bad, the act is wrong. Moralists who argue this way are called consequentialists. *When we speak of consequential theories, we mean theories that measure the morality of actions on the basis of their nonmoral consequences.* Consequentialists determine what's right by considering the ratio of good to evil that the action produces. The right act is the one that produces, will probably produce, or is intended to produce at least as great a ratio of good to evil as any other course. The wrong act is the one that does not.

When consequentialists evaluate the nonmoral consequences of an action, they consider what lies outside the realm of morality. For example, if Frank Grogan was a consequentialist, he would evaluate the nonmoral consequences

---

1.   See Jacques Thiroux, Ethics (Encino, Calif.: Glencoe Press, 1977), p. 21.

2.   For a full discussion of these theories, see Vincent Barry, Personal and Social Ethics (Belmont, Calif.: Wadsworth, 1978).

of his choices. Thus, if he were to speak out at a stockholders' session or go to the press, he would jeopardize the whole project. Certainly he would hurt subsequent sales of the aircraft and undoubtedly incur the wrath of his superiors. Grogan might even lose his job or be blackballed in the industry. On the other hand, he might be recognized as a conscientious worker. Consumer groups might applaud Grogan's sense of social responsibility. This could increase the image of the industry and of business in general. If Grogan chooses not to go public, the aircraft would be completed as proposed. It would probably sell very well and Icarus's stockholders would profit handsomely. Of course, if Grogan's right, the JLP-23 will pose a threat of injury or death because of its structural weaknesses. If an accident did occur, the company might be sued. Grogan himself might be held legally accountable.

We could go on introducing additional consequences. The point is: in determining the morality of an action, consequentialists evaluate its nonmoral consequences and eventually choose the course that would seem to produce the most good.

An obvious question arises in regard to the consequences. In deciding what to do, should Frank Grogan consider the consequences only for himself? Or should he consider them with respect to everyone involved? His decision hinges on two distinct concepts of consequential ethics: egoism and utilitarianism.

Egoism

Egoism, a consequential theory, contends that an act is moral when it promotes the individual's best long-term interests. In determining the morality of an action, egoists use their best long-term advantage to measure the action's goodness. If an action produces, will probably produce, or is intended to produce a greater ratio of good to evil for the individual in the long run than any other alternative, then that action is the right one to perform. Indeed, the individual must take that course.

Moralists often distinguish between two kinds of egoism: personal and impersonal. Personal egoists claim that they should pursue their own best long-term interests, but they don't say what others should do. Impersonal egoists, in contrast, claim that everyone should follow their own best long-term interests.

A number of misconceptions haunt egoism. One is that egoists do what they want, that they are of the "eat, drink, and be merry" school. This is just not so. Undergoing unpleasant, even painful experiences, is compatible with egoism providing it is consistent with advancing long-term happiness. Another misconception is that egoists necessarily eschew virtues like honesty, generosity, and self-sacrifice. Again, this isn't always so. Whatever is compatible with one's long-term best interests—including self-giving acts—is compatible with egoism. A final misconception is that all egoists are exponents of hedonism, the view that only pleasure is good in itself and worth seeking. True, some egoists are hedonistic, as was the ancient Greek philosopher Epicurus (341-270 B.C.). But other egoists identify the good with knowledge, power, rational self-interest, and with what is known in modern psychology as self-actualization. The fact is that ethical egoists may hold any theory of what's good and what's bad.

Having gained some insight into what egoism is and involves, we should now attempt to put it in the business context. Specifically, does egoism have any merits that recommend it as an ethical theory to facilitate moral decision making in business?

EGOISM IN THE BUSINESS CONTEXT.   Two features in particular make ethical egoism an attractive moral theory in the business context.

First, egoism provides a basis for formulating and testing policies. Regardless of size, all firms must, to some degree, take responsibility for regulating their business practices. Regulation usually takes the form of directives, guidelines, explicit policies, and codes of conduct. The purpose of such injunctions is clear: to ease individual decision making by discouraging certain kinds of actions and encouraging others. But on what grounds are actions to be evaluated?

Egoism provides an answer. A policy is legitimate when it promotes the best long-term interests of the firm. Put another way, a good policy advances the self-interests of the company to a greater degree than any other alternative would. To test the efficacy of existing policies, then, one need only show whether it's advancing or retarding the firm's best interests. For example, suppose corporate leaders were debating whether or not to formulate a policy about environmental pollution. Whether to have such a policy, as well as its contents, would be determined by appealing to the best long-term interests of the firm. In brief, egoism facilitates the process of formulating and testing business policies, decisions, and actions.

Second, egoism provides moral decision making in business the flexibility it needs. Egoism does not acknowledge any action, such as truth telling, as always being the right action. On the contrary, all actions and rules for actions must be evaluated in terms of best long-term interests. As a result, egoism allows a firm to sculpt codes of conduct to suit the complexities that characterize its business dealings. It allows them to say—if they choose to—that in some instances concealing facts about products is right, in other circumstances it's wrong; in some cases bribery is right, in other situations it's wrong. Furthermore, this flexibility is achieved without arbitrariness, for the principle of best long-term self-interests serves as the ruling standard.

Although egoism exhibits these two strengths, it also reveals decided weaknesses in theory and in the business context, which we should be aware of before wholeheartedly endorsing it as a solid ethical theory for business.

WEAKNESSES IN ETHICAL EGOISM.   *First, ethical egoism ignores blatant wrongs.* By reducing everything to the standard of the best long-term self-interests, ethical egoism would take no stand on principle against even the most outrageous business practices. In egoism, discrimination in the work place on the basis of race or sex, distribution of unsafe products, pollution of the environment, and all such actions are morally neutral until the litmus test of self-interest is applied.

Second, ethical egoism is incompatible with the nature and role of business. As we've already indicated, business is part of a social system, part of a combination of interrelated parts functioning as a whole and relating to people. Like any other system, (business receives important input from its environment,) which it then processes and relates to the environment in the form of output. Because of this reciprocal arrangement, it's inadvisable, if at all possible, for business to operate egoistically.

Third, egoism cannot resolve conflicts of egoistic interests. To grasp the implications of this weakness, suppose that two people, Smith and Brown, are competing for a promotion within a firm. Presumably it would be in both their best interests to get the job, but only one can. Ethical egoism would have both do whatever was necessary to secure the job. In short, Smith ought to dispose of Brown by whatever means, and Brown ought to do the same with Smith.

But what Smith is supposed to do is incompatible with what Brown is supposed to do. Apparently there are two opposing ethical obligations here. Are both right? Egoists might insist that egoism is not intended to arbitrate ethical conflicts. Nevertheless, a moral code must at least help do that, certainly in business where conflicts arise all the time. Any moral code, by definition, is supposed to tell us how we ought to act. If egoism can't, how useful is it?

Fourth, egoism introduces inconsistency into moral counsel. An apparent related weakness arises when we suppose that Smith goes to personnel director Jones for advice on the matter. Jones advises Smith to do everything he can to dispose of Brown. A few minutes later, Brown seeks Jones's counsel, whereupon Jones tells him to do all he can to dispose of Smith. Here Jones is recommending as right two conflicting courses of action.

Finally, egoism undermines the moral point of view. Still another objection to egoism is that it does not allow a person to consider a moral dilemma in a dispassionate, impartial way—from what is called the moral point of view. The moral point of view is a necessary part of moral decision making. *By the moral point of view, we mean the attitude of a person who sees, or attempts to see, all sides of an issue without being committed to the interests of a particular individual or group.* If we accept the legitimacy of the moral point of view, we must look for it in any proposed ethical theory. But ethical egoism does not allow for the moral point of view. The judgments of ethical egoists will always be colored by their own self-interests. Thus if personnel director Jones is an ethical egoist, he can't advise either Smith or Brown in any but a self-serving way. Likewise, if Frank Grogan is an egoist, he can't ask what a disinterested third party would do. The question contradicts ethical egoism.

Utilitarianism

Whereas egoism maintains that promotion of one's own best long-term interests should be the standard of morality, utilitarianism—another consequential theory—emphasizes the best interests of everyone concerned, the general good. *Specifically, utilitarianism is the consequential doctrine that asserts we should always act so as to produce the greatest ratio of good to evil for everyone.*

As philosophy professor Thomas McPherson has indicated, utilitarianism has a special interest for students of society because it is the philosophy underlying the modern welfare state. As originally formulated by notable reformers

Jeremy Bentham (1748–1832) and John Stuart Mill (1806–1873), utilitarianism has been associated with reform or social improvement.[3]

The term *utilitarianism* usually refers to pleasure or hedonistic utilitarianism, the doctrine that pleasure or happiness is the ultimate good thing, and conduciveness to human happiness is the criterion for judging the rightness of an action. But utilitarians can differ on this point. Modern utilitarians believe that things other than happiness have intrinsic worth (for example, knowledge, power, beauty, and moral qualities). Since our primary consideration is classical utilitarianism, we will use *itrinsic good* to mean happiness. Nevertheless, what we say about classical utilitarianism applies equally to modern utilitarianism, with, of course, the qualification on what counts as the good.

Whatever their position on what's good, utilitarians agree on a number of points. First, in referring to the "greatest possible ratio of good to evil," they don't indicate a preference for immediate or remote good. The emphasis is on greatest. Second, all utilitarians agree that in evaluating for the greatest possible good, we must consider unhappiness as well as happiness. Thus if it were possible to calculate accurately pleasure and pain (as Bentham proposed to do in devising his "hedonistic calculus" or six criteria for evaluating the goodness and badness of our actions), we would subtract the total unhappiness from the total happiness our action would produce. The result would accurately measure the action's worth. Finally, when choosing between two actions, utilitarians agree that we should choose the one that produces the greatest net happiness.

While both the original and modern utilitarians agree on the principle of utility—that is, the greatest happiness (good) for the greatest number—they disagree on how this principle should be applied. Some utilitarians would apply it to the act itself; others, to the rule the act falls under. Thus there are two distinct schools of utilitarian thought—act and rule.

Act utilitarianism maintains that the right act is the one that produces the greatest ratio of good to evil for all concerned. In performing an action we must ask ourselves what the consequences of this particular act in this particular situation will be for all concerned. If the consequences produce more general good than those of any other alternative, then that action is the right one and the one we should perform. In the twentieth century, act utilitarianism has found a novel twist in what is termed situational ethics. Before considering this, however, let's say a little more about act utilitarianism and distinguish it from rule utilitarianism.

Were Frank Grogan an act utilitarian, he would consider the consequences of the alternatives facing him not only for himself but for the firm, the aircraft industry, business generally, fellow employees, and society at large. He would let an evaluation of all the consequences to all the parties suggest the course of his action.

But what about actions that, in themselves, seem questionable? Suppose, for example, that Grogan's calculations led him to believe that the greatest good would be served by his not doing anything further, despite his conviction that faulty wing design could, under just the right conditions, kill someone. Or

3. *Thomas McPherson,* Social Philosophy *(London: Van Nostrand Reinheld Company, 1970), p. 41.*

suppose that a used-car dealer sets back the odometer on a car, not really to deceive or defraud but to get a quick sale. The dealer knows that the car's in good shape, and the odometer reading played no part in setting the sticker price, which, in fact, is highly competitive. And there is no question that whoever buys the car is getting an exceptionally good deal. In short, it is more to everyone's advantage that the car be sold rather than sit on the lot.

Although act utilitarians might agree that under such circumstances Grogan would be justified in remaining quiet and the car dealer in setting back the odometer, not all utilitarians would concur. These other utilitarians might say that Grogan and the dealer acted wrongly. In their evaluation, they might appeal not to the action itself but to the rule under which the action falls.

According to rule utilitarianism, we should not consider the consequences of a particular action but rather the rule under which the action falls. Rule utilitarians still appeal to the greatest good for the greatest number but on the basis of rules, not acts. *In effect, rule utilitarians ask us to determine the worth of the rule under which an action falls. If keeping the rule produces more total good than breaking it, we should keep it.* In the case of the used-car dealer, rule utilitarians might argue that the rule which enjoins dealers to represent a car's mileage accurately is a good one because it generally produces a greater ratio of good to evil than breaking such a rule. Reasoning thus, they might call the dealer's action immoral.

What, if anything, do rule and act utilitarianism offer in the way of moral directives for business?

UTILITARIANISM IN THE BUSINESS CONTEXT. There are several features about utilitarianism that make it appealing as a standard for moral decisions in business.

First, like egoism, utilitarianism provides a basis for formulating and testing policies. By utilitarian standards, a business policy, decision, or action is good if it promotes the general welfare more than any other alternative. To show that a policy is wrong (or needs modification) requires only that it does not promote the principle of utility as well as some alternative would. In short, utilitarians do not ask us to accept rules, policies, or principles blindly. On the contrary, they not only require us to test the worth of these concepts but also indicate the testing standards.

Second, utilitarianism provides an objective way of resolving conflicts of self-interests. This feature of utilitarianism dramatically contrasts with egoism, which seemed incapable of resolving conflicts of self-interest not only between firms but also between individuals and firms, and individuals and individuals. By proposing a standard outside self-interests, utilitarianism greatly minimizes and may actually eliminate such disputes. Thus, individuals within firms make moral decisions and evaluate their actions by appealing to a uniform standard: the general good.

Third, utilitarianism recognizes the four primary claimant groups in business activity: owners, employees, customers, and society. This feature follows from utilitarianism's concern with the greatest happiness for the greatest number of people. As we saw earlier, business activity inevitably involves complex transactions that involve multiple interests. This is especially true since today's economy is characterized by interdependent economic and social interests. An ethical standard that does not address this network of interdependency seems woefully lacking. This principle of utility, however, broadens the scope of business decisions, policies, and actions. Indeed, it requires that people in business make moral decisions against the background of collective interest.

Fourth, like egoism, utilitarianism provides the latitude in moral decision making that business seems to need. By recognizing no actions of a general kind as inherently good or bad, both schools of utilitarianism allow business people to tailor policies and make personal decisions to suit the complexities of the situation. This facet of utilitarianism provides business the moral elasticity it needs to make realistic judgments.

Despite the strengths of utilitarianism, this moral theory exhibits several limitations which we should consider before unequivocally endorsing it.

WEAKNESSES OF UTILITARIANISM. *First, both act and rule utilitarianism ignore actions that appear to be wrong in themselves.* We've already seen how act utilitarianism may approve of actions which, in themselves, seem questionable. But the same criticism (which we initially raised of egoism) also applies to rule utilitarianism. Like act utilitarianism, rule utilitarianism focuses on the ends of an action, not the means employed to achieve the end. In ethics, *ends* refers to the consequences or results of an action, whereas *means* refers to the action itself, its nature and characteristics. In effect, for all utilitarians, the end justifies the means. To them, no action or rule, or characteristic of either, is in itself objectionable. It's only objectionable insofar as it leads to a lesser ratio of good than evil. Thus intentionally deceiving the consuming public or willfully falsifying bills for work rendered is not in and of itself wrong. Such an action could be good. It all depends on the total consequences of the action.

Second, the principle of utility may come into conflict with that of justice. Critics of utilitarianism have pointed out that mere increase in total happiness is not of itself good. On the contrary, the distribution of happiness is a further and most important question. Surely, it's not unreasonable to argue for a state of affairs in which fewer people—the most deserving—were happy instead of one in which more people—the most undeserving—were happy.[4] In fact, this apparent weakness in utilitarianism relates to the preceding one; in both cases utilitarians seem to associate justice with efficiency rather than fair play. In effect, what is just is determined by a calculation of total benefit rather than by appeal to merit and desert. If action A is efficient in the sense that it's calculated to produce more total good than any other alternative, then it's thereby just. Critics dispute this concept of justice, which seems implied in the traditional doctrine of utilitarianism.

Third, it is very difficult to formulate satisfactory rules. With respect to rule utilitarianism, consider a rule that might govern the use of privileged information for personal gain. The rule might read: "Never use privileged information for personal gain." This rule sounds fine, but we can imagine circumstances that would strain its efficacy. Suppose, for example, that Stan Fremont, board

4. *Ibid., p. 43*

member of Johnson Tools, has just learned that his company is about to an-
nounce a two-for-one stock split and an increase in dividends. Fremont is a
father of four young children and is facing personal bankruptcy. A quick gain of
a few thousand dollars could rescue him, at least temporarily, from the jaws of
financial and, perhaps, social ruin. He has no intention of feathering his own
financial nest, merely surviving. He has never done anything like this before,
deplores even the thought of it now, and vows never to do it again. In deciding
to rescue himself and his family, Fremont reasons that the harm he'll do them by
not using the information is qualitatively greater than the harm he'd do stockholders and the general public by using it. Is Fremont morally wrong if he acts
on the privileged information? True, he violated the rule governing privileged
information. But why couldn't we devise another rule? This one would read:
"Never use privileged information for personal gain *unless you face bankruptcy*."
The point is that rules are often difficult to formulate. Frequently we make rules
so general that they are unrealistic. At other times, rules may be so narrow that
they have only pinpoint application. And, as in our example, very often we face
the problem of deciding which of two similar but significantly different rules
produces the more desirable results.

Having broadly sketched and evaluated rule and act utilitarianism, let's
examine a widespread moral view rooted in act utilitarianism that is called situational ethics.

Situational Ethics

In our time, act utilitarianism has provided the basis for a view proposed by
a Christian moralist named Joseph Fletcher, who is principally identified with
the ethical position termed situational[5] ethics.

Fletcher views situational ethics as one of three primary avenues for making
moral decisions. The other two are the *legalistic*, which contends that moral rules
are absolute laws that must always be obeyed; and the *antinomian* or existential,
which contends that no guidelines exist, that each situation is unique and requires a new decision. According to Fletcher, legalism is overly directive and
antinomianism unacceptably nondirective. Both are unworkable. As an alternative, Fletcher proposes situational ethics, which falls somewhere between these
two extremes but is closer to antinomianism than to legalism.

Like utilitarians, Fletcher is very much concerned with the consequences of
actions. But rather than acting in a way that produces the greatest happiness for
the greatest number, Fletcher advocates acting in a way that produces the most
Christian love, that is, the greatest amount of love fulfillment and benevolence.
Situational ethics, then, contends that the moral action is the one that produces the
greatest amount of Christian love of all the alternatives available.

For Fletcher, rules and principles are valid only if they serve love in a specific
situation. Therefore it's crucial when making moral decisions to be fully ac-
quainted with all the facts surrounding the case, as well as the probable
consequences that would attend each possible alternative. In this Fletcher is

5. *Interchangeable with the term situation.*

decidedly consequential, in fact, utilitarian. But he also argues that after all calculation has been completed, one must choose the act that will best serve love as it is defined by Christian tradition in the concept of *agape* (AH-gah-pay).

Christianity teaches that *agape* is unselfish love, epitomized by Jesus, who made the ultimate sacrifice for love of humankind. Agape is a principle expressing the type of actions that Christians are to regard as good. It's not something we are or have; it's something we do. Agape is a purpose, a preference, a disposition; it's an attitude, a way of relating to persons and of treating them. In a word, agape is loving concern, characterized by a love for God and neighbor.

Fletcher contends that agape is the one unexceptionable principle. In this he distinguishes himself from consequentialists generally and utilitarians particularly. For Fletcher everything but agape is valid only if it serves love in any situation. That includes the proscriptions of the Ten Commandments and the ideals of the Sermon on the Mount. According to Fletcher these should be viewed as cautious generalizations, not as absolutely binding moral principles. In this respect, Fletcher would agree with Martin Luther's statement that ". . . when the law impels one against love, it ceases and should no longer be a law. But where no obstacle is in the way, the keeping of the law is a proof of love, which lies hidden in the heart. Therefore you have need of the law, that love may be manifested; but if it cannot be kept without injury to the neighbor, God wants us to suspend and ignore the law."[6] In effect, Fletcher's position is that traditional Christian moral laws are fine and even obligatory but only if they serve love. When they don't, we can—we must—break them.

It's easy to misconstrue Fletcher. His agape principle is not a limp standard that can be used to justify anything. On the contrary, the hallmarks of agape are prudence and careful evaluation, characterized by a willing of the neighbor's good. As such, justice is an integral part of Fletcher's doctrine. But Fletcher doesn't seem to associate justice with the efficiency espoused by utilitarians. Rather, he sees justice as giving people their due. When we truly love, we must be practicing justice. If we separate justice from love, Fletcher claims that we make love sentimental. "*Agape* is what is due to all others," he writes, "justice is nothing other than love working out its problems."[7]

Fletcher believes that in formulating social policies, the Christian should join with the utilitarian in trying to produce the greatest good for the greatest number, or as he calls it, "the greatest amount of neighbor welfare for the largest number of neighbors possible." Thus, the hedonistic calculus of utilitarianism becomes for Fletcher the "agape calculus."[8]

In sum, for Fletcher nothing is good in itself except love, taken to mean Christian love, or agape. Love becomes the standard of moral decision making. It is identical with justice, justice being love distributed. We love when we will the good of our neighbor. Love's decisions are determined by particular situations, nothing but the end ever justifying the means.[9]

6. *Martin Luther,* Works, *ed. J. N. Linker (St. Louis: Luther House, 1905), 5:175.*

7. *Joseph Fletcher,* Situation Ethics: The New Morality *(Philadelphia: Westminster Press, 1966), p. 95.*

8. *Luther Binkley,* Conflict of Ideals *(New York: Van Nostrand, 1969), p. 265.*

9. *Ibid., p. 254.*

SITUATIONAL ETHICS IN THE BUSINESS CONTEXT.   There are at least a couple of features about situational ethics to recommend it as a standard for moral decisions in business.

First, situational ethics humanizes business decisions. By focusing on loving concern through the prism of justice, Joseph Fletcher brings to business a much needed emphasis on the primacy of individuals and their welfare. Too often, especially under strictly utilitarian doctrines, the centrality of human beings in business decisions can be lost. Homage can be paid more to computer printouts than to genuine human need. In contrast, Fletcher's situational ethics decisively restores the human dimension to business decisions with its emphasis on "willing of the neighbor's good."

Second, in rejecting moral legalism, situational ethics unmasks what is business's chief method of avoiding moral responsibility. Implicit in situationalism's rejection of moral legalism seems to be a concern about individuals' avoiding moral accountability. Because legalism dictates moral decisions, individuals really needn't grapple with them. At the same time, legalism leaves individuals with the impression that the law, whether civil or moral, represents the extent of their moral obligations. In effect, then, legalism undermines moral accountability by removing moral decision making from individual control. All the individual must do is conform with some moral law. We've already noted this tendency in business and cautioned against it. Situational ethics, in rejecting legalism, seems to energize the whole concept of moral accountability in business.

Despite its strengths, situational ethics is not without flaws. Let's consider them.

WEAKNESSES OF SITUATIONAL ETHICS.   *First, Fletcher's situational ethics is not a definite decision procedure.* In illustrating how love's decisions are determined by particular situations, Fletcher cites the example of a young woman who is asked by an American intelligence agency to use sex to blackmail an enemy spy. The problem is whether she should value her chastity more than patriotism and service to her country. Fletcher's answer is no.

But why not? Why couldn't she appeal to the same patriotic motives to preserve her chastity? She might reason that her country should not exploit a person sexually, whatever the reason. She might feel that it's high time to put government agencies on notice that information gathering is not a blanket justification for demanding any kind of behavior. In other words, she might as easily interpret her refusal to use her sex as bait as being more patriotic and rendering a greater service to her country than her consent. In short, she might see her refusal as the most loving thing to do. That the same motives could produce different behavior suggests a problem with Fletcher's situational ethics: as a decision-making procedure, it lacks definiteness.

Second, Fletcher actually espouses the antinomianism that he rejects. To understand fully this objection to situational ethics, we must distinguish between two kinds of rules: summary and general. *A summary rule is one which contends that following the practice advocated or avoiding the practice prohibited is generally the best way of acting.* Summary rules might be: "Telling the truth is *generally* love fulfilling" or "Paying your debts is *generally* love fulfilling." Summary rules clearly allow for exceptions. General rules, on the other hand, do not. *A general rule is one which contends that you must always follow the practice advocated and avoid the one prohibited.* Thus, "Telling the truth is *always* love fulfilling" and "Paying your debts is *always* love fulfilling."

Now it seems that Fletcher must deny the existence of general rules lest he fall into the legalism he condemns. If, on the other hand, he espouses summary rules, then he leaves individuals to their own devices in determining when the interests of loving concern transcend the summary rule. Of course, should he deny summary as well as general rules, then he would be advocating the antinomian or existentialist position, which contends that no guidelines exist, that each situation is unique and requires a new decision. The fact is that in his situational ethics Fletcher does express rules: "No unwanted and unintended baby should ever be born"; "Exploiting persons is always wrong"; "Sex which does not have love as its partner, its senior partner, is wrong." Presuming these are summary rules, under what conditions does loving concern allow one to transcend these rules? We could ask the same question concerning summary rules in a business context: "Intentionally misleading the consumer is wrong"; "Racial and sexual discrimination in employment practices is wrong"; "Using privileged information for personal gain is wrong." If these aren't general rules, under what conditions may an individual violate them?

Single-Rule Nonconsequential Theories

Whereas consequential theories argue that we should consider the consequences alone in evaluating the morality of an action, nonconsequential theories contend that we should consider other factors. Some nonconsequentialists have even argued that we should not consider consequences at all. One such moralist was Immanuel Kant, who proposed a single rule to determine the morality of actions. Before considering Kant's thought, we should examine another single-rule nonconsequential theory, one that's found considerable acceptance in business: the Golden Rule.

Golden Rule

Studies indicate that the vast majority of business managers propose the Golden Rule as the most important guide for ethical behavior in business. The Golden Rule has existed in some form throughout the major religions of the world. Indeed, it can be detected in some form in nonreligious ethics as well.

In our culture, the Golden Rule is most commonly interpreted as, "Do unto others as you'd have them do unto you." *It commands us to treat others the way we would want to be treated.* If you want to be treated fairly, treat others fairly; if you want to be told the truth, tell others the truth; if you want your privacy respected, respect the privacy of others.

The core of the Golden Rule is impartiality, the doctrine that you should never make an exception of yourself. Do not do to others what you are unwilling to have them do to you. Given our Judaeo-Christian backgrounds, it is understandable why this principle plays such a prominent role in personal and business ethics.

GOLDEN RULE IN THE BUSINESS CONTEXT.   Even as superficial an examination of the Golden Rule as we've presented indicates several features about it that make it more attractive than teleological theories.

First, the Golden Rule personalizes business relations. It's difficult to conceive of a directive for better regulating our dealings with other people than one that asks us to treat them as we would want them to treat us. What fairer standard exists for regulating human relationships in business, especially within complex modern organizational settings? As practiced in business, the Golden Rule personalizes what otherwise are highly impersonal decisions based almost exclusively on a cost-benefit analysis. By enjoining business people to put themselves in the other person's shoes, the Golden Rule returns to business that personal human element that many business leaders and academic scholars continue to note as the missing ingredient in today's business ethos.

Second, the Golden Rule brings fairness-ethics into business. So many moral problems in business today involve the question of fairness. Pricing, contracts, competitive practices, personnel management, all raise questions of fair treatment and cannot be resolved by the efficiency concept of, say, utilitarianism. What's needed is a concept of fairness grounded not in efficiency but in a recognition of the inherent worth of human beings and a respect for their rights. By charging us to treat others as we would want to be treated, the Golden Rule provides this emphasis.

Although these two features may give the Golden Rule advantages over strict consequential theories, the Golden Rule still evidences weaknesses that make its usefulness in the work place questionable.

WEAKNESSES OF THE GOLDEN RULE.   *First, the Golden Rule fails to recognize that inequalities often exist between the parties in an exchange situation.* Do you think that the Golden Rule is an adequate moral guide in the Grogan case? If yes, Grogan would ask himself if he were in the position of Kravits, would he want an employee going public with the information? The answer is undoubtedly no. But what if Grogan asks, "If I were a potential purchaser of the JLP, would I want an Icarus employee to reveal publicly such a serious defect?" Unquestionably, the answer is yes. Even if the Golden Rule implies that theoretically only one party need object to make an action wrong, it still must address the problem that's evident here. Simply put, parties in an exchange are rarely equal. This is particularly true in business, where parties to an exchange are seldom equally capable in terms of organizational power they command. Quite likely if Grogan were in Kravits's shoes, he wouldn't want his engineer spouting off to the press. But all that proves is that Grogan and Kravits represent unequal quantities with different and conflicting interests. In brief, when applying the Golden Rule to business decisions, people often overlook the fact that the "others" in the exchange situation frequently are in no position to return the behavior.

Second, the Golden Rule falsely assumes that we can know how others actually feel and think. To illustrate this objection, consider the case of computer expert Maria Ellis, new to a firm, wondering whether to include certain critical information in her first report to a superior. Maria fears that it might jeopardize her position. Not only is she, like Grogan, on an uneven organizational level with her superior, but now she's asked to imagine how that person thinks and feels. That is very difficult to do. Maybe her superior will become angry and hold it against her; maybe the person will consider her an upstart who's trying to rock the organizational boat. On the other hand, the superior may commend her work and recognize her conscientiousness. Or possibly the superior may show no feeling one way or the other. The point is that it's very hard to determine how someone will feel and think. This problem is further compounded by the multitude of others who are often involved in business decisions: owners, employees, customers, society. Can we know what each of these people will feel and think?

Kant's Categorical Imperative

One of the most influential thinkers in the history of philosophy was the eighteenth-century German philosopher Immanuel Kant (1724–1804). Kant's ethical theory stands as the premiere illustration of a purely deontological theory, one that attempts to exclude a consideration of consequences in moral decision making. To understand Kant's thought as expressed in his important *Foundations of the Metaphysics of Morals,* it is essential to grasp his idea of a good will.[10]

Kant believed that nothing was good in itself except a good will. Contrast this with the utilitarian assertion that only happiness is good in itself. But don't misunderstand Kant. He is not saying that numerous facets of the human personality are not good and desirable, such as intelligence, sensitivity, talent, and so on. But their goodness resides in the will that makes use of them.

By will *Kant meant the uniquely human capacity to act according to the concept of law, that is, principles.* It's this emphasis on will or intention that decisively sets Kant apart from consequential thinkers. For Kant these laws or principles operate in nature. A good will is one that acts in accordance with nature's law.

In estimating the total worth of our actions, Kant believed that a good will took precedence over all else. Contained in a good will is the concept of duty. Only when we act from duty does our action have moral worth. When we act only out of feeling, inclination, or intended results, our actions—though otherwise identical with ones that spring from a sense of duty—have no true moral worth.

To illustrate, merchants have a duty not to shortchange their customers. But simply because merchants don't shortchange customers, need we say that they're acting from a good will? They may be acting from an inclination to promote business or to avoid legal entanglement. Thus they would be acting in accordance with duty but not *from* duty. In other words, their apparently noble gesture happens to coincide with duty. But they have not willed the action from a sense of duty to be fair and honest. Their action, therefore, would not have true moral worth. For Kant, actions have true moral worth only when they spring from a recognition of a duty and a choice to discharge it.

Still we're left wondering what duties we have and how do we know them.

10. *Immanuel Kant,* Foundations of the Metaphysics of Morals, *translated by Lewis White (New York: Bobbs-Merrill, 1959).*

Let's suppose that Frank Grogan truly wishes to act from duty. What is his duty? How can he discover it?

Kant believed that through reason alone we could arrive at a moral law, based not on any religious injunctions like the Golden Rule, nor on empirical evidence relating to similar situations, or to consequences as in utilitarianism. Just as we know, seemingly through reason alone, that a triangle has three sides and that no triangle is a circle, so by the same kind of reasoning Kant believed that we could arrive at absolute moral truths.

For Kant, an absolute moral truth had to be logically consistent, that is, free from internal contradiction. To say, for example, that a triangle has four sides or that a square is a circle is to state a contradiction. Kant aimed to ensure that his absolute moral law would be free from such contradictions. If he could formulate such a rule, he contended, it would oblige everyone without exception to follow it. Kant believed that he formulated such a logically consistent rule in his categorical imperative.

In Kant's view there was just one command or imperative that was categorical, that is, one which presented an action as of itself necessary, regardless of any other considerations. He argued that from this one categorical imperative, this universalizable command, we could derive all commands of duty. *Simply stated, Kant's categorical imperative says that we should act in such a way that we could wish the maxim of our action to become a universal law.*

By *maxim*, Kant means the subjective principle of an action, the principle that people in effect formulate in determining their conduct. For example, suppose building contractor John Martin promises to install a sprinkling system in a project but is willing to break that promise if it suits his purposes. His maxim can be expressed: "I'll make promises that I'll break whenever keeping them no longer suits my purposes." This is the subjective principle, the maxim, that directs his action. Kant insisted that the morality of any maxim depends on whether we can wish it to become a universal law. Could Martin's maxim be universally acted upon?

That depends on whether the maxim as law would involve a logical contradiction. In fact, the maxim "I'll make promises that I'll break whenever keeping them no longer suits my purposes" could not be universally acted upon because it involves a contradiction of will. On the one hand, Martin's willing that it be possible to make promises and have them honored. On the other, if everyone intended to break promises when they desired to, then promises couldn't be honored in the first place. In other words, it's in the nature of promises that they be believed. A law that allowed promise breaking would contradict the very nature of a promise. This is true even if desirable consequences resulted from breaking the promise.

According to Kant, there's only one categorical imperative. But it can be stated in different ways so as to reveal a special aspect of it. One very important formulation of the categorical imperative is to always act so as to treat yourself and other individuals as ends in yourselves, and never as means to ends. This formulation underscores Kant's belief that every rational creature has inherent worth. This worth doesn't result from any quality other than the sheer possession of rationality. Rational creatures possess what Kant termed an "autonomous, self-legislating will." In other words, they can evaluate their actions, make rules for themselves, and direct their conduct according to these self-imposed rules. For Kant, then, the human's intrinsic worth lies in this rationality.

KANT IN THE BUSINESS CONTEXT. Like egoism, utilitarianism, and situationalism, Kant's categorical imperative has application for business.

First, the categorical imperative takes the guess work out of moral decision making in business. Business people rightly complain that professional codes of conduct are often so vague as to be useless. Worse, these codes of conduct leave much up to individual interpretation, thus making of morality a kind of guessing game or at best an exercise in public relations. In contrast, Kant's ethics remove much of this uncertainty and subjectivity. To act morally is to act on principle. No matter what the consequences may be, some actions are always wrong. Lying is an example. Thus, no matter how much good may come from misrepresenting a product, such deliberate misrepresentation is always wrong. Wantonly injuring others again would be always wrong. Thus, no matter how much personal or professional suffering Grogan might cause in speaking out on the serious dangers in the JLP wing design, he has a duty to do all he can to ensure the safety of its potential flyers.

Second, Kant's ethics introduce a needed humanistic dimension into business decisions. We saw that one of the principle objections to egoism and utilitarianism is that they treated humans as means to ends. Kant's ethics clearly forbids this. As a result it brings to moral decisions in business a needed humanistic flavor. This is especially needed today in business situations where encroaching technology and computerization tend to dehumanize people under the guise of efficiency. Kant's ethics also put the emphasis of business decision making where it belongs: on individual persons. Business, after all, involves individuals working in concert to provide goods and services for other individuals. The primacy Kant gives the individual reflects this essential function of business.

Third, Kant's concept of duties implies the moral obligation to act from a respect for rights and a recognition of responsibilities. According to Kant, we act morally when we behave dutifully, that is, according to a concept of law. But the formulation of laws involves demarcating among entities—individuals and other individuals, individuals and groups, groups and groups. While the lines of demarcation must constantly be drawn anew, fundamental to any demarcation is a concept of rights and responsibilities. This process is as true of business relationships as it is of social ones. Indeed, it is particularly needed in business because part of business's moral quandary is its inability to define and assign rights and responsibilities. Subscribing to Kant's ethics would necessitate clearly defining and specifying rights and responsibilities and then following the moral imperative to act with respect to them.

Undoubtedly, Kant's thinking raises needed dimensions in business ethics. Nevertheless, as was true of the theories previously discussed, his categorical imperative is not without weaknesses.

WEAKNESSES OF KANT'S CATEGORICAL IMPERATIVE. *First, Kant's principles provide no clear way to resolve conflicts of duties.* A company and its members have a duty to maximize stockholders' profits. They also have a duty to help people in need. Suppose that a firm is in a position to render a public service. In the long run this service may increase stockholders' earnings, but there's no assurance. In fact, the expenditure seems strictly unredemptive. What should the firm do? Kant doesn't provide a decisive way to resolve a problem like this.

Second, there's no compelling reason that the prohibition against certain actions should hold without exception. Frequently critics of Kant question or reject his principle of universalization. Why, they ask, should prohibitions against actions such as lying, breaking promises, and injuring others hold without exception? That individuals should not make themselves exceptions to rules, they argue, does not mean that a rule itself has no exceptions.

Suppose, for example, we decide that lying is sometimes right, as in the cases of little white lies secretaries are expected to tell for their bosses' convenience and sometimes for the good of the firm. Universalizing this maxim, we might arrive at something like, "Never lie, except when more harm than good would result from telling the truth." Perhaps this rule could be refined, but the point remains that this rule seems just as capable of being universalized as one which reads, "Never lie." The phrase "except when more harm than good would result from telling the truth" can be viewed not as an exception, in which case it would contradict the rule, but as a qualification of the rule. Why, then, isn't a qualified rule just as good as an unqualified one? If a qualified rule is as good, then we needn't state rules in the simple, direct, unqualified manner Kant did. And, as a result, we'd provide moral decision making in business the flexibility it apparently needs.

Multiple-Rule Nonconsequential Theories

Unlike single-rule nonconsequential theories, some nonconsequential theories, while relying on factors other than consequences in determining the morality of an action, appeal not to one rule but to several. Among these theories are three that warrant special attention because of their acknowledged place in the history of moral philosophy and of their applicability to the business context. They are prima facie duties, the maximin principle of social justice, and the proportionality, or limited responsibility, theory.

Ross's Prima Facie Duties

A half century ago, the English philosopher William David Ross published *The Right and the Good,* in which he presented an ethical theory that can be viewed as an attempt to join aspects of utilitarianism with those of Kantianism.[11]

Although Ross dismisses the utilitarian belief that what makes an act right are consequences, he does not agree with Kant's absolute rules. Clearly Ross is a nonconsequentialist, but unlike Kant he believes that it is necessary to introduce consequences into moral decision making while insisting that consequences alone do not make an act right.

11. *William David Ross,* The Right and the Good *(Oxford: Clarendon Press, 1930).*

The linchpin of Ross's theory is his belief that there are duties or obligations which bind us morally. In any moral decision, we must weigh options with respect to the duties involved and from the alternatives determine the duty that is most obligatory. As Ross explains, an act may fall under a number of rules at once. For example, as in the Grogan case, a business person may have the duty to maximize stockholders' profits and, at the same time, be obliged to refrain from injuring people. Invariably in such cases, each act is accompanied by a number of motivational reasons which, in turn, appeal to a moral duty: to be faithful to a contract, to help someone, to render justice, to be loyal. Each of these moral duties provides grounds for doing a particular action, but no single one provides sufficient grounds. The problem lies in choosing the most obligatory duty. Before we can do this, we must know what duties we have. To know our duties we must first understand what Ross terms *prima facie duties.*

The term *prima facie* means "at first sight" or "on the surface." By *prima facie duties,* Ross means ones that at first sight dictate what we should do when other moral factors are not considered. Stated another way, prima facie duties are ones that generally obligate us, that is, ones that ordinarily impose a moral obligation but don't apply in a particular case because of additional circumstances. Specifically, Ross considers a prima facie duty to be the characteristic an act has in virtue of its being a certain kind, for example keeping a promise or telling the truth. A prima facie duty is one we recognize at first sight as being obligatory when all other things are equal and when there are no conflicting duties. Thus, prima facie duties must be distinguished from an actual duty, that is, what one actually ought to do in a given situation. An actual duty is what one should do after considering and weighing all the prima facie duties involved.

One question that arises at this point refers to prima facie duties. What are they? Ross answers this by citing six categories of prima facie duties.

1. *Duties of fidelity are those which rest on prior acts of our own.* Included under duties of fidelity would be the duty not to lie (which Ross views as implied in the act of conversation), the duty to remain faithful to contracts, the duty to keep promises, the duty to repair wrongful acts. Thus, Grogan has a duty of fidelity to honor the terms of his work contract, which includes maximizing the stockholders' profits.

2. *Duties of gratitude are those which rest on acts of other people toward the agent.* Ross argues that we are bound by obligations arising from relationships that exist between persons, such as those between friends or between relatives and those between employers and employees. For example, suppose personnel director Fran Jefferson must fill a job opening with one of two qualified applicants. One is a stranger, the other a loyal member of the firm who has repeatedly rendered the firm services at great personal cost. Jefferson has a duty of gratitude toward the loyal employee, and this should be an important factor in making the decision.

3. *Duties of justice are those that rest on the fact or possibility of distributing pleasure or happiness in a manner which is not in accordance with the merits of the people concerned.* Imagine giving a job to a nonqualified, incompetent young man

simply because he is the nephew of a company's vice-president. Clearly the young man does not deserve the job; others do. Justice is not being served.

4. *Duties of beneficence are those that rely on the fact that there are other people in the world whose virtue, intelligence, or happiness we can improve.* For example, board members of a firm can improve the happiness of the firm's pensionees by voting a cost of living increase in retirement funds. It's worth noting that society seems to be becoming increasingly aware of duties of beneficence as the concept of social responsibility broadens. Thus people both in and out of business argue that business is obliged to help fight crime, restore cities, relieve poverty, ease unemployment, and cure pollution because it is in a position to do so.

5. *Duties of self-improvement are those that rest on the fact that we can improve our own condition of virtue, intelligence, or happiness.* For example, suppose Susan Moore, who's paid handsomely by her firm, receives an offer that promises opportunities for personal growth and enrichment that her present job does not. The catch is that Moore must take the position immediately, thus not allowing her present employer time to train a replacement. Clearly a number of duties operate here, including fidelity and gratitude. At the same time, Moore has a pressing duty to improve herself. As you might imagine, insults to duties of self-improvement frequently arise in cases of talented, intelligent people who, through slothful indifference, fail to develop their potential.

6. *Duties of noninjury (nonmaleficence) are those that do not injure others.* Ross includes this obligation to contrast it with duties of beneficence. Although not injuring others incidentally means doing them good, Ross interprets the avoidance of injuring others as a more pressing duty than beneficence. Thus Grogan can likely effect more company good by repressing further critical comments than by expressing them. On the other hand, he risks injuring the innocent, a duty that would override the beneficence he owes the firm.

In summary, Ross presents six categories of prima facie duties. He doesn't claim that they represent a complete list of recognizable duties, but he does insist that these are duties we acknowledge and willingly accept without argument. In the case of two conflicting prima facie duties, Ross tells us to follow the more obligatory duty. Where more than two duties are involved, our actual duty is the one with the greatest amount of prima facie rightness over wrongness.

ROSS'S PRIMA FACIE DUTIES IN THE BUSINESS CONTEXT. There are two principal features about Ross's theory that make it useful in the business context.

First, Ross's list of duties can play an important role in the moral education of persons in and out of business. His list exhorts each person to ponder the prima facie duties to primary claimants and to set duties aside only when others take precedence. Ross's categories can find concrete expression and application in business terms. Thus we can speak of employers as having duties of noninjury which bind them to provide sufficient notice before dismissing an employee. Likewise we can speak of employees as having duties of fidelity which bind them to give an honest day's work for a day's pay. Likewise, we can view business's social responsibilities to attack the problem of minority unemployment as stemming from a duty of beneficence. In short, Ross's categories of duties provide a useful framework for ordering business's responsibilities to its primary claimants.

Second, Ross's ethics brings to business the utilitarian sensitivity to consequences without ignoring apparent duties of undeniable moral force. Recall that one of the advantages of utilitarianism was that it provided business with a certain amount of moral flexibility. Utilitarianism did not lock moral agents into actions that were in themselves considered right or wrong. Everything depended on the circumstances and the probable outcome of the action (or the rule). Such a flexibility seems especially appealing in the complex world of business. But at the same time, utilitarianism seems to overlook things that in themselves appear highly questionable: misrepresenting products, violating work contracts, ignoring social problems. Ross recognizes this problem. His ethics can suffer evident wrongs but only when more pressing duties are present. Ross allows for a healthful consideration of consequences, while remaining mindful of the means taken to effect the ends.

Despite these two attractive features, Ross's ethics remains controversial. Specifically, it suffers from two principal weaknesses.

WEAKNESSES OF ROSS'S PRIMA FACIE DUTIES. *First, people disagree about moral principles.* How do we know what prima facie duties we have to begin with? How do we know that we have an obligation to tell the truth, to improve ourselves, or not to injure others? Ross claims that these are self-evident truths to anyone of sufficient mental maturity who has given them enough attention. But what if people disagree with Ross's list of duties? Surely we disagree about the relative weight they deserve. Suppose that people didn't think they had an obligation to keep a promise, or honor a contract, or accurately represent a product in advertisements? Ross must say that such individuals lack "sufficient mental maturity" or that they didn't give the proposition "sufficient attention." But the question arises as to the nature of "sufficient mental maturity." We must also wonder when we've given "sufficient attention" to a moral statement. In Ross's view, people have attended sufficiently to a moral proposition when they recognize his list of duties. This argument appears to involve circular reasoning.

Second, it is difficult, if not impossible, to determine the relative weight and merit of conflicting duties. When faced with a situation that presents one or more conflicting prima facie duties, how do we determine what our actual duty is? In the case of two conflicting prima facie duties, the act is one's duty which is in accord with the more stringent prima facie obligation. In cases of more than two conflicting prima facie duties, the act is one's duty that has the greatest balance of prima facie rightness over prima facie wrongness. But without assigning weights to duties, how can we determine the "most stringent" obligation or "the greatest balance of prima facie rightness over prima facie wrongness?" This is not to belittle or minimize Ross's theory. The fact is that in numerous cases we face no particular difficulties about resolving conflicts of duties. Thus most people would probably agree that when faced with telling a harmless lie and saving someone from serious injury, we have a more pressing obligation to prevent the injury than to tell the truth. And often in cases where the choice doesn't appear as clear, thoughtful reflection underscores the efficacy of Ross's approach. But what about other cases when the actual duties are not as clear? Ultimately, it seems that Ross must be judged at best inconclusive about the relative priorities of duties.

Rawls's Maximin Principle of Justice

We have seen that consequentialists and nonconsequentialists are fundamentally at odds. Specifically utilitarianism suggests the greatest happiness principle as the standard of morality, which in theory seems to allow injustices. Kant and Ross, in contrast, make intention and characteristics of acts fundamental moral concerns and emphasize the intrinsic worth of human beings. In 1971 Harvard Professor of Philosophy John Rawls published *A Theory of Justice* in which he proposed a theory of justice that tries to use the strengths of consequential and nonconsequential ethics while avoiding their pitfalls. At the same time, Rawls hoped to offer a workable method for solving problems of social morality. Because his theory attempts to maximize the lot of those minimally advantaged, it's termed the *maximin principle*.

Central to Rawls's theory is the question of establishing principles of justice. What principles will serve as a basis for justice in society? In answering, Rawls asks us to imagine a "natural state," a hypothetical state of nature in which all persons are ignorant of their talents and socioeconomic conditions. He calls this the "original position." Rawls claims that in the original position, people share certain characteristics. The people are mutually self-interested; rational, that is, they more or less accurately know their interests; and similar in their needs, interests, and capacities. Given these assumptions Rawls then asks what people in the original position would be likely to formulate when asked to choose a fundamental principle of justice to be followed. He surmises that they would choose two principles to ensure justice: the liberty principle and the difference principle.

By the *liberty principle* Rawls means that people in the original position would expect each person participating in a practice or affected by it to have an equal right to the greatest amount of liberty that is compatible with a like liberty for all. And by the *difference principle* Rawls means that people in the original position would allow inequality only insofar as it serves each person's advantage and arises under conditions of equal opportunity.

Before examining these concepts further, we should mention that by *person* Rawls means not only particular human beings but also collective agencies. And by *practice* he means any form of activity that a system of rules specifies, such as offices, roles, rights, and duties. Now let's examine the heart of Rawls's theory: the principles of equal liberty and difference.

Equality means that all persons are to be treated the same. Specifically, by *equality* Rawls means the impartial and equitable administration and application of rules which define a practice. The equal liberty principle expresses this concept.

When Rawls terms equality "impartial," he's referring to the spirit of disinterestedness that should characterize the distribution of goods and evils, to the fact that no person should receive preferred consideration. When he speaks of "equitable administration," Rawls seems to mean that the distribution must be fair and just to begin with. Let's apply these two characteristics of equality to a concrete situation.

Suppose a firm draws up job specifications for a particular position. The equal liberty principle decrees that everybody be judged by these criteria. The rule would not be impartially administered if the firm made an exception for an applicant. Nor would it be equitably administered if it excluded candidates from consideration on non-job-related criteria, perhaps on grounds of color or sex. Remember that Rawls is defining liberty with reference to the pattern of rights, duties, powers, and liabilities established by a practice. In this case, anyone applying for the job has a right to expect equal treatment insofar as the job specifications will be applied and to expect that the distribution is fair and equal to begin with.

But Rawls's equal liberty principle expresses the idea of equality in another, more important way. An intrinsic part of all regulations is that they infringe on personal liberty. Suppose, for example, the job specifications in question call for a college education. Those persons lacking a college education therefore can't compete equally for the job. In his equal liberty principle, Rawls recognizes this inherent characteristic of all laws and other practices: by nature they encroach on the equal liberty of those subject to them. Thus when a bus company will not consider anyone older than thirty-five years for the position of bus driver, it infringes on the equal liberty of the many persons older than thirty-five who may not only wish to apply for such a job but, in fact, are capable of doing the work required. Some argue that justice would only require an equal liberty, that is, as long as everyone over thirty-five is denied consideration by the bus company, justice is being served. Or, as long as college education is required of everyone applying for a job, then such a requirement is just.

Rawls appears more philosophically perceptive on this point, however, than his opponents appear to be. He notes that if a more extensive liberty were possible for all without loss, damage, or conflict, then it would be irrational to settle upon a lesser liberty. In the bus company case, for example, an argument could be made for a more extensive liberty than is allowed by the thirty-five-year-old age cut-off. Indeed, such an argument partially has contributed to the extension of the mandatory retirement age, and in some cases (for example, California) to its abolition.

Crucial to any theory of social justice is the determination of when inequality is permissible. After all, a just society is not one in which all are equal, but one in which inequalities are justifiable. Rawls addresses this problem with his difference principle.

Rawls's difference principle defines what kinds of inequalities are permissible. It specifies under what conditions the equal liberty principle may be violated.

For Rawls, equality is not contingent. It doesn't depend on something else, such as on the greatest happiness for the most people, for its justification. For Rawls, equality is fundamental and self-justifying. This does not mean that equality can never be violated. It means that inequality is permissible only if in all likelihood the practice involving the inequality works to the advantage of every individual affected or to the advantage of the least well-off. In other words, Rawls arranges inequalities so that ideally they advantage all affected or at least those most in need. Suppose, for example, that the bus company establishes a minimum corrected vision level for all bus drivers. Although this works against those who can't reach the minimum, the standard can be justified by showing how such a rule works to the advantage of all concerned, even those excluded. (After all, they won't be in a position of risking their own safety or of having it risked by others.)

Although such a rationale may appear to be a case of the greatest happiness principle, it isn't. The difference principle, in fact, doesn't allow inequalities generally justified on utilitarian grounds, that is, on the grounds that the disadvantages of persons in one position are outweighed by the advantages of those in another. On the contrary, the difference principle allows inequality ideally only when it works to *everyone's* advantage. Thus the key point in the hypothetical example: even those excluded from consideration are advantaged by the inequality.

The fundamental difference, then, between utilitarianism and Rawls's theory of justice is in their concepts of justice. In utilitarianism, the concept of justice rests on some notion of efficiency. What is just is what produces the most happiness for everyone. Sometimes this ethic is apparent in business. Frequently it takes an egoist bent, as in the old slogan, "What's good for General Motors is good for the U.S.A." Thus, what's just is what's best for me. At other times it takes the form of what's best for the social good.

In contrast to these consequential concepts of justice, Rawls's is best described by his own word "reciprocity." Reciprocity is the principle that requires that a practice be such that all members who fall under it could and would accept it and be bound by it. It requires the possibility for mutual acknowledgment of principles by free people, having no authority over one another, that makes the idea of reciprocity fundamental to justice and fairness. Without this acknowledgment, Rawls claims, there can be no basis for a true community. Thus a fair business contract would be one in which all affected can and will accept it and be bound by it.

In effect, then, where there is conflict between his two principles, Rawls relies on his first principle of justice, the equal liberty principle. He insists that it is logically prior to the difference principle. In contrast, the utilitarian sees liberty as contingent on social productivity. In other words, liberty is desirable insofar as it produces the most happiness for the most people. Obviously, the utilitarian position does not allow the loss of liberty if the greatest number aren't served. But Rawls would argue that any position that even allows the possibility of the loss of equal liberty is unacceptable. As Rawls puts it, "Each person possesses an inviolability founded on justice that even the welfare of society as a whole cannot override. . . . Therefore . . . the rights secured by justice are not subject to political bargaining or to the calculus of social interests."[12]

Besides agreeing on these basic principles of justice, Rawls claims that people in the original position would also recognize "natural duties" that generate one's obligations to another. The duties that Rawls lists are identical with those noted in discussing Ross's prima facie duties. Moreover, Rawls acknowledges the need to rank these as being of higher and lower obligations, although he doesn't undertake this task, presumably because his primary concern is with justice in social institutions.

Finally, Rawls recognizes the legitimacy of paternalism. By *paternalism* he means that occasions arise when people are not in a position to make decisions for themselves, that others must make the decisions for them. In business decisions, for example, consumers still exercise little influence over the planning, manufacturing, and marketing of goods and services. Rawls's recognition of paternalism requires that those in a decision-making capacity introduce the concerns, interests, and values of those who will be affected by decisions but don't have any substantive input to make their feelings known.

Undoubtedly Rawls's theory of ethics brings to business ethics nuances that other theories do not. Several features in particular are worth noting.

RAWLS'S MAXIMIN PRINCIPLE IN THE BUSINESS CONTEXT.   *First, Rawls's principle of justice provides business with an inherent respect for individual persons.* Just as Kant's and Ross's ethical theories focus on the primacy of the individual, so does Rawls's. According to Rawls, it would never be right to exploit one group of people or even a single person for the benefit of others. The business implications of this are vast, touching on various aspects of personnel management, contracts, warranties, advertising, employee privacy, and literally a multitude of other business concerns. For example, employers who hire individuals without providing a complete listing of job specifications and duties, and advertisers who conceal significant facts about their products violate the basic liberties of individuals and the absolute respect for persons that the principles of justice require. A potential employee has a right to know precisely what's expected of him or her *before* being hired. Similarly consumers have the right to know precisely what may be unfavorable about the product they're about to buy. Lacking this, both groups operate in an atmosphere which is more constrained than if they had the information.

Second, Rawls outlines areas of broad social responsibility for business. We have noted Ross's listing of prima facie duties and pointed out how they can be applied in specific business situations. Similarly Rawls's concept of "natural duties" can be used to outline broad areas of social responsibility for business.

Third, Rawls's concept of paternalism requires business to consider the preferences of individuals and groups who cannot act for themselves. In general, Rawls's paternalism could find broad application in business. Although hardly the only area that suggests its consideration, consumer-related problems represent perhaps

---

12.   *John Rawls,* A Theory of Justice *(Cambridge, Mass.: Harvard University Press, 1971), p. 4.*

the most graphic. From the earliest design stages of a product through production to marketing and retailing, consumers have relatively little input in the manufacture of a product. Yet consumers are the ones who will buy and use the product. So consumer views should be represented. Rawls's concept of paternalism could be extended to fill this need by morally obliging business people to collect and analyze consumer input and subsequently act on it in place of consumers. The same principle can be applied to other broad areas of social responsibility.

In sum, Rawls's maximin principle infuses needed life into the investigation of business ethics. It provides a justification for business involvement in numerous social issues and problems and provides a broad outline of areas for involvement. At the same time, Rawls's principle has several weaknesses that make it a most controversial theory of justice.

WEAKNESSES OF RAWLS'S MAXIMIN PRINCIPLE.   Since its formulation in 1971, Rawls's maximin principle has been the center of a highly technical philosophical debate. At this point it's impossible to isolate objections that all critics would share. But three criticisms recur often enough to bear mentioning.

First, Rawls's theory is based on several questionable assumptions. Recall that according to Rawls, when we don the veil of ignorance we are mutually self-interested, that is, we establish practices normally on the basis of self-advantage. But this is so only because Rawls assumes that humans would be rational. When Rawls describes people as rational, he implies a great many things that seem questionable: (a) that we more or less know our own interests, (b) that we can trace the likely consequences of one course over another and resist temptation of personal gain, (c) that we're not greatly bothered by the perceptible difference between our own condition and someone else's. Rawls also assumes that people have similar enough needs, interests, and capacities so that fruitful cooperation among people is possible. At the same time, he conceals from people in the original position any knowledge of their interests, talents, purposes, plans, and conceptions of the good. How can people so ignorant of these important aspects of their identities and personalities agree on principles to regulate their lives? But even conceding these assumptions, we can detect other weaknesses in Rawls's theory.

Second, Rawls's principle brings a measure of whim to moral decision making. Although Rawls is clear about the primacy of the equal liberty principle, differences in emphasis and interpretation might elevate the difference principle to the position of whim and thus lead to a contrasting moral decision. Take, for example, the case of sexual discrimination in employment practices. Under ideal conditions—those that Rawls describes as part of his definition of rationality— no one would agree to introduce the practice of sexual discrimination into employment for fear of being victimized by it. But this seems certain only if we assume a kind of germ-free, vacuum-like decision-making context; we must assume that there is no sexual discrimination to begin with.

But what would occur if you asked those same rational, self-interested, uncoerced people how they would redress already existing discriminatory employment practices? Perhaps they might emphasize the need to redress this injustice as quickly as possible through a program of preferential hiring that favored the discriminated-against group over the non-discriminated-against one. In so doing, they might employ Rawls's difference principle, by arguing that this temporary discrimination in employment would ultimately benefit all and therefore was permissible. But would it be altogether *irrational* for someone to object that such a defense is purely speculative, that in fact there are bound to be individual persons who will find themselves decidedly worse off under such a practice than not under it? It is unthinkable that reasoning this way, at least some people would refuse to be bound by a preferential hiring program?

It doesn't seem to be stretching a point for such people to invoke Rawls's equal liberty principle by claiming that preferential hiring programs on face value violate this principle. Unless we've warped Rawls's position, it appears that reasonable people could disagree on their interpretations and emphasis of Rawls's theory of justice. This evident weakness suggests another one.

Third, Rawls assumes that people would agree with the principle of difference only because he takes the view of the worst off in society. In his difference principle, Rawls claims that inequalities are permissible as long as at least the worst off benefit. Let's again consider sexual discrimination in employment. What is the just way to resolve existing sexually discriminatory practices? If the view of the worst off in the group is taken—females, in this case—we might easily support a program that would favor females in employment. But if the view of the better off males is taken, then we might not. Rawls, of course, takes the view of the worst off. But why? Critics wonder whether Rawls abandons the objectivity that justice requires and, in fact, permits some individuals (the better off) to be used as means to social ends (the improvement of the worst off).

Principle of Proportionality

In attempting to give business people explicit guidance in moral decision making, Thomas Garrett in his book *Business Ethics* has distilled the views of ethical theorists into the principle of proportionality or limited responsibility, another multiple-rule, nonconsequentialist ethic. In order to understand the principle, it's necessary to consider the nature of moral decisions.

Any moral decision involves three elements of moral import: what we intend, how we carry out our intention, and what happens (or: intention, means, and end). We've seen that consequentialists are primarily concerned with the end of an action, whereas nonconsequentialists generally put more emphasis on the intention behind it (as in Kant's case) or on one or more characteristics of the means itself. In the proportionality principle Garrett brings together intention, means, and end to form a synthesis.

Intention refers to a person's motives, to the reasons behind his or her actions. Rarely can we isolate motives with ease, probably never with certainty. Yet it seems safe to say that when people inquire about what's the right thing to do in a particular situation, they are attempting to purify their motives or intentions. When, for example, a camera company asked in 1971, "Is it right or wrong to do business in South Africa?" it appeared to take the first step toward intention cleansing. (Unless, hypothetically, the whole thing is a public relations gambit, in which case the company should ask: "Is it right or wrong to use business in South Africa as a promotional ploy?") Recognition of intention as an element in moral choice acknowledges the emphasis of Kant and most religious moralists, including Fletcher, who have pointed out that intentions are fundamental in determining morality.

Means refers to the way, the method, the procedure, or the action taken to effect the intention, to accomplish the ends. A bank teller facing personal bankruptcy and social ruin for himself and his family begins to embezzle money from the bank. Most people would agree that his intention—to save him and his family from ruin—was good. But the means he took, stealing, were deplorable. Therefore no one could approve of his action without reservation. Consideration of means in moral decisions takes heed of the importance that Ross and Rawls give it, and, of course, it recognizes Kant's emphasis on good will.

By ends is meant the results, effects, or consequences of actions. Consequentialists are correct in arguing that humans rarely approve of an action that produces evil results. The action that we approve without reservation is one whose results are good. This does not guarantee that an action with good consequences is automatically right or that we approve of it. An auditor conceals a bribe in a firm's audit. No one ever finds out, the firm never does anything like it again, and no one is injured. Still some people would question the morality of the auditor's action, not on grounds of consequences but on the basis of means.

By including consequences among the criteria for judging an action right without reservation, we recognize in moral decisions the objective element that is evident in utilitarianism. This step is crucial, for in the last analysis, whether an action is right or wrong must be determined by appealing to human experience and to all the evidence at hand. Experience may be limited, vision constrained, perception incomplete, but that's part of the human condition we must deal with.

Proportionality theorists recognize the importance of these three elements in moral decisions and use that insight to synthesize traditional ethical thought. Garrett has attempted to apply this synthesis directly to business affairs. His synthesis is summed up in the principle of proportionality, which states: "I am responsible for whatever I will as a means or an end. If both the means and the end I am willing are good in and of themselves, I may ethically permit or risk the foreseen but unwilled side effects if, and only if, I have a proportionate reason for doing so."[13] Conversely, "I am not responsible for unwilled side effects if I have a sufficient reason for risking or permitting them, granted always that what I do will as a means or an end is good."[14]

This principle of proportionality needs elaboration, which can be provided by viewing it as embodying three rules of negative obligation.

First, it is unethical to will, whether as a means or an end, a major evil to another or to oneself. Although short on specifics, by *major evil* Garrett means the destruction of goods necessary for an individual, institution, or a society to function and

13. *Thomas Garrett,* Business Ethics *(Englewood Cliffs, N.J.: Prentice-Hall, 1966), p. 8.*

14. *Ibid.*

survive. Thus individuals have basic physical and psychological needs, such as the needs for food, shelter, and safety. They also have basic rights to be treated fairly and equally, to have their freedoms respected, to be told the truth. Garrett contends that institutions similarly have vital needs, such as the need for cooperative effort, finances, and their reputations. Likewise society needs such things as citizen involvement and respect for laws. Although Garrett does not supply a list of these needs, he does contend that a willful violation of them, either as a means or end, is a major evil and therefore always wrong. A business that deliberately sets out to destroy a competitor's good name wills a major evil. A bank teller who embezzles from a bank does the same. Understandably, incidences of willing major evils are hardly as common as risking or permitting them.

Second, it is unethical to risk or permit a major evil to another or to oneself without a proportionate reason. By *risk* Garrett means to foresee as probable but not to will as a means or end. By *permit* he means to allow to happen but not to will. The key phrase in this second obligation, however, is "proportionate reason." This is the heart of the proportionality doctrine, for according to it we may risk or allow a major evil when we have a proportionate reason. A proportionate reason exists when the intended good result of an action is equal to or greater than the evil involved. Or more simply: we're not morally responsible for the side effects not willed providing significant reason exists for risking or allowing them.

Third, it is unethical to will, risk, or permit a minor evil without a proportionate reason. As previously suggested, by *minor evil* Garrett means harm to purely physical goods or to some means that are useful but not necessary for the individual and society. Thus stockholder dividends and employee stock options would be useful goods, not necessary ones. In most cases, neither owners nor workers need them to survive. A firm is justified in willing the destruction of a useful good if it has proportionate reason. Certainly the survival or financial integrity of the firm would justify a firm's not willing to vote a stockholder dividend or provide employees with stock options. Of course this distinction between necessary and useful goods, and major and minor evils remains elusive. Garrett believes that such distinctions are further complicated for Americans by our tendency to evaluate things in quantitative terms, whereas rights are qualitative. Indeed, he admits that it may take years of study to determine the exact nature of some acts and of their effects.

In sum, Garrett holds that it's unethical to will a major evil as either a means or an end. On the other hand, a minor evil may be permitted or risked—even willed—if there is proportionate reason. In applying these principles, Garrett provides a three-step method that's helpful in working through business decisions. Step 1 consists in determining what is willed as a means or as an end. If what's willed involves a major evil, we can stop at this step and declare the proposed action wrong. Step 2 involves determining the foreseen but unwilled side effects. If there is no proportionate reason for risking or allowing the major or minor evil, or of willing the minor evil, then we can stop at this step and declare the action wrong. Step 3 entails a consideration of alternatives. If there is an equally good method of attaining the good with less evil or risk of evil, we must pursue that course; not to pursue it would be unethical.

Obviously, since Garrett has tailor-made the principle of proportionality or limited responsibility for business, it should and does have wide application there. Two features in particular bear mentioning.

PROPORTIONALITY IN THE BUSINESS CONTEXT. *First, the principle of proportionality provides a synthesis of the most influential ethical theories.* We've already seen how specific consequential and nonconsequential theories could function in the business context. A significant problem with each, however, is that they take a limited view of moral decision making. Utilitarianism focuses on consequences, Kant on the goodness of the will, Ross on duties. Undoubtedly each of these is an important consideration for a moral decision in the business context. It seems to follow, then, that a synthesis of these emphases provides the strengths of each without its apparent constraints. By addressing intention, means, and end, the principle of proportionality provides business people with a comprehensive ethical theory that incorporates the three elements of any moral decision. It apprises them of the ennobling ethical principle that the action we regard as right or good without qualification is the one that springs from a good intention, is implemented by a good means, and produces good results.

Second, the principle of proportionality provides business ethics with needed flexibility, while not approving apparent immorality. We noted earlier that one of the advantages of consequential theories is that by not locking into concepts of intrinsic wrong, they provide business with a flexibility to match the complex nature of its decisions. At the same time, however, we noted the double-edged nature of this feature: it can also be used to justify what appear to be blatant wrongs. The principle of proportionality appears to provide a good amount of decision-making latitude without this liability, because it doesn't rely exclusively on consequences to determine the morality of an action. Proportionality allows ends to justify means providing that neither the means nor the end involves the willing of a major evil. In effect, the principle of proportionality incorporates the utility principle within the context of a nonconsequential ethic.

Despite these features, the proportionality theory suffers from at least two major weaknesses.

WEAKNESSES OF THE PRINCIPLE OF PROPORTIONALITY. *First, the principle of proportionality is vague on the subject of major and minor evils.* As suggested earlier, one of the most disquieting aspects of the principle of proportionality is its apparent fuzziness on the precise nature of major and minor evils. Although Garrett explains that a major evil is one that "robs a man of a quasi-absolute right or goes against his basic dignity . . . or does harm to necessary social goods,"[15] we're still left wondering about the precise nature of quasi-absolute rights, our basic dignity, and necessary social goods. Of course, Garrett himself admits this difficulty and concedes that much of his own book is "an attempt to decide what evils are major and therefore unethical when willed as a means or

15. *Garrett, p. 20.*

end."[16] Nevertheless, the issue begs for resolution in the same way in which ranking Ross's prima facie duties does.

Second, the factors affecting proportionality remain unspecific and open to an unacceptable amount of subjective interpretation. Crucial to the proportionality theory is the concept of "proportionate reason." It is proportionate reason that allows us to risk or permit major evils, or to will minor ones. And yet, the conditions bearing on proportionate reason remain at best ill-defined. Let's consider Garrett's claim that a necessary good will outweigh a useful one.

The first problem with such a claim lies in defining *necessary* and *useful*. If a necessary good is one that an entity needs to survive, then what does it need to survive? Human beings have not only biological but psychological and ego needs as well. The biological needs pertain to maintenance and safety; the psychological to security; the ego to status, fulfillment, achievement, and realization. Are all these to be considered "necessary" goods? If so, when conflicts arise among them, which predominate? Complicating the question of goods is their idiosyncratic nature. What is necessary for you may be only useful for me and vice versa. Money may be a necessary good in contemporary American society. But at what point does money cease to be necessary and begin to be useful? Can this question be answered objectively or only by appeal to personal need, life-style, and values? The same applies to firms. What's "necessary" for a firm to "survive" is open to a wide variety of interpretations, from meeting costs to mind-boggling profits. Even a superficial look at the history of corporate enterprise in America indicates that business people consider "growth" an essential feature of survival. If a company isn't growing, is it dying? If it is, then how much growth can be justified as "needed to survive"? The point is that whether the factor affecting proportionality is a necessary versus a useful good, the urgency of the good, or the certainty of the good, in each instance much is left to subjective interpretation. As a result, a decision on proportionality in many cases boils down to a personal value judgment.

Choosing a Theory

This completes our overview of major consequential and nonconsequential ethical theories. Which, if any, of these theories ought business to adopt? As a business person, which, if any, would you endorse?

There is no one principle that we can apply in choosing from among these various ethical codes. So, perhaps the whole enterprise of trying to formulate and justify moral principles is futile and should be abandoned. Such a reaction is thoroughly understandable. After all, the very diversity of imperfect ethical theories can be just as confusing and unhelpful as having none. Nevertheless, there are good reasons for not acting on this impulse of despair. To say that an ethical theory is imperfect is not to say that it is empty or that the search for a satisfactory theory is futile. Human relationships present a tangled web of frequently subtle, ill-defined problems. The world of business not only reflects

16. *Garrett, p. 12.*

problems common to human relationships but also adds ones peculiar to its own concerns. It is little wonder that we don't have a single theory that wins everyone's acceptance.

Each ethical theory discussed has an impressive range of application. In criticizing each theory, philosophers invariably focus on its weaknesses. This approach is consistent with the philosophical enterprise of pursuing truth and certainty. Philosophers cite cases that tend to break the theory down, that test its strength at the most fundamental levels. Failing to grasp this aspect of the philosophical enterprise, one could conclude that there's little worth in these ethical theories. This judgment would be a gross overstatement which not even the theories' harshest critics would agree with. It would be as indefensible as scrapping the theory of biological evolution or of quantum mechanics because these are incomplete or unsatisfactory in important ways. As in the world of science, so in the realm of human relationships which ethics deals with, we face complex realities that by nature seem to preclude total success.

Granting that these theories, though imperfect, are extremely useful, is not a selection of one theory ultimately arbitrary? Since none can be proved correct, doesn't it matter little which one we choose? Again, such a reaction is totally understandable, but before deciding that the choice of an ethical theory is arbitrary, we should reflect on the meaning of that word.

It probably would be an arbitrary decision to conclude that, since all ethical codes generally agree on basic ideals, it doesn't matter which code is followed. This position would be incorrect because each code commits us to different principles. The thoughtful person recognizes these differences and chooses. Such a choice, rooted as it is in a consideration of the alternatives, cannot be arbitrary. Instead it's based on the best available evidence, on a consideration of everything it could possibly be founded on.

> To describe such ultimate decisions as arbitrary . . . would be like saying that a complete description of the universe was utterly unfounded, because no further fact could be called upon in corroboration of it. This is not how we use the words "arbitrary" and "unfounded." Far from being arbitrary, such a decision would be the most well-founded of decisions, because it would be based upon a consideration of everything upon which it could possibly be founded.[17]

The selection of an ethical theory for business situations is only arbitrary for frivolous and unthinking people who have never undertaken a serious investigation into ethical theory. For those persons who have, the choice—far from being arbitrary—is often slow, methodical, and agonizing. The process suggests not the impudence of those who say it doesn't matter but the courage of those who say it does. It is an individual choice, not an arbitrary one.

Finally, we should note that the fundamental worth of studying and understanding ethical thought is not that we thereby have definitive guides to moral conduct. Rather, the value lies in becoming aware of the moral options available to us, of the general paradigm within which moral inquiry can take place as concrete human beings grapple with real-life issues. This is particularly evident

17. R. M. Hare, The Language of Morals (Oxford: Clarendon Press, 1952), p. 69.

in business, where individual choice is frequently not between obvious right or wrong, good or bad, but between actions and values that contain elements of both. The challenge for business people, then, is not so much one of finding an ethical standard to use, but of applying a reputable standard in a specific instance.

The chapters that follow are designed toward meeting that challenge. They not only raise specific issues and problems that arise in business's relationship with its employees and with society at large, but they also show how these ethical theories might be applied to these concerns. We'll discover that all theories are of some use but that some prove more useful than others in particular situations. It's hoped that such an exposure proves valuable in helping business people recognize the various kinds of ethical systems that may be employed in given situations and in determining what values override others in a conflict.

Summary

We've viewed ethical theories as dividing into consequential and nonconsequential. Under consequentialism, we discussed egoism, act and rule utilitarianism, and situational ethics; under single-rule nonconsequentialism, the Golden Rule and the categorical imperative; under multiple-rule nonconsequentialism, prima facie duties, maximin principle, and the theory of proportionality or limited responsibility. Although each of these theories has weaknesses in theory and in the business context, they nevertheless have a wide range of application for moral decision making in business. In the last analysis, the value of being exposed to ethical thought lies not so much in that we may discover a definitive guide for moral conduct but that we may develop a framework within which to pursue moral inquiry.

Is Business Bluffing Ethical?

Albert Z. Carr

In the preceding chapter we discussed a number of general ethical theories and their usefulness to business decisions. As we have indicated, the point of examining these theories is to develop some conceptual framework within which moral inquiry can occur. We must admit that our treatment has been loaded since we have assumed that general ethical theories are relevant to business decisions. It could very well be that maxims derived from moral philosophy or religion are not suited to the business world.

In the following essay Professor Carr, whom we met earlier, raises just this point. In essence, he observes that business has the impersonal character of a game that demands both special strategy and an understanding of its special ethics. Just as the game of poker poses its own brand of ethics—which can be far different from the ethical ideals of human relationships—so does business. And no one should think any the worse of business because its standards of right and wrong may differ markedly from prevailing traditions of morality.

In effect Professor Carr raises a most fundamental concern for our study of business ethics: whether traditional

Albert Z. Carr, "Is Business Bluffing Ethical?" Harvard Business Review, 40 (January–February 1968). Copyright ©1968 by the President and Fellows of Harvard College; all rights reserved.

moral theories, including values and standards, constitute appropriate paradigms within which to conduct moral inquiry. In responding to this concern, think seriously about the differences between business and a game, specifically poker. Ask yourself what characteristics business and a game do not share, for major differences would blunt the point of Carr's thesis.

A respected businessman with whom I discussed the theme of this article remarked with some heat, "You mean to say you're going to encourage men to bluff? Why, bluffing is nothing more than a form of lying! You're advising them to lie!"

I agreed that the basis of private morality is a respect for truth and that the closer a businessman comes to the truth, the more he deserves respect. At the same time, I suggested that most bluffing in business might be regarded simply as game strategy—much like bluffing in poker which does not reflect on the morality of the bluffer.

I quoted Henry Taylor, the British statesman who pointed out that "falsehood ceases to be falsehood when it is understood on all sides that the truth is not expected to be spoken"—an exact description of bluffing in poker, diplomacy, and business. I cited the analogy of the criminal court, where the criminal is not expected to tell the truth when he pleads "not guilty." Everyone from the judge down takes it for granted that the job of the defendant's attorney is to get his client off, not to reveal the truth; and this is considered ethical practice. I mentioned Representative Omar Burleson, the Democrat from Texas, who was quoted as saying, in regard to the ethics of Congress, "Ethics is a barrel of worms"—a pungent summing up of the problem of deciding who is ethical in politics.

I reminded my friend that millions of businessmen feel constrained every day to say *yes* to their bosses when they secretly believe *no* and that this is generally accepted as permissible strategy when the alternative might be the loss of a job. The essential point, I said, is that the ethics of business are game ethics, different from the ethics of religion.

He remained unconvinced. Referring to the company of which he is president, he declared: "Maybe that's good enough for some businessmen, but I can tell you that we pride ourselves on our ethics. In 30 years not one customer has ever questioned my word or asked to check our figures. We're loyal to our customers and fair to our suppliers. I regard my handshake on a deal as a contract. I've never entered into price-fixing schemes with my competitors. I've never allowed my salesmen to spread injurious rumors about other companies. Our union contract is the best in our industry. And, if I do say so myself, our ethical standards are of the highest!"

He really was saying, without realizing it, that he was living up to the ethical standards of the business game—which are a far cry from those of private life. Like a gentlemanly poker player, he did not play in cahoots with others at the table, try to smear their reputations, or hold back chips he owed them.

But this same fine man, at that very time, was allowing one of his products to be advertised in a way that made it sound a great deal better than it actually was. Another item in his product line was notorious among dealers for its "built-in obsolescence." He was holding back from the market a much-improved product because he did not want it to interfere with sales of the inferior item it would have replaced. He had joined with certain of his competitors in hiring a lobbyist to push a state legislature, by methods that he preferred not to know too much about, into amending a bill then being enacted.

In his view these things had nothing to do with ethics; they were merely normal business practice. He himself undoubtedly avoided outright falsehoods—never lied in so many words. But the entire organization that he ruled was deeply involved in numerous strategies of deception.

Pressure to Deceive

Most executives from time to time are almost compelled, in the interests of their companies or themselves, to practice some form of deception when negotiating with customers, dealers, labor unions, government officials, or even other departments of their companies. By conscious misstatements, concealment of pertinent facts, or exaggeration—in short, by bluffing—they seek to persuade others to agree with them. I think it is fair to say that if the individual executive refuses to bluff from time to time—if he feels obligated to tell the truth, the whole truth, and nothing but the truth—he is ignoring opportunities permitted under the rules and is at a heavy disadvantage in his business dealings.

But here and there a businessman is unable to reconcile himself to the bluff in which he plays a part. His conscience, perhaps spurred by religious idealism, troubles him. He feels guilty; he may develop an ulcer or a nervous tic. Before any executive can make profitable use of the strategy of the bluff, he needs to make sure that in bluffing he will not lose self-respect or become emotionally disturbed. If he is to reconcile personal integrity and high standards of honesty with the practical requirements of business, he must feel that his bluffs are ethically justified. The justification rests on the fact that business, as practiced by individuals as well as by corporations, has the impersonal character of a game—a game that demands both special strategy and an understanding of its special ethics.

The game is played at all levels of corporate life, from the highest to the lowest. At the very instant that a man decides to enter business, he may be forced into a game situation, as is shown by the recent experience of a Cornell honor graduate who applied for a job with a large company:

> This applicant was given a psychological test which included the statement, "Of the following magazines, check any that you have read either regularly or from time to time, and double-check those which interest you most. *Reader's Digest, Time, Fortune, Saturday Evening Post, The New Republic, Life, Look, Ramparts, Newsweek, Business Week, U.S. News & World Report, The Nation, Playboy, Esquire, Harper's, Sports Illustrated.*"
>
> His tastes in reading were broad, and at one time or another he had read almost all of these magazines. He was a subscriber to *The New Republic,* an enthusiast for *Ramparts,* and an avid student of the pictures in *Playboy.* He was not sure whether his interest in *Playboy* would be held against him, but he had a shrewd suspicion that if he confessed to an interest in *Ramparts* and *The New Republic,* he would be thought a liberal, a radical, or at least an intellectual, and his chances of getting the job, which he needed, would greatly diminish. He therefore checked five of the more conservative magazines. Apparently it was a sound decision, for he got the job.
>
> He had made a game player's decision, consistent with business ethics.

A similar case is that of a magazine space salesman who, owing to a merger, suddenly found himself out of a job:

> This man was 58, and, in spite of a good record, his chance of getting a job elsewhere in a business where youth is favored in hiring practice was not good. He was a vigorous, healthy man, and only a considerable amount of gray in his hair suggested his age. Before beginning his job search he touched up his hair with a black dye to confine the gray to his temples. He knew that the truth about his age might well come out in time, but he calculated that he could deal with that situation when it arose. He and his wife decided that he could easily pass for 45, and he so stated his age on his résumé.

This was a lie; yet within the accepted rules of the business game, no moral culpability attaches to it.

The Poker Analogy

We can learn a good deal about the nature of business by comparing it with poker. While both have a large element of chance, in the long run the winner is the man who plays with steady skill. In both games ultimate victory requires intimate knowledge of the rules, insight into the psychology of the other players, a bold front, a considerable amount of self-discipline, and the ability to respond swiftly and effectively to opportunities provided by chance.

No one expects poker to be played on the ethical principles preached in churches. In poker it is right and proper to bluff a friend out of the rewards of being dealt a good hand. A player feels no more than a slight twinge of sympathy, if that, when—with nothing better than a single ace in his hand—he strips a heavy loser, who holds a pair, of the rest of his chips. It was up to the other fellow to protect himself. In the words of an excellent poker player, former President Harry Truman, "If you can't stand the heat, stay out of the kitchen." If one shows mercy to a loser in poker, it is a personal gesture, divorced from the rules of the game.

Poker has its special ethics, and here I am not referring to rules against cheating. The man who keeps an ace up his sleeve or who marks the cards is more than unethical; he is a crook, and can be punished as such—kicked out of the game or, in the Old West, shot.

In contrast to the cheat, the unethical poker player is one who, while abiding by the letter of the rules, finds ways to put the other players at an unfair disadvantage. Perhaps he unnerves them with loud talk. Or he tries to get them drunk. Or he plays in cahoots with someone else at the table. Ethical poker players frown on such tactics.

Poker's own brand of ethics is different from the ethical ideals of civilized human relationships. The game calls for distrust of the other fellow. It ignores the claim of friendship. Cunning deception and concealment of one's strength and intentions, not kindness and openheartedness, are vital in poker. No one thinks any the worse of poker on that account. And no one should think any the worse of the game of business because its standards of right and wrong differ from the prevailing traditions of morality in our society.

Discard the Golden Rule

This view of business is especially worrisome to people without much business experience. A minister of my acquaintance once protested that business cannot possibly function in our society unless it is based on the Judeo-Christian system of ethics. He told me:

> I know some businessmen have supplied call girls to customers, but there are always a few rotten apples in every barrel. That doesn't mean the rest of the fruit isn't sound. Surely the vast majority of businessmen are ethical. I myself am acquainted with many who adhere to strict codes of ethics based fundamentally on religious teachings. They contribute to good causes. They participate in community activities. They cooperate with other companies to improve working conditions in their industries. Certainly they are not indifferent to ethics.

That most businessmen are not indifferent to ethics in their private lives, everyone will agree. My point is that in their office lives they cease to be private citizens; they become game players who must be guided by a somewhat different set of ethical standards.

The point was forcefully made to me by a Midwestern executive who has given a good deal of thought to the question:

> So long as a businessman complies with the laws of the land and avoids telling malicious lies, he's ethical. If the law as written gives a man a wide-open chance to make a killing, he'd be a fool not to take advantage of it. If he doesn't, somebody else will. There's no obligation on him to stop and consider who is going to get hurt. If the law says he can do it, that's all the justification he needs. There's nothing unethical about that. It's just plain business sense.

This executive (call him Robbins) took the stand that even industrial espionage, which is frowned on by some businessmen, ought not to be considered unethical. He recalled a recent meeting of the National Industrial Conference Board where an authority on marketing made a speech in which he deplored the employment of spies by business organizations. More and more companies, he pointed out, find it cheaper to penetrate the secrets of competitors with concealed cameras and microphones or by bribing employees than to set up costly research and design departments of their own. A whole branch of the electronics industry has grown up with this trend, he continued, providing equipment to make industrial espionage easier.

Disturbing? The marketing expert found it so. But when it came to a remedy, he could only appeal to "respect for the golden rule." Robbins thought this a confession of defeat, believing that the golden rule, for all its value as an ideal for society, is simply not feasible as a guide for business. A good part of the time the businessman is trying to do unto others as he hopes others will *not* do unto him. Robbins continued:

> Espionage of one kind or another has become so common in business that it's like taking a drink during Prohibition—it's not considered sinful. And we don't even have Prohibition where espionage is concerned; the law is very tolerant in this area. There's no more shame for a business that uses secret agents than there is for a nation. Bear in mind that there already is at least one large corporation—you can buy its stock over the counter—that makes millions by providing counterespionage service to industrial firms. Espionage in business is not an ethical problem; it's an established technique of business competition.

"We Don't Make the Laws"

Wherever we turn in business, we can perceive the sharp distinction between its ethical standards and those of the churches. Newspapers abound with sensational stories growing out of this distinction:

We read one day that Senator Philip A. Hart of Michigan has attacked food processors for deceptive packaging of numerous products.

The next day there is a Congressional to-do over Ralph Nader's book, *Unsafe At Any Speed*, which demonstrates that automobile companies for years have neglected the safety of car-owning families.

Then another Senator, Lee Metcalf of Montana, and journalist Vic Reinemer show in their book, *Overcharge*, the methods by which utility companies elude regulating government bodies to extract unduly large payments from users of electricity.

These are merely dramatic instances of a prevailing condition; there is hardly a major industry at which a similar attack could not be aimed. Critics of business regard such behavior as unethical, but the companies concerned know that they are merely playing the business game.

Among the most respected of our business institutions are the insurance companies. A group of insurance executives meeting recently in New England was startled when their guest speaker, social critic Daniel Patrick Moynihan, roundly berated them for "unethical" practices. They had been guilty, Moynihan alleged, of using outdated actuarial tables to obtain unfairly high premiums. They habitually delayed the hearings of lawsuits against them in order to tire out the plaintiffs and win cheap settlements. In their employment policies they used ingenious devices to discriminate against certain minority groups.

It was difficult for the audience to deny the validity of these charges. But these men were business game players. Their reaction to Moynihan's attack was much the same as that of the automobile manufacturers to Nader, of the utilities to Senator Metcalf, and of the food processors to Senator Hart. If the laws governing their businesses change, or if public opinion becomes clamorous, they will make the necessary adjust-

ments. But morally they have in their view done nothing wrong. As long as they comply with the letter of the law, they are within their rights to operate their businesses as they see fit.

The small business is in the same position as the great corporation in this respect. For example:

In 1967 a key manufacturer was accused of providing master keys for automobiles to mail-order customers, although it was obvious that some of the purchasers might be automobile thieves. His defense was plain and straightforward. If there was nothing in the law to prevent him from selling his keys to anyone who ordered them, it was not up to him to inquire as to his customers' motives. Why was it any worse, he insisted, for him to sell car keys by mail, than for mail-order houses to sell guns that might be used for murder? Until the law was changed, the key manufacturer could regard himself as being just as ethical as any other businessman by the rules of the business game.

Violations of the ethical ideals of society are common in business, but they are not necessarily violations of business principles. Each year the Federal Trade Commission orders hundreds of companies, many of them of the first magnitude, to "cease and desist" from practices which, judged by ordinary standards, are of questionable morality but which are stoutly defended by the companies concerned.

In one case, a firm manufacturing a well-known mouthwash was accused of using a cheap form of alcohol possibly deleterious to health. The company's chief executive, after testifying in Washington, made this comment privately:

We broke no law. We're in a highly competitive industry. If we're going to stay in business, we have to look for profit wherever the law permits. We don't make the laws. We obey them. Then why do we have to put up with this "holier than thou" talk about ethics? It's sheer hypocrisy. We're not in business to promote ethics. Look at the cigarette companies, for God's sake! If the ethics aren't embodied in the laws by the men who made them, you can't expect businessmen to fill the lack. Why, a sudden submission to Christian ethics by businessmen would bring about the greatest economic upheaval in history!

It may be noted that the government failed to prove its case against him.

Cast Illusions Aside

Talk about ethics by businessmen is often a thin decorative coating over the hard realities of the game:

> Once I listened to a speech by a young executive who pointed to a new industry code as proof that his company and its competitors were deeply aware of their responsibilities to society. It was a code of ethics, he said. The industry was going to police itself, to dissuade constituent companies from wrongdoing. His eyes shone with conviction and enthusiasm.
>
> The same day there was a meeting in a hotel room where the industry's top executives met with the "czar" who was to administer the new code, a man of high repute. No one who was present could doubt their common attitude. In their eyes the code was designed primarily to forestall a move by the federal government to impose stern restrictions on the industry. They felt that the code would hamper them a good deal less than new federal laws would. It was, in other words, conceived as a protection for the industry, not for the public.
>
> The young executive accepted the surface explanation of the code; these leaders, all experienced game players, did not deceive themselves for a moment about its purpose.

The illusion that business can afford to be guided by ethics as conceived in private life is often fostered by speeches and articles containing such phrases as, "It pays to be ethical," or, "Sound ethics is good business." Actually this is not an ethical position at all; it is a self-serving calculation in disguise. The speaker is really saying that in the long run a company can make more money if it does not antagonize competitors, suppliers, employees, and customers by squeezing them too hard. He is saying that oversharp policies reduce ultimate gains. That is true, but it has nothing to do with ethics. The underlying attitude is much like that in the familiar story of the shopkeeper who finds an extra $20 bill in the cash register, debates with himself the ethical problem—should he tell his partner?—and finally decides to share the money because the gesture will give him an edge over the s.o.b. the next time they quarrel.

I think it is fair to sum up the prevailing attitude of businessmen on ethics as follows:

We live in what is probably the most competitive of the world's civilized societies. Our customs encourage a high degree of aggression in the individual's striving for success. Business is our main area of competition, and it has been ritualized into a game of strategy. The basic rules of the game have been set by the government, which attempts to detect and punish business frauds. But as long as a company does not transgress the rules of the game set by law, it has the legal right to shape its strategy without reference to anything but its profits. If it takes a long-term view of its profits, it will preserve amicable relations, so far as possible, with those with whom it deals. A wise businessman will not seek advantage to the point where he generates dangerous hostility among employees, competitors, customers, government, or the public at large. But decisions in this area are, in the final test, decisions of strategy, not of ethics.

The Individual and the Game

An individual within a company often finds it difficult to adjust to the requirements of the business game. He tries to preserve his private ethical standards in situations that call for game strategy. When he is obliged to carry out company policies that challenge his conception of himself as an ethical man, he suffers.

It disturbs him when he is ordered, for instance, to deny a raise to a man who deserves it, to fire an employee of long standing, to prepare advertising that he believes to be misleading, to conceal facts that he feels customers are entitled to know, to cheapen the quality of materials used in the manufacture of an established product, to sell as new a product that he knows to be rebuilt, to exaggerate the curative powers of a medicinal preparation, or to coerce dealers.

There are some fortunate executives who, by the nature of their work and circumstances, never have to face problems of this kind. But in one form or another the ethical dilemma is felt sooner or later by most businessmen. Possibly the dilemma is most painful not when the company forces the action on the executive but when he originates it himself—that is, when he has taken or is contemplating a step which is in his own interest but which runs counter to his early moral conditioning. To illustrate:

The manager of an export department, eager to show rising sales, is pressed by a big customer to provide invoices which, while containing no overt falsehood that would violate a U.S. law, are so worded that the customer may be able to evade certain taxes in his homeland.

A company president finds that an aging executive, within a few years of retirement and his pension, is not as productive as formerly. Should he be kept on?

The produce manager of a supermarket debates with himself whether to get rid of a lot of half-rotten tomatoes by including one, with its good side exposed, in every tomato six-pack.

An accountant discovers that he has taken an improper deduction on his company's tax return and fears the consequences if he calls the matter to the president's attention, though he himself has done nothing illegal. Perhaps if he says nothing, no one will notice the error.

A chief executive officer is asked by his directors to comment on a rumor that he owns stock in another company with which he has placed large orders. He could deny it, for the stock is in the name of his son-in-law and he has earlier formally instructed his son-in-law to sell the holding.

Temptations of this kind constantly arise in business. If an executive allows himself to be torn between a decision based on business considerations and one based on his private ethical code, he exposes himself to a grave psychological strain.

This is not to say that sound business strategy necessarily runs counter to ethical ideals. They may frequently coincide; and when they do, everyone is gratified. But the major tests of every move in business, as in all games of strategy, are legality and profit. A man who intends to be a winner in the business game must have a game player's attitude.

The business strategist's decisions must be as impersonal as those of a surgeon performing an operation—concentrating on objective and technique, and subordinating personal feelings. If the chief executive admits that his son-in-law owns the stock, it is because he stands to lose more

if the fact comes out later than if he states it boldly and at once. If the supermarket manager orders the rotten tomatoes to be discarded, he does so to avoid an increase in consumer complaints and a loss of good will. The company president decides not to fire the elderly executive in the belief that the negative reaction of other employees would in the long run cost the company more than it would lose in keeping him and paying his pension.

All sensible businessmen prefer to be truthful, but they seldom feel inclined to tell the *whole* truth. In the business game truth-telling usually has to be kept within narrow limits if trouble is to be avoided. The point was neatly made a long time ago (in 1888) by one of John D. Rockefeller's associates, Paul Babcock, to Standard Oil Company executives who were about to testify before a government investigating committee: "Parry every question with answers which, while perfectly truthful, are evasive of *bottom* facts." This was, is, and probably always will be regarded as wise and permissible business strategy.

For Office Use Only

An executive's family life can easily be dislocated if he fails to make a sharp distinction between the ethical systems of the home and the office—or if his wife does not grasp that distinction. Many a businessman who has remarked to his wife, "I had to let Jones go today" or "I had to admit to the boss that Jim has been goofing off lately," has been met with an indignant protest. "How could you do a thing like that? You know Jones is over 50 and will have a lot of trouble getting another job." Or, "You did that to Jim? With his wife ill and all the worry she's been having with the kids?"

If the executive insists that he had no choice because the profits of the company and his own security were involved, he may see a certain cool and ominous reappraisal in his wife's eyes. Many wives are not prepared to accept the fact that business operates with a special code of ethics. An illuminating illustration of this comes from a Southern sales executive who related a conversation he had had with his wife at a time when a hotly contested political campaign was being waged in their state:

> I made the mistake of telling her that I had had lunch with Colby, who gives me about

half my business. Colby mentioned that his company had a stake in the election. Then he said, "By the way, I'm treasurer of the citizens' committee for Lang. I'm collecting contributions. Can I count on you for a hundred dollars?"

Well, there I was. I was opposed to Lang, but I knew Colby. If he withdrew his business I could be in a bad spot. So I just smiled and wrote out a check then and there. He thanked me, and we started to talk about his next order. Maybe he thought I shared his political views. If so, I wasn't going to lose any sleep over it.

I should have had sense enough not to tell Mary about it. She hit the ceiling. She said she was disappointed in me. She said I hadn't acted like a man, that I should have stood up to Colby.

I said, "Look, it was an either-or situation. I had to do it or risk losing the business."

She came back at me with, "I don't believe it. You could have been honest with him. You could have said that you didn't feel you ought to contribute to a campaign for a man you weren't going to vote for. I'm sure he would have understood."

I said, "Mary, you're a wonderful woman, but you're way off the track. Do you know what would have happened if I had said that? Colby would have smiled and said, 'Oh, I didn't realize. Forget it.' But in his eyes from that moment I would be an oddball, maybe a bit of a radical. He would have listened to me talk about his order and would have promised to give it consideration. After that I wouldn't hear from him for a week. Then I would telephone and learn from his secretary that he wasn't yet ready to place the order. And in about a month I would hear through the grapevine that he was giving his business to another company. A month after that I'd be out of a job."

She was silent for a while. Then she said, "Tom, something is wrong with business when a man is forced to choose between his family's security and his moral obligation to himself. It's easy for me to say you should have stood up to him—but if you had, you might have felt you were betraying me and the kids. I'm sorry that you did it, Tom, but I can't blame you. Something is wrong with business!"

This wife saw the problem in terms of moral obligation as conceived in private life; her husband saw it as a matter of game strategy. As a player in a weak position, he felt that he could not afford to indulge an ethical sentiment that might have cost him his seat at the table.

Playing to Win

Some men might challenge the Colbys of business—might accept serious setbacks to their business careers rather than risk a feeling of moral cowardice. They merit our respect—but as private individuals, not businessmen. When the skillful player of the business game is compelled to submit to unfair pressure, he does not castigate himself for moral weakness. Instead, he strives to put himself into a strong position where he can defend himself against such pressures in the future without loss.

If a man plans to take a seat in the business game, he owes it to himself to master the principles by which the game is played, including its special ethical outlook. He can then hardly fail to recognize that an occasional bluff may well be justified in terms of the game's ethics and warranted in terms of economic necessity. Once he clears his mind on this point, he is in a good position to match his strategy against that of the other players. He can then determine objectively whether a bluff in a given situation has a good chance of succeeding and can decide when and how to bluff, without a feeling of ethical transgression.

To be a winner, a man must play to win. This does not mean that he must be ruthless, cruel, harsh, or treacherous. On the contrary, the better his reputation for integrity, honesty, and decency, the better his chances of victory will be in the long run. But from time to time every businessman, like every poker player, is offered a choice between certain loss or bluffing within the legal rules of the game. If he is not resigned to losing, if he wants to rise in his company and industry, then in such a crisis he will bluff—and bluff hard.

Every now and then one meets a successful businessman who has conveniently forgotten the small or large deceptions that he practiced on his way to fortune. "God gave me my money," old John D. Rockefeller once piously told a Sunday school class. It would be a rare tycoon in our time who would risk the horse laugh with which such a remark would be greeted.

In the last third of the twentieth century even

children are aware that if a man has become prosperous in business, he has sometimes departed from the strict truth in order to overcome obstacles or has practiced the more subtle deceptions of the half-truth or the misleading omission. Whatever the form of the bluff, it is an integral part of the game, and the executive who does not master its techniques is not likely to accumulate much money or power.

The Golden Rule and Business Management: Quo Vadis?

Craig C. Lundberg

Limitations of space, as well as sheer unavailability, make it impossible to provide essays that directly address the usefulness of all the ethical theories we've discussed. But it seems that we should take a closer look at one which business people claim is the most useful for business: the Golden Rule. A great many people in America believe that in business, as in private affairs, they should treat others as they would want to be treated. But is this practicable? Does the nature and structure of business allow for the application of this widely acknowledged rule of moral behavior? Is the Golden Rule, or some reasonable facsimile of it, a useful guide to business decision making? In the following essay, Professor of Behavioral Science and Administration Craig C. Lundberg claims that it is not. Some of his reasons correspond to the two weaknesses we observed earlier. Professor Lundberg concludes that we must be very careful in applying the Golden Rule in business. Do you agree?

As I have talked with business managers I have been impressed that the vast majority of these men propose the Golden Rule as the most important guide for organizational behavior. Certainly this maxim is well-known as a guide for human conduct, yet regardless of its popularity we might question its adequacy as a business policy. Let me focus this paper by contrasting two sets of reasoning:

> The Golden Rule is the best general prescription for regulating human relationships, therefore, it is a good maxim for behavior in business especially within complex modern organization settings.

> The Golden Rule is a guide for human relations which is very limited in its applications in modern society. It must be applied with caution or not at all in contemporary business practice.

In the pages to follow I will note how the reasoning supporting the first assertion is generally believed, but will rely on my frame of reference as a social scientist to argue in favor of the second position. To do this I will differentiate between the Golden Rule as a religious norm and as a guide to ethical fairness in exchange relationships. Then I will examine some assumptions implicit in the rule and underline aspects which are simply unclear.

Religious Universality of the Golden Rule

While familiar the Golden Rule is stated in numerous forms. The book of Matthew, for instance, states that: "All things whatsoever ye would that men should do to you, do ye so unto them: for this is the Law and the Prophets." The medieval Biblical injunction, "Love thy neighbor as thyself" has of course been most commonly interpreted with the contemporary maxim, "Do unto others as you would like them to do unto you."

We should not assume that the Golden Rule is primarily associated with Christianity for most other religions carry some version of it. In the Talmud, for example, we find, "What is hateful to you, do not do to your fellow man. That this is the entire law; all the rest is commentary." Confucianism, too, in the Analects has, "Surely it is the maxim of loving kindness: do not unto others

Craig C. Lundberg, "The Golden Rule and Business Management: Quo Vadis?" Economic and Business Bulletin, 20 (January 1968), 36–40. Reprinted by permission of the author.

that you would not have them do unto you." Buddhism in the Udana-Yarga says, "Hurt not others in ways that you yourself would find hurtful." Islam joins the chorus with, "Not one of you is a believer until he desires for his brother that which he desires for himself." And in the Mahabharata the Brahman injunction says, "This is the sum of duty: do not do unto others which would cause you pain if done to you." And so we see that the Golden Rule exists throughout the major religions of mankind.

The Rule as a Guide for Exchanges

We must at this point distinguish between the Jewish-Christian norm of brotherly love and the Golden Rule of fairness-ethics. The Biblical

Love thy neighbor as thyself,

is a norm of Jewish-Christian brotherly love; it means love your neighbor, that is, to feel responsible for and at one with him. The Golden Rule as interpreted today is quite different. Perhaps it is no accident that the Golden Rule has become one of the most popular religious maxims of today because it can be interpreted in terms of fairness-ethics, which sounds a great deal like the religious maxims, but which in fact has quite a different meaning, namely, be fair in your exchanges with others. Contrast with the religious norm is complete for fairness-ethics means do not feel responsible and at one, but feel distant and separate; respect the rights of your neighbor, but do not love him. This differentiation between religious norm and a maxim of fairness-ethics is made so that we can focus on the latter, which is the principle or generalization in the fields of human relations as conceived by business management today.

Distortions and Changes in Meaning

The Golden Rule is very well known in western culture; it is a fairness-ethics injunction; and it is usually accepted unquestioningly. Although probably the most revered of common sense generalizations handed down by our industrial forebears, the Golden Rule has not gone unthought about or completely unchallenged. As our society has become more liberal and the value of individual work has been widened to include a value of individual differences, the Golden Rule

has been revamped. The playwright Bernard Shaw, for instance, has rewritten the Golden Rule:

Don't do unto others as you would have them do unto you because their tastes may be different.

Even Shaw's version has been altered. A well-known psychologist has rephrased the Golden Rule to serve as a guide for ethical conduct or as a guide for amiable relations among men:

Do unto others as you would have them do unto you if you were they.

This last statement of the rule seems to take Shaw's point that one man's meat is another man's poison, and adds the contemporary concern we have for empathy, the usefulness of putting ourselves in another person's place so we can appreciate how he thinks and feels.

In a recent graduate course and in a recent executive development program for middle managers, I asked participants to write out the versions of the Golden Rule known to them. The response was overwhelming and reflects and shows how far the Golden Rule has pervaded the mainstream of our business culture, everything from "an eye for an eye, a tooth for a tooth" to "every girl has a father"; from "You pat my back, I'll pat yours but you pat me first" to "drive carefully, the life you save may be your own"; from "The only way to have a friend is to be one" to "owe no man anything." Variations are reported implicit in our everyday petitions for help, such as "Share the United way" or "Give blood, the gift of life"; and we find variations in advertising such as one card manufacturer who asks that you give his card to show you care enough to send the very best, and of course there are even business philosophies such as the Murray D. Lincoln's "Intelligent selfishness."

We often hear people talk about the imperatives of life, and of course the Golden Rule is often promoted in just that way. It was the German-Scottish philosopher Immanuel Kant who conceived of the categorical imperative, the unconditional command of nature. It, too, sounds much like the Golden Rule:

Act so that the principle of your action could be made a universal law.

When men act on the Golden Rule as if it were

such an imperative, . . . then we can expect confusion and perhaps even injustice to occur.

On Applying the Golden Rule

We see that from a religious origin strained through the web and woof of an industrial society the Golden Rule has come to reside in humor, in philosophy, and common sense, in fact nearly all arenas of contemporary life. The question still remains, however, is it a useful imperative? Can we take it as a generalized principle of, or guide for, human relationships? Let us now examine a few simple situations which, while hypothetical, could very well exist, and as we look at them let us ask ourselves about the utility of applying the Golden Rule in each case.

> Picture a janitor and the president of a major corporation approaching the lobby doors of the corporation's downtown headquarters building. The two men approach the doors simultaneously. Who will open the door for whom and with what effects on the men?

> Consider the marketing vice-president of a major American business firm promptly arriving at the stated time for an appointment with an executive of potentially the largest purchaser of his product in Venezuela. After an hour and a half of waiting the v.p. actively considers leaving.

> Consider the personnel manager of a local company picking up his telephone to hear his counterpart in a competitor's firm asking if he would provide a summer job for the other man's high-school age son.

> Picture a computer expert who is new to a business deciding not to include certain critical information in his first report to his superior because he thinks it might jeopardize the existence of his function in the firm.

In the hypothetical examples above the parties have represented different organizational statuses, different cultures, different personal needs and capabilities for action, and different constraints on their behavior. In each example a literal application of the Golden Rule would be rather difficult for most reasonable people—they would feel the pressures of expectations and no doubt worry about the consequences to their responses to these situations. Perhaps these examples force us to wonder as to the universal application of the rule, and perhaps to question the assumption on which it is based. Let us now turn to this latter aspect.

Assumptions Behind the Golden Rule

One assumption in the Golden Rule is that the "others" in an exchange situation are in fact capable of reciprocating the behavior. We quickly remember that persons are not equal in terms of abilities, at least adults, and clearly are not equally capable in terms of the organizational power they command. You might go on with this assumption and ask whether the "others" are in fact motivated to reciprocate, that is, whether they would want to return similar behaviors if it were possible to. A second assumption would be that either party to an exchange really understands the consequences to the behavior—how, in fact, will the others really feel and think. This is of course contingent on their having similar goals or aims, and in most cases this seems extremely unlikely. A third major assumption is that the Golden Rule assumes that other rules are not being violated whether they be formal, explicit rules or other implicit perhaps informal ones, such as custom. Take the privilege and duty which come with certain statuses in our society, perhaps illustrated in the first example above. Today, too, we have a widespread understanding that business practice should not include reciprocity in regard to purchasing, for example, and this may in certain instances conflict with the Golden Rule injunction. A fourth assumption has to do with the assumed similarity of preference or taste of the parties to the Golden Rule. One could confuse or sadden, hurt, or disadvantage another who did not have somewhat similar preferences or tastes, that is, values and interests like ours. Cross cultural examples often make this point clearly.

Let us now examine the Golden Rule in terms of its clarity. Unless it is specific and explicit it becomes a maxim hard to follow. We might begin by asking about the unit of action. Are the actions implied in the rule a person or persons, groups or some larger social? Are you and the others in the Golden Rule to be seen as representatives of various social units or as independent citizens or persons in their own right, or does it make a difference? Of course the word "do" in the Golden Rule can mean many things too, and as usually interpreted all behaviors are included. Another thing which is not too clear has to do with the adequacy of resources. In most human situations there is a scarcity of resources. A major unclear aspect of the Golden Rule has to do with the amount and/or frequency of the exchange. Most people read the Golden Rule as implying some kind of equality. It would seem in our discussion of assumptions above that people are not equally capable or motivated to enter into an equal kind of exchange. In fact, we know from the new field of equity theory that the equality of exchange is almost never really expected. The act implied in the Golden Rule is of course conditioned by the perception of the parties, and we know from the research in psychology that emotional and situational factors among others, can alter and distort what is perceived to be done to oneself, this seemingly inviting considerable creative distortion and error. And of course the Golden Rule is not very clear as to how one measures the consequences which arise by using it. Do we look at both mental and physical consequences, how does the time dimension come in, and so on?

Evaluation of the Golden Rule

We have seen that the Golden Rule, at least as a maxim of fairness-ethics, is extremely popular, and widely applied in our industrial society. By means of some hypothetical illustrations and by examining more directly the assumption behind and the lack of clarity in the Golden Rule we have also been able to offer some comment on the adequacy of this rule as a general principle of organizational behavior. I believe that we have demonstrated that the Golden Rule cannot be taken as a categorical imperative, that in fact one would have to be extremely careful in applying it in business and other human affairs. I do not want to appear as relegating all common sense knowledge to the dustbin for in fact the scientific study of human relations is able to confirm a lot of the tried and true folklore and rules of thumb. It is crucial, however, to know when injunctions from the past are no longer applicable or to be able to identify the conditions when they do not apply. Such has been our intent in examining the Golden Rule's validity for contemporary business management.

For Further Reading

Bartels, R. (Ed.). *Ethics in business.* Columbus, Ohio: Ohio State University Press, 1963.

Baumhart, R. *Ethics in business.* New York: Holt, Rinehart and Winston, 1968.

Bowen, H. R. *Social responsibilities of the businessman.* New York: Harper & Brothers, 1953.

Clark, J. W. *Religion and the moral standards of American businessmen.* Cincinnati: South-Western, 1966.

Corson, J. J. *Business in the humane society.* New York: McGraw-Hill, 1971.

Golembiewski, R. T. *Men, management, and morality.* New York: McGraw-Hill, 1965.

Houser, T. V. *Big business vs. human values.* New York: McGraw-Hill, 1957.

Johnson, H. L. *Business in contemporary society: Framework and issues.* Belmont, Calif.: Wadsworth, 1971.

Selekman, S. K., & Selekman, B. M. *Power and morality in a business society.* New York: McGraw-Hill, 1956.

Sporn, P., Hickman, L. E., & Hodges, L. M. *The ethics of business: Corporate behavior in the marketplace.* New York: Columbia University Press, 1963.

Towle, J. W. (Ed.). *Ethics and standards in American business.* New York: Harper & Row, 1964.

Part II
BUSINESS AND THE PEOPLE IN IT

As we suggested earlier, one of the primary claimants on business is its employees. The relationship between a firm and those it employs is laced with moral concerns.

Having said something about the moral climate of business and about ethical theory, we turn to some specific issues that relate to business and the people in it, specifically to the relationship between the firm and its employees. Understandably the issues we could raise are legion, ranging from those peculiar to each profession (such as accountancy or marketing) to those common to each industry (such as construction or automotive). But our purpose here is not to prescribe moral behavior in specific professions, trades, or industries. Rather, it is to show how we can pursue moral inquiry in business generally, within the context of ethical thought. A good way to do this, it seems, is to focus on issues in which a vast number of business people have a stake. With this in mind, we'll confine our remarks to topics that cut across occupations and industrial lines. We'll examine issues which the widest variety of business people can identify with and can benefit from exploring.

Thus Chapters 3, 4, and 5 present subjects dealing with personnel administration. Specifically, in Chapter 3 we will examine questions relative to hiring, promotions, discipline, and discharge; in Chapter 4 we consider the issue of job atmosphere, including the function of work, work environment, and job content; in Chapter 5 we raise questions about organizational intrusion into the private lives of employees. Whereas these three chapters generally consider the firm's responsibilities to employees, Chapter 6 looks at employee responsibilities to the firm. Again, in an attempt to give our discussion the broadest base of appeal, we have centered the discussion on conflicts of interest, which seem to lie at the heart of most problems dealing with employee responsibilities to the firm. Within this context, we consider financial investments, use of official position for private gain, bribes and kickbacks, gifts and entertainment. Our intention is not to exhaust all pertinent topics or even to present those which a consensus of business people considers the most important. It is, instead, to show how we can pursue moral inquiry in business within a framework of ethical theory.

3

HIRING, PROMOTIONS, DISCIPLINE, AND DISCHARGE

In July 1963 a young black man named Leon Myart applied for a job as an analyzer and phaser at Motorola's plant in Franklin Park, Illinois. After Myart had filled out an application form, he was given General Ability Test No. 10, a test designed to measure candidates' abilities to acquire technical information by evaluating their verbal comprehension and simple reasoning skills. Myart scored four, two points below the minimum requirements. As a result, personnel gave Myart no further tests. They briefly interviewed, then dismissed him, the entire process taking about fifteen minutes.

Through his lawyers Myart, who had an extensive background in electronics, sued Motorola, charging discrimination in its hiring practices. Specifically Myart charged that Test No. 10 was discriminatory because it did not take trainability into account and because it tested for education and skills that were not actually needed on the job or could easily be learned or compensated for by other skills.

On March 14, 1966, the Supreme Court of Illinois found Motorola innocent of discrimination in its hiring practices. But, most important, the court did not decide whether Test No. 10 was discriminatory.[1]

Apart from its legal implications, the Myart case raises some important moral questions about how firms treat persons during the hiring process. It makes us wonder whether the use of testing as a criterion for hiring can ever be immoral. If so, how and when? What responsibilities does a firm have for the validation and administration of tests it uses in the recruitment process?

The Myart case indirectly invites speculations about other aspects of personnel management: promotions, discipline, and discharge. If management can deal unfairly with prospective employees during recruiting and hiring, how does it deal with present employees in other areas?

1. *See Thomas M. Garrett et al.,* Cases in Business Ethics *(New York: Appleton-Century-Crofts, 1968), pp. 47–50.*

This chapter will focus on moral concerns of the employer-employee relationship during hiring, promotion, discipline, and discharge. We will attempt to sort out what rights employees have in these areas and what responsibilities employers have. Finally, we'll show how the ethical theories we've presented might be applied in general ways to the topics discussed.

Hiring

A basic function of the employer or personnel manager is hiring. Persons responsible in this area generally hire people who will best maximize the efficiency of the firm. In discharging these obligations, personnel managers have to be very careful to be fair. Most moral questions about hiring—as well as promoting, disciplining, and discharging—involve a judgment of fairness. Moral decisions in these areas inevitably boil down to the fair thing to do. As you might imagine, determining the fair approach is seldom easy. It's helpful, though, to be aware of the steps in hiring that most frequently raise questions of fairness: screening, testing, and interviewing.

Screening

When firms are serious about recruiting employees, they attempt to screen them, that is, to attract only those applicants who have a good chance of qualifying for the job. When done properly, screening ensures a competent pool of candidates and guarantees that everyone has been dealt with fairly. Conversely, when the screening process is implemented improperly, it undermines effective recruitment and invites injustices into the hiring process.

Screening begins with a job description and specification. *A job description lists all pertinent details about a job, including its duties, responsibilities, working conditions, and physical requirements. A job specification describes the qualifications an employee needs to possess, such as skills, educational experience, appearance, and physical attributes.* Completeness is important. When either the job description or job specification is inadequate or unspecific, firms risk injuring candidates. Suppose, for example, candidate Rita Cox takes a day off from work and travels 200 miles at her own expense to be interviewed for a position as a computer programmer with Singleton Computer Company. During the interview Cox discovers that Singleton needs someone with IBM background, not Sperry Rand. Mentioning that detail in the job specification could have prevented Cox's loss of time and money. But even when specifications don't directly injure candidates as in this case, they could cause indirect injury by depriving candidates of information they're entitled to know in order to make informed decisions about their job prospects.

Questions of more serious moral concern arise when job specifications contain requirements irrelevant to job performance. In general, age, race, national origin, religion, sex, and other extraneous factors should not appear in a job specification nor figure in the hiring. Such irrelevant requirements have the effect of excluding candidates from consideration on non-job-related grounds. This clearly raises an important moral concern about justice. But there is another aspect of hiring that raises the question of justice even more dramatically, and it is the one this chapter began with: testing.

Tests

Testing is an integral part of the hiring process, especially with large firms. Tests are generally designed to measure the applicant's verbal, quantitative, and logical skills. Aptitude tests help determine job suitability; skill tests measure the applicant's proficiency in specific areas such as typing and shorthand; personality tests help determine the applicant's maturity and sociability. In addition, some firms engaged in the design and assembly of precision equipment administer dexterity tests to determine how nimbly applicants can use their hands and fingers.

To be successful, a test must be valid. *Validity* refers to the quality of measuring precisely what a test is designed to determine. Just as important, tests must be reliable. *Reliability* refers to the quality of accurately determining an applicant's ability to learn a desired function. Thus, if a test predicts that most applicants can learn a desired function when in fact they can't or don't, the testing device isn't reliable. Neither is a test reliable if it determines an applicant's ability to do a job without training rather than his or her ability to *learn* the desired function.

Clearly not all tests are valid or reliable. Many tests are not able to measure desired qualities, others exhibit a woefully low level of forecast accuracy. Moreover, some companies use tests that haven't been designed for the company's particular situation. The point is that legitimizing tests is frequently an expensive and time-consuming prospect. But if tests are used, the companies using them are obliged to ensure their validity and reliability. Otherwise, companies risk injuring applicants, stockholders, and even the general public. At the same time, companies must be cautious about the importance they place in such tests. In the last analysis a test is only one of many factors in an overall evaluative process. Ignoring these things, firms can easily introduce injustices into the hiring process.

But even when tests are valid and reliable, they can be both unfair and unjust. They could still be unfairly discriminatory. Take, for example, intelligence tests. Many students of such tests contend that they favor a white, middle-class test taker. since the questions contain points of reference which this group relate to well because of their cultural and educational background. For ghetto-bred blacks, however, the tests could be as mystifying as if they were composed in a foreign language because they don't relate to black culture. As a result, such tests can measure one's mastery of cultural assumptions more than one's intellectual capacity or potential. This was precisely the issue in the Myart appeal. Although the case was never clearly settled, in 1971 the United States Supreme Court took a decisive stand on testing in the case of Griggs v. Duke Power Company. The case involved thirteen black laborers who were denied promotions because they scored low on a company-sponsored intelligence test involving verbal and mathematical puzzles. In the ruling the Court found that the Civil Rights Act prohibits employers from requiring a high-school education or the passing of a general intelligence test as a prerequisite for employment or promotion without demonstrating that such conditions relate directly to job performance. Many firms responded by eliminating such tests. A more constructive response would have been to ensure that the tests were not culturally discriminatory.

Finally, we should mention the use of statistics as they enter into the overall evaluation of applicants. There's virtually no aspect of life today that doesn't show some evidence of the computer revolution and its accompanying blizzard of statistics. When applied directly to groups, statistics ordinarily prove justifiable and useful. Thus, Betty Rinehold is justified in not locating her tool and dye plant in an area that statistical analysis reveals to be one of generally low worker production. Problems arise, however, when she applies statistical generalizations to individuals. Thus Rinehold's use of those statistics as a basis for not hiring Bob Armstrong, who happens to come from that area, raises serious questions of justice. In so doing, she judges him guilty by association with the group of which he happens to be a part. She treats him unfairly.

A third aspect of the hiring process that raises questions of fairness is the inevitable job interview. Together with screening and testing, interviewing constitutes a principal part of recruitment.

Interviews

When moral issues arise in interviewing, they almost always relate to the manner in which the interview was conducted. The literature of personnel management rightly cautions against rudeness, coarseness, hostility, and condescension in interviewing job applicants. In guarding against these qualities, personnel managers would do well to focus on the humanity of the individuals who sit across the desk from them, mindful of the very human need that has brought those people into the office. But having done this, interviewers still risk treating applicants unfairly when they remain oblivious to their own personal biases, a subject which personnel management literature seems surprisingly unmindful of.

In interviewing, the human tendency is to like and prefer persons we identify with. Thus, Greg Tremont feels especially sympathetic to applicant George Horner because George has recently graduated from Tremont's own alma mater. Tremont feels this way despite ample evidence indicating that the institution from which one has been graduated has no material effect on job performance. As a result of this bias, Tremont treats Horner preferentially, treats other applicants unfairly, and renders harm to the firm by abandoning his objectivity.

Management bias, therefore, can raise moral issues in interviews. Those in a hiring position should recognize their own biases, what the English philosopher Francis Bacon (1561–1626) once termed the idols of the mind. As Bacon put it: "The human understanding is like a false mirror, which, receiving rays irregularly, distorts and discolors the nature of things by mingling its own nature with it."[2] In short, we view things, people included, through the lens of our own

2. *Francis Bacon,* The New Organon, *ed. Fulton H. Anderson (New York: Bobbs-Merrill, 1960), p. 48.*

preconceptions. It's true that Bacon's remarks were addressed to the nature of scientific method, but his observations seem appropriate here as well. For failing to heed Bacon's "idols," interviewers can easily sacrifice the objectivity that both the nature of their jobs and fairness require of them.

Before concluding these comments about hiring, we should indicate that there is a substantial cluster of issues that raise additional moral concerns. Among these is the treatment of women and other disadvantaged groups. So important and complex are the moral issues that this area raises that we will devote all of Chapter 8 to them.

For now let it suffice to underscore that hiring involves more than simply acquiring the best people for a job. Implicit in any hiring process is the moral concern of fairness. Just as important as how a firm treats potential employees is how it treats present employees. The area of on-the-job treatment is fraught with moral concerns, only a handful of which will occupy us at this point.

On the Job

The second major facet of personnel management involves how managers treat employees on the job. Many of the problems in this area relate to work environment and content. *Work environment* refers to such things as wages, working conditions, and company policy. *Work content* refers to the work itself insofar as it provides workers with autonomy, a sense of accomplishment, an opportunity to develop talents and skills, personal fulfillment, and related experiences. So numerous and important are the moral issues that these facets of job atmosphere raise, the next chapter will be spent on these subjects. Here we wish to focus on one aspect of the working experience that raises substantial moral concerns, namely, promotions.

Promotions

In theory, essentially the same criterion that applies to hiring also applies to promotions: job qualifications. But generalizations about standards for decisions in the work place need ample qualification. This especially applies to job qualifications as the standing determinant of promotions.

Let's face it: other things besides job qualifications often determine promotions. How long you've been with a firm, how well you're liked, whom you know, even when you were last promoted—all these influence promotions in the real business world. As with hiring, the key moral concern here is fairness. Nobody would seriously argue that promoting the unqualified is fair or justifiable. It's a serious breach of duty to owners, employees, and ultimately the general public. But many reasonable people debate whether promoting by job qualification alone is the fairest thing to do. Are other criteria admissible? If so, when, and how much weight should those criteria carry? These are tough questions with no easy answers. They require a well-honed concept of fair play, an ability to compare and contrast the courses available, and even a fertile imagination for devising alternatives. To highlight the problem, let's consider seniority, inbreeding, and nepotism.

SENIORITY. *Seniority refers to longevity on a job or with a firm.* Frequently job transfers or promotions are made strictly on the basis of seniority; individuals with the most longevity automatically receive the promotions. But problems arise.

To illustrate, personnel manager Manuel Rodriguez needs to fill the job of quality control supervisor. Carol Martin seems better qualified for the job than Jim Turner, except in one respect. Turner's been on the job for three years longer than Martin. Whom should Manuel promote to quality control supervisor?

The answer isn't easy. Those who'd argue for Carol Martin, that is, opponents of seniority, would undoubtedly claim that the firm has an obligation to fill the job with the most qualified person. In this way the firm is served and the most qualified are rewarded. Those advancing Turner's promotion, that is, proponents of seniority, would contend that the firm should be loyal to its senior employees, that they should reward them for faithful service. In this way, employees have an incentive to work hard and to remain with the firm.

When company policies indicate how much part seniority should play in promotions, the problem abates, but does not vanish. We can still wonder about the morality of the policy itself. In cases where no clear policy exists, the problem begs for an answer. Should seniority play a role in promotions and job transfers?

The question may seem to have a simple answer until we reflect on a few facts. First, seniority in itself does not necessarily indicate competence or loyalty. Simply because Jim Turner's been on the job three years longer than Carol Martin, we needn't therefore assume that he's more competent or more loyal. Moreover, promotions strictly by seniority can in some instances harm the promoted worker. Personnel manager Rodriguez is especially sensitive to this because of the experience of his friend Rob Walsch.

Walsch was assistant director of security at National Storage, Inc. In that job he related well with maintenance crews, plant operation staff, and just about everyone he dealt with on a regular basis. Walsch also showed keen judgment in distinguishing between the letter and the spirit of the law. Since National had a policy of promoting by seniority, barring egregious incompetence, when the director of security retired, Walsch was promoted to that position. Unfortunately he didn't perform as well as expected. He continued to perform many of his former duties, rarely delegated authority, and balked at the need to direct subordinates. He even showed an inflexibility few would have thought him capable of. In brief, Walsch wasn't ready or prepared for this leadership role. He seemed to be promoted beyond his level of competency. In fact Walsch has complained bitterly to Rodriguez about his experience with the new job, the substantial pay increase and new title notwithstanding.

Of course, there are instances when seniority may be a real indicator of job qualifications as well as length of service. A pilot who has logged hundreds of hours of flying time with an airline is conceivably more qualified for captaincy than one who hasn't. Then there's the question of employee expectations. If personnel expects seniority to count substantially, management can injure morale and productivity by discounting it. True, worker morale might suffer equally should seniority solely determine promotions. Ambitious and competent workers might see little point in refining skills and developing talents when positions are doled out strictly on a longevity basis.

It seems, then, that an unqualified answer to the question of what part, if any, seniority ought to play in promotions is impossible. This does not mean that managers thereby escape any responsibilities in this area. On the contrary, precisely because the issue defies simple resolution, management must give its policies careful consideration. Of paramount importance in any decision is that management remember its twin responsibilities here of promoting on the basis of qualifications and of recognizing prolonged and constructive contributions to the firm: fidelity to the firm and loyalty to workers. A policy that provides for promotions strictly on the basis of qualifications seems heartless, while one that promotes by seniority alone seems mindless. The challenge for management, then, is how to merge these dual responsibilities in a way that is beneficial to the firm and fair to all concerned. It is no easy task.

INBREEDING.   *All that we've said about seniority applies with equal force to in-breeding, the practice of promoting exclusively from within the firm.* In theory, whenever managers must fill positions, they should look only to competence. The most competent, whether within or without the firm, should receive the position. In this way responsibilities to owners are best served.

In practice, however, managers must seriously consider the impact of outside recruitment on in-house morale. Years of loyal service, often at great personal expense, invariably create a unique relationship between employer and employee. The eighteen years that Becky Thompson has worked for National Textiles creates a relationship between her and the firm that does not exist between the firm and an outsider it may wish to hire for the job that Thompson hopes to be promoted to. Some persons would argue that management has a moral obligation to remember this loyalty when determining promotions, especially when outside recruitment departs from established policy.

NEPOTISM.   *Nepotism is the practice of showing favoritism to relatives and close friends.* Suppose a manager hired a relative strictly because of the relationship between them. Such an action would raise a number of moral concerns; chief among them would be disregard both of managerial responsibilities to the organization and of fairness to all other persons aspiring to the position.

Clearly not all instances of nepotism raise serious moral concerns. For example, when a firm is strictly a family operation and has as its purpose providing work for family members, nepotistic practices are generally justified. Also, that a person is a relative or friend of firm members should not summarily exclude him or her from job considerations. Nevertheless even when such people are qualified for a position, responsible management must consider the impact of nepotistic hiring. Will the appointment breed resentment and jealousy among other employees? Will it discourage qualified outsiders from seeking employment with the firm? Will it create problems in future placement, scheduling, remunerations, and general dismissal?[3]

In general, then, management should not look on close relationships as

---

3.   *See Garrett,* Business Ethics, *p. 44.*

either an asset or a liability. Ethical decisions in this area will be characterized primarily by two considerations: (1) the qualifications of the candidate and (2) the potential impact of hiring that person on interests both inside and outside the firm.

In sum, the primary concerns in promotions are similar to those in hiring. Management must promote the most qualified, while at the same time ensuring fairness to all concerned. The moral question of fairness presents itself in discussing the third principal aspect of business's relationship with employees, namely, discipline and discharge.

Discipline

In order for the firm to function in an orderly, efficient, and productive way, personnel departments establish guidelines for behavior based on such factors as appearance, punctuality, dependability, efficiency, and cooperation. We don't intend to debate the morality of specific rules and regulations here, only the firm's treatment of employees when infractions occur.

At the outset, let's note that managers should discipline workers who violate behavioral standards because it is necessary for the firm, other employees, and society at large. This having been said, we can note that most moral issues in this area relate to how the manager imposes the discipline. For example, it's one thing to speak with a person privately about some infraction, quite another to chastise or punish the person publicly. Also, trying to correct someone's behavior on a graduated basis, from verbal warning to dismissal, is different from firing someone for a first infraction. The point is that discipline, while perhaps desirable and necessary, raises moral concerns in the way it's administered.

By far most problems involving the administration of discipline relate to fairness. Fairness is ordinarily thought to exist in the work place when rules and standards are themselves fair and when all parties are subjected to them in the same way. But to ensure the existence of such an atmosphere the principles of just cause and due process must operate.

JUST CAUSE. *Just cause* refers to reasons for discipline or discharge that deal directly with job performance. In general, whatever leads directly or indirectly to employee infractions of the job description may be considered a job-related reason. Thus, Phil Bruen's boss Charlie Whyte is justified in disciplining Bruen for chronic tardiness but not for voting Republican.

Of course, the distinction between a job-related and nonrelated issue is not always as apparent as we've made it out to be. How a person behaves outside work is often incompatible with the image a company wishes to project. In such cases does the firm have a right to discipline its employees? The answer depends largely on one's concept of company image and private lives, on precisely where the company image stops and the private life begins, and on the extent of organizational influence over individual lives. Such concerns involve complex questions of personal and group rights that we'll consider thoroughly in the next chapter. Suffice it here to repeat that *just cause* refers to reasons directly related to job performance.

DUE PROCESS.   Another prominent topic in discussions about worker discipline and discharge is the principle of due process. *Due process* refers to the specific and systematic means workers have of appealing discipline and discharge. It deals with the step-by-step procedure by which an employee can appeal a managerial decision. Where employees are unionized, such a procedure usually exists. When the procedure does not exist, serious moral questions of justice regarding employee discipline inevitably arise.

Discharge

All that has been said about discipline can also be applied to firing and discharge. In most cases, work contracts prescribe termination procedures. But strict reliance on the contract may fall short of moral behavior. For example, unless it is stated in the contract or employees have union representation, a company is not obligated to give reasons for firing an employee nor must it give advance notice. When employers fire someone without notice or cause, they may have been strictly faithful to contractual agreement, but have they been fair?

In answering this question, it's helpful to distinguish between two employer responsibilities. On the one hand, employers bear the responsibility of terminating the employment of workers who don't discharge their contractual obligations. But employers are also obliged to terminate these workers as painlessly as possible. In other words, although employers have the right to fire, this does not mean they have the right to fire in whatever way they choose. In fact, firing can be so materially and psychologically destructive to employees that we should consider what management can do to ease its effects. Relying on unemployment compensation laws may be a good beginning in determining where one's obligations lie, but such laws hardly constitute the last moral word.

One obvious thing employers can do to ease the trauma of firing is to provide sufficient notice. Just what constitutes sufficient notice depends primarily on the nature of the job, the skill involved, the availability of similar jobs, even the longevity of employees. Where employers have reason to suspect that employees will react in a hostile, destructive way to notice of their terminations, "sufficient notice" might take the form of severance pay. Ideally, the length of notice should be spelled out in a work contract. But even when it is not, management still has responsibilities in this area.

Today, with the frequency of plant shutdowns and relocations, sizable layoffs, and automation, moral management requires careful study of responsibilities to workers in times of termination. It is important to realize that the realities just mentioned affect not only workers but their families and communities as well. Obviously we can't specify what measures can or should be taken to ease the effects of displacement. Different circumstances suggest different measures. In some instances, job retraining might be appropriate, together with adequate notice and sufficient severance pay. Where mergers are involved, firms might notify workers well in advance and provide them with alternatives. Whatever the approach, the point remains that when firms terminate workers, serious moral questions arise.

Ethical Theories

In applying ethical theories to the questions of hiring, promotions, discipline, and discharge, we find a significant difference between consequential and nonconsequential theories that will be mentioned now and in subsequent chapters. Accounting for this difference are essentially conflicting notions of justice. On the one hand is the consequential view that associates justice with efficiency; what is just is what produces the most happiness for me (egoism) or for everyone (utilitarianism). In contrast, nonconsequential theories do not associate justice with consequences. They don't appeal to the net effects of an action to determine whether or not it's just. Rather, nonconsequentialists generally associate justice with giving others their due or with some concept of fair play. As such, justice is noncontingent; it doesn't depend on results or effects.

Specifically, egoism would view problems in these personnel management areas from the perspective of self-interest. In effect, the firm has no responsibilities outside those to itself. It should act in a way that best advances its long-term self-interests. This approach would also apply to individuals within the firm. Whether or not it is moral to administer a discriminatory intelligence test to job applicants depends on whether that act advances self-interests more than any other alternative. Egoists would apply a similar rationale to other questions relative to hiring, promotions, discipline, and discharge.

Utilitarianism would be concerned with the consequences of actions in these areas, but consequences for all concerned not just the individual. Specifically the act utilitarian would examine the individual act and determine whether it would produce more total happiness than any other alternative. Act utilitarianism would not offer a blanket indictment or approval of any kind of action but would want to appraise the individual act itself. For example, if asked whether they disapproved of hiring someone strictly on the basis of friendship or relationship, act utilitarians would not commit themselves. They'd ask for all the circumstances surrounding a particular case. On the basis of the total good produced for everyone, they would make a moral judgment. Obviously, they might decide that such flagrant nepotism in that instance was wrong. But they wouldn't say it was wrong because it didn't treat people equally. It was immoral because the total consequences for all concerned were less favorable than another alternative's.

The rule utilitarian, on the other hand, would examine the consequences of keeping the rule such an action falls under. Rule utilitarianism would respond directly to the original question about the morality of hiring someone strictly on the basis of friendship or relationship. The rule here might be stated: "Never hire people exclusively on the basis of friendship or relationship." If keeping this rule produced more total good than not keeping it, then rule utilitarians would support as moral an action that kept the rule and condemn as immoral one that broke it. Again, however, as with egoism and act utilitarianism, rule utilitarians would evaluate behavior in these areas on the basis of efficiency, not fair play.

Joseph Fletcher's situational ethics, while decidedly consequential, tempers its appeal to consequences with a concept of justice rooted not in efficiency but in loving concern, that is, giving people what is due them. We'll have many occasions in the chapters ahead to underscore this nuance in situationalism which distinguishes it from pure act utilitarianism, although some moralists would argue that the distinction is more theoretical than actual. It's true that Fletcher claims that only the end justifies the means, but at the same time a close reading of him reveals a committed concern for the means since only by acts of love can we hope to produce the greatest amount of loving concern. Such a concern with the means of an action or with its motivational impulse is not apparent in utilitarianism; both versions are preoccupied with ends.

Certainly Fletcher is concerned with ends, but he also seems mindful of the justice of the means employed to achieve those ends. By *justice* Fletcher means providing people with their due. How then might Fletcher react to the flagrant nepotism mentioned earlier? First, like the act utilitarian, he would not offer any general rule concerning it, as the rule utilitarian might. On the contrary, he would inquire into the total amount of loving concern that such an act exhibited or was calculated to produce. Unless we're warping Fletcher's position, it seems that in this he strikes a somewhat different pose from the utilitarian's.

Recall that the hedonistic calculus of utilitarianism requires an assessment of the total happiness produced for all concerned. It could very well be that flagrant nepotism as described earlier could in some instances produce more total happiness than any other alternative and therefore would be moral according to act utilitarians. Although Fletcher's situationalism allows such a verdict in theory, at the same time it uses an "agape calculus," that is, a standard which measures greatest loving concern. Such a standard necessitates a consideration of the purpose of the action. If unbridled nepotism is practiced in love, then it is right and good. For the situationalist what makes an action in any of these areas right is its loving purpose. If the act is performed lovingly, it is right; if it's performed unlovingly, it's wrong. Thus, even though a nepotistic practice did produce the most happiness for the most people, situationalists would question its morality if it did not find its impulse in loving concern. They would find themselves agreeing with Kant that the only really good thing is a good will. With Kant, a good will is expressed in commitment to legalism; with Christian situational ethics, the good will is the one that follows the path of loving concern, a path that sometimes leads in one direction, other times in a different one.

When we apply nonconsequentialist theories to issues in hiring, promotions, discipline, and discharge, we notice the sharpness of the distinction between their concept of justice and the nonconsequentialists'. The Golden Rule, for example, introduces the element of reciprocity into moral decision making: we should do to others as we would have them do to us. Thus, if you were a bona fide job applicant, would you want the position to go to someone else strictly on a friendship or relationship basis? Would you want to be treated this way? If no, then you shouldn't engage in such unvarnished nepotism.

Looking at Immanuel Kant's ethical theory, we can note that Kant's prohibition against using individuals as means to ends would preclude an approach to justice based on efficiency. One could never justify hiring someone on the basis of friendship or relationship even if by so doing one could produce more total happiness for those concerned than by following any other alternative. Specifically, an application of Kant's categorical imperative would require that we could wish the maxim of our action to become a universal law. In this case, we could state the maxim as, "Be nepotistic in hiring." In analyzing such a maxim for logical consistency, a Kantian might suggest that the nature of the hiring process requires that individuals applying for a job be judged by criteria that are job-related and by the same criteria. But by definition nepotism would violate this process. In effect, then, a strict application of the categorical imperative suggests that the practice of nepotism is logically incompatible with the hiring process. If this analysis is correct, then giving preferential hiring treatment to friends or relatives is always immoral. Likewise, to exclude friends or relatives from job considerations simply because of the close relationships would also be wrong. Notice the decisiveness of Kant's positions. Having ascertained that the maxim under discussion could not be logically universalized, we are then forbidden to perform acts reflective of it. Contrast this rigidity with Fletcher's position, which, while introducing the purpose of the will, as does Kant's, does not restrict the will to the adherence to universals. Kant would consider nepotism always wrong. Fletcher would not take such a stand. He could approve of a nepotistic act if it sprung from loving concern.

Both Ross and Rawls would be mindful of justice as fair play and not as efficiency. For Ross justice is a prima facie duty. An act that is not in accord with what people deserve violates this duty to justice. Thus, in applying for a job, people have a right to be evaluated in the same way based on the same job-related criteria. As a result, tests that discriminate in non-job-related ways, positions that are secured on the basis of favoritism, discipline which is administered arbitrarily and unevenly, all pose serious violations of Ross's duty to justice, apart from any consideration of consequences. This doesn't mean that such actions are never justifiable. In fact, they may represent only one of many duties operating in a given situation. Ultimate moral judgment rests on an analysis of all the prima facie duties involved. In theory, then, Ross could tolerate an act of injustice in these personnel management areas when it was demonstrated that more pressing duties warranted it. This theoretical qualification shouldn't minimize the fact that in recruitment, promotion, discipline, and discharge, duties of justice would play a major part in the moral resolution.

John Rawls's maximin principle would call for a similar nonconsequential view of justice. Especially appropriate to consider in examining questions of hiring, promotions, discipline, and discharge would be Rawls's equal liberty principle. Recall that by *equality* Rawls means the impartial and equitable administration and application of the rules which define a practice. The injunction to treat everyone the same cuts to the heart of the principal moral concern in these personnel management areas: fair play. In dealing with specific problems such as flagrant nepotism, biased tests, and arbitrary discipline, Rawls's equal liberty principle seemingly allows for the establishment of some broad moral guidelines. Thus, Rawls would ask whether rational, self-interested creatures in the original position would agree to the practices under consideration. Would they agree to be bound by a policy, rule, or system that allowed for nepotism as described, discriminatory tests, and arbitrary discipline? Taking Rawls's perspective of the least well-off, we're inclined to answer no, for the simple reason that people would realize that they could be victimized by such procedures; rational, self-interested creatures would never agree to this victimization. Another way of looking at this is through the lens of a fundamental aspect of the equal liberty principle: Rawls's concept of reciprocity.

By *reciprocity* Rawls means that a practice be such that all members could and would accept it and be bound by it. Thus, would those who hire exclusively on the basis of friendship or relationship accept and be bound by such a procedure themselves? Would those who administer biased tests willingly sit for tests that were biased against them? Would those who fire without notice or severance choose to be subjected to the same practices? In this way it seems that Rawls would attempt to carve out some general moral directions in these areas. He would not, however, work his way into an unbending, inflexible stand on them. Rather he would develop broad outlines of fair play relative to particular issues. Where possible exceptions to these broad moral outlines arise, they would have to pass the test of the difference principle. In other words, any violations of rules derived from Rawls's equal liberty principle would have to be shown to work ideally to the advantage of every individual affected, or at least of those most disadvantaged. Under no circumstances could a violation be justified on grounds of the social good.

Finally, proportionality theorists would favor a view of justice associated with fair play, just deserts, and the inherent worth and dignity of human beings. Put in other words, proportionalists would consider fair and equal treatment in the work place an inherent human right and basic human need. Violations would constitute a major evil.

Thus, under no circumstances could a firm or its representatives will as a means or an end that employees be treated unfairly or unequally. For example, to deliberately screen out an applicant on a non-job-related factor such as race or sex would be immoral. In cases where the evil is not willed as a means or an end but permitted or risked, then questions of sufficient reason or proportionality arise. Suppose, for example, that faced with dire financial prospects, a firm must shut down one of its plants, thereby putting several hundred employees out of work, not to mention the hardship which the shutdown will cause the small community where it's located. (Suppose that over the years the town has grown almost completely dependent on the jobs and economic resources that the firm generates.) Nevertheless, the firm must either close down this particular plant or seriously risk the jobs of the thousands of its other employees at some future date. In such a case, the firm does not will evil as a means or end. It merely wishes to survive and preserve the jobs of the vast majority of its employees. To do this, it will shut down a plant, which of itself is not evil. However, the unfavorable side effects surely constitute major evils, which the firm will permit to occur. The morality of such a decision, then, depends on a complete evaluation of all the facts involved in order to determine whether or not more probable good than harm will result from the firm's decision. We're assuming, of course, that it has no other alternative than to remain open. If it had a less harmful alternative that would accomplish the same result, proportionalists would argue that the firm would be obliged to pursue it. To do otherwise would be immoral. Since there are major evils involved, the firm would be required to develop a greater degree of sufficient reasons than if only a minor evil were being permitted or even willed.

Obviously, we've been able to provide only the barest outline of some of the ways in which these moral theories might find use in the personnel management areas of hiring, promotions, discipline, and discharge. Here, as in the forthcoming chapters, our remarks are intended to be nothing more than suggestive. As in all areas of business ethics, the issues raised require working out the application of these theories in great detail. Also, whatever we've said in applying each theory bears the qualifications that the theory as a whole does. These qualifications were raised in discussing the weaknesses of each theory. In short, our remarks should be viewed as a jumping off point for a full-scale discussion of these and related issues and to a more satisfactory application of ethical theories.

CASE PRESENTATION
The President's Son

Bob Watson, twenty-five-year veteran with General Auto Corporation and its senior sales executive, read the request with some concern. He sensed trouble.

It wasn't that such requests were uncommon. Quite the reverse: the cars were selling well; so naturally almost all of G.A.'s dealers had requested more. But the company had strict dealership allotment regulations, and Bob had regretfully turned down every request. Yet he wondered whether he could handle this request so routinely. It was from Bob Mitchell, Jr., son of Robert A. Mitchell, president of General Auto.

Watson gazed at the letter, thinking more about the feelings of the senior Mitchell than about the request. He knew that while Mitchell never actively solicited the interests of relatives within the firm, he wasn't above it. In fact, Mitchell had made an exception to the company's prohibition against the employment of managers' children when he permitted another Mitchell son, Ted, to start with G.A.

"Permitted," thought Watson, "that's a kind word for it." He folded the letter neatly along its creases. It was common knowledge that an executive with a G.A. supplier had been reassigned to make room for Ted Mitchell. What's more, everyone believed that the president was now grooming son Ted to take over the company some day.

Bob Watson didn't want to be "reassigned." At fifty he had recently secured the position that he'd aspired to from his earliest days with General Auto, a quarter of a century before. Maybe it wouldn't happen, Watson told himself. Maybe Mitchell wouldn't expect him to show any favoritism toward Bob, Jr. But then he thought about his own two kids in college, how much he and wife Anne were enjoying the new house . . . and about that other executive and what *he* was doing these days.

1.   *Apply each of the ethical theories to the decision that Watson must make. What course, if any, does each prescribe? Explain.*

2.   *What do you think Watson ought to do? Give reasons.*

CASE PRESENTATION
Shutdown at Withrow

Bill and Barbara Redding first met while working at Withrow Cabinets Company in their small hometown of Derwent. They subsequently fell in love, married, and began saving for their first home. Their future seemed assured.

But not any more. The grapevine has it that Withrow plans to move its operations to a state where labor is cheaper. The rumor has caused much concern and bitterness in Derwent where Withrow Cabinets has been the town's main work place for generations.

"I don't know what we're going to do," Bill tells his wife, who is expecting their third child in a few months. "You just start getting ahead of the game and they pull the rug out from under you."

In addition to the Reddings, about half of Derwent's two thousand workers will lose their jobs if Withrow Cabinets relocates. What's more, residents not employed by Withrow are small business people or self-employed contractors, mechanics, and plumbers; all are dependent on the presence of the plant for their livelihood. And to make matters worse, a local bank vice-president has predicted that such a move would severely hamper local government, which is largely dependent on the sizable real estate tax that the company currently pays.

Company owner Gary Withrow knows there is one alternative to moving. It would involve laying off older workers who receive high wages and replacing them with cheap labor who would accept the minimum wage level or below. He realizes that few displaced employees could get jobs elsewhere in the town and would probably be forced to move. But it is an alternative. Since Withrow Cabinets is not a union shop, he could take such action without fearing reprisals from organized labor.

1.   *Which of the two alternatives might the ethical theories prescribe? Apply each theory to the Withrow decision.*

2.   *Do you think Withrow ought to lay off older workers or move the plant? (Qualify your response with information you think is relevant, even though it is not provided.)*

3.   *If Withrow moves, does it have any responsibilities to its workers and the community at large? If it does, what are they?*

CASE PRESENTATION
Job Offer Withdrawn at Evergreen

Ronald Parsons felt good. And why not? As the personnel coordinator he was about to fill the final job vacancy in Evergreen Recreation's summer camp program. The program was an increasingly popular and profitable outgrowth of the firm's principal interest: the manufacture of sporting goods and recreational equipment.

What made Parsons particularly happy was the quality of the man he was about to hire: Henry Phillips, a thirty-year-old college graduate and successful 114-pound Amateur Athletic Union wrestler who had nearly qualified for the 1980 U.S. Olympic wrestling team. Phillips surely would round out Evergreen's athletic program, which already had received widespread commendation as an exceptional training ground for young people seriously interested in athletics. Before placing the call to Phillips, Parsons looked through the letters of recommendation that had arrived on the young man's behalf. Parsons couldn't wait to meet him. He picked up his office phone and eagerly placed the transcontinental call to Henry Phillips at his home in California.

Phillips was elated at the news. And Parsons's own enthusiasm was thereby increased. During the conversation, Parsons couldn't help being distracted by a machine noise in the background. At first he ignored it, but when it persisted he asked Phillips about it.

"Oh, that," Phillips said matter-of-factly, "I'm typing our conversation in Braille."

Parsons felt his stomach fall. Hesitantly he asked how much vision Phillips had.

"I can tell you that without blinking an eye," Phillips laughed. "None." Then he added, "I've been blind since I was two."

Parsons asked Phillips why he hadn't mentioned this in his application.

"No one asked," Phillips said. "Besides, you would have told me you had no openings just as everyone else has."

"Oh I wouldn't say. . ." Parsons stopped in mid sentence. The young man was right.

"To tell you the truth, Mr. Parsons," Phillips added, "I thought those recommending me would have mentioned it. If they didn't, they mustn't have thought it relevant." Parsons could anticipate Phillips's next question: "So why should you?"

The conversation ended awkwardly a few minutes later. In the days ahead Ronald Parsons gave the matter serious consideration, rereading the numerous letters of recommendation and poring over Phillips's transcripts. He felt his enthusiasm for Phillips rekindled when he read the sheaf of newspaper clippings testifying to Phillips's wrestling ability and achievements. In the end, Parsons concluded that there was no sound reason Phillips shouldn't get the job.

He even felt guilty about having doubted him simply because he was blind. Still, he thought he should bring the matter to Evergreen's board of directors.

While agreeing with Parsons that Phillips certainly had much to recommend him for the job, the board expressed grave reservations about employing him. Several members expressed doubt that Phillips could do the work satisfactorily. "How can he tell kids what they do wrong if he can't see what they're doing?" one asked. Another wondered about Evergreen's liability if one of their charges suffered an injury while under Phillips's supervision. Still others mentioned the additional responsibilities that all camp instructors, coaches, and counselors were expected to assume on occasion. Could Phillips adequately discharge them? As a result of their skepticism, the board regretfully instructed Parsons to rescind his job offer to Henry Phillips.

Parsons left the meeting disconsolate. He was more convinced than ever that Phillips should get the job, that Phillips was being assumed incompetent when all the evidence indicated otherwise. If he had his way . . . but what could he do? He had his orders.

1. *Do you approve of the board's decision?*

2. *Apply each of the ethical theories to the decision that faced the board. What courses of action might they prescribe?*

3. *Was Parsons right in going to the board? Should he just have hired Phillips?*

4. *What do you think Parsons ought to do now? What courses of action might our ethical theories prescribe?*

The Effect of the Supreme Court's Seniority Decisions

Stephen C. Swanson

In recent years the practice of job placement by seniority has become intertwined with the nation's attempt to root out racial and sexual discrimination in the work place. As we indicated earlier, in Chapter 8 we'll examine problems peculiar to women and other disadvantaged groups. But since we discussed seniority in this chapter without having raised the racial and sexual discrimination aspects of it, it seems appropriate to focus attention on how the unit seniority principle can carry over the effects of past discrimination by locking minority employees into the jobs they had been given under the old, discriminatory regime. Morally at stake here are conflicting rights: seniority rights versus equal opportunity rights. Which take precedence? Probably any reply would need to be qualified by the circumstances that enshroud the specific case. But, as with most moral decisions, it's nonetheless helpful to develop general guidelines which could facilitate moral decision making. Although the following essay deals with legalities, the discussion can at least initiate the process.

In the essay, Stephen C. Swanson, lawyer and consultant for Equal Employment Opportunities Services in New York, discusses how the Supreme Court's seniority decisions affect employer responsibility in conjunction with past discrimination. As Mr. Swanson indicates, in essence the decisions found that a seniority system that serves as a vehicle to carry over the effects of past discrimination is not necessarily unconstitutional. Why it isn't and when it is serve as nice departure points to launch a full-scale moral inquiry into the issues involved when seniority rights and equal opportunity rights clash.

In 1971, the United States Supreme Court established a principle that became one of the foundations of EEO law. Under Title VII, said the Court, "Practices, procedures or tests neutral on their face, and even neutral in terms of intent, cannot be maintained if they operate to 'freeze' the status quo of prior discriminatory employment practices."[1] This meant that *employers were to be responsible for the present effects of past discrimination.*

The principle remains, but its operation in relation to seniority systems has been modified.

How Is Past Discrimination Carried Into the Present?

Discrimination occurring in the past can be carried into the present through a variety of "vehicles." For example:

Nepotism (a union's policy of excluding all applicants not related to incumbent members carries forward the effect of a discontinued policy that excluded minorities from membership);[2]

Experience Requirements (a trucking company's policy of requiring three years' long haul experience for long haul truck drivers carries forward the effect of a discontinued policy excluding blacks from long haul jobs);[3]

Employee Referrals (an employer that depends upon incumbent employees to refer applicants carries forward a discontinued policy against hiring blacks);[4] and,

Chilling Effect (an employer's discriminatory hiring policy over a long period of years leads blacks to feel that applying for work would be futile, even after the policy may have been discontinued).[5]

The courts have consistently found that when these vehicles carry over discrimination from the past, they violate Title VII. As a result, employers and unions have been ordered to abandon the policies that create such vehicles, and they have been ordered to take affirmative steps to remedy the continuing discrimination.

It is important to note that the principle of employer responsibility for the present effects of past discrimination remains untouched in relation to these and other non-seniority vehicles. Modification of the principle has come only where a vehicle involves seniority.

Unit Seniority and the "Lock In Effect"

Seniority systems provide another vehicle for carrying over the effects of past discrimination. Before passage of Title VII, it was common in many industries to have organizational units[6] segregated on the basis of race. Typically, units with the least desirable, lowest-skilled and lowest-paying jobs were reserved for minorities.[7]

With passage of Title VII, the pattern of segregated departments began to break down. But in unionized industries, *unit seniority* was the principle criterion of selection for job assignment, promotion, layoff, recall and so forth. This meant that minority employees who transferred out of formerly all-minority units into newly integrated units sacrificed the seniority they had earned in their old jobs, and started at the bottom of the seniority list in their new units. Thus, minority transfers into the newly integrated units were discouraged. The unit seniority system carried over the effects of past discrimination because minority employees were "locked into" the jobs they had been given under the old, discriminatory regime.

"Adjusted Seniority" to Relieve the Lock In Effect

When the lock in effect was challenged, courts initially found that unit seniority systems which perpetuated past discrimination through the lock in effect violated Title VII.[8] As a result, employers and unions were ordered to modify the offending systems. Specific modifications differed to suit the situation in each case, but common to all was an order that minority employees transferring into formerly segregated units keep all or part of the seniority they had earned in their old jobs. Thus, instead of being forced to sacrifice the seniority they had earned previously, minority employees were granted "adjusted seniority." This served to defeat the lock in effect.

A very important aspect of this relief was that it was granted to all employees in the class that had been subject to past discrimination. Individual class members were not required to demonstrate that they personally had suffered discrimination.

Of course, transferring minority employees gained this relief at some expense to incumbents in formerly all-white units. The seniority rights of white incumbents—guaranteed under the terms of labor-management contracts—were watered down by the introduction of adjusted seniority. In competition for promotions, job assignments and so forth, a white incumbent's unit seniority would be compared with the adjusted seniority that a transferred minority brought from another unit. This infringement on established seniority rights was a constant source of friction, and eventually served as the basis for reinterpretation of the law.

The Supreme Court's Decisions Supporting Seniority Rights

On May 31 of this year, the United States Supreme Court issued two decisions, *Teamsters v. U.S.*[9] and *United Air Lines v. Evans*,[10] that rejected the approach initially taken by the courts. Essentially, the Supreme Court's decisions said that:

> Title VII includes a special provision protecting the legality of seniority systems and existing seniority rights.[11] Because of this provision, *the fact that a seniority system serves as a vehicle to carry over the effects of past discrimination does not mean that the system violates Title VII.*

Courts that had considered the question earlier had not ignored the special provision protecting seniority, but they had interpreted it differently. In its new ruling, the Supreme Court said that Congress meant to maintain the integrity of the seniority concept when it passed Title VII. Indeed, the Court said that Congress intended that minorities be locked in, if necessary, to protect existing seniority rights. Seniority systems were not to be modified in order to relieve the lock in effect.

These decisions will certainly have an impact on the results of future discrimination actions that involve seniority. They may have an impact on some actions that were settled or decided in the past.[12] The degree of impact will depend upon how EEO enforcement agencies and the courts interpret the Supreme Court. Already we see moves to restrict the decisions' effect.

When Can Seniority Rights Be Modified?

Although it provided strong support for seniority rights, the Supreme Court's *Teamsters* decision pointed out that two approaches are still available for attacking a seniority system to modify existing seniority rights:

Is It a *Bona Fide* Seniority System?

Only *bona fide* seniority systems—that is, systems that were neither established nor maintained with an intent to discriminate—are protected under Title VII. Systems used to intentionally discriminate still violate the law, and are subject to modification. But this avenue of attack can be successful only when challengers demonstrate the necessary discriminatory intent. Such intent is often difficult to prove.[13]

Shortly after publication of the Supreme Court's *Teamsters* decision, the EEOC issued an interpretive memorandum, ". . . to provide guidance to the Commission's District Offices in processing . . . charges and to apprise respondents and charging parties as to their rights and obligations under Title VII."[14]

Pursuant to this memorandum, it is the EEOC's position that a unit seniority system is *bona fide* only if it was established "prior to the effective date of Title VII[15] and only if the evidence shows that there was no discriminatory intent in the genesis or maintenance of the system."

Recognizing that intent can be difficult to prove, the memorandum goes on to point out when the EEOC will infer discriminatory intent:

> Where unions or units were previously segregated, discriminatory intent in the institution of a unit seniority system will be inferred; *and,*
>
> When a unit seniority system is in effect and the employer or union is made aware that it is locking in minorities or females, discriminatory intent will be inferred if the system is maintained . . . when an alternative system is available.

In sum, only *bona fide* seniority systems are protected under Title VII. With its memorandum, the EEOC has tried to make it easier to show that a seniority system which perpetuates past discrimination is not *bona fide,* and therefore not entitled to protection. It remains to be seen whether the courts will accept the EEOC's position.

Seniority Override as a Remedy for Individuals

The seniority override approach is available only for *individuals,* and only when *discrimination occurred after the effective date of Title VII.*[16] For example, this approach might be applicable when:

> an employer maintained a segregated units policy after July 2, 1965, even though the policy is no longer in effect, *and,*
> a unit seniority system perpetuates the effect of the post-Title VII discrimination by locking minorities into the jobs they had while the policy was still in effect.

When this occurs, employees who were victims of the post-Title VII discrimination, and who are locked in by unit seniority, can be granted adjusted seniority when they transfer to a formerly segregated unit.

This sounds much like the relief granted by the courts before the Supreme Court's decision in *Teamsters,* but there is a big difference in the burden of proof. *Before Teamsters,* individual employees in the class that had been subject to past discrimination were not required to show that they personally had suffered discrimination. *After Teamsters,* adjusted seniority can be granted only on an individual basis to minority employees who can show, among other things, that after the effective date of Title VII they:

> actually applied for and were denied transfer to an all-white unit; *or*
> that they would have applied for transfer, if they had not been discouraged from doing so by the chilling effect of the employer's old segregated units policy.

Thus, the seniority override is available only where those challenging unit seniority meet a demanding burden of proof. However, a recent decision of the Seventh Circuit Court of Appeals[17] suggests that in some situations this burden might be made relatively easy to carry. In *EEOC v. United Air Lines,* the Seventh Circuit said that minority

employees who successfully applied for transfer *after* the court had ordered adjusted seniority, met the burden of proving that they would have applied *earlier,* but for the chilling effect. In other words, the act of applying later was in itself sufficient to prove that the employee would have applied earlier.[18]

In sum, the seniority rights protected under Title VII are subject to seniority override as a remedy for individual victims of discrimination. This remedy is available only when the challengers meet a demanding burden of proof. But a recent Seventh Circuit decision accepted an easy method of carrying that burden. If many decisions adopt this method of proof, the override could become much more readily available. This would seriously undermine seniority's newly won protection.

The OFCCP's Position

Like the EEOC, the OFCCP has issued a memorandum responding to the Supreme Court's *Teamsters* decision.[19] In its memorandum, the OFCCP said that the contract compliance program is not affected by the decision, and that, ". . . compliance officers conducting compliance reviews . . . shall continue to require adjustments in . . . (unit) seniority systems if they perpetuate the effects of past discrimination."

The OFCCP operates under Executive Order 11246. *Teamsters* was decided under Title VII. It is the OFCCP's position that Title VII decisions do not determine what can be done under the Executive Order.

The Supreme Court's recent seniority decisions have created an important exception to the principle that employers are responsible for the present effects of past discrimination. This exception reinforces the integrity of seniority rights. It prohibits courts from compromising seniority rights in order to remedy the effects of past discrimination.

But the exception is limited in scope, and there appear to be several approaches that challengers can use to circumvent its effect:

1. The exception is limited to those situations in which seniority provides the vehicle for carrying past discrimination into the present. The principle remains untouched in relation to vehicles that do not involve seniority.

2. The exception can be circumvented if those challenging a seniority system successfully attack its *bona fides*, and show that the system is used intentionally to discriminate. The EEOC's memorandum aids challengers in carrying out this attack.

3. The exception can be circumvented for each employee who proves that he or she was a victim of post-Title VII discrimination. For some situations, a recent decision of the Seventh Circuit Court of Appeals provides an easy method for meeting this burden of proof.

4. The exception is limited to actions brought under Title VII. The exception does not apply to EEO enforcement under the OFCCP's contract compliance program, and the OFCCP says it will continue to demand modification of unit seniority that perpetuates the effects of past discrimination.

Recognizing that the scope of the Supreme Court's decisions is limited, and that the decisions can be circumvented, it remains to be seen how the courts will deal with attempts to avoid the decisions' impact.

Notes

1. *Griggs v. Duke Power Co.,* 401 U.S. 424 (1971).

2. *Asbestos Workers Local 53 v. Vogler,* 407 F. 2d 1047 (5th Cir. 1969).

3. *Rodriguez v. East Texas Motor Freight, Inc.,* 505 F. 2d 40 (5th CVir. 1974).

4. *Parham v. Southwestern Bell Telephone Co.,* 433 F. 2d 421 (8th Cir. 1970).

5. *Lea v. Cone Mills Corp.,* 301 F. Supp. 97 (M.D. N.C. 1969). See *Teamsters v. U.S.,* No. 75–636 (U.S. Sup. Ct., May 31, 1977).

6. *Organizational unit* means any unit by which an employer is organized. For example, it can refer to a particular *job, department* or *line of progression.* It follows that *unit seniority* means seniority within an organizational unit which is used in selection for job assignment, promotion, layoff, recall, and so forth.

7. Most EEO actions involving seniority are based on race or national origin discrimination. That is the discrimination we speak of here. The same concepts apply, however, in actions based on sex discrimination. *EEOC v. United Air Lines, Inc.,* No. 76–1769 (7th Cir., June 28, 1977).

8. The seminal decision is *Quarles v. Philip Morris, Inc.,* 279 F. Supp. 505 (E.D. Va. 1967). See cases cited in *Teamsters v. U.S.,* No. 75–636 (U.S. Sup. Ct., May 31, 1977), dissenting opinion n. 2.

9. *Teamsters v. U.S.,* No. 75–636 (U.S. Sup. Ct., May 31, 1977).

10. *United Air Lines, Inc. v. Evans,* No. 76–333 (U.S. Sup. Ct., May 31, 1977).

11. 42 U.S.C. Sec. 2000e–2(h).

12. *Key Job Bias Cases May be Reconsidered,* N.Y. Times, June 2, 1977. But see *Interpretive Memorandum Concerning International Brotherhood of Teamsters v. United States,* Equal Employment Opportunity Commission, July 12, 1977.

13. The *Teamsters* opinion suggests that in earlier decisions, seniority systems which were found to violate Title VII may have been systems adopted with an intent to discriminate. *Teamsters v. U.S.,* No. 75–636 (U.S. Sup. Ct., May 13, 1977) n. 28. To the extent that this is true, the earlier decisions can be made consistent with *Teamsters.*

14. *Interpretive Memorandum Concerning International Brotherhood of Teamsters v. United States,* Equal Employment Opportunity Commission, July 12, 1977.

15. The effective date of Title VII was July 2, 1965.

16. Ibid.

17. *EEOC v. United Air Lines, Inc.,* No. 76–1769 (7th Cir., June 28, 1977).

18. It is important to note that in this case, minority employees who transferred received adjusted seniority only for purposes of layoff and recall. Straight unit seniority applied for all other purposes. The Seventh Circuit felt that a willingness to start at the bottom of the seniority list for all purposes except layoff and recall, ". . . says much 'about what choice an employee would have made had he previously been given the opportunity freely to choose (the job).' "

19. *Policy Clarification Memorandum to Heads of All Compliance Agencies Re: Teamsters v. United States,* Office of Federal Contract Compliance Programs, Department of Labor, July 20, 1977.

Providing Equal Opportunities for Promotion

Robert M. Fulmer and William E. Fulmer

Not too long ago management alone determined who would receive a promotion. Not so today. Voices from various sectors of society are pressing American industry to adopt more open promotion systems. When firms yield to this pressure, as many already have, the choice of a promotional system will raise fundamental questions of fairness that involve management, employee, union, and societal interests.

In the following article Professors Robert M. Fulmer (Trinity University) and William E. Fulmer (Harvard University) examine and compare the major selection methods for promotional consideration. While their focus is on production employees, their conclusions apply equally to all employees. Professors Fulmer give special attention to the historical development of selection methods for promotion in the American industrial setting, the extent of current usage, and the experiences of major industrial users. In reading their analysis, pay particular attention to the strengths and weaknesses of the methods they discuss. Decide whether the authors are correct in saying that the employee request method represents the best alternative available. Would you say it's the fairest? Why?

The area of personnel administration abounds with areas where traditional prerogatives of management have been successfully challenged. Pressures from the public, unions, and government agencies have all had major impact. In our pluralistic society, there seems to be no such thing as an exclusive franchise for management.

The choice of who is to receive a particular promotion was once almost universally recognized as an exclusive management prerogative. Now, the various pressure groups have created new complexities for business managers seeking to reward loyalty or outstanding contribution. Because there are far more union members seeking advancement than there are opportunities for a promotion, and perhaps because companies often abused their early promotion freedoms,[1] organized labor has been particularly vigorous in seeking to make the criteria for promotion a matter of collective bargaining. Few companies have been able to completely withstand union pressure for these changes. Although most firms have made concessions in the area of promotions, many have resisted going to a completely open system in which an employee has guaranteed consideration for any job opening that occurs.

In recent years, with increasing public demands for openness in all aspects of society, renewed pressure for more open promotion systems in American industry is being exerted. Govern-

ment agencies with responsibility for civil rights enforcement have joined unions in the push for such systems. Although the objective of government is to facilitate the upgrading and promotion of minorities, many businessmen see the last frontier of management's prerogatives being destroyed by increased governmental regulation.

Although management may be faced with the loss of a traditional right, it must, at the same time, be prepared to make optimum utilization of the options still available. In order to investigate the major alternatives still available, extensive research was conducted to determine what has been said on this important subject. Because of the surprising dearth of publications dealing with the practical dimensions of this problem, approximately thirty hours of interviews were conducted with industrial relations representatives from ten major U.S. corporations, most of whom had some experience with open promotion systems, particularly job posting. The objective was to learn their experience and to determine their personal opinion of the basic concept of providing equal employment or equal promotion opportunities.

Historical Development

Prior to 1940 the selection of employees for promotion was considered by most companies and unions to be a management function. The role of the union in promotions was merely to prevent discrimination and caprice in the exercise of management's right. Unions were more concerned with matters of wage improvements, protection of employees from arbitrary disciplinary action and the development of seniority systems.[2]

Only in the railroad industry was there early concern about promotion policies and procedures. As early as 1901 the Illinois Central Railroad was considering an employee request system which would apply to the selection of conductors.[3] By 1924 some railroad contracts were beginning to require a very general posting and bidding procedure.[4]

During the 1940s promotions became a much more important collective bargaining issue. Consequently, the posting of job vacancies, often as a result of union demands, began to gain acceptance as a method of selecting employees for promotional consideration. It was not unusual for the contract provisions of the early 1940s to specify such factors as the location for vacancy notices, notice content, bidding and selection time and the criteria for selection. In addition, some unions began to demand a direct role in the process by being formally notified of all vacancies and the names of successful bidders.[5]

By the late 1940s the practice of job posting had become fairly common. Although the basic provisions of the early 1940s continued to be found, new restrictions were being imposed. Frequently, promotion procedures specified subsequent steps to be taken when jobs were not immediately filled. In addition, the role of unions increased in some industries where the company was required to confer with a union committee prior to making a selection, as well as requiring employees to officially notify the union of bids.[6]

Although formal promotion provisions were almost exclusively adopted as a result of union pressure, the federal government has now become a catalyst for industry's acceptance of these programs. The Office of Federal Contract Compliance (OFCC) is currently suggesting that posting is one way of achieving equal opportunity for promotion.[7] In addition, the Equal Employment Opportunity Commission (EEOC) has become an advocate of posting procedures.[8]

Although the lack of posting or similar arrangements is not illegal per se, in cases of complaints of discrimination one of the things looked for by the EEOC investigator is the presence of posting. In the absence of this, the company must demonstrate that its procedure is nondiscriminatory. Although there are few EEOC cases that deal specifically with posting, it is generally concluded that the absence of posting may be considered illegal within the context of the total selection system. The burden of proof is upon the company to justify its procedure. Where job posting is found, the main requirement seems to be that it must be "appropriate to the institution." Thus, it may be via such means as an internal plant paper or notices posted along main avenues or within departments. Since employees must have direct access to the information, word of mouth is insufficient.[9]

As an indication of the pressure being brought to bear, in an October 6, 1972 decision by the U.S. District Court for Southern Georgia, Baxter vs. Savannah Sugar Refining Corporation, the defendant was ordered to "post on bulletin boards in conspicuous places throughout all departments . . . notices of all job vacancies available for promotion or transfer of current employees." It was further emphasized that these notices were to "contain a specific job description for each vacancy, the rate of pay, and information with respect to the qualifications required and how and where application can be made." The court felt that because information regarding job vacancies was disseminated through supervisory personnel, there was a tendency to "channel and limit information regarding vacancies to those employees within segregated job classifications where such vacancies occur." Thus, because employees were not notified of promotion opportunities or the qualifications necessary for promotion, the court found that the defendant's promotion procedures violated Title VII of the Civil Rights Act in that particular.

The extent to which promotional consideration has now become an integral part of labor negotiations is indicated by a survey published in 1970 by the Department of Labor.[10] In this survey of 1,851 collective bargaining agreements which covered 1,000 or more employees, 45% (834) identified a specific method of selecting employees for promotional consideration. The frequency of the major methods considered in this article is summarized below:

834 Contracts Covering Promotional Consideration

Method	Number of Contracts	Percentage
Job Posting (exclusively)	437	52%
Job Posting (plus other method)	131	17%
Employee Request	90	11%
Automatic Consideration	81	10%
Company Discretion	10	1%
Other Combination	47	5%
Other Methods	38	4%
Total	834	100%

Criteria for Evaluating Selection Procedures

The development of criteria by which to evaluate selection procedures is a very subjective process and depends upon the assumptions made concerning the various participants in the system. The following criteria, although not exhaustive, will hopefully contain the basic objectives sought by the participants.

Management's basic objectives for a selection system are:

1. fill the manpower needs of the organization;
2. administrative efficiency;
3. satisfaction of governmental requirements; and
4. employee satisfaction.

Employees are primarily interested in a system that:

1. treats them equitably and fairly;
2. is easily understood; and
3. provides them with the opportunity to participate in their career development.

The union desires a system that:

1. allows easy policing of management's promotional decisions;
2. treats all members uniformly.

The federal government's basic objective is a system that aids in the upgrading and promotion of minorities.

Evaluation of Approaches

Because of its greater popularity, the practice of job posting should be considered first. Clearly, the majority of national agreements, if they specify a promotion procedure at all, contain some reference to job posting. Although specific details will vary from plant to plant, depending upon local negotiations, the following items are frequently found in local or supplementary agreements:

1. Locational requirements of the notice
2. Notice content
3. Eligibility for bidding
4. Temporary measures for filling vacancies
5. Specific promotional steps to be followed
6. Alternative methods to be used when posting does not provide suitable candidates
7. Time constraints for posting and selection
8. Selection criteria
9. The union's role
10. Consideration to be given bids by mail
11. Methods of filling subsequently created vacancies.

The details of a typical posting requirement might require the company to post a notice of each job vacancy on bulletin boards within a specific organizational unit for two to four days. Anyone within that unit could submit a bid to the personnel office during the term of the post. At the close of the time requirement, only those employees who have submitted a bid are considered by the personnel office and/or supervisor. The final decision will depend on the criteria previously agreed on by the various parties. The successful employee is then notified of his selection.

Nine of the ten companies interviewed in this study had some experience with a posting system. Six of the nine currently had a posting arrangement at most if not all plants, two currently posted for certain jobs, and one had recently eliminated posting from its one plant with such a history.

The six companies currently using posting on

a wide scale expressed great satisfaction with their systems. Four of the six had gone to posting as a result of union demands, whereas the other two had done so primarily as a union resistance effort. The latter two were either completely non-union or largely so and were the most enthusiastic about their programs.

Advantages

The primary advantage of the posting system, as perceived by all companies currently using the system, is its "fairness" to employees. The IR representatives felt that this system allows employees to keep informed as to promotion opportunities and assures them of consideration. A closely related advantage was that young employees, as well as minorities, seem to prefer this system. This preference was even acknowledged by one company that was strongly opposed to posting. Younger employees and minorities are believed to be particularly interested in maximum job information. Additionally, a posting system may be good for morale since employees are kept informed of job developments. Posting is also believed to help prevent difficulties with the EEOC and prevent management from inadvertently overlooking the employee with the most seniority. Finally, one interviewer saw the posting system as an aid to supervisors since they only have to consider those applicants who have expressed a specific interest in the job.

Disadvantages

The most consistently reported disadvantage was the delay created in filling jobs. Although no company had figures to support this contention, almost all considered this to be the primary disadvantage. The actual length of the delay varies from plant to plant and perhaps job to job, depending on such factors as the required time of posting and the time necessary to make a decision. Of course, decision time depends upon the selection criteria involved and the number of bids received. At a minimum, the filling of jobs would be delayed the length of time required for the notice to be posted.

A second problem frequently reported was the existence of administrative difficulties. All companies reporting this problem had initially adopted a very open system which allowed either

plant-wide bidding in large plants or company-wide bidding for each job. This type of system frequently created a need for relatively large administrative staffs or encouraged supervisors to circumvent the system which created morale problems and numerous grievances.

Other disadvantages reported included:

1. unions constantly seek to expand the areas and levels of posting (from departmental to plant to company-wide bidding and chain posting and bidding),

2. the tendency toward "seniority only" selection criterion since a large volume of bids is likely to cause management to seek a selection criterion that is easy to evaluate, such as seniority,

3. more grievances are stimulated since more people are aware of their consideration and therefore likely to be unhappy if not selected,

4. it hinders minority advancement since the great number of bids from white employees is likely to dilute the number of minority bids,

5. it results in an increase in training costs, and

6. it encourages spur-of-the-moment decisions concerning the employee's career.

Employee Request

Of the 834 collective bargaining agreements referred to earlier, 90 or approximately 11 percent identified an employee request system. This system was almost exclusively found in manufacturing industries and was particularly common among manufacturers of transportation equipment and machinery (both electrical and non-electrical). Major variables among contract provisions seemed to be the number and frequency of requests an employee could make.

The details of a request system are generally very simple. For example, a company may occasionally publish a list of all plant jobs in the plant newspaper or post such a list on plant bulletin boards. Employees will then have the right to submit bids to the personnel office for a specified number of jobs for which they would like to be considered. Whenever a vacancy arises, the appropriate supervisor is given only those bids which have been previously submitted for that specific job. From that number a decision is made based on the accepted selection criteria.

A request system has many of the advantages of a posting system but fewer disadvantages. The major advantage is its relative ease of administration and, relatedly, its time saving nature. As soon as a vacancy arises, supervisors can begin making their selection. An additional advantage is that such a system does not encourage instantaneous career decisions, but allows employees to give greater consideration to their decisions. The major disadvantage over a posting system is the added storage cost of maintaining a record of employee requests.

As far as the objectives for a selection system are concerned, a request system seems to satisfy all, at least as well if not better than a posting system, with the possible exception of satisfying governmental preferences. In actual practice, the request system seems just as advantageous for minorities as a posting system. The posting system, however, seems to be currently in favor with the EEOC and the courts. Whether or not a request is just as acceptable is unknown at this point.

Automatic Consideration

This procedure was the sole method specified by 81 contracts or approximately 10 percent of the agreements containing specific promotion methods. The procedure simply requires that when a vacancy occurs in a particular job, a promotion is offered to the employee next in the line of progression, assuming he meets the selection criteria.

The use of this procedure is normally dependent on the organizational structure of the work force. Generally, automatic consideration or progression is confined to smaller or narrower units—usually an occupational classification, a line of progression, or a job family. In 47 percent of the agreements which specified both automatic consideration and a seniority unit for promotion, job or occupational classification was the sole unit specified. The number of automatic consideration clauses specifying a unit other than a job or occupational classification declined substantially as the seniority unit increased. This system is particularly common in such industries as paper and petroleum.

Automatic consideration does not accomplish

as many objectives of the various parties as the more open systems. Its one major advantage is its ease of administration. Of all the major systems, it is one of the easiest, if not the easiest, to administer since the company limits its search to the next lower level of jobs. On the negative side, it is unlikely to appeal to certain segments of the work force since employees have little career influence once they get into a specific job ladder. In addition, the EEOC will find it less desirable than a more open system. If, however, the organization can justify its system and prove that it does not discriminate against minorities, under the present guidelines it is unlikely to encounter significant EEOC problems. In general, the system, because of its highly structured nature, is somewhat limited in application.

Company Discretion

Under this system the employer has sole authority to select the employee to be promoted. Only after the decision is made can the decision be challenged by the union. Out of 834 agreements, only 10, or one percent, gave management this right. Generally, even in these cases some limitations on management's authority did exist, such as the right of unions to file grievances or require promotions to be based on certain skills.

Of the objectives specified above, few are satisfied by a company discretion system. Its primary advantage is the flexibility it gives management in the use of its work force. Few, if any, objectives of the employees, unions, or the government are satisfied by this system.

Recommendations

If an organization desires to develop a selection process which results in the achievement of a maximum number of the objectives listed above, an employee request system would seem preferable. No doubt the details of the system would need to be tailored to local plant needs. This is particularly true in regard to the size of plants. Although unlimited requests might be feasible in small to medium size plants, very large plants would require some frequency restrictions in order to make it administratively efficient.

A good employee request system should provide employees with information concerning the jobs available in the organization and the necessary qualifications. This is perhaps best accomplished by publishing a list of those jobs so employees can have it for detailed study. In creating this list, management should counsel employees to realistically assess their abilities so as not to waste their allotted number of requests. In addition, employees should be reminded that they are under no obligation to use all granted requests.

Once employees have made their decisions, requests should be submitted either to the personnel office or dropped in bid boxes. Each bid should remain in effect until the employee withdraws it (at which time he would be entitled to request consideration for another job) or until he has rejected an offer for that job on a specific number of occasions—perhaps twice. A definite cutoff time for bid consideration should be established (such as one week before a job becomes vacant) so complete processing of all requests is possible. A backup procedure should be identified so that everyone can know what steps management will take if no qualified requests are received.

Potential Problems

If an employee request system is adopted, several relatively minor problems should be anticipated. First, some initial administrative problems can be expected. As is true of any new system, there will be some confusion over the correct procedures. This, as in any major change, will produce some administrative problems until the system is fully understood. In addition, a request system is likely to generate a large number of requests shortly after the program is inaugurated. A second probable problem is a continuing storage cost. The extent of this cost will depend on variables, such as plant size, the number of requests allowed each employee, and the degree of job satisfaction of employees. All in all, the employee request system, although far from perfect, does seem to satisfy most if not all of the basic objectives sought by management, the union, employees, and the government. Therefore, its advantages

seem to outweigh the problems that are likely to occur.

To sum it up, although there is increasing interest in the development of more open promotion procedures, attention should not be solely restricted to the popular concept of posting. Posting is far from being an optimum system. Despite the fact that it offers several advantages to the interested parties, it contains the potential for management problems—an aspect often overlooked by proponents. If a more open system is desirable, an employee request system has much to recommend it. This system contains most, if not all, of the advantages of a posting system, and also reduces some of the potential problems for management.

Notes

1. Sumner H. Slichter, James L. Healy and Robert Livernash, *The Impact of Collective Bargaining on Management* (Washington: The Brookings Institution, 1960), pp. 178–79.

2. *Ibid.*

3. Samuel M'Cune Lindsay, "Railway Employees in the United States," *Bulletin of the Department of Labor* (Washington: Government Printing Office), No. 37, November 1901, p. 1050.

4. U.S. Department of Labor, *Trade Agreements 1920 and 1924* (Washington: Government Printing Office), Bulletin No. 393, September 1925, p. 113.

5. U.S. Department of Labor, *Union Agreement Provisions* (Washington: Government Printing Office), Bulletin No. 686, 1942, p. 135.

6. U.S. Department of Labor, *Collective Bargaining Provisions* (Washington: Government Printing Office), Bulletin No. 908–7, 1948, pp. 6–17.

7. U.S. Department of Labor, "Affirmative Action Programs," *Federal Register*, Vol. 36, No. 234, December 4, 1971, p. 60–2.24 (f) (1).

8. Interview, May 1972.

9. Interview, June 1972.

10. The statistics used in this and following sections are taken from the following source: U.S. Department of Labor, "Seniority in Promotion and Transfer Provisions," *Major Collective Bargaining Agreements,* No. 1425–11 (Washington: Government Printing Office, March 1970), pp. 15–22.

For Further Reading

Drucker, P. *Preparing tomorrow's business leaders today*. Englewood Cliffs, N.J.: Prentice-Hall, 1969.

Dubin, R. *Human relations in administration*. Englewood Cliffs, N.J.: Prentice-Hall, 1961.

_____. *The world of work: Industrial society and human relations*. Englewood Cliffs, N.J.: Prentice-Hall, 1958.

McGregor, D. *The human side of enterprise*. New York: McGraw-Hill, 1960.

Mintzberg, H. *The nature of managerial work*. New York: Harper & Row, 1973.

Petit, T. *The moral crisis in management*. New York: McGraw-Hill, 1967.

4
JOB ATMOSPHERE

The Pet Food plant of General Foods in Topeka, Kansas, was troubled with low worker morale, frequent shutdowns, and serious worker dissatisfaction. When incidences of sabotage and violence erupted, officials at Pet knew it was time to take action.

Rather than adopting an adversary or punitive stance toward its employees, Pet decided to enrich their jobs by permitting its workers a greater degree of responsibility and autonomy. Specifically, it formed work teams of from eight to ten employees and gave them responsibility for various stages of the production process. The teams decided who would perform which tasks, trained one another for jobs, and assumed responsibility for support functions, such as maintenance, quality control, engineering, and personnel. In addition, Pet made a concerted effort to upgrade tasks; they were made more challenging and demanding, less dull and routine. When team members performed well, they were recognized both by the team and by the rest of the plant. The role of team leader replaced the traditional one of supervisor. Status symbols, such as preferred parking space and special office decor, were eliminated. Plant rules were relaxed and allowed to evolve out of the work experience. In short, Pet attempted to make the work more meaningful from the viewpoint of the employees.

The results were heartening for both Pet and its workers. Whereas Pet had anticipated a work force of 110 for operations, less than 70 employees were needed once the teams started functioning. In addition, the company experienced major economic benefits in terms of waste minimization and efficiency of operations. Most important, worker attitudes improved measurably. Morale rose, absenteeism decreased, shutdowns ceased, acts of violence disappeared.[1] In this case job enrichment—a program designed to make job content more satisfying—had worked.

Discontent with work is hardly a new phenomenon. It's been around as long as people have had to work. Nevertheless, it's a cause for some wonder today.

1. *Special Task Force to the Secretary of Health, Education, and Welfare,* Work in America *(Cambridge, Mass.: MIT Press, 1972), pp. 960–999.*

Why should today's workers be discontented? In general, they enjoy the highest pay ever and unprecedented job security. Furthermore, the growth of unionism has ensured them shorter working hours; generally healthful work conditions; attractive medical and dental benefits; ample sickness, emergency, and bereavement leaves; fair treatment; and due process. While technology has sometimes eliminated jobs, it has just as often created others. Most important, it has eliminated the drudgery of much manual labor.

And yet increasing numbers of workers at all levels express dissatisfaction and frustration with their work. All too often job motivation has decreased while indifferentism has risen. The results are high employee turnover, poor productivity, inferior product quality, general unrest, and even worker sabotage.

Business managers must be as concerned with problems relating to work atmosphere as they are with problems in hiring, promotions, discipline, and discharge. The health and survival of the firm are at stake; thus, persons determined to behave morally in a business context must attend to questions of work atmosphere. Furthermore, issues relative to work atmosphere raise fundamental questions about the relationship between business and its employees. Questions about health and safety of workers, wages, stability of employment, working conditions, and work satisfaction are potential sources for many a moral dilemma.

Everyone agrees that employers have responsibilities and that workers have rights in this area of work atmosphere. Almost everyone disagrees about the precise nature of responsibilities and rights. The disagreement begins with a very fundamental question. What constitutes proper work atmosphere?

At one time, the employee solution to any problem in this area was quite predictable: a fatter paycheck. Some workers still respond this way. But the Pet experience is hardly an isolated one. It testifies to the general inadequacy of this response today.

The fact is that any response to what constitutes proper work atmosphere must involve some concept of human need. Reflect on the Pet experience. When human needs went unmet, trouble erupted. When needs were satisfied, harmony returned. So basic to the question of work atmosphere are human needs that this chapter begins with an examination of what constitutes human needs. How does work function to fill these needs? Is there a connection between work atmosphere and worker needs? We'll try to answer these questions in the hope that by so doing we'll throw some light on business responsibilities to workers in the area of work atmosphere.

Needs

Let's define a need as a basic requirement that must be met for the normal functioning of a human being. Granted, establishing universal needs is not easy. Nor is it any easier to define what normal is. As a result, any exploration of needs must carry implicit qualifications to account for individual differences. At the same time, psychologists today talk about two basic kinds of needs: maintenance and actualizing.

By *maintenance needs* psychologists mean the biological and psychological requirements for the normal functioning of human beings. Among these would be the needs to be nourished, to sleep, to avoid pain and injury, to be stimulated and active, and to have sex. Among the psychological needs would be the needs for order, security, adequacy, competency, self-esteem, meaning, and feeling of belonging and approval.

Actualizing needs are tougher to pin down. In using the term, modern psychologists generally mean the peculiarly human strivings for personal growth and improvement, life enrichment, self-expression, and the realization of one's potential.

Levels of Needs

Psychoanalyst Abraham H. Maslow, in his book *Motivation and Personality*,[2] presented a hierarchy of human needs. Although he applied this hierarchy to general human needs, we can also apply them to worker needs.

SURVIVAL.   At the lowest level workers are motivated by physiological needs such as hunger and thirst. People out pounding the pavement in search of work are primarily concerned with satisfying needs related to survival. In brief, they need and value the food and shelter that the money from a job will provide.

SECURITY.   Maslow's great insight is that as one level of needs is satisfied, it is replaced by the next level. Thus, as workers have their physiological needs met, they generally progress to the next level, the security level. Workers begin to wonder about what would happen if they were injured on the job or lost it, or were stricken by enormous expenses. How would they provide? In short, they become preoccupied with questions relating to safety and security. In business these needs are generally met by various fringe programs, such as health and accident insurance, pension plans, unemployment benefits, and savings programs.

SOCIAL INTERACTION.   Maslow points out that when people satisfy security needs, they generally progress to the level characterized by the need for social interaction. Money and security may simply not be enough for workers. They may need a satisfactory relationship with others at work. They require group interaction, friendship, and affection. Thus it's not unusual for workers to leave well-paying and secure jobs when their social needs aren't met.

STATUS.   Once social needs have been met, workers may develop what Maslow terms status needs. At this level workers seek out self-respect and esteem, recognition by others, and feelings of importance. This largely explains why business liberally confers so many status symbols on its employees, from parking places to frosted windows.

SELF-FULFILLMENT.   At this point workers progress to the highest level of needs. When all other needs have been relatively satisfied, only needs for self-fulfillment remain. Maslow calls these self-actualizing needs. They include the needs to achieve one's potential for self-development, creativity, and self-expression. Business people at this level may seek appointments to government

2.   *Abraham H. Maslow*, Motivation and Personality, *2nd ed. (New York: Harper & Row, 1970).*

office or decide to head philanthropic drives, often at great personal expense. As you might expect, relatively few people ever reach this ultimate stage in Maslow's hierarchy.

It seems, then, that any concept of proper work atmosphere must be rooted in an awareness of human needs. This doesn't mean that business has obligations to fulfill all the needs of its workers or that a failure to meet a need results in immorality. Rather, human needs propose a theoretical framework within which business can begin to meet its responsibilities in work atmosphere. Although this framework is general, it assumes a more concrete form when related to the function of work, the work environment, and job content.

Function of Work

In general, work functions to fill human needs. Traditionally work accomplished this primarily on an economic level. People worked to live. They still do. But increasingly people work for other reasons. More and more, work performs important personal and social functions as well as economic ones.

On the personal level work functions to provide people with self-identity and esteem. Because workers spend at least half their waking adult lives and most of their energy, skills, and talents, at work, they invariably identify themselves with the work they do. People who work derive self-worth and esteem from their jobs. If the work does not meet these needs, workers can easily suffer diminished personal regard.

Work also functions socially by identifying the roles one has in society. In Maslow's terms it provides status, not only to the workers but to their families as well. When workers are made to feel that their work is without status, they begin to lose touch with society. They don't fit in. Because business does not ordinarily confer the social status on its members that professions with admitted business overtones such as medicine and law do, management has a greater burden to devise ways of providing workers with a sense of social importance stemming from the work they do. Finally, work serves to provide people with social contacts, feelings of belonging, and the chance to establish meaningful human relationships.

Research confirms the importance of these noneconomic functions of work for today's workers. One analysis indicates that people don't reduce the time and energy channeled into work even when they increase their earnings and acquire more wealth.[3] Another study suggests that individuals would continue to work even if financially they didn't have to.[4] Still another report finds that poor blacks and whites, males and females, identify their self-esteem with work as much as nonpoor persons do.[5]

Unfortunately, it seems that most managers still don't understand worker needs. Consequently, managers stand little chance of meeting needs and court

3. Morgan, J., *Survey Research Center findings, reported in* Work in America.

4. R. Morse and N. Weiss, *"The Function and Meaning of Work and the Job,"* American Sociological Review, 20 (1955) 191–198.

5. L. Goodwin, *"A Study of Work Orientations of Welfare Recipients,"* reported in Work in America.

grave risks of not discharging their basic responsibilities to workers as human beings. To illustrate the depth of this ignorance, consider a study that was conducted to find out whether what managers think workers need corresponds to what workers think they need. The study was conducted by asking workers to rank order from one (highest) to ten (lowest) what they wanted from their jobs. Supervisors were also asked to rank these items in the order in which they thought workers would rank them. The results revealed that supervisors had a tremendous ignorance of worker desires. Specifically, supervisors rated good wages, job security, and promotion and growth with the company as the top three worker choices. In contrast, workers rated these fifth, fourth, and seventh respectively. Similarly, while workers rated full appreciation of work done, feeling "in" on things, and sympathetic understanding of personal problems as their top three choices, management rated these the three lowest.[6]

When management overlooks the importance of jobs in meeting basic worker needs, or doesn't appreciate precisely what worker needs are, then how can it create proper job atmosphere or avoid injuring employees? We can understand the moral issues better if we look at work environment and work content.

Work Environment

Work environment refers to factors that are extrinsic to the job and which are often associated with producing worker dissatisfaction. These factors include company policy and administration, supervision, interpersonal relations, working conditions, salary, status, and security. Generally speaking, research indicates that when workers are dissatisfied with the jobs, it's usually because of problems in one or more of these areas. Although we can't cover all aspects of work environment, we will explore three areas that seem to raise many significant moral issues: wages, working conditions, and leadership styles.

Wages

Every employer faces the problem of setting wage rates and establishing salaries. From the moral view it's very easy to say that firms should pay a fair and just wage, but what constitutes a fair and just wage? There are so many variables involved that no one can say with mathematical precision what a person should be paid for a job. The contribution of the firm, the market for labor and products, the competitive position of the company, the creative power of the firm and unions, seasonal fluctuations, individual needs, all conspire to make a simple answer to the fair and just wage issue impossible.

The impossibility of determining precisely what a fair wage is, does not mean that employers may pay workers anything they choose. In general, if work functions to fill human needs, then employers should seek to pay a wage that significantly helps individuals satisfy their basic needs. Obviously, this directive is vague. A wage of significant help in one case may be rather meager in another. Moreover, as suggested earlier, factors sometimes impinge on the employer's

6. *See Paul Hersey and Kenneth H. Blanchard,* Management of Organizational Behavior *(Englewood Cliffs, N.J.: Prentice-Hall, 1969), p. 35.*

ability to pay an ideal wage. Fortunately, though, the issue of a *fair wage*—one that significantly helps individuals satisfy their basic needs—is not as morally insoluble as it appears to be. Frequently the fairness of the wage depends almost entirely on the means firms have taken to arrive at it. In short, *what* did they do and *how* did they do it? Determining this issue will shed considerable light on the legitimacy of the wage. Just as important, it will help firms and their representatives decide whether or not they have properly discharged their responsibilities to workers in this area of job environment.

With respect to the question of what firms or their representatives do to arrive at the wage rate, we can isolate a number of factors that bear on fairness. Surely none of these alone is enough to determine a fair wage. Indeed, all of them taken together can't guarantee it. But at least introducing these factors minimizes the chances of unfairness creeping into wages and salaries, and provides the well-intentioned business manager some ethical guidelines for arriving at a wage.

1. *What is the prevailing wage in the industry?* Although this factor is not foolproof or even a moral barometer, what similar positions in the industry earn can provide some direction for arriving at a fair wage.

2. *What is the community wage level?* This point recognizes that some communities have a higher cost of living than others. New York City, for example, is more expensive to live in than Los Angeles. The cost of living relates to basic maintenance needs and must be considered very seriously in establishing a wage. To ignore the cost of living would be to seriously jeopardize worker welfare.

3. *What is the nature of the job itself?* Some jobs require more training, experience, and education than others. Some jobs are physically or emotionally more demanding than others. Some jobs are downright dangerous; others socially undesirable. Frequently, risky or unskilled jobs attract the least well-educated and the most desperate for work. As a result, the occasions for worker exploitation can be nearly irresistible. Although it is impossible to draw a precise correlation between the nature of the job and what someone should be paid, a relationship exists which should be taken into account.

4. *Is the job secure?* A job that promises little or no security offends a basic worker need. In such cases employers might seek to compensate workers for this deprivation. Compensation could take the form of higher pay, fringe benefits, a sensible distribution of the two, or something else.

5. *What are the firm's financial capabilities?* What can a firm afford to pay? A firm's profit margin may be so narrow that it cannot afford to pay higher than a minimum wage. Another's may be so large that it can easily afford to pay more than it does.

6. *What is the law?* Federal law requires that businesses pay at least minimum wage. Even when a particular business is exempt from the law, this minimum can serve as a guide in setting wages. At the same time, we should repeat our general caution about relying on law to determine ethical

practice. As we've said elsewhere, one can satisfy the minimum requirements of the law and still not act morally. This should be kept in mind with respect to wage setting. Considering all factors involved, and not just legislative guidelines, will help business people do this.

Naturally there are other factors that employers consider in determining wages. Some of these factors include supply and demand, the wage philosophy of the firm, and comparative rates of various key jobs within the organization.

Equally important in determining what the wage will be is *how* the wage is established. In general we can say that the fairness of a wage is largely determined by a fair work contract. Just what makes up a fair work contract, in turn, demands a consideration of how the contract was wrought. Was it arbitrarily imposed? Did management unilaterally draw up a contract and present it to workers on a take-it-or-leave-it basis? Did a union present it to management with a take-it-or-else ultimatum? Or was the contract arrived at through mutual consent of employer and employee? Answering these questions will prove invaluable in determining the fairness of a contract and, by implication, the fairness of the wage.

Invariably the fairness of a work contract hinges on free and fair negotiations. These negotiations exhibit several characteristics. Obviously they must be representative of the interests of those persons directly concerned and sometimes of persons who are indirectly concerned. Also all parties should enjoy the freedom to express themselves openly without coercion or fear of reprisal. And, of course, all parties should operate in good faith, carefully avoiding the use of fraud, deceit, power, or institutional blackmail in effecting agreements.

In sum, a consideration of the factors upon which a wage is based and of the procedure that was followed in establishing the wage usually determines the fairness of the wage, which is the primary moral concern in discussions about wages. Establishing wages in this way will positively affect work environment by removing a potential cause of job dissatisfaction. Just as important, wages so established go a long way toward helping management discharge its responsibilities to employees in this area.

In recent years, two unique forms of wages, or remuneration, have become increasingly popular in business. They are incentive programs and secret pay policies. Both raise unique moral concerns.

INCENTIVE PROGRAMS.   Some employees work on an incentive program. *Under incentive programs employees receive a specific amount of money for each unit of product they produce.* The purpose of an incentive program is to increase production and efficiency. Although there's nothing inherently objectionable about incentive programs, they can raise moral questions.

Sometimes, in order to earn incentive pay, employees do inferior work, or they work slowly while incentive rates are being set and then faster afterward. Workers have also been known to develop short-cut methods that they conceal from management. In such instances, rather than advancing the welfare of the firm, employers are unwittingly retarding it with incentive programs.

Furthermore incentive programs can create disharmony among employees.

Thus, Bill Wilson, a particularly slow worker, is a source of amusement to other employees when all are working under an hourly wage system. When incentives are set, however, Bill quickly becomes a source of irritation and bitterness to co-workers who depend on his work to produce their own.

A related problem with incentive programs is the impatience workers often show when unavoidable delays caused by machine breakdowns or late arriving raw materials retard worker productivity. Workers can easily feel that they're being penalized through no fault of their own, and perhaps they are. The potential for charges of injustice should be clear, as well as the likelihood of strained employer-employee relations and its subsequent negative impact on work atmosphere.

So, while not in themselves objectionable, incentives pose potential problems for work atmosphere. Managers should consider the potential negative impact of incentive programs before enacting them. Problems ordinarily revolve around the increased pressures workers feel. Related to incentive programs are secret pay policies that some companies use.

SECRET PAY POLICIES.   A *secret pay policy* refers to a management policy of covertly rewarding employees on the basis of merit. Such a policy is thought to increase individual productivity. It also gives management great flexibility in granting raises. Thus, rather than giving every clerk in the furniture department a periodic raise, Berkeley Furniture singles out individual salespeople for raises based on their job performance. For example, salesperson Eileen Wellard is told secretly that she has received a fifty-dollar raise, while co-worker Dick Watson receives nothing. Unlike the incentive system, secret pay policies contain a number of elements that may be inherently objectionable. To grasp these objections requires an understanding of the nature of a raise.

The purpose of a *raise* is not only to reward the deserving but to stimulate and motivate other workers. But if workers are to be motivated, they must know precisely what warrants a raise and must understand what the criteria are. We should mention that this knowledge is required not only by sound motivational theory but also by fairness. Some would contend that one of the best ways to ensure that raises function fairly and motivate is for workers to see individuals like themselves getting them. In this way workers see abstract goals in the form of concrete achievements. If Watson knew about Wellard's raise, he might think, "If Eileen Wellard can earn a raise, so can I!"

By definition, however, secret pay policies short-circuit the motivational purpose of wage and salary adjustments. As a result, the firm can be injured. At the same time they can injure employees by depriving them of the concrete knowledge and experience they need to qualify for a raise. Thus, although Dick Watson may be aware of Berkeley's secret pay policy, he may not have a clear-cut idea of what warrants a pay increase. If he knew that Eileen Wellard had received a pay increase, then he could compare her performance with his own to learn precisely where he was deficient. Is it reasonable to deny him this knowledge, when being denied it can place him at a singular disadvantage?

Another observation raises additional moral concerns. Secret pay policies can actually encourage the giving of unearned rewards. Maybe Eileen Wellard has a friend "upstairs." Maybe she graduated from the same institution as the boss. Maybe she's a "company person." Maybe any number of things. The point is, when co-workers don't know about merit raises, they are in no position to question the deservedness of such raises. As a result, the potential for favoritism and unmerited raises is great. At the very least, such policies seem likely to breed worker suspicions that management is capricious or downright unfair, rewarding only their favorites. When employees harbor such sentiments, work environment suffers.

Another fact about secret pay policies that raises moral concern is that they almost always cause employees to spend too much time worrying about money. This can easily detract from job performance. Worse, when employees unearth the fact that a colleague is making substantially more than they, they can experience needless ego deflation. In reality the unrewarded employees' work may be adequate. It just isn't outstanding or good enough to warrant a raise. This is no reason for despair. But try explaining this to employees who may already feel they're being underpaid when they discover that their salary is substantially lower than that of a colleague doing the very same job.

It seems crucial to question why some companies have secret pay policies. Why should a merit raise be kept secret? Notice that we're not questioning the morality of merit raises, but rather how they are granted. The fact is that such secrecy almost automatically creates suspicions, ill will, needless distractions, destructive competitiveness, and biased treatment. These are hardly ingredients for increased productivity and efficiency, which raises should encourage.

So much for the wages aspect of the work environment. Another vital aspect of this subject, one that figures prominently in the creation of proper work atmosphere and raises serious moral consideration, is working conditions.

Working Conditions

The conditions under which people work are as significant as wages in meeting basic human needs. Fortunately considerable legislation and enlightened business leadership have significantly reduced the dinginess that often characterized the work place in former years. Nevertheless, problems remain. Safety laws and company policies cannot keep pace with the dangers that employees face as a result of modern technology and equipment.

For example, at a Shell location not too long ago, a refinery employee nearly lost an arm while using a high-pressure lubricating gun. The incident began harmlessly enough when the worker inadvertently got his forearm in the way of the spray jetting from the gun's nozzle. He wiped the grease off, unmindful of the serious injury he had just sustained. Later the arm swelled and became painful. Surgery was required. For a while serious doubt loomed as to whether the arm would have to be amputated.

What had happened? Grease is usually a soft substance, but when propelled to high velocity it can become like needles that penetrate the skin. In this instance the grease penetrated the skin, depositing foreign material well up to the worker's elbow. The material, insoluble in blood, could be removed only by surgery.

Was this a bizarre, remote occurrence? Not exactly. With the widespread use of a similar tool, the high-pressure airless paint gun, such incidents have become common enough for concern. Indeed, a recent survey by the Consumer Product Safety Commission's Bureau of Epidemiology indicated that an estimated 847 surgeons and hand specialists have treated at least one injury caused by injection from high-pressure grease guns or airless spray paint guns. Ninety-six percent of the patients were professional painters.[7]

Modern technology has also introduced another threat to worker health and safety heretofore unacknowledged: noise. So serious a threat has noise become in many occupational settings that the 1970 Occupational Safety and Health Act proposed that 85 decibels be the maximum noise level to which a worker may be exposed during an eight-hour day. Many companies don't think this goal is enforceable or realistic. Nevertheless, the fact remains that worker health and safety is an ethical concern that employers must address themselves to, even in the absence of legislation.

Despite legislation the scope of occupational hazards remains awesome and generally unrecognized. Thus, although the thrust of the 1970 Occupational Safety and Health Act is ". . . to ensure so far as possible every working man and woman in the nation safe and healthful working conditions," implementation of the act has been spotty. Consider the fact that there are fewer than one hundred qualified Occupational Safety and Health Administration (OSHA) industrial hygienists and approximately five hundred OSHA inspectors for about four million work places. Add to this the fact that OSHA has established only one permanent standard, for asbestos, recognizing the epidemic of asbestosis and asbestos-induced lung and other cancers, especially among insulation workers. What's more, of 80 million workers, there are over 7 million annual work-related diseases and injuries, of which 2 million are disabling and 14,000 fatal. Furthermore, estimates of losses run as high as 250 million person-working days, costing $1.5 billion in wages and an annual loss to the gross national product (GNP) of $8 billion.[8] Before presuming that things are getting better, reflect on the fact that the incidence of disabling injuries in manufacturing industries was 20 percent greater in the late 1970s than it was in 1958.

Although of paramount importance, worker health and safety represent just two facets of working conditions that both affect the work environment and raise moral questions. There are numerous others: forcing employees to participate in questionable legal or moral activity, showing favoritism in dealing with employees, transferring workers great distances without sharing costs. In some cases, working conditions can raise multiple moral concerns. Take, for example, forced overtime, the practice of compelling workers to work beyond their regular hours or shifts. Occurring on an occasional, infrequent basis, forced overtime is rarely injurious. In fact, it can be highly beneficial in helping workers meet basic maintenance needs. But what about when forced overtime becomes a regular practice? In some instances workers must put in so much overtime that they lack

7. Reported in Robert E. Swindle, Fundamentals of Modern Business (Belmont, Calif.: Wadsworth Publishing Co., 1977), p. 72.

8. See Rollin H. Simonds, "OSHA Compliance: Safety Is Good Business," Personnel, July–August, 1973.

time to fill vital personal needs, such as tending to their families or restoring themselves through recreation. The implications are serious not only for workers but for the firm and consumers as well because efficiency and productivity usually suffer. The moral implications of forced overtime grow even more serious when the practice is used to avoid hiring additional workers. Here questions of justice invariably crop up, as well as social responsibility.

There is another aspect of work environment that is so far-reaching in its implications that we will consider it separately; it involves leadership styles.

Leadership Styles

How managers conduct themselves on the job can often do more to enhance or diminish the work environment than any other facet of employer-employee relations. Partially influencing this conduct are the general assumptions that managers make about human beings and the subsequent leadership styles they adopt.

The late Douglas McGregor proposed two basic sets of assumptions about human beings that he observed many managers take.[9] He called these Theories X and Y. We describe them here because so many moral problems that arise relative to managerial treatment of employees have their roots in these assumptions. In order to evaluate intelligently the morality of specific behavior, it's frequently necessary to evaluate the underlying assumptions about people that give rise to it. For example, if a male chauvinist manager treats female subordinates unequally and unfairly, the immorality of his behavior ultimately lies in his assumptions about women generally. In a word, if he weren't sexually prejudiced, he probably wouldn't behave the way he does. Given his assumptions about women, however, his behavior is altogether consistent and, in his mind, moral. After all, he believes women are inherently unequal and inferior to men. If, on the other hand, you would consider his behavior immoral, it's likely because you believe his assumptions are unsound and lead to immoral behavior.

According to McGregor managers who espouse Theory X believe that workers essentially dislike work and will do everything they can to avoid it. As a result, such workers must be coerced and bullied in order to make their efforts conform to organizational objectives. Such managers insist that the average person wishes to avoid responsibility, lacks ambition, and primarily values security above everything else.

In contrast, managers who espouse Theory Y believe that workers essentially like work, that they view it as something natural and potentially enjoyable. As a result, they don't believe that strict control and direction is the only way to achieve organizational goals. Similarly, they view workers as being motivated by higher level needs as well as by maintenance ones. Workers don't eschew responsibility but accept it and seek it out. In this way workers partially realize the self-fulfillment that they believe work can hold out for them.

These assumptions inspire different and often divergent managerial conduct toward employees. This is perhaps best observed in the leadership styles that

9. Douglas McGregor, The Human Side of Enterprise (New York: McGraw-Hill, 1960).

managers adopt. For example, Theory X managers likely provide autocratic leadership. They closely shepherd employees by giving orders and directions to subordinates. They rarely solicit ideas about how tasks should be performed. They tell employees what to do and how to do it. They expect little more of employees than that they follow orders. Theory Y managers, on the other hand, are likely to be more democratic. While informing employees of the tasks to be performed, they also solicit new ideas from them regarding the execution of the tasks. They use this input to refine their own ideas about how to perform tasks. Theory Y managers might also tend to be laissez-faire in their approach to work. In other words, they provide minimum direction for employees. Decisions on work methods are left to employees. Laissez-faire managers generally view themselves as resource persons, trouble shooters, and supporters rather than directors of the work force.

As suggested, many moral problems in management-employee relations can be traced to basic managerial assumptions about workers. Specifically, moral issues crop up when managers routinize themselves to a leadership role regardless of the idiosyncrasies of the employees they deal with. This is analogous to the question of justice that arises in subjecting everyone to the same intelligence test despite the fact that the test has been devised with a select group in mind. In both cases not only are legitimate individual differences overlooked, but these differences become the basis of punitive treatment. Thus, it's very tempting for managers, even of the non–Theory X variety, to assume an autocratic style for unskilled workers, laissez-faire for highly skilled ones, and democratic for employees who fall somewhere in between. But unfortunately human nature defies such glib pigeonholing and stereotyping. People differ. Some employees at whatever level respond to and need little managerial orchestration; others need and want close supervision. When managers overlook this, they overlook people's needs. They run risks of creating a work atmosphere that's not only hostile to workers but unconducive to optimum productivity. They also invite injustice into the work place, for injustice can arise as much from treating people identically as treating them unequally. If these problems are to be avoided, it seems that managers must choose a style of leadership suitable to the needs, abilities, and predilections of those in their charge.

In sum, wages, working conditions, and leadership roles are three aspects of the work environment. Simply because of their general effect on proper work atmosphere they are of moral concern. But in addition, as we've seen, these factors frequently raise specific moral concerns in the management-employee relationship. But even when wages, working conditions, and other environmental factors are not effecting job dissatisfaction, there still may remain reasons for lack of job satisfaction. The reasons lie not in the job environment but in the job content.

Job Content

As early as the 1920s researchers began to realize that employees would be more productive if management fulfilled those needs that money cannot satisfy.

Managers at the Hawthorne factory of Western Electric Company were conducting experiments to determine the effect of the work environment on worker productivity. In the literature of work motivation, these studies have become known as the Hawthorne studies. What they discovered has been termed the Hawthorne effect.

Researchers in the Hawthorne studies chose a few employees to work in an experimental area, apart from the thousands of employees in the rest of the factory. Every effort was made to improve working conditions, from painting walls a cheerful color to making lights brighter. Worker productivity increased with each improvement.

Then experimenters decided to reverse the process. For example, lights were made dimmer. To everyone's surprise productivity continued to increase.

The conclusion researchers drew was that workers were producing more because they were receiving attention. Instead of feeling that they were cogs in the organizational wheel, they felt important and recognized. The attention had the effect of heightening their sense of personal identity and feeling of control over their work environment. Recognition of this Hawthorne effect signaled the beginning of what we now know as the science of human relations. Morally, it represents an insight into how management can effectively discharge its responsibilities to the firm and to employees in terms of worker motivation and job satisfaction.

More recent studies tend to corroborate and deepen the application of the Hawthorne effect. In a most important study conducted to shed light on the problem of poor worker motivation, Frederick Herzberg discovered that factors producing job satisfaction differed from those producing job dissatisfaction. Herzberg found that job dissatisfaction invariably arises from problems relating to the work environment: pay, worker supervision, working conditions, leadership styles. But a satisfactory work environment does not translate into satisfied workers. They can still express little or no job satisfaction. The reason, Herzberg contends, is that worker satisfaction is a function of work content, not the work environment. And work satisfaction depends on such factors as a sense of accomplishment, responsibility, recognition, self-development, and self-expression.

A survey conducted in 1970 lends credence to Herzberg's findings. When 1,533 workers at all occupational levels were asked to rank in order of importance to them some twenty-five aspects of work, they listed: interesting work; sufficient help, support, and information to accomplish the job; enough authority to carry out the work; good pay; opportunity to develop special skills; job security; and seeing the results of their work.[10]

These studies suggest that although lower level, maintenance needs may have been met, workers are not necessarily satisfied with their jobs. In other words, higher level needs are not being met. Clearly, managers have an economic interest in job satisfaction, namely, the good of the firm. This alone would suggest the moral overtones of the job content–worker satisfaction

---

10. *Survey Research Center,* Survey of Working Conditions (*Ann Arbor: University of Michigan, 1970*).

phenomenon. But there are deeper human and moral considerations involved, stemming from the fact that human needs are at stake.

To dramatize the moral import of the work content question, consider a study conducted in 1972 by the Institute of Social Research. In studying a cross section of American workers, it found numerous mental health problems directly attributable to lack of job satisfaction. These problems included psychosomatic diseases such as ulcers and hypertension, low self-esteem, anxiety, and impaired interpersonal relations.[11] Similarly, in an exhaustive study of industrial workers, A. W. Kornhauser found that about 40 percent of all autoworkers exhibit some symptoms of mental health problems related to job satisfaction.[12] In general, studies indicate that greater mental health problems occur in low-status, boring unchallenging jobs that offer little autonomy. These findings are of particular relevancy to today's work force, characterized as it is by persons of relatively high educational achievement in comparatively low-status jobs.

How workers attempt to cope with work that offers little satisfaction raises another concern. We're probably all familiar with the hard-driving, hard-drinking executive stereotype. But the Special Task Force report of 1972 indicated that significant numbers of industrial workers drink heavily during the lunch hour to help manage the boredom or pressure of their jobs. It also found that many younger workers do the same, perhaps substituting drugs for alcohol.

One of the most intriguing studies done not only suggests a correlation between longevity and job satisfaction but contends that job satisfaction is the strongest predictor of longevity.[13] The second major factor for longevity is happiness. Both job satisfaction and happiness predict longevity better than either the physical health or genetic inheritance of individuals.

The moral thrust is that the content of work materially affects the total well-being of workers. This fact makes work content and job satisfaction issues of vital moral concern. Ignoring these issues or treating them indifferently invites profound injury to workers, to owners, and to society at large. Determining how firms should attempt to effect job satisfaction is beyond the parameters of this book. For some firms it may mean providing workers with less supervision and more autonomy. For others it may mean providing workers opportunities to develop and refine skills. Still others might try to provide workers with greater participation in the conception, design, and execution of their work, with greater responsibility and a deeper sense of achievement. Perhaps all companies ought to examine the impact of technology on job satisfaction. While generally increasing efficiency of operations and eliminating the physical drudgery that plagued yesterday's workers, today's technology just as often results in repetitive and boring tasks. So serious is this problem that the Special Task Force on Work in America recommended sweeping reforms and innovations in the work place

11. *H. Sheppard and N. Herrick,* Where Have All the Robots Gone? *(New York: The Free Press, 1972).*

12. *A. W. Kornhauser,* Mental Health of the Industrial Worker: A Detroit Study *(Huntington, N.Y.: R. E. Krieger, 1965).*

13. *E. Palmore, "Predicting Longevity: A Follow-Up Controlling for Age,"* Gerontologist, *9 (1969) 247–250.*

aimed at recapturing the spirit, sense of commitment, and enthusiasm of today's workers at all occupational levels. The report cited with optimism attempts by various companies such as Texas Instrument, Travelers Insurance, and Corning Glass to provide workers with greater autonomy and responsibility for managing work tasks. All of this notwithstanding, it's neither the charge nor the intent of this book to spell out how business ought to go about providing job satisfaction. Rather, it's to suggest that business has responsibilities in this area.

In conclusion, we want to note that business can act most irresponsibly in this area by doing nothing; for neglect and practiced indifference can be as morally suspect as an overt act. In general, then, it seems that concerned management at all levels might design appropriate managerial strategies to create conditions that allow individuals to achieve their own goals while at the same time achieving organizational goals. One student of management has put it succinctly. He writes: "The leadership and other processes of the organization must be such as to ensure a maximum probability that in all interactions and all relationships with the organization each member will, in the light of his background, values, and expectations, view the experience as supportive and one which builds and maintains his sense of personal worth and importance."[14]

Ethical Theories

There are far too many individual cases involving job atmosphere to begin to apply ethical theories to all of them. In the last analysis, moral concerns involving the work environment and content demand separate analyses within particular theoretical frameworks. Nevertheless, we can speculate about the general direction in which these ethical theories are likely to take us in the area of work atmosphere.

It is helpful to keep in mind the general attitudes toward and emphases on the individual that these theories convey. Consequentialists generally don't cultivate the inherent respect and worth of the individual that nonconsequentialists generally do, although in the case of situational ethics this observation needs careful qualification. Broadly speaking, then, consequentialists would not champion the cause of improved job atmosphere on grounds of human need, rights, or dignity. This doesn't mean that consequentialists would not acknowledge management's responsibility in these areas. It's just that consequentialists generally would rationalize these responsibilities on the basis of consequences for self (egoism) or for everyone (utilitarianism). Put in other words, under no circumstances would either egoists or utilitarians morally justify an increase in wages, improved working conditions, or an enriched job program on the basis of what workers deserve as human beings. Rather the justification would lie strictly in a consideration of results: whether these actions produce more favorable consequences than any other alternative. If they don't, then these actions lack moral justification. In contrast, nonconsequentialists would likely tie job atmosphere considerations to basic human rights. With their emphasis on the pri-

14. *Rensis Likert,* New Patterns of Management *(New York: McGraw-Hill, 1961), p. 103.*

macy of the individual, they'd take a dim view of any action, policy, or practice that inhibited workers from satisfying their basic needs, despite the favorable consequences that such phenomena might elicit.

Having said this, it's curious to note that each of these theories could provide a philosophical basis for business responsibilities in these areas. Take, for example, the issue of work content. Does business have any responsibilities for trying to ensure that work content functions to help workers satisfy higher level needs, such as autonomy and self-fulfillment? Such a basic question is a useful one because it's unlikely that moral debates about specific programs and policies could even arise prior to a resolution of this question.

Given the apparent connection between work content and worker motivation, egoists could argue that business has a responsibility to do what it can to improve the quality of work content. After all, if workers are more motivated and productive when doing work that they can relate to, then it's in the best long-term interests of business to do what it can to effect that atmosphere. At the same time this doesn't commit egoists to blind endorsement of any policy or program designed to improve job content, for a specific implementation of this commitment may not be in business's best interest. For example, the Pet program was fine for Pet, but it might not be appropriate for the interests of another concern. In short, egoism could provide a philosophical basis for a general business responsibility to at least investigate the prospects of improving the quality of job content, since it appears that that aspect of work atmosphere affects the interests of the firm.

Likewise, act utilitarians, while avoiding endorsement of anything that smacks of a rule, could at the same time use its theory as a philosophical basis for business responsibilities in the area of work content. We say this because given the direction and findings of current research and thought on the matter, it seems that if business acknowledged responsibilities in this area, it would take the first step toward improving the quality of work content, which, in turn, would apparently produce more good for all concerned than any other alternative. Again, however, as with egoism, this in no way would commit act utilitarians to an unquestioning implementation of any decision calculated to improve the quality of work content. At that point each proposal must be examined in terms of its own impact on all concerned. It could turn out that in a particular instance doing nothing to improve the quality of work content or actually doing something to retard it might be the moral thing to do, if it were attended with the most good for the majority of people.

Rule utilitarianism, likewise, could provide philosophical underpinnings for commitment to the proposition that business has a responsibility to do what it can to help satisfy workers' higher level needs with respect to work content. Proponents of this theory could argue that implementing a rule which embodied this proposition would likely lead to more total good than breaking such a rule would. Again, however, this doesn't mean that rule utilitarians would thereby be committed to approval of any program designed to improve work quality, for some programs obviously are attended with greater benefit and less harm than are others. But given the current nature of the research, it seems that utilitarians could enthusiastically endorse the proposition that business has responsibilities in the area of work content as it relates to worker satisfaction.

In a similar vein, Fletcher's situationalism, while generally eschewing rules and principles, endorses the law of Christian love, the greatest amount of neighbor welfare. The question, then, is whether business generally acts more or less in harmony with this principle of love by acknowledging and accepting responsibilities in the area of work content than it does by rejecting it. It's hard to imagine how situationalists would argue that being oblivious to workers' higher level needs is compatible with loving concern, while it's relatively easy to see how it is not. It seems as safe to say, therefore, that situationalists would be sympathetic to the proposition that business does have responsibilities for worker satisfaction, as it does to say that situationalists are sympathetic to the propositions that business ought to pay a fair wage and provide safe working conditions. Again, however, actions serving to subtract from a fair wage, create unsafe working conditions, or reduce the quality of work content would not necessarily be immoral. If these actions spring from loving concern, they would in fact be right and good. On the surface this may appear to be inconsistent. But a closer look reveals the consistency of the commitment and the actions in that both follow love's lead.

Moving to nonconsequentialist theories, it seems that the Golden Rule would acknowledge business responsibilities for improving work content. An application of the rule itself leads to this conclusion. For should those in a position to affect work content ask themselves whether they'd want such initiatives were they in the position of subordinates, they'd undoubtedly say they would. Notice, however, that Golden Rulists would not arrive at this conclusion by appealing to consequences, but by appealing to a principle of fair play.

Similarly, Kantians would avoid concern with consequences in this matter. They would primarily consider the inherent worth and dignity of rational creatures. They would condemn any action that militated against what they perceived as proper to the functioning of rational creatures. Applying the categorical imperative to a maxim such as "Business may be unconcerned with worker satisfaction," Kantians would examine the logical consistency of such a proposition when universalized. Since worker satisfaction is intimately conjoined with human needs, universalizing such a maxim would undermine the functioning of rational creatures. They might add that such a rule would also subvert the institution of business itself if we assume that worker satisfaction is intimately connected to worker motivation and thus to productivity and efficiency.

Similarly, Ross's prima facie duties and Rawls's natural duties would be mindful of business's responsibilities to workers as human beings. Of uppermost importance here would be duties of justice, beneficence, and noninjury, which in a general way would commit intuitionists like Ross and social justice theorists like Rawls to the cause of improved work atmosphere.

Also noteworthy here is Rawls's notion of reciprocity that characterizes his concept of justice. Thus, considering the work environment at the Pet plant before it instituted a job-enrichment program, Rawls might ask: "Would plant supervisors accept similar boredom, frustration, and general emptiness in their own work?" Or Rawls might inquire into the positions of employees confronted with such work content in relation to their superiors. If such workers were in an unequal position with respect to determining the work content, then they wouldn't be in a position to acknowledge the work content as it exists. In that event, Rawls might say that the practice violated his equal liberty principle. Furthermore, he could argue that his principle of paternalism binds managers to represent the interests of those workers who are not in a position to represent their own.

Proponents of the proportionality principle, likewise, would support the claim that business has obligations in the area of work satisfaction. Garrett is clear on this point: "Work occupies a large part of a man's day," he writes. "Unless his job is humanly satisfying, not only his productivity but his whole life is diminished. Man needs to find significance in what he does. Unconsciously, at least, he needs to feel that he has created something, served others, and left his mark upon the world. Work should provide the opportunity for this sense of fulfillment."[15] (We, of course, extend Garrett's remarks to embrace women, as well as men!)

Under no circumstances could firms willfully diminish work content. At the same time, however, the proportionality principle would condone risking or allowing a diminishment of work content providing that sufficient reason existed to warrant it. Nevertheless, there's no question that proportionalists would underscore management's moral obligations to seek imaginative and inventive ways of making the work place a stimulating rather than a stultifying place. As Garrett puts it: "Lack of imagination and initiative can contribute to moral failures as well as business losses. . . . it would certainly appear that the businessman has a real obligation to study and utilize the vast literature concerned with motivation."[16]

In applying these theories, we've obviously focused on just the work content facet of job atmosphere. We've done so because work content is of increasing concern and study now that the work place ordinarily satisfies basic needs. At the same time, the subject of worker satisfaction and relative organizational responsibilities remains rather amorphous. We should point out that although each of these theories could provide a logical basis for improved quality of work content, this doesn't mean that it necessarily would. As always, our interpretations and applications are open to challenge, correction, and amendment. Thus, some moralists might detect in one or more of these theories overlooked subtleties which suggest different inferences. At the same time, all of what we've said must ultimately be placed within the context of the general theories as explained in Chapter 2. This might prove a significant task when the weaknesses of the theories are brought to bear on these applications. If you are seriously concerned with business ethics, we encourage you to pursue alternative interpretations for the ethical theories we have presented.

15. *Garrett,* Business Ethics, *p. 61.*

16. *Ibid, p. 62.*

CASE PRESENTATION
The First Job

Trenton's young vice-president in charge of labor relations had received mail from disgruntled employees before but none had been like this. Sarah Wainwright's correspondence was in the form of a diary, which recorded her impressions during the five months she was employed at Trenton.[17] Vice-president Pedigrew read it with interest.

May 11: Went for the Trenton interview today at the U. placement center. Lots of others there. All job hungry, like me. Trenton's rep. says the firm's involved primarily in oil exploration, also various natural resource development programs. They anticipate needing about a half-dozen chemical engineers to work on projects they'll be developing over the next year. Hope I'm one (of the engineers, that is, not the projects!). Sounds like a good opportunity. Who can be fussy these days?

June 11: Got the job! Congratulations, me! Knew you could do it all the time, and all that rot.

June 25: First day on the job. A bit scary. No, a whole lot! Met my supervisor, Bill Ryan—quiet, businesslike. He assigned me to a project; implied that it was new and useful.

July 1: Still feel disoriented at Trenton. Lost, anxious. Probably first-job jitters. Not sleeping right. Pressing too much, I think—the bane of all over-achievers. Still enthusiastic, though. Really want to make a good impression on Bill Ryan.

July 19: Floundering. This is awful. Project's going badly. Getting no direction from Bill. Feel helpless. Know I can do the job. Just don't know the ropes— where things are, what facilities are available, how to get information, who to ask for what I need, where to get it, etc., etc., etc.!

August 10: Things no better at work. Should really talk with Bill. Don't want him to think I'm incompetent or lazy, though. Wish he were more approachable. Has his own work, probably. Not around much. Whenever I've asked something, he's been terse, evidently feeling put upon. Sometimes he doesn't answer at all; just does the thing himself. That's got to be the pits. Sure he doesn't mean it personally. Probably just his way. Ugh! What a way!

Sept. 1: Eureka! Found some sympathetic ears! Good resource people, too. Don't mind helping me.

Sept. 28: Directed to Jack Justin today for help on an aspect of the project. Jack expressed bewilderment, not with the problem but with the project itself. Said a similar project had been tried and abandoned several years before. Can't believe it. Must see Bill about this.

Oct. 15: Learned that Tom Anatole has received a raise. We were hired together. Didn't even know that I might get a performance review, let alone be considered for a raise so early. This whole thing is getting Kafkaesque. Feel confused, hurt, and angry.

Nov. 1: Been fishing around for two weeks trying to land some hard info.

17. *Adapted from John P. Kotter, "Managing the Joining-Up Process," Personnel, July–August, 1972.*

about salary administration and employee evaluation. It's hopeless. Nobody knows anything for sure. Can't believe it. Must see Bill.

Dec. 1: Finally got up the gumption to see Bill. Must be the most inaccessible person I've ever met. Worse than some professors. Vaguely understanding, sympathetic. But utterly uninformative. May have to go above him.

Dec. 5: Saw Fred Garcia today. Assistant division head. Told him I wanted a transfer. Didn't seem to hear me. Seemed more concerned with organizational chain of command. Seems I leaped above two levels of management in expressing my gripes. Made it sound like I had to go directly to jail without collecting two-hundred bucks!

Dec. 12: Quit.

Pedigrew glanced through the diary the first time but then read it carefully several times before slipping it into his desk drawer. But he couldn't dismiss its impact on him. In the days ahead he was drawn back to several more readings, which left Pedigrew with the distinct impression that Sarah Wainwright had been treated unfairly, assuming the accuracy of her account.

But what should Pedigrew do? There wasn't a whole lot he could do for Wainwright now that she had quit. Besides, he had enough work handling in-house complaints and disputes channeled to him through the due-process procedure without embracing the gripes of former employees. What's more, Ryan and Garcia were veterans of proven ability whose contributions to Trenton needed no documentation. The chances of making a dent in the operating methods of either of them were nil. Why stir up a hornet's nest? And yet, at the same time, he couldn't help wondering whether he should do something.

1. *Should Pedigrew do nothing, in effect forget he ever received Wainwright's correspondence?*

2. *What direction do the ethical theories provide?*

3. *If Pedigrew should do something, what do you suggest?*

4. *How would you assign the blame in the Wainwright case? Who or what's responsible for this episode?*

5. *Does Pedigrew have an obligation to ensure that something like this does not occur again?*

6. *Assuming the accuracy of Wainwright's account, and that she was treated unfairly, do you think Trenton owes her anything? If so, what form would you suggest this reparation take?*

CASE PRESENTATION
The Burden of Atlas

"I don't mean to sound ruthless," Atlas Mining board member Ralph Thomas was saying to a packed meeting of stockholders as he held up a copy of the letter that the board had recently received. "But Hank Ingstrom knew of the implied risk he was taking when he chose to be a uranium miner. Furthermore, he was well compensated for those risks for the nearly thirty years he was in our employ. Naturally, like all of you, I deplore the fact that Hank now suffers from lung cancer. But I don't think it's fair to expect Atlas Mining to compensate him for his personal tragedy."

The room was silent, those in attendance undoubtedly expecting stockholder Thurman Blomberg to reply. After all, for the past hour Blomberg had been arguing that Atlas did have a responsibility to Hank Ingstrom, even though Ingstrom had been retired for nearly three years and his cancer had been diagnosed only six months before.

"Did Ingstrom know he was risking lung cancer?" came Blomberg's voice from the middle of the room. "The fact of the matter is that Ingstrom no more appreciated the risks he was running than most of us did twenty years ago."

"Does that make Atlas responsible for Ingstrom for as long as he lives and for whatever he incurs?" Thomas shot back.

"Yes," insisted Blomberg, "if he or anybody else contracts a disease that is directly related to uranium mining."

"But how do we know that for sure?" Thomas demanded.

"Do you realize, Mr. Thomas, that about one-sixth of Western uranium miners will probably die of lung cancer in the next twenty years? That's over one thousand workers. Now, I hope you don't mean to tell me that in all likelihood these people would have contracted lung cancer had they been teaching school or frying hamburgers in some hash house."

"No, maybe they'd have developed hypertension or arteriosclerosis," Thomas replied. A nervous laugh exploded in some quarters of the room. "All right," Thomas continued, raising a conciliatory hand, "let's assume that Hank Ingstrom has developed lung cancer directly as a result of his working as a uranium miner for Atlas. Nevertheless, the fact remains that we didn't intend that. In fact, until very recently, as you suggest, none of us was aware of the full impact of uranium exposure over the long haul. Now that we do know, we've taken measures to ensure the safety of today's miners. I'm sure I needn't remind you, Mr. Blomberg, that just last year Atlas was one of the first companies to agree to joint management-labor responsibilities for protecting workers' health. This means periodic inspection of plants by independent consultants, medical examination of workers at company expense, and availability to the Oil, Chemical, and Atomic Workers International Union of all future company records on workers' sickness and death. Now, I think that that shows a deep sense of responsibility on behalf of the ownership of Atlas for worker health and safety."

"I couldn't agree more," Blomberg replied. "But that doesn't discharge our responsibilities to those unfortunates who are already suffering or will suffer the consequences of uranium exposure."

"But what do you expect us to do?" Thomas asked irritably, "canvas all our retirees and discharged, and compensate them for deferred illnesses?"

"If those illnesses are directly related to uranium mining, yes," Blomberg answered.

"Do you have any idea what that would cost? I'm not talking only about medical costs but about our general liability," Thomas explained. "Do you have any idea of the impact that such an initiative would have on this industry? On business generally?"

The room fell silent until Thurman Blomberg said, "Tell that to Hank Ingstrom."

At that point the matter of compensating Hank Ingstrom was put to a vote.

1. *If you had a vote in the decision, what would it be? Why?*

2. *Apply each of the ethical theories to the decision facing Atlas. What courses of action would they suggest?*

3. *Would you argue for or against a general principle of corporate responsibility for deferred job-related illnesses?*

Twenty-Two Arguments Against Job Enrichment

Robert H. Schappe

In this chapter we talked about the apparent connection between intrinsic factors and job satisfaction. Thus achievement, recognition for achievement, the work itself, level of responsibility, and advancement all seem a fundamental part of job satisfaction. We noted that in recent years some companies, like Pet, have attempted to provide these intrinsic work experiences through programs of job enrichment. But often such programs meet staunch organizational resistance. Such resistance raises moral concern, for if job enrichment is the most expeditious way to provide job satisfaction, then to resist it is to thwart the satisfaction of higher level human needs. The question then is when, if ever, is resistance to enrichment programs justifiable? The answer largely depends on the validity of the common arguments offered by management and labor to the organizational change effort of job enrichment. In the following article, Robert H. Schappe, senior staff assistant in the organizational research and development department with General Motors, outlines and discusses these arguments. By anticipating and using these arguments, we should be better able to formulate a position on the morality of resisting job-enrichment programs, and also to develop a clearer rationale for job enrichment and to create a better understanding of what it is and what it can and cannot do.

The arguments against job enrichment which are presented here have arisen primarily in industrial organizations with assembly line processes and a long history of organized labor. The information has been collected from such diverse sources as management seminars, industrial consulting situations, academic classrooms, the mass media and informal discussions and is divided into management and labor positions, because the arguments reflect much of the prevalent political philosophy of each side of the organization. These arguments vary along organizational dimensions such as department, function, level and job, as well as along socioeconomic, cultural and personality dimensions. It cannot be said that they represent or typify any particular management or labor position. Sometimes labor and management agree and sometimes they disagree, or at times there is disagreement within labor or within management on the concept of job enrichment. Some of the twenty-two arguments arise as unadulterated resistance while others arise more as inquiries about job enrichment and its implications. It is not likely that all of these reasons would be heard in the same organization, but over many organizations these twenty-two are the ones which recur and persist.

The job enrichment under discussion is essentially that proposed and discussed by Herzberg (1968), Ford (1973) and Myers (1964). It involves modifying job content so that the individual has increased responsibility and autonomy, a wider variety of tasks and more opportunities for achievement and recognition in his work. In effect the work itself becomes a source of motivation for the individual.

Myers (1971) examined union opposition to job enrichment as a *general* phenomenon in labor-management relations, but was not directly concerned with the *specific* union arguments against enrichment. He suggested four "models" or processes whereby both sides of the organization could more easily attain goals in the common interest of the organization. But in the main, he was concerned with solutions to a *general* problem of union resistance.

An underlying assumption in this article is that if a job enrichment effort is to be implemented, it will be done only after a thorough analysis of the organization has been made and this analysis indicates that enrichment would be a workable solution to existing problems. The next step would be one of explaining job enrichment, clarifying questions about it, and convincing certain individuals of its potential. This is in contrast to situations where job enrichment is being "sold" to an organization as a program, regardless of existing needs.

Management Arguments Against Job Enrichment

In the course of discussing job enrichment with management and trying to show how it can solve certain kinds of problems, some very predictable arguments and forms of resistance are offered and when committing these to paper, they can be sequenced or organized in a variety of ways. Those arguments appearing early in this section tend to be general in nature and could apply to other change efforts as well as job enrichment, while those appearing later in the list tend to be arguments peculiar to job enrichment. Usually, when the subject of job enrichment is discussed, members of management assume that it is hourly-rated jobs that are under consideration. Many of the management arguments are presented here from this perspective.

1. General Argument Against Change Through Job Enrichment

This is mentioned mainly because of its pervasiveness and ubiquity in organizations. It may be regarded as some global resistance to change or viewed as a sum of several specific arguments. Underlying this resistance seems to be the feeling that if change is suggested for the way things are to be done in the future, something must have been wrong with the way things were done in the past.

Admittedly, the possibility for needed change may be psychologically painful insofar as it means admitting error. Overcoming this kind of resistance is especially difficult because of the diffusion of the resistance. Treating this general resistance as a summation of several specific arguments makes it more vulnerable as each argument can then be examined and dealt with as a concrete, specific item.

2. No Felt Need for Job Enrichment

If an analysis of the organization reveals that job enrichment could be a meaningful answer to existing problems, the next step is to get certain members of management to admit they have problems which can be dealt with by job enrichment. When there is no felt need or a lack of willingness to admit the need for help, it is common to hear "horror stories" and requests for motivational "Band-Aids." The former are anecdotes about expensive, time-consuming, motivational efforts which the organization tried sometime in the past and which weren't successful. The latter are requests for motivating certain individuals; the 63 year-old sweeper or the chronically absent female assembler. Both of these tactics are commonly used for saving face and keeping problems out of sight. One approach that has been successful in dealing with this type of resistance is to initiate an organizational change strategy (before that of job enrichment) which will promote and foster an atmosphere of trust and mutual acceptance. This is not easy, but it is only when individuals feel free to discuss problems, rather than try to hide them, that solutions can be brought to bear on them.

3. Job Enrichment Is Incompatible With Profits

This is perhaps the oldest and most common reason to be found in any organization. The traditional conception of man at work embodies the notion of a trade-off between satisfaction and earnings. The worker can have it one way or the other, but cannot expect to have both. This has been perpetuated by programs or efforts to increase satisfaction which have not been reflected in organizational earnings. This may be the cardinal item for the success not only of job enrichment, but for any motivational effort designed to change the organization. When the improvement of work content is viewed as an integral aspect of profits rather than something in competition with them, job enrichment can be successful. Satisfaction gained from meaningful work is a means by which the organization can achieve the goal of profits. In short, the amount of change produced by job enrichment ultimately must get translated into the scale of measurement by which the organization is appraised—dollars and cents.

4. Job Enrichment Costs Too Much, Takes Too Much Time

With little research on the cost of job enrichment and its expected financial return, it becomes necessary to turn from empiricism to persuasion to respond to this argument. Job enrichment is an investment which will require an initial expenditure of time (money) by the organization. As an investment it will be some time, probably months, before there is any visible return. This return may be reflected in different ways: greater productivity, better quality, less scrap, less absenteeism, or other measures of performance. In the long run, it just might cost *less* to motivate people through meaningful work than through extrinsic work context factors which cost real money, but which don't seem to motivate. The entire issue of cost, investment, and profits as they relate to a motivational effort like job enrichment is very complex and cannot be satisfactorily examined here, but treating job enrichment as an investment has met with success in the past when the argument of cost has arisen.

5. Job Enrichment Is Just Another Program

This is related to Argument 3, but is mentioned because of the word, "Program." This word has a connotation of something starting one day and stopping a few days later. In industry these programs typically involve technical training or behavior modification, with the former concerned

with very specific, practical goals and the latter concerned with broader and frequently more elusive goals. People in the plant tend to regard these programs as something extra and not as an integral aspect of their work. If job enrichment is regarded as "just another program," it will be placed well down on the priority list. When this happens, the effort is usually regarded as a personnel department activity and operating managers feel neither identification with it nor commitment to it. Unless there is involvement of operating managers and commitment by them, job enrichment *will* be "just another program."

6. Job Enrichment Hasn't Proven Itself Yet

The cold pragmatism and practicality that pervades many manufacturing organizations today produces a fear of failure and discourages risk-taking. Members of management are rewarded for producing. This system reduces risk-taking, losses, innovating and maybe profits, and breeds an understandable reluctance to attempt any change strategy like job enrichment. The evidence for the positive effects of enrichment usually is questioned on the grounds of non representative worker composition and work processes. There is a reasonable quantity of research available to argue for job enrichment, but more is needed in heavy industry, especially where there are assembly-line operations.

7. Lack of Power to Enrich Jobs

Members of lower and middle management frequently state that they feel impotent to alter job content because they are too far down in the organization, while members of upper management maintain that they feel impotent because they are too far removed from the work itself. The greater the adamance with which these positions are held, the greater the probability that something must be done to prepare the climate before job enrichment is attempted. Management must be ready for job enrichment or it cannot be successfully implemented. When these two groups are able to meet and talk with feelings of mutual trust and confidence, and can begin to share ideas about job design and work content, the authority and knowledge needed to modify certain jobs materializes. This stated feeling of impotence can itself be treated as a symptom of job design problems within lower and middle management and job enrichment can be used effectively for entree into these levels of the organization.

8. Job Interdependency

This is a very real and complex problem and deserves considerably more space than is available here, but it is touched on briefly for the sake of closure. If the job to be enriched is independent of other jobs, its redesign and enrichment are not so difficult. However, many jobs, especially in assembly, are highly interdependent, and altering one job can change the entire work flow. In this case, several interdependent jobs might be considered simultaneously for enrichment. This does not mean there has to be confusion and chaos when it is introduced. Job redesign can be dealt with by modifying just certain aspects of each job initially, but gradually adding to them over time, with the enrichment process occurring in phases over a period of several months. Another way of handling the redesign of several interdependent jobs is that of setting up a long term plan so that when one of the enriched jobs is operating smoothly, another of the jobs is phased in for enrichment. It frequently happens that as the enrichment process of interrelated jobs evolves, rethinking and redesigning the whole work flow and work process for that area occurs. If the whole process of job enrichment of interdependent jobs is carefully planned, its execution will be more orderly and the outcome more stable. Research concerned with basic parameters of change is needed in this area.

9. Job Enrichment Infringes on Management Prerogatives

When an employee's job is enriched, he is given increased autonomy and responsibility. This means that certain aspects of his superior's job are now going to be a part of his job. To the extent that the employee is viewed as having a voice in the decision-making, the superior may regard this as an infringement on his job. In a more subtle way the superior will see his job role of "purveyor of rewards" undermined because now, if the work itself provides more rewards, he as the superior will suffer a perceived reduction in power. With enrichment of the subordinate's jobs, the supervisor's job content and role will undergo change and there will be a need for educating individuals to this new role. The supervisor will spend less

time checking work and "bossing" people and will be able to spend more time on the real supervisory aspects of his job such as coordinating, communicating, developing and planning.

10. Workers Don't Want Increased Job Enrichment

This is a very tantalizing assertion because it contains just enough "truth" to make it seem like a good argument. While it is mentioned by both labor and management, the latter tends to use it much more frequently. Furthermore, when it is used by production management, it is as though job enrichment is always for the other guy, the worker. The seductiveness of this argument is that there is, in fact, a significant percentage (which varies with numerous factors including functional area, department, shift, company, and personal matters) of the work force which states that it does not desire the increased responsibility of job enrichment. However, the fallacy here is that many of the people comprising this percentage are not aware of the full meaning of increased responsibility. From the worker's perspective, the typical example of increased responsibility is the harried, overburdened, first-line production supervisor. Usually the worker does not see increased responsibility as an opportunity for advancement, achievement, recognition or fulfillment on manual or blue collar work. Thus, when a worker is asked if he wants an enriched job and increased responsibility, it is essential that an adequate explanation of its meaning, as well as the alternatives to it, are made available. When this is done, greater confidence can be placed in the interpretation of data on worker attitudes about more responsibility and enriched work.

11. Subtle Punitiveness

This argument against job enrichment takes the form of a disdainful attitude toward or contempt for low-skill employees. Certain members of management maintain that since these people have virtually no personal investment of education, training, or experience and are earning high wages, they should be willing to put up with the work they have been assigned. In short, they don't deserve enriched jobs. If you do have some personal investment and have been through the organization's initiation, then the job you're on might be considered for enrichment. When it is shown that a department has its absenteeism rate reduced by 40 percent due to the enrichment of jobs, this subtle punitiveness is less evident.

12. Constrained by the Union Contract

This argument seems to come up toward the end of a discussion and always sounds like a final management plea for the status quo. It can be a good argument because as a form of resistance, it brings about a coalition of labor and management against the threat of change. Some members of management are aware of this, others are not, but if labor is not invited to contribute to rethinking the jobs of its members, they will undoubtedly oppose job enrichment. Why labor would choose to do this is not the issue. However, it must be recognized that labor does have a say about the content of its members' jobs and should be represented in any enrichment effort of these jobs. When this is done, many of the arguments about contract restraints dealing with job content disappear.

13. Constrained by Company Policy

This is another "last-ditch" argument, but it has more the appearance than the substance of an obstacle to job enrichment. If top management is sincere about facing its problems and is genuinely interested in having real changes made, company policy is more likely to accommodate than to impede the enrichment of jobs. Sincerity of commitment can be demonstrated by active involvement and participation of staff members. Without this support, any broad or long range effect of job enrichment is doubtful.

Labor Arguments Against Job Enrichment

Labor's response to the enrichment of hourly-rated jobs is a product of the labor-management conflict model and reflects labor's traditional mistrust and skepticism for management "motivation programs." Today, the response of some union officers is to dismiss extrinsic factors such as a shorter work week, more time off, and early retirement. In effect, these individuals maintain that workers will tolerate existing working conditions, but only for shorter periods of time. When the management position on job enrichment was outlined, several of the reasons were

really inextricably related but for analytical purposes they were parceled out. This also applies to labor arguments against job enrichment.

14. Job Enrichment Is Confusing

There is a continuing lack of resolution in the collective mind of organized labor about the definition, objectives, and rationale behind job enrichment. This is not surprising in light of the many things which have been labeled job enrichment. Keeping people busy has been called job enrichment. Rotating workers through a series of boring jobs has been labeled job enrichment. Giving people more work has been called job enrichment. Adding more of the same kind of boring tasks to a job has been called job enrichment. This confusion about job enrichment is shared by many members of management, but it is mentioned in this section because labor more than management has expressed puzzlement about it. In the sense that it is used by Herzberg (1968), Myers (1964), Ford (1973) and in this article, the preceding definitions are *not* job enrichment. Job enrichment is the redesign of a job for the purpose of introducing a wider variety of tasks, increasing individual autonomy and responsibility, and creating the opportunity to achieve on the job so that work will become intrinsically rewarding and more meaningful to the individual.

15. Job Enrichment Is Not Bread and Butter

This could be argued, but it's probably true. It's not tangible like a dollar bill, not apparent like a day off; it doesn't say anything about job security and doesn't mention fringe benefits. It is not an easily understood concept and its implications seem abstract when conventional concrete measuring devices are employed. The challenge is to translate job enrichment into bread and butter terms.

16. Job Enrichment Is Just Another Manipulative Device

Various efforts at organizational change have been manipulative. Some have been conceived to attain that end while others began honestly, but were later subverted. This is closely related to the line of thinking in Argument 14. Different devices have been called "Job Enrichment," but beneath the verbal veneer could be found the core of manipulation. Job enrichment is seen by many as just another attempt to get more work for no more reward. As the mutual trust of labor and management increases, manipulation and suspicion about manipulation are less likely to occur.

17. Job Enrichment Is Just a Substitute for Tangible Rewards

Used as a substitute for money or other tangible reward, job enrichment would be just another manipulative device, but it is not the intent of job enrichment to be used as a replacement for money. While it is true that job enrichment is based on the hypothesis that the motivation to work comes from the work itself and that money is not an effective motivator, money is a prerequisite for avoiding dissatisfaction on the job.

18. Job Enrichment Means Something Else Will Be Taken Away

Management and labor have historically adhered to a conflict model. This has worked well at some times and ill at others, but unfortunately, prolonged conflict breeds mistrust and suspicion. Every gesture becomes an attack or a feint. Nothing is done without an ulterior motive. Every action of the other must be scrutinized and questioned. If labor softens a demand today, it is merely a set-up for tomorrow. If management gives up something this week, they will take away something next week. Does the enrichment of jobs mean something will be taken away from labor? Job enrichment, per se, does not mean that members of labor must give something up. Activities referred to as job enrichment have been used for abusive purposes and underhanded tactics, but this is not a problem with job enrichment per se. This is a problem of management style and labor-management relations. Having one's job enriched does not mean that something else must be taken away.

19. Job Enrichment Is a Threat to Job Security

The threat that job enrichment poses for labor insofar as it threatens job security is more imaginary than real. Again, labor's rationale would appear to emerge out of the traditional mistrust for any change which management might seek to introduce. To remain competitive, companies have increased efficiency and productive capacity through the introduction of technological devices or processes which have made certain jobs or classes of jobs obsolete. Job enrichment, as an organizational change technique, has not proven its worth to a company as a competitive strategy by eliminating jobs. Rather, it pays off by making work more satisfying and this increased job satisfaction is reflected by monetary savings produced by increased quality, less scrap, or decreased absenteeism, etc. Job enrichment does not have job elimination as a goal.

20. Job Enrichment Conflicts With Contract Job Descriptions

This position asserts that particular jobs have specific boundaries which are inviolable and immutable. This is basically the same argument offered by management in Argument 12, but is used by labor for a different reason. While management tends to use this for arguing against change and for maintaining existing organizational processes, labor uses it for job protection and security. Unfortunately, while a worker's job is indeed protected, the worker himself may be locked into a boring, repetitive, demeaning job. If it can be recognized that management and labor are working toward common goals, both sides should be willing to discuss and share in the enrichment of jobs.

21. Management Is Trying to Undercut Union Influence

This springs from the very depths of the union as a political power bloc and is most likely to be heard in those places where job enrichment has been introduced, or is being considered, and the union has not been invited to participate in the effort. It is viewed as a threat to the worker's allegiance to labor because management is seen as vying in an underhanded way with the union for the workers' attention. If it appears that a job enrichment effort is having some payoff and is getting good press, the union is going to insist strongly on union involvement in the effort. It is beneficial and productive for labor and management to sit down at the earliest stages and start cooperating in the enrichment effort.

22. Job Enrichment Threatens the Union Institution

If job enrichment were to achieve everything that it was supposed to, people would find their work rewarding and meaningful, management philosophy would change, and unions as known today would have no reason to exist. The need for a union as originally conceived and historically maintained would simply not be there. This kind of thinking is more likely to be heard at the highest levels of the union structure and not phrased in those words. Furthermore, it is only in the long run that organized labor would feel a real threat from job enrichment, and the long run impact of job enrichment is yet to be felt and assessed.

Toward Effective Job Enrichment

For job enrichment to be effective it must meet the needs of the organization, not the needs of someone who has taken a fancy to it. Only after a thorough analysis of the organization reveals a need for it, should it be attempted. It has met with failure at times and places in the past because it was imposed on a system rather than emerging out of the needs of that system.

Job enrichment won't work if people don't want enriched jobs. This presupposes that the worker rejecting the increased responsibility of an enriched job knows what enrichment is and is aware of some of the alternatives.

When it is introduced to an organization, job enrichment is most usefully regarded as an aid to achieving organizational goals rather than as a "now" or "right" approach which suggests the old approach was in error. It should be regarded as a natural and needed component of the change process in the organization.

Job enrichment will need the support of both top management and labor if it is to be a viable force for change. Lacking either of these will reduce the effort to an exercise to be terminated at the end of the budget year.

The *sine qua non* of a job enrichment effort is its eventual translation into the ultimate measuring scale of the organization—money. This may seem crass and mercenary, but it is reality. To have satisfied people who are proud of their work place because the work is meaningful is not enough. Eventually, this must be reflected somewhere with a dollar sign, whether it be by reduced absenteeism, improved quality, greater productivity, reduced scrap or whatever. If it does not get translated, then it will not become a part of the existing system.

Job enrichment might profitably be regarded as an investment. As such no immediate payoff should be expected. It will take some time for a return. If we look at industrial history and the length of time it has taken to create some of the existing problems, we can't realistically expect to reverse this course of events within a six-week time period. There is a need for well-conceived and well-designed studies in heavy industry and in large organizations. These must include sensitive measures which reflect both short and long term trends, as well as measures which detect time lags between cause and impact on the organizational system. Adequate controls must be provided and awareness must be created of such problems as the old Hawthorne effect and the new Experimenter effect.

After reading through this list of twenty-two arguments against job enrichment, an expected comment might be, "If there's so much resistance to job enrichment, maybe there's good reason not to get involved in it." For several years we have heard about the reasons for introducing job enrichment and the ways of overcoming resistance to it, but the specific arguments for resisting it have not been spelled out. Perhaps by using the negative approach to positive thinking, by enumerating these reasons and becoming aware of them, it will be less difficult to persuade labor and management that job enrichment can provide a possible solution to the continuing problem of motivating people to work.

References

1. Ford, R. N. Job enrichment lessons from AT&T. *Harvard Business Review*, 1973, 51 (1), 96–106.

2. Herzberg, F. One more time: How do you motivate employees? *Harvard Business Review*, 1968, 46 (1), 53–62.

3. Myers, M. S. Who are your motivated workers? *Harvard Business Review*, 1964, 42 (1), 73–88.

4. Myers, M. S. Overcoming union opposition to job enrichment. *Harvard Business Review*, 1971, 49 (3), 37–49.

Cost vs. Human Values in Plant Location

Kurt R. Student

One aspect of job atmosphere that we didn't consider in this chapter is plant location. In locating a plant, management gives due attention to economic factors aimed at profit maximization, but often fails to consider the impact of quality of life factors on its employees. Can site location raise moral concerns relative to quality of life? Does management have a moral responsibility to consider the impact of its plant location on the lives of its employees? If it has, what is the basis of that responsibility?

While the following essay by management psychologist Kurt R. Student does not directly answer these questions, in arguing for quality of life considerations it provides ample stimulating data for us to formulate our own responses. The essence of Dr. Student's thesis is that an assignment to a new plant must be seen as a family transfer. As a result, management must consider human values along with cost factors when choosing the new site.

Although the author's defense for this proposition is based on principles of shrewd management (for example, it makes "bottom line sense"), try to place the subject within the context of ethical theory by focusing on this question: In site selection, must management consider the impact of its choice on the lives of its employees? Using Dr. Student's analysis as background, apply the various ethical theories to this question.

Overlooking human considerations in plant site selection can be very costly. Surprisingly, some managements forget that figures do not control men and forecasts do not produce results. *People make organizations work, not vice versa.* People are the means by which an organization produces the results which are the reason for the organization's existence.

A new plant's success is largely in the hands of the twenty to thirty people who make up the new plant's management team. It is their drive, ambition, initiative and judgment which determine whether the plant's projected results will be achieved. Performance remains a function of both ability and motivation; when motivation to work is optimized, productivity increases. Consequently, managers with demonstrated ability will not achieve expected results in a new plant if their environment creates dissatisfactions that adversely affect motivation. The Swiss novelist and playwright Max Frisch has written, "We sought workers, and human beings came instead." One might paraphrase Frisch and say, "We sent managers to run the new plant, and human beings came instead."

When a new plant fails to reach projected profit and production standards, the cause can frequently be found not in the investment deci-

sion, but in management's failure to give proper consideration to quality of life factors in site selection. This failure may be attributed to the decision process itself.

One can usually observe sharp differences between top management's approach to decisions in capital investment and decisions on plant location. Establishing a new facility is usually considered only after the less costly alternatives of modernizing or expanding present facilities have been thoroughly explored. Intricate mathematical models have been developed to guide management in making capital spending decisions. These models require reliable and valid information, although such information can only be obtained through time-consuming, complex and costly measurement techniques. In most cases, staff is made available, and neither time nor cost is a constraint. Frequently, members of top management become personally involved in the analytical efforts as well as in decision making. Since such decisions usually require board of director approval, top management is motivated to be totally familiar with all aspects of the proposed investment. The climate in which capital decisions are made stresses deliberation, thoroughness and appropriate attention to detail.

Once the capital expenditure has been approved, the effort shifts to site selection. Interestingly, one can usually observe a shift in the decision climate as well as a shift in effort. Top management quickly reduces its direct involvement and delegates responsibility for site selection recommendations to a second echelon executive. In most cases management makes the final site selection directly from the recommendations. Since top management is less experienced and less involved in site selection processes, it may underestimate the time and the staff needed to make sound recommendations. Frequently a site selection group consists of specialists in taxation, facilities engineering and personnel. The personnel specialist is assigned to the group to assess community attitudes toward business and to study the local labor market. If time allows, he explores some of the quality of life factors. However, site survey groups tend to function with little or no staff support and have insufficient time to study the critical factors. If location consultants are used, they too are pressed for results and must function under time constraints. The sense of urgency which surrounds location decisions is understandable. There may be compelling competitive and strategic reasons for building the plant and getting it into operation quickly. Inflation makes delay increasingly costly; consequently financial considerations place a premium on speed once capital has been allocated.

Quantitative Location Criteria

The fundamental location criteria have changed very little in the past two decades. Labor costs, transportation costs, utility costs, tax incentives and other dollars-and-cents criteria are the most commonly used factors. The location decision seeks to combine these factors to give the lowest cost per unit output. Maurice Fulton has observed that while plant location decisions continue to be based on economic factors aimed at profit maximization, environmental, ecological and social influences are growing in significance.[1]

I thoroughly endorse the goal of profit maximization in plant location, but I question whether this goal can be achieved by most current decision processes which exclude nonquantitative, intangible quality of life considerations. Optimization models and other management science techniques such as linear programming can analyze the interrelationships between economic variables, but it does not take a computer program to tell executive management that men and women will be neither well motivated nor effective if they are sent to a community that is not satisfying. Allen Sweeney acknowledges the limitations which the money measurement principle imposes on business decisions:

> As the old saying goes, "Money isn't everything." Accounting reports include only those events which can be reduced to a monetary basis, and thus may ignore some of the most important facets of a business. Recognition of this fact is the beginning of the wise and intelligent use of accounting information.[2]

Similar caution appears necessary when using monetary data in plant siting decisions. Cost data are readily available from many quarters, and a site study group can get them quickly from state and local development agencies. Published rate schedules and governmental statistical data are other convenient sources for cost data. However, quality of life factors are less accessible and far more difficult to evaluate. Many quality of life factors are intangible and unmeasurable and can be examined only by making experiential judgments based on an in-depth study of a community. It is difficult to make comparative analyses with qualitative data; the results are never as clear cut as when only quantifiable data are used. Who then can blame a site study group for relying on quantitative (cost) data and giving only passing consideration to intangible quality of life issues?

The philosopher Abraham Kaplan relates the story of a drunkard searching under a street lamp for his house keys which he had dropped some distance away. When asked why he didn't look where he had dropped them, he replied, "It's lighter here." In his insightful book, *The Conduct of Inquiry*, Kaplan suggests that much inquiry, whether in physics, civil disorder or law, has the characteristics of the drunkard's search.[3] Plant sitings, too, are frequently based on inquiry similar to the drunkard's search. The contention that nonquantifiable factors must play an important part in plant location decisions finds support in recent research on another management decision. Larry Greiner, Paul Leitch and Louis Barnes found that in judging unit performance, quantitative criteria were less important than assumed.[4] They reported that the most effective judgments were made by management groups which used considerably more qualitative than quantitative criteria in making their decisions. More statistics, computers, information specialists and more centralized information systems were no substitute for management intuition in using qualitative factors in the decision process.

Qualitative Factors

In recent years the quality of life has become a concern for many Americans who fear our society is neglecting environmental and human values in favor of technological achievement, industrial production and economic growth. Quality of life as used here is an eclectic term for a number of separate factors which together affect one's life.

Research being conducted by the Survey Research Center at the University of Michigan has indicated that the following cluster of items have the greatest influence on overall quality of life: oneself (one's competence, efficacy and accomplishments); one's family (spouse, children and relatives); financial resources; housing; fun in life (usually associated with family); friends; and the use of time.[5] It should be obvious that community factors have a direct bearing on five of these seven item clusters. Although differences in culture, social class, family rearing, education and personality create diversity in human preferences, the Michigan group found that the seven factors held for the population as a whole as well as for major subgroups. This research underscores a point which does not always receive full recognition from management: *assignment to a new plant must be viewed as a family transfer.* The company must understand the implications of not only transferring a manager but also of moving a spouse, children, and occasionally relatives, and it must remember that the wife's views are crucial in matters of life style.

Management often harbors another misconception regarding quality of life factors. Contrary to conventional wisdom which tells us that men and women can learn to like almost anything, dissatisfactions with community life remain salient for years. Dissatisfactions with schools, housing and community services receive almost daily reinforcement; consequently, these dissatisfactions do not go away easily.

The interaction between work satisfaction, satisfaction with a new community and the motivation to leave or seek other employment is another important consideration. Vincent Flowers and Charles Hughes found that when employees are sent to new locations that are not highly attractive, they have little motivation to stay should their work become dissatisfying.[6] Any manager who has had experience with a plant start-up knows the high potential for work dissatisfaction during start-up activities. The hours are unusually long, the work unusually hard and frustrating. Sixteen-hour work days and seven-day work weeks can be the norm for many months. The new management team is usually under strong pressure for results in spite of inadequate staff support, incomplete offices and support facilities, unclear policies, no precedents and no history of past practice in labor-management relations, and other associated handicaps. Some work dissatisfaction is expected even among the most dedicated managers during plant start-up. If the manager, and especially his wife and children, have special difficulty in accepting life in their community, these dissatisfactions create serious personal and organizational problems.

Finally, it must be acknowledged that the correlation between a satisfying quality of life for the management team, management performance and plant effectiveness is neither direct nor automatic. Many factors play a role in these relationships. Nonetheless, there need be no conflict between important human values and organizational goals in the matter of plant location. With proper attention to both economic and human values, an effective plant can be located in a community which provides opportunities for a satisfying life style for the assigned management team as well as for the plant personnel recruited locally.

Quality of Life Factors

With this brief discussion of the interaction between plant effectiveness, management performance and quality of life, let us consider the four essential quality of life factors: sociocultural, health, educational and residential. Sociocultural elements are particularly crucial when the plant is to be located in a small community or a rural area and the management team is transferred from one or more metropolitan plants, as is often the case. No small community or rural setting can be expected to match the diversity and conveniences that metropolitan living offers. No wife and no child can be expected to want to alter dramatically tastes and preferences just because the husband and father is moved to a new position in a different kind of home environment. General continuity in family quality of life is the key to a satisfactory relocation. Continuity must be maintained if the new environment is to provide basic sociocultural satisfaction to every member of the management family. The critical question is therefore: Can the new community support sociocultural continuity and avoid a dramatic change in living habits, and at what cost in time and effort as well as in dollars and cents?

No specific answer can be forthcoming without an understanding of the individual preferences of those involved. However, my experience with plant location problems leads me to suggest the following needs of the typical management family. Good restaurants are important. The community should have a theater showing movies of interest to all members of the family. It is frustrating to read movie reviews in national magazines or watch movies discussed on television that never reach the community. Major network television should be available. Many families place importance on educational television and public service broadcasting, and these channels should be available. Shopping for basic necessities should not be a problem. I worked in a community which has no national chain supermarket, only two small groceries where prices are high and selection is limited. As a result, most wives drive thirty miles over poor roads to a larger community with several supermarkets where nationally advertised brand name foods are available. The wives hate the trip but they reason it is easier to do this than to change the families' well-established eating habits and food preferences.

The community should have a library with business reference material and business magazines as well as general reading material. Many communities point with pride to a golf course, but offer few other facilities for those who do not play golf and seek other recreation. Frequently communities have organized recreational programs for the youngsters but practically no recreational outlets for adults.

Transportation, particularly accessibility to airports, is important. Must one drive two or three hours to a small regional airport where connections to major cities are few and far between? In such cases it may take almost an entire day just to meet relatives and friends who wish to visit the family. I have observed a cavalier attitude on the part of top managers who encounter no such problems because they use the corporate airplane to fly directly to almost any community. When the grandparents wish to visit their children and grandchildren, they have no such luxury, and such a trip can create considerable family difficulties.

Those men and women interested in civic, social or political activity may experience difficulty adjusting to the climate of a small community. Politically, such communities are often one-party towns where only well-established native families are accepted and trusted. Plant management people are frequently viewed as outsiders who will stay only a few years. Where such attitudes exist, achieving continuity in the level of community involvement will not be easy.

Finally, how far is the drive to watch college or professional sports, go to a museum, see a play, watch a ballet, hear a symphony, visit a zoo, or just walk through a public garden? For those who would question the importance of such matters, I offer an eloquent answer from an unexpected source. Michael Manley, the prime minister of Jamaica and a leading Third World statesman, heads a post-colonial country with all the problems one would expect from a history that includes three centuries of slavery and a century of colonial exploitation. However, these problems do not keep Manley from raising his sights to a concern for the quality of life of his people when he writes:

> The development of the individual who can enjoy not only being entertained by a football or boxing match but who can also explore the human condition, and his own, through reading, looking at sculpture and painting, listening to music, or coming to grips with a play or a dance recital, is vital to a fully developed experience of life.[7]

Can American industry afford to be any less interested in the life experiences of all its members when making plant location decisions, as well as in all its management processes?

Health Care

Good health is taken for granted and health care elements are often not given the weight they deserve in evaluating a community for plant location. Expert opinion differs broadly regarding what constitutes good health care, but it is not difficult to agree upon minimum criteria for medical and hospital care. A community should have physicians who provide ambulatory, outpatient or clinic care. These physicians could be general practitioners, family practice specialists or internists. A community should also have a pediatrician. Small communities need not have a hospital where surgery is performed, provided a hospital is located no more than a thirty minute drive from the community. Even in cases of emergency surgical care, a thirty minute wait is usually acceptable.

Having a hospital in the community, even a new one with excellent facilities, is no guarantee of good community health care. The Hill-Burton Act and other federal funding encouraged the building and modernizing of hospitals in small communities. However, experts agree that much of this funding was unnecessary and inappropriate. Many such hospitals are very underutilized; beds are empty, whole wards are closed, and expensive equipment stands idle because the communities do not have the professional personnel to operate the facility. A hospital also needs registered nurses, licensed practical nurses and nurse aides as well as physicians to provide care. Skilled technicians must also be available to staff such ancillary services as radiology and pathology. I have worked in a plant community with a modern hospital but no resident anesthesiologist. As a result, no surgery could be performed without bringing in an anesthesiologist from fifty miles away. In another plant community wives must drive more than an hour over poor country roads to take their children to a pediatrician for routine care. As one might expect, they are angered when they recall the convenience of the medical office centers in their former suburban locales.

The ages of the local physicians is another important factor. If all the physicians in the community are in their sixties, the future of community health care is in jeopardy. Small communities have great difficulty attracting young physicians when older practitioners retire, and the resulting maldistribution of medical professionals is a growing national problem.

These health care elements should be candidly discussed with the hospital administrator and with members of the local medical society. Public information available in any public health library or medical library should be studied before such interviews are conducted. The services and facilities of any hospital can be determined from the guide issue, published each August, of *Hospitals* magazine. If a hospital meets minimum criteria of organization, structure, services and facility, it is accredited by the Joint Commission on Accreditation of Hospitals, and hospitals in communities being considered for plant location should have such accreditation. In states that have hospital licensure laws, the hospital should be licensed. The hospital should also be certified to provide services for Medicare and Medicaid patients. The local medical directory is a public document and lists the training, residency, board specialty certification and age of all local physicians. If a physician is a member of the American Medical Association, his background will also be listed in the AMA's directory of specialists.[8]

Education

The education of their children is of universal importance to men and women, and it is certainly a major concern for the American management family. Yet in one southern plant community, both the primary and secondary schools are badly overcrowded and more than half of the primary classes are held in makeshift metal trailers with little or no ventilation. Not surprisingly, the children complain of unbearable heat and classes are often cancelled. A member of the team that selected this plant site said they simply assumed that the local schools were adequate. Education is too important for mere assumptions. The school system of any community considered for a plant location should be studied carefully. As in the case of the sociocultural elements, the key consideration is continuity in the educational experience of each child. This means that if a child attended a school where the quality of education is considered average, the family expectations for the new school will be different from the expectations of a family whose child transfers from a school that is truly outstanding. Generally speaking, those children who transfer from suburban schools will have had an above average educational experience and their parents will be rather demanding in evaluating the new school system.

"Stone walls do not a prison make," nor do walls make a school. The educational process is largely a combination of intangibles, thus it is difficult to establish guidelines for rating primary and secondary schools. One loving and truly dedicated teacher can have far more impact on a child's development than such technical tangibles as class size, special programs and library facilities. Nonetheless, it should be remembered that social services, and especially education, are directly related to the state and local tax base. Moreover, it is often said that the willingness of a community's citizens to pay taxes is a measure of the strength of that community. In education, the percentage of state funding for local education is a very important factor. States which have an income tax tend to have a more equitable distribution of funds than states without such a tax. The latter states rely heavily on local property taxes to fund education. A large percentage of local tax funding usually means that poorer areas must struggle to support even inadequate education while affluent areas have good schools and little interest in helping the poorer communities.

A detailed analysis of a school system should include such matters as per capita outlay for education, the student to teacher ratio, spending per student, students per room, teacher pay scales, the library budget for both new and replacement books, the availability of special programs such as music and art, intramural athletic programs, extracurricular programs and the condition of the facilities themselves. These figures can then be compared with figures representative of the schools from which the children will transfer. Such a comparison will quickly predict whether the children will experience a sense of displacement or disjunction in their new schools and whether their parents will question the quality of education in the new community.

I have found a rather high degree of stress and tension in families that are not satisfied with the educational standards of their communities. Particularly affected are those parents who plan to send their children to college when few native families have similar aspirations for their children. Such parents are often debilitated from worrying whether a son or daughter will be accepted by a top rank college after graduation from a high school with questionable standards. Unlike executive families, middle management families can rarely afford private education. In one case, a family sent their only child, a high school age daughter, to live with relatives so that she might receive the kind of education the family deemed necessary. This arrangement proved to be unworkable, and the manager requested a transfer. The transfer could not be quickly arranged; consequently, this highly regarded man left to join a competitor whose plant was located in a much more desirable community.

Housing

It hardly requires repeating that satisfaction with housing is a significant quality of life consideration. Buying or building a home is one of the first important interactions between a family and a new community, and this experience has broad implications for how well the family will accept life in their new locale. For those families who have lived previously in metropolitan or suburban areas, differences in home availability and residential choices can be traumatic. Such families expect to find an active housing market with real estate brokers anxious to show a selection of homes. They also expect to find bankers anxious to provide mortgage financing. Instead, they may discover that the community has no active housing market and that homes are bought and sold only informally through established friendships. They discover it is difficult for an outsider to even learn which, if any, homes are for sale. They also find a small bank with limited financial resources and a reluctance to make loans to strangers. In a number of plant communities managers report they had to choose between two homes, neither of which was really desirable. Many communities have only small homes, and larger homes so common in suburbia are often not available. In too many cases, home selection becomes a very unsatisfactory Hobson's choice.

If the family wants to buy or build a new home, the potential problems are even larger. Frequently, homes are not built for sale, but are built only on demand to order and specification. In such cases, timing is a serious problem and a family may be separated six months or more while their new home is being built. If this is the family's first experience in home building, inexperience in negotiating with contractors and builders as well as sheer naivete can lead to costly mistakes. Moreover, the builders may have no experience with plans for larger homes, and building errors are not uncommon. Unfortunately some builders are unscrupulous and cannot resist the temptation to cheat the unsophisticated. In too many cases building a home in a new community results in a very unhappy family. The day-to-day dissatisfaction with their new home colors their feelings about the community and its people to a point where the family has little chance of ever being really happy in their new setting.

Residential patterns may create additional pitfalls. Often the company will buy a tract of attractive residential land and encourage the managers to build their homes side by side. Occasionally the new plant manager will be the first to build a home in an undeveloped area, and his subordinate managers will tend to build their homes nearby. Because plant start-up is so demanding and because so much of a manager's time and interest is occupied by his work, each manager needs a private life with different concerns, different values, and, most important, different personal ties and friendships. Wives have an equally compelling need to establish friendships beyond the husband's work circle. Too often, residential arrangements in small towns make social outreach difficult. In one plant community almost all of the management team live on the same street within view of each other. Social relationships and visiting patterns are discussed almost daily in the plant and in the homes. All of the managers, and especially the wives, have come to regret this unwise residential pattern. Consequently, the company must recognize the problems inherent in buying residential land for its personnel, and managers should receive counsel regarding the impact residential patterns can have on their social relationships.

Problem Plants

Industry's failure to place proper emphasis on human values and quality of life questions in plant location is a major reason why it takes years for new plants to reach projected profit and production standards. A plant management team must have an unusually high degree of motivation and dedication if a plant start-up is to be successful. If community elements erode this dedication, plant problems as well as personal and family problems can be expected. Dissatisfactions within the family and in the community at large have their impact on management performance. Long hours at the plant combined with hours in an unhappy home with an unhappy wife and unhappy children spell trouble and turnover.

I have seen several cases in which a carefully selected management team did not remain intact through the start-up, not because of dissatisfaction with the work, but because of dissatisfaction with the community. Some men request transfers to other plants, some leave their companies and return to their home communities to work for other firms, often for competitors. Some men remain at the plant, but their dissatisfactions continue to affect their work and they never perform up to their expected potential. Meanwhile, the plant becomes known throughout the company and the industry as a "problem plant." The company soon finds it difficult to attract new managers to the plant, and corporate personnel are even reluctant to take short assignments at the plant because of low morale and a generally unattractive work setting.

Many of the human problems in plant siting can be avoided through attention to the following guidelines:

Executive management should recognize the importance of noneconomic, intangible, quality of life factors in plant location, and senior executives should be as involved in the location decision as they are in the investment decision.

A personnel specialist or a consultant should be a contributing member of any site selection committee. This specialist should make an in-depth study of each potential site community and should develop detailed reports on the four quality of life factors for each community.

After the plant site is selected, the detailed report for the chosen community should be made available to every manager being considered for assignment to the new plant. Each manager and spouse should then meet with the specialist and discuss the family's mobility and its interest in the new community.

Only after these discussions should the company sponsor a visit to the community for both the manager and spouse. The visit should not be a grand tour. It should allow as much free time as needed for both of them to study the community themselves and to pursue any specific issues in the company's report which they consider particularly critical.

The manager should be offered a position in the new plant only if both the manager and spouse are satisfied with what developed during their visit to the community.

I would make a final, and admittedly controversial, recommendation. A "critical mass" in community size is necessary before one can expect a community to meet the quality of life expectations outlined. This mass appears to be about 10,000. A company planning to locate a plant in a community with less than 10,000 people should proceed cautiously, particularly if personnel are to be transferred from metropolitan areas. If the community is small, it should be within an hour's drive to a major metropolitan center. Preferably, this drive would be on expressways or the interstate highway system. A comfortable driving proximity to a major population center would assure access to those quality of life elements that one cannot expect to find in a community of less than 10,000.

A former executive observed recently that despite forty years of behavioral science research, most companies continue to manage the daylights out of their physical and financial resources while considering their human resources as a luxury or a frill.[9] Fortunately, changes are being observed.

Management is beginning to acknowledge that its people are a conspicuously underutilized resource and that a greater emphasis on people can undoubtedly have positive results. My experience with plant location problems strongly supports this new concern for human resource management. Striking a balance between cost considerations and human values in plant location is not altruistic; it is astute management and makes bottom line sense.

Notes

1. Maurice Fulton, "New Factors in Plant Location," *Harvard Business Review* (May–June 1971), pp. 4–17, 166–168.

2. Allen Sweeney, *Accounting Fundamentals for Nonfinancial Executives* (New York: American Management Association, 1972), p. 24.

3. Abraham Kaplan, *The Conduct of Inquiry* (San Francisco: Chandler, 1964).

4. Larry E. Greiner, D. Paul Leitch and Louis B. Barnes, "Putting Judgment Back into Decisions," *Harvard Business Review* (March–April 1970), pp. 59–67.

5. Stephen B. Withey, "Assessing Quality of Life," *Economic Outlook USA* (Spring 1975), pp. 10–11.

6. Vincent S. Flowers and Charles L. Hughes, "Why Employees Stay," *Harvard Business Review* (July–August 1973), pp. 49–60.

7. Michael Manley, *The Politics of Change: A Jamaican Testament* (London: Andre Deutsch, 1974), p. 58.

8. I am indebted to Howard S. Zuckerman, assistant director of the Program and Bureau of Hospital Administration at the University of Michigan, for his assistance in the discussion of health care.

9. Marvin R. Weisbord, "What, Not Again! Manage People Better?" *Think* (January–February 1970), pp. 2–9.

For Further Reading

Davis, L. E., & Taylor, J. C. *Design of jobs.* London: Penguin Books, Ltd., 1972.

McGregor, D., Bennis, W. G., & McGregor, C. (Eds.). *The professional manager.* New York: McGraw-Hill, 1967.

Madden, C. H. *Clash of culture: Management in an age of changing values.* Washington: National Planning Association, 1972.

Mintz, M., & Cohen, J. S. *America, inc.* New York: Dial, 1971.

National Industrial Conference Board. *Challenge to leadership: Managing in a changing world.* New York: Free Press, 1973.

Survey Research Center. *Survey of working conditions.* Ann Arbor, Mich.: University of Michigan Press, 1970.

Tarnowieski, D. *The changing success ethic.* New York: AMACOM, American Management Association, 1973.

Taylor, J. C., et al. *The quality of working life: An annotated bibliography.* Los Angeles: Center for Organizational Studies, Graduate School of Management, UCLA Press, 1973.

Tilgher, A. *Homo faber: Work through the ages.* Chicago: Henry Regnery, 1964.

5
ORGANIZATIONAL INFLUENCE IN PRIVATE LIVES

In April 1977, 1,400 workers at the Adolph Coors brewery in Golden, Colorado, walked off the job. Although technically the result of disputes over seniority, protection from layoffs, a definition of the work week, and who was to work preferential shifts, as discussions continued month after month the walkout seemed as much explained by other basic issues.[1]

Union representatives increasingly charged that Coors wanted workers to leave their rights at the plant gate. For example, they objected to the company's use of lie-detector tests to screen job applicants. Representatives also balked at Coors's policy of asking prospective employees questions not specifically job-related, such as those regarding the use of drugs and alcohol. The union saw these activities as invasions of privacy.

Assuming that Coors was engaging in the activities cited, was it justified? Does a company have the right to subject job applicants to lie-detector tests, to make them answer questions about their private lives? Not too long ago a newspaper reported that an office worker was fired because she wouldn't give more than ten dollars to the United Way. Does a company have the right to force employees to give to a charity? Is it moral for a company to bug employee rest rooms, lounges, and locker rooms? Can it ethically dictate the political, social, and civic activities of its employees?

What makes questions like these nettlesome is that they involve conflicting rights. On the one hand, employers are rightly interested in whatever affects job performance in a significant way. On the other hand, employees have the right to freedom in areas traditionally considered private. To answer these questions, then, demands some idea of where a company's control and influence over an employee ends. In effect, it requires deciding to what extent a company may legitimately limit the employee's freedom in areas that have traditionally been considered private.

This chapter attempts to throw some light on the question of what are

1. *Facts cited based on: Larry Pryor, "Beer Firm Dispute Spills Into California," L.A. Times, Oct. 26, 1977, Part 1, p. 32. Also: Larry Pryor, "Labor World Watching Coors," L.A. Times, Nov. 21, 1977, Part 1, p. 3.*

considered legitimate areas of organizational influence over employees. It's an important issue to confront since many moral issues are rooted in it, as the problems we've just mentioned suggest. Any answer to this question necessarily involves an exploration of privacy, for in the last analysis conflicts between organizational influence and personal freedom hinge on the value one attaches to privacy. Just what is privacy? What forms does it take? Do individuals ever have an absolute right to privacy? The chapter begins with such ponderings, and goes on to use them as a basis for exploring the question of legitimate organizational interference in private lives. In order to give this discussion some concrete, contemporary flavor, we'll examine the use of polygraph tests, personality tests, and intensive group experiences as illustrations of how the issue of privacy arises in the business context. Finally, we'll apply the ethical theories to the subjects raised in order to deepen our insight into how abstract moral principles can be used in practical situations.

Privacy

Other writers in the fields of ethics and business have devised a convenient way to speak about privacy. They speak of spheres of privacy to which every person has a basic right. Such an approach seems fruitful, for it avoids the distracting vagaries into precisely how the right to privacy is to be defined. Since the literature of law and philosophy exhibits sharp division of opinion on that question, it seems best to leave it to more theoretical concerns and immediately launch into an area which elicits a consensus, that being, the spheres of privacy.

Spheres of Privacy

Thomas Garrett is particularly well organized on the topic of privacy; so we'll follow his outline for the purposes of explication.[2] This should not be construed, however, as an endorsement of the proportionality theory. Rather it is as an acknowledgment of a well-developed and succinctly presented treatment of the topic. In general, we can isolate three areas which manifest the value of privacy: the psychic, physical, and social.

PSYCHIC. *Psychic privacy is the privacy of the inner sphere, the privacy of one's thoughts, ideals, ambitions, and feelings.* It represents an intensely personal area of the human personality. "Indeed," writes Garrett, "so intimate is the union between this sphere and the person that it is often impossible to distinguish them."[3] Because of its nature, then, the psychic sphere of privacy demands special respect.

It's true that we sometimes glimpse a person's inner life and psychic sphere through gestures, handwriting, facial expressions, and language. Indeed, individuals often reveal themselves profoundly, as when with loved ones or with professionals who are attempting to help them. Nevertheless, most of us gener-

2. *See Garrett,* Business Ethics, *pp. 64–67.*

3. *Ibid., p. 65.*

ally conceal large portions of this inner sphere from the public. In this way we protect ourselves from exploitation and injury. Just as important, by so doing we frequently provide ourselves rich opportunities for personal growth and actualization. Because of the inextricable bond between our innermost thoughts and our self-identities, it seems safe to propose that we have a right to psychic privacy, sometimes even an obligation to protect it. As an outgrowth of this right, others have the obligation to respect our psychic privacy.

PHYSICAL. Psychic privacy is enlarged and actually made possible by physical privacy. *Physical privacy is secrecy or seclusion from view or contact with others.* All humans need physical privacy at some time to function as human beings. Human beings need times and places to share their innermost feelings with others, if they so choose. Without such times and places individuals would be deprived of a great human need and of the potential good resulting from such intimate social intercourse with others. Think for a minute of the many relationships that require physical privacy in order to function: the relationship between husband and wife, lawyer and client, doctor and patient, counselor and client, employer and employee. Thus all humans have a right to physical privacy, and others have an obligation to respect it.

SOCIAL. *Social privacy refers to the roles people are called upon to play in their daily lives.* To illustrate, business people are not just business people. They are often spouses, parents, religious adherents, political activists, and idealists. Thus, Mike Collins wants to protest what he believes is an immoral national policy. But in so doing, he must be critical of his own firm. If his roles as a business person and responsible citizen/civic leader cannot be separated, then the community will be deprived of important social commentary. Moreover, Collins's self-expression and opportunity for self-definition will be severely hampered. *Social role privacy refers to the need to keep insulated and separate from each other the social roles that we must play.* Because individuals require social privacy to function as complete, self-governing entities, they have a right to it and others the obligation to respect it.

Conflicts between privacy rights and organizational influence underscore the contention that none of these rights is absolute. In fact, the reason conflicts arise is that reasonable people recognize two rights: the right of the organization to protect and advance itself and the right of individuals to their privacy. Just when an organizational infringement on personal privacy is morally justifiable is precisely the issue at stake here.

In general, it seems that whenever an organization infringes on the personal spheres of privacy, it bears the burden of justifying the reasonableness of that infringement. This consists in appealing to the interests of the firm. Thus, the aforementioned brewery allegedly subjected its prospective employees to lie-detector tests in order to ferret out potential threats to the welfare and integrity of the organization. That a firm thinks that such an action or policy is justifiable, however, does not demonstrate that it is. The firm must prove legitimate interest. What, then, distinguishes the legitimate interest from the illegitimate one? What are the areas of legitimate organizational influence over the individual?

Legitimate Areas of Organizational Influence

The work contract; the firm's responsibilities to owners, consumers, and society at large; and the purpose of the firm itself, all support the proposition that the firm is legitimately interested in what significantly influences work performance. But does a firm have the right to demand that its employees contribute to a charity? Can it legitimately compel them to participate in civic activities or engage in partisan politics? Is it moral to bug employees' dressing rooms and lounges? To answer these questions adequately, we must give considerable thought to what constitutes a significant influence on work performance.

No precise definition of a significant influence on work performance can be given because the connection between an act or policy and the job is often fuzzy. Take, for example, the area of dress. Ace Construction seems to have a legitimate interest in the kind of shoes Doug Bell wears while framing its houses because the quality of the shoes could affect his safety and job performance as well as the firm's liability. On the other hand, whether executive Margaret Rheingold may forbid her secretary Peg Morrison to wear slacks or a pant suit to the office is not as clear. Does wearing a pant suit significantly affect the work that Peg does? Maybe it does. Perhaps good public relations underlies Margaret's demands. On the other hand, maybe her demands are narrow-minded, provincial, and idiosyncratic.

The same rule applies to off-the-job conduct. What occurs off-the-job might relate significantly to the job. For example, how would you decide the following case?

In an off-the-job fight, a plant guard drew his gun on his antagonist. Although no one was injured, when the guard's employer learned of the incident, it viewed it as grounds for dismissal. It reasoned that such an action indicated a lack of judgment on the part of the guard in his use of firearms. Do you think that the firm had a right to fire the guard under these circumstances? The courts did.

Then there's the amorphous area of company image. Determining where company image ends and individual privacy begins isn't always easy. For example, the political activities of a firm's corporate executive could significantly affect the image a firm wishes to project. On the other hand, what an obscure worker on the firm's assembly line does politically might have a comparatively insignificant impact on the company's image.

The point is that we can't spell out precisely what constitutes a significant influence on job performance. But that doesn't weaken the proposition that the firm is legitimately interested in whatever significantly influences work performance any more than the highly generalized nature of the law which enjoins drivers to use reasonable caution when driving makes that injunction useless. A measure of subjectivity usually determines what constitutes a significant influence, as much as what constitutes "reasonable caution." But the judgments are not arbitrary or capricious. In fact, when judgments in this area are whimsical, they invariably court immorality and illegality.

In the last analysis, it seems that areas of legitimate organizational interest will depend on the connection between an act or policy and the job. Available research indicates that there's cultural agreement about general areas of legitimate organizational influence relating to an act or policy and the job. The results of administering the Schein-Ott legitimacy questionnaire to labor leaders, managers, persons in development courses, university students, and company managers demonstrate this point.

The questionnaire covers fifty-five areas of organizational influence, ranging from decidedly job-related areas, such as working hours, to highly personal ones, such as the political party which employees belong to. Those surveyed saw areas of high legitimacy related to the work environment and work performance. For example, most would agree that a restaurant can reasonably limit employee choice of working hours by setting the time that the firm will be opened for business. In the view of the respondents, areas of moderate legitimacy related to off-the-job conduct that might affect organizational interest. Thus, the persons being interviewed would probably agree that a firm manufacturing women's apparel would be legitimately interested in the off-the-job conduct of one of its top executives if it involved open and active campaigning against the Equal Rights Amendment (ERA), which is supposed to guarantee women equal rights. Finally, those surveyed related areas of low legitimacy to private acts and beliefs.[4] Thus, what that executive in question personally felt about the ERA would be no concern of the firm's. Nor would it be the firm's concern if that individual anonymously contributed funds to the campaign opposing ERA.

But even when a firm is legitimately interested in off-the-job conduct, issues of moral concern remain. One involves whether or not to interfere.

Interference

Suppose that corporate executive Patricia Ruiz strongly opposes the decided favorite in a gubernatorial contest. Her firm feels that criticism of the candidate may jeopardize its preferred status in the state should the candidate be elected, and we will assume this constitutes a legitimate interest in Ruiz's expression of her political views on the gubernatorial race. Does this, then, mean that the firm is ethical in interfering with her right to free and open political expression?

Although this question defies a simple answer, we can say that the firm's having a legitimate interest does not automatically justify the interference. Such interference may be thoroughly unethical. After all, more is involved than the company's interests. Obviously at stake are Ruiz's rights to free speech and to unhindered political intercourse with fellow citizens. The social need in a democracy for free and open airing of public issues, especially among persons who assume leadership roles in the community, is also at issue. The point is that even after an organization has ascertained an area of legitimate interest, it must determine whether or not its interference would be ethical.

What's more, having determined that the interference is ethical, the firm

4. *Edgar Schein and J. Steven Ott, "The Legitimacy of Organizational Influence,"* American Journal of Sociology, *May, 1962, pp. 682–689.*

must evaluate how it will interfere. Thus, a firm has a legitimate interest in determining the character of the people it will employ. Likewise, it is proper to take measures to find out. But does it behave morally in subjecting job applicants to lie-detector tests in order to find out what kind of people they are? This is an entirely different question but one of equal moral importance with determining legitimate areas of organizational influence and whether or not to interfere.

Although organizational interference in individual privacy takes numerous forms, two predominate. In the first form, organizations frequently seek, store, or communicate knowledge about employees without their consent. In the second form, they interfere in personal decisions. The remainder of the chapter will deal with these two principal forms of organizational interference with privacy.

Obtaining Information Without Consent

It's no secret that firms frequently seek, store, or communicate information about employees without their consent. Thus, without consulting with or informing its employees, a firm bugs employee lounges, hoping to discover who's responsible for the widespread pilfering that's been occurring. Another firm uses a managerial grapevine: supervisors meet once a month to exchange anecdotal material about employees, some of it obtained in confidence, all of it gathered with the hope of anticipating potential troublemakers. Still another company keeps detailed files on the personal lives of its employees to ensure compatibility with organizational image and reputation. Of special interest to our study are three common practices organizations engage in: subjecting employees to polygraph tests, using personality tests to place employees, and monitoring employees to discover sundry information.

Polygraph Tests

Scientific technology in the form of a polygraph shows that when people lie, certain detectable physiological changes frequently occur. Their hearts may begin to race, their blood pressure may rise, their respiration may increase. The polygraph is an instrument that simultaneously records changes in these physiological processes; it is sometimes used in lie detection.

Firms offer several reasons to justify their use of the polygraph to detect lying. The first reason given is the astronomical annual losses a company suffers through pilferage. The problem seems to defy control in any way other than subjecting employees to polygraph tests. Also, firms argue that in certain decentralized retail operations, such as small chain groceries, the use of polygraph tests allows business to abolish audits and controls that would be oppressive. In other words, they claim that using polygraph tests allows workers greater freedom than not using them would allow. Finally, firms frequently claim that using polygraph tests represents a sound way of screening candidates for employment. Used in this way, the tests can help reveal personal philosophy, behavioral patterns, or character idiosyncrasies that would be incompatible with the organization's purpose, function, and image.[5]

---

5. *Keith Davis and Robert L. Blomstrom,* Business and Society *(New York: McGraw-Hill, 1975), p. 319.*

But polygraphs raise moral concerns. By far the chief moral concern with polygraph tests is that they infringe on psychic privacy. This in itself may not always make their use wrong. There could be times when employers have the right to abridge psychic privacy, when employees have an obligation to reveal themselves. In cases involving excessive pilferage, firms may be justified in resorting to polygraph tests. But the threat to psychic privacy remains. Even when firms feel morally justified in resorting to polygraph tests, they must be judicious in how they administer them. This suggests a second and related concern about the use of polygraph tests.

Often a sinister impression accompanies the usage of a polygraph test. Firms can lead workers to believe that they will be judged by a machine or that they are being presumed guilty until the polygraph proves them innocent. Giving such impressions raises serious questions of justice as well as worker morale. Furthermore, in using the polygraph the ever-present danger is to extend the sphere of questioning and investigation to non-job-related issues, such as marriage, sex, politics, religion, personal philosophy, alcohol, and drug use.

Moral concerns suggest three points worth remembering in evaluating the justice of polygraph usage.

1. The information which the organization seeks should be clearly and significantly related to the job. This brings us back to a determination of the legitimate areas of organizational influence over the individual.

2. Since the polygraph intrudes on psychic freedom, those applying it should consider whether they have compelling job-related reasons for so doing. Some persons contend that among the reasons must be the fact that the polygraph represents the *only* way that the organization can get information about a significant job-related matter. They claim that a firm should think seriously about the morality of subjecting employees to polygraph tests without having first exhausted all other means of preventing pilferage and discovering its source.

3. We must be concerned with how the polygraph is being used, what information it's gathering, who has access to this information, and how it will be disposed of.

All of this notwithstanding, it's conceivable that under certain circumstances individuals may retain the right to protect their psychic privacy and refuse to submit to such tests. Indeed, there are those persons who would contend that the individual always retains this right.

Personality Tests

Companies often wish to determine whether prospective employees are emotionally mature and sociable and whether they would fit in with the organization; so they sometimes administer personality tests. Personality tests concern us here because essentially they are character probes that can reveal highly personal information. Such tests can easily invade psychic privacy by collecting data about employees without their full consent. Consent is usually lacking because personality tests are rarely taken on a strictly voluntary basis. They generally function as part of a battery of tests that job applicants must take if they wish to be considered for a position.

Used properly, personality tests serve two purposes in the work place. First, they help screen applicants for jobs by indicating areas of adequacy and inadequacy. Second, in theory, they simplify the complexities of business life by reducing the amount of decision making involved in relating to others. For example, if a firm knows that Frank Smith is an introvert, it would hardly place him in personnel or public relations.

But there are observations about personality tests relevant to evaluating their morality. The whole premise underlying the use of such tests is highly questionable. That premise is that all individuals can usefully and validly be placed into a relatively small number of categories in terms of personality and character traits. In other words, people are pure personality types, such as the classic introvert or extrovert. In fact, the pure type is the exception, not the rule. Most of us are neither purely introvert nor purely extrovert. We possess a mixture of these traits in varying degrees.[6] When organizations attempt to categorize employees, they force them into oversimplified and artificial arrangements that may be fair neither to employees nor to the firms.

Another observation is that personality tests screen for organizational compatibility. This has serious moral implications. From the firm's view, it is ironic that such a function can eliminate prospective employees whose creativity may be exactly what the firm needs. Thus personality tests can actually injure the firm. More important, when used in this way personality tests elicit a pressing moral issue in the employer-employee relationship: conformity of the individual to organizational ideals.

More than twenty years ago, William H. Whyte, Jr., wrote *The Organization Man*,[7] still a widely read work. In this book, Whyte observed the growing tendency in business to elevate organizational conformity and loyalty to the level of moral imperatives. Organization people, argued Whyte, are ones who dedicate themselves totally to the firm; unquestioningly accept its maxims, standards, and ethos; and unflinchingly believe that ideas and creativity emanate not from the individual but from the group. In other words, Whyte shows concern not only for the organizational threat to individual autonomy but also for individuals' using the organizational ethic to rationalize away a sense of personal responsibility, a subject we alluded to in Chapter 1.

In 1957, one year after Whyte's publication, Chris Argyris published *Personality and the Organization*, which gave some credence to Whyte's organization man theory. Argyris's study dealt with psychological problems of work, specifically things like alienation, frustration, and suppression of self-actualization. Argyris concludes that the basic goals of individuals and organizations are at odds. This incongruence creates conflict, frustration, and failure for the participants. In other words, according to Argyris, blind conformity to organizational

6. *James M. Sawrey and Charles W. Telford,* Adjustment and Personality *(Boston: Allyn & Bacon, 1975), pp. 500–501.*

7. *William H. Whyte,* The Organization Man *(New York: Simon & Schuster, 1956).*

standards can be self-destructive. And the organization that requires it cultivates this subversion of personal meaning and self-fulfillment. These are reasons enough for moral concern.

We mention Whyte's organization man theory and Argyris's psychological findings not to characterize business as a thoroughgoing vehicle of conformity. On the contrary, there are a number of indications that business today significantly fosters individualism. The point is that organizations by nature represent a danger to individual freedom and independence. When personality tests are used to screen for conformity to organizational values, goals, and philosophy, they can catalyze this natural tendency into a full-blown assault on the human personality; its moral implications can't be overlooked. For this reason the use of such tests must always be viewed as raising moral concerns, much as polygraph tests do.

But polygraph and personality tests are only two ways that organizations secure information about employees without their full consent. A third way is by monitoring them.

Monitoring Employees

Where incidences of in-house theft, sabotage, or other behavior that threatens the firm occur, organizations frequently install monitoring devices both to apprehend employees responsible and to curtail the problem. These devices take the forms of mirrors, cameras, or electronic devices. They can be used to monitor either suspected trouble spots or private acts. As with personality and polygraph tests, monitoring gathers information about employees without their consent.

Frequently, firms confuse notification of such practices with employee consent. Notification does not constitute consent. When employee rest rooms, dressing rooms, locker rooms, and other private places are being bugged, an obvious and serious threat to physical and psychic privacy exists, posted notices notwithstanding. It's true that in some cases such surveillance devices may be the only way to apprehend the guilty. Nevertheless, they can do more harm than good by exploiting and victimizing the innocent, who are the vast majority of employees. An evaluation of the morality of using these devices must include a careful analysis of the circumstances they're employed under. Even when the circumstances are extraordinary, some persons argue that monitoring employees without their full and informed consent is not justified. Obviously even more serious moral questions arise when monitoring devices are not used exclusively for the purposes intended but for cajoling, harassing, or snooping on employees.

In sum, then, polygraph tests, personality tests, and monitoring devices constitute three principal ways organizations collect information about employees without their full and informed consent. Use of any of them always raises moral concerns. Together with other forms of information gathering, they represent one facet of organizational influence over the individual. Another facet is invading the sphere of personal decisions.

Invasion of Personal Decisions

Although organizational invasion of personal decisions takes many expressions, we'll concentrate on two; one is traditional, the other modern. Traditionally organizations have invaded employee privacy in such seemingly harmless ways as encouraging employees to participate in civic service activities and to contribute to charities. Much more recently, the growth of modern psychology has influenced organizational policies. Specifically, modern psychology's interest in enlarging one's potential for personal growth has prompted some organizations to exhort executives and others to participate in such exercises. Let's consider each of these forms of invasion of personal decision more closely.

Business organizations continue to try to influence employees' off-the-job behavior to accommodate company image. Sometimes organizations urge employees to participate in civic activities, such as running for the local school board or heading up a commission on the arts. At other times business will encourage employees to join civic service organizations, such as Kiwanis, Lions, or Rotary. Still other times, firms may not only encourage but compel employees to contribute to charities. In the case of a worker previously mentioned, the woman was fired because she gave only ten dollars to the charity. Such a "meager" contribution violated the firm's policy of requiring each employee to give the equivalent of an hour's pay each month. For this employee, a $2.30 an hour desk clerk, the donation would have amounted to $27.60. True, in this case the firm compelled workers to contribute; in many other instances organizational "urgings" or "suggestions" have the impact of orders.

Attempts by companies to influence off-the-job behavior frequently represent invasions of privacy, specifically the privacy of personal decisions, psychic privacy. By explicitly or implicitly requiring employees to associate themselves with a particular activity, group, or cause, firms are telling workers what to believe, what values to hold, what goals to seek outside work. There also arises a question of social privacy. Rather than keeping separate and distinct the roles individuals must or choose to play in society, organizational exhortations mix them. Thus, executive Bob Rodriquez may be joining the Rotary Club not because of a social commitment on his part to the community but because his supervisor has strongly recommended it for public relations reasons. Likewise, Sharon Borstein doesn't contribute to the United Way because she is a responsible citizen but because she considers it an extension of her job obligations.

In recent years company interference has taken a more subtle form. Modern psychology has made us aware that most people never realize their potential for perceiving, thinking, feeling, creating, and experiencing. Attempts to enlarge the potential for personal growth have resulted in the human potential movement. The focus of this movement is on developing ways to help people lower their defenses, remove their masks, become more aware and open to experience, feel more deeply, express themselves more efficiently, be more creative, and become everything they can be.[8] The human potential movement has affected

8.   See James C. Coleman and Constance L. Hammen, Contemporary Psychology and Effective Behavior (Glenview, Ill.: Scott, Foresman, 1974), p. 424.

virtually every aspect of contemporary life, business included, as has one of its most important tools, intensive group experience.

INTENSIVE GROUP EXPERIENCE.   Intensive group experience goes by various names such as sensitivity training groups, encounter groups, T-groups, awareness groups, creativity groups, or workshops. Industry frequently employs a form of intensive group experience called team-building groups in order to facilitate the attainment of production and related goals as well as to provide opportunities for improved human relations and personal growth.[9] Whatever form it takes, the intensive group experience brings together a group of people who through various exercises attempt to realize the goals of the human potential movement.

Although the potential benefit of such experiences in the work place are exciting, especially in terms of filling higher level needs, they nevertheless pose a threat to psychic privacy. This occurs when groups lay bare a participant's innermost feelings. Although this doesn't always occur, it can. When it does, is intended to, or can easily occur, then we must be concerned with psychic privacy.

Obviously, as with most questions about organizational interference with individual privacy, the issue of voluntary participation arises. When employees are genuinely free to participate or not, then such group sessions are provided by management primarily as a means of job enrichment and function as legitimate vehicles to job satisfaction. But where coercion exists, infringement on personal decision making arises, and we must be morally concerned. The coercion may take an oppressive form, as when employers demand that employees participate in such group activities. At other times it can take a subtle form, for example, when participation in such groups becomes an unwritten prerequisite for job promotion. Sometimes, the coercion can take an apparently munificent form, as when employers—rather than discharging workers for reprehensible behavior—order participation in an encounter group. Whatever the form, the presence of coercion raises moral concerns relative to privacy.

In summary, then, organizational attempts to influence personal decisions raise as many serious moral questions as organizational attempts to gather information about employees. Both areas underscore the continuing need in business to define and assign rights and responsibilities and to heighten sensitivity to their relative merits.

Ethical Theories

The more one sorts out the many cases involved in the area of employee privacy and organizational influence, the more one becomes impressed with a central concern: the relative weights given to the principle of privacy and to the general freedom of inquiry and interference. One scholar has expressed the problem quite succinctly: "It's whether a principle of privacy extends immunity in inquiry to all human activities, to be overridden only by special consideration, or [whether] . . . there is a general freedom to inquire, observe, and

9.   *Ibid.*, p. 425.

report on human affairs as on other things, unless a special case can be made for denying it with respect to certain activities that are specifically private."[10]

Benn's question is worth raising and reacting to in our application of ethical theories to organizational influence over individuals because so many moral decisions will depend on the comparative emphasis a firm gives to privacy or to its general freedom of inquiry and interference in areas that significantly affect job performance. What directions, then, do the ethical theories point to on these two values?

Both egoism and utilitarianism would base their response, as well as their determinations of the morality of cases involving organizational interference with personal privacy, on an evaluation of the consequences involved. Looked at another way, neither of these theories considers privacy, of whatever sphere, an absolute value. Nor, of course, would it view the general freedom of inquiry as a nonnegotiable value. Thus, taking the view of the firm, egoists would argue that eavesdropping on employees without their full and informed consent is moral if it produces the most good for the firm in the long run. If it doesn't, it's wrong. Utilitarians would introduce consequences for all concerned. According to the act utilitarian, if a particular act of eavesdropping was calculated to produce the most good for the most people, then it would be morally justifiable. If another alternative was likely to produce more total good, then it should be chosen. The rule utilitarian would inquire into the consequences of following the rule the act falls under. Thus the rule might read: "Never eavesdrop on employees without their full and informed consent." Would following this rule likely produce more good than not following it? If so, then it would be immoral to eavesdrop on employees without their consent. It's easy to see in this case how act and rule utilitarianism can lead to conflicting moral judgments.

Although it's true that in theory neither version of utilitarianism would consider either privacy or the freedom of inquiry an absolute value, the utilitarian philosopher John Stuart Mill argued that freedom of choice was so important that it could be justifiably abridged only when unregulated free choice would cause people harm. Mill insisted that forcing people to act in prescribed ways "for their own good" was never legitimate. He believed that such a position was compatible with the principle of utility. Despite his respect for individual freedom, Mill leaves resolutions to moral questions concerning it to the greatest happiness principle. In a word, utilitarianism does not offer a straightforward answer to whether privacy or inquiry is more important.

Similarly, situationalism would not show an obvious preference for one or the other of these values. If an organizational invasion of privacy is calculated to produce more loving concern than any other alternative action, then it's moral. At the same time, however, the situational concern with justice, which consists of love working out its problems or of a willing of the neighbor's welfare, would incline its members to be more sensitive to the innocent victimization that often accompanies organizational interference in private lives than other consequential theories might be. Thus, not only are those responsible for organizational

10. Stanley I. Benn, "Privacy," in Nomos, ed. J. Roland Pennock and John W. Chapman (New York: Atherton Press, 1971), 13:4.

pilfering foiled by the electronic eavesdropping, but a majority of innocent workers may be compromised as well. However, situationalism, like other consequential theories, does not provide a decisive answer to the question of which value takes precedence, privacy or the general freedom of inquiry.

Moving to nonconsequential theories, the Golden Rule really is not much clearer. After all, if supervisors wish to bug employee lounges without employee notification and approval, the Golden Rule enjoins them to consider whether they would want to be bugged if the positions were reversed. The question defies a precise answer. Nevertheless, in introducing the element of reciprocity, the rule provides a standard other than consequences for determining the morality of such cases. This has the effect of personalizing the decision, which other theories might be less inclined to do. Thus, a utilitarian corporate executive might argue, "Since it's in the majority's best interests to bug employee lounges without employee notification and consent, we're right in doing it." An application of the Golden Rule, however, would require a more existential involvement in the decision. Thus, "Given these circumstances, if I were in the place of employees, I would want to be bugged." In order to validly draw such a conclusion, the executive would have to demonstrate why employees would want to be bugged. This could be a tougher task than demonstrating that such bugging is in everyone's best interests, since employees are the ones to be directly victimized, should such victimization occur.

Kant's position on the conflict between privacy and inquiry seems more clear-cut. For Kant every person is a rational and autonomous agent. An intrinsic part of human nature is to be self-governing—people can make the fateful decisions that affect their lives. Kantians might argue then that personal autonomy is something we're inclined to by nature and thus something we should aim for in our social institutions. Indeed, autonomy is what our social institutions should aim at fostering. This basic right and social ideal cannot flourish or even survive in an atmosphere in which individuals must guard themselves for fear of being monitored, observed, and spied upon. Because privacy is necessary to the concept and functioning of personal autonomy, Kantians might argue for the importance of the principle of privacy. This doesn't mean that Kant would not consider the general freedom of inquiry a significant value. On the contrary, it could be argued that inquiry is often necessary for social institutions, business included. Nevertheless, if our analysis is correct, Kant would not allow this general freedom of inquiry to justify using individuals as a means to desirable institutional goals. Thus, the firm that faced deciding whether to bug employee lounges without employee notification and consent ultimately must base its decision on whether or not the universalization of this maxim would involve a logical inconsistency. In fact, the implied rule, "Bug employee lounges without employee notification and consent," undermines the autonomous nature of rational creatures. If so, Kant would disapprove of it.

Like Kant's, Ross's principles acknowledge that all persons have the moral right to be treated as autonomous agents who are entitled to make decisions affecting their lives. Specifically, in the cases of monitoring employees or subjecting them to polygraph and personality tests without their full and informed consent, Ross would probably note that prima facie they violate duties of justice and noninjury. But, of course, it's possible to imagine circumstances that would justify any of these. The right course is the one that's determined by a complete evaluation of all the prima facie duties involved. Ross's principle may rule out various forms of organizational influence over individuals but not in any absolute way.

Since Rawls's general theory endorses Ross's account of prima facie duties, while rejecting Ross's intuitionism, it seems safe to surmise that Rawls's view on the question of privacy would be essentially the same as Ross's. Like Ross, Rawls would appeal to an evaluation of duties (natural duties in his case) to make a moral determination. But Rawls would also make an application of his original position. How would rational, self-interested creatures operating behind a veil of ignorance evaluate the practice of monitoring employees without their consent? Since they'd likely realize that approving it could lead to gross violations of their own privacy, they'd probably deplore it. In a similar way it seems safe to conjecture that they'd probably endorse the inherent value of privacy itself. This doesn't rule out that they would reject all violations of privacy in the work place or even being monitored without their full and informed consent. Then it would have to be shown that everyone, or at least the most disadvantaged, would likely benefit from such a practice. This is no easy task since it calls for an evaluation of the interference, of the information unearthed, of the disposition of that information, and of anything else that could negatively affect those whose privacy would be invaded. Nevertheless, as with Ross, it's possible to imagine conditions that justify acts of organizational invasion of individual privacy and general interference in employee lives.

As for proportionalists, they would highly regard the principle of privacy, recognizing it as a necessary good for every human being. Any case of willing, as a means or end, an invasion of privacy would be a major evil. At the outset, proportionalists would raise the question of intention. Is bugging an employee lounge intended to improve or guarantee a state or condition consistent with the entire well-being of the organization? Or is it intended to invade employee privacy? If the former is the case, then it needs justification. In cases like this one, which involve psychic privacy as well as physical, the justification must be commensurate with the seriousness of the sphere of privacy being invaded, psychic requiring the most justification. In contrast, the placement of a television camera or mirror may invade physical, not psychic, privacy and therefore not need as much justification.

The foregoing arguments take the means into account. Especially relevant here would be the conditions affecting proportionality such as a consideration of the good involved. Is the good the organization seeks a necessary or useful good? Remember: employee privacy represents a necessary good; the organization must seek a good of comparable value, which a useful good would not be. Then there's the question of likelihood. How likely is the proposed action to accomplish the intended result? Is the electronic eavesdropping likely to catch the thieves? Is the personality test demonstrably reliable? Proportionalists also would be mindful of available alternatives. And, in the case of monitoring devices, they would determine whether a private act or a location is being observed. The former presents more serious infringements of privacy than the latter.

Finally, in evaluating the consequences, proportionalists, in addition to determining how likely the action or policy would be to accomplish its purpose, would introduce the effects on all concerned, the possibility and probability that numerous innocent people may be victimized, and the total impact on work performance, especially on morale, the reputation of the firm, and society at large. The proportionality principle clearly places a high premium on the principle of privacy over the general freedom of inquiry. It falls short, however, of endorsing it in an absolute way. It could justify risking or allowing a violation for sufficient reason.

Obviously, we've only been able to sketch the likely directions that these theories might move in ranking a principle of privacy and a general freedom of inquiry. We've tried to comment on these principles by tying them to specific acts such as monitoring or testing employees. We realize, however, that we've only scratched the surface of moral concerns. Much additional groundbreaking is necessary. And, as always, the views presented here are open to challenge, since undoubtedly none of them has been worked out in an altogether satisfactory way. But, hopefully, as tentative as this exposure has been, it will serve to quicken interest and ardor in the task of devising a morality of privacy in the work place.

CASE PRESENTATION
Speak, If You Dare

Martin Davis, senior vice-president for the National Power Company, wrote an article for a widely circulated magazine. It wasn't just any article. It questioned his company's social responsibility in intending to put a nuclear power plant near a small California town.

Davis not only raised serious doubts about the safety of nuclear power plants in general but suggested that a plant in the proposed location would seriously undermine agricultural interests in that area by diverting much-needed water to the power plant. It was the kind of article that could only hurt National Power.

Obviously, there were those who wholeheartedly supported Davis's position and told National that. But also responding were those who didn't support Davis and were irritated that National apparently had succumbed to political and social pressure to abort a project that would ease the country's energy burden and provide an alternative that might stabilize or even reduce the costs of soaring fuel bills. In addition, National received a large outpouring of local labor resentment. The company, the charges ran, was preventing the creation of perhaps thousands of much-needed jobs in the area.

Needless to say, none of this was lost on the top management at National. They felt that as vice-president, Davis had acted irresponsibly. They thought that such a plant was not only safe but absolutely vital to the national welfare. And yet Davis had entirely overlooked these points. He had even suggested awesome legal responsibilities National might incur should some remotely possible accident occur.

As an upshot, National's chief operating officer, at the request of the board, instructed Davis never again to so comment publicly without first clearing his remarks with the firm. Davis was outraged. National was way off base and was "invading," as he termed it, his duties as a responsible citizen. He wouldn't have it and told the officer as much. In fact, Davis intended to honor several speaking engagements to air further what he viewed as "a matter of conscience."

The chief operating officer relayed Davis's feelings to the board, which, in turn, issued Davis an ultimatum. Either he would conform with their order or Davis would submit his resignation immediately.

The chief operating officer delivered the message. "They expect your answer by the end of the week, Marty," he told the vice-president.

1. *Do you think that National has a right to abridge Davis's freedom of expression on this issue?*

2. *Do you think that Davis acted irresponsibly as the board charges?*

3. *What do you think Davis ought to do?*

4. *Apply each of the ethical theories to determine the morality of National's action and the course that Davis should take. Supplement the scenario with any information that, though unprovided, you feel is pertinent.*

CASE PRESENTATION
Foreign Cars: Keep Out

Opinion among both management and union leadership was sharply divided, but they all agreed on one point: they deplored the debilitating impact that imported steel and steel products had had on domestic production. Thousands of steelworkers had lost their jobs; profit margins were sagging. Something had to be done. And whatever it was, it had to be aimed at the major cause of the problem: the imported automobile.[11]

What should be done about it? It had been proposed at a major steel producing plant that no imported cars be allowed inside the gates. Anyone arriving in a foreign car would be provided with transportation inside the plant. And that meant *anyone:* workers, executives, visitors, delivery people. Under no circumstances would any imported car be permitted to pass through the gate. Naturally, the ban did not apply to American cars.

11. *See "Foreign Cars Get Bumped in Birmingham,"* Business Week, *January 10, 1970, p. 29.*

Those sponsoring the motion claimed it was necessary because steelworkers and the steel industry had a significant interest in the success of American automobile companies. Those opposed contended that such an action was merely symbolic, and such symbolism was too expensive a price to pay for the abridgment of a personal freedom. Opponents also argued that it would lead to ill will at the plant between owners of domestic and imported cars. The issue went to a vote.

1. *If you had a vote on this issue, what would it be? Explain.*

2. *Apply each of our ethical theories to the decision at hand. Which choice do they prescribe? (Introduce additional facts, if you wish.)*

CASE PRESENTATION
She Snoops to Conquer

Jean Fanuchi, manager of a moderately large department store, was worried.[12] Shrinkage in the costume jewelry department had continued to rise for the third consecutive month. In fact, this time it had wiped out the department's net profit in sales. Worse, it couldn't be attributed to damage or improper handling of markdowns, not even to shoplifting. The only other possibility was in-house theft.

Fanuchi ordered chief of security Matt Katwalski to instruct his security people to keep a special eye on the jewelry department employees as they went about their business. She also instructed that packages, purses, and other containers employees carried with them be searched when workers left the store. When these measures failed to turn up any leads, Katwalski suggested they hire a couple of plainclothes officers to observe the store's guards. Fanuchi agreed. But still nothing turned up.

"We're going to have to install a hidden camera at the check-out station in the jewelry department," Katwalski informed the manager.

"I don't know," Fanuchi replied.

"Of course," said Katwalski, "it won't be cheap. But you don't want this problem spreading to other departments, do you?" Fanuchi didn't.

"One other thing," Katwalski said, "I think we should install some microphones in the rest room, stockroom, and employee lounge."

"You mean snoop on our own employees?" Fanuchi asked, surprised.

"We could pick up something that could crack this thing wide open," Katwalski explained.

"But what if our employees found out? How would they feel, being spied on? And then there's the public to consider. Who knows how they'd react? Why, they'd probably think that if we were spying on our own workers, we were

12. *Adapted from a case reported in* Cases in Business Ethics, *Garrett et al., pp. 9–10.*

surely spying on them. No, Matt," Fanuchi decided. "Frankly, this whole approach troubles me."

"Okay, Ms. Fanuchi, but if it was my store—"

Fanuchi cut in, "No."

"You're the boss," said Katwalski.

When the shrinkage continued, Fanuchi finally gave in. She ordered Katwalski to have the camera and microphones installed. Within ten days the camera had nabbed the culprit.

The microphones contributed nothing to the apprehension of the thief. But because of them Fanuchi and Katwalski learned that at least one store employee was selling "grass" and perhaps hard drugs, that one was planning to quit without notice, that three were taking food stamps fraudulently, and that one buyer was out to discredit Fanuchi. In solving their shrinkage problem, the pair had unwittingly raised another: What should they do with the information they had gathered while catching the thief?

1. *Do you think Jean Fanuchi acted immorally in ordering the installation of the viewing and listening devices?*

2. *What would each ethical theory likely say about her action?*

3. *How should Fanuchi and Katwalski handle the information they've gathered about their employees? Would the ethical theories prescribe specific courses of direction?*

Your Employees' Right to Blow the Whistle

Kenneth D. Walters

Earlier in our study, and by implication in this chapter, we discussed the double bind business people sometimes find themselves in: organizational demands don't always accord with personal values. Individuals must either go along and be untrue to themselves, or be true to themselves and buck the system. Neither choice is attractive, the first inducing self-contempt, the second joblessness.

In the past when such conflicts arose, management resolved them. Those who couldn't abide by management's decision were expected to resign. To go outside the organization or over the superior's head was at least improper and, more likely, considered disloyal. Increasingly, however, employees are claiming their right to speak out publicly on matters of conscience, to blow the whistle. Such behavior raises a cluster of concerns, some with moral overtones. Chief among them are the nature and extent of employee loyalty to the firm, responsibility to society, and fidelity to one's own values.

When are acts of whistle blowing morally justifiable? When ought employees blow the whistle? Under what conditions would employees be irresponsible if they didn't blow the whistle? The following essay does not answer these questions, but it does provide data and observations that should help interested parties to answer those questions for themselves.

The author, Kenneth D. Walters, is a lawyer and professor of business administration at the University of Washington. In assessing the current status of laws applicable to whistle blowing, Walters focuses on the factors that should determine whether an employee who protests company practices should be protected against organizational

Kenneth D. Walters, "Your Employees' Right to Blow the Whistle," Harvard Business Review, July–August 1975, copyright © 1975 by the President and Fellows of Harvard College; all rights reserved.

reprisal. It's true that in so doing Professor Walters is speaking in legal terms, but these factors enter into a moral judgment of any act of whistle blowing, though admittedly they don't exhaust them. His legal analysis can help us begin an intelligent moral analysis of a phenomenon that is a direct outgrowth of this chapter's concern with organizational influence in the private lives of its employees. Upon completing the essay, you might reconsider the case presentation entitled "Speak, If You Dare" to determine whether Professor Walters's remarks support or detract from your analysis.

A recent manifestation of the perpetual tug-of-war between employees and employers is the new phenomenon known as whistle blowing. A whistle blower has been called a "muckraker from within, who exposes what he considers the unconscionable practices of his own organization."[1] Having decided at some point that the actions of the organization are immoral, illegal, or inefficient, he or she acts on that belief by informing legal authorities or others outside the organization. Such a public denunciation of policies or practices that an employee deems intolerable has been characterized as a deed of "courage and anguish that attend[s] the exercise of professional and personal responsibility."[2]

Organizations have always had to contend with outside muckrakers and critics, but the current movement emphasizes the responsibility of inside critics to uncover and report organizational misconduct. Within the last three years several books that emphasize the importance and frequency of employee whistle blowing have been written.

The first published and still the best general treatment is the report, *Whistle Blowing*, edited by Ralph Nader, Peter J. Petkas, and Kate Blackwell. This report describes the dilemmas faced by employees in deciding to tell the public about their companies' defective products, concealed hazards, pollution, corruption, or law breaking. Nader insists that "loyalties do not end at the boundaries of an organization."[3] The defense of "just following orders" was rejected at Nuremberg, he argues. In addition to spelling out the rationale underlying the whistle-blowing ethic, the report also contains a series of cases in which employees have blown the whistle. According to a reviewer in the *Wall Street Journal*, this report "probably deserves far wider readership at all levels of the corporate ladder than it is likely to get."[4]

A. Ernest Fitzgerald, the Pentagon cost specialist who revealed cost overruns in the production of C-5A transport planes and whose job

was therefore abolished, wrote *The High Priests of Waste*.[5] He recounts numerous official attempts to hush up what he calls bureaucratic bungling, chiseling, waste, collusion, and fraud on the part of defense contractors. As a result of taking legal action, he has been reinstated to his position.

In *Blowing the Whistle: Dissent in the Public Interest*, Charles Peters and Taylor Branch present several case studies of government employees who have revealed organizational abuses or deceptions.[6] Peters and Branch, editors of *Washington Monthly*, see whistle blowing as a notable new development in the history of American reform movements.

Louis McIntire, who worked as a chemical engineer for Du Pont, claims he was fired for writing *Scientists and Engineers: The Professionals Who Are Not*,[7] a fictional account of a chemical corporation's attitude toward its professional employees.

In *Advise and Dissent: Scientists in the Political Arena*, Joel Primack and Frank von Hippel urge scientists to assume a wide variety of professional and ethical responsibilities, including whistle blowing.[8]

The Whistle Blower: Judas Iscariot or Martin Luther?

Reflecting a radical departure from long-held organizational beliefs, the basic assumption behind this new genre of literature is that employees who disagree with organizational policy on grounds of conscience are obliged not to quit their jobs but to remain in their organizations and act as forces for change from within. This stance is very different from the traditional role of the employee whose "preeminent virtue is loyalty" and whose "principle is 'your organization, love it or leave it.'"[9] Some businessmen hold to this traditional view and strongly oppose any effort to dilute the undivided loyalty expected from employees. In 1971, James Roche, then chairman of the board of General Motors Corporation, warned against what he considered to be the insidious effects of whistle blowing:

> Some critics are now busy eroding another support of free enterprise—the loyalty of a management team, with its unifying values of cooperative work. Some of the enemies of business now encourage an employee to be disloyal to the enterprise. They want to create suspicion and disharmony, and pry into the proprietary interests of the business. However this is labelled—industrial espionage, whistle blowing, or professional responsibility—it is another tactic for spreading disunity and creating conflict.[10]

Roche's views reflect the fact that from the time we are children we are taught the value of "playing on the team." Learning to get along by showing loyalty to others is a vital social lesson, especially in a society where more and more earn their livelihood in an organizational environment. This institutional loyalty, coupled with a general loathing for traitors and tattletales, casts the whistle blower more in the role of Judas Iscariot than in that of Martin Luther. Peters and Branch have remarked that "in fact, whistle blowing is severely hampered by the image of its most famous historical model, Judas Iscariot. Martin Luther seems to be about the only figure of note to make much headway with public opinion after doing an inside job on a corrupt organization."

Some organization theorists seem to agree that employees should have undivided loyalty to their employers. Paul R. Lawrence says, "Ideally, we would want one sentiment to be dominant in all employees from top to bottom, namely a complete loyalty to the organizational purpose."[11] Harold J. Leavitt comments that Likert's ideal organization has loyal employees who see no conflicts between personal goals and organizational purposes.[12] In his critique of organization theory, Robert Presthus appears to regret but to admit that "organizational logic . . . has been essentially authoritarian."[13]

Other theorists stress the idea that employees in a free society should not be obligated to restrict their loyalty to only one institution or cause. Clark Kerr advocates allowing plural loyalties as a necessary guarantee against totalitarianism: "A pluralistic system assumes a 'pluralistic person,' that is, one who is willing to work with divided loyalties

and set his own pattern of activities, rather than have it set for him by a single external institution."[14] Kerr's fears have proved to be well-founded. We have recently been reminded of the consequences of following a Nixonesque pattern of demanding complete loyalty from subordinates. It is one thing to expect employees to commit themselves to pursuing broad organizational objectives; it is quite another to see the contract of employment as a Faustian bargain in which employees suspend all critical judgment to serve their superiors.

The Informer in Public Organizations

Advocates of whistle blowing point out the need for legal protection of critics within an organization. In "Whistle Blowing and the Law," Arthur S. Miller, a specialist in constitutional law, notes that the present legal system offers little protection to such informers.[15] While it is true that most employees undertake to blow the whistle at their own risk, a fact that has received little notice is that employees in public organizations do have substantial legal protection in this regard. It arises from the First Amendment's provision that government may not deny citizens freedom of speech. Although current legal protection for whistle blowers extends mainly to employees in government organizations, managers in private organizations as well should be aware of these new legal trends. Whistle blowers in private organizations are steadily gaining legal support and may someday enjoy essentially the same rights as employees in government organizations.

In *Pickering* v. *Board of Education* in 1968, the U.S. Supreme Court established legal protection for certain kinds of whistle blowing by public employees. In a letter to the editor of a local newspaper, Pickering, an Illinois high school teacher, criticized the school board for its policies, particularly for its allocation of funds to athletic programs. Pickering was fired for this act of disloyalty, which the school board found "detrimental to the efficient operation and administration of the schools of the district." Pickering sued, alleging a right to free speech. The U.S. Supreme Court found that Pickering's "right to speak on issues of public importance may not furnish the basis for his dismissal from public employment." The right to raise such an issue publicly is protected by the First Amendment:

> The question whether a school system requires additional funds is a matter of legitimate public concern on which the judgment of the school administration, including the School Board, cannot, in a society that leaves such questions to popular vote, be taken as conclusive. On such a question free and open debate is vital to informed decision making by the electorate.

The Court went on to say that teachers like Pickering have special competence and interest in speaking out on issues that affect the organizations for which they work:

> Teachers are, as a class, the members of a community most likely to have informed and definite opinions as to how funds allotted to the operation of the schools should be spent. Accordingly, it is essential that they be able to speak out freely on such questions without fear of retaliatory dismissal.[16]

A survey of cases involving public employees since the *Pickering* case shows that nearly all whistle blowers who have been punished for their outspoken views do win their cases when they challenge such punishment in court.[17] The courts appear to be agreeing with an assessment that Peters and Branch have made, which is that the "strength on which whistle blowers have relied is basically that they have been judged *right* by most of the people who have studied the conflicts from outside the battle area." Such a consensus seems rather ironic if we contrast it with the specter of treachery that shadows whistle blowers. The nearly unanimous conclusion that they "did the right thing" perhaps testifies to the morality of the positions they have taken.

Disloyalty or Legitimate Dissent?

As Peters and Branch point out, not all organizational loyalty is bad, and not all whistle blowing is good. What factors, then, should determine whether an employee who protests company practices should be protected against sanctions that are imposed by the organization?

Perhaps the best way to answer this question is to look at the legal cases that have arisen from public employees' criticizing their bosses. The courts have outlined some general guidelines that are helpful in distinguishing between whistle blowing that deserves protection and that which does not. It should be stressed that these rules currently apply only to whistle blowers in government and public organizations, but some legal scholars believe that similar rules will soon be applied to organizations in the private sector, a matter I will examine later in this article.

Motive

The employee's motive for blowing the whistle has been an important factor used by the courts in determining whether or not the employee's freedom of speech should be protected. Usually an informer attempts to publicly expose misconduct, illegality, or inefficiency in an organization.

Several cases fit this pattern. In *Rafferty* v. *Philadelphia Psychiatric Center*, for instance, Mrs. Rafferty, a psychiatric nurse, was fired following the publication of a news article in which she was quoted as being critical of patient care and medical staff behavior at the state mental hospital where she was employed. Her comments caused great controversy at the hospital, and the staff appeared to resent her statements. The court concluded, however, that Mrs. Rafferty "was engaging in precisely the sort of free and vigorous expression that the First Amendment was designed to protect."[18]

In *Muller* v. *Conlisk*, a policeman discovered that other policemen had taken stolen property they had recovered in the course of their duties into their own use. He reported this fact to his superiors, waited, and saw no indication that they were investigating the charge. Finally, he appeared on a television news program and suggested that the fact he had reported was being covered up. He was fired for making "derogatory comments reflecting on the image or reputation of the Chicago Police Department." The court ordered him reinstated on the ground that the rule prohibiting derogatory comments was "unconstitutionally overbroad," and that the First Amendment protects "some speech by policemen which could be considered 'derogatory to the department.'"[19]

Sometimes the issues addressed may seem so trivial that they can hardly be characterized as whistle blowing. Nevertheless, superiors who are the objects of even mild criticism sometimes react (or overreact) defensively, and then the courts are forced to step in and protect the employee's freedom of speech.

For example, in *Downs* v. *Conway School District*, an elementary school teacher with over 25 years of experience publicly voiced concern over the use of an open incinerator on the playground during school hours. She also assisted students in composing a letter to the school cafeteria director that requested that raw instead of cooked carrots be served occasionally. For these and other similarly innocuous activities, the superintendent decided not to recommend Mrs. Downs for renewal of her teaching contract. The court found that "the superintendent demanded blind obedience to any directive he gave, whether illegal, unconstitutional, arbitrary or capricious." It ruled that Mrs. Downs's activities were constitutionally protected by the First Amendment:

> When a School Board acts, as it did here, to punish a teacher who seeks to protect the health and safety of herself and her pupils, the resulting intimidation can only cause a severe chilling, if not freezing, effect on the free discussion of more controversial subjects.[20]

Internal Channels

Does it make a difference if whistle blowing takes place inside or outside an organization? Perhaps the employee owes his or her employer enough loyalty to try to work first within the organization to attempt to effect change. This is a sound general rule to follow, but the Supreme Court in the *Pickering* case did not sanction organizational rules requiring that employees always resort first to internal grievance procedures:

> There is likewise no occasion furnished by this case for consideration of the extent to which teachers can be required by narrowly drawn grievance procedures to submit complaints about the operation of the schools to their superiors for action thereon prior to bringing the complaints before the public.

In fact, employees usually do seek change within the organization first. Perhaps this is an indication that most employees appreciate the harm that could be done to the organization if every problem were aired publicly before attempts to solve it inside were made.

The organization's internal environment for free speech should be a key consideration in deciding whether employees must exhaust internal channels of communication before they seek outside help. In general, employees will probably tend to go through organizational channels before going public if they have not had too much trouble with bureaucratic red tape in the past, if their superiors have demonstrated some empathy with them for legitimate grievances in the past, and if the employees perceive their superiors to be more or less colleagues. Whistle blowers are most likely to go directly to the public when their earnest criticisms are met with bureaucratic runarounds, deaf ears, or hostility.

The subject matter of the grievance may also determine whether it is reasonable to expect employees to resort to internal grievance channels before going public.

In *Tepedino* v. *Dumpson*, social investigators in the New York City Department of Welfare wrote a letter to an HEW official in Washington. In it, they criticized existing procedures and asked for information they had been unable to receive from superiors. The suspended employees' superior argued before the New York Court of Appeals that the social investigators had violated the grievance procedure mandated by the department. The court held that in many cases it is reasonable that employees be required to follow grievance procedures, but that the nature of some grievances are such that they need not be raised through established procedures: "The subject matter of the letter, critical though it may have been of the Welfare Department's operations, could not be appropriately raised or dealt with through its grievance machinery." The court distinguished between "individual problems of employees" and "broad issues" and ruled that the latter need not be carried through grievance procedures.[21]

One can also foresee cases in which whistle blowers should not be required to go through internal channels when time is important. They may be warning against an imminent danger, and, by the time they have gone through a complex and time-consuming bureaucratic maze, the harm of which they warn may have already occurred.

Another problem is that the requirement that all employees go through organizational channels before speaking in the forum of their choice conflicts with the constitutional principle that prior restraints on speech are "impermissible with but the narrowest of exceptions."[22]

One can see that it is impossible to lay down a simple yet fair rule on the issue of whether employees must exhaust internal remedies before making public allegations. Each case must be examined on its own merits. This matter will be clarified further as the courts look at a wider variety of cases raising the issue.

Organizational Friction

One of the major concerns of the courts in adjudicating whistle-blowing cases has been the question of harm done to personal relationships in an organization because of such actions. Aside from the aspect of possibly damaged public relations, the organization must often deal with upset working relationships between the informer and his or her co-workers and superior.

The Supreme Court in *Pickering* noted that the public statements were "in no way directed towards any person with whom appellant would normally be in contact in the course of his daily work as a teacher" and "thus no question of maintaining either discipline by immediate superiors or harmony among co-workers [was] presented." Pickering's relationships with the school board and the superintendent were "not the kind of close working relationships for which it can persuasively be claimed that personal loyalty and confidence are necessary to their proper functioning." The court therefore held Pickering's speech to be protected but warned that "significantly different considerations" could apply if "the relationship between superior and subordinate is of such a personal and intimate nature that certain forms of public criticism of the superior by the subordinate would seriously undermine the effectiveness of the working relationship between them."

The problem that must be squarely faced in deciding whether speech that disrupts personal relationships should be protected is that, in virtually all whistle-blowing cases, these relationships are already upset to one degree or another. The very nature of whistle blowing implies the presence of conflict or disagreement. A comment by the California Supreme Court in *Adcock* v. *Board of Education* recognizes this fact and points out that all organizational conflict is not necessarily dysfunctional:

> Disharmony and friction are the healthy but natural results of a society which cherishes the right to speak freely on a subject and the resultant by-products should never prevent an individual from speaking or cause that individual to be penalized for such speech.[23]

Because of this unavoidable friction in relationships, the real task of the courts is to balance the benefits from the employee's freedom of speech (which are often quite substantial in whistle-blowing cases) with the costs or harm from the speech. Only after this careful weighing of the employee's and the employer's interests do the courts reach a decision.

In both the *Downs* and the *Rafferty* cases, the courts obviously felt that the whistle blowers had not harmed their organizations seriously but had performed a public service. In *Rafferty*, one of the alleged reasons for the nurse's discharge was the "staff anxiety" created by her public criticism of hospital conditions. The court found this anxiety to have been overstated by the employees and not an acceptable reason for firing Mrs. Rafferty. And in *Downs*, although the superintendent and the school board were upset by what they regarded as Mrs. Downs's impertinence, the court felt that for her not to have warned of the open incinerator on the school grounds "would be violative of her moral, if not legal, duty to protect the health and safety of her students."

Courts have sometimes ruled that the employer's assertion that working relationships have been seriously harmed have simply not been proved from the facts. In *Dendor* v. *Board of Fire and Police Commissioners*, a fireman said that the village's fire marshal did not know how to manage the fire department and predicted that his lack of direction would "end in disaster." The employer discharged Dendor because his continued presence "would be seriously detrimental to the discipline, morale, and efficiency of the Fire Department." But the court said that the employer "has the burden of proving that the forbidden speech rendered the speaker unfit for public service or so adversely affected the public service involved that it justifies impairment of free speech." The employer, the court said, "did not find, and describe by such finding, the kind of harm inflicted on the village fire department by Dendor's derogatory statements."[24]

Other courts have concluded that the disharmony resulting from an employee's speaking out is the result of "oversensitivity to criticism" on the part of the superior or "bureaucratic paranoia."[25]

Discretion

There are other factors that courts will obviously have to consider as new whistle-blowing cases arise. Whether the allegations are true or false is certainly relevant, as is the degree of care exercised in gathering the data on which the charges are based. A negligent dissenter who harms an organization by recklessly making serious charges that are false does not deserve to be protected.

A further factor to consider is confidentiality. On the one hand, unauthorized disclosures of confidential information obviously cannot be permitted every time an employee personally feels the public would benefit from having such information. On the other hand, organizations should not be allowed to hide a multitude of sins under the guise that the matters are proprietary or confidential. Individual cases will have to determine the delicate balance between revealing misconduct and maintaining legitimate requirements of confidentiality.

When Whistle Blowers Lose

We have already suggested that a whistle blower who seriously damages personal relationships in an organization by saying things that have no countervailing benefit to the organization or to society would probably not be given legal protection. We also saw that some situations may require that a critic exhaust internal remedies before going outside the organization. No court, however, has actually held that a whistle blower's freedom of speech would be unprotected in such situations.

In only two cases have the courts held that the public employee's criticisms were not protected by the First Amendment. In *Kelly* v. *Florida Judicial Qualifications Commission*, the Florida Supreme Court split four to three over whether a Florida district court judge could be disciplined for criticizing his fellow judges in public for their alleged failure to establish procedural reforms in judicial administration. Saying that he was motivated by personal vanity and political ambition rather than by genuine concern for the public interest, the majority upheld the censure of Judge Kelly. In essence, the majority seemed to feel that Judge Kelly lacked the true whistle-blowing ethic—a desire to improve the performance and quality of public service. The dissenting judges disagreed with the majority's finding that Judge Kelly was motivated by self-interest.[26] The *Kelly* case illustrates that determining an employee's motive can be a difficult but critical task, since it differentiates the true whistle blower from the employee whose real object is harassment or blackmail.

In *Watts* v. *Seward School Board*, a teacher publicly criticized the school administration in an open letter to the school board and as a result was not rehired.[27] The case is interesting in that its facts are quite similar to the landmark *Pickering* case, decided by the U.S. Supreme Court. The Supreme Court of Alaska distinguished Watts's case from Pickering's (unpersuasively, a dissenting judge said) when it noted that the teacher's letter in *Watts* was not met with "massive apathy and total disbelief" by the general public as in *Pickering* but became a very disruptive force in this small Alaskan community.

Whistle Blowing in Private Organizations

As we have seen, employees in public organizations can generally engage in open dissent within certain reasonable limits. The issue remaining is: What will be the future for whistle blowers who work for private organizations? Speculation on future trends and laws is risky, but certain forces that could greatly expand the legal rights of whistle blowers are already at work.

Professor Thomas I. Emerson, perhaps the nation's foremost First Amendment scholar, has made the following observation:

> A system of freedom of expression that allowed private bureaucracies to throttle all internal discussion of their affairs would be seriously deficient. There seems to be general agreement that at some points the government must step in. In any event the law is moving steadily in that direction.[28]

Another legal scholar, Phillip I. Blumberg, has explored in detail the current law on the employee's duty of loyalty to the employer. Blumberg predicts that whistle blowing "will become an area of dynamic change in the corporate organization and in time will produce significant change in established legal concepts."[29]

A complete discussion of the legal trends to which Professors Emerson and Blumberg refer is impossible here, but I can briefly cite three of them:

Collective Action

First, if unionism spreads to new employee groups, one can expect that legal protection for whistle blowers will include these groups. Union contracts generally specify that employees may only be discharged for just cause or good cause. Whistle blowing is not usually considered to be just cause for firing. Edward A. Gregory, a perennial thorn in General Motors' flesh for his whistle blowing on auto design safety, credits his union with protecting him from attempted disciplinary actions by General Motors.[30]

A second but related development involving collective employee action is the banding together of employee groups who refuse to work for organizations that condition employment on the sacrifice of basic rights. This appears to be a course of action appealing particularly to professional and scientific employees. For example, the American Chemical Society is proposing to set up a legal aid fund for members who are punished for criticizing their organizations' policies and to institute sanctions against offending employers.[31] The Federation of American Scientists has a similar program and goal.[32]

Rights of Employment

Another trend that in the long run may produce more fundamental changes in employee rights is the movement of courts away from the time-honored rule that an employee who has no formal contractual rights to employment may be fired for any reason or for no reason, within the limits of statutory law (for example, civil rights laws). This rule has been uniformly applied in all states and has been described by Lawrence E. Blades as "what most tends to make [the employee] a docile follower of his employer's every wish."[33]

But in *Petermann* v. *International Brotherhood of Teamsters* an employee fired for testifying against his employer (a labor union) at a legislative hearing was found to have been unlawfully discharged. The court ruled that the firing was "against public policy" even though there was no formal contract of employment.[34] And in 1974 the New Hampshire Supreme Court in *Monge* v. *Beebe Rubber Co.* ruled that a married employee with three children could recover damages when she claimed she was fired because she refused to go out on a date with her foreman. The court declared:

> We hold that a termination by the employer of a contract of employment at will which is motivated by bad faith or malice or based on retaliation is not in the best interest of the economic system or the public good and constitutes a breach of the employment contract.[35]

The decisions in the *Petermann* and the *Monge* cases do not seem revolutionary given the facts involved, but the basic rationale underlying the decisions reveals the willingness of some courts to examine the circumstances surrounding discharges of nonunion employees, an inquiry that the courts previously have studiously avoided in all cases. *Petermann* and *Monge* may be harbingers of future employee claims that whistle blowing is not a ground for discharge and that discharge of a whistle blower can be "against public policy."

Regulatory Provisions

A final legal development is the appearance of specific statutory provisions that prohibit employers from discharging or disciplining an employee who discloses conduct that the statute forbids. An example of this kind of provision is Section 110(b) of the Coal Mine Safety Act:

> No person shall discharge or in any other way discriminate against or cause to be discharged or discriminated against any miner or any authorized representative of miners by reason of the fact that such miner or representative (A) has notified the Secretary or his authorized representative of any alleged violation or danger, (B) has filed, instituted, or caused to be filed or instituted any proceeding under this Act, or (C) has testified or is about to testify in any proceeding resulting from the administration or enforcement of the provisions of this Act.[36]

Making Whistle Blowing Unnecessary

How can an organization work with its employees to reduce their need to blow the whistle? Here are five procedures that might be kept in mind:

First, managers should assure employees that the organization will not interfere with basic political freedoms. Management theorists have increasingly stressed that organizations should encourage an open environment in which employees freely express their often controversial views.

Second, the organization's own grievance procedures should be streamlined so that employees can get a direct and sympathetic hearing for issues on which they are likely to blow the whistle if their complaints are not heard quickly and fairly. Much whistle blowing occurs only because the organization is unresponsive to early warnings from its employees. A sincere commitment to an "open door" policy makes much whistle blowing unnecessary.

Third, the organization should take a look at its concept of social responsibility. Too often social responsibility is seen as being limited to corporate gifts to charity parceled out by top management and the board of directors. But the organization's interface with society is far more complex than this, and employees at all levels have a stake in the organization's social performance. Keeping the internal channels of communication open, not only on personal issues affecting employees but also on these larger questions of corporate social policy, decreases external whistle blowing.

Fourth, organizations should formally recognize and communicate to employees a respect for the individual consciences of employees. Jay W. Forrester has proposed that the modern enterprise "should develop around a 'constitution' that establishes the rights of the individual and the limitation of the power of the organization over him."[37]

Fifth, the organization should recognize that dealing harshly with a whistle-blowing employee could result in adverse public reaction and publicity. Respecting an employee's right to differ with organizational policy on some matters, even if the law does not currently require it, may be in the best interests of the organization in the long run.

Notes

1. Charles Peters and Taylor Branch, *Blowing the Whistle: Dissent in the Public Interest* (New York: Praeger, 1972), p. 4.

2. Ralph Nader, Peter J. Petkas, and Kate Blackwell, eds., *Whistle Blowing, The Report of the Conference on Professional Responsibility* (New York: Grossman, 1972), p. 10.

3. Ibid.

4. Richard Martin, "Why People Inform on Their Bosses," *Wall Street Journal*, 17 October 1972.

5. A. Ernest Fitzgerald, *The High Priests of Waste* (New York: Norton, 1972).

6. Peters and Branch.

7. Louis V. McIntire and M. B. McIntire, *Scientists and Engineers: The Professionals Who Are Not* (Lafayette, La.: Arcola Communications, 1971).

8. Joel Primack and Frank von Hippel, *Advise and Dissent: Scientists in the Political Arena* (New York: Basic Books, 1972).

9. Nader et al., p. 26.

10. James M. Roche, "The Competitive System, To Work, To Preserve, and To Protect," *Vital Speeches of the Day*, 1 May 1971, p. 445.

11. Paul Roger Lawrence, *The Changing of Organizational Behavior Patterns. A Case Study of Decentralization* (Boston: Division of Research, Harvard Business School, 1958), p. 208.

12. Harold J. Leavitt, "Applied Organizational Change in Industry," in *Handbook of Organizations*, ed. James G. March (Chicago: Rand McNally, 1965), p. 1156.

13. Robert Presthus, *The Organizational Society* (New York: Vintage Books, 1962), p. 321.

14. Clark Kerr, *Labor and Management in Industrial Society* (Garden City, N.Y.: Anchor Books, 1964), p. 17.

15. Arthur S. Miller, "Whistle Blowing and the Law," in *Whistle Blowing*, ed. Nader et al., p. 25.

16. Pickering v. Board of Education, 391 U.S. 563 (1968).

17. Tepedino v. Dumpson, 249 N.E. 2d 751 (1969); Muller v. Conlisk, 429 F.2d 901 (1970); Brukiewa v. Police Commissioner of Baltimore, 263 A.2d 210 (1970); Downs v. Conway School District, 328 F.Supp. 338 (1975); Donahue v. Staunton, 471 F.2d 475 (1972), *cert. den.* 93 S.Ct. 1419 (1973); Turbeville v. Abernathy, 367 F.Supp. 1081 (1973); Dendor v. Board of Fire and Police Commissioners, 297 N.E. 2d 316 (1973); Rafferty v. Philadelphia Psychiatric Center, 356 F.Supp. 500 (1973); Adcock v. Board of Education, 513 P.2d 900 (1973). The current United States Supreme Court has also recently upheld the whistle-blowing concept in Perry v. Sindermann, 408 U.S. 593 (1972), where a college professor

alleged that his termination was the result of testimony he gave before the state legislature and other public criticism of the school administration.

18. Rafferty v. Philadelphia Psychiatric Center, 356 F.Supp. 500 (1973).

19. Muller v. Conlisk, 429 F.2d 900 (1970).

20. Downs v. Conway School, 328 F.Supp. 338 (1971).

21. Tepedino v. Dumpson, 249 N.E. 2d 751 (1969).

22. Board of Education v. West Hempstead, 311 N.Y.S.2d 708, 710 (1970).

23. Adcock v. Board of Education, 513 P.2d 900 (1973).

24. Dendor v. Board of Fire and Police Commissioners, 297 N.E.2d 316 (1973).

25. Roberts v. Lake Central School Corporation, 317 F.Supp. 63 (1970); Murray v. Vaughn, 300 F.Supp. 688, 705 (1969).

26. Kelly v. Florida Judicial Qualifications Commission, 238 So.2d 565 (1970).

27. Watts v. Seward School Board, 454 P.2d 732 (1969).

28. Thomas I. Emerson, *The System of Freedom of Expression* (New York: Vintage Books, 1970), p. 677.

29. Phillip I. Blumberg, "Corporate Responsibility and the Employee's Duty of Loyalty and Obedience," *Oklahoma Law Review,* August 1971, p. 279.

30. "Lonely Causes: For Edward Gregory, General Motors Corp. Is Employer and Target as Assemblyline Inspector, He Publicly Raises Issues About Standards, Defects," *Wall Street Journal,* 31 December 1973.

31. Nicholas Wade, "Protection Sought for Satirists and Whistle Blowers," *Science,* 7 December 1973, p. 1002.

32. "New Ethical Problems Raised by Data Suppression," *Federation of American Scientists Professional Bulletin,* November 1974, p. 1.

33. Lawrence E. Blades, "Employment at Will vs. Individual Freedom: On Limiting the Abusive Exercise of Employer Power," *Columbia Law Review,* December 1967, p. 1405.

34. Petermann v. International Brotherhood of Teamsters, 344 P.2d 25 (1959).

35. Monge v. Beebe Rubber Co., 316 A.2d 549 (1974).

36. Coal Mine Safety Act, §110(b), Public Law 91-173.

37. Jay W. Forrester, "A New Corporate Design," *Industrial Management Review,* Fall 1965, p. 14.

Polygraph Usage Among Major U.S. Corporations

John A. Belt and Peter B. Holden

As we've already noted, the manner, purpose, and rationale for performing an action frequently affect its morality. This fact is undoubtedly true in the area of organizational influence in the private lives of employees, where the morality of organizational invasion hinges on justification. Specifically, such considerations are important in determining when the lie-detector test is a morally justifiable means of judging employee integrity.

In the following article, Professor John A. Belt and Peter B. Holden report the results of an empirical investigation designed to measure: (1) how many major firms use the polygraph in personnel matters, (2) how these firms administer the tests, and (3) why these firms use them. Their findings, while not addressing directly the moral justification of polygraph usage, do provide a basis for moral debate and inquiry. In short, the data provided help us formulate parameters within which we can evaluate the morality of polygraph usage and more generally the morality of obtaining information about and from employees without their free and informed consent.

During the past decade many business people, union leaders, legislators and civil libertarians have expressed concern over private industry's increasing use of the polygraph (or lie detector) for preemployment screening as well as for other personnel-related purposes. It is estimated that anywhere from 200,000 to half a million such tests are administered yearly in the private sector, and observers generally conclude that the number of tests given and the number of firms giving them are increasing rapidly.

The polygraph has become a particularly attractive method of personnel selection largely because of its low operating cost—typically running from $25 to $50 per test—and the speed with which results can be obtained when compared

"Polygraph Usage Among Major U.S. Corporations," by John A. Belt and Peter B. Holden. *Reprinted with permission of* Personnel Journal, *copyright February 1978.*

with more conventional methods of background investigation. Opponents of the polygraph, however, stress that the technique may be an invasion of individuals' privacy and that the results of the tests are not as valid or reliable as most polygraph operators claim.

Over the course of its 50-plus years of existence, the polygraph has become the object of an intensifying controversy. As concerns its use in the personnel field and in employment practices, there appear to be two general schools of thought. On the one hand, there are those who contend that with internal business losses due to pilferage, theft and embezzlement estimated at some six billion dollars annually,[1] employers are entitled to all the information they can gather on prospective employees, and that they should be allowed to do so by the most expeditious means available. In seeking to secure or continue employment, they argue, the applicant or employee is in fact seeking the employer's faith and trust. In return for this trust, the applicant or employee should be willing to waive some small portion of his or her "right to privacy" by submitting to a polygraph exam when asked to do so. Members of this school of thought seem to think that both the employers and the employees benefit through this admitted trade-off.

Many employers who favor the polygraph also feel that applicants or employees who refuse to submit to the tests have something to hide and are therefore not worthy of the trust they seek in employment.

The polygraph's opponents, however, contend that such testing is too great an imposition on employees' individual rights and dignity and that the traditional methods of personnel selection are more than adequate to accomplish the task of selection. Many of these people also question the validity of the tests as well as the legal and ethical implications of their use.

It should also be noted that the controversy is not confined solely to the business sector. The American Civil Liberties Union (ACLU) has taken an active stance against the use of polygraph tests in employment settings, as has the AFL-CIO. Former Senator Sam Ervin (D-N.C.) introduced a number of bills while in Congress that would have prohibited any such practices by industry, but all failed to become law. Senator Birch Bayh (D-Ind.) and Rep. Edward Koch (D-N.Y.) both introduced

similar legislation to the 94th Congress. Most recently, the Federal Privacy Protection Study Commission recommended that the use of polygraphs by private businesses be curtailed.

Leading the battle against any proposed ban of the polygraph is the industry's professional organization, the American Polygraph Association (APA). While simultaneously seeking to upgrade the professionalism of its some 1,500 members and working for the passage of licensing legislation for polygraph examiners by state and municipal governments, the APA has pledged to fight any measures which would deny organizations or individuals the right of access to polygraph examinations. Moreover, the APA has gained considerable support from lawyers, law enforcement officials and academicians in pursuing its goals.

Many state governments have already enacted their own laws designed to regulate or control the use of polygraph examinations in the area of employment. Nineteen states[2] and the Department of Defense have established formal laws or standards prescribing licensing and training requirements for polygraph examiners. In addition, 15 other states[3] have effected legislation which in one way or another limits or restricts the use of the polygraph in employment practices. While there are many variations among these respective prohibiting statutes, they may be generally categorized in one of two basic formats: those that forbid employers' requiring employees to undergo polygraph exams, and those that prohibit employers from even requesting such a procedure. Ten of the states fall under the former category and the remaining five under the latter. Furthermore, several of the states leave open the possibility of voluntary submission on an employee's part. Thus, while the battle lines seem to have been rather clearly defined, the dispute is far from resolved.

Frequently, as a controversial issue gains the attention of the general public and the media, conflicting reports, statistics and conclusions emerge. The issue of business and the lie detector is no exception. Although the APA claims that one-fourth of all major corporations now use the polygraph,[4] a recent study of background verification techniques found that less than 2% of the respondents used it regularly.[5] Similarly, while the polygraph is thought to be used primarily in preemployment screening, many firms also use the technique to periodically assess employee honesty and company loyalty and as an investigative tool in regards to specific thefts and other alleged irregularities.

A Survey of Polygraph Usage

Given the emotional nature of the controversy, the conflicting reports of polygraph usage, the variety of legislation found at the state level, the possibility of new federal legislation which might ban the polygraph from industrial applications, and the lack of any recent studies aimed at establishing the actual frequency of polygraph usage in the private sector, it was apparent that an empirical investigation of the issue would be most helpful. A survey was designed and undertaken to measure: (1) the proportion of *major* firms now using the polygraph as a part of their personnel programs; (2) the manner and purposes of the tests administered by (or for) these firms; and (3) the firms' rationale for using (or not using) such methods.

The method of survey was a questionnaire which was mailed to the corporate personnel directors of major U.S. corporations nationwide. The questionnaire was divided into two sets of questions: one to be completed by those firms which were utilizing polygraph tests, and the other by those firms which were not. The first set investigated the following: (1) how long the firm had been using the polygraph; (2) the most frequent types (purposes) of tests administered and the proportion of employees to whom they were given; (3) whether the tests were required, requested or voluntary; and (4) a ranking of five characteristics of polygraph testing which are generally considered the method's greatest benefits or faults (depending on one's particular point of view).

The second set of questions covered different territory:

whether the firm had *ever* used the tests;

a brief explanation of why the polygraph was not used;

an estimate of use by other firms in the respondent's industry;

whether the firm would consider using such tests and under what circumstances;

and a ranking of the same five characteristics included in the first set.

The Sample

Since the study was directed toward major corporations, the sample of 400 firms was drawn from *Fortune*'s lists of largest companies. There is general agreement that certain industries (e.g., transportation, retail and finance companies) are more prone to polygraph testing than others, such as durable goods manufacturers. To compensate for this tendency, the sample was composed as follows: the 50 largest retailers, the 50 largest life insurers, the 50 largest transportations, the 50 largest commercial banks, the 50 largest diversified financials and 150 of the 500 largest industrials. The number of industrials was greater because the *Fortune* index includes such a wide variety of concerns, ranging from lumber to steel to food processing. To avoid overweighting the sample toward the largest corporations, the 150 firms in the industrial category included those ranked 1-50, 101-151, and 201-250, rather than just the top 150. By thus delineating the various industries to be surveyed, the authors felt that both those firms which were considered major in absolute terms, as well as those corporations which were deemed major within their own industry, could be queried. Similarly, this particular industry mix was believed to be representative of those firms more inclined to use polygraph testing as well as those which were less likely to.

No attempt was made to segregate the sample along geographic lines in consideration of the various state regulations regarding polygraph testing for employment purposes. Each questionnaire was coded prior to mailing, however, as to whether the particular firm was located in a state which had no regulations or restrictions, in one which prescribed licensing and training requirements, or in a state which had statutory prohibitions of usage, however limited. In this respect, the sample was composed as follows: 39.8% of the firms were located in states which had no regulations or restrictions; 23.7% were in states which prescribed licensing and training requirements; and 36.5% were in states which had statutory prohibitions of usage.

Survey Results: Use of Polygraph Testing

Of the 400 major U.S. corporations surveyed, usable responses were received from a total of 143, or 35.7 percent. In response to the key question, "As a part of your firm's personnel program, are you currently utilizing polygraph examinations?" 29 of the corporate personnel directors (20.3%) replied yes and 114 (79.7%) replied no. The response to the key question immediately indicates that the APA's contention that "one-fourth of all major corporations now use the polygraph" would seem reasonably supported. Further analysis of these data by type of industry suggests that usage is most common among commercial banks and retail companies (see Figure 1); 50% of them replied in the affirmative. These two industries were followed in order by transportations with 25% affirmative response, industrials with 12%, and life insurance companies with 4%. None of the diversified financial firms reported using the polygraph in their employment and personnel programs.

As a means of investigating the growth rate of polygraph testing in employment settings, those firms which had responded positively to the key question were asked to indicate the length of time that they have used the polygraph examination in this respect. Thirteen firms (48.1%) indicated that they have used polygraph tests for five to ten years, another seven respondents (25.9%) for ten to fifteen years, and four firms (14.8%) for over fifteen years. Only three of the firms responding to the question (11.1%) indicated that they have used the polygraph for less than five years, and the mean for all respondents was approximately ten years of continued usage. Investigating this aspect further, the respondents reporting that they do not use the polygraph were asked to say whether they had previously used it and since discontinued usage, or have never used it at all. A substantial majority of 90 respondents (93.8%) indicated that they have never used the polygraph, while only six firms (6.2%) said that they have discontinued usage. It would seem, then, that those major corporations which do use the polygraph have been doing so for an extended period of time, with only a few firms turning to the practice recently, and fewer still discontinuing it. These data, at least, belie the notion that polygraph usage is increasing rapidly, at least among the major firms.

Purposes for Polygraph Testing

Since a prime objective of the study was the determination of just what purposes the polygraph test serves in industry, the next question addressed to the firms using it was, "In general, what are your most frequent uses of polygraph test results?" The question was followed by three purposes which are acknowledged by the APA to be among the most common:[6] (1) verification of employment applications; (2) periodic surveys to assess employee honesty, loyalty and compliance with company policy; and (3) investigation of specific instances of theft or other alleged irregularities. For each applicable purpose, the respondents were also asked to indicate whether such tests were administered to all applicants/ employees or only a sampling of them.

In the case of employment application verification, ten firms which reported using the polygraph (34.5%) declared that they use it for this purpose, but of these, only three firms (10.3%) administer the tests to *all* applicants. Further, all three of these firms were retail companies. An identical proportion of respondents reported using the polygraph in periodic surveys of employee honesty, and again, only three of the respondents indicated administering the tests to all employees. In this case, two of the three were retail firms and the third a commercial bank. Overall, only firms in four of the six industries surveyed (transportations, retails, commercial banks and industrials) reported using the polygraph for either of these two purposes.

In the case of the third common purpose, however, that of investigation of specific thefts or other irregularities, 26 (89.6%) indicated using the polygraph, but yet again, only a small portion of them (15.4%) administer the tests to all employees. Taking the affirmative respondents as a whole, only three firms (10.3%) said they use the polygraph solely to verify employment applications or to periodically check employee honesty; ten firms (34.5%) use it only in specific instances of theft or other irregularities; and 16 firms (55.1%) use polygraph tests in specific instances as well as for one or more of the other purposes. Clearly, while the specific instances test is by far the most common in use, a majority of firms still use the polygraph for more than one personnel-related purpose. The tests, however, are generally ad-

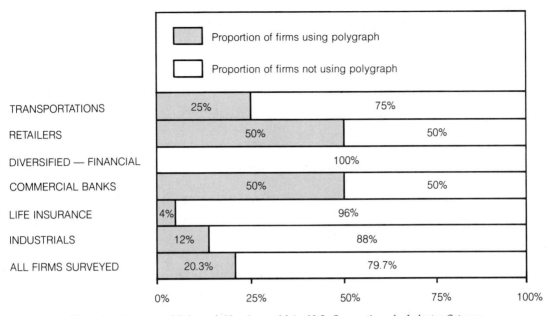

Figure 1. *Frequency of Polygraph Use Among Major U.S. Corporations, by Industry Category*

ministered only to a sampling of applicants or employees.

Effect of State Licensing and Training of Operators

In light of the APA's drive to effect state licensing legislation and in an attempt to measure any effects of such legislation, the corporate personnel directors were asked whether the polygraph tests administered by their firms are required, requested or voluntary in terms of applicants' or employees' securing or continuing employment. These data were then cross-tabulated with the respondents' location so far as degree of state legislation is concerned. Subsequent analysis suggests a tendency for employers in states which have licensing and training requirements established by law to require the tests more and request them less than do employers located in states which have no statutory regulations or controls. In the former case, 38.5% of the firms responding to the survey require their employees to submit to polygraph examinations and 23.1% of the firms request submission. In states which have no regulations, only 25% of the firms require the tests be taken, while 37.5% request them. In both cases, voluntary tests are permitted by the remaining firms. Further analysis of the three industries which appear to use the polygraph most frequently (retailers, commercial banks and transportation companies) reveals that a significantly greater proportion of firms located in states which have licensing statutes use the polygraph than do firms which are located in states without such controls (Figure 2). It thus appears that the existence of state regulatory statutes may be an important factor in firms' consideration of polygraph examinations as a viable personnel selection technique, and such legislative stipulations have probably also done much to increase firms' awareness of the degree of professionalism and expertise attained by polygraph examiners.

Reasons for Use/Nonuse

The final question directed to firms which do utilize polygraph testing in their personnel programs consisted of a scaled ranking of five characteristics that might justify use of the polygraph: cost, as compared with other selection methods; speed of obtaining results; availability of trained operators; validity and reliability of the tests; and

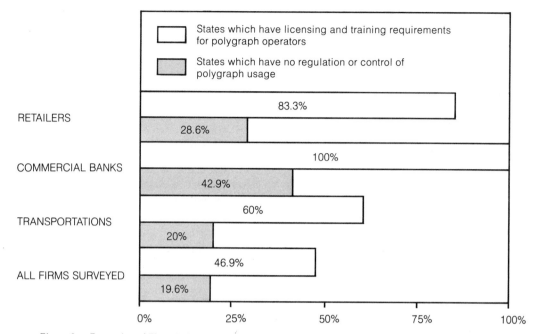

States which have licensing and training requirements for polygraph operators

States which have no regulation or control of polygraph usage

RETAILERS
83.3%
28.6%

COMMERCIAL BANKS
100%
42.9%

TRANSPORTATIONS
60%
20%

ALL FIRMS SURVEYED
46.9%
19.6%

0%   25%   50%   75%   100%

Figure 2.   Proportion of Firms Using Polygraph Which Are Located in Regulated and Non-Regulated States

moral or ethical implications of the polygraph as used in industry. This same question was also put to the personnel directors of the firms which reported not using the polygraph. In the latter case, however, the question was reworded slightly, requesting the respondents to rank the characteristics in order of their importance as reasons for *not* using the procedure. Analysis of the response to these questions reveals that two items—speed and moral or ethical implications—are ranked exactly opposite by the personnel directors in the two groups (Table 1). Those whose firms are using the polygraph rate speed as the most important factor and offer the least consideration to moral or ethical implications. Conversely, personnel directors whose firms are not using the polygraph rate moral or ethical implications as the most objectionable characteristic of the method, but do not consider the speed of obtaining results to be of any major significance. It is interesting to note that a rather substantial disparity exists in the ratings given to the issue of moral implications by the respondents who reported using the polygraph. While nearly one-half (47.8%) of them rated the item as being of least importance, another 21.7% of the respondents in this group rated the issues as

either first or second in importance. This divergence of opinion is perhaps explained by what the propolygraph forces refer to as "the right of the innocent to prove their innocence."[7] They note quite emphatically that the polygraph works both ways; that is, not only does it identify the guilty, but it also absolves the innocent, a characteristic which many seem to consider a prime benefit. It would appear from the survey results that a number of personnel directors of major U.S. corporations which are currently using the polygraph also subscribe to this notion and regard it rather highly.

In the cases of the three remaining ranked items, both groups of respondents ranked each item identically.

Those questions to firms which don't use polygraph methods were primarily designed to investigate why the technique is not being used. One such question asked respondents to briefly explain why they had rejected the idea of polygraph testing. While the question was open ended, almost all of the responses could be categorized into one of three groups: (1) the tests were considered unnecessary and inappropriate in the business setting by 51 (79.7%) of the respon-

Table 1. *Major Characteristics of the Polygraph Method Ranked According to Their Relative Importance As . . .*

Characteristic	Benefits of Using* the Method			Objections to Using** the Method		
	Rank	Mean	Std. Dev.	Rank	Mean	Std. Dev.
Speed of Obtaining Results	(1)	1.760	.831	(5)	4.163	.717
Cost, as Compared to Other Methods	(3)	3.391	1.406	(3)	3.264	1.195
Availability of Qualified Operators	(4)	3.636	.902	(4)	3.415	1.134
Validity and Reliability of the Tests	(2)	2.125	1.154	(2)	2.167	.994
Moral or Ethical Considerations	(5)	3.739	1.484	(1)	1.408	.982

*Ranked by personnel directors whose firms do use the polygraph.

**Ranked by personnel directors whose firms do not use the polygraph.

dents; (2) legal implications of polygraph usage were the primary cause of reluctance on the part of ten personnel directors (15.6%); and (3) cost was the paramount objection in the case of three respondents, or 4.7%.

Asked what procedures were used in lieu of polygraph testing for personnel selection, the overwhelming response was the personal interview and the traditional reference check, as indicated by 49 firms (79.0%). Less than 5% of the firms indicated a reliance on psychological testing, and the remaining respondents offered a myriad of alternatives ranging from checks of credit files and police records to fingerprinting and ". . . a very perceptive personnel manager."

Another question put to the personnel directors not currently using the polygraph was, "Are there any conditions under which you would consider using polygraph testing?" Again, the open-ended responses could be grouped among three general replies. Fifty-five respondents (62.5%) replied with a definite no or none. Seventeen others (19.3%), however, reported that they would only consider such tests as a "last resort," while 16 of the respondents (18.2%) noted that they would consider using the polygraph under certain conditions. An examination of these data based on firms' type of business reveals some rather diverse opinions among the respondents. For instance, while one-half of the commercial banks responding to the questionnaire reported using the polygraph, 85.7% of those banks which do not use it said that they would not consider doing so under any circumstances. On the other hand, although only 12% of the industrials reported using the

polygraph, almost one-half (47.1%) of those who do not said that they would consider it under certain conditions. Further, while none of the diversified financial firms responding to the survey used the polygraph, one-third of these firms indicated that they would be receptive to the idea in certain cases. Less than a quarter of the personnel directors of firms engaged in transportation or life insurance said that they would consider the polygraph as a viable alternative, but 71.4% of the retail firms not now using the method replied that they would consider such use. Among other things, the data suggest that a rather extensive pool of potential polygraph users exists in some areas of business which have not been thought likely to utilize such services.

The final item which personnel directors not using the polygraph were asked to complete was an estimate of the proportion of firms within their own industry they thought might be using the polygraph in personnel-related areas. The question was prompted to a large degree by the observation that "companies that use the polygraph to screen employees tend to be reticent about it,"[8] and the data collected seem to support the observation. Asked to indicate whether they thought most firms, more than half, less than half, or only very few firms in their respective industries were presently using the polygraph in the personnel area, none of the respondents replied with either of the first two choices. Only three of the personnel directors (3.4%) opted for less than half, and 85 (96.6%) of the respondents believed only a very few firms in their industry were actually using the polygraph. Among the three business categories indicating high use of polygraph (transportations, retailers and commercial banks), the perceptions of personnel directors whose firms are not using the technique are markedly different from the actual usage frequency found by the study. As an example, the view was unanimous among commercial banking personnel directors that only a very few of their peers use the polygraph, but the data collected during the survey reveals that 50% of commercial banks do in fact use it. Similarly, respondents in the retail trade were 83% in agreement that only a very few retailers use the method, while 50% of the retail respondents noted that they do use the polygraph. Among the personnel directors of transportation companies, 88.9% replied that they thought only a very few firms in their industry were using the polygraph, whereas the actual usage rate was found to be 25%.

Summary

Upon examination and analysis of all of the data collected during the study, several factors emerge from the survey as characteristic of the use of the polygraph by private business today. Most notable of these must surely be the implication that one-fifth of major corporations are presently using the polygraph in personnel-related areas; a fact that seems substantially amplified when one considers that the firms surveyed represent the largest and most influential corporations in the country. Of course, this finding may be viewed in the opposite respect as well, and many may find somewhat greater satisfaction in the impression that four-fifths of the major firms are *not* using the polygraph.

So far as the practice in general is concerned, the study also revealed the following patterns of polygraph usage:

While it may be said that polygraph tests are most frequently administered as a means of investigating specific instances of theft or other irregularities, it is important to note that a majority of firms which utilize the technique use it for *more than one* of the three most common purposes. Thus, if a firm has no objections to using the polygraph for security purposes, it will probably have no objections

to extending the practice to the employment function.

Polygraph examinations are generally given only to a sampling of applicants or employees, although some industries (e.g., retail firms and commercial banks) appear more prone to administering the tests to all job applicants or employees than do others.

According to the survey results, corporate personnel directors whose firms engage in polygraph testing feel that the major incentives for using the technique are: the speed with which results may be obtained, the validity and reliability of the testing procedure, and the low cost of such tests. Personnel directors whose firms do not use the method, however, indicated that they abstain for much the same reasons, citing moral or ethical implications, validity and reliability, and cost as their main objections, coupled with the notion that the use of the polygraph in the business setting is both unnecessary and inappropriate.

Most corporations which are now using the polygraph as a part of their personnel programs have been doing so for at least five years, and in contrast to earlier reports, usage among major firms does not seem to be increasing rapidly. Rather, there are indications of a small but sustained growth rate among large corporations. Although the absolute magnitude of this growth in usage may seem slight, it should not be construed as indicative of limited polygraph testing in the future. While 60% of the respondents not now using the polygraph reported that they would in no way consider the practice, the other firms indictated that they *would* consider the method under certain conditions.

Among all firms surveyed, there is a substantially greater proportion of firms using the polygraph in states which legally prescribe licensing and training requirements for polygraph examiners than there is in states which do not regulate the practice in any way. Furthermore, there is a greater tendency for firms in regulated states to require (as opposed to request) the tests as a condition of employment or continued employment than exists in states where such regulation has not been effected. On the other hand, it would appear that state licensing legislation has had the net effect of generating a greater confidence in polygraph examiners and establishing a higher degree of credibility for the profession as a whole.

While the study was not intended to offer any direct resolution of the polygraph controversy, it does present a clear empirical picture of the frequency and purposes of polygraph testing among major U.S. corporations today. Perhaps this information will be used to supplant the estimates, conjecture and suppositions which now surround the issue, and to form the basis for objective debate and legislative action in the future.

Notes

1. David T. Lykken, "The Right Way to Use a Lie Detector," *Psychology Today*, March 1975, pp. 57–60.

2. Alabama, Arizona, Arkansas, Florida, Georgia, Illinois, Kentucky, Michigan, Mississippi, Nevada, New Mexico, North Carolina, North Dakota, Oklahoma, South Carolina, Texas, Utah, Vermont, Virginia.

3. Alaska, California, Connecticut, Delaware, Hawaii, Idaho, Maryland, Massachusetts, Minnesota, Montana, New Jersey, Oregon, Pennsylvania, Rhode Island, Washington.

4. "Corporate Lie Detectors Come Under Fire," *Business Week*, January 13, 1973, pp. 88–89.

5. George M. Beason and John A. Belt, "Verifying Applicant's Background," *Personnel Journal*, July 1976, pp. 345–348.

6. J. Kirk Barefoot, ed., *The Polygraph Story* (Hyattsville, Maryland: American Polygraph Association, 1974), pp. 9–16.

7. See note 6.

8. See note 4.

Privacy vs. Intrusion: Darkness at Noon?

David W. Ewing

It is obvious that a conflict often exists between organizational and private interests. As noted in this chapter, organizations sometimes feel compelled to take actions for self-defense or self-preservation that are incompatible with individual rights to privacy. Stating this problem is simple. But how can it be resolved?

In Freedom Inside the Organization *author David W. Ewing addresses both this problem and its resolution. Ewing calls for an employee bill of rights, guaranteeing workers basic rights to freedom and privacy within an organizational context. These rights are principles derived from guidelines that Mr. Ewing suggests would balance employee interests with employer needs. The following essay, a chapter from his book, primarily deals with those guidelines. The moral value of the author's guidelines is that they establish possible principles to facilitate moral inquiry and decision making when organizational needs clash with employee interests. Although Mr. Ewing's guidelines are open to debate, modification, even rejection, they do provide a starting point for discussions. In closing his essay, the author turns to the question of employee manners, dress, and life-style. He suggests that there, too, a balance must be struck between organizational and employee rights.*

When employees talk candidly about their jobs in business and public organizations, they often criticize management for snooping and bureaucratic harassment. This is one of the themes running through Studs Terkel's book *Working*.[1] Of course, management doesn't see its activity this way. To management, detection practices are part of an effort to control employee output and assure productivity. Most supervisors, middle managers, and other executives share Samuel Johnson's opinion—they fear that where there is mystery, roguery is not far off.

Traditionally, the law has favored employer attitudes of "the less employee privacy, the better." Thus, the personnel records of employees are not confidential. Authorities agree that the constitutional concept of a right to privacy has had little influence on personnel relations. Even when an employer misuses personal information about an employee and the employee is fortunate enough to find out, the way to a remedy can be very difficult. "Claims by an employee who has been injured by misuse of his personal information may fall between the effective privacy and defamation causes of action," states Mordechai Mironi, an attorney and researcher at the University of Minnesota.[2]

An employee's privacy is invaded twice in organizations that exercise the full freedom given them by the traditional law. First, it is invaded when the employer collects data about the worker. Exhaustive questionnaires about the person's life and habits, psychological tests, and electronic tests—even their enthusiastic supporters in personnel departments admit that they raise a legitimate question of unfair invasion. But they insist that the benefit to management and society outweighs the invasion. Second, the employee's privacy is invaded when the information collected is put to use. Managers make decisions on the basis of information the employee may not know about, including hearsay comments and off-the-cuff opinions gleaned from quick interviews. The organization uses the same information to answer inquiries from social workers, credit bureaus, union officials, insurance companies, lawyers, government agencies, and other sources.

"What is common to all these episodes," writes Mironi, "is that personal information initially revealed by a job seeker in order to get a job, or collected by an employer throughout and as part of the employment relationship, is released for a purpose that has nothing to do with the job and perhaps is against the employee's interest."[3] Thus a whole block of an employee's private life may bob to the surface at an unexpected place downstream, for other viewers along the bank to see. What follows is a sampling of both types of invasions.

An assistant professor had a personal falling-out with the dean of his graduate school. According to observers, the rift had to do with an outside consulting assignment and did not concern the professor's teaching or personal habits, both of which were generally regarded

as above criticism. The dean vowed that the professor would never find a good job in another university. To make sure, he inserted in the man's file some fabricated assertions that he was a homosexual and a possible danger to students. When the professor applied for jobs elsewhere, he received what was (for him) an inexplicable lack of interest in considering his application.

While a sales supervisor was away on business, her boss went through all the folders in her desk drawers and file cabinets, including those marked "Personal." Queried about this by another manager who happened to hear about it, the boss responded that the employee was believed to have some cost figures that would be useful. While judges have cautioned management that it has no right to prowl through an absent employee's desk on a fishing expedition, it appears that any pretext will suffice, so long as a senior manager does the prowling. In one case, this rule was upheld in court even though the employee's locked desk was pried open.[4]

When one company recently decided, on its own initiative, to revise its personnel files in favor of more light, less secrecy, and better safeguards on use, it was discovered by an alert administrator that information on two employees with similar names—let us call them "Robert Anderson" and "Robert Andersen"—had become mixed, years earlier, as a result of carelessness. On each employee there were various items that could have been embarrassing. When inquiries came from insurance firms, credit agencies, and other such sources, the answers were based on the garbled data. Neither Robert Anderson nor Robert Andersen knew what was going on.

In 1974 the American Civil Liberties Union did a report on privacy and computer data banks. The authors of the investigation concluded that California was "closer to 1984 than the rest of the nation." For instance, California was the first state to have a county clerk's office continuously bugged. Conversations that employees of the Los Angeles County Office in Pomona had with visitors were recorded because, according to the explanation of the county legal counsel, workers in that office "have no reasonable expectation of privacy."[5]

In all but two states, company managers are free to monitor employees' conversations on company telephones without telling the employees. The two exceptions are California, which requires a beeper to be used on monitored phones, and Georgia, where the Public Service Commission requires that monitored phones be marked with a bright orange label and that monitoring supervisors obtain licenses.

The Government Information Subcommittee of the U.S. House of Representatives found numerous government agencies monitoring secretly in 1970, but no federal legislation resulted. A great many companies apparently monitor secretly. As the House subcommittee concluded, electronic equipment for monitoring has become quite sophisticated, and an employee cannot know whether, to what extent, or for what purpose he or she is unwittingly sharing telephone calls with a supervisor or higher-up.

Incidentally, there is no legal restriction on a supervisor's putting any notes thus gathered in the personnel folder of the individual monitored, locked up from that person's view but available to senior management people and, if organization policy allows, outside groups.

In 1974 the *Wall Street Journal* reported that Combustion Engineering, its management incensed by a *Journal* article describing certain terms of nuclear power contracts negotiated by the company, was requiring officers and employees to submit to lie detector tests. "Do you know anybody at the *Wall Street Journal*?" was one question asked by the polygraph operator. "Did you give any information to anybody at the *Wall Street Journal*?" was another.[6]

According to Ralph Nader, a U.S. Senate study in 1974 estimated that between 200,000 and 300,000 lie detector tests are administered each year in companies. Nader also reported that two surveys showed that the loyalty of about one worker in every five is checked by eavesdropping or other means.[7]

According to an old Chinese saying, the buyer needs a thousand eyes, the seller but one. Personnel officials apparently have another version of this thought. Some of them say: the employer needs a thousand eyes, the employee but one.

However, neither this philosophy nor the present law sits well with the public mood. It is becoming increasingly obvious that Americans, old and young alike, object to the no-privacy-is-good-policy tradition. Former Supreme Court Justice William O. Douglas once said, "The right to be let alone is indeed the beginning of all freedom." This statement comes close to mirroring the national mood.

For instance, many national legislators are disturbed by reports that there are nearly 900 federal data banks containing more than 1.25 billion records with personal information about individuals. The U.S. Senate Government Operations Committee and other Congressional committees have shown dismay over the sharing of information that goes on among federal agencies. Various groups of experts have been studying ways to control this situation. The Pentagon, after complaints about information filed on discharged military personnel, has agreed to omit from discharge papers certain coded data that previously permitted prospective employers to identify misfits, drug abusers, and alcoholics.

Universities and schools face a similar change in attitude. Responding to college students' complaints about secret information in their files, Congress in 1974 enacted a law giving students the right to inspect their records. In that same year, a schoolteacher who lost her job after the school superintendent, without her consent, obtained a doctor's report that she was pregnant, went to court and got reinstated. The federal court held that her privacy could not thus be invaded.

In the business sector the wind has been blowing in the same direction. Reacting to employees' complaints about alleged invasions of their privacy, unions have been protesting more vigorously. The AFL-CIO has mounted a drive against lie detectors; partly because of its pressure, thirteen states have laws prohibiting the use of lie detector tests for employees or prospective employees. Some leading companies have seized the initiative in changing their policies (more about this presently).

Some Paths to Privacy

What guidelines might be suggested that would balance employee interests with employer needs? The question has two parts: (a) collection of information; (b) use of information already collected.

In drawing up the guidelines that follow, I have taken advantage of the innovative work of International Business Machines. According to Professor Alan Westin of Columbia University, perhaps no company has spent more management time and money on the privacy question than IBM. Its commitment to greater protection of employee interests began in the middle 1960s, and intensified when Frank T. Cary became board chairman in 1973. He has encouraged special exploratory task forces, training sessions, help from outside consultants, and other efforts; he has written directives to managers on standards to be followed.[8] "The privacy issue is IBM's issue," Cary says. "It is the large data processing systems that have made privacy so pressing an issue. Given the kind of business we're in, we ought not to sit back and let someone else take the lead in trying to do something about it."

First, what about the *collection and retention* of information? The rules that follow are proposed for all organizations, public or private. I make no attempt to state the rules in a legal manner so as to cover all quarks and possibilities, but only to make the general intent clear.

1. Management can collect and keep in its personnel files only those facts about employees that are required by law or that are necessary to manage operations. Thus, IBM's job application forms no longer ask for previous addresses, or whether the employee has relatives working for IBM, or about prior mental problems, or about convictions more than five years back, or about more recent criminal charges that did not result in conviction.

2. Performance evaluations more than three years old must be weeded out from an employee's file. Other out-of-date information should also be removed on schedule. For instance, if an employee had a hassle over his expense account in February, 1970, why keep any notations made then by an irritated boss?

3. Employees are entitled to know what information about them is on file and how it is being used. As Cary notes, employees should understand that "there's no great mystery about it."

4. An employee is entitled to see *most* of the information on file about him or her. Only in this way can he share in the responsibility for accuracy. Of course, there is some information that management usually wishes to be withheld. An example is a confidential discussion of an opportunity for promotion that was never given, or a boss's personal reactions to an unusual request that an employee brought in for discussion.

   In IBM's case, comments of supervisors and fellow workers about an employee's effort to correct an alleged grievance are not available for him to see, either. If this data were available, the company's "Open Door" procedure for appealing grievances would not work so well, management feels, for other employees would not provide the candid reactions needed in handling the case.

   Since enactment of the Privacy Act of 1974, federal government employees have been entitled to examine their personnel files. The Privacy Protection Study Commission is investigating the need for further protection of personal information.

5. Employees' conversations (including telephone) and meetings may not be taped or monitored without their knowledge and consent.

6. A boss is not entitled to use *any* available means of checking up on an employee, say, to confirm a reason given for an absence, or to find out the reason for an unscheduled absence. For instance, calling the employee's home and "cross-examining" whoever answers the phone is not permissible. Neither is sending an investigator out to peer at the home with binoculars, peep in the windows, or follow an employee on a trip.

7. Personality and general intelligence tests are not permissible. However, aptitude tests and skill tests may be legitimate, for they give an employer relevant knowledge about an applicant's ability. For example, typing tests

may be given at IBM. At a company where delicate manual assembly is important, manual dexterity tests may be useful. At the *Harvard Business Review*, applicants for some editorial positions are given a "test article" to edit.

8. When an employee is absent or has left the organization, regular mail addressed to him may be opened only by a person in authority (e.g., his immediate boss or the personnel manager), and envelopes marked "Personal" may not be opened by anyone in the organization, unless the employee authorizes someone to do so.

9. When an employee is away, his desk and personal office files may be opened only by someone in authority who is looking for specific items of information needed for operations. For instance, it would be permissible for a boss to search for a letter containing a price quotation relevant to negotiations the boss is conducting. But if the boss's eye falls on some letters on another matter, as he hunts for the price quotation, he may not say, "Hm-m-m, these look interesting," and take them, too. Nor may he look through the employee's desk on a fishing expedition, that is, when he is not sure what he is after. In other words, we want to apply the principle of the Fourth Amendment, the guarantee in our Bill of Rights, that a person's house may not be searched by officers without a warrant indicating why and for what evidence the search is being conducted.

10. It is not permissible to use polygraphs ("lie detectors") or psychological stress evaluators (PSEs) in interviewing applicants for jobs, candidates for transfer or promotion, or employees who may have knowledge of a problem being investigated, except with their permission. If they do not give permission, that decision must not be held against them. It may be true, as the polygraph and PSE buffs insist, that the innocent person has nothing to fear. But the very mystique of these impersonal, police-type instruments makes them fearsome to many people. They look too much like a device of "pathological professionalism" in the personnel department.

11. If an employee's conversation is taped with his or her permission, the tape may not be run later through a PSE or other black plastic machine without his permission.

Now what about the *uses made* of information about employees on file? As indicated, what organizations do with the data may be as serious a breach of privacy as the manner of collection. I propose the following rules.

1. All information on file about an employee is confidential, and an employer may furnish no fact to an outsider without the employee's consent or a court order. In other words, the employer has a fiduciary relationship to the employee, much as a lawyer does to his client or a doctor to his patient. No distinction may be drawn (as some lawyers have suggested) between personnel information that is "tangible" property and information that is "intangible" property.

One of many advantages of such a clear and decisive rule is that an employee need have no fear of saying something in the employment interview, or in an interview for possible promotion, that he will regret later on. I recall the case of a corporate planner who confided in some detail to his prospective employer about an emotional problem he had, giving names of doctors, hospitals, and so on. His frankness helped him to get the position he wanted. However, several years later he became greatly concerned that the information might be made available to another organization that had inquired about him. "I'm killed if it is," he said.

2. Within the organization, the use of files must be classified. This is one of the principles IBM follows. It divides information about an employee into job-related files and personal information files. The employee's supervisors can see the first type of data, but they cannot look at the personal information files, which contain facts and statements about medical insurance claims, life insurance beneficiaries, criminal convictions, wage garnishments, applications for home loan guarantees, and so forth. Only personnel officials can see this second type of data.

3. No information about an employee may be
    destroyed without his consent (unless the or-
    ganization is simply following a standard pro-
    cedure, such as the removal of out-of-date
    data mentioned earlier). The purpose of this
    rule is to prevent "mysterious disappear-
    ances" of information that might be helpful to
    an employee in a controversy.

Do these rules unfairly fetter management?
They do make it more difficult for managers to get
a "complete picture" of an employee. There are
times when it would indeed be helpful, let us say,
to a sales executive if he could see information in
the personal information folder that he is forbidden to see, or if he could go back eight or ten years
in the file and find "clues" to an employee's puz-
zling behavior. This is the debit side. However, on
the credit side of the ledger is the importance of
privacy. Many employees feel strongly about it,
and a "bill of rights" would be reassuring.

Another debit is that outsiders may not be
able to get information that would be quite helpful
to them. In the example of the planning official, for
instance, the facts about his mental illness would
undoubtedly have been interesting to the outside
group. But, again, the debit is offset by the value
of greater privacy to individuals.

Also, it should be noted that these rules
would not hobble management in security efforts.
Where the checking of purses, briefcases, and
bundles is legal today, it would still be legal.
Moreover, where the law today authorizes a boss
or employer to give frank opinions about an
employee to an outsider, in answer to questions
about the person's competence and character,
those opinions could still be provided.

Finally, it is important to note that the main
impact of these rules is not to reduce the amount
of accurate, relevant, verifiable information available to bosses concerned with a person's on-the-
job record. The main loss is of flimsy information.
Arthur R. Miller was referring to commercial credit
bureaus when he concluded, "The resulting reports usually contain hearsay narratives and off-
the-cuff opinions gleaned from quick interviews
with neighbors, landlords, employers and
'friends.' "[9] But he could have been referring to
personnel folders on file in many other business
and public organizations. One personnel executive
reported that more than three-fourths of the comments about one employee recently reviewed
came from persons who could no longer be con-
tacted, and were apparently collected in haste.
"It's impossible to read them without getting prejudiced against Mrs. ———," he remarked, "yet
most of the stuff is unreliable and has nothing to
do with her work here."

Employees à la Mode

Now let us turn from the privacy of information issue to the question of employee manners,
dress, and life style. Few organizations want their
staffs to look like students in a military academy,
or bow and curtsy, or speak without splitting in-
finitives. At the same time, few managements feel
indifferent about personal habits and style. Appearance can affect morale, customers, and public
opinion. Sometimes, therefore, a line must be
drawn. But where? And by whom?

In general, the law says that managers may
set "reasonable" bounds for dress, hair styles, and
grooming. For instance:

A young man employed by a marketing research organization began reporting to work
in colorful sport shirts and no neckties. When
a supervisor told him he would have to wear a
necktie, the employee refused and was fired.
The employee went to court. The company
had violated the Civil Rights Act, he
charged—female employees were not required to wear ties. Also, the company was
old-fashioned; many young men found ties
uncomfortable and regarded them as outmoded. But in late 1975 a U.S. district court
ruled in favor of the company. Considering
the nature of its business—its need to appear
"professional," the expectations of potential
customers, and so forth—management was
making only a reasonable demand when it insisted on neckties for male workers.[10]

When a switchboard operator turned up at
work wearing tattered, faded, soiled blue
jeans, her supervisor exclaimed, "Really now!
You ought to know better than that. We won't
have it here." The operator said she felt more
comfortable in jeans and refused to change.
When told she had forfeited her job, she went

to the union and began a grievance proceeding. Her case was built on the popularity of jeans among young women in 1975, her desire to be comfortable, and the fact that she could not be seen by the people whose calls she handled. Management countered with the belief that sales people, delivery men, customers, and others did on occasion pass through the switchboard area and get an impression of the company. Besides, it had a long-standing rule about dress which the operator knew about when she took the job. The arbitrator agreed with the company. The woman got her job back when she agreed to conform in the future, but she was not awarded back pay for the time she was laid off.[11]

In 1974 Ken Kunes, the county assessor in Phoenix, Arizona, insisted that his female employees wear dresses. In 1975 he ordered male employees not to let their hair grow within one inch above the collar. Four men let their hair grow longer than that. Kunes fired them. The men went to court, claiming their rights of free expression had been violated. The court ruled in favor of Kunes; his order was reasonable.

In 1975 the New Hampshire Supreme Court ruled that the New Hampshire State Hospital could require a security guard to shorten his hair as a condition of keeping his job. The guard had argued that his hair was neat and, though it came down to the level of his collar, was no longer than women's hair. The court did not agree with him that his rights of free expression were at stake.

Presumably most managers feel this general line of decisions by arbitrators and judges is sound. In my surveys of several thousand executives' opinions on employee rights, I found a heavy majority favoring restrictions of the type just described. These were the same liberal respondents who felt employees should be entitled to refuse to obey unethical orders and to speak out on issues of social responsibility where they disagreed with top management.

As civil liberties advocates have long noted, censorship is not only oppressive but it looks ridiculous when a historical perspective is taken. Today in Michigan mustaches are well accepted,

even prized by many well-groomed men; yet in the early 1960s the case of a senior high student who chose to wear a neat mustache caused an uproar in Saginaw, Michigan.

Again, modern art was forbidden in many public halls not so long ago. Now it is a public relations plus for Chase Manhattan, Reynolds Tobacco, S. C. Johnson, and other well-known companies that buy and display expensive modern paintings and sculpture for all visitors to see. Books by James Joyce, Henry Miller, and other authors were forbidden distribution in the U.S. a few years ago because they were considered obscene. Now *The Joy of Sex* and *More Joy* are best-sellers in leading bookstores. One can go on and on with such examples.

Yet it is a fact that the people an organization serves, buys from, and does business with are affected by employee appearance. Whether these people's attitudes, and the censors who influence them, are rational or irrational is beside the point from an economic standpoint. The organization *can* be hurt. Keeping in mind that managers and organizations have rights which must be balanced against the rights of a dissident employee group, it would seem fair to accept intrusions like those described so long as there are solid checks and balances on management's power. In other words, the dissidents must have some effective way of challenging the intrusion.

Just as employees' hair styles and choice of clothes may be their own business, up to a point, so may their "personality styles"—their angers and frustrations, their feelings about alcohol and sex, their patriotism, and other attitudes. When does their own business become the organization's business?

For instance, a few years ago a supervisor in a state agency of California was sitting in a restaurant watching two other male employees dining with a female employee whom he much admired. When the men escorted the young lady to a motel room, the supervisor could stand his frustration no more. He jerked out a pistol and threatened to kill the two Lotharios if they did not stop "ruining" the young lady whom he so much admired. Next week the supervisor was fired. He petitioned to get his job back, going first to the state personnel board. There he lost on the ground that his conduct had a harmful effect on the staff. Next he went to the California Court of Appeals. Taking into account his record of long service, the court said that discharge was too severe a punishment. It gave him his job back.[12]

Sexual morality is a bottomless pit of problems. A competent employee with ten years of experience in one company happened to be a young woman who dated lots of men, including other workers. Her amours were a favorite subject of office gossip. On two occasions a jilted sweetheart stomped into her office and threatened her. Management got so irritated it told her to leave: She was a loose woman and a danger to morale. Rushing to her defense, the union claimed that her private life was her own business and that it was management's job to keep out intruders, not hers. When the case went to arbitration, the union's argument prevailed over management's and the young woman got her job back.[13]

However, the moment a person's life style becomes a possible threat to the organization as an economic whole—that is, to customer and public relations rather than to a group of employees—the decision is likely to go to management. For instance, a bank teller was called in one day and told that various customers had noticed him at a local bar early in the morning. The teller said yes, this was true, but he always got to work on time and did his job. But what would the bank's customers think? It was a small town, wasn't it? When the teller refused to change his habits, he was given a pink slip. Applying for unemployment compensation, the teller argued that his dismissal was not due to disobedience because the bank had no right to run his private life. The unemployment agency did not agree with him. When an employee's behavior affects the organization's image, controls are justified, the agency ruled.[14]

What about searching an employee's purse, carrying case, or other belongings when he or she comes to work or leaves? So long as the search is done in a reasonable way for an understandable purpose—plant security, for instance—the law says there is no invasion of privacy. In fact, in a recent arbitration case a Wisconsin coal mine company was allowed to have its supervisors "pat down" miners to see if prohibited smoking articles were being carried.[15]

The law today is characterized by its concern for the rights of owners, managers, creditors, and

agents. This preoccupation is not wholly materialistic. Indeed, it is not completely inconsistent with humanistic concern for life, liberty, and individualism. For unless organizations survive and prosper, people cannot rise much above the subsistence level. Even the most liberal society must recognize this.

On the other hand, little is gained if organizations prosper while the souls within them vie, in John Donne's phrase "to watch one another out of fear." In the long run no organization can achieve much at the expense of the quality of life in its offices, plants, and stores. This is why it is so important to extend and expand the right of privacy. Much more can be done before we need to worry about threatening the ability of managers to manage.

Notes

1. Studs Terkel, *Working* (New York: Pantheon, 1974).

2. Mordechai Mironi, "The Confidentiality of Personnel Records: A Legal and Ethical View," *Labor Law Journal*, May 1974, p. 286.

3. Mironi, p. 273.

4. N.Y., U.I.A.B. Appeal #169,246. Also see *Protection Management* (New York, N.Y., Man & Manager), September 1, 1974.

5. *Boston Globe*, February 24, 1974, p. 8.

6. *Wall Street Journal*, March 21, 1974.

7. *New York Times*, May 9, 1976.

8. See "IBM's Guidelines to Employee Privacy," an interview with Frank T. Cary conducted by David W. Ewing and Wanda A. Lankenner, *Harvard Business Review*, September–October 1976, p. 82.

9. Arthur R. Miller, *The Assault on Privacy* (Ann Arbor: University of Michigan Press, 1971), p. 69.

10. 9 EPD Sec. 10, 197 (1975). Also see *White Collar Management* (New York, N.Y., Man & Manager), January 15, 1976.

11. 62 LA 1107 (1975). Also see *White Collar Management*, April 15, 1975.

12. 102 *Cal. Reporter* 50 (1972). Also see *White Collar Management*, January 1, 1973.

13. 67–1 ARB 3262 (1967). Also see *White Collar Management*, April 15, 1967.

14. N.Y., U.I.A.B. Appeal #A-750-1185 (1971). Also see *White Collar Management*, October 15, 1971.

15. *In re Wisconsin Steel Coal Mines*, June 30, 1976, 67 LA 84.

For Further Reading

Anshen, M. (Ed.). *Managing the socially responsible corporation.* New York: Macmillan, 1974.

Blough, R. *Free man and the corporation.* New York: McGraw-Hill, 1959.

Enberg, E. *The spy in the corporate structure.* Cleveland: World Publishing Co., 1967.

LeMond, A. *No place to hide.* New York: St. Martin's, 1975.

Long, E. V. *The intruders: The invasion of privacy in the computer age.* New York: Praeger, 1966.

Reiss, A. H. *Culture and company.* New York: Twayne, 1972.

Riesman, D. *The lonely crowd.* New Haven, Conn.: Yale University Press, 1950.

Sayles, L. *Individualism and big business.* New York: McGraw-Hill, 1963.

Westin, A. *Privacy and freedom.* New York: Atheneum, 1967.

6
EMPLOYEE RESPONSIBILITIES

Remember Bert Lance? He was the amiable Georgian who directed the Office of Management and Budget—but not for long. In the fall of 1977, less than a year after being appointed by President Carter, Lance resigned under fire.

The several factors that led to Lance's departure can be summed up with the phrase "highly dubious banking practices." You may recall that before assuming his governmental post, Lance was president of the Calhoun First National Bank in Georgia. During that time Lance apparently drew large personal loans from banks with which his own bank had established correspondent relationships. One such bank was Georgia's Fulton National Bank.

Between 1963 and 1975 Lance and his wife LaBelle apparently received nearly twenty loans totaling close to $4 million from Fulton National. In documents related to these loans, the Fulton bank noted that "satisfactory balances are maintained by Calhoun National Bank,"[1] thus implying a direct connection between the loans and the interest free deposits that Lance's bank had placed with Fulton to establish the correspondent relationship. In his report, Comptroller of the Currency John Heimann concluded that there was reason to believe that Lance would not have received the loans had it not been for the correspondent accounts. Heimann further indicated that Lance had established a similar pattern of personal loans with two smaller Georgia banks in which he had an interest.

Investigators also discovered that Lance might have profited from a series of sales of a Beechcraft airplane, which the Calhoun bank had purchased while Lance was its president. The bank subsequently sold the plane to Lancelot Company whose owners were Bert and LaBelle. When Lance later became president of the National Bank of Georgia, that bank purchased the Beechcraft from Lancelot.

Apparently Lance also used the Calhoun bank to help finance and promote

---

1. "Lance: Going, Going . . ." Newsweek, September 19, 1977, p. 7. The details reported here can be found in this article.

his bid for governor in 1974. His campaign accounts at the bank, which he then headed, were at one point overdrawn by $99,529. Further investigation indicated that the bank may have paid for entertainment, supplied computers for sending out campaign literature, and provided time to help with Lance's campaign. Evidently the Calhoun bank also paid many of Lance's campaign bills, although listing them as business expenses. Lance later reimbursed the bank.

In a related issue, Lance and his family ran up overdrafts at the Calhoun bank while he was its president. Comptroller Heimann reported that Lance's account was overdrawn by about $50,000 at least twenty-five times between 1972 and 1975. Furthermore, LaBelle Lance overdrew her account by up to $110,000 in 1974. And between September 1974 and April 1975, nine Lance relatives were overdrawn by $450,000.

It's easy to become disoriented by the dizzying effect of the figures and financial razzle-dazzle in the Lance case. On top of this are the political overtones that can easily bruise objectivity. Yet most people both in and out of the banking profession would likely agree that the evidence indicates that at various times Bert Lance used his professional banking status to advance his own interests. In other words, he seems to have engaged in practices that many bankers would consider irregular and not in the best interests of one's bank.

Was Lance's behavior immoral? Before this question can be answered, another more general one must be posed. When employees put their own interests ahead of the interests of their firms, is their behavior wrong? Such a question clearly suggests the primary difference between this chapter and the preceding three. Essentially, earlier chapters dealt with the firm's responsibilities to its employees; this one concerns the employee's responsibilities to the firm. Just what does an employee owe the firm? Obviously the interests of the firm and those of the individual aren't always compatible. How are employees to resolve clashes of interests morally?

In this chapter we'll discuss conflicts of interest inherent in financial investments, use of official position, insider dealings, bribes and kickbacks, gifts, and entertainment. The chapter is not intended as a complete examination of the many ways conflicts of interests can arise, but focusing on some of their most common expressions can initiate the thorough investigation that the topic of employee responsibilities to the firm deserves.

Conflicts of Interest

You don't have to work for a firm for very long, either at a management or nonmanagement level, before realizing that your interests often collide with the interests of the company. You want to dress one way, the firm wants you to dress another way; you'd prefer to show up for work at noon, the firm expects you to be present at 8 A.M.; you'd like to receive $50,000 a year for your labor, the firm gives you a fraction of that figure. Whatever the value in question, attitudes toward it can differ. Thus the reward, autonomy, and self-fulfillment that workers seek aren't always compatible with the worker productivity that the firm desires.

Sometimes this clash of values can take a serious form as in what is officially termed in business a conflict of interest. *In business a conflict of interest arises when employees, at any level, have an interest in or are parties to an interest in a transaction substantial enough that it does or reasonably might affect their independent judgment in acts for the firm.*[2] Looked at another way, the firm has the right to expect employees to use independent judgment on its behalf. Conflicts of interest arise when employees jeopardize this independent judgment.

The primary source of the firm's right to expect independent judgment on its behalf and the concomitant employee responsibility to respect that right is the work contract. When one is hired, one agrees to discharge contractual obligations in exchange for pay. Thus one does specific work, puts in prescribed hours, expends energy, all in return for remuneration, usually in the form of money. Implicit in any work contract is that employees will not use the firm for personal advantage. This doesn't mean that individuals shouldn't seek to benefit from being employed with a firm, but that in discharging their contractual obligations, employees will not subordinate the welfare of the firm to personal gain.

Both students of business practice and moralists agree that conflicts of interest may be either actual or potential. An *actual conflict of interest* arises when employees allow their interest in a transaction to becloud their independent judgment on behalf of the firm. For example, Bart Williams, sales manager for Leisure Sports World, gives all his firm's promotional work to Impact Advertising because its chief officer is Bart's brother-in-law. The transaction costs Leisure World about 15 percent more in advertising costs than comparable work with another agency would. The conflict here is actual: Bart has allowed his judgment on behalf of Leisure Sports World to be influenced by his own interest in Impact. Note that Williams's interest is not a financial one. He doesn't profit financially from the transaction. This underscores the point that an interest conflict can take various forms. The key thing is always whether the transaction functions to hamper one's independent judgment on behalf of the firm.

But even if Bart Williams does not actually compromise himself in this way, he still faces a potential conflict of interest just by being in a position where he could compromise the interest of the firm. Thus, *a potential conflict of interest* arises in cases in which employees might reasonably be expected to sacrifice independent judgment on behalf of the firm. Williams could easily throw some business his brother-in-law's way at the expense of Leisure Sports World.

A conflict of interest can arise in all sorts of ways and take many forms. Its most common expressions, however, seem to involve actions related to financial investments, the use of official position, insider dealings, bribery, kickbacks, gifts, and entertainment. Although these phenomena don't necessarily involve conflicts of interests as defined, they often do and always raise moral questions.

Financial Investments

Conflicts of interest can be present when employees have financial investments in suppliers, customers, or distributors with whom their firms do busi-

---

2. *Davis and Blomstrom, p. 182.*

ness. For example, Fred Walters, purchasing agent for Trans-Con Trucking owns stock with Timberline Paper. When ordering office supplies, Fred buys exclusively through a Timberline affiliate, even though he could get the identical supplies cheaper from another supplier. This is an actual conflict of interest, but, again, even if Walters never advantages himself in this way, he is potentially conflicted.

How much of a financial investment compromises one's independent judgment in acts for the firm? The question defies a precise answer. Ordinarily it's acceptable to hold a small percentage of stock in a publicly owned supplier that's listed on a public stock exchange. Some firms often state what percentage of outstanding stock in a company employees may own. This varies from 1 to 10 percent. Firms may also restrict the percentage of the employee's total investment funds that are involved in an investment. Some companies even require key officers to make a full disclosure of all outside interests or of other relationships which could cloud their judgment on behalf of the firm.[3] Obviously, then, company policy will have a material effect on the morality of outside investments and of conflicts of interests.

But financial investments aren't the only area of conflict of interests. Another conflict is the use of one's official position in a strictly self-serving way.

Use of Official Position

A serious area of conflict of interest involves the use of one's official position for personal gain. Cases in this area can range from using subordinates for non-business-related work to using one's important position with an influential firm to enhance one's own financial leverage and holdings. Some persons claim that this latter form of conflict of interest was most evident in the Lance case. Lance apparently used his bank's correspondent account to float personal loans upward of $4 million. Also he seemingly used his position to overdraw his Calhoun bank account by about $100,000 while financing his gubernatorial campaign. Similarly, Lance's relatives seem to have benefited directly from Lance's position.

Although not apparent in the Lance case, many abuses of official position arise from capitalizing on privileged information. Capitalizing on such information is called insider dealings.

INSIDER DEALINGS. *Insider dealings refers to the ability of key employees to profit from knowledge or information that has not yet become public.* Thus, Marie Kellogg, vice-president of Target Investments, learns at a board meeting that the firm is interested in developing a large parcel of land in a remote corner of the city. In the weeks following, Kellogg purchases a number of acres of the land inexpensively. Sure enough, some months later Target's forecast is borne out. And just as predictably Kellogg makes a tidy profit.

Participants in deals like these ordinarily defend their actions by claiming that they didn't injure anyone. It's true that trading by insiders on the basis of nonpublic information seldom directly injures anyone. But moral concerns arise

---

3. *Davis and Blomstrom, p. 182.*

from indirect injury. As one author puts it, "What causes injury or loss to outsiders is not what the insiders knew or did, rather it is what they themselves [the outsiders] did not know. It is their own lack of knowledge which exposes them to risk of loss or denies them an opportunity to make a profit."[4] Consider, for example, the Texas Gulf Sulphur stock case.

In 1963 test drilling by Texas Gas Company indicated a rich ore body near Timins, Ontario. In a press release of April 12, 1964, insiders at Texas Gulf attempted to play down the potential worth of the Timins property by describing it as "a prospect." But on April 16 a second press release termed the Timins property "a major discovery." In the interim, insider investors made a handsome personal profit through stock purchases. At the same time, stockholders who unloaded stock based upon the first press release lost money. Others who might have bought the stock lost out on a chance to make a profit.

In 1965 the Security and Exchange Commission (SEC) charged that a group of insiders, including Texas Gulf directors, officers, and employees, violated the disclosure section of the Securities and Exchange Act of 1934 by purchasing stock in the company while withholding information about the rich ore strike the company had made. The courts upheld the charge, finding that the first press release was "misleading to the reasonable investor using due care."[5] As a result, the courts not only ordered the insiders to pay into a special court-administered account all profits they made by trading on the inside information but also ordered them to repay profits made by outsiders whom they had tipped. The courts then used this account to compensate persons who had lost money by selling their Texas Gulf Sulphur stock on the basis of the first press release. We mention these facts to illustrate how indirect injury can result from insider dealings and also to note the risk that insiders run in capitalizing on privileged information, both of which facts bear on the morality of such trading.

In addition, insider dealings clearly raise moral questions not easily resolved. When can employees buy and sell securities in their own companies? How much information must they disclose to stockholders about the firm's plans, outlooks, and prospects? When must this information be disclosed? Also, if people in business are to operate from a cultivated sense of moral accountability, it's important for them to understand who is considered to be an insider. In general, an *insider* would be anyone who has access to privileged information. In practice, determining precisely who this is isn't always easy. On the one hand, corporate executives, directors, officers, and other key employees surely are insiders. But what about outsiders whom a company temporarily employs, such as a contractor doing work for a firm? It seems reasonable to say that such outsiders in their temporary roles bear the same responsibilities as insiders do with respect to privileged information.

Related to but distinct from information that's privileged is information

4.   John A. C. Hetherington, "*Corporate Social Responsibility, Stockholders, and the Law,*" Journal of Contemporary Business, *Winter, 1973, p. 51.*

5.   "*Texas Gulf Ruled to Lack Diligence in Minerals Case,*" Wall Street Journal *(Midwest Edition), February 9, 1970, p. 1.*

that's secret or classified. How employees use such proprietary data can raise important moral concerns.

PROPRIETARY DATA. *Proprietary data is classified or secret information which employees are exposed to in discharging their obligations to the firm.* Moral questions involving the disposition of proprietary data sometimes arise when an employee leaves a firm. A classic case involved Donald W. Wohlgemuth, who was a worker in the spacesuit department of B. F. Goodrich Company in Akron, Ohio. Eventually Wohlgemuth became the general manager of the spacesuit division and was privy to Goodrich's highly classified spacesuit technology for the Apollo flights. Shortly thereafter Wohlgemuth, feeling his salary insufficient, joined Goodrich's competitor, International Latex Corporation in Dover, Delaware. His new position was manager of engineering for the industrial area that included making spacesuits in competition with Goodrich. As you might expect, Goodrich protested by seeking an order restraining Wohlgemuth from working with Latex. In 1963 the Court of Appeals of Ohio denied Goodrich's request for an injunction, respecting Wohlgemuth's right to choose his employer. But it did provide an injunction restraining Wohlgemuth from revealing Goodrich's trade secrets.[6]

Cases like Wohlgemuth's are fundamentally different from those involving insider dealings, for they pit a firm's right to protect its secrets against an employee's right to seek employment wherever he or she chooses. This doesn't mean that moral problems don't arise in proprietary data cases or that they're easily resolved. After all, one can always ask whether Wohlgemuth was moral in what he did, the legality of his action notwithstanding. Such a question seems especially appropriate when one learns that Wohlgemuth, when asked by Goodrich management whether he thought his action was moral, replied, "Loyalty and ethics have their price and International Latex has paid this price."[7]

Clearly, then, considerably more moral groundbreaking is needed in the areas of insider dealings and use of proprietary data. But one thing seems clear: both areas raise serious ethical questions. Similar questions surround practices involving bribes and kickbacks.

Bribes and Kickbacks

A bribe is a consideration for the performance of an act that's inconsistent with the work contract or the nature of the work one has been hired to perform. The consideration can be money, gifts, entertainment, or preferential treatment.

Bribes constitute another area where conflicts of interest arise. To illustrate, in exchange for a "sympathetic reading of the books," a firm gives a state auditor a trip to Hawaii. Or a sporting goods company provides the child of one of their retailers with free summer camp in exchange for preferred display, location, and space for their products. In both instances, individuals have taken considera-

---

6. *This case is treated in "Trade Secrets: What Price Loyalty?" the first reading of this chapter.*

7. *Michael S. Baram, "Trade Secrets: What Price Loyalty?"* Harvard Business Review, November–December, 1968, p. 67.

tions inconsistent with the work contract or the nature of the work they contracted to perform.

Bribery sometimes takes the form of *kickbacks, a practice which involves a percentage payment to a person able to influence or control a source of income.* Thus, Alice Farnsworth, sales representative for Sisyphus Book Co., offers a book-selection committee member a percentage of the handsome commission she stands to make if a Sisyphus civics text is adopted. In a word, the committee member receives a kickback for the preferred consideration.

There are a number of noteworthy observations to make that bear on the morality of bribes and kickbacks. First, since they are ordinarily illegal, they raise the same general moral issues as any act of law breaking does. This observation applies to bribes and kickbacks that American companies and their overseas subsidiaries might give to foreign officials. Such acts were declared illegal in 1977, following the admission that nearly 400 American companies had made payments to foreign officials and political leaders amounting to about $300 million. Note that this legislation does not outlaw so-called "grease payments," payments designed to prod foreign officials into carrying out policies set by their governments. Nevertheless, such payments raise moral questions about cooperation in extortion. Moreover, questions of illegality arise even when a firm gives gratuities without asking for or expecting favors in return. An important case was Gulf's pleading guilty in 1977 to giving trips to an Internal Revenue Service auditor who was in charge of the company's tax audit. According to government sources, Gulf's plea marked one of the first times a major U.S. corporation acknowledged that gifts to public officials are illegal even when no favors are asked or expected.

In addition to the legal ramifications of bribes and kickbacks, there's the morally relevant fact that such practices can easily injure the firm. Employees who take bribes can conveniently overlook the interests of the firm in pursuit of their own gain. But even when bribes appear to hurt no one, moral concerns arise. In the case of the sporting goods company that wanted special treatment let's suppose that the product is a good, fairly priced one. People buy it and are satisfied with it. The manufacturer is happy, the retailer is happy, the consumer is happy. In brief, it appears that everyone's interests are served. So what's wrong, if anything? Perhaps nothing. But before reaching a conclusion, note that bribery always involves cooperation with others who are seeking to gain preferential treatment through an act that undermines the free market system. True, such an economic system might be inherently immoral. In that case, an act that undermines it is not necessarily wrong; it may be right. We will not debate this thesis here but will raise it in a later chapter. For now, we wish to note that bribes tend to subvert the free enterprise system, because they function to give advantage in a way that is not directly or indirectly product-related. Bribes attack the foundation of the free market system, which is competition.

As suggested by our examples, gifts are often given as bribes. But even when they're not intended or received as bribes, gifts and entertainment often involve conflicts of interest.

Gifts and Entertainment

In determining the morality of gift giving and gift receiving in a business situation and in deciding whether a conflict of interest exists, a number of factors must be considered.

1. *What is the value of the gift?* Is the gift of nominal value, or is it substantial enough to influence a business decision? Undoubtedly definitions of *nominal* and *substantial* are open to interpretation and are often influenced by situational and cultural variables. Nevertheless, many firms consider a gift of ten dollars or less given infrequently—perhaps once a year—a nominal gift. Anything larger or more frequent would constitute a substantial gift. Although this standard is arbitrary and inappropriate in some cases, it does indicate that a rather inexpensive gift might be construed as substantial.

2. *What is the purpose of the gift?* Dick Randall, a department store manager, accepts small gifts, like pocket calculators, from an electronics firm. He insists that the transactions are harmless and that he doesn't intend to give the firm any preferred treatment in terms of advertising displays in the store. So long as the gift is not intended or received as a bribe and it remains nominal, there doesn't appear to be any actual conflict of interest in such cases. But relative to the purpose of the gift, it would be important to ascertain the electronic firm's intention. Is it to influence how Randall lays out displays? Does Randall himself expect it as a palm-greasing device before he'll ensure that the firm receives equal promotional treatment? If so, extortion may be involved. Important to this question of purpose is a consideration of whether the gift is directly tied to an accepted business practice. For example, appointments books, calendars, or pens and pencils with the donor's name clearly imprinted on them serve to advertise a firm. Trips to Hawaii rarely serve this purpose.

3. *What are the circumstances under which the gift was given?* A gift given during the holiday season, or for a store opening, or to signal other special events is circumstantially different from one unattached to any special event. Whether the gift was given openly or secretly should also be considered. A gift with the donor's name embossed on it usually constitutes an open gift, whereas one known only to the donor and recipient would not.

4. *What is the position and sensitivity to influence of the person receiving the gift?* Is the person in a position to affect materially a business decision on behalf of the gift giver? In other words, could the recipient's opinion, influence, or decision of itself result in preferential treatment for the donor? Another important point is whether the recipients have made it abundantly clear to the donors that they don't intend to allow the gift to influence their action one way or the other.

5. *What is the accepted business practice in the area?* Is this the general way of conducting this kind of business? Monetary gifts and tips are standard prac-

tice in numerous service industries. Their purpose is not only to reward good service but to ensure it again. But it's not customary to tip the head of the produce department in a supermarket so that the person will put aside the best of the crop for you. Clearly, where gratuities are an integral part of customary business practice they are far less likely to pose conflict of interest questions.

6. *What is the company's policy?* Many firms explicitly forbid the practice of giving and receiving gifts in order to minimize even the suspicion that a conflict may exist. Where such a policy exists, the giving or receiving of a gift would constitute a conflict of interest.

7. *What is the law?* This consideration is implicit in all facets of conflicts of interest. Some laws, for example, forbid all gift giving and receiving among employees and firms connected with government contracts. Again, where the gift transaction violates a law, a conflict of interests is always present.

Related to gift giving is the practice of entertaining. In general, entertainment should be interpreted more sympathetically than gifts because it usually occurs within the context of doing business in a social situation. Some companies distinguish entertainment from gifts as follows: If you can eat or drink it on the spot, it's entertainment.

Ordinarily the morality of entertainment may be evaluated on the same basis as gifts, that is, with respect to: value, purpose, circumstances, position and sensitivity to influence of recipient, accepted business practices, company policy, and law. In each case the ultimate moral judgment often hinges on a decision as to whether an objective party could reasonably suspect that the gift or entertainment could blur one's independent judgment. Similarly, the donor often must ask whether an objective party could reasonably suspect that the gift or entertainment was aimed at blurring the recipient's independent judgment.

Ethical Theories

Obviously cases involving conflicts of interest are too numerous and diverse to show how each ethical theory might apply to them. We'll confine our remarks, therefore, to the general direction that these theories seem to point on the broad question of whether being party to a conflict of interest is ever morally justifiable.

Consistent with its approach to any moral issue, egoism allows individuals to serve their own best long-term interests. This means that business people may be parties to transactions that affect their independent judgments on behalf of the firm. Of course, egoists would strongly warn individuals about the pitfalls of accepting bribes, making investments outside the firm, and engaging in other conflicts of interest. People can and do lose their jobs, pay substantial fines, even go to jail. In fact, for these reasons egoists might eschew conflicts of interest. But in the last analysis egoists view such factors as strictly cautionary. In other words, if individuals ultimately judge it to be in their own best interests to accept or give gifts and kickbacks, then they are not only morally right in involving themselves, but they're morally obliged to. In short, for egoists being party to a conflict of interest may be morally justifiable.

Utilitarianism would also make use of the nonmoral consequences of conflicts of interest situations. Unlike egoism, however, utilitarianism would introduce consequences for all concerned: stockholders, customers, other employees, competitors, creditors, society at large. On the basis of an evaluation of these nonmoral consequences to those concerned, utilitarianism would decide what to do. Although it's conceivable that either act or rule utilitarianism could condone a specific act of bribery or insider dealings, or other conflicts of interest, in practice it seems that act utilitarianism would be more likely to approve it than rule would. The reason is that act utilitarianism considers each situation as a separate and distinct act. This means that one can't appeal to any general principle or rule for moral direction in the area of conflicting interests, not even to company policy or law except insofar as keeping or breaking either would have desirable or undesirable consequences. Relying on one's own devices and viewing situations in isolation, one is more likely to engage in a conflict of interest than if one asked: "What if everyone did this?" It is this question that the rule utilitarian usually asks in evaluating the total consequences of the rule under which the action falls. Suppose, for example, we're considering an insider dealing. The rule might read: "Don't engage in insider dealings." The rule utilitarian would inquire into the consequences of breaking this rule. Would breaking it likely produce more total good than keeping it? If everyone went around using privileged information for personal gain, would the total effect be more or less desirable than if everyone kept this rule?

Put in these terms and considered within a contemporary business context, the unfavorable consequences probably loom more ominously than they would in the isolation that act utilitarianism calls for. I'm probably not as likely to think that my isolated use of privileged information for personal gain would materially affect the free enterprise system, stockholders, or the general public as I'd be if I were forced to consider the impact of everyone's using privileged information for personal gain whenever they so desired. The rule utilitarian might apply the same logic to a more general rule that forbade being party to any conflict of interest, in contrast with the act utilitarian who would not take a position on any such rule.

If our analysis is correct, rule utilitarianism would likely support a rule forbidding one's involvement in conflicts of interest, given the climate of contemporary business. On the other hand, act utilitarianism could not consistently support or oppose such a rule but would consider each act individually. In conflict of interest cases, therefore, the philosophical difference between act and rule utilitarianism is apparent.

Like utilitarianism, Fletcher's situational ethics contends that nothing but the end justifies the means. For Fletcher the end consists of the greatest amount of neighbor welfare, that is, loving concern. However, as we've pointed out previously, the situational ethic seems to view intention and consequence on a continuum. In other words, the act that *produces* the most loving concern cannot be separated from the one that springs from a *willing* of loving concern, from a love of God and neighbor. Situationalists, therefore, could not consistently approve of someone's using privileged information exclusively for personal gain, presuming that such an intention was divorced from loving concern. Indeed, it seems that most conflict of interest cases by nature pit self-interest against the greater neighbor welfare. At the same time, we pull up short of asserting that situational ethics would hold that being party to a conflict of interest would never be justifiable. For one thing, situationalists oppose such legalisms. For another, it's conceivable that loving concern could indeed justify an act that constitutes a conflict of interest.

Moving to nonconsequential theories, the Golden Rule, "Do unto others as you would have them do unto you," enjoins us to take into account the positions, circumstances, and interests of all parties involved in a conflict of interest. In conflict of interest cases, it's vital to understand who the others are. Surely others would be all parties with a legitimate interest in the action. In determining whether it's right to offer a bribe, for example, it's not enough to ask whether or not I would want to be offered a bribe if I were in the other person's position. I must also ask: if I were in my employer's position, would I want one of my employees to offer a bribe; if I were in the position of the recipient's employer, would I want one of my employees to accept a bribe? The same questions would be asked from the view of customers and competitors. The decision would be made on the basis of the answers to these questions, but not on a consensus standard. Offering a bribe wouldn't be right or wrong because the majority of interests favored it. It would be right only if, having assessed the position of each interested party, I could conclude that each would want the bribe to be offered. Put in other words, offering the bribe would be wrong if just one party whose position I've assumed would object. Since by definition conflicts of interest always violate the interest of at least one party—the firm—we can surmise that the Golden Rule would generally prohibit it.

According to Immanuel Kant, the moral action is the one that springs from a good will, one that aims to act from duty to law. What's one's duty in conflict of interest cases? Let's suppose again that we're contemplating the use of privileged information for personal gain. In order to determine our duty, that is, what's the right thing to do, we must first formulate the maxim of our action. Our proposed action could be stated thus: "I may use privileged information for personal gain." Could we want this maxim to become a universal rule of behavior? We could if and only if it is not self-contradictory. Examining the maxim reveals an internal contradiction. It's in the nature of privileged information to include matter that stockholders and investors have a right to. A rule that would allow an individual to use privileged information for personal gain—in this case to capitalize on information before it becomes public—would violate the very nature of privileged information. Therefore, it would be wrong to use privileged information for personal gain. We might apply the same line of reasoning to conflicts of interest generally. A rule that would approve of being party to a conflict of interest, it could be argued, would undermine the institution of business itself and for that reason would be immoral. (We should note here that according to Kant an action calculated to avoid conflicts of interest out of fear of censure or prosecution could not be considered altogether moral. Only those actions stemming from a recognition of the logical inconsistency in being party to a conflict of interest would have moral import.)

In applying Ross's prima facie duties and Rawls's maximin principle, we should note the role that a sensitivity to duties would play in determining the morality of conflicts of interest. Both theorists would be sensitive to violations of fidelity that conflicts of interest raise. Thus, in contracting to do a job, one implicitly agrees to exercise independent judgment on behalf of the firm. A conflict of interest invariably violates this duty. Also at stake are other duties such as justice and noninjury. For example, in using privileged information for personal gain, one treats stockholders and investors unfairly. In offering or accepting bribes, one usually jeopardizes the interests of competitors and of the free enterprise system itself. In Rawls's case, one could also argue that the equal liberty principle is compromised in conflicts of interest cases. Recall that Rawls's fundamental principle guarantees the greatest amount of liberty compatible with a like liberty for all. The liberty that an individual extends to self in a conflict of interest issue isn't compatible with a like liberty for all, since all interested parties don't have access to the privileged information, the bribe, the gift, and so on. More to the point, by so putting oneself in an advantageous position, one thereby puts others in a disadvantageous position. For these reasons it seems that both Ross and Rawls could not justify one's being party to a conflict of interest.

In determining the morality of conflicts of interest, proportionalists would first determine whether a major evil were being willed as either a means or end. To illustrate, let's again use the example of privileged information. Insider dealings undoubtedly are cases of individuals' willing their own good. There's certainly nothing wrong with this. At the same time, though, they're willing, as means, the violation of the firm's trust and the rights of stockholders, investors, and the general public. We feel safe in saying this because in the absence of these violations such individuals would not stand to profit. According to proportionalists, a major evil is an act that deprives an entity of a major good, what it needs to survive and function. It could be argued that firms must be able to trust their employees, because as in any human relationship those in business cannot survive long in an atmosphere of distrust and suspicion. Similarly, proportionalists could argue that stockholders, investors, and the general public must have equal access to privileged information in order to function fully as economic beings. It seems, then, that the use of privileged information for personal gain would constitute willing a major evil as a means and therefore would be immoral. In terms of conflicts of interest generally, proportionalists would follow a similar line of argument. Are major evils being willed as means or ends? If so, the action's wrong. If a major evil is being permitted or risked, or if the evil involved is not major, then sufficient reason must exist for performing the action.

As is always true of our analyses, we must concede latitude for divergent interpretations and for qualifications. Indeed, we encourage these as a constructive way to make inroads into the area of business ethics. At the same time, we must emphasize that the crucial question in conflict of interest issues is determining precisely when one exists, actually or potentially. After all, it's of little value to have a general idea of the directions in which various ethical theories would likely move in determining the morality of conflicts of interest if one isn't first sensitized to where a conflict of interest exists. The business practices that we've outlined inevitably raise conflicts, but there are others of an occupationally idiosyncratic nature that employees face. Thus, any employee who is serious about behaving morally would do well to compose an inventory of conflicts of interest cases in his or her area of specialty.

CASE PRESENTATION
Catching Up With a Lucky Star

"You understand, of course," the island's representative was saying, "that a modest gratuity would—how shall we put it?—*speed things up?*"

Ellen Reuster smiled charmingly, but she was thinking: *"This is extortion."* Not that his proposition shocked her. On the contrary, officials at Lucky Star Bottling had warned her and other negotiators who'd be involved in securing outlets for Star's soft drinks abroad to be prepared for such demands. "Officially," the firm's president had remarked, "we must disapprove of and resist such overtures." Then he added wryly, *"Officially."* The unanswered laughter which met this comment underscored the clear intent of the president's message: while publicly condemning such practices, Lucky Star nonetheless expected its negotiators to "deal constructively" with the "peculiar nature" of host country customs and practices in order to ensure that Star would make substantial inroads into the international soft-drink market.

"How modest?" Reuster asked the jolly, robust representative.

"Oh," he said, folding his hands contentedly over his ample paunch, "a few hundred American dollars."

"Not even the cost of my air-fare here," Reuster thought as she produced her checkbook.

It was thus that Lucky Star captured the exclusive right to market its soft drinks on the island. A truly insignificant investment when one realizes that other island neighbors quickly followed suit. Within three years Lucky Star had not only established itself in the island chain but was doing a far more profitable business than it had ever dreamed.

In the interim, Lucky Star was engaging in a round of corporate musical chairs at home. The result was a new president, Winston Arnett. Not long after assuming his new position, Arnett learned of how opportunistic the firm had been in securing its enviable trade in the islands. What's more, he discovered that what were once "modest gratuities" had developed into a full-scale greasing and bribing operation, consisting of a wide variety of favors and services bestowed on local officials instrumental in perpetuating Star's lucrative position.

Arnett immediately sent for Ellen Reuster who by this time had risen to chief operations officer in the islands. While informing Reuster that without doubt her initiatives had vastly enriched the firm's international interests, Arnett thoroughly deplored what she had done and continued to do. In her defense, Reuster indicated that Lucky Star was paying a small price for the huge dividends it was reaping. "Furthermore," she told Arnett, "we're doing no more down there than what's expected of anyone who wishes to fit in with local custom and practice." Nevertheless, Arnett was intent on suspending all activities that smacked of bribery.

"You realize, of course," Reuster pointed out, "it would mean the end of Lucky Star's interests in the islands," a point that wasn't lost on the new president who wished to avoid anything that would seriously undo the firm's profits.

Arnett still was not convinced. He wanted to take a strong stand against bribery.

"If you won't think of the firm," Reuster finally cautioned, "consider the catastrophic impact that our withdrawal will have on those island economies." She reminded Arnett not only of the number of natives that the firm employed but also of the sizable taxes it was paying, which almost single-handedly underwrote many social welfare programs the islands desperately needed.

1. *Was Reuster wrong in initiating the bribes?*

2. *Do Reuster's current payments constitute a conflict of interest? Are they morally questionable?*

3. *What should Arnett do?*

4. *What moral direction does each ethical theory provide for Arnett?*

5. *To what extent did company policy implemented by the first president contribute to Lucky Star's present dilemma?*

6. *Would Arnett be morally justified in disciplining or dismissing Reuster?*

7. *If you were a stockholder whose counsel Arnett sought, what would you advise as the moral thing to do? Why?*

CASE PRESENTATION
Spying on the Boss

"I don't know," Fred Watson said to Ted Moore, the well-dressed man sitting across the table from him. "Old man Barnett's been pretty good to me."[8]

Watson was right. When jobs were hard to get, especially for ex-cons, Milt Barnett, president of Barnett's Drug Exchange, had employed Watson as a shipping clerk. "Others are more qualified than you are," Barnett had told Watson while examining his job application, "but you seem to need the job more than

8. *Adapted from a case that came before a U.S. Senate subcommittee as reported in* Cases in Business Ethics, *Garrett et al., pp. 182–183.*

they do." Watson was understandably impressed with Barnett's concern for him, an impression that Barnett did nothing to tarnish in the two years that Watson had been in his employment. In fact, Barnett had recently intimated to Watson that he was next in line for the job of purchasing manager that promised to open in the next year. Now he was being asked to violate Barnett's trust and to endanger his own livelihood.

"Let's get this straight," Watson said to Moore, "you want me to spy on my boss."

"What we at Schilling Laboratories would like you to do, Mr. Watson, is to help us determine whether or not our suspicions of irregularities in Barnett's distribution of drugs is founded."

As he explained it, Schilling's franchised distributors were entitled to specific discounts for selling directly to retailers. But Schilling had reason to believe that these distributors were getting their discounts while actually selling to Barnett. "What we'd like you to do," he told Watson, "is to report to us the contents of the cartons shipped to and from the Barnett company."

"Well, the whole thing strikes me as pretty underhanded, if you want to know the truth," Watson told him.

"Let me assure you, Mr. Watson, that we find such surveillance equally as repugnant as you do. But at the same time we've an obligation to enforce wholesale distribution agreements under law, and since we've exhausted every other means of doing this short of espionage, we're left with no alternative." Then he added, "I should point out that what you're doing will be kept in the strictest confidence and should you in any way suffer as a result of your activities, Schilling will adequately compensate you for the inconveniences."

Watson shook his head slowly before muttering, "I don't know."

1. *What should Watson do in deciding between loyalty and social responsibility?*

2. *What moral directions do the ethical theories provide for Watson?*

3. *Is Moore acting morally in placing Watson in this dilemma?*

4. *If Barnett is violating wholesale distribution agreements, could his activities in any way be said to be unethical to his employees?*

5. *Would Barnett be morally justified in disciplining or firing Watson should he discover that Watson's spying on him?*

CASE PRESENTATION
The Costs of Keeping a Secret

Phillip Cortez reread the engineering director's memo with considerable anxiety. It read: "Call me at your earliest convenience about design specs for new radial."

"New radial"—that could mean only one thing: that his employer, National Rubber and Tire, wanted to beat its biggest competitor, Lifeworth, in getting an 80,000-mile, puncture-proof tire on the market.

Ordinarily such a memo would signal a challenge for an employee as conscientious and industrious as Phil Cortez. But until six months ago Cortez had
been employed by Lifeworth. While there, he had been instrumental in drawing
up designs for a similar tire that Lifeworth was not only interested in producing
but was also counting on to revitalize its sagging profit posture. In fact, so
important did Lifeworth consider Cortez's work that when he announced his
departure, Lifeworth's president reminded him of an agreement which Cortez
had entered into when undertaking his work with Lifeworth. He had promised
to refrain from disclosing any classified information directly or indirectly to
competitors for a period of two years after his termination with Lifeworth. In no
uncertain terms the president indicated that he considered Cortez's work on the
new radial highly classified. Cortez assured the president that he anticipated no
conflict of interests since National had given him every reason to believe that it
wanted him primarily in a managerial capacity.

And now, the memo was staring him in the face. Cortez responded to it that
very afternoon and had his worst fears realized. As he'd suspected, the engineering director solicited Cortez's input on the matter of a new radial.

Cortez unhesitatingly explained his dilemma. While sympathetic to Cortez's
predicament, the director broadly hinted that refusal to provide constructive
input would not only result in a substantial disservice to National but was bound
to affect Cortez's standing with the firm. "After all," the director said, "it's very
difficult to justify paying a man a handsome salary and expediting his movement
up the organizational ladder when his allegiances obviously lie elsewhere."

The conversation ended icily with the director's advising Cortez to "think
about it."

1. *What should Cortez do?*

2. *What moral direction do the ethical theories provide to assist Cortez in his
    decision?*

3. *Was Cortez morally obliged to disclose to National the agreement he had signed
    with Lifeworth?*

4. *What do you think of the morality of policies that oblige workers to conceal
    classified information for a specified period after their termination with a firm?*

5. *Is National acting morally in pressing Cortez to reveal what he knows?*

Trade Secrets: What Price Loyalty?

Michael S. Baram

---

*As suggested in this chapter, the problem of employees leaving firms and taking with them proprietary data raises a
number of operational and moral concerns. Obviously, this problem is especially troublesome in the research and
development (R&D) sector of the economy. As Michael S. Baram, attorney and executive officer of the graduate*

*Michael S. Baram, "Trade Secrets: What Price Loyalty?" Harvard Business Review, November–December 1968, copyright © 1968
by the President and Fellows of Harvard College; all rights reserved.*

school of Massachusetts Institute of Technology, points out in the following article, employee mobility and high personnel turnover rates in R&D threaten industrial reliance on trade secrets for the protection of certain forms of intellectual property. There's no question that safeguarding the right of the corporation to its trade secrets while safeguarding the rights of employees to depart for what they view as more favorable job opportunities poses difficult legal, practical, and ethical questions. Of special importance is the protection of these rights without detriment to either party. In this reading the author examines these seemingly irreconcilable interests, and presents a five-step management approach to meet the challenge.

In 1963, the Court of Appeals of Ohio heard an appeal of a lower court decision from The B. F. Goodrich Company. The lower court had denied Goodrich's request for an injunction, or court order, to restrain a former employee, Donald Wohlgemuth, from disclosing its trade secrets and from working in the space suit field for any other company.

This case, as it was presented in the Court of Appeals, is a fascinating display of management issues, legal concepts, and ethical dilemmas of concern to research and development organizations and their scientist and engineer employees. The case also represents an employer-employee crisis of increasing incidence in the young and vigorous R&D sector of U.S. industry. Tales of departing employees and threatened losses of trade secrets or proprietary information are now common.

Such crises are not surprising when one considers the causes of mobility. The highly educated employees of R&D organizations place primary emphasis on their own development, interests, and satisfaction. Graduates of major scientific and technological institutions readily admit that they accept their first jobs primarily for money and for the early and brief experience they feel is a prerequisite for seeking more satisfying futures with smaller companies which are often their own. Employee mobility and high personnel turnover rates are also due to the placement of new large federal contracts and the termination of others. One need only look to the Sunday newspaper employment advertisements for evidence as to the manner in which such programs are used to attract highly educated R&D personnel.

This phenomenon of the mobile employee seeking fulfillment reflects a sudden change in societal and personal values. It also threatens industrial reliance on trade secrets for the protection of certain forms of intellectual property. There are no union solutions, and the legal framework in which it occurs is an ancient structure representing values of an earlier America. The formulation of management responses—with cognizance of legal, practical, and ethical considerations—is admittedly a difficult task, but one which must be undertaken.

In this article I shall examine the basic question of industrial loyalty regarding trade secrets, using the Goodrich-Wohlgemuth case as the focal point of the challenge to the preservation of certain forms of intellectual property posed by the mobile employee, and then offer some suggestions for the development of sound management policies.

The Appeals Case

Donald Wohlgemuth joined the B. F. Goodrich Company as a chemical engineer in 1954, following his graduation from the University of Michigan, and by 1962 he had become manager of the space suit division. As the repository of Goodrich know-how and secret data in space suit technology, he was indeed a key man in a rapidly developing technology of interest to several government agencies. Nevertheless, he was dissatisfied with his salary ($10,644) and the denial of his requests for certain additional facilities for his department.

A Goodrich rival, International Latex, had recently been awarded the major space suit subcontract for the Apollo program. Following up a contact from an employment agency hired by Latex, Wohlgemuth negotiated a position with Latex, at a substantial salary increase. In his new assignment he would be manager of engineering for industrial products, which included space suits. He then notified Goodrich of his resignation, and was met with a reaction he apparently did not expect. Goodrich management raised the moral and ethical aspects of his decision, since the company executives felt his resignation would result in the transfer of Goodrich trade secrets to Latex.

After several heated exchanges, Wohlgemuth

stated that "loyalty and ethics have their price and International Latex has paid this price. . . ." Even though Goodrich threatened legal action, Wohlgemuth left Goodrich for Latex. Goodrich thereupon requested a restraining order in the Ohio courts.

At the appeals court level, the Goodrich brief sought an injunction that would prevent Wohlgemuth from working in the space suit field for *any* other company, prevent his disclosure of *any* information on space suit technology to *anyone*, prevent his consulting or conferring with *anyone* on Goodrich trade secrets, and finally, prevent *any* future contact he might seek with Goodrich employees.

These four broad measures were rejected by the Ohio Court of Appeals. All were too wide in scope, and all would have protected much more than Goodrich's legitimate concern of safeguarding its trade secrets. In addition, the measures were speculative, since no clear danger seemed imminent. In sum, they represented a form of "overkill" that would have placed undue restraints on Wohlgemuth.

The court did provide an injunction restraining Wohlgemuth from disclosure of Goodrich trade secrets. In passing, the court noted that in the absence of any Goodrich employment contract restraining his employment with a competitor, Wohlgemuth could commence work with Latex. With ample legal precedent, the court therefore came down on both sides of the fence. Following the decision, Wohlgemuth commenced his career with Latex and is now manager of the company's Research and Engineering Department.

Common-Law Concepts

The two basic issues in crises such as the Goodrich-Wohlgemuth case appear irreconcilable: (1) the right of the corporation to its intellectual property—its proprietary data or trade secrets; and (2) the right of the individual to seek gainful employment and utilize his abilities—to be free from a master-servant relationship.

There are no federal and but a few state statutes dealing with employment restraints and trade secrets. The U.S. courts, when faced with such issues, have sought to apply the various common-law doctrines of trade secrets and unfair competition at hand to attain an equitable solution. Many

of these common-law doctrines were born in pre-industrial England and later adopted by English and U.S. courts to meet employment crises of this nature through ensuing centuries of changing industrial and social patterns. In fact, some of the early cases of blacksmiths and barbers seeking to restrain departing apprentices are still cited today.

To the courts, the common legal solution, as in *Goodrich v. Wohlgemuth*, is pleasing because it theoretically preserves the rights of both parties. However, it is sadly lacking in practicality, since neither secrets nor individual liberty are truly preserved.

The trade secrets which companies seek to protect have usually become an integral portion of the departing employee's total capabilities. He cannot divest himself of his intellectual capacity, which is a compound of information acquired from his employer, his co-workers, and his own self-generated experiential information. Nevertheless, all such information, if kept secret by the company from its competition, may legitimately be claimed as corporate property. This is because the employer-employee relationship embodied in the normal employment contract or other terms of employment provides for corporate ownership of all employee-generated data, including inventions. As a result, a departing employee's intellectual capacity may be, in large measure, corporate property.

Once the new position with a competitor has been taken, the trade secrets embodied in the departing employee may manifest themselves quite clearly and consciously. This is what court injunctions seek to prohibit. But, far more likely, the trade secrets will manifest themselves subconsciously and in various forms—for example, as in the daily decisions by the employee at his new post, or in the many small contributions he makes to a large team effort—often in the form of an intuitive sense of what or what not to do, as he seeks to utilize his overall intellectual capacity. Theoretically, a legal injunction also serves to prohibit such "leakage." However, the former employer faces the practical problem of securing evidence of such leakage, for little will be apparent from the public activities and goods of the new employer. And if the new employer's public activities or goods appear suspicious, there is also the further problem of distinguishing one's trade secrets from what may be legitimately asserted as the self-generated technological skills or state of the art of the new employer and competitor which were utilized.

This is a major stumbling block in the attempt to protect one's trade secrets, since the possessor has no recourse against others who independently generate the same information. It is therefore unlikely that an injunction against disclosure of trade secrets to future employers prevents any "unintentional" transfer (or even intentional transfer) of information, except for the passage of documents and other physical embodiments of the secrets. In fact, only a lobotomy, as yet not requested nor likely to be sanctioned by the courts, would afford security against the transfer of most trade secrets.

Conversely, the departing employee bears the terrible burden of sensitivity. At his new post, subconscious disclosure and mental and physical utilization of what he feels to be no more than his own intellectual capacity may result in heated exchanges between companies, adverse publicity, and litigation. He is marked, insecure, and unlikely to contribute effectively in his new position. In fact, new co-workers may consider him to be a man with a price, and thus without integrity. Frequently, caution on the part of his new employer will result in transfer to a nonsensitive post where he is unlikely to contribute his full skills, unless he has overall capability and adaptability.

The fact that neither secrets nor individual liberty will be truly preserved rarely influences the course of litigation. Similarly, these practical considerations are usually negligible factors in the out-of-court settlements which frequently terminate such litigation, because the settlements primarily reflect the relative bargaining strengths of disputing parties.

Finally, there is the full cost of litigation to be considered. In addition to the obvious court costs and attorney's fees, there is the potentially great cost to the company's image. Although the drama enacted in court reflects legitimate corporate concerns, the public may easily fail to see more than an unequal struggle between the powerful corporate machine and a lonely individual harassed beyond his employment tenure. Prospective employees, particularly new and recent graduates whose early positions are stepping stones, may be reluctant to accept employment with what appears to be a vindictive and authoritarian organization.

Practical and Legal Aspects

Trade secrets are, of course, a common form of intellectual property. Secrecy is the most natural and the earliest known method of protecting the fruits of one's intellectual labors. Rulers of antiquity frequently had architects and engineers murdered, after completion of their work, to maintain secrecy and security. The medieval guilds and later the craftsmen of pre-industrial Europe and America imposed severe restraints on apprentices and their future activities.

Recognition and acceptance of the practice of protecting intellectual property by secrecy is found throughout Anglo-American common or judge-made law, but statutory protection has not been legislated. Perhaps the failure to do so is because of the recognition by the elected officials of industrial societies that secrecy is not in the public interest and that the widest dissemination of new works and advances in technology and culture is necessary for optimal public welfare.

Coincidentally with the industrial revolution, British and U.S. copyright and patent legislation was enacted and represents to this day enlightened efforts to diminish the practice of secrecy. Such legislation was designed to stimulate creativity and disclosure by providing limited commercial monopolies of copyright and patent to authors and inventors, in exchange for immediate public disclosure of their works following acceptance by copyright and patent agencies. However, the copyright and patent systems have failed to meet changing technologies, societal concepts, and industrial practices. A current example is the inadequate response of both agencies to computer software.

Dual standards for patent and copyright protection have arisen, since courts have applied strict standards of validity to the patents and copyrights that are challenged and litigated. The result is a high incidence of findings of subsequently invalid patents and copyrights issued by the federal systems. Further, the 17-year period of patent protection is often insufficient because inventions normally require a longer period of time, following reduction to practice and patentability, before commercial acceptance occurs. Thus early disclosure of the invention through the award of a patent only serves to inform the competition of one's state of the art. Industry has therefore continued to rely on secrecy and the persistent and ill-defined concepts of the common law of trade secrets and unfair competition to protect its intellectual property.

To summarize this common law briefly, virtually all information—ranging from full descriptions of inventions to plant layouts, shop know-how, methods of quality control, customer and source lists, and marketing data—is eligible for protection as trade secrets. No standards of invention or originality are required. If such information is not known to the public or to the trade (or it is known but its utility is not recognized), and if such information is of value to its possessor, it is eligible for protection by the courts.

Further, and of greatest importance in terms of favorably impressing the courts, there must be evidence that the possessor recognized the value of his information and treated it accordingly. In the context of confidential relationships, "treatment" normally means that the possessor provided for limited or no disclosure of trade secrets. This means many things: for example, total prohibition of disclosure except to key company people on a need-to-know basis; provision of the information to licensees, joint ventures, or employees having contractual restraints against their unauthorized disclosure or use; division of employee responsibilities so that no employee is aware of more than a small segment of a particular process; and use in labs of unmarked chemicals and materials.

There must also be evidence that particular efforts were expended for the purpose of preserving secrecy for the specific data claimed as trade secrets. General company policies indiscriminately applied to data and employees or licensees will not suffice in the legal sense to convince the courts of the presence of trade secrets.

When the possessor and his information do fulfill such criteria, court recognition and the award of compensation to damaged parties, or injunctive restraints to protect parties in danger of imminent or further damage, will follow. If there is evidence of (a) breach of confidential relationships (contracts or licenses) which were established to preserve the secrecy of company information, (b) unauthorized copying and sale of secrets, or (c) conspiracy to damage the possessor, the courts will act with greater certitude. But in many cases, such as in the Goodrich-Wohlgemuth litigation, no such evidence is present.

Finally, the courts will not move to protect trade secrets when an action is brought by one party against another who independently generated similar information, or who "reverse-engineered" the publicly sold products of the party petitioning the court, unless there is some contractual, fiduciary, or other relationship based on trust connecting the parties in court.

Other Considerations

In addition to the foregoing practical and legal aspects, basic questions of industrial ethics and the equitable allocation of rights and risks should be examined to provide management with intelligent and humane responses to employer-employee crises that involved intellectual property. The patent and copyright systems for the stimulation and protection of such property are premised on dissemination of information and subsequent public welfare. These systems reflect public concern with the proper use of intellectual property, which the common law of trade secrets lacks.

Will the courts continue to utilize common-law concepts for the protection of trade secrets, when such concepts are based solely on the rights of the possessors of secret information, and when the application of such concepts has a detrimental effect on both the rights of employees and the public welfare? Since current court practice places the burden of industrial loyalty solely on the employee, the skilled individual has to pay the price. In other words, the law restricts the fullest utilization of his abilities. And the detrimental effect on public welfare can be inferred from recent federal studies of technology transfer, which indicate that employee mobility and the promotion of entrepreneurial activities are primary factors in the transfer of technology and the growth of new industries.

The continuation of trade secret concepts for the preservation of property rights in secret information at the expense of certain basic individual freedoms is unlikely. The law eventually reflects changing societal values, and the mobile R&D employee who seeks career fulfillment through a succession of jobs, frequently in sensitive trade secret areas, is now a reality—one not likely to disappear. Thus it is probable that the courts will eventually adopt the position that those who rely on trade secrets assume the realities or risks in the present context of public concern with technological progress and its relationship to the public good, and with the rights of the individual. Resulting unintentional leakage of secret information through the memory of a departing employee is now generally accepted as a reasonable price to pay for the preservation of these societal values. However, the courts will never condone the theft or other physical appropriation of secret information, nor are the courts likely to condone fraud, conspiracy, and other inequitable practices resulting in some form of unfair competition.

The failings of the statutory systems serve, not as justification for the inequitable application of medieval trade secret concepts, but as the basis for legislative reform. Injunctive restraints against the unintentional leakage of secrets and the harassment of departing employees through litigation should not be part of our legal system. This is especially true when there is a growing body of evidence that management can respond, and has intelligently done so, to such crises without detriment to the individual employee, the public good, or the company itself.

Management Response

How then shall managers of research and development organizations respond to the reality of the mobile employee and his potential for damage to corporate trade secrets?

Contractual Restraints

Initial response is invariably consideration of the use of relevant contractual prohibitions on employees with such potential. For a minority of companies, this means the institution of employment contracts or other agreements concerning terms of employment. For most, a review of existing company contracts, which at a minimum provide for employee disclosure of inventions and company ownership of subsequent patents, will be called for to determine the need for relevant restraints.

Contractual prohibitions vary somewhat, but they are clearly of two general types: (1) restraints against unauthorized disclosure and use of company trade secrets or proprietary information by employees during their employment tenure or at any time thereafter; (2) restraints against certain future activities of employees following their employment tenure.

A restraint against unauthorized disclosure or use is normally upheld in the courts, provided it is limited to a legitimate company concern—trade secrets. But it is usually ineffective, due to the unintentional leakage and subconscious utilization of trade secrets, and the difficulties of "policing" and proving violation, as discussed earlier. In fact, several authorities feel that this type of restraint is ineffective unless coupled with a valid restraint against future employment with competitors.

Restraints limiting future activities are more difficult to generalize since little consistency—and hence, predictability—as to validity is provided by the common law. Nevertheless, when held valid, a limitation on employment with competitors can be totally effective. In the past, such restraints limited certain activities of the departing employee for a period of time and within a geographical sector. Thus, such a restraint as "no competing activities for five years, and thereafter not within a 50-mile radius of Cambridge" may have served a colonial craftsman. But now that corporate interests are nationwide, a geographical limitation is meaningless to the employer. It is therefore the reasonableness of the scope of restricted activities and of the time limitation that is at issue in all such cases today.

Is enforced abstinence from competing activities of, say, five years, or three, or one, a reasonable price to exact from the departing employee to protect his former employer's trade secrets? Let me point out that the trend over the last several decades has been toward a position that no time limitation is a reasonable one.

The *Encyclopedia of Patent Practice and Invention Management*, in discussing "restrictions on future employment," states:

> It is understood that no contract is valid that withdraws from a man the right to earn a living. This may be expressed in the words that a man's tools cannot be taken for debt or that the operations of his brain may not be mortgaged. . . . Such limitation as that an engineer may not accept other work in the

engineering industry or a chemist in chemistry is obviously improper and void. Restrictions on future employment, if they are to have any chance for enforceability, must define the forbidden field clearly and with severe limitations.

One company is reported to have attempted to modify its research chemists' contracts, so as to require approval by the company of any employment accepted by the chemist for two years after leaving the company. Employment within two of the less industrialized states was excepted . . . the attempt was unsuccessful.[1]

In *Donahue* v. *Permacil Tape Corporation*, the court said in regard to an ex-employee's knowledge and overall capability:

> They belong to him as an individual for the transaction of any business in which he may engage, just the same as any part of the skill, knowledge, information or education which was received by him before entering the employment. . . . On terminating his employment, he has a right to take them with him.[2]

Courts have been naturally reluctant to extend protection to trade secrets when the freedom of an individual to use his overall capability is at stake. In addition, the former employer faces the practical difficulty of convincing almost any court that a prohibition of future employment is necessary, since the court will look for clear and convincing evidence that the ex-employee has, or inevitably will, exercise more than the ordinary skill a man of his competence possesses. A few states—such as California by statute and others by consistent court action—now prohibit future employment restraints.

It therefore appears that a contractual prohibition of future employment in a broad area, which prevents an ex-employee from using his overall capability, is invalid in most states. And a request for an injunction to prohibit such employment, without a prior contractual provision, stands an even poorer chance of success, as Goodrich learned when it sought to prevent Wohlgemuth from working in the space suit field for any other company.

Nevertheless, there are occasional cases in which provisions in employment contracts restraining a narrow scope of activity—i.e., work on a particular process or machine—for up to two

years have been upheld. These cases are often distorted by the presence of highly charged factors such as the employee's departure with copies of company trade secrets in his possession, or evidence of his enticement by a competitor to garner the trade secrets he bears, to the direct detriment of his former employer. In the absence of such distortions, and in the presence of evidence that even such narrowly defined prohibited activities would prevent the individual from a reasonable pursuit of his career, it is doubtful if even the most skillfully drawn contractual prohibition would prevail.

Few scientists and engineers possess sufficient strength at the time of negotiating a new position to demand excision of contractual restraints on their post-employment futures. Yet the restraint is a deterrent, and its impact, though unmeasured, on the sensitivities of the creative, highly motivated employees in demand by R&D organizations can be anticipated.

Management must therefore consider the opprobrium connected to contractual restraints on employees. It is worth noting that in the most intensive trade secret area—the chemical industry—a recent survey revealed that only 1 of 24 companies utilized contractual restraints on future employment.

Government classification of company contract work serves no purpose toward the protection of company trade secrets. The intellectual property arising from government-funded work is, in Department of Defense terminology, "unlimited rights data." Since it is the property of the government, it is available to other cleared government contractors who are competitors and potential employers.

In sum, there is low predictability and low security in management reliance on the employment contract as protection against the loss of trade secrets through the departure of key employees.

Internal Policies

Another response of R&D management to the mobile employee and his potential for damage to corporate trade secrets is the formulation of internal company policies for the handling of intellectual property of trade secret potential. Such policies may call for the prior review of publications and addresses of key employees, prohibition of consulting and other "moonlighting," dissemination of trade secrets on a strict "need to know" basis to designated employees, and prohibitions on the copying of trade secret data. More "physical" policies may restrict research and other operational areas to access for designated or "badge" employees only and divide up operations to prevent the accumulation of extensive knowledge by any individual—including safety and other general plant personnel. Several companies I know of distribute unmarked materials—particularly chemicals—to employees.

Although internal policies do not necessarily prevent future employment with competitors, they can serve to prevent undue disclosures and lessen the criticality of the departure of key personnel. All must be exercised with a sophisticated regard for employee motivation, however, because the cumulative effect may result in a police state atmosphere that inhibits creativity and repels prospective employees.

Several farsighted R&D organizations are currently experimenting with plans which essentially delegate the responsibility for nondisclosure and nonuse of their trade secrets to the key employees themselves. These plans include pension and consulting programs operative for a specified post-employment period. In one company, for example, the pension plan provides that the corporate monies which are contributed to the employee pension fund in direct ratio to the employee's own contributions will remain in his pension package following his term of employment, provided he does not work for a competing firm for a specified number of years. In another company, the consulting plan provides that certain departing employees are eligible to receive an annual consulting fee for a given number of years following employment if they do not work for a competitor. The consulting fee is a preestablished percentage of the employee's annual salary at the time of his departure.

Obviously, such corporate plans are subject to employee abuse, but if limited to truly key employees, they may succeed without abuse in most cases. They not only have the merit of providing the employee with a choice, an equitable feature likely to incur employee loyalty, but they also have no apparent legal defects.

Another valid internal practice is the debrief-

ing of departing employees. The debriefing session, carried out in a low-key atmosphere, affords management an excellent opportunity to retrieve company materials and information in physical form, to impart to the employee a sense of responsibility regarding trade secrets and sensitive areas, and to discuss mutual anxieties in full.

External Procedures

Several management responses relating to external company policies are worth noting, as they also serve to protect trade secrets in cases involving employee departures. Among several industries, such as in the chemical field, it is common to find gentlemen's agreements which provide mutuality in the nonhiring of competitor's key employees, following notice. Employees who have encountered this practice have not found the experience a pleasant one. This same practice is also found in other areas, such as the industrial machinery industry, that are in need of innovation; and it appears that the presence of such agreements helps to depict these industries in an unappealing fashion to the types of employees they need.

Another external response for management consideration is company reliance on trademarks. Given a good mark and subsequent public identification of the product with the mark, a company may be able to maintain markets despite the fact that its intellectual property is no longer a trade secret. Competitors may be hesitant about utilizing the former trade secrets of any company whose products are strongly identified with trademarks and with the company itself.

Some trade secrets are patentable, and management faced with the potential loss of such secrets should consider filing for patent protection. The application is treated confidentially by the U.S. Patent Office and some foreign patent offices up to the time of award. Moreover, if the application is rejected, the secrecy of the information is not legally diminished. In any case, the subject matter of the application remains secret throughout the two-to-three year period of time normally involved in U.S. Patent Office review.

Conclusion

A major concern of our society is progress through the promotion and utilization of new technology. To sustain and enhance this form of progress, it is necessary to optimize the flow of information and innovation all the way from conception to public use. This effort is now a tripartite affair involving federal agencies, industry, and universities. A unique feature of this tripartite relationship is the mobility of R&D managers, scientists, and engineers who follow contract funding and projects in accordance with their special competence. Neither the federal agencies nor the universities rely on trade secret concepts for the protection of their intellectual property. However, industry still does, despite the fact that trade secret concepts bear the potential ancillary effect of interfering with employee mobility.

It is becoming increasingly clear that new societal values associated with the tripartite approach to new technology are now evolving, and that the common law dispensed by the courts has begun to reflect these values. A victim of sorts is trade secret law, which has not only never been clearly defined, but which has indeed been sustained by court concepts of unfair competition, equity, and confidence derived from other fields of law. The day when courts restrict employee mobility to preserve industrial trade secrets appears to have passed, except—as we noted earlier—in cases involving highly charged factors such as conspiracy, fraud, or theft.

In short, it is now unwise for management to rely on trade secret law and derivative employee contractual restraints to preserve trade secrets. Companies must now carefully weigh the nature and value of their intellectual property, present and potential employees, competition, and applicable laws in order to formulate sound management policies.

Programmed Approach

Regarding the challenge to the preservation of trade secrets posed by the mobile employee, sophisticated management will place its primary reliance on the inculcation of company loyalty in key employees, and on the continual satisfaction of such key employees. For example, management might consider adopting the following five-step basis for developing an overall approach to the challenge:

1. Devise a program for recognition of employee achievement in the trade secret area. At present, this form of recognition is even more neglected than is adequate recognition of employee inventions.

2. Make an appraisal of trade secret activities. This should result in a limitation of (a) personnel with access to trade secrets, (b) the extent of trade secrets available to such personnel, and (c) information which truly deserves the label of trade secret.

3. Review in-house procedures and the use of physical safeguards, such as restrictions on access to certain specified areas and on employee writings for outside publication. Restrictions may tend to stifle creativity by inhibiting communication and interaction conducive to innovation. Striking the balance between too few and too many safeguards is a delicate process and depends on employee awareness of what is being sought and how it will benefit them.

4. Appraise the legal systems available for the protection of intellectual property. Utility and design patents may be advisable in some cases. The copyright system now offers some protection to certain types of industrial designs and computer software. Trademarks may be adroitly used to maintain markets.

5. Recognize that all efforts may fail to persuade a key employee from leaving. To cope with this contingency, the "gentle persuasion" of a pension or consulting plan in the post-employment period has proved effective and legally sound. A thorough debriefing is a further safeguard. Other cases wherein employee mobility is accompanied by fraud, unfair competition, or theft will be adequately dealt with by the courts.

The problem of the departing employee and the threatened loss of trade secrets is not solved by exhortations that scientists and engineers need courses in professional ethics. Management itself should display the standards of conduct expected of its employees and of other companies.

Finally, let me stress again that success probably lies in the inculcation of company loyalty in key employees, not in the enforcement of company desires or in misplaced reliance on the law to subsidize cursory management. Better employee relations—in fact, a total sensitivity to the needs and aspirations of highly educated employees—

requires constant management concern. In the long run, total sensitivity will prove less costly and more effective than litigation and the use of questionable contractual restraints.

Notes

1. R. P. Calvert, editor (New York, Reinhold Publishing Company, 1964), p. 230.
2. 127 N.E. (2), p. 235.

The Phenomenon of International Bribery

Jack G. Kaikati

Any discussion of bribery in business today would be incomplete if the issue of international bribery were not raised. In recent years U.S. multinational companies have openly admitted paying hundreds of millions of dollars abroad in various forms of bribery. The problem of international bribery raises a fundamental ethical concern generally absent in concerns about domestic bribery: the relativity of ethical standards. While bribery may be illegal and unethical in the United States, in some other countries it's customary and considered moral. Thus many business people, while deploring the immorality of domestic bribery, see nothing wrong with "doing as the Romans do" with respect to bribery overseas. As Jack G. Kaikati, member of the marketing faculty at Southern Illinois University, demonstrates in the following article, international bribery and its implications are rapidly becoming issues of major concern in business and government. Particularly relevant for our purposes are the national and international proposals dealing with the ethical nature of this phenomenon, since these proposals might help us formulate an opinion on the morality of international bribery.

Improper payments by U.S. multinational companies to foreign officials have spread a darkening stain over the global reputation of American business. A Library of Congress study conducted in November 1975 reported that since January 1, 1974, American companies had publicly admitted making more than $300 million in illegal political payments or other forms of kickbacks.

The objectives of this article are four-fold. First, it provides a basic definition of bribery and contrasts it with other forms of payments. Second, it outlines the findings of at least three research studies that have been conducted since the advent of the current wave of questionable overseas payments. Third, it traces the growing list of federal agencies and congressional committees that have been investigating improper payments. Finally, it discusses in detail the national and international proposals and recommendations dealing with the ethical problem.

Basic Definition

The phenomenon of corporate bribery which is now agitating both the government and the corporate world is as old as sin itself. Although the patterns of bribery are essentially the same throughout the world, there exists a variety of regional epithets describing the phenomenon. Almost every country has a name for it—"la mordita" in Latin America, "baksheesh" in the Middle East, "bustarella" in Italy, "hai yo" or "hung pao" in Hong Kong, "dash" in some parts of Africa, "pot de vin" in France and "schmiergelder" in Germany. Thus, no country has developed an immunity to bribery.

Although U.S. statutes and judicial interpretations vary, the legal essence of bribery is a payment voluntarily offered for the purpose of inducing a public official to do or omit doing something in violation of his lawful duty, or to exercise his official discretion in favor of the payor's request for a contract, concession or privilege on some basis other than merit. Many forms of payments now under attack do not constitute "bribery" under this definition.

First, there is a distinction between bribery and extortion.[1] The former type of payments are voluntarily offered by someone who seeks an unlawful advantage while the latter payments are extracted under genuine duress and coercion from an innocent victim seeking only the treatment to which he is lawfully entitled. For example, Gulf Oil's ex-chairman has explained to Senator Frank Church's Subcommittee on Multinational Corporations that the payment of $4 million to help finance the reelection of President Chung Hee Park in South Korea was not so much a bribe as an extortion wrung from the company by threats against its $350 million investment in that country.

This author believes such extortion tactics may well jeopardize the existence of the company in the host country, and it is difficult to find a subject more important to the board's responsibilities than knowledge of such blackmail threats. The board may be compelled to take action which could easily involve both risk to the corporation and to the directors. Defining the best interests of the corporation and its shareholders may be difficult, but the board would seem obligated to face the issues and record its conclusions.

Second, there is a distinction, not always easily determined, between a "lubrication bribe" and a "whitemail bribe."[2] The former involves a relatively small sum of cash or other gift or service made by a businessman to a low-ranking government official in a country where such offerings are not prohibited. The purpose of these payments is to facilitate, expedite or express appreciation for normal, lawful performance of ministerial or procedural duties by the government official. The whitemail bribe, however, involves an elaborate system of concealing the use of large sums of corporate cash. These payments are invariably accompanied by false accounting, fictitious bookkeeping entries and bogus documentation. Based on the above two definitions, this author urges that "lubrication" payments should not be condemned since these payments are similar to the American and European customs of paying tips for prompt and efficient services. Lubrication payments should not be confused with bribing an official *not* to do his job.

Third, there is a distinction between a bribe and agents' fees. A company contemplating business arrangements in a foreign country where it is not known may seek out an agent. Of course, a good agent's role is not restricted to bribing government officials. He can set up appointments between important government officials and company representatives, help the firm chart its investment strategy, advise it on how to shape its bid, as well as funnel back useful intelligence on government needs. It is next to impossible to determine how much of the agent's fee is a legitimate business expense and how much is passed on in bribes. Indeed, one well-known foreign commission agent now states that although he reported to the American company that he used certain sums to bribe a government official, in fact he kept the money for himself. Since there is no easy way to get the truth, this author believes company executives can treat the agent's fee as a tax-deductible business expense. In these circumstances, if bribes become public knowledge, company executives can categorically deny having ever knowingly authorized them.

It is clear that there are a wide variety of practices, differing in both degree and intent. Consequently, it is not easy to determine with certainty what constitutes a bribe, and gray areas of interpretation will always remain. The size, form and timing of payment, the adequacy of its disclosure as well as other pertinent facts must bear on the conclusion in a doubtful case.

Since the advent of the current wave of questionable or improper overseas payments, at least three research studies have been conducted. An examination of these studies reveals that large numbers of business executives believe that companies should pay bribes and kickbacks overseas if such practices are routine in the host country.

Conference Board Study

This research study surveyed seventy-three U.S. business leaders in the fall of 1975 to assess their policies and practices regarding unusual foreign payments.[3] Nearly half of the business leaders surveyed said that companies should make payoffs in countries where such practices are accepted. Three-quarters of the executives indicated that they had encountered demands from foreign officials or others for unusual payments, and 25% added that such demands were a problem for their industries as a whole.

The study also revealed that payoff pressures were more of a problem for certain types of companies than for others. The industries which seem most able to avoid payoff pressures are the consumer goods companies which do not deal with government agencies, and those best able to resist pressures are those with technology products or with especially strong market positions. Conversely, aerospace arms, whose customers often are governments, and pharmaceutical companies, often regulated by governments, are two industries which are subject to heavier than normal pressures for payoffs.

Payoff pressures are apparently heavier in certain parts of the world than others. The leading areas where U.S. companies encountered such pressures were Latin America and the Middle East, with the Far East, Africa and the developing countries not far behind.

Although the study was restricted to overseas payments, a few of the executives said that they believed there was no significant difference between U.S. business standards and those found in other countries. Moreover, 75% of the companies surveyed did not have written policy statements or guidelines on requests for unusual payments abroad.

The Conference Board report cautioned that while its survey of senior international executives represented a broad spectrum of companies across the nation, it should not be interpreted as being representative of all American companies. Nevertheless, the survey provided a rare indication of the extent of overseas bribery and of corporate attitudes toward foreign payoffs and bribery.

Opinion Research Study

The above startling results were confirmed by the Opinion Research Corporation study which was commissioned by Pitney-Bowes, Inc.[4] This study polled 531 top and middle managers on how they viewed the bribing of foreign officials by employees of U.S. corporations in attracting and retaining contracts. Although half of the business executives surveyed said that bribes should not be paid to foreign officials, 18% believed the latter should be paid if such practices were prevalent in the host country. Of those who condoned the practice, 47% indicated it was a cost of doing business in certain countries and 32% believed it was an established practice. In addition, 92% of the respondents did not believe legislation would effectively stop these practices. However, the executives believed that publicity would be effective in discouraging such bribery.

Marketing Management Study

A third survey was conducted by the *Sales and Marketing Management* (SMM) magazine.[5] This study polled 146 members of SMM's Leadership Panel in April 1976 to assess their attitudes and practices regarding overseas and domestic bribery. Slightly more than 40% of the panel's members responded to the survey.

The results were startling. When quizzed whether they or someone else in their company had been asked to make payments either abroad or in the United States, 22% of the respondents confirmed the overseas requests and almost 50% confirmed domestic requests. However, the overwhelming majority of respondents indicated that they would disapprove such requests domestically. The majority of respondents believed that U.S. firms would be put at a serious disadvantage should they be restricted from making such payments. In addition, though one-third of the respondents opposed governmental action to control overseas bribery, the majority believed that companies should attempt to agree voluntarily not to make such payments.

Currently, the Federal Trade Commission (FTC) and the Robinson-Patman Act prohibit commercial bribery in the United States on grounds of unfair methods of competition. Even though the SMM study revealed the existence of domestic commercial bribery, the FTC is reluctant to initiate a probe, claiming that it would duplicate other federal agency activities.

Although the fact of bribery has been admitted by some American multinational companies, the specifics in most cases remain ill defined. They remain obscure because law enforcement agencies in the United States have not yet completed their investigations. Yet some of the abuses detailed by the various investigations include illegal political contributions, huge payoffs made to foreign officials to gain sales or favorable treatment abroad, secret company slush funds, dummy foreign subsidiaries, numbered Swiss bank accounts and doctored corporate books. For example, the Securities and Exchange Commission (SEC) accused General Tire and Rubber Co. of a wide array of foreign and domestic payoffs, including some to get off the Arab boycott list.

SEC Investigations

The SEC has uncovered many bribery activities in following up domestic illegalities in the Watergate affair. Even though there is nothing in U.S. law that prohibits the payment of a bribe to a foreign official, there is a great deal of legislation that makes it a criminal offense for a company to disguise or omit such payments from its shareholders' accounts. More specifically, it is illegal for any corporation subject to the jurisdiction of the U.S. securities acts to fail to include and to describe accurately all payments, including bribes, payoffs, kickbacks, or other improper payments to foreign government officials, or any political contributions, in its various statements and periodic reports to the SEC and shareholders required by those acts. It is also illegal for any such corporation to finance such payments through secret slush funds or phony offshore corporate entities outside the normal system of financial accountability described by those acts.

Unfortunately, it cannot be said that the practice of making questionable payments abroad is confined to a few wayward companies. In early March 1976, the SEC was investigating eighty-four publicly held companies, whose 1974 revenues amounted to more than $200 billion. Forty-five of these companies were included in the *Fortune* 500 list of the largest enterprises in the United States.

More recently, the SEC introduced its "voluntary" program, which urges corporations to disclose illegal, improper or questionable payments abroad rather than be discovered by investigators. The SEC clearly held out the prospect that it might go easy on those that volunteered. A company had to pledge that it would not repeat the offending acts; and it had to undertake a thorough investigation of what had occurred. As a result, many companies have opened their books to complete reauditing of their financial returns over the last several years. Though this voluntary program applies only to companies listed on the American stock exchanges, there is reason to believe that this policy will have widespread effects and result in a general raising of ethical standards.

Prodded by the SEC, the New York Stock Exchange also is becoming a leader of the antibribery campaign. The NYSE has proposed that each listed company should be ordered to have an audit committee that is dominated by outside directors by the end of 1977. This would be a fierce deterrent to the use of bribery as a business practice. Under existing securities laws, members of audit committees who conceal improper payments risk going to jail for withholding material facts from shareholders.

IRS Audits

Escaping prosecution from the SEC does not mean the companies are free from prosecution by the IRS. According to the IRS, it is illegal for a U.S. corporation to deduct as an ordinary business expense on its U.S. income tax returns any improper payments to foreign government officials, whatever the label or justification, or any political contributions, whether lawful or not. Currently, the IRS is pushing a "large case audit" program against companies with more than $250 million in assets.

There is reason to believe that rulings by the SEC and IRS put American companies at a disadvantage in international competition. Both Britain and Germany, for example, allow companies to deduct on their tax returns at least some kind of payoffs abroad. But the IRS will not allow deduction of any payments abroad that would be illegal in the United States, even though they may be legal where they are paid. The SEC's disclosure requirements also make it difficult for U.S. companies to pay large bribes or kickbacks abroad.

Justice, Defense Warnings

The Departments of Justice and Defense also are warning companies that they are considering bribing charges outside the realms of breaking the tax or securities laws. The Antitrust Division of the Justice Department is likely to examine whether payments abroad by U.S. firms were used to block out other American companies or tie up a scarce commodity. The Department of Defense launched its own probe to ascertain the legitimacy of commissions paid to middlemen in negotiating the sale of military aircraft and hardware. The Defense Department also is reviewing its agreement with some two dozen companies to determine whether any may have charged Defense for "overhead expenses" under their contracts to provide some of the money they poured into political payoffs.

Congressional Inquiries

The Senate Foreign Relations Subcommittee was quick to hold public hearings on the leads developed by the SEC. Moreover, a parade of companies is being brought before the Senate Subcommittee on Multinational Corporations as well as the Senate Banking Committee. Testimonies before the committees have revealed specific cases of huge payoffs to foreign officials and concealed donations to foreign political parties, including the Italian Communists.

Cabinet-Level Task Force

To the growing list of federal agencies and congressional committees investigating improper payments made overseas by American corporations, President Gerald Ford added his own blue-ribbon, cabinet-level panel. Its chairman is Secretary of Commerce Elliot Richardson. The panel will supervise the investigations going on at the SEC, the IRS and the Justice Department, as well as recommend what, if anything, can be done to stop such practices in the future.

Legislative Action

Since the advent of the current wave of bribery scandals, there has been a growing outcry in Washington for a new law that would prohibit U.S. corporations from engaging in bribery and political payoffs abroad. Currently, there are at least four antibribery measures that have either been enacted or are being considered by Congress.[6]

The Arms-Sales Measure

Congress has passed an arms-sales law compelling disclosure of consultant fees to the State Department and in some cases to law enforcement agencies and Congress. The law covers government-to-government sales as well as company-to-government transactions. Business representatives claim that the new law will adversely affect U.S. corporations because foreign

firms can bribe at will. Where arms are not involved, a variety of measures have been proposed, and one has been included in the Tax Reform Act. Currently, only two antibribery bills are under serious consideration: one is sponsored by the U.S. Senate, and another is from the Ford Administration.

Tax Reform Act

The Tax Reform Act requires that earnings equal to the bribe be repatriated and taxed by the United States. Previously, the law stipulated that such bribes were not deductible but it permitted deferral of tax on the money. The bribery provision was one of two related Senate proposals denying tax benefits for U.S. companies abroad. The other proposal would deny three foreign tax benefits to the U.S. companies that comply with the Arab boycott of Israel—the foreign tax credit, tax deferral on overseas earnings and DISC benefits for exports.[7]

Senate's Antibribery Bill

The Senate approved a bill outlawing bribery of foreign officials by U.S. companies. The bill, sponsored by Senate Banking Committee Chairman William Proxmire, would outlaw: (1) any payments to induce foreign officials to assist a company by not carrying out their duties, (2) payments to third parties when the U.S. company knows "or has reason to know" that the ultimate recipient will be a government official, and (3) payments to foreign political parties and candidates with the aim of influencing government business transactions. There is reason to believe that the wording is intended to exempt any foreign payments "extorted" from U.S. companies or the lubricating payments traditionally demanded by foreign government officials to speed up customs clearance, mail delivery and other routine government functions.

The Justice Department will enforce the legislation as it applies to unregistered companies by imposing criminal penalties of up to $10,000, two years in prison, or both. In addition, SEC-registered companies would be subject to the civil and criminal penalties already available to the commission under its existing authority. But Roderick Hills, SEC chairman, opposes such an enforcement role for the agency for two major reasons. First, during its forty-year history, the

SEC has been concerned basically with adequate disclosure by corporations of information deemed important to investors. Second, it would be difficult for the SEC to judge whether foreign payments actually represented bribes.

In another action, the Senate rejected a payments disclosure proposal introduced by Senator Frank Church. The proposal would have required companies whose stock is registered with the SEC to tell the agency about any "contribution, payment, gift, commission or anything of value" disbursed abroad in connection with a sale. The SEC would have been required to keep these reports in a public file. The proposal also would have given a U.S. company the right to sue a bribe-paying domestic competitor for triple damages on grounds it lost foreign business because of the competitor's bribes.

The Administration's Bill

Secretary of Commerce Elliot Richardson, who headed the administration's task force on questionable corporate payments abroad, objected that the Senate's bill was unworkable. Enforcement of a criminal bar against foreign bribes would be very difficult, if not impossible. Witnesses and information might prove to be beyond the reach of U.S. courts, and foreign governments might refuse to cooperate on grounds of national sovereignty. Therefore, the Ford Administration presented its own antibribery bill.

The administration's bill would not outlaw payoffs to foreign officials. It would require U.S. corporations operating abroad to report to the Commerce Secretary both proper and improper payments, although it is intended the Secretary of Commerce would issue regulations exempting small payments and taxes. Reports of payments, including names of recipients, would be kept confidential by the Commerce Secretary for one year, although they would be available earlier to the State and Justice Departments, the Internal Revenue Service, and the Securities and Exchange Commission, and could be made available earlier to foreign governments.

By confessing its misdeed, the U.S. corporation would gain immunity from prosecution at home. However, the administration's bill proposes a $100,000 civil penalty for failing to disclose payments or to keep certain records and up to

$500,000 criminal fine for deliberately failing to disclose. Corporate officers convicted of deliberate violations could get up to three years in jail. In reality, the administration's bill suffers the weakness of expecting companies to report their own misdeeds, and the Senate's bill is probably unenforceable.

Self-Regulation

Some analysts acknowledge that bribery disclosure by the SEC and other government agencies, as well as corporate investigations triggered by those disclosures, have been accompanied by an increased demonstration of corporate self-regulation. Consequently, they argue that the government has done enough and that business, at least for now, should be left to reform itself. Indeed, the advent of the current wave of bribery scandals has led to an upsurge in self-regulatory activity on several levels.

National Code of Business Ethics

The idea of a national code of business ethics has drawn a number of supporters. W. Michael Blumenthal, chairman and president of Bendix Corp., proposed that a group of business executives devise such a national code of conduct. The code would correspond to the standards of other professional associations such as the American Medical Association, which sets minimal standards of behavior.

Reactions to drafting such a national code are mixed. Theologians and academic experts generally applaud the idea, but some sympathetic observers, including this author, wonder if many corporations are really ready to embrace a national code of ethics and make it stick. There is reason to believe that most executives will pay little attention to codes other than the ones companies formulate for themselves.

The idea of a national code of business ethics is not new, of course. For instance, the electrical equipment price-fixing scandals of the early 1960s triggered a barrage of criticism from the press and the public, and soon afterwards an ethics advisory council of top business leaders was set up under the Commerce Department. In 1962, the group presented a proposed code to President John F. Kennedy, but after his assassination, the Johnson

Administration, seeking business support, let the code die.

Company Codes of Ethics

In more recent years, company codes have come into fashion, as they do after nearly every major business scandal. Responding to the current wave of corporate payoff scandals, dozens of major companies are issuing written rules governing corporate ethical questions, or are revising long-standing codes of conduct to cover new problems. Most of the codes being drafted now concentrate on two areas of current controversy: political contributions and overseas payments to increase sales.

The existing codes of conduct vary widely in form and content. They range from the terse, one-page "Statement of Business Principles" recently issued by Gulf's new chairman, to the handsomely packaged, ten-page "Code of Worldwide Business Conduct" issued by Caterpillar Co. in late 1974. As one of the earliest comprehensive codes, the Caterpillar document has become a model of sorts for some of the companies currently drafting codes.

Codes of ethics require something more than the recent public relations announcements of companies rushing to "reemphasize long-standing policy." To develop effective codes of business ethics, companies should ascertain that the sales and profit goals can be attained by current ethical business practices. Unrealistic goals might induce subordinates to resort to under-the-table deals in order to attain the chief executive's targets. A study by the American Management Association of 3,000 executives showed that most felt they were under pressure to compromise their personal standards to meet company goals.[8] Pressure for results, as narrowly measured in money terms, has increased. As firms become larger, more decentralized, and under absentee ownership, performance is measured in numbers and not by broader or more humane criteria.

The real test of codes will come in their strenuous enforcement and prompt disciplinary action. Any code of ethical behavior is unlikely to be observed unless the chief executive declares that violators will be punished. When a company fails to take strict action, many employees may assume that unethical acts are accepted standards of corporate behavior. One strict disciplinary measure may include dismissal at any level, commensurate with the degree of transgression. For instance, except for a few spectacular resignations of top executives at companies such as Gulf Oil and Lockheed, very few executives involved in briberies have been fired, demoted or even transferred. Another control measure may require all responsible members of management to sign annual pledges that they have followed the rules in the company's ethics code.

Public Speeches by Executives

A number of business leaders, sensing rising public hostility and fearing that all companies could be tarred with the same brush if business merely closes ranks and shrugs off the subject, have begun to speak out for business to reform itself and raise its ethical standards. For example, Fred T. Allen, chairman and president of Pitney-Bowes, took a challenging position in his speech to the American Chamber of Commerce in Zurich, Switzerland.[9] He emphasized that corporate morality begins at the top and added, ". . . those of us who have devoted our lives to the responsible growth and profitability of large corporations are, again, thought of—collectively—as little if any better than 'the robber barrons' of an earlier era."

Trade Associations' Views

The International Trade Club of Chicago, the nation's largest professional association of international trade executives, recently issued a position paper condemning illegal and unethical conduct in international trade and investment. Since its founding in 1919, the club has encouraged international trade management on a high ethical plane; it repeated its policy because of current public attitudes triggered by revelations of alleged corrupt practices involving U.S. multinationals abroad. In addition to the above position paper, several other trade associations, including the U.S. Chamber of Commerce, have issued policy statements on business payments abroad.

International Cooperation

No amount of U.S. regulation of companies subject to the jurisdiction of the SEC and the IRS can achieve a comprehensive long-run solution to the problem of transnational bribery. Consequently, some analysts believe that solutions to such problems can only be achieved through international cooperation. The United States has taken a number of initiatives that might lead to such cooperation.

OECD Guidelines

The Ministerial Conference of the Organization for Economic Cooperation and Development (OECD) recently adopted a document concerning rules for multinational corporations on issues ranging from bribery to restrictive business practices and disclosure of information. These voluntary guidelines are a product of more than a year's work by an OECD committee. The bribery section has been notably strengthened due to the insistence of the United States. Consequently, the guidelines call on multinational corporations not to render "any bribe or other improper benefit, direct or indirect, to any public servant" and to "abstain from any improper" political involvement. While this code of ethics does not possess statutory binding power or punitive rules, its significance lies in the fact that this is the first time that an international organization has worked out such guidelines for multinational corporations.

International Chamber Commission

The Paris-based International Chamber of Commerce, which represents multinational companies, has set up a commission headed by Lord Showcross, chairman of the City of London's panel on take-overs and mergers, to recommend guidelines for ethical business practices.

United Nations' Role

The United States proposed an international agreement at a meeting of the U.N. Center on Transnational Corporations in March 1976 in Lima, Peru. More specifically, the United States supplied the initiative for negotiations to curb bribery. It called for steps by governments to punish violators, to establish clear guidelines on the use of business agents, and to cooperate in exchanging information. Governments of developing nations seem anxious to sidestep the question, which they turned over to the U.N. Economic and Social Council for discussion as a separate issue.

Stringent Auditing Standards

According to official rules of the SEC and the American Institute of Certified Public Accountants (AICPA), an auditor is not required to disclose il-

legal political contributions or massive slush funds made by his client.[10] Consequently, when Price Waterhouse discovered that United Brands paid a bribe of $1.25 million to a Honduras official, the auditors did not require disclosure for fear of jeopardizing the company's operations in Latin America. As a matter of fact, when the auditors' decision was discussed with the SEC, the commission did not object.

AICPA Proposals

In light of this incident, the AICPA auditing standards executive committee has drafted guidelines governing auditors' conduct upon the discovery of illegal payments by a corporation during the course of an audit.[11] In addition to reiterating traditional auditing procedures, the proposed guidelines discuss the controversial questions of "materiality"—what is important enough to require disclosure or special provision in the financial statements. The guidelines direct auditors to consider not merely the dollar amount of an illegal payment but also "the related contingent monetary effects" such as fines, penalties and damages, and such "loss contingencies" as expropriation. The guidelines also indicate that if a substantial amount of business depends on paying a bribe, that risk might have to be disclosed.

The proposed guidelines stipulate that when an auditor comes across a "material" illegal act, he must promptly report it to a company official who can do something about it. If the illegal act then is not properly disclosed or accounted for, the auditor should give a qualified or adverse audit opinion, which presumably would bring the illegal act to light. When an auditor stumbles upon illegal acts that are "immaterial" financially, he should consider resigning if he fails to persuade the client company to take remedial action.

Overall, the proposed guidelines do not extend the traditional auditing doctrine very far. They explicitly state that the auditor is under no legal obligation to notify outside parties. The proposed guidelines rely on the company to reveal any "immaterial illegal act to the authorities or other outsiders."

Recent IRS Measures

The IRS decided to direct eleven questions on bribery, slush funds and overseas bank accounts to corporate managers when reviewing a company's tax return, hoping to get honest answers. As a check, the agency decided to put the same questions to the outside accountants who audit the company's books. However, accountants strongly opposed the idea of bringing auditors under the IRS investigatory umbrella. They were so infuriated that AICPA sent a delegation to Washington to protest to the IRS commissioner. Consequently, the IRS backed off on its new policy and accepted a compromise under which the accountants are to sign a letter stating that, to the best of their knowledge, belief and recollection, management's answers to the eleven questions are accurate.

Recent SEC Guidelines

After over a year of study, the Securities and Exchange Commission has put in writing its guidelines for disclosure of illegal or questionable corporate payments and practices. The report lists several factors which should be considered when deciding if disclosure is necessary, including the amount of payments, their legality and the awareness or participation of top management. Also important is whether accounting records were falsified and whether the questionable conduct has ceased.

When disclosure is appropriate, the SEC believes these matters should be discussed:

the existence, amount, duration and purpose of payments

the role of management

tax consequences

information as to lines of business to which the payments relate

the company's intention to continue or terminate payments

potential impact on the business of cessation of payments

method of effecting the payments.

To help curb questionable corporate conduct, the SEC proposes an amendment to the Securities Exchange Act of 1934, requiring registrants to maintain accurate accounting records and an adequate system to internal accounting controls, and making it unlawful to falsify records or give false information to an accountant.

Because of the current wave of bribery scandals, this author speculates that the U.S. government will introduce stringent antibribery regulations which go far beyond the actions of any other country, and that American firms will pursue at least six strategies in dealing with the overseas bribery issues.

Strategy 1. Companies will continue to sell their products abroad without bribery because of their strong market positions, their advanced technology, and/or because their products are greatly in demand. Due to their unique positions, these firms will continue to resist payoff pressures.

Strategy 2. Some companies will not be pressured to pay bribes abroad due to their low profiles and indistinct images. For example, Ingersoll-Rand Co. claims that it is relatively immune from direct solicitations of bribe-takers due to its low profile. However, this immunity may fade away in the long run as these corporations become more conspicuous.

Strategy 3. Companies will continue to pay bribes to minor officials overseas whenever the practice is considered a normal way of conducting business. For example, Vetco Offshore Industries, Inc., adopted a corporate policy prohibiting payments to foreign officials in countries whose governments begin prosecuting the practice. However, in countries where "grease" is a normal practice, Vetco considers such payments legal, even if, in fact, illegal by law. More specifically, Vetco will continue its payments under three circumstances: where payments are widespread and an acceptable business practice; where reasonable alternatives do not exist; and where discontinuance of the payments might inhibit the conduct of Vetco's business.

Strategy 4. As a result of the proposed antibribery regulations, some companies will cease paying bribes abroad even where it is acceptable practice. By ceasing to conform to payoff customs of host countries, these American companies complain that they will suffer a competitive disadvantage because foreign competitors in the same markets will continue to offer bribes. Consequently, the SEC and the U.S. Treasury Department are studying three alternatives to make foreign companies as clean as American ones:

Disclosure. The 116 foreign companies listed on stock exchanges in the United States can, under securities laws, be required to disclose improper payments the same as domestic corporations are required to do. Thus far, a half-dozen companies have volunteered such reports. For example, Imperial Chemical Industries Ltd., a British concern, has disclosed "questionable" payments of $2.4 million since 1972 through mid-1976.

Retaliatory Trade Practices. The President's existing powers can be used to discourage or prevent the import of products of foreign entities which have engaged in unfair competitive practices, or products of those countries which tolerate or encourage such conduct.

Federal Procurement Practices. The federal government could boycott foreign companies that make improper payments while competing with American companies. The SEC notes that executive branch agencies have sufficient economic authority to reject, as against the public interest, bids and offers from such companies.

The SEC concedes that reliance on the disclosure rules has several limitations; obviously, only firms registered with the commission would be affected. The commission also admits that it has limited investigative and enforcement powers over transactions between foreign parties. The chief sanction against a foreign issuer of shares or bonds in the United States would probably be to suspend trading in its securities or rescind the securities' registration.

Consequently, trade reprisals as well as a blackball by the federal government on corrupt companies might be the most compelling means of discouraging bribery by foreign firms. Most major government procurement contracts contain a clause granting the comptroller-general direct access to the books and records of the contractor. This requirement is usually waived for foreign contracts, but the SEC suggests the President could direct government agencies to insist on inspection, thereby providing additional enforcement leverage.

Strategy 5. Companies will avoid the antibribery regulations in the United States by exporting through their foreign subsidiaries in Western Europe where antibribery statutes are less stringent. For example, even though the German domestic antibribery regulations correspond to those in the United States, the Germans are far more tolerant of foreign bribery, which is deductible from income tax.

There is strong reason to believe that some American business abroad may be lost as a result of this strategy, and a reduction in foreign trade may have at least two serious economic consequences. First, the United States may lose a portion of its foreign exchange earnings which are badly needed to pay for the ever-increasing purchases of imported oil. Second, since many American jobs are related to international trade, unemployment may reach unnerving peaks.

Strategy 6. The aerospace and defense-related industries could take advantage of the Webb-Pomerene Act which allows consortia of American exporters to enter joint bids in seeking foreign contracts. This would avoid the ironic and unethical use of commissions and kickbacks given to foreign buyers by one American company to beat out another American firm in a field where little if any real competition exists.

Corporate directors and officers are finding themselves in a vulnerable position as a result of the ongoing ballyhoo over questionable overseas payments. Though bribery is illegal and unethical in the United States, it is both customary and ethical in other countries. Consequently, American executives are being caught between the ethical standards of two cultures. American executives who pay bribes when local conditions seem to demand it can scarcely be accused of degrading the pure, since corporate payoffs are seen in many countries as venial sins, or even normal courtesies.[12] On the other hand, a few countries have implemented various antibribery measures. For example, foreign investors in Iran are confronted with a new anticorruption regulation that requires foreign companies to sign an affidavit testifying that no payoffs or kickbacks would be made to brokers or agents connected with a contract award.[13] Though this antibribery measure applies only to foreign investors in Iran, there is reason to believe that this policy will have widespread effects and result in a general raising of ethical standards if other countries follow Iran's footsteps.

Notes

1. Joseph M. Waldman, "A Primer on Corruption," *Business Studies* (Spring 1973), p. 28.

2. Peter Nehemkis, "Business Payoffs Abroad: Rhetoric and Reality," *California Management Review* (Winter 1975), pp. 7 and 9.

3. James R. Basche, Jr., *Unusual Foreign Payments: A Survey of the Policies and Practices of U.S. Companies* (New York: The Conference Board Record, 1976).

4. *Executive Attitudes Toward Morality in Business* (Princeton, N.J.: Caravan Surveys, Opinion Research Corporation, July 1975); and Fred T. Allen, "Corporate Morality: Executive Responsibility," *Atlanta Economic Review* (May–June 1976), p. 9.

5. James D. Synder, "Bribery in Selling: The Scandal Comes Home," *Sales and Marketing Management* (May 10, 1976), pp. 35–38.

6. Editor's note: As indicated in the chapter, bribery overseas is now illegal.

7. Jack G. Kaikati, "The Challenge of the Arab Boycott," *Sloan Management Review* (Winter 1977).

8. "After Watergate: Putting Business Ethics in Perspective," *Business Week* (September 15, 1973), p. 178.

9. Allen, "Corporate Morality."

10. "Are Auditors Required to Report Their Clients' Bribes?" *The CPA Journal* (September 1975), p. 59.

11. *Proposed Statement on Auditing Standards: Illegal Acts by Clients* (New York: The Auditing Standards Executive Committee of the American Institute of Certified Public Accountants, April 30, 1976).

12. See, for example, Ronald Wraith and Edgar Simpkins, *Corruption in Developing Countries* (New York: W. W. Norton, 1964); and Victor T. LeVine, *Political Corruption: The Ghana Case* (Stanford, Calif.: Hoover Institute Press, 1975).

13. Jack G. Kaikati, "Doing Business in Iran: The Fastest Growing Import Market Between Europe and Japan," *Atlanta Economic Review* (September–October 1976), p. 19.

For Further Reading

Behrman, J. N. *Some patterns in the rise of the multinational enterprise.* Chapel Hill: University of North Carolina Press, 1964.

Dymsza, W. A. *Multinational business strategy.* New York: McGraw-Hill, 1972.

Folsom, M. R. *Executive decision making.* New York: McGraw-Hill, 1962.

Vernon, R. *Sovereignty at bay: The multinational spread of U.S. enterprises.* New York: Basic Books, 1971.

Wright, M. A. *The business of business.* New York: McGraw-Hill, 1967.

Part III
BUSINESS AND SOCIETY

In Part II we considered some important recurring moral concerns that face business people as they function within organizations. But business people must deal with other concerns born from the relationship between business and society. Specifically, business people, on both personal and organizational levels, confront issues of moral concern that relate directly to the role that business plays in the social system.

In this part of the book we will consider some social issues with profound moral overtones for business. We will concentrate our energies on three major social issues: consumerism, women and other disadvantaged groups, and the environment. We will attempt to establish organizational responsibilities in these areas and, in keeping with the thrust of this text, try to develop some parameters within which business can define and assign responsibilities for tackling these issues of high social concern.

7

BUSINESS AND THE CONSUMER

On July 2, 1973, the Food and Drug Administration (FDA) removed Pertussin Medicated Vaporizer from market shelves because the product was suspected in the deaths of eighteen people.

In the ten years that Pertussin Medicated Vaporizer had been available, shoppers who read the can's label found nothing to make them wary of the product's contents. On the contrary, Pertussin spray claimed to "build a roomful of relief" from colds and hay fever. Its directions encouraged the spraying of the product on handkerchiefs, in rooms, and even on pillows and sheets. "Repeat as often as necessary" and "safe even in the nursery" seemed to reassure even the most skeptical of shoppers. For its ingredients, Pertussin listed the harmless menthol and oil of eucalyptus.

How could eighteen people possibly die after using such an innocuous product? They apparently ingested the propellants and solvents the product contained. It seems that Pertussin failed to indicate that menthol and oil of eucalyptus made up only 12 percent of the total ingredients. The remaining 88 percent consisted of propellants and solvents. Nor did the manufacturer mention that these chemicals broke down about equally between fluorocarbons and trichloroethane, which tend to upset the heartbeat and depress other vital activities such as breathing. It was these chemicals that were implicated in the deaths of eighteen people.

The Pertussin case raises a host of questions, among them whether consumers had a right to know that the vaporizer contained propellants and solvents. It's easy to respond with a vigorous yes *after the fact*. But what about before these tragedies occurred? Were the manufacturers of Pertussin morally obliged to provide this information to consumers, even if they sincerely believed that the risks consumers were running were minimal and remote? Any answer to this specific question must involve some general concept of business responsibilities to consumers, of consumer rights. In other words, before we can determine whether the manufacturer of Pertussin was morally bound to inform consumers completely about its product, we must first determine whether business has a general obligation to provide such information to consumers.

This chapter focuses the question of business's responsibilities to consumers. If business does have responsibilities, what are they and how can business discharge them morally? In effect, we'll be examining the relationship between business and one of its primary claimants, the consumer. In so doing, we'll look at many of the techniques and practices apparent in the marketplace, and examine the moral issues that they raise. But essentially we'll be trying to isolate broad areas of business responsibility to consumers.

Consumerism

The relationship between business and the consumer is one that has come under intense scrutiny in recent years with the growth of consumerism. *Consumerism is a movement to protect consumers from the products they buy and use.* Consumer advocates seek protection not only against dangers and frauds but also against deceptive advertising, concealed facts, gross distortions, mislabeling or incomplete labeling, fine print warranties and guarantees, and any business practice that could endanger consumer interests. In earlier days the watchword in the marketplace was *caveat emptor* ("Let the buyer beware"), but today the responsibility for consumer interests is more and more the realm of business.

The literature of consumerism is generally agreed on broad areas of business responsibility to consumers. We can conveniently structure our discussion around these areas and suggest the moral concerns that arise within them.

Areas of Business Responsibility to Consumers

Most consumer advocates and commentators on the business scene view business responsibilities to consumers as falling into four main categories: needs, information, safety, and quality. Let's consider each of these.

Needs

Business's responsibility for understanding and providing for consumer needs derives from the fact that citizen-consumers are completely dependent on business to satisfy their needs. This dependence is particularly true in our highly technological society, characterized as it is by a complex economy, intense specialization, and urban concentration. Contrast these conditions with those prevailing in the United States when the country was primarily agrarian, composed of people who could satisfy most of their own needs. In those times one had little difficulty practicing the virtues of self-reliance, independence, and rugged individualism in providing for oneself and one's family.

Today, however, we find ourselves parts of an economic and social network of interdependency. More and more we rely on others to provide the wherewithal for our survival and prosperity. We no longer make our own clothing, produce our own food, provide our own transportation, manufacture our own tools, or construct our own homes. At one time Americans could provide their own entertainment, but today's urban sprawl has in many instances covered recreational commons. Whereas once opportunities for exercise and recreation were as near as the front door, now they're often only as near (or as far) as gyms, health spas, tracks, bike paths, or other designated zones of exercise. In short, today's citizen-consumers are utterly dependent on the goods and services business provides to satisfy their maintenance and actualizing needs. This dependency makes business responsible for understanding and providing for these needs.

Obviously business alone does not shoulder the responsibility for our total well-being, but it does carry the lion's share for determining what commodities to produce and in what numbers, how these will be produced and for whom. But responsibilities for production decisions in the operation of a market economy cannot be divorced from the problems of procuring raw materials to sustain the consumer's society. Already the United States lacks the domestic reserves to meet more than only a small and shrinking fraction of American needs. Where will we get the raw materials U.S. industry needs to provide for domestic needs? The answer seems to lie in the Third World nations of Asia, Africa, and Latin America. If this is so, serious moral concerns will inevitably arise.

To catch the flavor of these concerns, consider that in 1952 the President's Materials Policy Commission opened its report with the question: "Has the United States of America the material means to sustain its civilization?" Its answer was that the United States depended on foreign sources for all important industrial resources with the exceptions of molybdenum and magnesium. The commission, headed by then Chairman of the Board of Columbia Broadcasting System (CBS) William S. Paley, attempted to predict American demand for natural resources over the next quarter of a century and to counsel the president on measures necessary to secure them. In essence, the commission forecast that materials would be available but our domestic reserves would not be enough to meet our needs. Presumably what we lacked would be furnished by Third World nations. This is precisely what's occurring today, and we assume will continue. But in numerous Asian, African, and Latin American countries native populations are making intense demands on available natural resources. Imagine what would happen if those countries' standards of living rose significantly. Their own demands for natural resources would rise commensurately, thus leaving less to be exported to satisfy our needs. In effect, we're faced with a situation in which increased living levels for Third World countries cannot be sustained while assuring the same standards for developed countries like the United States.[1] Securing the continued availability of foreign resources, then, may require political and economic domination of Third World countries, a domination exercised against the fundamental rights and perhaps interests of their populations.

So, while business's responsibility to understand and provide for consumer

1. *For a discussion of these matters, see Heather Dean,* Scarce Resources: The Dynamics of American Imperialism *(Detroit: The Radical Education Project, 1966).*

needs seems a harmless abstraction, it is fraught with serious moral overtones, which often spill beyond our own territorial limits. In the years to come, these moral overtones seem destined to become a full-fledged moral dilemma at home and abroad, a dilemma that business will and must play a large part in resolving.

Information

The responsibility to provide consumers with product information derives from much of what we've just said. The complex and highly specialized nature of today's economy makes it impossible for consumers to become self-made experts on all the products and services they need. Without enormous business input consumers can't even become knowledgeable. Because business is often the sole source of consumer information, it has an obligation to provide *clear*, *accurate*, and *adequate* product and service information.

When business communicates clearly, it does so in a direct, straightforward way, relying neither on deception nor psychological manipulation. When it communicates accurately, it provides truths, not half-truths; it avoids gross exaggeration and innuendo. When it communicates adequately, it provides consumers enough information to make the best choice with respect to quality and price. The nature of these descriptions should indicate that determining what's clear, accurate, and adequate communication isn't easy. Perhaps the best way of illuminating these obligations is to consider marketing areas where moral issues relative to information are present. Two of the main areas are advertising and labeling.

ADVERTISING.   Most moral issues related to advertising exist because of a conflict between its informative and persuasive functions. On the one hand, advertising functions to provide consumers information about the goods and services available to them. On the other hand, it serves to persuade them to purchase one product rather than another. These two functions are not always compatible. In an attempt to persuade, advertisers often obfuscate, misrepresent, or even lie. Specifically, moral issues arise when, in an attempt to persuade, advertisers are ambiguous, conceal facts, exaggerate, or employ psychological appeals. Let's look at each of these aspects of advertising.

AMBIGUITY.   *When ads are ambiguous, they can be taken to mean more than one thing.* Suppose, for example, a government study found that Grit filter cigarettes were lower in tar and nicotine than its filter-tip competitors. As part of its advertising, Grit claims, "Government Supported Grit Filters." "Supported" here is ambiguous. It can not only mean that government research supports Grit's claim that it's lower in tar and nicotine than its competitors but also that the government endorses the use of Grit. The Continental Baking Company was charged with such ambiguity by the Federal Trade Commission (FTC). In advertising its Profile Bread, Continental implied that using the bread would lead to weight loss. The fact was that Profile had about the same number of calories per ounce as other breads but each slice contained seven fewer calories only because it was sliced thinner than most breads. Continental issued a corrective advertisement.

In all aspects of advertising, much potential moral danger lies in the interpretation. The Profile ad is a good example. A large number of people interpreted that ad to mean that eating Profile bread would lead to a weight loss.[2] Likewise, for years consumers have inferred from its advertisements that Listerine mouthwash effectively fought bacteria and sore throats. Not so; in 1978 the FTC ordered Listerine to run a multimillion-dollar disclaimer. In such cases, advertisers and manufacturers invariably deny intending the inference that consumers draw. But sometimes the ad is so ambiguous that a reasonable person couldn't infer anything else. Thus, when a cold tablet advertises, "At the first sign of a cold or flu—Coricidin," what is the consumer likely to infer? The fact is that neither Coricidin nor any other cold remedy can cure the common cold. At best they can only provide temporary symptomatic relief. The point is that consumers are left to draw their own conclusion, and it is likely to be the incorrect one.

Aiding and abetting ambiguity in ads is the use of "weasel" words, words used to evade or retreat from a direct or forthright statement or position. Consider the weasel *help*. *Help* means "aid" or "assist" and nothing else. Yet, as one author has observed, " 'help' is the one single word which, in all the annals of advertising, has done the most to say something that couldn't be said."[3] Since the word *help* is used to qualify, once it's used almost anything can be said after it. Thus, we're exposed to ads for products that "help us keep young," "help prevent cavities," "help keep our houses germ free." Consider for a moment how many times a day you hear or read phrases like these: "helps stop," "helps prevent," "helps fight," "helps overcome," "helps you feel," "helps you look." And, of course, "help" is hardly the only weasel. "Like," "virtual" or "virtually," "can be," "up to" (as in "provides relief *up to* eight hours"), "as much as" (as in "saves *as much as* one gallon of gas"), and numerous other weasels function to say what can't be said.

The fact that ads are open to interpretation doesn't exonerate advertisers from the obligation to provide clear information. Indeed, this fact intensifies the responsibility because the danger of misleading through ambiguity increases as the ad is subject to interpretation. At stake is not only people's money but also their health, loyalties, and expectations. The potential harm a misleading ad can cause is great, not to mention its cavalier treatment of the truth. For these reasons ambiguity in ads is of serious moral concern.

A final word about this topic. As far back as 1944 the United States Supreme Court, speaking about the issue of truthful advertisement, proposed a standard whose spirit might still be used in evaluating ads. In insisting on the literal truthfulness of an ad, the Court recommended "a form of advertising clear enough so that, in the words of the prophet Isaiah, 'wayfaring men, though fools, shall not err therein.' "[4]

2. See "Mea Culpa, Sort Of," Newsweek, *September 27, 1971, p. 98.*

3.   Paul Stevens, "Weasel Words: God's Little Helpers," *in* Language Awareness, *ed. Paul A. Eschhol, Alfred A. Rosa, Virginia P. Clark (New York: St. Martin's Press, 1974), p. 156.*

4.   "Charles of the Ritz District Corporation v. FTC, 143, F. 2d 276 (2d Cir. 1944)," *in David A. Aaken and George S. Day,* Consumerism: Search for the Consumer Interest *(New York: The Free Press, 1974), p. 140.*

CONCEALED FACTS. *When advertisers conceal facts, they suppress information which is unflattering to their products.* Put another way, a fact is concealed when its availability would probably make the desire, purchase, or use of the product less likely than in its absence. The case of Pertussin is a case in point. Surely if consumers had known of the potentially fatal ingredients that the vaporizer contained, they'd have been less likely to purchase the product than they apparently were. Concealed facts concern us in ethics not only because they can exploit by misleading as much as ambiguity can but also because they wantonly undermine truth telling.

Truth rarely seems foremost in the minds of advertisers. As Samm Sinclair Baker writes in *The Permissible Lie:* "Inside the agency the basic approach is hardly conducive to truth telling. The usual thinking in forming a campaign is first what can we say, true or not, that will sell the product best? The second consideration is, how can we say it effectively and get away with it so that (1) people who buy won't feel let down by too big a promise that doesn't come true, and (2) the ads will avoid quick and certain censure by the FTC."[5] In this observation we see the business person's tendency to equate what's legal with what's moral, an attitude we previously alluded to. It's precisely this outlook that leads to advertising behavior of dubious morality.

One needn't look far to find examples of concealed facts in ads. You may recall the old Colgate-Palmolive ad for its Rapid Shave Cream. It showed Rapid Shave being used to shave "sandpaper": "Apply, soak, and off in a stroke." This was an impressive ad for any man who's ever scraped his way awake. Unfortunately, what Colgate concealed was that the sandpaper was actually plexiglas and that actual sandpaper had to be soaked in Rapid Shave for about eighty minutes before it came off in a stroke.[6]

More recently Campbell vegetable soup ads showed pictures of a thick, rich brew calculated to whet even a gourmet's appetite. Supporting the soup were clear glass marbles deposited into the bowl to give the appearance of solidity.

Then there's the whole area of feminine deodorant sprays (FDS), one rife with concealed facts. Currently an industry in excess of $55 million, FDS ads not only fail to mention that such products in most cases are unnecessary but that they frequently produce unwanted side effects: itching, burning, blistering, and urinary infections. A Food and Drug Administration (FDA) "caution" now appears on these products.

If business has obligations to provide clear, accurate, and adequate information, we must wonder if it meets this charge when it hides facts relevant to the consumer's need and desire for or purchase of a product. Hiding facts raises serious moral concerns relative to truth telling and consumer exploitation. This exploitation takes the form of real injuries that can result to users of products and also of abridgements to consumers' personal freedom. When consumers are deprived of comprehensive knowledge about a product, their choices are constricted.

EXAGGERATION. *Advertisers can mislead through exaggeration, that is, making*

5. *Samm Sinclair Baker,* The Permissible Lie *(New York: World Publishing Co., 1968), p. 16.*

6. *Ibid.*

claims unsupported by evidence. For example, claims that a pain reliever provides "extra pain relief" or is "50% stronger than aspirin," that it "upsets the stomach less frequently," or that it's "superior to any other non-prescription pain killer on the market" fly in the face of evidence which indicates that all analgesics are effective to the same degree.[7]

In recent years the FTC has been making numerous companies substantiate their claims, as in the Profile and Listerine cases. In the tire industry, the FTC has questioned Goodyear's claim that its Double-Eagle Polysteel Tires can be driven over ax blades without suffering damage. It's also asked Sears, Roebuck and Company to prove its claim that its steel-belted radial tires can give 60,000 to 101,000 miles of service. In the auto industry, the FTC has questioned Volkswagen's claim that its squareback sedan gets about 25 miles per gallon and that it gives drivers 200 gallons of gas more a year compared with the average domestic compact. In addition, the FTC has asked General Motors to verify its claim that its Vega's ground beams provide more side-impact collision protection than those of any other comparable compact. And it has questioned Chrysler's claim that its electronic system never needs tuning.[8]

Clearly the line between deliberate deception and what advertising mogul David Ogilvy has termed "puffery" is not always clear. By *puffery* Ogilvy seems to mean the use of "harmless" superlatives. Thus advertisers frequently boast of the merits of their products by using words such as *best, finest,* or *most.* In many instances the use of such puffery is indeed harmless, as in the claim that a soap is the "best loved in America." Other times, however, it's downright misleading, as in the Dial soap ad which claimed that Dial was "the most effective deodorant soap you can buy." When asked to substantiate that claim, Armour-Dial Company insisted that it was not claiming product superiority; all it meant was that Dial soap was *as effective as* any other soap.

Of moral importance in determining the line between puffery and deliberate deception would seem to be the advertiser's intention and the likely interpretation of the ad. Are the claims intended as no more than verbal posturing, or are they intended to sell through deceptive exaggeration? Are advertisers primarily interested in saying as much as they can without drawing legal sanction or in providing consumers with accurate information? But even when the intention is harmless, advertisers must consider how the ad is likely to be interpreted. What conclusion is the general consuming public likely to draw about the product? Is that conclusion contrary to likely performance? Without raising questions like these about their ads, advertisers and manufacturers run risks of warping truth and injuring consumers, two significant moral concerns.

PSYCHOLOGICAL APPEALS.   *A psychological appeal is one that aims to persuade by appealing to human emotions and emotional needs, not to reason.* This is potentially the area of greatest moral concern in advertising. An automobile ad that presents the product in an elitist atmosphere peopled by members of the "in" set appeals to

7. *The editors of* Consumer Reports, The Medicine Show *(Mt. Vernon, N.Y.: Consumers Union, 1972), p. 14.*

8. *Fred Luthans and Richard M. Hodgetts,* Social Issues in Business *(New York: Macmillan, 1976), p. 353.*

our need and desire for status. A life insurance ad that portrays a destitute family woefully struggling in the aftermath of a provider's death aims to persuade through pity and fear, not sound argumentation. Reliance on such devices, while not per se unethical, raises moral concerns because rarely do such ads fully deliver what they promise.

Ads that rely extensively on pitches to power, prestige, sex, masculinity, femininity, acceptance, approval, and so on aim to sell more than a product. They're calculated to dispense psychological satisfaction. Some students of marketing claim that such ads appeal to the unconscious mind by taking a subliminal form. *Subliminal advertising would be advertising that communicates at a level beneath our conscious awareness, where some psychologists claim that the vast reservoir of human motivation primarily resides.* Most marketing people would likely deny that such advertising occurs. Author Wilson Bryan Key, who has extensively researched this topic, disagrees. Indeed, he goes so far as to claim: "It is virtually impossible to pick up a newspaper or magazine, turn on a radio or television set, read a promotional pamphlet or the telephone book, shop through a supermarket without having your subconscious purposely massaged by some monstrously clever artist, photographer, writer or technician."[9]

Concern with the serious nature of psychological appeals is what the California Wine Institute seemed to have in mind when it adopted an advertising code of standards. The following restrictions are included:

No wine ad shall present persons engaged in activities with appeal particularly to minors. Among those excluded: amateur or professional sports figures, celebrities, or cowboys; rock stars, race car drivers.

No wine ad shall exploit the human form or "feature provocative or enticing poses or be demeaning to any individual."

No wine ad shall portray wine in a setting where food is not presented.

No wine ad shall present wine in "quantities inappropriate to the situation."

No wine ads shall portray wine as similar to another type of beverage or product such as milk, soda, or candy.

No wine ad shall associate wine with personal performance, social attainment, achievement, wealth, or the attainment of adulthood.

No wine ad shall show automobiles in a way that one could construe their conjunction.

As suggested, the code seems particularly sensitive to the subtle implications that wine ads often carry. In a more general sense it alerts us to the psychological nuances of ads. In adopting such a rigorous code of advertising ethics, the California Wine Institute recognizes the inextricable connection between *what* is communicated and *how* it is communicated. In other words, as media expert Marshall McLuhan has for so long insisted, content cannot be distinguished from form, nor form from content. Sensitivity to this proposition

9. *Wilson Bryan Key,* Subliminal Seduction *(New York: New American Library, 1972), p. 11.*

would go far toward raising the moral recognition level in advertising and toward alerting business people to the moral overtones of psychological appeals.

In sum, people would agree that business has general responsibilities in the area of consumer information. It should provide clear, accurate, and adequate information about goods and services. Moral problems related to this obligation arise most frequently in advertising, specifically in the use of ambiguity, concealed facts, exaggeration, and psychological appeals. In addition to advertising, the area of labeling and packaging is the second primary area that raises consumer information concerns.

LABELING AND PACKAGING.   Business's general responsibility to provide clear, accurate, and adequate information undoubtedly applies to product labeling and packaging. The reason is that, despite the billions of dollars spent annually on advertising, a product's label and package remain the consumer's primary source of product information. Specifically, a product's label and package either succeed in providing or fail to provide information that consumers need to make the best choice of price and quality.

To illustrate the nature and dimensions of the moral overtones in this area, consider a representative study made up of five randomly selected housewife-shoppers.[10] Each shopper shared the characteristics of a college education and extensive family marketing experience. The five women were taken to a supermarket, where they were handed ten dollars each and asked to purchase fourteen items, the average number of purchases that shoppers make. When they finished, their selections were compared with the merchandise available in the supermarket. Of the seventy items chosen, thirty-six were the "best buys," that is, the most economical selections available of products of comparable quality. Even granting that the sample here is too small to draw firm conclusions, the results suggest that some shoppers are fooled by such things as labeling and packaging.

Language abuse partly accounts for consumer bewilderment in the marketplace. Frequently shoppers are mystified by terms such as *small*, *medium*, and *large*, by *economy size* and *serving*, as well as by the net quantities of the contents (ounces, pints, quarts, grams, etc.). Without a pocket computer consumers often find it difficult to calculate the relative prices of items. They can fall victim to terms and numbers, even though unit pricing is doing much to alleviate the problem.

What's more, although the Truth in Packaging Act (Fair Packaging and Labeling Act, 1966) empowers representative agencies to rank and list all ingredients in the order of decreasing percentage of total contents, wily marketers can sometimes circumvent this at the consumer's expense. For example, since sugar is the predominant ingredient in Shazam! breakfast cereal, it must be listed first. But breaking down sugar into its various forms—sucrose, glucose, fructose, lactose—by "precising" the sugar contents, the manufacturer of Shazam! can minimize the appearance of sugar in the product. Indeed, it can avoid the word

10.   E. B. Weiss, *"Marketers Fiddle While Consumers Burn,"* Harvard Business Review, July–August, 1968, p. 48.

sugar entirely. As a result, a consumer must not only guess at the amount of sugar in the product but must be something of a chemist to accomplish even this.

As with product information in advertising, the moral issues that packaging and labeling raise relate primarily to truth telling and consumer exploitation. Many persons would argue that sound moral judgments in this area must root in a profound desire to provide consumers information about the price, quality, and quantity of a product, so that they can make an intelligent choice. When marketers are interested primarily in selling a product and only secondarily in providing relevant information, then morally questionable practices are bound to follow. At the same time, those responsible for labeling and packaging would be well advised to consider at least the following questions, a negative answer to any of which could signal a moral problem. Have we clearly and specifically identified the product in an appropriate part of the label? Is the net quantity prominently located? Is it readily understandable to those wishing to compare prices? If a term such as *serving* is used, as in soups or puddings, is the net quantity of the serving stipulated? Are ingredients so listed as to be readily recognized and understood? (Some soft drinks crowd the ingredients list on their bottle caps in such small type that almost perfect eyesight is needed to read it.) Have we indicated and represented the percentage of the contents that is filler, for example, the bone in a piece of meat?

These questions represent only some that a moral person might ask. Obviously, product idiosyncrasy could raise others, as with meats when terms such as *prime, choice, graded,* and *ungraded* continue to mystify consumers. In the last analysis, moral evaluation of problems relative to labeling and packaging must be based on how well or poorly either provides clear, accurate, and adequate consumer information.

Together with advertising, then, product labeling and packaging represents an area of uppermost concern relative to consumer information. Although this responsibility is an important one, there are others that deserve equal consideration. One is consumer safety.

Safety

We have seen that the increasing complexity of today's economy and the growing dependence of consumers on business for their survival and enrichment have heightened business responsibilities in the area of consumer information. The same factors apply to product safety. From toys to tools, consumers use products believing that they won't be harmed or injured by them. Since consumers are not in a position of technical expertise to judge the sophisticated products which are necessary for contemporary life, they must rely primarily on the conscionable efforts of business to ensure consumer safety. This extreme dependency underscores business's obligations in the area of consumer safety.

Unfortunately, statistics indicate that the faith consumers must place in the manufacturers of products to ensure consumer safety is often misplaced. Currently over 20 million Americans per year require medical treatment from product-related accidents. Of these persons, 110,000 are permanently disabled and 30,000 die; in addition, roughly $5.5 billion is lost to the economy.[11] These figures are reason enough for emphasizing business's responsibility in this area, but there's another reason that bears directly on the self-interests of the firm.

Today consumers who suffer product-related injuries and sue have a good chance of winning. In recent years courts have become especially liberal in awarding damages. A remarkable example is the recent case of a California youth who was tragically burned over 80 percent of his body as a result of an auto accident in which the gas tank of his car exploded. A court held Ford Motor Company accountable for the potentially dangerous location of the tank and awarded the young man in excess of $20 million. Ford is appealing the decision.

In addition, today under the doctrine of privity of contract, an injured consumer may sue any or all persons in the product distribution chain of command. The doctrine once stressed direct contractual relationships, holding that producers could avoid responsibility for product failure if a product was purchased from someone other than the producer. But the doctrine of privity of contract has been expanded. Today it includes persons who endorse products, such as celebrities. Also, under strict liability laws, manufacturers have limited liability for unfit or unsafe products that injure consumers or workers. What's more, negligence does not have to be proved. Suit can be brought as long as it can be established that the manufacturers made a defective or unsafe product. In effect, strict liability laws ensure that the cost of product-related injuries will be borne by the manufacturers of a product rather than by the injured party. The point is, business owes it to itself and its stockholders to be safety conscious, apart from any concerns for protecting consumers.

When discussions of product safety arise, such glamour items as the automobile attract the most attention. While it's true that in the area of product safety consumerism has given considerable attention to automobile safety beginning with Ralph Nader's book *Unsafe at Any Speed* (1965), statistics show that numerous other products are associated with more injury-producing accidents than the automobile is. In 1973 the Consumer Product Safety Commission listed the most hazardous products as the bicycle and bicycle equipment: 372,000 accidents; stairs, ramps, and landings: 356,000 accidents; nails, carpet tacks, screws, and thumbtacks: 275,000 accidents; sports-related equipment and apparel: 750,000 injuries. Obviously not all or even the majority of these injuries and accidents resulted from defective products. But the point is that the potential for accidents and injuries is everywhere. Thus business bears a general responsibility to ensure the safety of all products.

Whether or not business people discharge their responsibility in the area of consumer safety depends almost entirely on what, if anything, they do to ensure a safe product. Abiding by the following steps would do much to help business behave morally with respect to consumer safety.

1. *Business can give safety the priority warranted by the product.* This is an important factor because businesses often base safety considerations strictly on

11. *Luthans and Hodgetts, p. 362.*

cost factors. Thus, if the margin of safety can be increased without significantly insulting budgetary considerations, fine. If not, then safety questions are shelved. Moreover, businesses frequently allow the law to determine to what extent they'll ensure safety. Although both cost and the law are factors in safety control, two other considerations seem of more moral importance. One factor is the seriousness of the injury that the product can cause. The automobile, for example, can cause severe injury or death. Thus it should be an item of the highest priority. Other products which can cause serious injury, such as power tools, pesticides, and chemicals, also deserve high priority. The second factor to consider is the frequency of occurrence. How often is a particular product involved in an accident? When a product scores high on both the seriousness and frequency tests, it would warrant the highest priority as a potential safety hazard.

2. *Business should abandon the misconception that accidents occur exclusively as a result of product misuse and abuse.* At one time such a belief may have been valid, but in using today's highly sophisticated products, numerous people have had the misfortune of following product instructions explicitly and still being injured or having been in an accident. For example, in the Greenman v. Yuba Power Products, Inc. case, plaintiff Greenman's lawyer was able to show that the power tool which caused Greenman serious head injury was unsafe when used in the manner recommended by the company. The point is that the company shares the responsibility of product safety together with the consumer. Rather than insisting that consumers' abuse of products leads to most accidents and injuries, firms could probably accomplish more by carefully pointing out how their products can be used safely. In some instances, if the product poses a potentially serious threat, a company may need to take extraordinary measures to ensure continued safe usage of it. Determining the extent to which the company must go, however, isn't an easy task. Doubtless there are times when a firm's moral responsibility for ensuring safety doesn't reach much beyond the sale of the product. Other times, it may extend well beyond that. Consider, for example, the case of a power tool company. Users of its products can easily fall into bad and dangerous habits while using the firm's machinery. Some would argue, therefore, that the company has an obligation to follow up the sale of such a product, perhaps by visiting consumers to see if they've developed hazardous shortcuts.

3. *Business must monitor the manufacturing process itself.* Frequently firms fail to control key variables during the manufacturing process, resulting in product defects. Of moral relevancy in this case is whether companies periodically review working conditions and the competence of key personnel. It's just as pertinent that at the design stage of the process personnel be able to predict ways that the product will fail and the consequences of this failure. Again, with respect to the materials used in production, companies ordinarily can select those that have been pretested or certified as flawless. If a company fails to do this, then a question is raised about the priority that company

gives safety. Similar questions arise when companies do not make use of research available about product safety. When none is available, a company really interested in safety can generate its own. In doing this, however, or in making use of safety research and studies, companies should rely on the findings of so-called independent research groups. Studies by these groups ensure impartial and disinterested analysis and are usually more reliable than studies by in-house programs.

Likewise, when a product moves into production, it can be changed in a variety of ways. It's important that these changes be documented and referred to some appropriate party, like the safety engineer, for analysis. This procedure means that the firm must be scrupulous about coordinating department activities to preclude one department's altering manufacturing specifications without consulting other departments to determine any potential dangers related to these changes.

4. *When a product is ready to be marketed, companies should have their product safety staff review advertising for safety-related content.* This step not only ensures accuracy and completeness but also provides consumers with vital purchase information. A corollary to this would be informing salespeople about the product's hazardous aspects.

5. *When a product reaches the marketplace, firms should make available to consumers in writing everything relative to the product's performance.* This information should include operating instructions, the product's safety features and under what conditions it will fail, a complete list of the ways the product can be used, and a cautionary list of the ways it should not be used.

6. *Companies should investigate consumer complaints.* This process encourages firms to deal fairly with consumers and to utilize the most effective source of product improvement: the opinions of those who use it.

Obviously, even if firms seriously tended to each of these safety considerations, they couldn't guarantee an absolutely safe product. Some hazards invariably will attach to numerous products, heroic efforts notwithstanding. But the point is that business acknowledge and discharge moral responsibilities in this area. Morally speaking, no one's asking for an accident- and injury-proof product, only that a manufacturer do everything reasonable to approach that ideal.

Product Quality

Most persons would agree that business bears a general responsibility to ensure that the quality of a product measures up to the claims made in its behalf and to reasonable consumer expectations. They would undoubtedly see this responsibility as deriving primarily from the consumer's basic right to get what one pays for. But it seems that business's obligation for product quality also stems from its general responsibility to protect owners' interests, for just as the burden of product safety has shifted to the producer, so has product performance. This realization means a toughening of product liability law and a softening of judicial resistance to consumer complaints. In increasing numbers consumers are going to court when products don't perform. What's more, the courts often uphold their complaints. As a result, the area of product performance raises serious financial risks to stockholders that must increase business's responsibility in this area.

One way that business tries to meet its responsibilities is through *warranties, obligations that sellers assure to purchasers.* We generally speak of two kinds of warranties, expressed and implied. Expressed warranties are the claims that sellers explicitly state. Expressed warranties include assertions about the product's characteristics, assurances of product durability, and statements that generally appear on a warranty card or statements placed on labels, wrappers, packages, or in the advertising of the product. Of moral concern here is that the manufacturer ensure that a product live up to its billing. Just as important morally, however, is the question of reparation. When a product fails to perform as promoted, whether and how the manufacturer "makes good" the consumer loss raises moral concerns. In some cases, the manufacturer may issue a refund or a new product; in others, much more reparation may be required.

In contrast to expressed warranties, implied warranties include the implicit claim that a particular product is fit for the ordinary use for which it is likely to be employed. Again, serious moral questions of reparation arise when injury or harm results from a failure of a product to perform as it should. Suppose, for example, that Eleanor Solano buys a new automobile. After she drives the car around for a few days under normal conditions, its steering mechanism fails and she is severely injured. In such a case, a company may bear far-reaching moral as well as legal responsibilities, even if on purchase Solano signed a disclaimer limiting the company's liability to replacement of defective parts.

Advertising can result in implied warranties which raise questions about consumer rights to reparation and concomitant manufacturer responsibility to honor them. For example, in one case a man named Inglis, relying on an American Motors advertising claim that a Rambler would be trouble free, economical to run, and a product of superior quality, bought one. Sadly, Inglis's expectations proved unrealistic. Not only was his Rambler's trunk out of line, it couldn't even be opened. Furthermore, the door handles were loose; the steering gear was improperly set; the oil pump was defective; the brakes squeaked and grated; the engine leaked oil; and loose parts inside the car occasionally fell on the floor. In short, if not a lemon, certainly Inglis's car was of the citrus variety. Unable to get satisfaction from his dealer, Inglis went to court. The court ruled that in cases where there is a difference between advertisement claims and a product's actual performance there was no sound reason that consumers shouldn't be permitted to recoup their losses.[12]

In sum, business has a general responsibility to ensure the quality of its product. Where discrepancies between explicit or implicit claims and performance arise, moral questions about reparation are present. At the same time, it is important to note that business's responsibility for product quality and its obligation to provide clear, accurate, and adequate information to ensure prod-

12. *David L. Rados, "Product Liability: Tougher Ground Rules,"* Harvard Business Review, *July–August, 1969, p. 148.*

uct safety are tied to questions that reach beyond consumer dissatisfaction with unsafe or inferior merchandise. Obligations in this area invite serious consideration by business about its attitude toward people in general, about its priorities, and about whether it's cultivating a marketplace atmosphere conducive to fair treatment for all consumers, no matter what their socioeconomic standings.

Ethical Theories

A great deal of how ethical theories apply to consumer-related issues depends on the comparative values they place on human beings and an accompanying recognition of basic rights. It seems easier to speculate about the application of ethical theories that inherently respect the dignity and worth of the human being and openly recognize fundamental human rights than those that don't or do so only contingently. This doesn't at all mean that representatives of the latter theories would not vigorously support the tenets of consumerism. Rather, it means that their support ultimately hinges on a calculation of the expectant good that might result from supporting the tenets of consumerism, in contrast to opposing or being indifferent to them. Such a calculation is at best problematic. On the other hand, it's easier to predict the position of a theory that openly endorses as intrinsically worthwhile virtues such as truth, honesty, and justice. In all likelihood, these theories will translate such abstract commitments into vigorous support for things like truth in labeling and packaging, and reparation when products fail to satisfy manufacturing claims. This having been noted, let's see how each of the theories might be applied to consumerism.

Egoism, as in all business issues, would approach consumer-related issues from the viewpoint of self-interest. As such, the question of consumer rights would never really arise for the egoist, since manufacturers and advertisers should do whatever is in their own best long-term interests. Of course, egoism advises consumers to do the same thing. If for business this means suppressing unflattering facts about products or exaggerating their merits, so be it. Egoism would not always chart such a course. It could certainly be in a business's best interest to advocate consumerism. Indeed, many business leaders assume this very posture. But notice that where egoism is involved, business champions consumerism not in recognition and acknowledgment of basic consumer rights but from concern for self-interest.

Utilitarianism, in contrast, would judge manufacturing, marketing, and retailing practices on the basis of the consequences for all concerned. In theory, the utility principle would be more representative of consumer interests than egoism would be. Specifically, act utilitarianism would evaluate the total consequences of each particular consumer-related action. Consider, for example, the practice of associating cigarette smoking with fun, romance, and adventure, while a consensus of medical opinion associates cigarette smoking with serious illness and early death. Act utilitarianism would not judge the morality of using such psychological appeals to sell cigarettes. Instead, it would concentrate on each individual marketing act or practice that involved selling cigarettes through these appeals. It would judge them right or wrong on the basis of the consequences for all involved. These would include not only the effects on the health of the potential smokers but the economic and social consequences as well. In some instances, act utilitarianism could approve of such a practice; in other instances, it could disapprove of it. Note that act utilitarians would not be morally alarmed by what some might term the manipulative and fraudulent nature of such ads but would concentrate exclusively on their effects. If the effects of an individual advertising practice are better than those of any alternative, then it is the right thing to do; if not, then it's the wrong thing.

Rule utilitarianism, on the other hand, would look at the rule under which the act falls. The rule here might read: "Never use psychological appeals to sell cigarettes." Does following this rule provide more total happiness than not following it? If not, then it's moral to use psychological appeals to sell cigarettes. Otherwise, it's not moral, and *any* act that violated this rule would be wrong, its attractive cost-benefit ratio notwithstanding. As with act utilitarianism, there are a multitude of factors which rule utilitarians would evaluate before judging the rule. Among them are the effects of such ads on cigarette sales and thus the tobacco industry, including owners, growers, cutters, packers, and retailers; the effects on business generally; and the effects on the revenue that cigarette sales provide for government to sponsor public services, including, ironically, cancer research. This doesn't mean to minimize the harm to individual smokers but to place it in perspective. Utilitarians consider *all* consequences. It seems safe to venture, then, that, while having the theoretical apparatus to evaluate a rule about the use of psychological appeals to sell cigarettes, rule utilitarianism would not condemn it on the basis of a violation of consumer rights.

The fact is that consumerism seems studded with "freedoms to," which the doctrine of classical utilitarianism addressed sparingly, if at all. Consider some of these freedoms: to receive clear, accurate, and adequate product information, to have safe, healthful products, to receive products that perform as advertised, to complain and be heard, to receive reparation. As we mentioned in a preceding chapter, classical utilitarians like Mill primarily addressed freedoms *from* interference, but such freedoms do not constitute the thrust of consumerism. One shouldn't conclude, however, that classical utilitarianism wouldn't support federal regulation of marketing and retailing practices. On the contrary, Mill argued eloquently for governmental interference in matters that involve more than oneself, that is, in so-called public matters. But government interference would evolve from a hedonistic calculus, a calculation of the greatest good for the greatest number; it would not evolve from an inherent commitment to any concept of basic consumer rights to truth, honesty, and justice in the marketplace.

Joseph Fletcher's situationalism, while relying on an evaluation of consequences as a moral standard, would do so within a context of loving concern. Analyzing some of the practices we've mentioned suggests a fundamental tension between them and the principle of loving concern, that is, giving to others what they deserve. For example, how could an ad of an essentially deceptive and manipulative nature constitute an act of loving concern? How could manufacturers who don't honor warranties be said to be acting out of loving concern? How could firms who produce goods while being unmindful of or indifferent to consumer safety be said to be acting out of loving concern? Granted, we must pull up short of asserting that situationalists would roundly condemn these practices, for we would then be committing situationalists to the legalism that they eschew. At the same time, however, it seems grossly misrepresentative of situationalism even to imply that it could equally swing one way or the other on consumer-related issues as outlined in this chapter. On the contrary, it seems decidedly more reflective of the spirit of situationalism to say that while in theory it would allow the individual case to dictate the moral thing to do, in practice the standard of loving concern would leave situationalists seriously questioning the morality of marketing and retailing actions and practices that include deception, lies, manipulation, and dishonesty. When placed in the context of one person or a group of people treating another, it's most difficult to imagine situations in which such business behavior would be inspired by loving concern. But fidelity to the letter of situationalism impels us to acknowledge the theoretical possibility that such behavior could be compatible with loving concern. Thus, a case could arise in which intentionally concealing serious product defects could be calculated to produce the greatest amount of neighbor welfare possible. All of which suggests that the central question for situationalism would be: is the action or practice intended to produce a greater amount of loving concern than any other alternative? If so, it's moral; if not, it's immoral.

Of the nonconsequential positions, the Golden Rule, like situationalism, implies a theory of justice based on an impartial distribution of desert. This is altogether relevant to consumer-related questions. Thus, adherents to the Golden Rule would ask manufacturers to ponder how they would want to be treated were they in the consumer's position. It's difficult to imagine one's responding to this query by saying, "Yes, I would want to be deceived, manipulated, and endangered." But such a response might be possible. While in theory the Golden Rule of itself seems noncommittal on the general question of consumer rights in the marketplace, in practice it probably would find itself firmly defending them in the vast majority of cases. Such a tentative evaluation strengthens when the Golden Rule is fleshed out, as it frequently is, with other moral principles and standards, such as the Ten Commandments.

Immanuel Kant's theory seems to leave no difference between theory and practice in most of the marketing and retailing practices we've outlined. We say this because Kant clearly condemned lying and dishonesty, while vigorously championing basic rights that he saw as inherent to rational creatures. As for his rationale, Kant condemned lying because it undermines the nature of serious communication, whose nature is to impart and exchange truth. Likewise Kant disapproved of dishonesty in all its forms because it undoes the fair and just treatment that individuals deserve simply because they are rational creatures. In specific issues, Kant undoubtedly would approach the case logically by asking whether a particular maxim when universalized contained a logical contradiction or inconsistency. Thus, does a rule which reads, "Use psychological appeals to sell cigarettes," contain a logical inconsistency? Kant would likely say it does, because psychological appeals undermine the personal freedom that rational creatures need and deserve. In other words, such a maxim, when universalized, would run counter to the nature of human beings. Most relevant here, of course, is Kant's fundamental respect for the dignity and worth of rational creatures. Given this, he could never justify using consumers as the means to some social end, such as greater employment or distribution of wealth.

Ross's prima facie theory would call for an examination of the characteristics of the consumer-related acts under discussion. It would entail an evaluation of the evident duties involved. Take, for example, the case of cigarette advertising. What duties are involved in the practice of using psychological appeals to sell cigarettes? Clearly, several duties are operative, some of which are conflicting. There are, on the one hand, duties to be faithful to owner interests, while on the other, duties to be truthful about the claims one makes. Specifically, an ad which increases cigarette sales by implicitly promising sexual satisfaction may coincide with owner interest but at the same time violate a duty of fidelity to truth by being unable to deliver what it promises. Undoubtedly other duties are involved, as there are in all consumer-related issues. But it seems safe to argue that Ross would be concerned primarily with the duty of noninjury, which invariably arises in these cases. Where conflicts of duties arise, Ross seems primarily sensitive to noninjury as the overriding moral obligation. Ross's theory seems to parallel the main thrust of consumerism, which is fundamentally concerned with business violations of what consumerism views as obligations of noninjury and beneficence, although admittedly not formulating its position in precisely this language. After all, even where consumer advocates call for accurate and adequate information in labeling, they do so within a context of the potential harm that ensues from anything less. In this, consumer advocates seem to reflect the prima facie theorist's primary concern in cases where these duties are clearly violated.

Rawls's concept of natural duties would indicate moral concerns similar to Ross's. An application of Rawls's original position concept sharply draws out these concerns. What would rational, self-interested people think about practices such as concealing product information, exaggerating product merits, making unrealistic product promises? Divested of any interests, as they are behind Rawls's veil of ignorance, most self-interested, rational creatures would likely disapprove of these actions because they could be victimized by them. In the original position, rational, self-interested creatures seem to champion basic consumer rights to truth, honesty, justice, and safety in the marketplace. Would they ever permit exceptions to these principles? For example, would they ever approve of subliminal advertising? In the original position, rational beings would permit exceptions only if everyone or at least those worst off, benefitted.

It taxes the imagination to conceive of a situation in which acts of subconscious manipulation could benefit everyone, or even those most disadvantaged. But it is possible since subliminal suggestions can sometimes advantage us. Suppose, for example, that a television commercial subliminally contained an antismoking message. Such a pitch could conceivably work to the ultimate advantage of all or at least of those most disadvantaged. This notwithstanding, by nature advertisers are not primarily interested in rendering this sort of social service. In fact, the admitted reason for the existence of advertisers is to sell products. Realizing this and remembering that Rawls is attempting to formulate a theory of social justice, we must conclude that he would enthusiastically support the principles of consumerism when they relate to basic consumer rights to truth, honesty, justice, and safety.

As for the theory of proportionality, its exponents would be vitally concerned with the rights of consumers. For proportionalists this means that people are entitled to truth, honesty, safety, and reparation in their shopping for, purchasing of, and using products. Proportionalists would view these rights as necessary goods, things individuals need to function in their roles as consumers. It follows that any willful abridgment of these rights, as either a means or end, is a major evil. Thus, manufacturers who conceal significant product defects in order to increase sales will, as a means, a major evil. In cases where such an evil is not willed but allowed or risked, then ample justification is needed to support its morality. How much justification depends on the situation. Relevant here would be whether there were less injurious alternatives available to the manufacturer or advertiser. For example, proportionalists would agree with the California Wine Institute that ads aimed at a young audience in which wine drinking is associated with status, prestige, and success are wrong, if for no other reason than that less potentially harmful ads are possible. In brief, although creators of such misleading ads would not be willing injury to consumers as a means or an end, their ads would be unjustified because less harmful options are available to them.

These, then, represent the general moral directions that the ethical theories might move in the area of consumerism. As usual we must qualify what we've said, pointing out that other applications might indicate different courses. Moreover, the usefulness of these theories is always subject to the weaknesses in them that we raised in previous chapters. All of this notwithstanding, the evidence points to the conclusion that most of these theories, at least in a general way, speak directly to the phenomenon of consumerism as we've discussed it in this chapter.

CASE PRESENTATION
Closing the Deal

Now that she had to, Jean McGuire wasn't sure she could. Not that she didn't understand what to do. Wright Boazman, sales director for Sunrise Land Developers, had made the step clear enough when he had described a variety of other effective "deal-closing techniques."

As Wright explained it very often people actually want to buy a lot, but at the last minute they're filled with self-doubt and uncertainty. The inexperienced salesperson can misinterpret this as a lack of interest in a property. "But," as Wright pointed out, "in most cases it's just an expression of the normal reservations everyone shows when the time comes to sign our names on the dotted line."

In Wright's view, the job of a land salesperson was "to help the prospect make the decision to buy." This didn't mean that salespeople should misrepresent a piece of property or in any way mislead people about what they were purchasing. "Law prohibits this," Wright pointed out, "and personally I find such behavior repugnant. What I'm talking about is helping them buy a lot they genuinely want and which you're convinced will be compatible with their needs and interests." In a word, for Wright Boazman, salespeople should serve as motivators, people who could provide whatever impulse was needed for prospects to close the deal.

In Wright's experience one of the most effective closing techniques was what he termed "the other party." It went something like this.

Suppose someone like Jean McGuire had a "hot" prospect, someone who was exhibiting a real interest in a lot but who was having trouble deciding. To motivate the prospect into buying, Jean ought to tell the person that she wasn't even sure the lot was still available, since there were a number of other salespeople showing the same lot, and they could already have closed a deal on it. As Wright put it, "This first ploy generally has the effect of increasing the prospect's interest in the property, and, more important to us, in closing the deal *pronto*."

Next Jean should say something like, "Why don't we go back to the office and I'll call headquarters to find out the status of the lot?" Wright indicated that such a suggestion ordinarily "whets their appetite" even more. In addition, it turns prospects away from wondering whether or not they should purchase the land and toward hoping that it's still available.

When they return to the office, Jean should make a call in the presence of the prospect. The call, of course, would not be to "headquarters" but to a private office only yards from where she and the prospect sit. Wright or someone else would receive the call, and Jean should fake a conversation about the property's availability, punctuating her comments with enough contagious excitement about its desirability. When she hangs up, she should breathe a sigh of relief that the lot's still available—but barely. At any minute, Jean should explain anxiously, the lot could be "green tagged," which means that headquarters is expecting a call from another salesperson who's about to close a deal and will remove the lot from open stock. (An effective variation of this, Wright had pointed out, would have Jean abruptly excuse herself upon hanging up and dart over to another sales representative with whom she'd engage in a heated, though staged, debate about the availability of the property, loud enough, of course, for the prospect to hear. The intended effect, according to Wright, would place the prospect in the "now or never" frame of mind.)

When Jean first heard about this and other closing techniques, she felt uneasy. Even though the property was everything it was represented to be, and the law allowed purchasers ten days to change their minds after closing a deal, she instinctively objected to the use of psychological manipulation. Nevertheless, Jean never expressed her reservations to anyone, primarily because she didn't want to endanger her job. She desperately needed it owing to the recent and unexpected death of her husband, which left her as the sole support of herself and three young children. Besides, Jean had convinced herself that she could deal with closures more respectably than Wright and other salespeople might. But the truth was that after six months of selling land for Sunrise, Jean's sales lagged far behind those of the other sales representatives. Whether she liked it or not, Jean had to admit that she was losing a considerable number of sales because she couldn't close. And she couldn't close because, in Wright Boazman's words, she lacked technique. She wasn't employing the psychological closing devices that he and others had found so successful.

Now as she drove back to the office with two "hot prospects" in hand, she wondered what to do.

1. *What should Jean do? Expand or qualify the facts however you choose.*

2. *What moral directions would the ethical theories provide?*

3. *In general, what do you think of the morality of psychological sales techniques? Would you always approve of them? Disapprove of them? Approve of them under certain conditions?*

CASE PRESENTATION
The Ad Too Hot to Touch

Jack Saroyan, vice-president in charge of advertising for *American Companion*, a family magazine with a multimillion circulation, had heard of Car/Puter, but he never imagined that it would pitch him into a dilemma that could cost him his job.

Saroyan knew that Car/Puter International Corporation was a firm based in Brooklyn, New York, that for ten dollars would provide any person interested in buying a specific car with a computer print-out of the list prices and the dealer's cost for the car and any accessories or options available. For another ten dollars, it would order the car from one of 900 participating dealers at $125 above the dealer's cost, far below the usual markup.

While Saroyan realized that millions of Americans had access to information about this unique service through newspaper and magazine articles and editorials, he also knew that rarely had Car/Puter ads appeared in the print media. Not that Car/Puter hadn't tried to place ads; dozens of periodicals had summarily rejected their ads.

Although to Saroyan's knowledge no periodical had ever expressed why it wouldn't sell Car/Puter some advertising space, he realized the rationale. Car/Puter's services directly competed with automotive dealers who pay millions of dollars annually for advertising space in newspapers and magazines. If a print medium were to advertise a service that car dealers disapproved of, automobile manufacturers would be highly reluctant to continue advertising in it. The result would be a tremendous loss of advertising revenue.

Most magazines simply couldn't risk losing such a considerable source of profit. For example, Saroyan's *American Companion* attributed more than half its annual advertising revenue to ads placed by Ford, General Motors, Chrysler, and American Motors. Saroyan was no fool. To jeopardize this income by running ads for Car/Puter struck him as the height of economic folly. What's more, if he lost even a fraction of these revenues by approving Car/Puter ads, Saroyan would be held personally accountable. He didn't wish to dwell on the career implications of that.

Unfortunately, Jack Saroyan had never been one to see things entirely in economic or self-interest terms. In this instance, for example, he felt sensitive to the significant social service that running Car/Puter ads would perform. No doubt, the ads would help consumers avail themselves of information they needed to make wise and prudent decisions about a car purchase. It also offered a service calculated to help them save millions of dollars annually. Besides, Saroyan was keenly aware of the economic disadvantage that Car/Puter suffered by being denied advertising space in the print media, by being denied its general right to make its service known to the public through advertising.

In the last analysis, Saroyan viewed his decision as a choice between rendering the public at large and Car/Puter in particular a service or doing what he thought to be in the best interests of *American Companion*. As hard as he tried, he didn't see these values as compatible.

1. *What should Saroyan do?*

2. *What moral direction do the ethical theories provide for resolving this dilemma?*

3. *If Saroyan decides to reject Car/Puter's request, does he have a moral obligation to explain to them why? (Keep in mind that anything he writes could be used in subsequent litigation that Car/Puter may wish to pursue.)*

4. *Do you think that the media ought to grant advertising space to all who desire it and can pay for it? If not, what limitations would you impose, and why?*

CASE PRESENTATION
The Skateboard Scare

Colin Brewster, owner of Brewster's Bicycle Shop, had to admit that his skateboard sales had salvaged his business now that interest in the bicycle seemed to have peaked. In fact, skateboard business was so brisk that Brewster could hardly keep them in stock. But the picture is far from rosy.

Just last week a concerned consumer group visited his shop to inform Brewster that it had ample evidence to prove that skateboards presented a real and immediate hazard to consumer safety. Brewster conceded that the group surely provided enough statistical support as to the shocking number of broken bones and concussions that had resulted directly and indirectly from accidents involving skateboards. But he thought the group's position was fundamentally unsound because, as he told them, "It's not the skateboards that are unsafe but how people use them."

Committee members weren't impressed with Brewster's distinctions. They likened them to saying that automobile manufacturers shouldn't be conscious of consumer safety because it's not the automobile that's unsafe but how we drive them. Brewster objected that the automobile presented an entirely different problem, because a number of things could be done to ensure their safe usage. "But what can you do about a skateboard?" he asked them. "Besides, I don't manufacture them, I just sell them."

The committee pointed out that other groups were attacking the problem on the manufacturing level. What they expected of Brewster was some responsible management of the problem at the local retail level. They pointed out that recently Brewster had run a series of local television ads portraying young but accomplished skateboarders performing flips and somersaults. The ad implied that anyone could easily accomplish such feats. Only yesterday one parent had told the committee of her child's breaking an arm attempting such gymnastics after having purchased a Brewster skateboard. "Obviously," Brewster countered, "the woman has an irresponsible kid whose activities she should monitor, not me." He pointed out that his ad was no more intended to imply that anyone could or should do those tricks than an ad for a car that shows it traveling at high speeds while doing stunt tricks implies that you should drive that way.

The committee disagreed. They said Brewster not only should discontinue such misleading advertising but also should actively publicize the potential dangers that lurk in skateboarding. Specifically, the committee wanted him to display prominently beside his skateboard stock the statistical data testifying to its hazards. Furthermore, he should make sure that anyone buying a skateboard had read this material prior to purchase.

Brewster argued that the committee's demands were unreasonable. "Do you have any idea what effect that would have on sales?" he asked them.

Committee members readily admitted that they were less interested in his sales than in their children's safety. Brewster told them that in this matter their children's safety was their responsibility, not his. But the committee was adamant. Members told Brewster that they'd be back in a week to find out what positive steps, if any, he'd taken to correct the problem. In the event he'd done nothing, they indicated that they were prepared to picket his shop.

1. *Whom do you agree with—Brewster or the committee? Why?*

2. *What should Brewster do?*

3. *What moral directions do the ethical theories provide to help Brewster decide?*

4. *In general, what responsibilities, if any, do retailers have to ensure consumer safety?*

The Morality (?) of Advertising

Theodore Levitt

At one point in this chapter we attempted to distinguish between advertising intended to misrepresent and that intended to exaggerate. The relatively short coverage we gave this topic doesn't mean that it is unimportant or that the two are easily distinguishable. In fact, as the following article demonstrates, quite the opposite is so.

Author Theodore Levitt, professor of business administration at Harvard, rightly points out that the issue of truth vs. falsehood, in advertising as in anything else, is "complex and fugitive." As a result, Levitt takes a long look at the difference between legitimate distortion and essential falsehood. Professor Levitt's look is appropriately philosophical, for, as he indicates, the issue at stake is basically a philosophical one. In brief, this article presents a philosophical treatment of the human values of advertising as compared with the values of other so-called imaginative disciplines.

This year Americans will consume about $20 billion of advertising, and very little of it because we want it. Wherever we turn, advertising will be forcibly thrust on us in an intrusive orgy of abrasive sound and sight, all to induce us to do something we might not ordinarily do, or to induce us to do it differently. This massive and persistent effort crams increasingly more commercial noise into the same, few, strained 24 hours of the day. It has provoked a reaction as predictable as it was inevitable: a lot of people want the noise stopped, or at least alleviated.

And they want it cleaned up and corrected. As more and more products have entered the battle for the consumer's fleeting dollar, advertising has increased in boldness and volume. Last year, industry offered the nation's supermarkets about 100 new products a week, equal, on an annualized basis, to the total number already on their shelves. Where so much must be sold so hard, it is not surprising that advertisers have pressed the limits of our credulity and generated complaints about their exaggerations and deceptions.

Only classified ads, the work of rank amateurs, do we presume to contain solid, unembellished fact. We suspect all the rest of systematic and egregious distortion, if not often of outright mendacity.

The attack on advertising comes from all sectors. Indeed, recent studies show that the people most agitated by advertising are precisely those in the higher income brackets whose affluence is generated by the industries that create the ads.[1] While these studies show that only a modest group of people are preoccupied with advertising's constant presence in our lives, they also show that distortion and deception are what bother people most.

This discontent has encouraged Senator Philip Hart and Senator William Proxmire to sponsor consumer-protection and truth-in-advertising legislation. People, they say, want less fluff and more fact about the things they buy. They want description, not distortion, and they want some relief from the constant, grating, vulgar noise.

Legislation seems appropriate because the natural action of competition does not seem to work, or at least not very well. Competition may ultimately flush out and destroy falsehood and shoddiness, but "ultimately" is too long for the deceived—not just the deceived who are poor, ignorant, and dispossessed, but also all the rest of us who work hard for our money and can seldom judge expertly the truth of conflicting claims about products and services.

The consumer is an amateur, after all; the producer is an expert. In the commercial arena, the consumer is an impotent midget. He is certainly not king. The producer is a powerful giant. It is an uneven match. In this setting, the purifying power of competition helps the consumer very little—especially in the short run, when his money is spent and gone, from the weak hands into the strong hands. Nor does competition among the sellers solve the "noise" problem. The more they compete, the worse the din of advertising.

A Broad Viewpoint Required

Most people spend their money carefully. Understandably, they look out for larcenous attempts to separate them from it. Few men in business will deny the right, perhaps even the wisdom, of people today asking for some restraint on advertising, or at least for more accurate information on the things they buy and for more consumer protection.

Yet, if we speak in the same breath about consumer protection and about advertising's distortions, exaggerations, and deceptions, it is easy to confuse two quite separate things—the legitimate purpose of advertising and the abuses to which it may be put. Rather than deny that distortion and exaggeration exist in advertising, in this article I shall argue that embellishment and distortion are among advertising's legitimate and socially desirable purposes; and that illegitimacy in advertising consists only of falsification with larcenous intent. And while it is difficult, as a practical matter, to draw the line between legitimate distortion and essential falsehood, I want to take a long look at the distinction that exists between the two. This I shall say in advance—the distinction is not as simple, obvious, or great as one might think.

The issue of truth versus falsehood, in advertising or in anything else, is complex and fugitive. It must be pursued in a philosophic mood that might seem foreign to the businessman. Yet the issue at base *is* more philosophic than it is pragmatic. Anyone seriously concerned with the moral problems of a commercial society cannot avoid this fact. I hope the reader will bear with me—I believe he will find it helpful, and perhaps even refreshing.

What Is Reality?

What, indeed? Consider poetry. Like advertising, poetry's purpose is to influence an audience; to affect its perceptions and sensibilities; perhaps even to change its mind. Like rhetoric, poetry's intent is to convince and seduce. In the service of that intent, it employs without guilt or fear of criticism all the arcane tools of distortion that the liter-

ary mind can devise. Keats does not offer a truthful engineering description of his Grecian urn. He offers, instead, with exquisite attention to the effects of meter, rhyme, allusion, illusion, metaphor, and sound, a lyrical, exaggerated, distorted, and palpably false description. And he is thoroughly applauded for it, as are all other artists, in whatever medium, who do precisely this same thing successfully.

Commerce, it can be said without apology, takes essentially the same liberties with reality and literality as the artist, except that commerce calls its creations advertising, or industrial design, or packaging. As with art, the purpose is to influence the audience by creating illusions, symbols, and implications that promise more than pure functionality. Once, when asked what his company did, Charles Revson of Revlon, Inc. suggested a profound distinction: "In the factory we make cosmetics; in the store we sell hope." He obviously has no illusions. It is not cosmetic chemicals women want, but the seductive charm promised by the alluring symbols with which these chemicals have been surrounded—hence the rich and exotic packages in which they are sold, and the suggestive advertising with which they are promoted.

Commerce usually embellishes its products thrice: first, it designs the product to be pleasing to the eye, to suggest reliability, and so forth; second, it packages the product as attractively as it feasibly can; and then it advertises this attractive package with inviting pictures, slogans, descriptions, songs, and so on. The package and design are as important as the advertising.

The Grecian vessel, for example, was used to carry liquids, but that function does not explain why the potter decorated it with graceful lines and elegant drawings in black and red. A woman's compact carries refined talc, but this does not explain why manufacturers try to make these boxes into works of decorative art.

Neither the poet nor the ad man celebrates the literal functionality of what he produces. Instead, each celebrates a deep and complex emotion which he symbolizes by creative embellishment—a content which cannot be captured by literal description alone. Communication, through advertising or through poetry or any other medium, is a creative conceptualization that implies a vicarious experience through a language of symbolic substitutes. Communication can never be the real thing it talks about. Therefore, all communication is in some inevitable fashion a departure from reality.

Everything Is Changed . . .

Poets, novelists, playwrights, composers, and fashion designers have one thing more in common. They all deal in symbolic communication. None is satisfied with nature in the raw, as it was on the day of creation. None is satisfied to tell it exactly "like it is" to the naked eye, as do the classified ads. It is the purpose of all art to alter nature's surface reality, to reshape, to embellish, and to augment what nature has so crudely fashioned, and then to present it to the same applauding humanity that so eagerly buys Revson's exotically advertised cosmetics.

Few, if any, of us accept the natural state in which God created us. We scrupulously select our clothes to suit a multiplicity of simultaneous purposes, not only for warmth, but manifestly for such other purposes as propriety, status, and seduction. Women modify, embellish, and amplify themselves with colored paste for the lips and powders and lotions for the face; men as well as women use devices to take hair off the face and others to put it on the head. Like the inhabitants of isolated African regions, where not a single whiff of advertising has ever intruded, we all encrust ourselves with rings, pendants, bracelets, neckties, clips, chains, and snaps.

Man lives neither in sackcloth nor in sod huts—although these are not notably inferior to tight clothes and overheated dwellings in congested and polluted cities. Everywhere man rejects nature's uneven blessings. He molds and repackages to his own civilizing specifications an otherwise crude, drab, and generally oppressive reality. He does it so that life may be made for the moment more tolerable than God evidently designed it to be. As T. S. Eliot once remarked, "Human kind cannot bear very much reality."

. . . Into Something Rich and Strange

No line of life is exempt. All the popes of history have countenanced the costly architecture of St. Peter's Basilica and its extravagant interior decoration. All around the globe, nothing typifies man's materialism so much as the temples in which he preaches asceticism. Men of the cloth have not been persuaded that the poetic self-denial of Christ or Buddha—both men of sackcloth and sandals—is enough to inspire, elevate, and hold their flocks together. To amplify the temple in men's eyes, they have, very realistically, systematically sanctioned the embellishment of the houses of the gods with the same kind of luxurious design and expensive decoration that Detroit puts into a Cadillac.

One does not need a doctorate in social anthropology to see that the purposeful transmutation of nature's primeval state occupies all people in all cultures and all societies at all stages of development. Everybody everywhere wants to modify, transform, embellish, enrich, and reconstruct the world around him—to introduce into an otherwise harsh or bland existence some sort of purposeful and distorting alleviation. Civilization is man's attempt to transcend his ancient animality; and this includes both art and advertising.

. . . and More Than "Real"

But civilized man will undoubtedly deny that either the innovative artist or the *grande dame* with *chic* "distorts reality." Instead, he will say that artist and woman merely embellish, enhance, and illuminate. To be sure, he will mean something quite different by these three terms when he applies them to fine art, on the one hand, and to more secular efforts, on the other.

But this distinction is little more than an affectation. As man has civilized himself and developed his sensibilities, he has invented a great variety of subtle distinctions between things that are objectively indistinct. Let us take a closer look at the difference between man's "sacred" distortions and his "secular" ones.

The man of sensibility will probably canonize the artist's deeds as superior creations by ascribing to them an almost cosmic virtue and significance. As a cultivated individual, he will almost certainly refuse to recognize any constructive, cosmic virtues in the production of the advertisers, and he is likely to admit the charge that advertising uniformly deceives us by analogous techniques. But how "sensible" is he?

And by Similar Means . . .

Let us assume for the moment that there is no objective, operational difference between the embellishments and distortions of the artist and those of the ad man—that both men are more concerned with creating images and feelings than with rendering objective, representational, and informational descriptions. The greater virtue of the artist's work must then derive from some subjective element. What is it?

It will be said that art has a higher value for man because it has a higher purpose. True, the artist is interested in philosophic truth or wisdom, and the ad man in selling his goods and services. Michelangelo, when he designed the Sistine chapel ceiling, had some concern with the inspirational elevation of man's spirit, whereas Edward Levy, who designs cosmetics packages, is interested primarily in creating images to help separate the unwary consumer from his loose change.

But this explanation of the difference between the value of art and the value of advertising is not helpful at all. For is the presence of a "higher" purpose all that redeeming?

Perhaps not; perhaps the reverse is closer to the truth. While the ad man and designer seek only to convert the audience to their commercial custom, Michelangelo sought to convert its soul. Which is the greater blasphemy? Who commits the greater affront to life—he who dabbles with man's erotic appetites, or he who meddles with man's soul? Which act is the easier to judge and justify?

. . . for Different Ends

How much sense does it really make to distinguish between similar means on the grounds that the ends to which they are directed are different—"good" for art and "not so good" for advertising? The distinction produces zero progress in the argument at hand. How willing are we to employ the involuted ethics whereby the ends justify the means?

Apparently, on this subject, lots of people are very willing indeed. The business executive seems to share with the minister, the painter, and the poet the doctrine that the ends justify the means. The difference is that the businessman is justifying the very commercial ends that his critics oppose. While his critics justify the embellishments of art and literature for what these do for man's spirit, the businessman justifies the embellishment of industrial design and advertising for what they do for man's purse.

Taxing the imagination to the limit, the businessman spins casuistic webs of elaborate transparency to the self-righteous effect that promotion and advertising are socially benign because they expand the economy, create jobs, and raise living standards. Technically, he will always be free to argue, and he *will* argue, that his ends become the means to the ends of the musician, poet, painter, and minister. The argument which justifies means in terms of ends is obviously not without its subtleties and intricacies.

The executive and the artist are equally tempted to identify and articulate a higher rationale for their work than their work itself. But only in the improved human consequences of their efforts do they find vindication. The aesthete's ringing declaration of "art for art's sake," with all its self-conscious affirmation of selflessness, sounds hollow in the end, even to himself; for, finally, every communication addresses itself to an audience. Thus art is very understandably in constant need of justification by the evidence of its beneficial and divinely approved effect on its audience.

The Audience's Demands

This compulsion to rationalize even art is a highly instructive fact. It tells one a great deal about art's purposes and the purposes of all other communication. As I have said, the poet and the artist each seek in some special way to produce an emotion or assert a truth not otherwise apparent. But it is only in communion with their audiences that the effectiveness of their efforts can be tested and truth revealed. It may be academic whether a tree falling in the forest makes a noise. It is *not* academic whether a sonnet or a painting has merit. Only an audience can decide that.

The creative person can justify his work only in terms of another person's response to it. Ezra Pound, to be sure, thought that ". . . in the [greatest] works the live part is the part which the artist has put there to please himself, and the dead part is the part he has put there . . . because he thinks he *ought* to—i.e., either to get or keep an audience." This is certainly consistent with our notions of Pound as perhaps the purest of twentieth-century advocates of art for art's sake.

But if we review the record of his life, we find that Pound spent the greater part of his energies seeking suitable places for deserving poets to publish. Why? Because art has little merit standing alone in unseen and unheard isolation. Merit is not inherent in art. It is conferred by an audience.

The same is true of advertising: if it fails to persuade the audience that the product will fulfill the function the audience expects, the advertising has no merit.

Where have we arrived? Only at some common characteristics of art and advertising. Both are rhetorical, and both literally false; both expound an emotional reality deeper than the "real"; both pretend to "higher" purposes, although different ones; and the excellence of each is judged by its effect on its audience—its persuasiveness, in short. I do not mean to imply that the two are fundamentally the same, but rather that they both represent a pervasive, and I believe *universal*, characteristic of human nature—the human audience *demands* symbolic interpretation in everything it sees and knows. If it doesn't get it, it will return a verdict of "no interest."

To get a clearer idea of the relation between the symbols of advertising and the products they glorify, something more must be said about the fiat the consumer gives to industry to "distort" its messages.

Symbol and Substance

As we have seen, man seeks to transcend nature in the raw everywhere. Everywhere, and at all times, he has been attracted by the poetic imagery of some sort of art, literature, music, and mysticism. He obviously wants and needs the promises, the imagery, and the symbols of the poet and the priest. He refuses to live a life of primitive barbarism or sterile functionalism.

Consider a sardine can filled with scented powder. Even if the U.S. Bureau of Standards were to certify that the contents of this package are identical with the product sold in a beautiful paisley-printed container, it would not sell. The Boston matron, for example, who has built herself a deserved reputation for pinching every penny until it hurts, would unhesitatingly turn it down. While she may deny it, in self-assured and neatly cadenced accents, she obviously desires and needs the promises, imagery, and symbols produced by hyperbolic advertisements, elaborate packages, and fetching fashions.

The need for embellishment is not confined to personal appearance. A few years ago, an electronics laboratory offered a $700 testing device for sale. The company ordered two different front panels to be designed, one by the engineers who developed the equipment and one by professional industrial designers. When the two models were shown to a sample of laboratory directors with Ph.D.'s, the professional design attracted twice the purchase intentions that the engineer's design did. Obviously, the laboratory director who has been baptized into science at M.I.T. is quite as responsive to the blandishments of packaging as the Boston matron.

And, obviously, both these customers define the products they buy in much more sophisticated terms than the engineer in the factory. For a woman, dusting powder in a sardine can is not the same product as the identical dusting powder in an exotic paisley package. For the laboratory director, the test equipment behind an engineer-designed panel just isn't as "good" as the identical equipment in a box designed with finesse.

Form Follows the Ideal Function

The consumer refuses to settle for pure operating functionality. "Form follows function" is a resoundingly vacuous cliché which, like all clichés, depends for its memorability more on its alliteration and brevity than on its wisdom. If it has any truth, it is only in the elastic sense that function extends beyond strict mechanical use into the domain of imagination. We do not choose to buy a particular product; we choose to buy the functional expectations that we attach to it, and we buy these expectations as "tools" to help us solve a problem of life.

Under normal circumstances, furthermore, we must judge a product's "nonmechanical" utilities before we actually buy it. It is rare that we choose an object after we have experienced it; nearly always we must make the choice before the fact. We choose on the basis of promises, not experiences.

Whatever symbols convey and *sustain* these promises in our minds are therefore truly functional. The promises and images which imaginative ads and sculptured packages induce in us are as much the product as the physical materials themselves. To put this another way, these ads and packagings describe the product's fullness for us: in our minds, the product becomes a complex abstraction which is, as Immanuel Kant might have said, the conception of a perfection which has not yet been experienced.

But all promises and images, almost by their very nature, exceed their capacity to live up to themselves. As every eager lover has ever known, the consummation seldom equals the promises which produced the chase. To forestall and suppress the visceral expectation of disappointment that life has taught us must inevitably come, we use art, architecture, literature, and the rest, and advertising as well, to shield ourselves, in advance of experience, from the stark and plain reality in which we are fated to live. I agree that we wish for unobtainable unrealities, "dream castles." But why promise ourselves reality, which we already possess? What we want is what we do *not* possess!

Everyone in the world is trying in his special personal fashion to solve a primal problem of life—the problem of rising above his own negligibility, of escaping from nature's confining, hostile, and unpredictable reality, of finding significance, security, and comfort in the things he must do to survive. Many of the so-called distortions of advertising, product design, and packaging may be viewed as a paradigm of the many responses that man makes to the conditions of survival in the environment. Without distortion, embellishment, and elaboration, life would be drab, dull, anguished, and at its existential worst.

Symbolism Useful and Necessary

With*out* symbolism, furthermore, life would be even more confusing and anxiety-ridden than it is *with* it. The foot soldier must be able to recognize the general, good or bad, because the general is clothed with power. A general without his stars and suite of aides-de-camp to set him apart from the privates would suffer in authority and credibility as much as perfume packaged by Dracula or a computer designed by Rube Goldberg. Any ordinary soldier or civilian who has ever had the uncommon experience of being in the same shower with a general can testify from the visible unease of the latter how much clothes "make the man."

Similarly, verbal symbols help to make the product—they help us deal with the uncertainties of daily life. "You can be sure . . . if it's Westing-house" is a decision rule as useful to the man buying a turbine generator as to the man buying an electric shaver. To label all the devices and embellishments companies employ to reassure the prospective customer about a product's quality with the pejorative term "gimmick," as critics tend to do, is simply silly. Worse, it denies, against massive evidence, man's honest needs and values. If religion must be architectured, packaged, lyricized, and musicized to attract and hold its audience, and if sex must be perfumed, powdered, sprayed, and shaped in order to command attention, it is ridiculous to deny the legitimacy of more modest, and similar, embellishments to the world of commerce.

But still, the critics may say, commercial communications tend to be aggressively deceptive. Perhaps, and perhaps not. The issue at stake here is more complex than the outraged critic believes. Man wants and needs the elevation of the spirit produced by attractive surroundings, by handsome packages, and by imaginative promises. He needs the assurances projected by well-known brand names, and the reliability suggested by salesmen who have been taught to dress by Oleg Cassini and to speak by Dale Carnegie. Of course, there are blatant, tasteless, and willfully deceiving salesmen and advertisers, just as there are blatant, tasteless, and willfully deceiving artists, preachers, and even professors. But, before talking blithely about deception, it is helpful to make a distinction between things and descriptions of things.

The Question of Deceit

Poetic descriptions of things make no pretense of being the things themselves. Nor do advertisements, even by the most elastic standards. Advertisements are the symbols of man's aspirations. They are not the real things, nor are they intended to be, nor are they accepted as such by the public. A study some years ago by the Center for Research in Marketing, Inc. concluded that deep down inside the consumer understands this perfectly well and has the attitude that an advertisement is an ad, not a factual news story.

Even Professor Galbraith grants the point when he says that ". . . because modern man is exposed to a large volume of information of varying degrees of unreliability . . . he establishes a system of discounts which he applies to various sources almost without thought. . . . The discount becomes nearly total for all forms of advertising. The merest child watching television dismisses the health and status-giving claims of a breakfast cereal as 'a commercial.' "[2]

This is not to say, of course, that Galbraith also discounts advertising's effectiveness. Quite the opposite: "Failure to win belief does not impair the effectiveness of the management of demand for consumer products. Management involves the creation of a compelling image of the product in the mind of the consumer. To this he responds more or less automatically under circumstances where the purchase does not merit a great deal of thought. For building this image, palpable fantasy may be more valuable than circumstantial evidence."[3]

Linguists and other communications specialists will agree with the conclusion of the Center for Research in Marketing that "advertising is a symbol system existing in a world of symbols. Its reality depends upon the fact that it is a symbol . . . the content of an ad can never be real, it can only say something about reality, or create a relationship between itself and an individual which has an effect on the reality life of an individual."

Consumer, Know Thyself!

Consumption is man's most constant activity. It is well that he understands himself as a consumer.

The object of consumption is to solve a problem. Even consumption that is viewed as the creation of an opportunity—like going to medical school or taking a singles-only Caribbean tour—has as its purpose the solving of a problem. At a minimum, the medical student seeks to solve the problem of how to lead a relevant and comfortable life, and the lady on the tour seeks to solve the problem of spinsterhood.

The "purpose" of the product is not what the engineer explicitly says it is, but what the consumer implicitly demands that it shall be. Thus the consumer consumes not things, but expected benefits—not cosmetics, but the satisfactions of the allurements they promise; not quarter-inch drills, but quarter-inch holes; not stock in companies, but capital gains; not numerically controlled milling machines, but trouble-free and ac-

curately smooth metal parts; not low-cal whipped cream, but self-rewarding indulgence combined with sophisticated convenience.

The significance of these distinctions is anything but trivial. Nobody knows this better, for example, than the creators of automobile ads. It is not the generic virtues that they tout, but more likely the car's capacity to enhance its user's status and his access to female prey.

Whether we are aware of it or not, we in effect expect and demand that advertising create these symbols for us to show us what life *might* be, to bring the possibilities that we cannot see before our eyes and screen out the stark reality in which we must live. We insist, as Gilbert put it, that there be added a "touch of artistic verisimilitude to an otherwise bald and unconvincing narrative."

Understanding the Difference

In a world where so many things are either commonplace or standardized, it makes no sense to refer to the rest as false, fraudulent, frivolous, or immaterial. The world works according to the aspirations and needs of its actors, not according to the arcane or moralizing logic of detached critics who pine for another age—an age which, in any case, seems different from today's largely because its observers are no longer children shielded by protective parents fom life's implacable harshness.

To understand this is not to condone much of the vulgarity, purposeful duplicity, and scheming half-truths we see in advertising, promotion, packaging, and product design. But before we condemn, it is well to understand the difference between embellishment and duplicity and how extraordinarily uncommon the latter is in our times. The noisy visibility of promotion in our intensely communicating times need not be thoughtlessly equated with malevolence.

Thus the issue is not the prevention of distortion. It is, in the end, to know what kinds of distortions we actually want so that each of our lives is, without apology, duplicity, or rancor, made bearable. This does not mean we must accept out of hand all the commercial propaganda to which we are each day so constantly exposed, or that we must accept out of hand the equation that effluence is the price of affluence, or the simple notion that business cannot and government should not try to alter and improve the position of the consumer vis-à-vis the producer. It takes a special kind of perversity to continue any longer our shameful failure to mount vigorous, meaningful programs to protect the consumer, to standardize product grades, labels, and packages, to improve the consumer's information-getting process, and to mitigate the vulgarity and oppressiveness that is in so much of our advertising.

But the consumer suffers from an old dilemma. He wants "truth," but he also wants and needs the alleviating imagery and tantalizing promises of the advertiser and designer.

Business is caught in the middle. There is hardly a company that would not go down in ruin if it refused to provide fluff, because nobody will buy pure functionality. Yet, if it uses too much fluff and little else, business invites possibly ruinous legislation. The problem therefore is to find a middle way. And in this search, business can do a great deal more than it has been either accustomed or willing to do:

> It can exert pressure to make sure that no single industry "finds reasons" why it should be exempt from legislative restrictions that are reasonable and popular.

> It can work constructively with government to develop reasonable standards and effective sanctions that will assure a more amenable commercial environment.

> It can support legislation to provide the consumer with the information he needs to make easy comparison between products, packages, and prices.

It can support and help draft improved legislation on quality stabilization.

It can support legislation that gives consumers easy access to strong legal remedies where justified.

It can support programs to make local legal aid easily available, especially to the poor and undereducated who know so little about their rights and how to assert them.

Finally, it can support efforts to moderate and clean up the advertising noise that dulls our senses and assaults our sensibilities.

It will not be the end of the world or of capitalism for business to sacrifice a few commercial freedoms so that we may more easily enjoy our own humanity. Business can and should, for its own good, work energetically to achieve this end. But it is also well to remember the limits of what is possible. Paradise was not a free-goods society. The forbidden fruit was gotten at a price.

Notes

1. See Raymond A. Bauer and Stephen A. Greyser, *Advertising in America: The Consumer View* (Boston, Division of Research, Harvard Business School, 1968); see also Gary A. Steiner, *The People Look at Television* (New York, Alfred A. Knopf, Inc., 1963).
2. John Kenneth Galbraith, *The New Industrial State* (Boston, Houghton Mifflin Company, 1967), pp. 325–326.
3. Ibid., p. 326.

The Product Liability Revolution

Conrad Berenson

Who is responsible if a defective product causes personal injury or damage? The question is of both legal and moral importance, and, as we mentioned, a tough one to answer. Traditionally, the individual who directly sells the product is considered at fault. This is no longer true. Today everyone in the production-marketing chain can be held liable for a product's shortcomings. While legal responsibility must be distinguished from moral responsibility, it nonetheless introduces a consideration in ascertaining moral responsibility. After all, if manufacturers or advertisers know that they

Conrad Berenson, "The Product Liability Revolution," Business Horizons, *October 1972. Copyright, 1972, by the Foundation for the School of Business at Indiana University. Reprinted by permission.*

are legally liable for a product's shortcomings, then morally they must operate and be judged within a different moral framework than if they were not liable or if the question of their liability were in doubt. What's more, knowing who is legally responsible and why they are helps in the task of defining and assigning moral responsibilities and in justifying those positions.

The following article by Conrad Berenson, professor of marketing and executive officer of the Ph.D. program at the City University of New York Baruch College, deals with the evolution of the concept of product liability. Professor Berenson points out that a number of recent product liability suits have elicited judicial observations that the burden of payment and the burden of pain should be shifted to those who can bear it best. Such comments are morally provocative, because they suggest a perspective that can be brought to the question of moral responsibility, in this case, a consideration of equity based on ability to shoulder the liability.

One of the more significant marketing developments of the last decade—both from the consumer's and producer's view—is the new concept of *product liability*.[1]

The age-old phrase, "let the buyer beware," has been changed to "let the manufacturer and the seller be sued." This is dramatically shown by the well over 100,000 product liability cases introduced in the United States courts in 1969. Estimates for 1971 range up to 250,000 cases. The figures themselves are only significant because they reflect an enormous increase from the few thousand cases of a decade ago; many of these cases amount to big money, with some individual awards exceeding $100,000.

The rise in legal activity against manufacturers and sellers of a broad variety of products and concomitant changes in the law are of grave importance to marketers. Marketing managers, advertising managers, sales managers, product managers, customer service supervisors, and others in the marketing organization are all affected by the changes in our society, by the proliferation of lawsuits, and by the changes in our laws which have resulted in these suits. This article will examine some of the product liability considerations which are important to marketers and consumers, and show how new attitudes toward product liability will affect marketing performance.

Causes of Liability Revolution

What are the reasons for this tremendous increase in legal activity and for the changes in the law?

1. Many products today, certainly far more than in prior decades, are packaged so that the consumer cannot examine them. Because the consumer is prevented from examining the merchandise, the courts have placed the responsibility on the vendor and the maker.

2. Many products today are so technically sophisticated that the average consumer simply cannot be expected to have the knowledge to properly appraise them and to reach reasonable conclusions as to safety, quality, price, suitability, and so on. Consider for a moment the complexity of a modern day television set, a hi-fi, or even an electric can opener.

3. Advertising has grown. In the United States it is now a more than $23 billion a year industry—much of this in the form of a wide variety of claims urging that the consumer take action and purchase Product A, B, or C, instead of E, F, and G, because of real or imagined attributes. Subjected to this enormous barrage in the media, the average person often does not know how to make a rational purchasing choice.

4. The transaction between the ultimate consumer and the one who immediately sells to him is usually a transaction between parties who often do not know each other, and, in fact, have never even seen each other. The day when you went to the local grocer, whom you had known well all your life and upon whose recommendation you could rely completely, is long past. Clerks in supermarkets may scarcely know where the merchandise is located, nor can they tell you anything about the nature of the contents of those glamorously designed packages, or the reliability of their manufacture.

5. The emergence of national distribution networks has perhaps caused some manufacturers to be less careful in the design and quality

of their product. Their business ethics may have changed too. Their feeling, for example, may have been conditioned by the fact that most of their customers do not know them and neither do their customers' friends, so there will be no personal problems due to a faulty product. This was not so 100 years ago, when many manufacturers sold within a very small geographic area and were known personally to many of their customers.

6. The plethora of product innovations makes even the most sophisticated buyer a loser in the race to keep informed about the attributes of new products. For example, the average supermarket contains between 7,000 and 9,000 different products—this includes different sizes of the same product. Therefore, even the most energetic supermarket manager who attempts to keep up with product information just in his own store must contend with these thousands of products, as well as the new ones each year, about 20 percent of his stock.

7. With such rapid product innovation, the innovators often make honest errors in design and quality. Since they have not had sufficient experience in producing what they are selling, this inexperience may from time to time injure consumers. Today's sophisticated consumer simply will not sit idly by and accept such injury, whether it be physical or economic.

8. The success of some attorneys who specialize in product liability claims has encouraged other attorneys to get into the field and injured parties to seek redress.

9. As a result of higher levels of consumer education, as well as political expediency of the moment, a new consumer attitude has developed, which encourages stiff resistance on the part of consumers. Also, consumer groups have organized which actively lobby and sue for legislation and redress.

10. Finally, there is a growing tendency by injured people to seek recovery for damages as assiduously as possible. Forty years ago someone who was bumped lightly by an automobile would dart quickly away in embarrassment, thinking he had been too clumsy. Today, such a bump would immediately be followed by cries for witnesses, ambulances, doctors, and attorneys.

Traditional Product Liability Approaches
Privity

From the time this nation was established until 1916 the *manufacturer* of most products had absolutely no liability (legal responsibility) for them, except to those customers to whom direct sales were made. The exceptions to this doctrine were those products which could seriously affect human life—food, chemicals, drugs, and firearms. If you had purchased an automobile from a dealer in 1915, and not from a manufacturer, you could have filed a lawsuit for negligence only against the dealer.

In 1916, however, a man named Donald MacPherson was driving a new Buick at 15 miles per hour when one of its wheels fell off. MacPherson was injured and sued Buick for negligence, claiming that the wheel had been defective. MacPherson won, and the case of MacPherson v. Buick Motor Company[2] represents a landmark in the philosophy of *privity of contract*.[3] The approach has since become more permissive in the range and scope of allowable lawsuits. Today, for example, if a wheel falls off your car, you have the opportunity of suing the auto manufacturer or the auto dealer, or both. For products in which the chain of distribution may be longer—for example, a chocolate bar that goes from the manufacturer to a wholesaler to a retailer to the ultimate user—any or all of these parties may be sued through the purchaser, and the possibility for a plaintiff's recovery of any damages awarded is consequently far higher.

The change in legal philosophy has developed because of the changes in marketing methods that have occurred in the past 40 years. The New York Court of Appeals made a statement about this several years ago: "The world of merchandising is, in brief, no longer a world of direct contact; it is, rather, a world of advertising and, when representations expressed and disseminated in the mass communications media and on labels (attached to the goods themselves) prove false, and the user or consumer is damaged by his reliance on these representations, it is difficult to justify the manufacturer's denial of liability on the sole ground of the absence of technical privity." Furthermore, continued the court, these manufacturers make a determined advertising effort to attest "in glowing terms to the qualities and virtues of their products, and this advertising is directed at the ultimate consumer, or at some manufacturer or supplier who is not in privity with them. Equally sanguine representations on packages and labels frequently accompany the article throughout its journey to the ultimate consumer and, as intended, are relied upon by remote purchasers."[4] Accordingly, "It is highly unrealistic to limit a purchaser's protection to warranties made directly to him by his immediate seller. The protection he really needs is against the manufacturer whose published representations caused him to make the purchase."[5]

The court also said: "The policy of protecting the public from injury, physical or pecuniary, resulting from misrepresentations outweighs allegiance to an old and outmoded technical rule of law which, if observed, might be productive of great injustice. The manufacturer places his product upon the market. By advertising and labeling it, he represents its quality to the public in such a way as to induce reliance upon his representations. He unquestionably intends and expects that the product will be purchased and used in reliance upon his express assurance of its quality and, in fact, it is so purchased and used. Having invited and solicited this use, the manufacturer should not be permitted to avoid responsibility, when the expected use leads to injury and loss, by claiming he made no contract with the user."[6]

The New York Court of Appeals is not alone in its attitude on privity—many more courts across the country are also taking views that permit the consumer to have legal access to the manufacturer. As one Connecticut court put it—after first emphasizing the fact that neither the retailer nor the consumer can examine a packaged product, and that both rely upon the product's glittering packaging, in riotous color, and the alluring enticement of the qualities as depicted on labels: "There appears to be no sound reason for depriving a purchaser of the right to maintain an action against the manufacturer. Where the purchaser alleges he was induced to purchase the product—by the misrepresentations in the manufacturer's advertising—and he sustained harm when the product failed to measure up to the express or implied representations, he has that right."[7]

Still another decision contained a lengthy statement about the necessity of protecting the consumer so that "the burden of losses consequent upon use of defective articles is borne by those who are in a position to either control the danger or make an equitable distribution of the losses when they do occur . . ."[8]

This comment by the court is typical of a growing tendency—even when there is no blame on either side—to hold responsible the party better able to bear a loss. In effect, this new philosophy creates a liability on the part of the producer or seller, even when there has been no fault and no departure from reasonable standards of production control.

In addition to the privity of contract concept, other legal parameters are involved in any consideration of product liability. Some of these are discussed briefly in this article.

Negligence

The concept of negligence, that is, that the product's producer made a mistake, or was careless in its manufacture, has been one of the traditional avenues through which the consumer could sue for injury sustained as a result of using that product. Negligence, however, is not easy to prove. For example, an unsafe product—if designed and produced with reasonable care, skill, and quality control—cannot be said to have been negligently manufactured.

Express Warranty

When selling a product, the manufacturer or retailer almost always represents it as having certain characteristics, and he makes various claims for it. Some of these claims are *express*, that is, explicitly stated to the buyer. It does not matter whether the express claims are written or oral. What is significant is that they are presented to the buyer in an unequivocal manner. The seller's or manufacturer's express warranty is not limited to the warranty card which may accompany the item. Statements of labels, wrappers and cartons, and in advertising, are also express warranties. Manufacturers of goods are liable to the buyer for express warranties even though the consumer does not buy the product directly from them.

Implied Warranty

Simply by selling a certain product to a customer the seller implies that the goods are fit for the ordinary purpose for which such goods are most likely to be used. In addition, those sellers who furnish the customer with a product suitable for his need find that this transaction also falls within the purview of implied warranty. Thus, if you went to a camera store, claimed ignorance, and put yourself under the guidance of a salesman, his statements are implied warranties of the fitness of the camera he recommends for the purpose for which you are buying it.

A landmark automobile case concerns a New Jersey housewife who, while driving the family car purchased less than two weeks previously, was injured when the car went out of control and hit a wall. Although there was *no* proof that the car's manufacturer had been negligent, the court directed the jury to reach a verdict in favor of the driver. The case was appealed, and again the auto manufacturer lost. The New Jersey Supreme Court said: "We hold that under modern marketing conditions, when a manufacturer puts a new automobile in the stream of trade and promotes its purchase by the public, an implied warranty that it is reasonably suitable for use as such accompanies it into the hands of the ultimate purchaser."[9]

Strict Liability in Tort— A New Approach[10]

In the last several years a new theory has evolved that allows lawsuits under the concept of *strict liability in tort*. According to this theory, the manufacturer is liable for unfit products that unduly threaten the consumer's personal safety. The traditional conditions of either negligence or warranty (express or implied) are not required. Now, the manufacturer simply by having produced an unreasonably dangerous defective product, regardless of any other consideration, can be held liable for harm caused to the ultimate user of that product. As with warranties, it does not even matter if the manufacturer took every possible precaution to prevent defects. The liability of the manufacturer does not stem from either contractual or promissory understanding; instead, *liability in tort arises from the fact that the courts are imposing a social responsibility on manufacturers and sellers.* Even if they have exercised all possible care in the preparation and sale of the product they are now held accountable for a consumer's injury; these injuries can be either physical, or, as a result of the physical damage, financial.

Strict liability applies to a seller, contractor, supplier, assembler and manufacturer of all or any components of the distributed product. Unfortunately for the links in the supply chain, contributory negligence is not an acceptable defense in a lawsuit based upon strict liability. The purchaser or user of the defective product usually has to show only that it was defective when it left the control of the seller, although there are even exceptions to this rule.[11]

The situation that established the concept of strict liability was a 1962 California case, Greenman v. Yuba Power Products, Inc.[12] The plaintiff, Mr. Greenman, was seriously injured when a combination power tool (one which could be used as a saw, lathe, and so on) let fly a block of wood that hit him in the forehead. The California Supreme Court said: "A manufacturer is strictly liable in tort when an article he places on the market, knowing that it will be used without inspection, proves to have a defect that causes injury to a human being."[13] The effect of this decision was immediate. All over the country other courts began to rule similarly, particularly in the most populous, industrialized parts of the nation. The case can be considered to have two major areas of influence, legal and social. Legally, its significance is that it obviates the necessity to prove fault on the producer's or seller's part—it is only necessary that the product was defective when sold and that it did cause an injury to person or property. Socially, its significance is found in a quote from the Greenman decision, "The purpose of [strict liability in tort] is to insure that the costs of injuries resulting from defective products are borne by the manufacturers that put such products on the market rather than by the injured persons who are powerless to protect themselves."

When Is a Product Defective?

For purposes of the strict liability rule how is a product defined? When is it unreasonably dangerous or defective? The Restatement of Torts says: "The article sold must be dangerous to an extent beyond that which would be contemplated by the ordinary consumer who purchases it with the ordinary knowledge common to the community as to its characteristics."[14] Thus, the emphasis is upon the unusual and unexpected dangers attendant to the use of the product. Whiskey, for example, would not be considered dangerous because it makes people drunk and deteriorates their livers. Nor would butter, even though it can cause excessive cholesterol levels; but a nail imbedded in the butter is unusual and if you ingest it and scratch your intestine, you have exceeded the ordinary danger contemplated by the Restatement of Torts. To prosecute successfully a claim for injury under this strict liability rule, a consumer has only to show that the product was defective when it left the producer's control and that it did, indeed, cause him damage.

Strict Liability Is Not Absolute Liability

The section on defective products should not be interpreted to mean that the producer is liable under all conditions. He does not have *absolute liability*. The product's defect must be proven by the consumer. If there is no defect in the product, but it has caused harm, there is no liability on the part of the maker of the product. Several key cases have zeroed in on the definition of "defect." The Supreme Court of Arizona, for example, ruled that "a defective article is one that is not reasonably fit for the ordinary purposes for which such articles are sold and used."[15] And the Illinois Supreme Court noted that a product is defective when it does not perform as one might reasonably expect it to in view of its characteristics and intended function.[16]

The concept of strict liability in tort does not state that anyone harmed by the use of a product can recover damages from the product's maker or seller. These links in the channel of distribution are not *insurers* of the ultimate consumer. The latter must first demonstrate that there was *fault* in the production or design of the product and that the defect was present when it left the control of the maker or seller.

What Products Are Included Under Strict Liability?

It is obvious from the many court decisions in the last few years that all types of products are included under the purview of the strict liability doctrine. There is no limit to the products which can, if defective, become dangerous to the user or to his property. What can one do, however, with products necessarily unavoidably dangerous to the user? In this category would fall such items as a knife, hammer, whiskey, cigarettes, and automobiles. Can we hold the manufacturer of an automobile liable for the way people drive it? Do we hold the producer of a hammer responsible if somebody smashes his thumb with it? The vaccine for rabies, for example, often causes intense suffering when it is administered, and sometimes even results in paralysis and death. It is used, of course, because the alternative is an extremely painful death, but what about the producer of this rabies vaccine? Is he responsible for the pain and suffering of those who use it?[17]

It is important to remember that selling a product of merchantable quality does not mean that one is selling a *perfect* product. What it means is that the product is free from serious and unusual defects. Accordingly, one could expect to find a fish bone in fish served in a restaurant, or chicken bones in chickens. In these examples one would not have a viable case against the producer or seller of the food. In reviewing a broad range of liability cases involving many, many products, William L. Prosser of the University of California, concluded: "There is no strict liability when the product is fit to be sold and reasonably safe for use; but it has inherent dangers that no human skill or knowledge has yet been able to eliminate."[18]

The Foreseeability Doctrine

As the law of product liability is currently being developed, it appears quite likely that not only will manufacturers and sellers be held responsible for known risks of harm to consumers, but also for those risks which may be reasonably foreseen. The logic behind this is demonstrated in a statement by Arnold B. Elkind, a noted negligence lawyer, when he was head of the National Commission on Product Safety. Mr. Elkind said: "A manufacturer is best able to evaluate the risks inherent in his product and figure out ways to avoid them."[19]

A recent decision of the Kentucky Court of Appeals provides further insight into the development of the foreseeability doctrine.[20] It held that a manufacturer of vacuum cleaners designed to be used in 115 volt outlets was liable when a user of its product plugged the vacuum cleaner into a 220 volt circuit. The vacuum cleaner blew up. Despite the fact that the label clearly stated that the vacuum was to be plugged into 115 volt outlets only, the court still held the producer responsible because of the latter's failure to warn that plugging it into greater voltage was to invite disaster. In short, it is not sufficient to say "Don't do it" but you have to say why you should not do it, and what will happen if you do. The analogy used by the court was "It may be doubted that a sign warning 'Keep off the grass' could be deemed sufficient to apprise a reasonable person that the grass was infested with deadly snakes."

How Good Must a Product Be?

It is reasonable to ask ourselves how good a product actually must be in order for the manufacturer to avoid many of the risks of product liability. Some insight into this can be obtained by examining the criteria proposed by Dickerson. Dickerson concluded that the product is legally defective if it meets the following conditions:[21]

1. The product carries a significant physical risk to a definable class of consumer, and the risk is ascertainable at least by the time of trial.

2. The risk is one that the typical member of a class does not anticipate and guard against.

3. The risk threatens established consumer expectations with respect to a contemplated use and manner of use of a product in a contemplated minimum level of performance.

4. The seller has reason to know of the contemplated use and possibly, where injurious side effects are involved, has reasonable access to knowledge of a particular risk involved.

5. The seller knowingly participates in creating the contemplated use or in otherwise generating the relevant consumer expectations in the way attributed to him by the consumer.

Who Is Responsible for Faulty Products?

It has been written that, "The housewife who sells a jar of jam to a neighbor, or the man who trades in a used car on the purchase of a new one will obviously stand on a very different footing so far as the justifiable reliance of third persons is concerned. It is also very probable that the rule will not apply to sales outside of the usual course of business such as execution sales, or the bulk sale of an entire stock of goods for what they will bring after bankruptcy or a fire."[22]

Who then is liable? Well, to begin with, the manufacturer of the item. He, of course, is the most obvious. On the other hand, one who merely assembles the parts as opposed to actually having the machinery which makes them is also responsible for the safe and suitable performance of the product.[23] Also, each one who makes a component part of a final product, assuming that that component does not undergo change (and this is an extremely frequent occurrence) is responsible. While in most jurisdictions the retailer has also been held accountable under the theory of strict liability, there are a few exceptions in which certain courts have ruled that if products are sold in sealed containers the retailer is not necessarily responsible.[24] Here too there has been occasional disagreement as to this general interpretation.

If a seller of a product advertises that he has "manufactured" that product, or he has, simply by not saying otherwise, represented himself to be the manufacturer, he finds that he has the same responsibilities as the manufacturer.[25] Sub-assemblers and component part manufacturers are responsible for the products in the same sense as a fully integrated manufacturer and seller of a product. The co-equal responsibility of the suppliers of raw materials, sub-assemblies, assemblies, and entire operating systems is such that a few years ago a product's marketers were able to select their vendors, materials and components on the basis of price, speed of delivery, quality, and service—today they can no longer do this. Times have changed. They now have to add to their original purchasing criteria the determination of whether or not the prospective vendors' insurance is sufficient to cover any claims for damage, which might reasonably result from the use of his products. After all, if there may be a lawsuit, and if the injured consumer has the choice of suing the marketer or his supplier, he is obviously going to pick the one who is financially able to pay his claim for damages. If the vendor of the components, raw materials, sub-assemblies, and so on skirts the thin edge of financial responsibility in this respect, then the seller is likely to be "it." The watchwords for him are: "Be careful."

At the same time that this new criterion has to be added to the traditional list of the intelligent purchaser, the time tested criterion of quality control must be put under renewed surveillance. Some buyers, in fact, have recently gone to the extent of placing inspectors in their suppliers' plants to see to it that those items which they buy are of consistently high quality. It is very difficult to produce an item which is trouble free if the raw materials or components are not up to the desired standards.

The Effect Upon the Producer

All that has been said in this article affects the producer of consumer goods and services. There are certain effects, however, which have not yet been described. One is the additional risk to the *innovative* producer and seller. Obviously, the first producer of a consumer good which can be potentially dangerous, for example, television sets and electric irons, is in a different position regarding product liability than those who follow him. The first one must expend a good deal more time, effort, and money to establish production controls. He has to design for safety (both in the product and in its labeling and packaging), advertise the product properly so as not to mislead the buyer, and so on. Those firms which copy innovations later on can also copy the safeguards and designs in packaging and labeling, advertising, and quality control. Hence, their risks and their costs of operation will be lower. The result may well be a considerable diminution of innovator enthusiasm. Indeed, this has certainly happened in the last several years in the domestic drug industry, where today to get a drug approved by the Food and Drug Administration a rather lengthy, costly, and risky procedure must be followed. This may all be to the good of society in the long run, since many drugs which came out in years prior were less useful than their producers claimed. On the other hand, it is likely that some useful consumer products may either never emerge on the marketplace, or if they do it will be at a later time than was technically possible.

For all producers and sellers, not just innovators, there has been, since the expansion of the concept of strict liability, an increase in cost. The next time the reader wonders why some consumer items have gone up in cost he should remember that someone has to pay for the product liability insurance that so many items now require. Due to production and quality control measures designed to minimize faulty product design and performance there are additional costs to all producers and sellers. Too, legal fees, which can be quite expensive, must be paid for by everyone in the channel of distribution, from the producer to the consumer. For example, prior to its distribution, many advertisers now have each advertisement checked by a lawyer.

Products Liability Insurance

The risk that a producer or seller of any product can be hit with a claim for a catastrophic sum—one which could wipe out the entire net worth of the firm—is a real one. Obviously, manufacturers and marketers have begun to turn to products liability insurance as a means of dealing with the probability that the company will be involved in a damaging lawsuit.

The concept of products liability insurance is about 50 years old. In its early days it was generally confined to products designed for human consumption. Its primary feature was to protect the producers of such products against the fact that an occasional insect, piece of metal, chunk of glass, and so on would be in the food or drink. With the recent increased scope and activity of product liability, the coverage of products liability insurance has been extended to virtually every product category. Indeed, the total annual amount of insurance premiums for such coverage is probably about $100 million just in the United States. This is a big business which has developed in response to a major problem. Both the business and the problem will enlarge considerably before a stable level of activity is reached.

The Future

In the past several decades the law of product liability has changed enormously. It is reasonable to assume that some time in the near future liability will be imposed on the producer's or marketer's product without regard as to whether or not there was a defect in that product. After all, a certain amount of precedence has already been set by the fact that "no fault" insurance is now in effect in some parts of the country and is likely to sweep the nation within the next few years.

In addition, a number of recent product liability suits have evoked comments from the courts to the effect that the burden for payment and the burden of pain should be shifted to those who can bear it best. This almost always is the manufacturer and the seller, not the consumer. The implications for marketers are clear. The number of inputs which together comprise the ingredients of the marketing mix must now be expanded by one. Consideration of product liability must be included. The failure to do so can have a catastrophic effect upon the financial security of the firm. While product liability considerations may reduce innovation for some, it is better for them to have a reduced rate of innovation than to be wiped out entirely.

Notes

1. *Product liability* simply means the legal responsibility of a manufacturer or marketer of a product to compensate a consumer who has been "harmed" by the product.
2. MacPherson v. Buick Motor Company, 217 N.Y. 382, 111 N.E. 1050 (1916).
3. Privity is a legal concept. Its effect was to allow lawsuits only between those who purchased an item and those who sold it *directly* to them. Users other than the purchasers, or sellers more distant in the channel of distribution, could not be parties to a suit for injury arising from the use of that product.
4. Randy Knitwear v. American Cyanamid Company, 181 N.E. 2d 402 N.Y. (1962).
5. *Ibid.*
6. *Ibid.*
7. Connolly v. Hagi, 188 Atl. 2d 884 (Conn., 1963).
8. Henningsen v. Bloomfield Motors, Inc., 161 A. 2d 81–84 (1960).
9. Henningsen v. Bloomfield Motors, Inc., *ibid.* 84.
10. Tort is the legal term used to denote one form of a personal injury.
11. Vandermark v. Ford Motor Company, 61 Cal. 2d 256 (1964).
12. Greenman v. Yuba Power Products, Inc., 59 Cal. 2d 57, 377 P. 2d 897, 27 Cal. Rptr. 697 (1963).
13. *Ibid.*
14. "Injuries Caused by Products: Effects of Strict Liability," *National Underwriter* (December 1, 1967), p. 11.
15. Baily v. Montgomery Ward, 431 P. 2d 108 (1967).
16. Dunham v. Vughan and Bushnell Manufacturing Company, 86 Ill. App. 2d 315 (1967); 42 Ill. 2d 339 (1969).
17. Carmen v. Eli Lilly & Company, 109 Ind. App. 76, 32 N.E. 2d 729 (1941).
18. William L. Prosser, "The Fall of the Citadel" (Strict Liability to the Consumer) *Minnesota Law Review*, Vol. 50, No. 5 (April 1966), p. 812.
19. "The Long Reach of Liability," *Business Week*, No. 2088 (September 6, 1969), p. 95.
20. *Ibid.*
21. Reed Dickerson, "Products Liability: How Good Does a Product Have to Be?" *Indiana Law Journal*, Vol. 42 (1967), p. 331.
22. Prosser, "The Fall of the Citadel" (Strict Liability to the Consumer) *Minnesota Law Review*, Vol. 50, No. 5 (April 1966), p. 812.
23. Putman v. Erie City Manufacturing Company, 338 Fed. 2d 911 (5th Cir. 1964).
24. Esborg v. Bailey Drug Company, 61 Wash. 2d P. 2d 298 (1963).
25. Ibbetson v. Montgomery Ward & Company, 171 Ill. App. 355 (1912).

Corporate Responses to Consumerism Pressures

David A. Aaker and George S. Day

Today all signs indicate that consumerism pressures will intensify. The result will be increased demand for governmental regulation, with its attendant problems of inflexibility, high costs, and new inequities created by uneven administration. The seriousness of the problems that these pressures create depends on the effectiveness of business

David A. Aaker and George S. Day, "Corporate Responses to Consumerism Pressures," Harvard Business Review, November–December 1972, copyright ©1972 by the President and Fellows of Harvard College; all rights reserved.

organizational response, and business's willingness to help the various agencies and legislative committees frame realistic and workable guidelines, rules, and regulations. In other words, business's moral response to consumers can be viewed in the nature of its response to the private and governmental bodies established to protect and advance consumer rights. In the following article, Professors David A. Aaker (School of Business Administration, University of California, Berkeley) and George S. Day (Graduate School of Business, Stanford University) stress the opportunities inherent in management responses to consumers and suggest how corporate managements can make future consumer-oriented programs more effective. Of particular interest is the authors' call for a new marketing orientation that focuses on long-run consumer interests instead of concentrating on what the market is looking for at the moment.

Until recently, observers of the consumer movement concentrated on understanding the scope and causes of consumerism and on forecasting probable future activity in this area. This emphasis was appropriate, given the rapid emergence of consumerism and the attendant confusion and uncertainty. The ground rules for business were changing rapidly, and it was easy for these observers to conclude that the initiative was with legislatures, regulatory bodies, consumer advocates, and the judiciary.

By contrast, the responses of business to these pressures often appeared passive and confused or reactive and misguided. This picture is changing as companies and trade associations accept the reality of consumerism and gain experience with positive programs.

Evidence on the success of these endeavors is sketchy; many programs are new, seem to be exploratory, and often lack adequate resources. However, it is not too early to attempt to generalize from these efforts to help management make future programs more effective.

This raises a whole series of questions: What approaches are promising? What are the barriers to developing effective response programs? How can the important problem areas and worthwhile opportunities be identified? Are existing decision-making processes and organizational forms inhibiting progress? What about industry-wide efforts? Finally, what is the role of government regulation?

In this article, we shall first take a look at these evolving corporate responses, then discuss the barriers to company initiatives, and finally examine the potential for industry action spearheaded by the leadership of trade associations.

Evolving Company Actions

In the early 1960's, consumerism was most often regarded by business executives as a transitory threat to be opposed at every turn by invoking ideology and denying the seriousness of the charges. Such approaches generally gave way to defensive responses wherein the apparent problems were usually identified by those outside the organization and managers were forced to react under pressure.

Increasingly, however, corporate managers are making efforts not only to identify and anticipate problems but also to view consumerism as a marketing opportunity, not as a threat. The result of such an orientation can be the optimal consumer program—one which addresses a real social problem and simultaneously demonstrates short-term value to the company.

Approaches and Programs

Whirlpool was perhaps the first corporation to take this positive approach aggressively through the development of a comprehensive consumer-problem-oriented program that has evidently been successful in terms of conventional measures. In recognizing the inherent problem of providing appliances which perform reliably, Whirlpool first invested in an improved service organization. This was followed by the introduction of the corporation's subsequently widely imitated "cool line," a program that permits customers with a complaint or problem to contact service consultants directly, and a radically simplified warranty. Later, the company experimented with tel-tags to improve the quality of Whirlpool's point-of-sale information. Equally important, these innovations were communicated to the consumer in a way that enabled Whirlpool to build a corporate image of genuine consumer concern—an image that was based on substance.

Several supermarket chains have since developed comprehensive programs that have had similar impact. Utilizing discounting, open dating, unit pricing, and nutritional information plans, they have been able to assert an aggressive consumer-oriented image.

Specific research. There is some evidence that programs are being increasingly evaluated and refined. Specific program research increases the probability that programs and company positions will be more defensible in the future both to internal and external challenges.

For example, Federated Department Stores has developed a series of experiments with tel-tags on small appliances. Safeway Stores and others have conducted research on unit pricing. Such research can sometimes uncover unexpected benefits. Thus Federated found that the tel-tags were of considerable value to sales clerks; the unit pricing research determined that costs for large stores were less than anticipated and were partially offset by the benefits of enhanced consumer confidence.

Research can also test often overly optimistic predictions of public interest. While program research is still not being conducted frequently enough, the situation has improved considerably in recent months.

Educational efforts. If there is an underlying theme to any analysis of consumerism, it is that consumers lack adequate information on which to base informed decisions. Various programs have been initiated which are responsive to this general problem. In particular, many national advertisers have been increasingly willing to undertake educational campaigns and to use longer, more informative copy than they were using only a few years ago.

For example, a Ford Motor campaign told consumers how to buy cars and offered a booklet with helpful details. Lee Carpets has run advertisements addressing questions faced by those purchasing carpets and offering a booklet. Hunt-Wesson Foods has decided to avoid advertising relatively immaterial product differences. Such a trend is most welcome since advertising has been under increasing attack—with some justification—as contributing to the information gap by emphasizing emotional appeals, with greater potential for deception, at the expense of comparative information. Undoubtedly, there is much room for further improvement.

Raymond A. Bauer and Stephen A. Greyser, in their study of Americans' attitudes toward advertising, had respondents categorize advertisements and found that only 5.8% of those ads noticed were perceived as being particularly informative—that is, "ads that you learn something from, that you are glad to know or know about . . . that help you in one way or another because of the information they provide."[1]

Countervailing influences. A further illustration of the increased responsiveness of some companies is their willingness to capitalize on the inability of related industries or suppliers to respond to consumerism. This has the dual benefit of (a) enhancing a company's image in this area by deflecting criticism to a new target and (b) solving problems that are otherwise out of the control of the company. This approach is seen in the recent announcement by Giant Food that it will not carry specific items in which the packaging or other aspects are perceived to be potentially unsafe or deceptive.

Other food chains (a) have unilaterally stopped stocking items whose contents have been deceptively reduced to avoid a price raise, (b) have marked the phosphate content of soaps and detergents with shelf signs, (c) have highlighted items that are ecologically better than others (such as glass instead of plastic and returnable rather than nonreturnable bottles), and (d) have instituted shelf-dating programs for products such as batteries and wristwatches when the supplier does not have such a program.

Insurance companies are putting pressure on automobile manufacturers to design automobiles that are safer and easier to repair in order to control the rising cost of damages. Allstate is advertising that it "will cut collision rates 20% for any car the manufacturer certifies, through independent tests, can take a five-mile-an-hour crash into a test barrier, front and rear, without damage."

Mobilization and Organization

The practice of creating consumer affairs departments is spreading as more and more companies search for ways to deal with consumerism problems. Some of these efforts are obviously blessed with top-management commitment, a key to short-run success. Others, however, appear less viable because the corporate focus is on gaining a public relations advantage or on presenting an aura of concern in order to forestall possible litigation.

A new or expanded consumer affairs department can provide the needed impetus. To be effective, however, it should have a clearly defined set of responsibilities and corresponding authority. The specific functions will depend on many factors, but they should generally be defined to incorporate these four related actions:

1. To receive customer complaints and problems, and to have sufficient authority to resolve them—if necessary, by overriding the desires of the operating groups. Such an effort would be close to the concept of an ombudsman, representing the individual complainant against the organization.

2. To develop and operate an information system with the dual functions of (a) monitoring the extent to which product-class buyers and users are satisfied with each element of the marketing programs of the company and its major competitors, and (b) detecting and predicting areas of basic consumer discontent that may possibly have a negative impact on the company or to which the organization may be uniquely qualified to respond.

   Obviously, such a system will be effective only to the extent that the output is interpreted and communicated to management so that policy implications are highlighted and follow-up is encouraged. In particular, profit opportunities through new products and/or services need to be identified and communicated to the appropriate decision makers.

3. To be a representative and advocate of the consumer interest during the policy-making process. Thus the new department should be in a position whereby it can provide an independent appraisal of the company's marketing programs.

   For example, do proposed new products represent a real contribution to the life-style of a market segment? Or are they simply an unneeded addition created to exploit current buying patterns? What will be the human and environmental side effects of proposed new products? Are the company's external communications (not only media advertising, but also product-label copy, warranties and guarantees, and so forth) as deception-free and informative as possible?

   The basic principle here is that the monitoring and control functions should be distinct from operating management. This suggests that the consumer affairs department ought to report to the chief executive officer who is ultimately responsible for the company's performance in the consumer affairs area. A further implication is that the new department might have direct responsibility for functions such as quality control and product service that are vital to the resolution of consumer problems. (Such functions generally tend to be compromised when carried out by operating groups.)

4. To contribute to the development of corporate social objectives, programs to implement those objectives, and operational measures by which the programs can be evaluated. The establishment of objectives will involve tough resource-allocation questions and consideration of nonprofit measures of performance.

Barriers to Initiatives

There are various inherent difficulties facing corporate executives who would develop response programs. Some arise from the nature of the decision area. It is not easy to identify and analyze the fundamental problems to be addressed. Others are due to the difficulty of adapting the organization and its decision-making process. Finally, there are external pressures from the marketplace to consider.

Understanding the Problems

Experience shows that many specific consumer difficulties and dissatisfactions are surface symptoms of more basic problems. If the symptom is eliminated, another will probably appear unless the underlying problem is identified and addressed. Without this recognition, a response program can too easily become a futile fire-fighting effort rather than a step on the road to resolving the fundamental problem.

There is evidence of this difficulty in the current flurry of interest in nutritional labels and charts. A wide variety of labeling plans has been proposed by industry and legislatures. Some cereal manufacturers have gone as far as to flash a list of nutrition contents on the television screen at the end of their commercial messages. Other companies have lengthy nutrition charts which they distribute to customers. Several companies are participating in races to turn bread products into vitamin pills.

Suppose, however, that such an analysis reveals the basic problem is that people are undernourished. One segment is undernourished because good food is not available to the people and/or because they do not know how to select proper diets; another larger segment has the means and perhaps the knowledge but lacks motivation to pursue proper diets. Neither segment will probably be influenced by nutritional labels or charts.

An example of a program that is likely to be more appropriate than labels or charts is Hunt-Wesson Foods' computerized menu service. Over 1.3 million people requested and received a month's supply of menus tailored to their food budget and family size. Another is Del Monte's experimental program to provide a computer-based analysis of diets of groups with special problems, such as alcoholism. It might be worthwhile to attempt to motivate people to consider nutrition more in their menu planning. Such efforts could be useful not only from a social viewpoint but also from the standpoint of increased profits for a food company.

A cool-line program to provide customers with telephone contact with factory service consultants may be difficult to justify as part of a service operation. In most cases, the customer can either call a service representative directly or else contact the company by letter.

However, assume that one of the basic problems underlying the consumerism movement is a dissatisfaction with the degree to which the institutions in our society are perceived as being impersonal and unresponsive. (The widespread use of self-service retailing, the low profile maintained by most executives, the entry of computers into the interface between the individual and the organization, and the inherent difficulties of dealing with bureaucracies—all contribute to this dissatisfaction.)

Then, a cool-line program appears in another perspective. It provides the customer with immediate personal contact with the company. The potential of calling a *real* person—*provided* that person can actually solve problems and is not simply another intermediary who increases the customer's frustration level—should dramatically alter people's perception of an institution as impersonal and unresponsive.

Pinpointing the Issues

If an organization is to address fundamental issues instead of symptoms, it must identify and analyze them. Such a task is most formidable for two reasons.

First, the basic issues are inherently difficult to understand. Issues tend to be dynamic and interrelated. The real problems are frequently not visible to the public; even significant symptoms often lie dormant until a startling report of a particularly misleading, unsafe, or unwholesome social situation serves to focus consumer discontent.

Second, the information systems of most organizations are neither oriented to nor effective in obtaining information that will enable the company to detect and predict underlying social issues. Market research groups are usually directed at short-term projects with relatively limited objectives—that is, projects which are primarily concerned with competitive considerations. They essentially research symptoms if, indeed, they do any research that is relevant to real consumer needs.

Some organizations do of course make good use of longitudinal analyses of consumer complaints, consumer surveys, and the positions of consumer advocates. But too often such analyses have neither the breadth nor the depth to provide adequate insights. What is needed is a more ambitious mission for the research group, and also the development of new measures.

There are some promising research efforts that suggest what is required. One is the emerging use of social indicators and the more directed life-style measures. Another is the application of focused group interviews systematically conducted over time and oriented to the identification of basic consumer problems rather than to specific product decisions. Still another is the effort to obtain futuristic subjective inputs. One organization is applying the Delphi technique, an iterative approach used to stimulate and refine ideas of a group of individuals working independently, using a number of futurists.

Whatever the difficulties, it seems clear that organizations need to divert resources in this direction. As Peter F. Drucker has observed, the responsibility of any institution in a period of rapid change is "the anticipation of social needs and their conversion into opportunities for performance and results."[2]

The Nature of Decision Making

An appropriate orientation toward basic problems and a capable information system are necessary but not sufficient conditions for an effective response program. In addition, program development requires a compatible decision-making process within a sympathetic organizational structure.

Cost-benefit analysis. The decision-making process within the company is not easily adjusted to encompass social consequences. Decision makers are not oriented to consider social implications. They have been trained and conditioned to think about more conventional determinants of profits. A related problem is that the benefits are difficult to quantify. There are two reasons for this.

First, the payoffs to the company are often largely deferred. It is difficult enough to identify cause-effect relationships and to solve troublesome measurement problems when the impact of a decision is immediate. When the implications are long run in nature, the uncertainties are magnified.

Second, the benefits are often indirect. A unit-pricing program or the installation of a tel-tag system will primarily have a direct impact even if it has a long-run component. However, the value to the organization of nutritional education programs in the ghetto areas, for instance, will have benefits that are more indirect. Although benefits are difficult to quantify, the costs are usually painfully obvious and appear to affect prices or profits directly. It is easy and natural to let the hard data dominate the decision-making process.

Operational objectives. Most corporations have well-developed planning processes that involve both short- and long-range time horizons, but relatively few explicitly include in their planning effort social goals and corresponding programs to implement them. Yet there is a clear need for consumer programs to be guided by operational objectives with accompanying nonprofit, short-run measures which will serve to reflect long-run and indirect benefits.

Other parts of the organization make similar use of objectives with nonprofit measures of success. Advertising, for example, usually has communication objectives which are often measured by constructs like awareness levels and attitude changes. Similarly, a consumer program should have objectives, as well as appropriate performance measures. An insurance company's program to reduce the number of drunk drivers might use indexes of drunk driving as program measures. A nutritional information campaign might be evaluated in terms of attitudes and motivations.

The need for objectives to guide consumer programs becomes particularly acute when the benefits seem far removed from the day-to-day operation of the company. In these situations, decisions are usually made in an ad hoc manner. Without operational objectives and implementation plans, the chances for real impact are slim. Further, if objectives and accompanying performance measures do not exist, resources devoted to social response programs cannot be held accountable.

A set of objectives and an accompanying implementation program provide four benefits: (1) the organization's efforts tend to be more integrated and focused, (2) the possibility that programs would be addressed to basic problems instead of symptoms is increased, (3) the potential of providing a rational means of allocating resources to alternative programs is created, and (4) the development of nonprofit measures as well as performance benchmarks and targets is stimulated.

Ethical considerations. Complicating the decision-making process are ethical considerations—standards which can result in costly self-imposed constraints on decisions. Ethical considerations assume importance when decisions must be made in the gray areas between what is legally permitted and what is morally and ethically wrong. There is a decided tendency in marketing to use the words "legal" and "honest" interchangeably.

There are also many situations in which the law is open to interpretation—with respect to deceit, misrepresentation, competitive disparagement, and so forth—so that legal compliance provides only a minimum ethical standard. Consequently, managers who resort to law as their justification look particularly graceless under public scrutiny.

The marketing concept can also serve as a convenient rationale for avoiding responsibility. This rationale is related to the ideological issue of whether marketers should lead or respond. Robert Moran, a researcher who is interested in the conflicts between marketers and their critics, has noted:

"... marketers perceive their role, or at least claim it to be, as *responding* to consumer wants, habits, interests, and abilities. They resist what they feel is a new role their critics would have them perform—namely, that of confronting consumers with products and policies designed to give the consumer what they believe he *needs* or *should want*."[3]

For this reason, there has been great resistance to the "paternalism" aspect of consumerism that encompasses the protection of consumers against themselves or, more simply, giving consumers what they need rather than what they want. There are encouraging signs that this resistance by industry is lessening, especially in the area of product labeling and performance claims.

Decentralization disadvantages. The leaders in the development of progressive consumer programs—such as retail food stores and manufacturers of large appliances—tend to be characterized by centralized decision making. In contrast, the "consumerism record" for those with highly decentralized decision making is much less impressive. There are several reasons why the decentralized corporation is at a real disadvantage when attempting to respond to consumerism pressures.

In organizations with decentralized profit centers, the short-run profit pressures are often intense. Decision makers at lower profit-center levels are likely to be relatively early in their careers, a time when competition for recognition is high. They are often systematically moved so that their tenure in a particular job may last for only one or two years. Thus it is natural for them to emphasize short-term considerations.

Further, these lower level managers are not always motivated to consider the whole organization when evaluating decision alternatives since they, themselves, are judged solely on the basis of their own profit center. Yet social consequences tend to operate at the level of the whole organization. For example, a department store buyer might—perhaps accidentally—authorize a deceptive advertisement that could affect the store's reputation but would have little impact upon his profit center.

Of course, those at higher levels of profit responsibility are also under pressure, but they normally have a broader perspective and can often afford to take a longer view.

We are not suggesting that organizations should reject decentralization, especially when such an approach has provided managerial motivation and good short-run response to consumer demand. However, one should recognize that an organization with a high degree of decentralized decision making has special problems in developing responses to consumerism pressures.

Thus it may be possible to develop a subsidy system to influence decision making without imposing external constraints. This system would recognize decisions that had demonstrable long-run or corporate benefits which would not ordinarily appear on the current profit statements. Such recognition could be negative as well as positive.

For example, if a branch manager authorized a deceptive advertisement, this too would be suitably and formally recognized. Just as the corporation needs to be measured by more than profitability, so does the manager of a profit center within that corporation.

Authority positions. We assume that sufficient authority could be conferred on the new consumer affairs positions to make them effective. Our assumption could be ill-founded, however, if the authority were to be obtained by supplanting that of existing positions such as the vice president of sales or marketing. Such loss of authority would likely be regarded as both an accusation of failure and a threat for the future. The result might be a withdrawing of vital support within the organization.

Thus it could be tempting for the holder of an ombudsman-like position, especially if he perceived it as a short-term position, to retain support by avoiding decisions that favored a complainant or outsider. This could be a very real threat to the potential of these new positions to achieve change within the organization.

An approach which will alleviate the problem is to make sure the manager involved is sufficiently respected by the organization so that he need not rely too heavily on formal authority. This implies that he must be a competent and broadly trained senior manager or outsider of the stature of Esther Peterson, the consumer adviser to the president of Giant Food.

Paul R. Lawrence and Jay W. Lorsch studied positions with cross-functional area "integrator" responsibilities.[4] They concluded that effective managers in such positions are influential because of their knowledge and expertise rather than because of their formal authority. They also noted that the assigning of young managers lacking in exposure to all facets of the business to such positions was a common failing.

Competitive considerations. The ultimate reality to be faced is that many potential initiatives will involve costs and risks of failure which can threaten the company's competitive position. Unless there is a fair certainty that competition will emulate the initiative, a great deal of the incentive to act independently is lost.

This was the position the automobile manufacturers found themselves in during the 1960's regarding the safety problem when consumers did not consider safety especially important. It is still a problem for companies considering extensive and costly improvements in safety, reducing advertising clutter, or eliminating nonreturnable bottles.

In this light, self-regulation looks very attractive, for it promises industrywide action with no loss in competitive position.

Industry-Action Potential

Until very recently, most trade associations were viewed by their members as defense mechanisms or negative lobbyists. This has changed with various pressures on them to be more responsive and with the increasing threat of government regulation. Individual companies are now turning to their trade associations for leadership in the four basic areas of (1) coordinating and disseminating research, (2) consumer and dealer education, (3) development of standards, and (4) complaint handling.

The first responsibility of trade associations is to keep their members properly informed by coordinating and disseminating research.

This activity may either supplement or be a substitute for the efforts of individual companies to become sensitive to consumerism problems and government initiatives. Without such information the members may pressure the association to take unrealistic and unattainable positions that work against the long-run interests of the industry.

Furthermore, if the information is objective, and not subject to restrictions because of confidentiality, it can be very useful in presenting industry arguments to governmental bodies. There is no question that research findings would be welcomed in both sectors, in preference to the "relatively unstructured and unscientifically assembled information which comes to us either out of our own experience or the experience of friends or in individual letters of complaint, in testimony of individual consumers and out of the experience of those who deal with and work with consumer problems."[5]

These considerations have led to the formation of the Consumer Research Institute by the Grocery Manufacturers of America, and the support of basic research on advertising by the American Association of Advertising Agencies and the Canadian Advertising Advisory Board.

The second responsibility of trade associations is to provide leadership in consumer and dealer education.

An industry association has an enormous comparative advantage over individual members in the educational function. This is most obvious in broad-scale controversies such as nutrition, where education can play a big role but no individual company can undertake the responsibility.

Associations are also in a good position to work through dealers, where the education function frequently fails. This was the experience of the Outdoor Power Equipment Institute in its efforts to acquaint users with the hazards and proper use of power mowers. The dealers should have been the most influential channel of information about safety, but they needed stimulation and education before their potential was achieved.

The third responsibility of trade associations is leadership in the development of standards.

The most common form of self-regulation is the product standardization and certification program in the areas of quality, reliability, safety, and/or healthfulness. Standards may also apply to size, shape, and style variations, where necessary to facilitate consumer comparisons, reduce product proliferation, or ensure interchangeability of parts. Certification is the mechanism for identifying whether the product conforms to the standard. This judgment is made by one of approximately a thousand laboratories that test products.

There are various explanations for the motives behind the development of standards. One view is that the subscribers to a standard do so out of a sense of public responsibility and professional ethics combined with a desire to prevent similar standards from being imposed from the outside.

The Federal Trade Commission has recently argued that the character of the market on the buying side is the major determinant of the extent and quality of standards. The FTC observed that most of the estimated 20,000 sets of industry standards in effect in the United States exist in industrial markets where the buyers are large and expert and can force the development of this kind of information. One outcome of this analysis is a proposal that the law itself must provide the incentive for the development of standards for consumer products.

In many ways, the standards for advertising and promotion practices are the most difficult to set because of the problems in deciding what is inappropriate, deceptive, tasteless, or not in the public interest. Such standards are frequently only recommendations or suggestions (e.g., those of the Proprietary Association for the advertising of medications).

The fourth responsibility of trade associations is to provide leadership in the area of complaint handling.

In an effort to forestall the aggrieved consumer from turning first to the government, many industries are considering or implementing their own hearing boards for processing complaints. These are similar to the efforts of individual companies to provide an independent ombudsman-like function.

As an illustration, the appliance industry, in conjunction with major retailers, has set up a major appliance consumer action panel which will act as a "court of last resort," should retailer and manufacturer contact fail to resolve a complaint problem.

A similar principle is followed by the National Advertising Review Board. This organization utilizes the resources of 140 local Better Business Bureaus to monitor national advertisements, evaluate complaints, and advise advertisers on planned campaigns. If a complaint cannot be resolved at the local bureau level, it is referred to a review board of five people (one of whom represents a consumer group). If the advertiser is found to be in violation of review board standards and refuses to change or withdraw his ad, the dis-

agreement is publicized and the case turned over to the Federal Trade Commission.

Problems With Self-regulation

Experience indicates that purely voluntary efforts at self-regulation are not likely to be successful. There must be some enforcement mechanism by which violations of regulatory norms can be punished through collective action against the violator.

Unfortunately, such private power can also be used to enforce product standards rigged in favor of one or two producers or to dictate a safety certification program that is too costly for small manufacturers. Such actions are clearly anticompetitive and therefore forbidden by antitrust legislation.

The courts have used the potential for such abuses as reason to declare many enforcement techniques illegal—including the circulation of blacklists, withholding of a seal of approval, and the use of indirect boycotts. Many of these judgments against self-regulation are made without reference to the social merit of restraint.

This presents a real dilemma. An industrywide agreement on standards is unlikely to be effective without inducements for compliance that are beyond the scope of a voluntary agreement. Yet the stronger the enforcement procedure, the greater the degree of potential coercion and danger of an antitrust violation.

This threat can be substantially diminished (a) by industry-government teamwork (in which industry proposes and implements the rules and standards by which the government regulates the industry), and (b) by the public and other interested parties playing a significant role both in developing and administering the rules and standards and in avoiding any discrimination against specific manufacturers.

Presuming that enforcement problems can be overcome, there remain four other barriers to the effectiveness of self-regulation (insofar as effectiveness means forestalling other forms of regulation):

1. The industry members may simply fail to see that there is an injustice in a practice and hence not take any regulatory action. Consequently, "such abuses as the advertisement in poor taste, unsolicited merchandise, the

engineered contest, shrinkage of package weight, the unsubstantiated claim, and the negative option sales plan are all defended by sellers who perceive no wrong in them."[6] Their insensitivity leaves room for government investigation if not regulation.

2. The quality of the decision making and leadership of the association is frequently weakened by the need for consensus among a majority of members. This has particularly weakened safety standards for many products to the point that they represent nothing more than an affirmation of the status quo. The antitrust question also complicates the search for consensus.

3. Virtually every industry or trade association is accused of, and complains of, having inadequate resources to carry out its responsibilities (with the probable exception of lobbying efforts). Inadequate resources mean outdated and inadequate standards, poor research and communications efforts, and complaint mechanisms that are inaccessible or unknown to the consumer.

One measure of the seriousness of the resource problem in the United States is found in the product-safety area. Although there are more than 1,000 standards covering 350 product categories, the National Commission on Product Safety found that industrywide voluntary safety standards applied to only 18 of the 44 categories that are highest in the number of estimated annual injuries.[7]

Efforts to provide complaint-handling mechanisms are particularly vulnerable. For example, the experience of Great Britain with "consultative machinery" in four major nationalized industries—gas, electricity, coal, and transportation—is sobering. After 22 years of publicizing these channels for complaints, a consumer study found that unaided recall awareness by industry varied from 4% to 12% of the population.[8]

The reason is that a complaint about the performance of a specific industry is a rare event for most consumers. Herein lies the strength of the Better Business Bureaus, for they are readily accessible and well-known to consumers as a place to register all kinds of complaints. The long-run prospects for specific industries to reach out and find aggrieved consumers (without an intermediary) appear slim.

4. Some problems may be beyond the scope of the responsibility that the industry is willing or able to accept. This seems to characterize many pollution-related issues, including nonreturnable bottles, auto emissions, and other currently intractable problems such as advertising clutter in all media.

The effectiveness of self-regulation ultimately depends on the public's willingness to accept industry regulations and standards in lieu of government intervention. This, in turn, requires that the public trusts the intention and effectiveness of business in solving consumer problems. Here, the climate is distinctly unfriendly.

A recent national probability sample of 1,613 adults, age 18 or over, found substantial support for new government restrictions and regulations. For example, 75% of the sample supported a regulation that would "require major companies to set strict standards of quality which would be enforced by government inspection."[9]

The context was certainly not one of complete mistrust of business; there was evidence of a "readiness to give the private sector credit for what it can do for itself" (it is interesting to note here that the much-maligned Better Business Bureau was given the highest proportion of positive ratings of any consumer protection group or individual), as well as distinct ambivalence about the effectiveness of government.

However, this standing is vulnerable to rising criticism, especially over the conflict of interest implications of financial dependence on the businesses being regulated. The big question is whether recent efforts at reform, including regional rather than local control, can offset this criticism.

Overall, the loss of confidence in the ability of business to adequately respond to the pressures of consumerism is the greatest threat to industry self-regulation as it is currently conceived. This does not preclude such efforts; it simply means that industry associations are going to have to demonstrate greater leadership and extend their efforts further than they appear to be doing.

This will almost certainly mean broadening the participation of the public in both the setting and enforcing of standards. Such a move, with all its threatening ramifications, is likely, on balance, to be superior to government regulation for most consumerism problems.

Conclusion

The evolution of business responses to consumerism is entering a new stage, with increasing recognition that—

consumerism pressures will continue at a high, although perhaps less frenetic, level in the future;

for some companies, consumerism has been an opportunity rather than a threat, and that responsive programs can yield dividends through increased consumer confidence;

a posture of resistance, coupled with purely defensive programs, is likely to be counterproductive in the long run, because it increases the probability of government regulation with all the attendant problems of inflexibility, high costs, and new inequities created by unworkable rules and uneven administration.

These factors have led companies—acting either autonomously, through their trade associations, or in conjunction with government agencies—to undertake efforts to identify and correct problems before they become too serious. The question is no longer whether the effort should be made, but how to make the effort effective. Some tentative generalizations as to how to achieve this end are now possible.

First, it is necessary to focus on underlying consumer problems instead of chasing symptoms of those problems. Such an orientation requires an extended information system involving new measures of the consumer—his attitudes, values, and life-styles—and a fresh interpretation of existing measures.

Second, it is useful to have an independent group in the organization charged with representing the consumer interest, but only if it has top-

management support and is staffed with people who are both knowledgeable and respected.

Third, attention must be given to the design and implementation of programs. Because of the difficulty in creating effective and appropriate programs, experimentation and testing should be employed. Further, operational objectives with distinct, measurable indicators of performance are required. These indicators are not easy to develop since they usually will not be closely linked to short-term profits.

Finally, a new orientation is required. The success of the organization cannot be measured by short-run sales or profits. The marketing concept must be interpreted in terms of long-run consumer interests instead of what the market is accepting at the moment. Products and supporting communication need to be carefully scrutinized to determine whether they actually provide the consumer with real utility and useful information.

Notes

1. *Advertising in America: The Consumer View* (Cambridge, Massachusetts, Harvard University Press, 1968), p. 183.

2. *The Age of Discontinuity* (New York, Harper & Row, 1969), p. 205.

3. "Formulating Public Policy on Consumer Issues: Some Preliminary Findings" (Cambridge, Massachusetts, Marketing Science Institute, 1971), p. 31.

4. "New Management Job: The Integrator," HBR November–December 1967, p. 142.

5. Mary Gardiner Jones, "Enough Talking—Let's Get on With the Job," address to Illinois Federation of Consumers, Chicago, Illinois, April 3, 1970, p. 12.

6. Louis L. Stern, "Consumer Protection via Self-Regulation," *Journal of Marketing,* July 1971, p. 49.

7. *Final Report of the National Commission on Product Safety* (Washington, Government Printing Office, June 1970), p. 48.

8. *Consumer Consultative Machinery in the Nationalized Industries,* A Consumer Council Study (London, Her Majesty's Stationery Office, 1968).

9. John Revett, "Consumers Endorse More Restrictions on Business," *Advertising Age,* October 25, 1971, p. 98.

For Further Reading

Bauer, R., & Greyser, S. A. *Advertising in America: The consumer view.* Cambridge, Mass.: Harvard University Press, 1968.

Levitt, T. *The third sector.* New York: AMACOM, American Management Association, 1973.

Nader, R. *Unsafe at any speed.* New York: Pocket Books, 1966.

_____ (Ed.). *The consumer and corporate accountability.* New York: Harcourt Brace Jovanovich, 1973.

O'Connell, J., & Myers, A. *Safety last.* New York: Random House, 1966.

Peterson, M. B. *The regulated consumer.* Los Angeles: Nash Publishing, 1971.

Winter, R. K., Jr. *The consumer advocate versus the consumer.* Washington, D.C.: American Enterprise Institute for Public Policy Research, 1972.

8

WOMEN AND OTHER DISADVANTAGED GROUPS

Manuel Ortega is manager of the design department of Quilling Engineering, a division of Universal Business Equipment (UBE). Although business within Quilling has been brisk, UBE is feeling the pinch of a sluggish economy. As a result, UBE management has asked all its divisions to cut back costs by 12.5 percent.

The president of Quilling, wanting to ensure his company makes this goal, raises the cutback costs to 15 percent. Although Manuel Ortega objects, the president insists. Ortega sees no other alternative than to implement the president's decision.

On the very day that he receives his orders, Ortega informs his section heads to draw up plans reflecting the proposed cutback. A few days later the plans come in, each listing projects cut and employees to be laid off. A note on one plan catches Ortega's eye: "One of the five engineers to be laid off is Barbara Marshall, the *only* female working in the design department." Ortega winces, immediately sensing a problem.

Without hesitating he removes from his desk a booklet containing UBE's policy about hiring members of minority groups and women. It reads: "Managers should realize that they are expected to meet the equal opportunity goals within their departments, while at the same time meeting profit goals." A glance at her personnel file informs Ortega that Marshall is a thirty-two-year-old divorced mother of two. Her progress reports indicate that she's cooperative, competent, and efficient, but at present she is the least effective of the engineers in the design department.

In the days ahead, Ortega tries every way to transfer Marshall to another department without having to bump someone else. It's impossible. He must either discharge Marshall and thus violate UBE policy or keep her and dismiss a more valuable employee.

The dilemma that Manuel Ortega faces is not an uncommon one today. On the one hand, managers are being asked to comply with governmental programs designed to give members of groups traditionally disadvantaged special consideration in personnel decisions. On the other hand, they must operate in a way that's fair and just to all concerned and in a way that is compatible with the best interests of the firm. This is not an easy task. Although these obligations needn't conflict, they frequently do. What's more, they raise fundamental concerns about justice.

In this chapter we'll consider the problem that the Ortega case raises. Specifically, we'll be inquiring about whether it's moral to give individuals preferential treatment in the work place because of their sexual, racial, or ethnic identities. Those persons who say it is moral base their reply partly on the traditional discrimination that has victimized women and minority-group members, arguing that business owes it to these groups to repair the damages of the past. To grasp this argument, it's important to understand the unequal and unfair treatment such group members have received. For this reason the chapter begins with an overview of the plight of women and minority-group members in the work place. In addition, it considers the condition of two other groups, older and younger workers, whose peculiar place and treatment in the work place raise unique moral concerns. All of this is intended as necessary exposition for a thorough airing of preferential treatment for the disadvantaged.

We would like to make one additional point. The plight of the disadvantaged in the work place raises some issues that we've indirectly addressed in our chapters (4, 5, 6) dealing with the relationship between the firm and its employees. Nevertheless, the moral questions that attach to this subject are so broad and profound, the subject itself so morally vital, that any coverage of the major issues involving business and society would seem incomplete without adequate chapter consideration of the state of women and other disadvantaged groups in the work place.

Women

In ever increasing numbers, women are expanding their traditional cultural roles as wives and mothers by entering the work force. Like their male counterparts, they seek an opportunity to develop themselves while making a constructive contribution in work outside the home. Yet, disquietingly large numbers of women face fundamental obstacles in the form of institutional sexism or socialization inadequate for the demands of the work place.

A number of work aspects illustrate this point, for example, salaries. At all occupational levels, women earn less money than men—even for the same work—despite legislation forbidding discrimination on the basis of sex. In 1955 the average female employee earned 64 percent of the wages paid to her male counterpart; in 1971, she earned 59 percent. The story is no different when you look at specific occupational groups. In 1966 salaries for women in sales were 41 percent of men's; in 1972, 42 percent. In clerical jobs women's income was 66.5 percent that of men's; in 1971, it had fallen to 61 percent.[1] A number of factors

---

1. *Luthans and Hodgetts, p. 126.*

explain, not justify, this discrepancy. One factor is of particular moral import: the practice of having women do the same work as men but under a different title and, therefore, for less pay.

Then there is the issue of job status, which further illustrates the plight of women in the work place. Despite strides forward in some occupations, women still find status in what are regarded as "women's jobs": teaching and nursing. In general, the work of large numbers of women continues to be dull, unfulfilling, and low in status, not to imply that teaching and nursing have any of these characteristics. Author Caroline Bird makes the point dramatically when she reports that in the middle of the 1960s women were:

> . . . less than 10% of all the professional or "knowledge" elites except classroom teachers, nurses, librarians, social workers, and journalists; 9% of all full professors; 8% of all scientists; 6% of all physicians; 3% of all lawyers; 1% of all engineers.
>
> Five percent of the income elite of the individuals with incomes of $10,000 or more. . . . Five percent of the prestige elite listed in *Who's Who in America* for 1967, down from 6% in 1930. Two percent of the power elite of business executives. . . . Less than 4% of all Federal civil servants in the six highest grades; 1% of Federal judges; 1% of the U.S. Senate.[2]

Add to this the facts that one-third of the entire female work force, about 9 million workers, consists of secretaries; that women hold the majority of least desirable white-collar jobs, such as keypunch operators and file clerks, and that they're overrepresented on assembly lines.

Are things getting better for females in the work place? In 1974 the *Harvard Business Review* asked this of 5,000 subscribers. Of the 5,000, 1,500, or 30 percent, said yes. Of more significance, however, the study revealed deep-seated anti-female bias within managerial ranks. Specifically, it indicated that managers expect male employees to put job before family when conflicting obligations arise, but they expect females to sacrifice their careers to family responsibilities. Also, when personal conduct threatens an employee's job, managers go to greater lengths to retain a valuable male employee than an equally well-qualified female. Finally, the survey discovered that in employee selection and promotion and in career-development decisions, managers clearly favor males.[3] Other research supports these tentative conclusions. One study, for example, has found that men prefer male supervisors and feel uncomfortable with female supervisors.[4] Another report indicates that major obstacles to equal work status for women continue to include myths about females, stereotypes, and false preconceptions.[5] This factor generates so many moral issues in the treatment of females that we should consider it a bit more closely.

2. I. M. Garskof, ed., The Sex Map of the Work World (Belmont, Calif.: Brooks/Cole, 1971), pp. 56–57.

3. Benson Rosen and Thomas H. Jerdee, "Sex Stereotyping in the Executive Suite," Harvard Business Review, May–June, 1974, pp. 45–58.

4. Bernard M. Bass, Judith Krusell, Ralph A. Alexander, "Male Managers' Attitudes Toward Working Women," American Behavioral Scientist, November, 1977, p. 223.

5. Charles D. Orth and Frederic Jacobs, "Women in Management: Patterns for Change," Harvard Business Review, July–August, 1971, pp. 139–147.

U.C.L.A. Professor of Psychology James Coleman has compiled a list of popular misconceptions about female workers that function to perpetuate their victimization.[6] One myth is that work outside the home is somehow inappropriate to the female's unique and proper role as wife and mother. If single, the assumption is that marriage will quickly steal her away. If already a mother, the woman will be chronically absent because of domestic demands. Yet, Coleman observes, a Public Health Service survey of work time lost due to illness or injury indicates insignificant differences between males and females, as well as comparable labor turnover rates. Note that where employer figures do reflect higher absenteeism among women, it could be explained by the low-status, dead-end jobs that most women continue to do.

Coleman also mentions the myth that "lady supervisors mean trouble." This bias is consistent with the findings of the study previously referred to which found males preferring male supervisors. Thus, it is frequently charged that both men and women respond unfavorably to female bosses. Yet, this flies in the face of evidence. A Department of Labor survey of executives who had *actually* worked for females determined that at least three-fourths of the respondents had favorable views of their female supervisors.[7]

Then there's the myth that "women are suited only for 'feminine jobs.' " What constitutes a "feminine job" is, of course, painfully vague. But according to this view, women are best employed in work appropriate to their homemaking roles or roles as men's helpmates. Such activities presumably include: classroom teaching, nursing, mental hygiene, dietetics, clerking, waitressing, cooking, and the like. But the correlation between occupational structure and sex difference is often one that custom and tradition have produced, not that nature has decreed. In fact, historically many of the roles deemed "feminine" were once male domains; among them: teachers, clerks, telephone operators, and bank tellers. Yet, as Coleman says, myths continue to crowd women into a limited number of jobs where the pressures of excess supply drive wages and status down.

The tendency to stereotype female workers has the same effect. Thus, the secretary is often viewed as a "gum-chewing sex kitten; husband-hunter, miniskirted ding-a-ling; slow witted pencil pusher; office go-fer; reliable old shoe."[8] Such stereotypes have the effect not only of minimizing the importance of the working female but also of degrading her as a human being.

Finally, Coleman mentions the belief that "men should have higher status anyway." This reflects a time-honored religious, sociocultural attitude that men deservedly should have higher status than women, that husbands need to support families, that males rightfully should supervise women. If, however, we accept the premise that women are human beings, then it makes little sense to argue that one group of human beings, males, *inherently* deserves higher status

6. *James C. Coleman and Constance L. Hammen,* Contemporary Psychology and Human Behavior *(Glenview, Ill.: Scott Foresman, 1974), p. 363.*

7. *Reported in Special Task Force,* Work in America.

8. *J. Klemesrud, "Secretary Image: A Tempest in a Typewriter,"* New York Times, *March 7, 1972, p. 34.*

than another, females. Furthermore, the vast number of household- and self-supporting women explodes the myth that males as primary providers deserve higher status than females.

The point is that these myths and stereotypes frequently underlie the inequities to women. Thus, unequal pay or employment placement can often be traced to business attitudes about women in general. As a result, any incisive moral analysis of the problems facing women today must at some point acknowledge the presence of these fundamental attitudes and scrutinize the moral legitimacy of them. Failing to do this, it's easy to overlook the foundational moral concerns that generate unfair and unequal treatment in the work place.

We said earlier that most of the problems arise primarily because of institutional sexism and socialization inadequate for the work place. We've illustrated the problem of institutional sexism as it relates to employment, placement, salaries, and promotion. We should now say a word about socialization.

Socialization may be defined as the process by which human beings are prepared to assume the roles they'll play as adults in society. It will come as no surprise to anyone that women in America have been primarily prepared to assume the role of wife and mother. This alone goes a long way toward explaining the lopsided male-female ratios in business. This preparation hardly qualifies women to function and flourish in the business world, where ambition and aggressiveness are of premium value. In other words, women's socialization has poorly equipped them in the qualities that business most highly prizes: ambition, achievement, productivity, assertion. It's not surprising, therefore, that research indicates that achievement in typically "male" occupations produces profound conflict in many women. On the one hand, women have been socialized to be submissive, nonassertive, and supportive. On the other hand, in business women are expected to be dominant, expressive, and independent. The ambitious, aggressive woman can easily find her femininity challenged, evidence of internal as well as external obstacles facing women who venture forth into the work place. Unless managers, especially men, realize this situation and develop ways and means of dealing with it, they can grossly underestimate and leave undeveloped the occupational potential of female employees.

While the problem of women in the work place raises many unique moral considerations, those facing other disadvantaged groups loom just as large. In particular, business must be mindful of the problems peculiar to minority groups, older workers, and younger workers.

Other Disadvantaged Groups

Minority Workers

The responsibilities that firms have to employees in the areas of hiring, promotions, discipline, and discharge, as well as in general treatment, cut across all levels of employment and include all workers. There are, however, particular groups of workers for whom occupational problems seem particularly prominent. Women are certainly one. Minority-group members are another.

Despite heightened social consciousness of the occupational needs of minority workers and of the obstacles to their satisfaction, as well as appropriate legislation to end discrimination in the work place, statistics continue to report the sad plight of minority workers (especially blacks, Hispanic-Americans, and American Indians). Of every three minority workers, one is employed irregularly or has given up looking for work. One in three minority workers is engaged primarily in a job which pays less than a living wage. The annual salary of employed minority males is significantly below the average salary of their white male counterparts. As for job satisfaction, a recent survey indicates that the most dissatisfied group of all blacks consists of young black workers in "white collar" jobs. The source of dissatisfaction is racial discrimination.[9] The problem of racial and ethnic discrimination is further confounded by the socialization process which has ill prepared many minority-group members to compete equally in the business world with their white male counterparts.

But minority groups aren't the only ones, in addition to women, who find themselves disadvantaged in the work place; so do older workers.

Older Workers

Older workers, like women and minority-group members, face peculiar problems in the work place. In the first place, unless they are already employed, the older worker's chances for employment are slim, since aging is generally associated with declining ability to perform or acquire new skills. This assumption, like the many about women, not only ignores the heterogeneity of individuals over sixty but is also groundless. On the contrary, evidence disputes the proposition that aging means inevitable intellectual decline.[10]

In addition to employment problems which face older workers are those that center on retirement. Although a law was passed in 1978 raising the mandatory retirement age to seventy in most occupations, the whole concept mandatory retirement deserves moral scrutiny. If a person performs competently and efficiently, why should he or she be forced to retire? The most frequent answer is to make room for younger workers. Before accepting this reason as adequate justification, you should think about its implications. First, there is the question of the inherently arbitrary nature of age as a criterion. If age can be a criterion, why not color or sex? Second, the effects on retired persons should be considered. In view of modern research which associates longevity, happiness, and general well-being with work satisfaction, forced retirement raises serious moral questions about employee injury. The following example graphically illustrates this point.

Mr. Winter had for some years single handedly run an operation for his company that no one else fully understood. As Winter approached his sixty-fourth birthday, the company assigned him a young man whose charge it was to learn Winter's operation so that he could replace the elderly worker on retire-

9. R. L. Kahn, "The Meaning of Work: Interpretation and Proposals for Management," in Human Meaning of Social Change, ed. A. A. Campbell and P. E. Converse (New York: Basic Books, 1972), p. 103.

10. H. Geist, The Psychological Aspects of the Aging Process (St. Louis: Warren H. Green, 1968).

ment. It was not that Winter wanted ro retire; company policy decreed retirement at sixty-four. Winter reluctantly complied.

Not long after his retirement, a significant change occurred in Winter, characterized by a withdrawal from people and a general diminution of his zest for life. Within a year of his retirement Winter was hospitalized. The diagnosis was senile psychosis. In a word Winter had become a vegetable.

As chance would have it, two years after assuming Winter's job the young worker suddenly died. The company found itself having to fill his vacancy but was at a loss to find a competent employee. Thus,

> a decision was made to approach Mr. Winter and see if he could pull himself together enough to carry on the job and train somebody to take over. Four of his closest co-workers were sent to the hospital. After hours of trying, one of the men finally broke through. The idea of going back to work brought the first sparkle in Mr. Winter's eyes in 2 years. Within a few days, this "vegetable" was operating at full steam, interacting with people as he had years before.[11]

Although dramatic, this illustration of the potential effect of forced retirement on workers' health should not be viewed as atypical. Indeed, in a society as youth-centered and future-oriented as ours, the problems facing older workers are serious now and promise to intensify in the next twenty years. At the same time, however, we must note that younger workers themselves confront work problems that also raise important moral concerns.

Younger Workers

For the most part, the problems that younger workers face in the work place can be traced to the amount and nature of the educational preparation they have received. As to the amount of education, it is true that today's younger workers are generally more educated than their counterparts of, say, fifteen or twenty years ago. For example, in 1960, 26 percent of white and 14 percent of black craftspersons had completed four years of high school; by 1969, 41 percent of whites and 29 percent of blacks had.[12] Today the percentages are even higher. Similarly, more younger workers today have had some advanced educational training (college or professional schools) than ever before.

Unfortunately, while increased education may remain a way to escape dull and boring jobs, in many cases it is just as great a source of job dissatisfaction. For example, a study conducted in 1972 revealed that the expansion of professional, clerical, and technical jobs absorbed only 15 percent of the newly educated workers. Where did the remaining 85 percent find employment? They obtained jobs which had been done by people with fewer educational credentials.[13] When the job one must do doesn't measure up in content, responsibility, or challenge to one's educational preparation, serious problems of job dissatis-

11. B. Margolis and W. Kroes, "Work and the Health of Man," in Work in America, Special Task Force, quoted in Coleman, p. 361.

12. For a full discussion, see R. Schrank and S. Stein, "Yearning, Learning and Status," in Blue Collar Workers: A Symposium on Middle America, ed. S. A. Levitan (New York: McGraw-Hill, 1971).

13. For a full discussion, see S. Levitan, G. Magnum, and R. Marshall, Human Resources and the Labor Market (New York: Harper & Row, 1972).

faction can arise, with noteworthy implications for worker morale and productivity. There are many social implications for a society that counts a substantial pool of young, dissatisfied employees, implications that can be as exotic as a young man's refusing to repay a several thousand dollar student loan. This was the case of a Ph.D. in history who could not find work in his profession and took a job selling refrigerators. When the time came to begin repaying his loan, he refused. "There was my university telling me to start paying $240 a year. For what? To pay off a degree they gave me so I could sell refrigerators?"[14] It is difficult to condone the young man's behavior (especially since he was making $18,000 a year in sales!), but it is easy to understand his feelings of disappointment and frustration, even of being defrauded. Such cases carry significant moral overtones for educational institutions who do little to counsel students professionally, but they also say much about businesses who do not engage in active dialogue with institutions about future occupational prospects.

Thus, the nature of a young person's educational preparation is as important a factor to consider in examining work problems for younger workers as is the amount of the education. Even for business majors in colleges problems loom, since their view of the business world results from what they've experienced in the classroom. Frequently, this involves examining business problems from the perspective of upper-management, which may be different from seeing things in terms of the mundane operational problems which younger workers must frequently deal with. Then there's the task of dealing with and managing other workers, for which younger workers' primarily technical education has inadequately prepared them. In addition, business recruiters often build up young recruits for serious on-the-job letdowns by exaggerating the nature of the work they will be doing and of the opportunities it holds for them.

Finally, we should emphasize that today's younger workers, while valuing work as much as their predecessors, bring into the work place different values and attitudes. Rarely do younger workers espouse the "Protestant work ethic" as much as their predecessors did. In general, they don't value work for its own sake or believe that hard work will always pay off. More and more young people view a job as a vehicle to self-identity, self-esteem, and self-fulfillment. In addition, they are far less likely to acquiesce to authority than workers in former times did. Finally, and perhaps most important, today's younger workers do not value job security and job promotion as much as workers of twenty years ago. In contrast, young workers betray far greater selectivity and exhibit a marked affinity for job autonomy and significance.[15]

In view of the amount and nature of their educational preparation, then, the challenge of managing younger workers is a major one for contemporary business managers. At stake is not only the general well-being of workers but also the productivity of business. Management that ignores the peculiar composition of its young work force, therefore, risks injuring workers, undermining owner interests, and jeopardizing the nation's economy.

14. Newsweek, *March 7, 1977, p. 95.*

15. *See American Institute for Research, "Project Talent: Progress in Education, A Sample Survey"* (Washington, D.C.: American Institute for Research, 1971).

At the present time almost everyone would agree that business must face up to the problems facing women and other disadvantaged groups in the work place. But precisely what these responsibilities are and how business ought to discharge them remains obscure and controversial. Even if we assume, for example, that business has an obligation to distribute jobs in a way that roughly reflects the sexual and ethnic makeup of the population at large, we're still faced with determining the fairest way to do this. In recent years government programs have prodded business into giving women and other disadvantaged groups preferred treatment in hiring and placement. It is such a policy that makes the decision facing Manuel Ortega an agonizing one, for it seems that in order to abide by the policy he must treat some white male unfairly. Indeed, some persons would argue that preferential treatment policies are inherently unfair precisely for this reason. Are they?

Affirmative Action: Preferential Treatment

As amended by the Equal Employment Opportunity Act of 1972, the Civil Rights Act of 1964 requires that businesses which have substantial dealings with the federal government undertake affirmative action programs. *Affirmative action programs are plans designed to correct imbalances in employment that exist directly as a result of past discrimination against women and minority groups.* Even though these acts do not technically require companies to undertake affirmative action programs, in recent years courts have responded to acts of discrimination in the work place by ordering the offending firms to undertake affirmative action programs to combat the effects of past discrimination. In effect, then, all business institutions must adopt affirmative action programs either in theory or in fact. They must be able to prove that they have not been practicing institutional sexism or racism, and when they can't prove this, they must undertake programs to ensure against racism or sexism.

What do affirmative action programs involve? The U.S. Equal Employment Opportunity Commission lists general guidelines as steps to affirmative action. Under these steps firms must issue a written equal employment policy and an affirmative action commitment. They must appoint a top official with responsibility and authority to direct and implement their program and to publicize their policy and affirmative action commitment. In addition, firms must survey current female and minority employment by department and job classification. Where underrepresentation of these groups is evident, firms must develop goals and timetables to improve utilization of women and minorities in each area of underrepresentation. They then must develop specific programs to achieve these goals, establish an internal audit system to monitor them, and evaluate progress in each aspect of the program. Finally, companies must develop supportive in-house and community programs to combat sexual and racial discrimination.

In implementing such programs, some companies have adopted a policy of preferential treatment for women and minorities. *Preferential treatment refers to the practice of giving individuals favored consideration in hiring or promotions for other than job-related reasons* (such as the person is female or black). Those espousing preferential treatment argue that such a policy is the only way to remedy traditional sexism and racism, or at least that it is the most expeditious and fairest way to do it. In some instances preferential treatment for women and minorities takes the form of a *quota system, that is, an employment policy of representing women and minorities in the firm in direct proportion to their numbers in society or in the community at large.* Thus a firm operating in a community which has a 20 percent black population might try to ensure that 20 percent of its work force be black.[16]

To unravel some of the complex moral issues that affirmative action programs can raise, let's look at a specific instance of quota hiring. Suppose that an equally qualified man and woman are applying for a job. The employer, conscious of affirmative action guidelines and realizing that the company has historically discriminated against women in its employment policies, adopts a quota hiring system. Since males are already disproportionately well-represented and females underrepresented, the quota system functions to give the female applicant a decided advantage over the male simply because she's a woman. As a result the employer hires the female. Is this action moral? Are affirmative action programs which operate in the preferential way moral?

Many persons argue that affirmative action programs are inherently discriminatory and therefore unjust. In this context, *discriminatory* should be understood to refer to policies that favor individuals on non-job-related grounds (for example, on the basis of sex, color, or ethnic heritage). It has been argued that quota hiring is unjust because it involves giving preferential treatment to women and minorities over equally qualified white males, a practice which is clearly discriminatory, albeit reverse discrimination.

Those in favor of affirmative action, on the other hand, generally attempt to rebut this objection by appealing to principles of *compensatory justice. In other words, since women and minorities clearly continue to be victimized directly and indirectly by traditional discrimination in the work place, they are entitled to some compensation.* This is the basis for preferential treatment. The soundness of this contention seems to rely on at least two factors: (1) that affirmative action programs involving preferential treatment will in fact provide adequate compensation; (2) that they will provide compensation more fairly than any other alternative.[17] Since the justice and the morality of affirmative action programs depend to a large degree on these assumptions, we should examine them.

The question that comes to mind in regard to the first assumption is: adequate compensation for whom? The answer seems obvious: for women and minorities. But does this answer mean *individual* women and minority-group members, or women and minorities taken *collectively*? University of Tampa Professor Herman J. Saatkamp, Jr., has demonstrated that this question, far from

---

16.   *Some institutions simply reserve a number of places for women and minority members. The University of California at Davis, for example, had such a policy in its medical school when it denied Alan Bakke admission. Bakke appealed to the Supreme Court, which—in a five to four decision—found in his favor. He was presumably more qualified than some "minority" students who had been admitted.*

17.   *Albert W. Flores, "Reverse Discrimination: Towards a Just Society,"* Business & Professional Ethics, *a quarterly newsletter/report (Troy, N.Y.: Center for the Study of the Human Dimensions of Science & Technology, Rensselaer Polytechnic Institute, Jan. 1978), p. 4.*

being merely a technical one, bears directly on the morality of affirmative action programs and how they are implemented.[18]

Saatkamp points out that the question of the conflict between individual and collective merit is one that typifies the debate between government agencies and business over employment policies. On the one hand, business is ordinarily concerned with the individual merit and deserts of its employees. In contrast, government agencies primarily focus on the relative status of groups within the population at large. To put the conflict in perspective, employment policies based solely on individual merit would try to ensure that only those individuals who could prove they deserved compensation would benefit and only those proved to be the source of discrimination would suffer. Of course, such a focus places an almost unbearable burden on the resources of an individual to provide sufficient, precise data to document employment discrimination, which is commonly acknowledged to exist at times in subtle forms at imperceptible organizational levels. Indeed, social policies recognize this difficulty by focusing on discrimination on an aggregate level. Individuals, then, need not prove that they themselves were discriminated against, only that they are members of groups that have traditionally suffered because of discrimination.

Taking the collective approach to remedying work-place discrimination is not without its own disadvantages.

1. Policies based on collective merit tend to pit one social group against another. Thus white males face off against all nonwhite males; women find themselves jockeying with other disadvantaged groups for priority employment status; even black females can end up contesting with white Hispanic males for preferred treatment. This factionalizing aspect of policies based on collective merit can prove detrimental to society.

2. Policies based on collective merit victimize some individuals. The individual white male who loses out on a job because of preferential treatment given a woman or minority is penalized.

3. In many cases the women and minority members selected under preferential treatment are, in fact, less deserving of compensation than those women and minorities who are not selected. In a word, those most in need may not benefit at all.

4. Some members of nonfavored groups may be just as deserving or more deserving of compensation than some women or members of minority groups. Many white males, for example, are more seriously limited in seeking employment than some women and minority-group members are.

5. From the viewpoint of business investment, policies based on collective merit can be prohibitively expensive. In order to enforce such programs, businesses must hire people to collect data, process forms, deal with government agencies, and handle legal procedures. From business's viewpoint this additional time, energy, and expense could have been channeled into more commercially productive directions.

18. Ibid., pp. 5–6.

In sum, those who argue that affirmative action programs will provide adequate compensation for the victims of discrimination must grapple with the problems of determining the focus of the compensation: on the individual or on the group. While both focuses have merit, neither is without disadvantages. What's more, it seems that neither approach can be implemented without first resolving a complex chain of moral concerns.

But even if we assume that affirmative action programs will provide adequate compensation, it is still difficult to demonstrate the validity of the second assumption of those who endorse affirmative action by appealing to principles of compensatory justice: that such programs will provide compensation more fairly than any other alternative. By nature affirmative action programs provide compensation at the expense of the white males' right to fair and equal employment treatment. In other words, affirmative action programs in the form of preferential treatment or quota systems undermine the fundamental principle of just employment practice that a person should be hired or promoted only on job-related grounds. Apparently, then, it presents an awesome undertaking to defend the proposition that affirmative action will provide compensation more fairly than any other alternative when such a proposition makes a non-job-related factor (membership in a group) a relevant employment criterion.

Although it would appear that reverse discrimination may not be justified on grounds of compensation, we should not conclude that it cannot be justified. In fact, some persons contend that a more careful examination of the principles of justice suggests an alternative defense. As we have mentioned, those who argue against affirmative action programs do so because such programs allegedly involve unequal treatment and are therefore unjust. The clear assumption here is that whatever involves unequal treatment is in and of itself unjust. But, as Professor Albert W. Flores points out, while justice would demand that equals receive equal treatment, it is likewise true that unequals should receive treatment appropriate to their differences. Hence, he concludes that "unfair or differential treatment may be required by the principles of justice."[19] In other words, unequal treatment is unfair in the absence of any characteristic difference between applicants which, from the viewpoint of justice, would constitute relevant differences. Following this line of reasoning, we must wonder whether being a female or a minority member would constitute a "relevant difference" that would justify unequal treatment.

To illustrate, let's ask how one could justify giving preferential consideration to a female job applicant over an equally qualified white male. Flores contends that while sex may be irrelevant to the job, it may be a relevant consideration as to who should be selected. In effect, he distinguishes between criteria relevant to a job and those relevant to candidate selection. He clearly bases this distinction on a concept of business's social responsibilities. As we have indicated and demonstrated elsewhere, business does not exist in a commercial vacuum. It is part of a social system and, as such, has obligations that relate to the welfare and integrity of society at large. Thus Flores argues that when a firm must decide between two equally qualified applicants, say a white male and a female, it is

19. *Flores, p. 4.*

altogether justified in introducing as a selection criterion some concept of social justice, which in this case takes cognizance of a fair distribution of society's resources and scarcities among competing groups. From the viewpoint of justice, business may be correct in hiring the qualified female or minority member. Notice, however, that this contention is not based primarily on principles of compensatory justice but on a careful examination of the nature of justice.

The moral issues that affirmative action programs raise with respect to justice are profound and complex. In this brief overview, we have been able to raise only a few, but these demonstrate that the morality of preferential treatment through affirmative action cuts to our basic assumptions about the nature of human beings, the relationship between business and government, and the principles of justice. Any moral resolution to the problem of discrimination in the work place will not only betray these assumptions but must justify them.

Ethical Theories

As in all business issues, application of ethical theories frequently leads to divergent moral decisions or, even more often, to identical ones for different reasons. This observation seems especially striking if we apply our theories to discrimination in the work place.

Turning our attention first to consequential theories, we can note that egoism could in theory defend discriminatory employment practices on the basis of best long-term interests of the firm (assuming the viewpoint of the firm as the moral agent). On the other hand, the same consideration might lead to a condemnation of a specific act of discrimination. In fact, given the current climate, this conclusion might be more likely, since business apparently stands to lose much more than it would gain by discrimination. As for preferential hiring programs, egoism cannot theoretically approve or disapprove of them without introducing the interests of the particular moral agent. But who is this? From the viewpoint of a woman or minority member, such programs might be readily justified egoistically. From the viewpoint of the white male, they might not. The crucial point here is that egoism lacks the theoretical wherewithal to provide some principles of social justice that, while perhaps not providing an irrefutable position, will at least provide some. Indeed, it is in areas of social justice that egoism appears most inadequate to provide moral direction.

Like egoism, act utilitarianism seems theoretically indisposed to taking an unqualified stand on discrimination practices in the work place. Thus, if a discriminatory practice was calculated to produce more social good than any other alternative, then it would be good and right. If not, then it would be wrong and bad. It's important to note here that where act utilitarianism would object to a discriminatory act, it would not do so because that act violated a basic human right or because it inherently treated people unfairly. The utilitarian calculus is based not on any inherent characteristic of an act but on its social productivity. Thus when human rights and unfair treatment enter into the calculation, they would do so on the basis of the consequences that follow upon supporting them and abridging them. In other words, any appeal to principles of justice would take root in efficiency, not fair play and would produce a rule such as, "Alice

Jones should have as equal a chance as any male to get a job because acting in that way will produce more total good than not acting in that way." It follows that if more total good could be attained by discriminating against Alice Jones, then an employer should discriminate against her. Similarly, act utilitarians would evaluate acts of preferential treatment. Again, where they'd object to them, they would do so not on the basis of the violation of any basic human rights or of a concept of fair play but because the specific act was not as productive of total happiness as some other alternative. On the other hand, act utilitarians could also support acts of reverse discrimination by appealing to the social good. Again, the criterion is justice as efficiency. Curiously, then, whereas in theory act utilitarianism can support discrimination, it also offers the theoretical basis to justify acts calculated to remedy discrimination.

While rule utilitarianism also would base its moral decision about employment discrimination on the social good, it would do so by appealing to the rule under which the particular practice or action falls. Thus, if Alice Jones is excluded from job consideration because she is a female, this action might fall under a rule formulated to proscribe one's ever excluding a person from a job on the basis of sex. If following this rule would likely produce more favorable consequences for more people than breaking it, then the employer who denied Jones consideration would have acted immorally. Similarly, the morality of preferential hiring programs must be determined on the probable consequences of following a rule which enjoins one to provide preferential treatment to members of groups traditionally discriminated against in the work place. If the probable consequences would likely produce more total good, then one must follow the rule; if it would not, then one must not follow the rule. Of course, determining the total good of such programs is far from easy. Thus, while in theory rule utilitarianism provides a moral direction, in practice that direction remains unclear and uncertain.

It is important again to note that rule utilitarianism, like egoism and act utilitarianism, is motivated by a concept of justice as efficiency, that is, the greatest good for the greatest number. Thus, rule utilitarians might consider affirmative action programs just insofar as they make better use of human resource, advance societal harmony, and produce more social good than any other alternative rule. In effect, such a concept of justice reduces to a cost-benefit analysis the efficacy of a rule. Undoubtedly, it is such a concept of justice that Professor Flores uses to defend affirmative action programs that include preferential hiring.

In contrast, Joseph Fletcher's situationalism, while appealing to consequences to determine the morality of an action, introduces a concept of justice which, at least in theory, is based on desert, not efficiency. We say "in theory" because in practice Fletcher's concept of justice may function similarly to the utilitarian's when ample attention is paid to consequences.

Nevertheless, for Fletcher, justice involves giving to people their due; it is "love working out its problems." The moral act is the one inspired by loving concern, that is, the one calculated to give others what they deserve. As mentioned earlier, it is important to distinguish this agape calculus, at least in theory, from the utilitarian hedonistic calculus, although in practice they may be indistinguishable. Frankly, it is very difficult to make sharp operational distinctions because Fletcher seems vague about the precise nature of "loving concern" and because he addresses himself primarily to the personal moral dilemmas that contemporary Christians must face (for example, premarital sex and abortion). If our reading of Fletcher has been careful enough, this one area of social justice flushes out germs of both concepts of justice inherent in Fletcher's thinking: justice based on fair play and justice based on efficiency. As a result, without further elaboration from Fletcher, it's difficult to say with assurance precisely what direction his situationalism would give us on the question of employment discrimination.

This having been noted, it seems safe to say that situationalism could in theory justify discrimination in the work place. Quota hiring is a good example. No matter how one analyzes quota hiring, or preferential treatment based on sex or race for that matter, the practice is discriminatory. Yet, if such an action were motivated by loving concern and calculated to produce the greatest amount of neighbor welfare, then it would be moral.

In contrast to consequential positions, central to nonconsequential theories is a concept of justice as fair play, not efficiency. Unlike utilitarians, for example, nonconsequentialists could not justify denying people their due on the basis of the total good produced by an action. Also note that nonconsequentialist views of what a person is due are associated with some concept of basic human rights. Finally, whereas consequential theories hedge on issues of discrimination in the work place, nonconsequential views seem decisive in their disapproval of discrimination as traditionally practiced in the work place, although sometimes they remain just as indecisive when it comes to judging reverse discrimination.

For example, the Golden Rule, in employing a standard of impartiality and reciprocity, would have those who practice employment discrimination ask themselves whether they would want to be so treated if the positions were reversed. Presumably the answer would be no. So the Golden Rule seems decisive enough in condemning traditional discriminatory actions, policies, and practices in the work place. But what about concepts like preferential treatment? Is the Golden Rule adequate in itself to determine the morality of affirmative action programs that include preferential treatment? The answer would have to be negative because the subjectivity of the Golden Rule makes a determination very difficult. Thus a woman might conclude that were she a male, she would not want to be subjected to reverse discrimination. But it is at least possible that she could conclude otherwise, reasoning that she would want to be subjected to it, given a heightened sense of compensatory justice and social responsibility.

Immanuel Kant would look at the practice of discriminatory hiring on the basis of sex or race as incompatible with the inherent worth, dignity, and equality of all rational creatures. Any rule that would legitimize such practices would be logically inconsistent with the nature of human beings and therefore immoral. More important, any rule that is self-contradictory and immoral doesn't become logical and moral in the presence of qualifiers. Thus, if discrimination is logically inconsistent and immoral, so is reverse discrimination. Looked at another way, Kant's theory prohibits the individual's being made a means to a social end. Any rule or practice, then, which attempts to use white males as a means of achieving a desirable social end violates a cardinal assumption of Kant's moral theory. If our interpretation is correct, Kant's categorical imperative and attending principles would not condone affirmative action programs that institutionalize preferential treatment.

While undoubtedly more morally flexible than Kant, both Ross and Rawls would nonetheless share his concept of justice based on desert. Ross would introduce all the duties that discriminatory employment practices would call up and base his moral decision on what appears as the compelling actual duty. Uppermost in his mind would probably be duties of noninjury and, of course, justice. Ross would undoubtedly condemn sexual and racial discrimination traditionally practiced in the work place, because they have injured and continue to injure individuals and groups, as well as to insult individuals' basic rights to fair and equal treatment. It's considerably more difficult, however, to apply his theory decisively to the issue of preferential treatment in affirmative action programs, because there duties of justice and noninjury can be applied to conflicting interests. Suffice it to say that Ross's moral principles do not lead to an actual condemnation of reverse discrimination, although they could easily recognize prima facie the questionable nature of such a practice. Indeed, Ross's theory could be used to justify reverse discrimination when one considers seriously the multiple duties that seem to impel it. There are, for example, duties of reparation: business is obliged to repair the past damage it has caused through institutional racism and sexism. There are also duties of beneficence: business is in a position to improve materially the lot of the least well-off. There are duties of self-improvement: business can improve its own moral stature by actively pursuing equal opportunity in the work place and by repairing the effects of past moral insensitivity. In addition, there are obvious duties of justice and noninjury involved in the issue of reverse discrimination that would apply to persons not immediately benefited as well as those who are.

There can be no doubt that Rawls's maximin principle would condemn discriminatory employment practices as they have traditionally operated. Just consider his original position. Knowing that they could be victimized by such practices, rational, self-interested creatures would hardly condone them.

As with Ross, however, the question of preferential treatment raises more complex problems, although as a theory of social justice Rawls's maximin principle generally provides more distinct direction. On the one hand, one could argue that in the original position preferential hiring in the form, say, of quota hiring would be condemned as a species of a discriminatory employment practice. On the other, Rawls's difference principle allows for unequal treatment as long as everyone is benefited by it or at least those most disadvantaged benefit. Since those most disadvantaged, women and minority members, would likely benefit from reverse discrimination, it seems that at least in theory Rawls's maximin principle could condone quota hiring. This conclusion is strengthened when one introduces Rawls's principle of paternalism by which he obliges those in a position of authority to introduce the interests of those unable to foster their own interests. This principle would obligate business leaders to pursue aggressively the equal employment and treatment of women and minorities, though admittedly not necessarily in the form of reverse discrimination.

Like Kant, Ross, and Rawls, proportionality theorists would decisively condemn traditional racism and sexism in the work place because it involves the willing of a major evil as an end, the major evil being the unequal treatment of human beings. As to the issue of preferential treatment through affirmative action programs, proportionalists would side with Kant in disapproving of it. It is not the intentional aspect of preferential treatment that proportionalists would object to, since providing advantage to the most disadvantaged is wholesome enough. But preferential treatment, by definition, in its means renders a major evil to other persons while achieving this end. Thus when a firm hires or promotes on the basis of sex or race, it discriminates against those who are not members of that particular sex or race. In effect, proportionalists would likely see no difference between discrimination and reverse discrimination. Both constitute major evils and, therefore, could not be willed as either a means or an end.

In summary, it seems that all nonconsequential theories would roundly condemn traditional discriminatory employment practices as immoral despite what the social consequences may have been or continue to be. But whereas imperativists and proportionalists would likely disapprove of reverse discrimination as well, prima facie theorists and maximin principle proponents in theory could justify the practice.

On the other hand, consequential theories seem to be a great deal more indecisive on these issues. Egoism and utilitarianism, for example, in theory could approve or disapprove of all forms of employment discrimination as long as efficiency were served. Similarly, Fletcher's concept of loving concern could be used, at least in theory, to justify or condemn acts of employment discrimination.

This having been said, we must indicate that as always these interpretations and applications are subject to correction and amendment based on a closer reading of the theorists involved. We can conclude, however, that while some of our theories do not adequately address issues of social justice, several do quite thoughtfully. This doesn't mean that more specific thinking through of the problems facing women and other disadvantaged groups in the work place isn't necessary. It does mean that those theories most equipped to deal with problems of social justice may provide a theoretical framework within which to conduct further moral study on the issues.

CASE PRESENTATION
First Hired, First Fired

Marvin Alcott knew it was foolish. But, as a personnel director faced with a sticky decision, he couldn't help wishing that Frank Stimson were anything but a white male.

Things had been going so well with the firm's pilot program for training the hard-core unemployed for positions as assistant machinists. Just a month before, Alcott had placed sixteen workers in the program, one of whom—indeed the first—was Frank Stimson.

Having been out of work for the better part of a year and having no specific skills, Stimson had easily met the program's minimal qualifications for training. A number of things about Stimson had impressed Alcott.

It seemed that since returning from his two-year stint in Vietnam, Stimson had found nothing but tough employment sledding. In fact, as Stimson told it, if it hadn't been for the meager income his wife earned waitressing, he would have had to apply for welfare, something he strongly objected to on principle. As Stimson had said in the interview, "I was brought up to believe that you should carry your own weight. Anything less was being a leech, if you know what I mean." Then Stimson explained how he didn't think it was right to expect society to bear the burden of what he termed a "misspent youth." Stimson had put it quite graphically: "Why should I expect others to pay for my screw-ups?" Predictably enough, when Alcott informed Stimson that he was the first trainee to be selected, Stimson was elated and expressed every desire to seize his opportunity to make something of himself.

Alcott chuckled on the first day of training when Stimson showed up for work a half hour before the prescribed time. He appreciated Stimson's enthusiasm especially since it contrasted sharply with the apparent indifference of some other trainees.

After the first week of training several instructors went out of their way to compliment Alcott on his selection of Stimson, while at the same time indicating that they'd had to admonish several other employees for being tardy, nonchalant, and generally uninterested in the opportunity that the program was providing them.

It's little wonder, then, that Marvin Alcott considered Frank Stimson his top job trainee. This is precisely what made the decision he faced so painful.

It seems that when the firm launched the program, it did so with the government's implicit promise to fund sixteen positions. When the grant was actually issued, it covered only fifteen trainees. Alcott was faced with having to drop one.

Being a thoughtful, sensitive, and fair man, Alcott was trying to determine the most equitable way to manage the cut. One possibility was a lottery. He'd simply put the names of the candidates into a hat and draw one to be dropped. He had also considered making the drop on the basis of apparent job potential. But whatever method he contemplated, Alcott was haunted by the fact that Stimson was a white male. The other fifteen trainees were divided among minority groups and women, and Alcott was keenly aware of affirmative action guidelines that prescribed benefits for members of traditionally disadvantaged groups. In a word, there was a real question in his mind whether he'd endanger the entire program should he decide to drop one of the fifteen disadvantaged members.

Above all else Alcott wanted to be fair. There was no doubt in his mind that from what he and other company officials had observed, Stimson was the most promising trainee in the program. At the same time, he felt the press of fairness to members of groups traditionally discriminated against, which left him questioning the fairness of perhaps the most obvious solution: drop the last selected.[20]

1. *What should Alcott do?*

2. *What moral directions do the ethical theories provide?*

3. *In the event that Alcott decides to drop Stimson, does he have an obligation to make a case to the firm for underwriting Stimson's training? Do you think the firm has a moral obligation to do this?*

CASE PRESENTATION
A Snag at Elton Textiles

"The point I'm trying to make," said Betty Farnsworth, production supervisor with Elton Textiles, "is that we simply can't afford to carry Barney Riles for another three years."

Farnsworth was referring to a sixty-two-year-old, thirty-year employee in her charge. In her view Barney Riles, while still exhibiting the same degree of competence he always had, in recent years had showed a marked decline in productivity. As Farnsworth put it, "In many cases Barney takes twice as long as necessary to do a task, twice as long as he took five years ago." She was pointing out to Elton's president that such a decline in productivity not only hurt the firm but also was undermining morale in her division. The president asked her to be specific.

"Well," she began, "as you know, we have a considerable complement of young, bright, ambitious people. I'm thinking of one in particular, Bill Matson, who's been with us seven years. He came to us right out of college. Bill shows considerable promise. But his morale recently has plummeted, primarily because of Riles. For one thing, Bill finds himself spending too much time doing Barney's job as well as his own, so that the division can meet production goals. What's more, Matson is eager for and deserving of advancement."

"Matson would like to be quality control engineer?" the president asked with pointed reference to Barney Riles's position.

"He's next in line for it," Farnsworth replied.

"Can't Bill be patient for a few more years?" suggested the president.

"I don't think so," Farnsworth said. "He's already alluded to offers he's had elsewhere, and I'm convinced they're genuine. Any firm would love to have him, and I can see why."

The president sat silently for a moment before saying, "As you know, Betty, our voluntary retirement age is sixty-five."

20. *Suggested by a case reported in* Social Issues in Business, *Luthans and Hodgetts, pp. 170-172.*

"But Barney's not going to retire voluntarily," Farnsworth said adamantly.

"You know that for a fact?" queried the president.

"He's said as much."

"Do you mean Barney wants to stay on till he's seventy?" the president wanted to know.

Farnsworth said he would. Then she added, "But even if Barney were going to retire at sixty-five, in my professional judgment we can ill afford to indulge him for another three years."

The president reminded Farnsworth of how much the company prided itself on its compassionate treatment of its senior members. He emphasized that this stemmed from the company's recognition of the invaluable contributions these employees had made to Elton's currently attractive profit picture. But he was quick to add, "Of course, that doesn't justify featherbedding."

Farnsworth acknowledged that forcing someone to retire presented delicate legal and moral problems. "I know," she said, "that Barney would suffer financially."

"In fact," the president pointed out, "he stands to lose about 50 percent in retirement benefits against mandatory retirement at seventy."

"But is that consideration enough to justify productivity losses?" Farnsworth asked him. "Is it enough to jeopardize losing a highly qualified and productive person like Bill Matson?"

"You've put the choice I face starkly," the president said, "but most accurately."

1. *What should the president do?*

2. *What moral directions do the ethical theories provide?*

3. *Suppose the president summons Riles for a conference at which he explains the situation to him. Upon reflection Riles agrees that he's not as productive as he once was, that he is a liability to the firm. Do you think Riles would then have a moral obligation to retire?*

CASE PRESENTATION
Raising the "Ante"

Having spearheaded the women's cause on behalf of equal pay for equal work, Phyllis Warren was elated when the board decided to readjust salaries in the light of that principle. Its decision was clearly important in the sense that Phyllis and other women employed by the crafts firm would receive pay equivalent to male employees. But in a larger sense it constituted an admission of guilt on the part of the board, acknowledgment of a history blemished with sexual discrimination.

In the euphoria that followed the board's decision, neither Phyllis nor any of the other campaign activists thought much about the implications of such an implied admission of female exploitation. But some weeks later, Herm Leggett, a sales dispatcher, half jokingly suggested to Phyllis over lunch that she shouldn't stop with equal pay *now*. Phyllis asked Herm what he meant.

"Back pay," Herm said without hesitation. "If they're readjusting salaries for women," he explained, "they obviously know that salaries are out of line, and have been for some time." Then he asked her pointedly, "How long you been here, Phyl?" Eleven years, she told him. "If those statistics you folks were passing around last month are accurate," Herm said, "then I'd say you've been losing about $500 a year or $5,500 over eleven." Then he added with a laugh, "Not counting interest, of course."

"Why not?" Phyllis thought. Why shouldn't she and other women who'd suffered past inequities be reimbursed?

That night Phyllis called a few of the other women and suggested that they press the board for back pay. Some said they were satisfied and didn't think they should force the issue. Others thought the firm had been fair in readjusting the salary schedule, and they were willing to let bygones be bygones. Still others thought that any further efforts might, in fact, roll back the board's favorable decision. Yet, there was a nucleus that agreed with Phyllis that workers who had been unfairly treated in the past ought to receive compensation. They decided, however, that since their ranks were divided, they shouldn't wage as intense an in-house campaign as previously but take the issue directly to the board while it might still be inhaling deeply the fresh air of social responsibility.

The following Wednesday, Phyllis and four other women presented their case to the board, intentionally giving the impression that they enjoyed as much support from other workers as they had the last time they appeared before it. Although this wasn't true, Phyllis suggested it as an effective strategic ploy.

Phyllis's presentation had hardly ended when board members began making their feelings known about her proposal. One called it "industrial blackmail." "No sooner do we try to right an injustice," he said testily, "than you take our good faith and threaten to beat us over the head with it unless we comply with your request."

Another member just as vigorously argued that the current board couldn't be held accountable for the actions, policies, and decisions of previous boards. "Sure," he said, "we're empowered to alter policies as we see fit, as new conditions chart new directions. And we've done that. But to expect us to bear the full financial liability of decisions we never made is totally unrealistic."

Still another member wondered where it would all end. "If we agree," he asked, "will you then suggest that we should track down all those women who ever worked for us, and provide them compensation?" Phyllis said no, but that the board should readjust retirement benefits for those affected.

At this point the board asked Phyllis if she had any idea what all of what she was proposing would cost the firm.

"Whatever it is, it's a small price to pay for righting wrong," she said firmly.

"But is it a small price to pay for severely damaging our profit picture?" one of the members asked. Then he added, "I needn't remind you that our profit outlook directly affects what we can offer our current employees in terms of salary and fringes. It directly affects our ability to revise our salary schedule." Finally, he asked Phyllis whether she'd be willing for the board to reduce everyone's current compensation in order for it to meet what Phyllis termed the board's "obligations to the past."

Despite its decided opposition to Phyllis's proposal, the board agreed to consider it and render a decision at its next meeting. As a final broadside, Phyllis hinted that if the board didn't comply with the committee's request, the committee was prepared to submit its demand to litigation.

1. *If you were a board member, how would you vote? Why?*

2. *What moral directions do the ethical theories provide?*

3. *Do you think Phyllis Warren was unfair in turning the board's implied admission of salary discrimination on the basis of sex against it? Why?*

4. *Do you think Phyllis was wrong in giving the board the impression that her proposal enjoyed broad support? Why?*

5. *If the board rejects the committee's request, do you think the committee ought to sue? Give reasons.*

EEO Compliance: Behind the Corporate Mask

Frances Lear

Can a company comply with the letter of equal employment opportunity legislation and not with its spirit? Can it operate legally while in fact continuing to discriminate? In the following article Frances Lear, founder and president of Lear Purvis Walker & Co., a Los Angeles executive search organization specializing in the placement of executive/professional/technical women and minorities, suggests that it can. Specifically, Lear argues that the considerable talk of equal employment opportunity cannot conceal either the openly intentional or the unconscious prejudice a business actually holds against women and other disadvantaged groups. As she points out, to female and minority candidates for employment, an organization's subtle prejudicial jargon and impossibly demanding or inflexible job specifications signal sexual and racial discrimination. Ms. Lear gives us a firsthand look at the variety of faces companies present in attempting to comply with the Equal Employment Opportunity Act of 1972 or in trying to avoid compliance. At the same time, the author apprises us of everyday occupational behavior that carries important moral overtones relative to discrimination in the work place.

At first glance, large American corporations bear a striking resemblance to one another. Housed in uniformly handsome buildings landscaped with flawless plants, these companies radiate cheerful well-being. The evidence of success is everywhere, from the thickly carpeted floors to the numbers in the annual reports that I carry in my briefcase. The *Fortune* "500" are irresistible.

They are also predictable. The receptionist who takes my card is always young, only occasionally black, never a man. The secretary whom I follow is also young, rarely Chicano, again never a man. She leads me past rows of offices inhabited exclusively by men. Hardly ever are they minority men. In front of the offices women sit behind secretarial desks. Never men.

I am introduced to my host, who is usually a senior vice president. In my experience, this position has never been occupied by a woman. To the best of my recollection, only twice has it been occupied by a black. The vice president listens attentively to my company presentation about how we specialize in the placement of women and minorities in management. But when I am finished, the collective corporate attitude toward women and minorities—the "face" I see—begins to emerge. Not all at once but slowly, as the dialogue develops.

For example, the face of McGraw-Hill, Inc. is warm and friendly. The company is genuinely anxious to fill a $40,000 job with a woman. The face of Quaker Oats Co. is tougher, but its intent is laudable. A minority male could get its $30,000 marketing position. Columbia Broadcasting System has a face that is impeccable. As proof, a 29-year-old woman has just become vice president of planning. But American Telephone & Telegraph Co. has a troubled face. Although basically committed, it shows signs of inner conflict.

Then there are the other corporate faces. Like the company that is seeking to employ more minority males. And it would, too, except for one "problem." Its executives say, "The minority male is fine here at corporate headquarters, but we can't control him out in the divisions. He goes to pieces."

Corporate Dances

For over two years I have been looking at the bogus face of a major drug company. Theoretically, it is open to women and minorities; in actuality, it has developed an intricate corporate dance to keep them out. Surprising in that the vice president of personnel confided to me that an important lawsuit is going to be brought against one drug company, probably his own. To him, a costly court case appears to be preferable to compliance. On the one hand, this company's face conveys cordiality, interest, and cooperation; on the other, the quality of impenetrability.

Fandango Footwork

Corporate dances vary. In one, the name of an exceptionally well-qualified woman is submitted, but she is not considered for the position. The question-and-answer period goes like this:

"Why?"

"Her salary is too high."

"But women have always been underpaid; she must be outstanding to have reached that level."

"We have other candidates with pretty much the same qualifications for less pay."

"Pretty much?"

"Yes."

"Men?"

"Yes."

"Isn't it reasonable to assume that she could be better qualified than they are?"

"Maybe."

"Then wouldn't you be willing to see her?"

"No, she is too expensive."

In another dance, a woman or a minority candidate qualifies for interviews with three or four managers. Mysteriously, only one manager has a positive reaction.

"McLellan liked the candidate, but he has three others under consideration."

Later: "McLellan chose somebody else."

"Sorry to hear that. Do you know why, so that I can give the candidate some feedback?"

"No, he just chose somebody else."

In still another dance, a woman or a minority candidate is chosen for a job. Then, a few days later:

"Tell him/her that Englehart changed his mind. He decided not to fill that job right now."

"When do you think it will open up again?"

"Don't know. Tell her/him to get something else."

Up-and-Down Shuffle

As a representative of women and minority candidates, I have often been engaged in a similar dance. But instead of going from manager to manager or hearing a direct turndown, I am shuffled up *or* down on the personnel administrative ladder. Each rung welcomes me. Yet I am not allowed to land on any one of them.

"When Bill gets things straightened out on his

desk, he will take good care of all your people."

"Hello, this is Bill. Listen, why don't you give Walter a call; you should really be working with him."

"Hello, may I speak with Walter, please?"

"He's away for a month recruiting."

Back up the ladder to the top. Then, an elegant lunch with Bill in which we again agree that we need each other.

"We've got to work this out. Your people are invaluable to us."

Again I believe. Again I am snowed. The *Fortune* "500" are irresistible. They also seem at peace with themselves. But are they really? I think not.

Company Faces

Beneath the superficial good looks of the majority of American companies are the scars and blemishes of the struggle to rid themselves of discriminatory habits. The struggle results not in bad faces but in interesting ones, very possibly as good as can be expected during this time of transition.

Uniform Commitment

Rarely is corporate commitment to affirmative action, or the lack of it, uniform throughout a large organization. Unique in this respect is Wells Fargo & Co., California's third largest bank. There are two women who sit on its board of directors. No other major California corporation has a woman as a board member for reasons other than nepotism (the niece of the founder of a rival bank) or ownership (two women who have founded their own companies).

During a recent visit with Wells Fargo's Daniel S. Livingston, senior vice president of personnel, I submitted the names of three candidates for his consideration. Among them was an exceptional woman now working in Washington, D.C. He expressed an interest in her as a possible board member. A third woman? Incredible. Can Wells Fargo really be that pure?

I asked a thinly disguised question to find out. "Mr. Livingston, does your bank already have sufficient numbers of women and minority employees in management?"

"No, there are never enough women and minorities in management in any company. We have an ambitious program to try to correct this situation here, however."

The perfect answer. Wells Fargo must have the purest face this side of the Mississippi.

No Commitment at All

The flip side of Wells Fargo is an aircraft parts company located in a midwestern city. On the day of my appointment, the temperature outside was four degrees. Inside, my reception was even colder. Mr. M, the senior personnel officer, was in a meeting. Would I wait? I waited.

The departure time for my plane drew near.

"I have to be at the airport in 30 minutes. Do you think Mr. M could see me now?"

The receptionist was a young Caucasian woman. Again.

"Mr. M is in a meeting."

"I came to see him at his request. I am sure he would want to see me before I leave."

"I can't interrupt him. See Mr. R. He isn't doing anything."

Mr. R was clearly embarrassed. Not by Mr. M's failure to show up. No, Mr. R was embarrassed by my presence.

When I explained that I specialized in the placement of women and minorities in management, he fairly shrieked, "Women and minorities? Women and minorities in *management*?" Obviously Mr. R had never heard of such a thing.

"Mr. L and I are thinking about hiring women into our sales force. Do you think they would do well in that field?"

"Mr. R, many women make excellent salespeople. A sales personality is easily identifiable, and you will discover it in teachers, housewives, in a variety of professional and nonprofessional women."

"Oh, really?"

"Yes. By the way, have you thought about training women to be sales managers?"

"*Women* sales managers?"

I remembered that we had been here before. Not wanting to go around full circle again, I left

Mr. R, Mr. L, and their bleak corporate face in that cold midwestern city and went elsewhere to seek a sunnier company face.

Candidates' Faces

Although I may see sunshine or bleakness, the applicants I send out for interviews may not. Often something other than what I see is visible during the interviews.

One of the northeastern states has an old, established insurance company with new, progressive ideas about affirmative action. Although much of its management has been around for years, the personnel manager is doing everything he can to hire and promote young talented men and women. Therefore, I was pleased to send a woman engineer to him for an interview.

He responded immediately with a job offer. I was shocked when she refused it.

"Andrea, can you tell me why?"

"He made lots of promises that didn't ring true. I was sure he was just telling me what I wanted to hear, especially after I had taken a look around the engineering department."

"But he's slowly trying to change all that."

"Maybe, but I have strong doubts. Also, I didn't see any path into management for me."

"Didn't you talk to several people in management who had started in the very same job you would be getting?"

"Yes, but none of them were women. Even though he insisted that he wanted a woman who could be promoted, I didn't believe him."

If I believe him, why doesn't she? I determined to find out what she had seen that I hadn't and went to see the personnel manager myself.

"Pete, would you mind showing me your engineering department?" He guessed what I was after and led me down the hall to a large, brilliantly lit room.

"This is the section Andrea will work in if she comes with us." It was true that most of the engineers were Caucasian males. It was also true that there was a predominance of gray heads in the room. But Andrea had forgotten to tell me that the department head was an Asian woman or that she would be working alongside a number of young men and women of all races.

Back in Pete's office, I asked him to repeat what he had said during Andrea's interview. I turned his answers to her questions over and over in my mind. As I was about to leave, still bewildered, a thought suddenly hit me—Andrea did not trust Pete because he was an old, established personnel man. She had been hearing promises from personnel men all her life, and all of them had been empty. Why would Pete's be any different?

Later, I called Andrea.

"Andrea, I think I understand why you refused Pete's offer. Could we talk about it over dinner tonight?"

"I don't want to talk about it. I know when someone is lying to me."

"Andrea . . ."

Click.

Some candidates have bad faces, too.

An Effective Technique

Could the poor communication between Pete and Andrea have been avoided? Probably, but not many companies would have known how to communicate more effectively. One that does is the Los Angeles headquarters of the Bank of America.

Thanks to a series of company training programs and a fine recruitment officer, Caroline Nahas, women candidates at the bank receive intelligent, thoughtful treatment. Caroline's success makes me wonder if too much can ever be said on behalf of women interviewing women, a simple technique that can eliminate many of the pitfalls that occur during the interview process. Witness the case of Greta, a Stanford MBA with several years of experience in the financial community and a highly desirable candidate to the bank.

Caroline first interviewed Greta alone. During that meeting, Greta was given an overview of her career path, an in-depth look at her entry position, a clear picture of what the bank would expect of her, and literature describing the divisions and services of the bank. On Greta's second visit, Caroline set up a series of three interviews—one with a former associate who was then working in the bank, one with an acquaintance from graduate school, and another with the hiring manager, Mr. S.

When she returned from the bank, Greta said, "The interviews went badly from my point of view. Nobody answered my questions, nor did they seem to care whether I was hired. Mr. S told me four times that he wanted to hire women in his department. I got the impression that being a woman was my only credential."

For reasons not evident to Greta, she was being given a soft sell. She began to question the wisdom of leaving her present job, which was a good one, and going to the bank.

I called Caroline, who said, "I know what happened. Mr. S is accustomed to interviewing young women right off the campus who don't need as much convincing as Greta. He really does want to hire women. I'll suggest to him that we take Greta out to lunch and talk with her again."

Caroline was right. At lunch, Mr. S assiduously answered all Greta's questions and gave her the assurance she needed to make the move.

Caroline's involvement at the critical point in this "courtship" was the difference between a hire and needless failure. Alone, Greta could not have penetrated the masked face of management, and her right to assess her future employer was no less legitimate than his right to assess her. Many managements unconsciously resent this right of the candidate. They believe that women and minorities will be grateful for any opportunities given them. In reality, quite the opposite reaction occurs. Those who have been discriminated against are highly suspicious of anything new.

The burden of proof in interviews rests heavily on women and minorities, lightly on the company. Will they measure up to job specifications as well as to irrelevant criteria applicable only to them? Male supervisors protest too much ("I love women") or too little ("What about your family obligations?").

As they assess minority candidates, nonminority managers are influenced by their own stereotypical attitudes. The purpose of the interview—to determine whether a candidate is qualified for a job and, if so, whether he or she wants it—is obscured by extraneous or inflammatory comments. Interviews take on added dimension when predispositions are introduced. Interviewing techniques now taught in management programs might well be expanded to include new methods of coping with this fundamental problem.

Reward vs. Punishment

Although the Bank of America is enlightened, other corporate faces are not so bright. Many companies form a solid barrier against hiring women and minorities at the first-line management level. "It is at that level," says Gordon Stagg, national sales manager of Avon Products, Inc., "that most of the wrongs are committed." Although much has been written and said in favor of commitment to affirmative action, the fact remains that such commitment becomes more and more diluted the further one progresses down the management line and out into the divisions.

The company's dilemma is the choice of means for implementation. On the one hand, there are managers who believe in a system of reward; on the other, there are advocates of punishment. Which choice is best?

When I asked a number of managers whether they approve of bonus incentives for hiring women and minorities, Avon's Gordon Stagg said, "Absolutely," and Bob LoPresto of Fairchild Camera and Instrument Corp. said, "When integrated with other performance goals, it's the only thing that works."

Tod Jagerson of Jagerson Associates Inc., EEO consultants, on the contrary, said, "No, I do not approve." And Jean Moore of Atlantic Richfield Co. said, "No. Equal opportunity employment should be a routine part of a manager's job."

The truth is that bonus incentive programs work minimally. If they had a clear record of success behind them, they might be tolerable to the women and minorities who now oppose them. The morality of rewarding someone for treating others equitably is doubtful. As Jagerson suggested, "Should an executive be rewarded for simply obeying the law?"

Good citizenship is often rewarded in our society, so Jagerson's view is open to rebuttal. Reward, the basic incentive in our system, might effectively be used for encouraging nondiscriminatory hiring practices, but the specifics for a workable system have yet to be developed. For example, how can performance be measured? The vagaries of good, bad, and better treatment of people defy quantifying.

Also, the fallout from a bonus incentive system must inevitably be hires and promotions made solely for reasons of race or sex. Few women and minority members approve of such reverse discrimination. The flawed system of cash incentives is unacceptable to the very people it is designed to help.

A Desirable System

In considering alternate possibilities for making change, special notice should be taken of government actions that have produced success. Penalties meted out by regulatory agencies are providing a sense of urgency in industry to reverse its discriminatory habits. The severe punishments that the courts have inflicted, plus the attendant publicity, have raised public awareness and private concern.

Harsh though such punitive procedure may be, it has made the only substantive inroad to date into the inequities of employment, promotion, and compensation. That some corporations are still failing to comply with EEO regulations after sustaining costly judgments is disappointing, but it testifies to the enormity of the problem.

Imposing penalties for discriminatory hiring practices on individual managers could accelerate beneficial results at all corporate levels. Tod Jagerson believes that "the manager should feel the same pressure from his company as the company feels from the government." A system involving both reward and punishment would be the most desirable of all (reward measured not by "head count" but by increased awareness, personal growth, and maturing attitudes).

Today's Dismal Picture

What are reasonable expectations for the hiring of management-level women and minorities these days, given the amount of retrenchment for survival that has been undertaken by so many companies and the resulting high level of professional unemployment? The year 1975 was to have been one of great promise for women and minorities in industry. Manpower plans were based on an increasing number of new hires and on the assurance that the door to management positions would be open. But the downturn in the economy has dealt these plans a severe blow. Consider the following scenarios, which are representative of situations I have encountered.

October 1974: A national consumer products company official is talking on the phone.

> "We are looking for a divisional marketing manager with three to five years' experience in a company like Bristol-Myers, Procter & Gamble, or General Foods. Location is in the Southwest, salary in the mid-30's. A graduate degree in marketing from a top school is required. I would like to fill it with a minority."

A recruitment drive produces a qualified minority candidate who is interviewed over a period of several weeks. As the details of his relocation are being worked out, the company is placed in a hiring freeze. The candidate is pressed to wait until the freeze is lifted.

January 1975: A woman who is a corporate loan officer is on the phone.

> "The bank is taking all women out of its line. I had better move before it happens to me, too."

February 1975: The national consumer products company official is speaking again.

> "We are looking for a divisional marketing manager with three to five years' experience in a company like Bristol-Meyers, Procter & Gamble, or General Foods. Location is in the Southwest, salary in the mid-30's, graduate degree in marketing from a top school required."

Something is missing. "Isn't this the same job you called in last October?"

"No. The specs are different this time."

Quite different. The minority preference is left out.

March 1975: An aerospace corporation manager is speaking.

"By the way, about that project director's job we gave you. Make it easy on yourself and fill it with a man."

Because of the continuing recession, affirmative action has slowed down to a crawl. Which issue is to take precedence—seniority or affirmative action—will eventually be ruled on by the Supreme Court. This gloomy picture results from companies laying off their most junior employees first, who include a high proportion of women and minorities during cutbacks. Less commonplace but frequent, nonetheless, is the demotion or firing of women and minorities from executive positions.

Regressions of the former kind are to be expected during an economic crisis, but the reason for the latter kind is particularly disquieting—a blossoming prejudicial attitude. Although most women and minorities who have reached a level of corporate responsibility have had to be exceptional to get there, confidence in them versus old-line employees lessens as business becomes harder and harder to get. Furthermore, as each new hire escalates in importance to companies balanced on top of a precarious economy, Caucasian men are considered to be less risky choices than either women or minority applicants.

Under our present economic uncertainty and staggering unemployment, is there any hope for women and minorities? While the concept of equal employment opportunity appears to be palatable to most companies, implementing it does not. This state of affairs will likely accelerate the corporate dance of avoiding compliance to rock-and-roll speed.

Lawsuits are a continuing horror. They provide handsome fees to attorneys, heavy fines to companies, and benefits—but not acceptability—to women and minorities. Misconceptions about women and minorities continue to blur the truth when they are considered for hire or promotion. Corporations are writing manuals by the hundreds to cover everything from women in the boardroom to the dreary problem of who is to get the coffee. Systems of reward, punishment, and combinations of both are being debated and redebated. Consultants are prospering, and so are affirmative action officers, but neither group has much clout. Being understaffed, federal and local government enforcement agencies are unable to cope with the many thousands of charges on file with them. Overall, it is a dismal picture indeed.

Tomorrow's Brighter Faces

But amid the gloom there shines a beam of light. As a result of this current struggle and others before it, the faces of America's corporations are becoming more human. Corporate anonymity is no longer sacrosanct. Consumerism, public demand for corporate responsibility to the community, and advocacy of equal employment opportunity are unmasking the faces of corporations. Reports of class-action suits brought by women and minorities and the final disposition of such cases are revealing the character of many corporate institutions. In living rooms across the country, people are discussing firsthand the employment experiences of women and minorities.

In short, the public is drawing well-delineated portraits of its corporations. The corporate faces people see—as consumers, employees, and citizens—will determine their future attitudes and actions.

Thus we come to the larger question: Will self-examination and public scrutiny, as consequences of the struggle for compliance, radically change the faces of U.S. business in the next decade? Hopefully, yes, as this final scenario suggests.

January 1985: "Hello, this is Jane Watkins, vice president of personnel for the International Corporation."

The name Jane Watkins rings a bell. She is also an officer of the NAACP and president of the local Kiwanis Club. She has been selected as Minority Woman of the Year for the Western Hemisphere for ten straight years. She sings contralto with the American Legion Glee Club, and she also serves on the boards of six major corporations.

"It certainly is a pleasure to hear from you, Ms. Watkins. Is there anything we can do to help you?"

"Yes. I am looking for either a man or a woman candidate—it doesn't matter which. If it's a woman, we absolutely do not want to know if she can type or take shorthand. We don't care if the person is married or single or how many children he or she has. A college degree is fine but not necessary if we find the right individual. We simply want someone who is capable, attuned, and sensitive to our needs."

"What is the salary range?"

"Whatever is equitable."

"Pardon me, Ms. Watkins, but I can hardly believe this. You're describing the ideal job."

"How did you guess? That's the job title—The Ideal Job. Can you recommend someone to fill it?"

"Yes, I can. I have an ideal woman candidate for you—785-40-9072, 213-553-4088."

"What are all those numbers?"

"My social security number and my phone number. My address is 255 Westview Avenue. My salary requirements are. . . ."

The International Corporation has a beautiful face.

Blacks vs. Women: When Victims Collide

Betsy Hogan

What happens when the rights and interests of blacks and women clash in the equal employment opportunity struggle? In attempting to resolve such a collision, it's tempting to introduce a sheaf of statistics in defense of coming down on the side of one group or another. While this may be inevitable and indeed necessary, an exclusive reliance on such a quantitative justification for an equal opportunity decision may, in fact, retard the implementation of an effective corporate affirmative action program. Put in other terms, if we assume that affirmative action programs are right and desirable, then we must be concerned with the ways and means employed in trying to effect them; for these can raise as many and serious moral issues as the problems that they attempt to correct.

In the following article, Betsy Hogan, equal employment opportunity consultant, raises the issue of implementing affirmative action programs. While vividly portraying how interests of disadvantaged groups can clash in the work place, she suggests additional questions of particular moral concern. One question involves the general unrest that underlies the job of a corporate EEO officer resulting from the tension created by divided loyalties. On the one hand, the officer has an obligation as a corporate executive to facilitate organizational operations. On the other, the officer must maintain credibility with corporate minority members and other disadvantaged employees. These twin obligations often collide. Hogan believes the only way to settle this unrest is through an unswerving commitment to an effective affirmative action program for every disadvantaged employee. Essential to this commitment is the breakdown of stereotypes, especially that of woman as white. Hogan underscores an issue we raised in this chapter; but in showing how stereotyping by and among members of disadvantaged groups can impede their own quest for fair and equal employment opportunities, she brings to the topic a nuance worthy of consideration. Finally, she argues that effective affirmative action programs can only be effective if all disadvantaged groups join a coalition to enlarge their gains, a coalition in which special interest groups remain intact but assist each other when the interests of several groups converge or when one group needs emergency help. We might view her call for intergroup unity as an endorsement of the proposition that in the area of equal employment opportunity for disadvantaged groups, one's self-interest is best served by attempting to advance the interests of women and minorities as a whole. In so doing, Hogan reminds us again that in the business world, as in many other areas of life, self-interest cannot be neatly separated from group interest, that a well-thought-through egoism may in fact be inextricable bound to some version of utilitarianism.

In the beginning was The Word. The black employee was not getting a fair shake in employment. The result: programs were sent forth for "minorities"—implicitly defined as black males.

Then there was The Second Word. There were other minorities abroad in the land—Spanish-

Reprinted from Business and Society Review/Innovation, *No. 10 (Summer 1974), pp. 71–77. Used with permission of the publisher.*

surnamed Americans, American Indians, Asian Americans, to name a few. *They* were not getting a fair shake in employment. Programs went forth for a broader group of "minorities"—implicitly defined as Third World males.

Then came The Third Word. Women—of all colors—were not getting a fair shake. This word was spoken primarily by white women, and everyone completely lost patience. Enough already! This was the *very last word*! Which women have always had, if you believe the myths.

"We've worked all these years for our place in the sun and now you want to take it away," said the minority male.

"We're told to worry about all the Third World people, the veterans, the hard-core unemployed, the handicapped, and now *you too*?" said the employer. To the woman, the whole scene was straight out of Alice in Wonderland's tea party:

> The table was a large one, but the three were all crowded together at one corner of it: "No room! No room!" they cried out when they saw Alice coming. "There's *plenty* of room!" said Alice indignantly, and she sat down in a large arm-chair at one end of the table. . . . "I didn't know it was *your* table," said Alice; "it's laid for a great many more than three."

The hostile tea party scene is familiar to every corporate equal employment opportunity officer. The battle between black minority groups, other Third World groups, women from all groups, and management is hot and getting hotter. Like the corporate EEO officer, I stand on the front lines in this battle. It's a distinctly volcanic job territory. From my consulting assignments, I have witnessed the depth and breadth of the inter-group hostility, its effect on all disadvantaged employees, and how it can be rechannelled to constructive action toward EEO for everyone. There is indeed room at the table. It's even possible to convince the warring groups of employees that there's room. But it's a long, rough road from here to there.

I have devised an approach for dealing with this situation which has repeatedly worked. It may serve as a model which other EEO officers can adapt to the needs of their own employees and

working environments. Let me illustrate with a typical consulting assignment.

The Client's Call

A manager calls from an organization which has a long history of war between minority and women employees. In the call, my assignment sounds deceptively easy. "Our EEO coordinators are familiar with the problems of minority workers," the caller explains, "but they need to be sensitized to the problems of women. Can you come?"

Of course. Have tranquilizers, will travel.

They are planning a five-day conference. We arrange for two days of "sensitizing"—an afternoon, a full day immediately thereafter, and a morning on the third day. The lid will blow off on day one, I figure. We'll spend day two analyzing the reasons and drafting the way to a truce. The third morning, we'll nail the new peace into place.

I form a panel of people mixed by race and sex and thoroughly knowledgeable about EEO. It will be their task to come in on the second day, after hostilities are out in the open, to help work out the battle lines toward the truce table.

On the afternoon of day one, the "woman" segment of the seminar opens with "Adam and Even," a consciousness-raising play performed by Plays for Living, a New York group. This was the client's plan. During the telephone conversation I had agreed, but warned, "Watch out for racism in the casting." The play consists of four characters—a manager, his wife, his secretary, and his receptionist. My warning apparently went unheard. The receptionist, the bottom of the office hierarchy, is played by a black actress; all other players are white.

The problem in the play is that the secretary wants to move into a vacant position as buyer for the firm. She is qualified, but the manager, who can't overcome his cultural stereotyping about women, fails to perceive her qualifications. The stages in this struggle provide an excellent rundown of the universal sex discrimination problems encountered by women. At the end, the secretary pulls off a miracle and saves her boss from disaster, and he promises to look at her résumé with the buyer's position in mind.

At the play's end I face the seminar group.

"Well, what do you think?" I ask brightly, knowing perfectly well what they think. The lid starts to blow.

"I don't hear anyone speaking for my black sister," says a black male.

"That play is a mirror of black and white society. The black woman is at the bottom of the heap. Who's worrying about getting a promotion for her?"

"The white woman has access to the man in power. Black women can't get that far up."

"The black woman won't be uplifted until the black man is uplifted," offers a black man. "You think they'd hire a black man as a buyer? No way. But a white woman can get the job."

"White women won't worry about us until the black man starts moving up and threatening the white women's jobs," says another black male.

Since the discussion threatens to fly off into fantasyland at this point, I inject a note of reality by writing on the board the Labor Department's statistics on median earnings of full-time, year-round workers broken down by sex and race. White male, $10,918 . . . Black male, $7,373 . . . White female, $6,172 . . . Black female $5,280.

The figures show the money effects of both racism and sexism, I point out, with sexism producing the dominant division. Men of both colors occupy the top two income categories, with black men under white. Women of both colors are at the bottom income levels, with black women under white. "Now do you want the white women's jobs?" I ask the black men in the group.

The figures are greeted with disbelief, and then ignored.

"The white woman can have any job she wants," says a black male. "She goes to Vassar or Smith. She marries the man with the power and gets to know his friends with the rest of the power. What she wants, she gets."

A white woman rises in dispute. She agrees that she has an education, a Ph.D., in fact. "What good does it do me?" she asks. "I'm a librarian and I've been refused every promotion. Sure, I married a white man. He knows important people. We entertain them. My husband gets favors and promotions from his friends. But you know what they bring me when they come to dinner? Aprons and gourmet cookbooks. That's how they see me. It would never occur to them to help me advance in my career. Until now, it never occurred to me."

"If you haven't moved up with all that education, baby, there's something wrong with you," says a black male.

"That's what my boss tells me," the woman says bitterly. "And that's what your boss tells you, right? It's not your color, you're just not qualified. There's something wrong with you. Well, I was counting on you to understand. You've been through this. If you don't understand, who will?"

"Suppose you start to move up," a black woman says. "Who's going to cook in your kitchen? Black women have been cooking in white women's kitchens all their lives. You want us to help put our black sister out of her own kitchen and back into yours?"

"That stuff about not understanding—that's a cute trick you pulled," says a black male. "You say we're keeping you down. But we're the victims, not you. The oppressed can't be the oppressors."

"The whole thing is, the black woman has layers and layers to go through," a black woman explains thoughtfully. "The black man has fought to get just a tiny 10 percent wedge of the pie. Along comes the women's movement and it moves faster than the black movement ever did. Just think about it—there weren't any goals or timetables until the women moved in. Now they're going to take away that 10 percent of the pie from our men. That just makes us mad!"

"I don't see the white woman helping us," says a black male.

"The white woman will fight to take away my typewriter," puts in a black woman, "but she's not fighting to take away my mop."

"Let's be realistic," says a black woman, "I don't see anybody moving in this EEO program. We go to the manager about minorities and he says 'Don't bother me, I'm busy with women's problems.'" She looks directly at me. "I'll bet when you go in he says 'Don't bother me, I'm busy with the minorities.' Am I right?"

"You're right," I answer.

"Okay, then. Who wants us to be fighting like this? The white man didn't get where he is by being dumb, you know. That's the reality."

End of day one. It is clear that of all the minority employees present, the black people are the only ones united enough to speak out forcefully—and their forceful message is that society is racist. The white woman is part of the ruling structure . . . she can make it on her own and in fact also has vicarious power, through the white male, to oppress other minority people. In addition, there is a class warfare going on in which the white woman is seen as affluent, wanting work for self fulfillment or a hobby, while minorities are seen as facing issues of pure survival. These are the negative themes which block coalition between black groups and women's groups. There are positive, pro-coalition statements, too. But before they can be pulled out, the administrative tangles descend upon me.

Ring Around the Officer

As everyone leaves the seminar room, the client is upset because the lid blew off—the day was "divisive." Minority participants lecture me about the mistakes whites always make such as casting the play with a black actress in the receptionist's part. Several white women who felt unable to speak for themselves in the seminar group are upset because I didn't speak for them. Several black men and women are upset because they feel I *did* speak for white women. This game is called "Ring Around the EEO Officer."

Since every EEO officer stumbles into the middle of the ring, it's worth examining. The dynamics express a good deal of the unspoken tension in that seminar room, and the same dynamics create the unrest which underlies the job of the EEO manager.

On the one hand, there is top management which wants to "own" the EEO officer in order to keep the peace. In fact, the in-house EEO person *is* owned by management to some degree, by the very fact that he or she is on the payroll. The dilemma was sensitively put by an experienced EEO executive when he asked a group of fellow EEO officers, "What do you do when a government compliance officer comes in the door? You know there's rampant discrimination in X, Y, and Z departments. You feel an obligation to the employees who are discriminated against. You have an obligation to yourself as a committed EEO officer—you *want* to point it out. But you're on the company's payroll, and you know damn well the company doesn't want the government to find out what's going on in those departments! What do you do?"

In general, it is the job of any executive to facilitate, negotiate, mediate, and keep the corporate wheels turning smoothly. Top managers are usually chosen for promotion precisely because of their ability to keep the peace. Thus the supervisor down the line who runs a dissident department is seen by top management as an inadequate supervisor. Equally, the EEO officer is measured by the peace with which an EEO program is run. When employees mount pressure for affirmative action, the EEO officer runs the risk of losing credibility at top management levels—or of being fired. Even the relatively mild threat of losing one's credibility can tie the EEO officer's hands. It is crucially important that an EEO officer be able to sit down with top management and negotiate for the changes which affirmative action inevitably requires.

On the other hand are the disadvantaged employees, with whom the EEO officer must maintain credibility. Employee "out" groups, knowing the pressure from management, are constantly suspicious that the EEO officer has been or will be co-opted by a paycheck, a need for job security, or promises of corporate advancement if the peace is kept. Their suspicion is deepened by their own past experiences. Every disadvantaged group has been betrayed by management's promises of action which never materialized. Impatient after a long wait, suspicious after many betrayals, the out groups telegraph one clear message to the EEO officer—"Prove whose side you're on." To the extent that any out group sees itself at war with another, as well as with management, it demands not only that the EEO officer prove loyal to the employees, but to one particular group of employees over other groups.

The game of "Ring Around . . ." is elaborate, and there seems to be no way out of the ring. In fact, there is a way. Every successful EEO officer has held firmly to center ground and refused to be owned by any single group.

To illustrate, after the "Ring Around" game had been played, a veteran of the minority/women war in this organization confided a piece of history to me. Several years ago this organization had an EEO officer who publicly declared, "Affirmative action in this organization means affirmative action for the black male."

The narrator of the story says to me, "I didn't want to hear that."

"Why not?" I ask, surprised because he is himself a black male.

"I knew where it would lead," he says quietly.

Indeed, it led to three years of unremitting war. The EEO officer instantly lost credibility with nonblack minority males and all women. Outcries from these groups, heard by management, led to a credibility gap between management and the EEO officer. Without credibility at top levels, the EEO officer could not negotiate with management even on matters which would help the black male. He then lost credibility with black males as well. This impasse inevitably led to the firing of the EEO officer.

The only ground which everyone can trust in the long term is that of unwavering commitment to an effective affirmative action program for every disadvantaged employee. In the short term, a center-ground stance inspires wholehearted mistrust from everyone, as we saw in the seminar room.

Breaking Down the Stereotypes

Now it's time to prepare for day two. The second day will be built on the muted subthemes which surfaced on day one. Meeting with the panelists, I review the positive factors—cries for help from one group to another. From a black male: "I don't see the white woman helping us." From a white woman: "If *you* don't understand, who will?" From a black woman: "I don't see *anybody* moving in this EEO program. That's the reality." These are cries for intergroup unity instead of war, a call for each group to help the others and to get on with EEO, a subliminal recognition that the program won't move until the employees stop fighting each other. On these subthemes we'll build a truce tomorrow.

The first order of business on the second day is to break down the stereotype of "woman" as "white." Women are half of the white population—and half of every minority group. As the needs of women are met, the needs of half the minority people are met. I generally set the theme with a litany that goes like this: "We are half the people in the ghetto, half the people in Appalachia, half the people on the Indian reservations, half the people in Chinatown, half of the blue collar workers. We are half of the people who live in Beverly Hills and half of the migrant workers."

The second step is to break down the stereotype of the woman who *is* white, a stereotype which emerged clearly in the seminar. Aside from being morally offensive, stereotyping is divisive and can bring an entire EEO program to a halt. So, as "woman" must be shown to come in all colors, "white woman" must be shown to come in all socio-economic brackets. She must be shown as she is, working because of economic need. And, like the working nonwhite woman, she needs EEO for sheer survival.

But what of the fear that women will take over that tiny wedge of pie where there is "no room"? Here the facts about affirmative action need to be explained. The ideal end result is that all jobs, *at all levels*, be divided in proportion to the racial, ethnic, religious, and sexual makeup of the work force. Thus, if white males comprise 40 per cent of the work force in a given company or labor area, eventually white males will fill 40 per cent of the janitorial, secretarial, clerical, professional, technical, and managerial jobs. Conversely, 60 per cent of all those jobs will be filled by minority males and women of all colors. Therefore, as a hypothetical minority group contingent is joined by other minorities and women, the wedge of pie expands in direct proportion to the number of people defined as disadvantaged. It is surprising how often the people most closely involved in EEO don't know, or have forgotten, this simple and very basic theory.

Far from feeling threatened by the expansion of EEO to cover women, minority men should see an advantage. There are more employees available to generate a strong push for a total EEO program. And here we should discuss the dynamics which will, finally, move EEO off paper into actuality.

Four pressure groups are theoretically available to move an EEO program—top management, the EEO officer, the disadvantaged employees themselves, and government enforcement agencies. Of these, only a few are actually effective.

Many people mistakenly look to top management to take the initiative. This is unrealistic if the major task of a manager is to keep the wheels turning smoothly. Since that *is* generally considered to be a manager's function, then it follows that top management will activate EEO only to keep the peace.

If government enforcement agencies mount a determined push, they do so from outside. They are potentially effective pressure points, though their effectiveness varies from one agency and region to another. The overall feeling is that government enforcement could be more effective.

The EEO officer can provide some pressure, but is hampered by the two factors previously mentioned—the need to remain on the payroll, and the need to maintain credibility with top management. The job ideally resolves to one of mediation between a strongly unified group of employees pressing for affirmative action, and the managers who will make the necessary changes when they must.

The strong inside push, therefore, must come from the disadvantaged employees themselves. This push inside, coupled with a government push outside, creates a strong force with which managers *must* negotiate. A strong in-house push can be mounted only by sizable numbers of employees. The larger their ranks, the stronger the dissidence and the stronger the pressure on management. As one experienced EEO officer puts it, "Make no mistake. We're running a numbers game."

Forming a Coalition

On day two of the seminar, then, the key word is *coalition*. We examine the power politics of EEO and the need for all groups to join in *coalition*. An experienced EEO person will never suggest that existing minority groups disperse to join a larger, generalized EEO group. It is vital to maintain the integrity, unity, and strength of the smaller peer groups already formed, particularly the groups of minority men and women so effective in making gains for minority employees. The strength and comfort offered by these peer groups would be diluted in a larger, more inclusive EEO group. This, too, has been an unspoken fear in the seminar room. The minority male and female alike have felt it. As the black woman identifies with the woman issue, the black male tries to call her back with phrases like, "I don't hear anyone speaking for my black sister"—a reminder that her place is with the black group. The black woman herself feels the threat of dispersion. More than once, black women have said to me, "If I identify with both blacks and women, I'll take half my strength, efforts, and time away from my black group. What happens then to my husband, my sons and

brothers, my community, and my rights as a black person?"

Coalition meets this problem. In a coalition, special-interest groups remain intact. But when the interests of several groups converge, or when one group needs emergency help from the others, the groups can call upon each other for help.

On day two of the seminar, then, we work through the stereotypes; we tackle the "no room" fear; we explain the need for coalition and how it can work to strengthen everyone without weakening anyone. But coalition doesn't seem quite real, its practicalities don't fall into place, until the group tackles a sample issue using coalition as a tool.

That afternoon, the workshops gather. An issue much on people's minds, and a natural for coalition comes up for discussion: There is a danger that 1,000 laundry workers, most of them minority women, will be laid off. There is no enforceable way to stop the layoff or guarantee other jobs for the workers. But workshop discussion brings out the fact that there are at least six separate employee groups in the organization whose interests bear upon this laundry problem. The workshop discussion centers around how to bring the employee groups together, to mount concerted pressure. Finally a resolution is drawn up which lays the groundwork for organizing an on-going coalition to tackle first the laundry situation and subsequently any other situation involving the rights of employees. That evening the resolution is brought before a general council meeting. The council responds with applause, cheers, and cries of "Beautiful!" from everyone present. Now the group is moving toward EEO at last. Elation fills the room.

In the morning of day three, participants gather to hammer out coalition plans in greater detail. Each special-interest group hears suggestions from other groups and adopts them as often as not. The climate is spontaneous, joyous, productive.

Is this a failure-proof plan for "getting it together"? There are never gilt-edged guarantees in any field, let alone a field as volatile as EEO. But it's a plan that has worked, more than once, where people have fought and had their fill of fighting.

Still, the war repeatedly breaks out in other organizations. The truce must be drawn and redrawn. Less than a week after my first successful minority women assignment, I was asked to address state and local officials in my home state about EEO for women.

I started and ended with the familiar litany: "We are half the people in the ghetto, half the people in Appalachia, half the people on Indian reservations, half the people in Chinatown. We are half the people in Beverly Hills, and half the migrant workers."

Came the first question off the floor.

"I don't hear anybody speaking for my black sister."

Why Stop at 65?

James W. Walker

Should a worker be forced to retire at a certain age, say sixty-five? Obviously, many factors are involved, including the nature of the job, the individual in question, the benefits available, and the company's policy. These and other factors must be considered in evaluating the morality of mandatory retirement. In the following article, specialist in human resource planning and development Dr. James W. Walker reviews the arguments for and against mandatory retirement. Implicit in his remarks is that the mandatory retirement issue must be approached within the framework of retirement programs generally. From the viewpoint of morality, any retirement program raises fundamental questions of fair treatment. Thus, it may be that the fairest policy includes mandatory retirement. On the other hand, mandatory retirement may be incompatible with the so-called fairest program. In considering the merits and liabilities of mandatory retirement, then, Dr. Walker provides us with a number of insightful ideas applicable to the general issue of fairness in retirement policies and programs.

Once a career milestone normally fixed at age 65, retirement is now becoming more of an individual career decision to be made earlier or later, depending on personal interests, abilities, health, and economic circumstances.

Change toward more flexibility has been under way for some time. For the past decade many companies have been modifying retirement policies to encourage early retirements, and today the prevalent retirement age is closer to 62, with early retirements particularly common among hourly workers and managerial employees. But prospective further easing of mandatory retirement policies, resulting from possible legislative actions, will give employees reluctant to stop working new opportunities for extending their careers beyond age 65.

Retirement timing has often been an emotion-charged issue, leading to adjustment difficulties for individuals in retirement. And removing or extending the present impartial age-65 standard for compulsory retirement will add to the difficulties experienced by both company and employee.

A wider range of retirement-age options also imposes new responsibilities on both employers and individuals. For employers, flexible retirement demands more objective and open judgment of individual capabilities to perform job duties. For employees, it imposes a greater degree of self-analysis and career planning.

Early-Retirement Practices

Age 65 has been considered the normal retirement age in most companies for decades, largely because of the arbitrary selection of age 65 for social security benefits. But when interest began developing in earlier retirement, pension plans were first modified to allow earlier departures with reductions in benefits ("actuarial reductions") to reflect the fact that employers would contribute for a shorter period of time to the pension plan while the early retiree would receive benefits for a longer period of time than would those retiring at the normal time. Then, to induce employees to elect early retirement, many em-

Reprinted by permission of the publisher, from Management Review, *September 1977.* ©*1977 by AMACOM, a division of American Management Associations. All rights reserved.*

ployers removed this discount for retirements at 62 and above and, in some cases, at earlier ages. This means that, while employees could retire early without the reduction in benefits, the retirement income level is based on service and salary levels attained at the actual age of retirement, not at the projected level that would be reached by age 65. In addition, some companies provide supplemental benefits in the form of lump sum payments, salary continuation arrangements, or special pension supplements—for example, "make up" payments until full social security payments become available.

Some companies introduced early-retirement liberalizations to induce retirements as a means of reducing staff levels without forced terminations. Also, it was felt that encouraging retirements of longer-service employees would create promotional opportunities for remaining employees and new room for "young blood," newcomers who might bring fresh ideas and new vitality to the organization.

Many workers and executives are opting to take advantage of early-retirement opportunities. At General Motors, for example, the mandatory retirement age for hourly employees is 68, but 89 percent of those retiring are leaving before age 65. In 1976, 60 percent of those retiring under the "30 and out" provision of the United Automobile Workers pension plan were in the 55-to-64 age group, and 29 percent were younger than 55. In other companies, retirements under pension arrangements have also shifted to earlier ages, and a Towers, Perrin, Forster & Crosby survey of 28 major corporations showed that most managers and executives were also retiring prior to age 65.

The initial popularity of early retirement has diminished somewhat, however, because of the effect of inflation on fixed retirement incomes and because attitudes toward retirement are changing. In many instances there was a surge of voluntary retirements under special early-retirement provisions ("window periods" during which unreduced early-retirement benefits are available) by those who were looking forward to retirement and saw the new provisions as an attractive inducement. But now many employees contemplating retirement are not at all sure they want to move into a life of leisure; many say they would prefer to continue working.

The Drive Against Mandatory Retirement

Many individuals who have retired before age 65 have subsequently felt that the timing was too early. Even though retirements were "voluntary" under programs where special compensation was provided, some persons believed they were pressured and forced out unfairly to make room for younger people.

Federal legislation enacted in 1967 generally bans job discrimination against employees aged 40 to 65 because of age. The Age Discrimination in Employment Act covers hiring, job retention, promotions, and other employment-related conditions, and under its provisions, early retirements must be purely voluntary decisions to avoid charges of age discrimination. (Many states have similar laws, some covering an even broader age range.) As a result, many companies have been hauled into court on charges they forced retirements prior to age 65, and in many cases the litigation has resulted in offers of reinstatement and payment of cash settlements.

Section 4(f) (2) of the Act, however, permits mandated retirements under an employee benefit plan (such as retirement, pension, or insurance) as long as the plan is not a subterfuge to evade the Act's rules against age discrimination. This means that an employer can set a mandatory retirement age under 65 if it is part of an established benefit plan.

This exception is under attack, however. In a case involving an airline technician, who sued United Airlines on charges of age discrimination after he was retired in 1973 at age 60, a federal court has ruled that even though the company's pension plan specifies 60 as the normal retirement age, arbitrary age discrimination may exist. The decision said there must be some basis other than age for compulsory retirement before age 65. The case, presently being reviewed by the Supreme Court, obviously has broad implications for compulsory "early" retirement policies in many companies.

Outside the courts, there is mounting public sentiment favoring a ban on mandatory retirement at any age. The latest in a series of proposed laws is H.R. 65, a bill that would remove the upper age limit of 65 from the Age Discrimination in

Employment Act (ADEA). Bills with the same basic purpose also have been introduced in the Senate and several state legislatures. H.R. 65 has more than 30 co-sponsors and is backed by increasingly strong public sentiment.

Another bill, H.R. 6798, would eliminate from ADEA the exemption for mandatory retirement under an employee benefit plan. A third bill (H.R. 5383) unanimously approved last June by the House Labor Subcommittee on Employment Opportunities would amend ADEA by prohibiting a mandatory retirement age for federal employees, and by raising the upper age limit of private sector employees covered by the Act from 65 to 70. In addition, the bill would mandate that employee benefit plans and seniority systems in the private sector not be used to force retirement because of age before the age of 70.

Opponents to mandatory retirement argue that individual abilities to perform a job vary greatly and that age alone is not a valid determinant. They say that performance and individual capabilities, not chronological age, should determine employment status. With increased longevity and improved health, many individuals are still highly productive in their sixties and seventies. Today's older employees are better educated, more highly skilled, and in better health than their counterparts of past generations.

The American Medical Association, in opposing mandatory retirement at any age, observes that the sudden shock of compulsory retirement and loss of earning power and productive work often leads to physical and emotional deterioration and premature death. Older people, through various organizations, are voicing their unwillingness to be cast on the "scrapheap of life" merely because of age. Comprising what may be our newest minority, older workers are demanding recognition of rights as a protected class, and their political influence, already significant, is growing as their number grows in relation to total population.

Corporate executives generally agree that the drive toward flexible retirement is strong and unrelenting. When asked to give their views on legislation banning mandatory retirement, a number of personnel officers said they regard it as inevitable and believe that corporations must accept the facts of social change and attune their employment policies to individual merit rather than chronological age. As difficult as this task may seem, these executives also see potential benefits—reduced retirement benefit costs, improved ability to retain needed skills and experience, and improved employment stability in their organizations.

Flexible retirement is also seen as an important benefit to society in general. Many have voiced concern about our ability to support growing numbers of retirees through the social security system, but these fears would be allayed somewhat by a larger proportion of older employees remaining in the workforce. Elderly, able persons who remain in their jobs would continue to earn wages and salaries, pay taxes, and contribute to productivity.

But in a broader sense, persons have a right to be judged on individual merit, regardless of age. Rather than set a goal of giving favorable treatment to the aged, we should strive to end age discrimination in all its forms. "Prejudice by age," says David Hackett Fischer, author of *Growing Old in America*, "is as unjust as prejudice by sex, race, and religion. Many changes must be made—chief among them the abolition of forced retirement at a fixed age."

The Case for Mandatory Retirement

Many companies are concerned about the difficulty of applying a flexible retirement policy evenhandedly. Speaking in opposition to H.R. 65, spokesmen for Exxon, General Motors, and CBS have argued that mandatory retirement programs protect workers against unequal treatment. They contend that a single, simple policy dictating retirement for all avoids the pitfalls of individual merit judgments and the possible stigma that would be associated with the selective termination of employees after age 65. It is difficult to develop and apply evenhandedly criteria for retirement other than age.

In addition to equitable treatment for employees, a major reason companies have applied mandatory retirement policies has been for administrative simplicity. A limit on employment tenure, based on age, makes it easy for the company to remove less qualified personnel, allows prediction of pension and other benefits costs, and prevents disputes with employees with regard to termination of employment after the age of 65.

The U.S. Chamber of Commerce, in opposing

elimination of mandatory retirement under H.R. 65, noted that eliminating an age limit may reduce the career opportunities for women and minorities in industry and business. The Chamber would rather support raising the mandatory retirement age than eliminate it. "Surely it is more rational for society to plan and allocate its finite resources based on a certain age at which people can be expected to retire," a Chamber spokesman said. "This legislation will possibly benefit a very small number of people who want to work beyond the traditional retirement age, 65, to the disadvantage of many other workers as well as greatly complicating the efforts of employers to provide jobs and opportunities."

Organized labor has stated a more ambivalent position, favoring retirement plans as a means of opening up job opportunities for newcomers in the labor force, but also seeking to preserve the right of older persons to keep working if they desire to do so and are physically and mentally capable. Unions seek to preserve the right of determining retirement provisions in collective agreements through the bargaining process.

Mandatory retirement programs have worked effectively for 40 or more years. Accordingly, any changes should be weighed very carefully, as this is a complex and highly important subject. It may be that raising ADEA's age limit to 70 will provide the desired range of retirement age flexibility while still retaining many advantages of an age limit.

Introducing Flexible Retirement

Proponents of the new legislation point out, however, that self-determined retirements have been the rule, not the exception in our society. Professionals, including physicians, lawyers, and dentists, and entrepreneurial businessmen and farmers all determine their own retirement timing. Some companies and specific plants within some companies have no mandatory age and have functioned effectively. Furthermore, within even the largest corporations, exceptions are frequently made to mandatory rules by providing post-retirement employment or consulting arrangements where needed skills or expertise would be lost through retirements.

Just as individuals make their own decisions regarding vocation, job choice, relocations, and other career decisions, they can make their own retirement timing decisions. Age itself is not a key determinant of the most appropriate time for an individual to retire. Individual capabilities, attitudes, and health are not strictly functions of age. Some persons at age 70 may be less ready for retirement than others at age 50. Hence a need exists for more flexible timing in retirement decisions. Among the factors that tend to push retirement age up (defer retirement timing) are fear of inflation, economic necessity, job satisfaction, fear of aging and death, and perceptions that retirement would not be satisfying. Factors that tend to accelerate retirement timing include adequacy of income and pension benefits, adequacy of social security benefits, job dissatisfaction, poor health, opportunity for a second career, decline in performance, threat of new technology and related obsolescence, pressures of competition from younger workers, and a generally positive view toward retirement.

To be workable, therefore, flexible retirement policies must help guide individual understanding and evaluation of these factors, so that individuals will opt for retirement at the times in their lives best suited to their interests and abilities, as well as the company's needs.

New Management Tools Required

To introduce flexible retirement effectively, employers need four basic tools: retirement planning resources, job requirements defined by skills and abilities, appraisals of individual performance and abilities, and modified work arrangements, such as gradual retirement. These tools are considered basic human resource management techniques in some companies and are being adopted for reasons of affirmative action programming or simply to enhance management effectiveness. Yet to many other companies these tools are new, or not yet fully applied, and thus must be implemented to make more flexible retirement a reality.

Assuming a retirement policy allowing an individual to retire at any age, or within a range of eligible ages, say 55 to 70, some form of *retirement planning resources* is needed to provide incentives for voluntary individual retirements. These may include:

Retirement benefit plans allowing an employee to retire with full benefits at any time after a minimum combination of age and service has been accrued (e.g., a combination totalling 80), or after a minimum age such as 50, with benefits adjusted by age and service. A typical company may have normal retirement benefits available at age 62 and above. Earlier than age 65, benefits are reduced actuarially.

Communication of retirement policy and benefits as part of a comprehensive self-analysis and career planning program; tools to help each employee evaluate personal abilities, limitations, interests, goals, and plans.

Counseling and guidance resources, either by company staff or by outside personnel. Some companies have cooperated in sponsoring community counseling centers to aid individual career and retirement planning, as well as to help solve alcoholism, drug, and other life adjustment problems.

Educational resources, such as the expanded tuition reimbursement program offered older employees at IBM, where employees as young as 52 can receive $500 a year to cover costs of courses taken in accredited institutions. The program begins three years before retirement and continues two years after retirement. Alternatively, more extensive in-house training and development resources could be provided to help equip individuals for retirement or second careers.

Defined job requirements are essential to establish corporate staffing and performance standards. As required under EEO regulations and many affirmative action programs, the needed skills, abilities, knowledge, and aptitudes necessary for satisfactory performance of job duties must be specified. Chronological age, sex, race, religion, and national origin are not legal job requirements (with rare bona fide exceptions). The requirements for a position need to be determined through empirical analysis, that is, through examination of the actual activities required on the position. All requirements must be demonstrably job-related, and not arbitrary. The tools needed to provide age-free job requirements include:

Job descriptions that are reasonably accurate and up-to-date and that are free of age bias;

Job specifications that do not exclude older

workers or make it impossible for older workers to be considered; and

Performance standards that are reasonable, job-relevant, and that do not arbitrarily exclude or discriminate against older workers.

Appraisals of individual performance and abilities have, of course, been desired by companies for decades, and renewed efforts to improve the objectivity of appraisals are needed to make flexible retirement work. Each employee should receive an impartial evaluation to determine the adequacy of current performance and capacity to continue performing on an assignment. This evaluation involves comparison of indicators of performance and abilities with the established standards. Appraisals need not be highly quantitative or complex, but they should be thoughtful, detailed, and impartial. Further, they need to be discussed openly with the individual to develop understanding regarding individual capabilities and career plans. The tools that are needed for effective appraisal include:

A system for defining performance against established standards, or against specific performance goals. Such systems exist and have been effectively applied by many companies.

Training and coaching of appraisers to ensure that the system is understood and fairly applied.

Monitoring of appraisal results to ensure that appraisals are free of bias relating to chronological age of employees.

A mechanism, as part of the appraisal process, for discussion of appraisal results with the individuals appraised. This is key if employees are to benefit from the results and apply them in personal career and retirement planning.

Formal documentation of appraisal results, so that necessary terminations or job reassignments (downgrading, particularly) can be justified on the basis of performance and ability to perform.

Additional assessments of individual abilities and knowledge through interviewing, testing, or other methods to determine qualifications for alternate job assignments and responsibilities. Performance alone may not determine individual ability to perform alternate duties or jobs.

As a practical matter, several companies are establishing procedures by which ability to continue working is reviewed by a panel or committee when each employee reaches normal retirement age. Additionally, many companies require annual medical examinations each year after age 65, as health is often a central factor in determining ability to continue working.

Modified work arrangements may be provided in instances where an older employee wishes to continue working, but at a reduced activity level. Among the common tools are:

Gradual retirement, involving a reduced number of hours at work per week or per day, at reduced pay, perhaps on a stepwise basis until fulltime withdrawal from work is achieved.

Leaves and sabbaticals, involving extended periods of time away from work. Increasing length of vacation periods also allows a gradual adjustment to retirement while maintaining ties with work.

Reduced job scope or the level of performance output required, with associated pay level adjustment or other modifications in job content to allow continued job performance under conditions of declining individual capabilities.

Special work assignments that allow older employees to serve in social or community projects considered worthwhile (at full or reduced pay) while gradually adjusting to retirement living.

Downgrading, involving reassignment to other positions, at lower levels of responsibility, difficulty, and pay, but which may be satisfying to the employee and which may result in productivity for the company. Examples include foremen who wish to return to shop work and senior executives who wish to continue with the firm in less demanding roles.

Some of these tools may be considered unconventional, but all are potentially useful means of introducing more flexible retirement

arrangements. Once applied, each can become an accepted, practical aspect of a company's management process. An employer should consider the scope of the task that lies ahead in getting ready for flexible retirement as a way of life and adopt the needed tools.

The Bottom-Line Impact

Because a large proportion of employees are opting to retire early and because many employees feel that the traditional retirement age of 65 is "normal," the actual number of cases that need to be handled under a flexible retirement policy may be extremely small. In one large company's analysis of the impact of a mandatory retirement ban, the number of prospectively affected employees was found to be fewer than a hundred each year. Of nearly 1,000 employees, two-thirds were expected to retire prior to age 65 and a majority of the remainder to leave at the traditional age 65, voluntarily. It was felt that these individual cases could be effectively handled through counseling and judgments based on individual circumstances.

As the number of prospective retirees grows during the next two decades, most employees will find retirement timing that suits their personal needs and circumstances. Many executives agree that individuals generally know what their abilities and interests are; the few cases where "Old Joe has been strung along for years" are relatively few and will probably become even more rare as companies adopt more objective performance appraisals and more extensive career planning programs. The emerging generation of older workers tend to be more affluent and more conscious of the factors involved in career and retirement planning, and are more likely to make the adjustment easily without relying on forced retirement.

If, as expected, it becomes more difficult to terminate employees under EEO and age discrimination regulations, companies will become far more selective in hiring and retaining talent and will work harder to build a fully competent and stable workforce. The tools identified above are all useful in effective human resource management. Many companies are already developing more objective job criteria and more open and objective appraisal processes, and career-planning programs are being widely adopted as development tools. Many companies see these as competitive necessities for attracting and retaining needed talent.

Whether a ban on mandating retirement is legalized or not, employers are well advised to get ready for flexible retirement.

For Further Reading

Epstein, E. M., & Hampton, D. R. *Black America and white business.* Belmont, Calif.: Dickenson Publishing Co., 1971.

Janger, A. R. *Employing the disadvantaged: A company perspective.* New York: National Industrial Conference Board, 1972.

_____ & Shaeffer, R. G. *Managing programs to employ the disadvantaged.* New York: National Industrial Conference Board, 1970.

Norgren, P. H., & Hill, S. E. *Toward fair employment. Part I.* New York: Columbia University Press, 1964.

Seashore, S. E., & McNeill, R. J. *Management of the urban crisis.* New York: Free Press, 1971.

Shaeffer, R. G. *Non-discrimination in employment: Changing perspectives, 1962–1973.* New York: National Industrial Conference Board, 1973.

Steiner, G. A. *Contemporary challenges in the business-society relationship.* Los Angeles: U.C.L.A. Press, 1972.

Young, R. A. *Recruiting and hiring minority employees.* New York: AMACOM, American Management Association, 1970.

9
ECOLOGY

The manager of a small dye-processing firm in an eastern city of 70,000 refuses to be influenced by local environmentalists who demand that his factory stop its minor pollution of a river that runs through the city. The manager insists that he is complying with all pollution-control laws; allocating any more money for pollution control would be bad business that would adversely affect not only profits but also the economic well-being of the 2,000 workers he employs.

The president of a mining company in a western state loudly objects to the state's board of health standards that far exceed federal air standards regulating sulfur dioxide emissions from mineral smelters. To comply with state standards would mean completely renovating the firm's antiquated smelter. The cost would be prohibitive. If the state insists, the president threatens to shut down the smelter and let the board deal with the calamitous economic impact it would have on local communities.

Members of a consumer group gather in front of the gates of a midwestern paper mill. Similar groups are simultaneously demonstrating at other paper mill firms across the country. Their purpose is to make the paper industry roll back its recent 50 percent increase in prices effected to absorb costs of pollution-control equipment. The consumer groups argue that it's unfair to put the burden of pollution-control costs on consumers. The paper industry points out that it's currently investing about 50 percent of its capital in pollution-control equipment in order to meet federal environmental quality regulations. Without exception, the consumer groups tell the paper industry to absorb such costs. The paper industry says it can't and won't; that if consumers want paper, then they'll pay the full price of its production.

Incidents like these are common as business and society attempt to deal with pollution of the physical environment. Although environmental pollution has always been with us, today many persons fear that we may not be able to survive unless we take immediate and extensive corrective measures. It's little wonder, then, that for the first time in history considerable attention is being given to business's responsibility for environmental improvement. Indeed, together with equal rights and consumerism, the integrity of the physical environment figures among the most pressing social issues facing business today.

As we are painfully aware, pollution to the physical environment can take many forms: foul air, impure water, solid waste, unhealthful noise, dangerous chemical pesticides. While this chapter deals with some of the moral dilemmas that environmental problems raise for business, it's not intended to provide a descriptive account of environmental pollution. The chapter will not argue how bad the problem is and how much industry may be contributing to it. Suffice it to say on this point that most persons believe that the problem is serious enough to bear correction and that business is a primary polluter.

Essentially this chapter is concerned with this question: given the problem of environmental degradation and the evident need to remedy it, what are business's responsibilities? We'll see that any satisfactory answer to this question begins with a recognition of how business functions as part of a global ecosystem. Moreover, it appears that if business is to deal constructively and morally with environmental problems, it must make attitudinal changes, which, in some cases, have begun to occur. This chapter will examine some traditional business attitudes that have contributed significantly to environmental pollution, have impeded pollution-control efforts, and have continued to worsen the condition. The chapter will then consider who should pay the costs of pollution control and how the clean-up costs should be allocated. It is difficult to imagine questions about the environmental crisis that are fraught with more moral overtones than these. Concerns about blame, benefit, and obligation introduce important questions of social justice and distribution of wealth.

Obviously we can't extract all the moral questions that environmental pollution and control raise relative to business. But we hope to raise enough questions to initiate a constructive debate about business ethics in this area, especially as it applies on the personal level. Finally, as in previous chapters, we'll reinforce this goal by attempting to apply ethical theories to the question of business's responsibilities for the environment.

Business and Ecosystems

In order to deal intelligently with the question of business's responsibilities for the environment, one must realize that business functions within an ecological system.

Ecology refers to the science of the interrelationships among organisms and their environments. The operative term is *interrelationships*, implying that an interdependence exists among all entities in the environment. In speaking about ecological matters, ecologists frequently use the term *ecosystem*, which refers to a total ecological community, both living and nonliving. An ordinary example of an ecosystem is a pond. It consists of a complex community of animal, vegetable, and geological life. Suppose the area where the pond is located experiences a prolonged period of drought; or someone begins to fish in the pond regularly; or, during a period of excessive rainfall, plant pesticides begin to spill into it.

Under any of these circumstances, changes will occur in the relationships among the pond's constituent members. Suppose that fewer fish can live in the pond; a particular kind may disappear. The change in the pond's ecosystem may affect other ecosystems. Thus a herd of deer that lived nearby may have to go elsewhere for water; their relocation may ensure an increased apple crop, which had previously been devoured by the hungry deer. The point is that in considering any ecosystem, one must remember its complex and interrelated nature, and the intricate network of interdependencies that bind it to other ecosystems.

It is apparent that in some sense every living organism affects its environment. The problem to be considered as we discuss business and the environment is that human commercial activities (for example, using pesticides, establishing oil fields) have unpredicted consequences for the ecosystem. Sometimes the effects are negative; other times they appear to be positive. So, while it may be true that no organism can live without affecting its environment, at the same time the species *Homo sapiens* possesses the power to upset drastically the stability of natural ecosystems.

A good example of the consequences of ecological ignorance can be found in the indiscriminate agricultural use of pesticides. Rachel Carson spoke eloquently about this problem in her classic book *Silent Spring*. She contended that we had put biologically dangerous chemicals into the hands of persons who were ignorant of their poisonous nature. These persons were using chemicals with no understanding of their effects on soil, water, wildlife, and human beings. Carson warned that tampering with ecosystems would have serious consequences. She predicted that future generations would indict our imprudence and deplore our insensitivity to the natural world.

Subsequent research and developments have confirmed Carson's worst suspicions. We now know that some pesticides can affect the reproductive capacity of animals and can reach such high concentrations in human fatty tissue that they cause brain damage and cirrhosis of the liver. Indeed, one study has revealed that a large percentage of terminal cancer patients has shown high concentrations of pesticide residues in their livers and brain tissues. Another study has observed that workers, such as crop dusters, who are exposed to certain pesticides exhibit dull reflexes and mental instability; they often die as a result of intolerable levels of toxicity.

The message to be learned from this aspect of environmental poisoning can be summed up in the facetious though pointed caution that a margarine commercial popularized a few years ago: "It's not nice to fool Mother Nature." Tampering with ecosystems does not always have the injurious effects evident in the use of pesticides. On the contrary, sometimes unforeseen benefits result, as was true of the expansive oil and gas drilling activity in the Gulf of Mexico. Much to everyone's surprise, the operational docks, pipes, and platforms provided a more beneficent place to which lower forms of life could be attached than the silt-laden sea ever did. As a result, oil drilling in the Gulf of Mexico has greatly increased the commercial fish catch in the area. But even in fortuitous instances like this, environmental intrusions affect the integrity of ecosystems. And that's the point. Because an ecosystem represents a delicate balance of interrelated entities and because ecosystems are interlocked, an intrusion into one will affect its integrity and the integrity of others.

In a word, we can't do something that has no effect anywhere else; we can't influence one part without influencing another. Dr. Paul Ehrlich, one of the best-known exponents of ecological awareness, has put the matter succinctly. "There are a number of ecological rules it would be wise for people to remember," Ehrlich has written. "One of them is that there is no such thing as a free lunch. Another is that when we change something into something else, the new thing is usually more dangerous than what we had originally."[1] Clearly everyone must learn the laws of interdependence and interrelationship, including an undeniably principal polluter, business.

In its role as the major economic instrument of production in our society, business must intrude into ecosystems. This does not mean, however, that all intrusions or any kind of intrusion is thereby justifiable. In fact, precisely because of the interrelated nature of ecosystems and because intrusions generally produce serious unfavorable effects, business must be scrupulous in its actions, practices, and policies that are calculated to have an impact on the physical environment. There's ample documentation to show that business traditionally has been remiss in both recognizing and adequately discharging its obligations in this area. We needn't spend time here retelling the sorry tale. But it does seem morally worthwhile to isolate some business attitudes which historically have supported this indifference, in much the same way that in the preceding chapter we tried to present some managerial attitudes toward women which functioned to perpetuate institutional sexism. In this case, we will try to understand business's attitudes and assumptions about its environment. For example, if a company wantonly pollutes a river because that represents the most economical way to manufacture a product, the morality of the behavior largely depends on the soundness of the assumption that the most economical way to produce something is necessarily the moral way to produce it. It's important, then, in discussing business's responsibilities to the physical environment to unearth some attitudes which have given rise to its behavior.

Business's Traditional Attitudes Toward the Environment

There are two principal attitudes which society in general and business in particular have held that bear directly on environmental pollution. One is viewing the environment as a "free good" and the other is considering business in strictly economic terms.

The Environment as a Free Good

Traditionally business has considered the environment to be a free good. In other words, aspects of the physical environment, especially air, water, and land, were available for business to use as it saw fit. These resources were

1.   "Playboy *Interview: Dr. Paul Ehrlich,*" Playboy, *August, 1970, p. 56.*

viewed as common entities, available to all. In economic terms, they represented an economic externality that business didn't have to account for in its reckoning of its costs of producing a good or service. Thus, steelmakers could use oxygen from the air for their blast furnaces or draw water from nearby rivers without having to pay a cent for them. Similarly, they could disgorge wastes into the atmosphere without incurring any additional production expenses. Both business people and society avoided paying costs for environmental pollution. Both were encouraged to pollute.

As long as the imposition on the environment remained light, few serious problems arose. In our time, of course, the environmental burden has become quite heavy, in some cases intolerably so. As a result, society is being forced to shoulder the social costs, the negative side effects, of having viewed the environment as a free good. This prevailing concept of the environment betrays a perception of business strictly as an economic enterprise.

Business as an Economic Enterprise

Traditionally business and society have viewed business's function in the strictly economic light of private industrial costs. In other words, business people have taken into account the cost of resources necessary for the manufacture of a good or service. They have not considered the full costs to society, the social costs.

To grasp this point fully, suppose a paper mill only partially treats the chemical wastes it emits into a lake that's primarily used for fishing and recreational activities. Should the amount of effluent be great enough to reduce the fishing productivity of the lake, then society, while paying a lower price for the mill's product, will pay a higher price for fish than it otherwise would. Moreover, the pollution may make the lake unfit for such recreational activities as swimming and boating or for use as a source of fresh water. The result is that the public must pay the cost of the mill's inadequate waste treatment system. *Economists term this disparity between private industrial costs and public social costs a spillover or externality.* In viewing things strictly in terms of private industrial costs, business overlooks spillover. As a result, business remains unmindful of serious moral questions involving social justice. What's more, without acknowledging or accepting responsibility for the social costs of production, business has little reason to cease its assault on the environment.

Both of these traditional attitudes have clearly contributed to the ecological problems we currently face. And they have given rise to serious questions of social justice concerning the costs of pollution control, who should pay them, and how the bill should be paid.

The Costs of Pollution Control

Now that environmental pollution has reached crisis proportions, the obvious question is what to do about it. The clearly evident reply is to do whatever is necessary to improve the environment. Before this answer has any operational worth, we must consider a number of things. One is the quality of environment that we want. This can vary from an environment restored to its pristine state to one minimally improved over the current state. Then there's the question of precisely what is necessary to effect the kind of environment we want. In some cases we may not at present have the technological capacity to improve the environment. But perhaps the overriding concern in any determination of what should be done to improve the environment is a calculation of what it will cost. This calculation will necessarily involve controversial value judgments that will affect the moral commitment, or lack of it, that business feels toward enhancing the environment.

To draw out this point, we must consider a technique that plays a major role in determining the total costs of environmental improvement: cost-effectiveness analysis. This analytical device is used to determine whether it's worthwhile to incur a particular cost, namely, the cost of employing a pollution-control and environment-improvement device. The general approach is to take a project and evaluate its direct and indirect costs and benefits, the difference being the net result for society. Take, for example, a national project undertaken to clean up the air.

In order to determine whether it's worthwhile to initiate such a program, a multitude of cost-benefit factors must be considered. For example, the Council on Environmental Quality estimates that air-pollution-control costs will run about $106.5 billion. Included here presumably would be such items as loss in corporate profits, higher prices for consumers, unfavorable effects on employment, and adverse consequences for the nation's balance of payments. These costs must be compared with the anticipated benefits. Thus, some persons calculate that a 50 percent reduction in the amount of particulates and sulfur oxide in the air over urban areas would reduce illness and premature death from bronchitis by at least 25 percent, perhaps as much as 50 percent. Also, deaths due to heart disease would decrease by 20 percent, from respiratory disease by 25 percent, from cancer by 25 percent or more. Moreover, a reduction in air pollution would add approximately three to five years to the life expectancy of an urban dweller. These facts can be translated into 5,000 fewer deaths per year from lung cancer and 16,000 fewer from heart disease. As for the savings in medical costs and personal effects, some conservatively estimate those at $2 billion. In addition, billions more may be saved in property and crop damages.[2] It would be on the basis of such an analysis that a decision for or against air-pollution control would be made.

Even granting this strictly consequential approach to determining whether or not to undertake a specific program, a cost-effectiveness analysis clearly involves value judgments which will affect the nature and extent of one's moral commitment. This is so because a cost-effectiveness analysis does not consider costs and benefits only in terms of money. Thus, costs relative to time, effort, and discomfort can and must be introduced. Benefits can take even more numerous forms: health, convenience, comfort, enjoyment, leisure, self-fulfillment, freedom from odor, visibility, psychological conditions, and so on.

2. *Steiner, pp. 242–243.*

Indeed, benefits are especially difficult to calculate in environmental matters because they often take the form of an aesthetic enhancement. Some environmentalists, for example, may campaign for the preservation of a remote forest visited annually by only a handful of stalwart backpackers, while developers wish to convert it into a more accessible and frequented ski resort. Should the forest be preserved or should it be converted into a ski resort? The answer largely depends on the aesthetic value one places on the forest as opposed to the more utilitarian value placed on the ski resort. Thus, those arguing against the ski resort feel it would be wrong to violate the forest; they attach an inherent value to it. Those arguing in favor of the ski resort attach a value to the usefulness of that project.

But even if business seeks a social result in which benefits of all types are greater than costs of all types, this formula isn't entirely satisfactory because, as in the case here, determination of the costs and benefits can depend foundationally on the value that one places on a pristine forest as opposed to a ski resort, a subject that is at least debatable. The fact is that the value one attaches to the forest cannot be as well quantified as the one attaching to the ski resort. It relies essentially on a qualitative judgment, which some environmentalists would argue outweighs the quantitative benefits of the ski resort. These same proponents might go further and claim that it was a strictly quantitative approach to the environment that has produced all the problems.

Clearly, then, an evaluation of costs and benefits is wed to values, assessments of worth, and to an ordering of those values. Compounding this fact further is that values are constantly being affected by changes in the environment itself. Thus, the high value that some environmentalists might attach to the forest is directly related to the fact that such wilderness areas are becoming rarer to the point of extinction. As a result, they might see the cost of obliterating it as prohibitive, whereas in former times they might not have. By the same token, others who are sensitive to the fact that recreational land is becoming scarce might consider a ski resort as a premium benefit. The point is that while the soundness of an environmental preservation or pollution-control project may reside in a cost-effectiveness analysis, an assessment of the costs and benefits can be significantly influenced by the values one holds. Thus, what value do society and business attach to clean air, pure water, space and privacy, silence? These values will play influential roles in the moral commitments made to environmental improvements. They will influence the moral judgments business and society form about the propriety of such programs. Finally, these values will affect who we think should pay the costs of pollution control and how these costs should be borne.

Who Should Pay the Costs?

One aspect of the environmental dilemma that raises questions of social justice is determining who should pay the costs of environmental improvements. Inherent in the answer to this question are some basic attitudes about equity and fairness, the relationship between business and government, and the proper distribution of wealth. Two popular answers to the question currently circulate. One is that those responsible for causing the pollution should pay for removing it. Another solution offers that those who stand to benefit from restoring the environment ought to pick up the tab.

Those Who Pollute

The claim that those responsible for causing the pollution ought to pay the costs of pollution control seems eminently fair until one asks a simple question. Just who is responsible for the pollution? Who are the polluters? Proponents of this theory observe that individuals and institutions with large incomes generally produce disproportionately more pollution than those with low incomes. Thus, big business is the chief polluter. This alone, the argument goes, is enough to justify the claim that business ought to bear the lion's share of pollution control. But there's another reason. Shifting environment-improvement costs to society or customers would only increase the economic disparity that already exists between polluters and those damaged by pollution. In effect, a policy of making polluters pick up the tab for environmental restoration would probably have the desirable social effect of shifting income from the richer to the poorer and thus provide for a more equitable distribution of wealth. In the minds of some persons, the question of who should pay the bill is connected with the fair and just distribution of wealth.

The validity of this position depends partially on the soundness of the proposition that large income entities produce disproportionately more pollution than those with low income. But even if this is true, income, whether large or small, is not generated in a vacuum. An automobile manufacturer does not come by its sizable wealth without the explicit and implicit cooperation of government, of millions of individuals, and of all sectors of society. Pinning the blame for atmospheric pollution on Ford, Chrysler, General Motors, and American Motors overlooks that government and people generally share the responsibility. While it's true that business probably has benefited financially more than any other group as a result of treating the environment as a free good, surely not all a firm's wealth or even most of it has resulted directly from this assumption. Moreover, consumers themselves have benefited to the tune of billions of dollars by not having had to pay higher costs for products. In fact, some people would argue that consumers are primarily to blame for pollution and therefore should pay the bill for its control.

This variation of this thesis sees customers as the culprits in environmental degradation, since they have used the goods or services. Because customers create the demand for the products whose production eventually impairs the environment, then customers ought to pay for the spillover. In this way, the argument goes, social costs are not unfairly passed on to those who have not incurred them, not unfairly given only to the manufacturer who, after all, is merely meeting a consumer demand and need. In a word, let those who want the products pay a price for them which includes all the costs of production without degrading the environment. But still, questions remain as to which customers ought to pay.

Consider this case, for example. The citizens of Massachusetts, wanting cleaner air, vote to pay higher prices for their electricity. It appears that they will pay the entire economic costs of the environmental improvement. But some of the costs of the cleaner air in Massachusetts may be borne by miners of high-sulfur coal in Pennsylvania who lose their jobs because this coal will no longer be used in Massachusetts. Is this fair? After all, they neither caused the pollution nor will they benefit from controlling it. At the same time, miners of low-sulfur coal in, say, some western state stand to reap a windfall benefit along with the railroad which hauls the coal.[3] This one example is enough to illustrate that the effects of assigning pollution-control costs to customers can, in fact, present an intricate network of economic interdependence that raises serious questions of social justice.

The fact is that those arguing either version of the polluter-should-pay-the-bill thesis, in attributing primary responsibility for pollution to big business or to customers, largely ignore the manifold deep-rooted causes of environmental degradation.

CAUSES OF POLLUTION. One important cause is the concentration of people who live in urban areas. In the sixty years between 1910 and 1970 the percentage of Americans living in urban areas of 2,500 or more rose from 45.7 percent to 70 percent, the numbers of people increasing from 42 million to 150 million. One need only spend a few hours in one American city to concede that this tremendous growth of urban population has resulted in staggering demands for goods and services. Thus, between 1960 and 1970 a 10 percent increase in the population (from 181 million to 205 million) resulted in a 14 percent rise in metropolitan population, with an accompanying 33 percent increase in vehicles, a 65 percent growth in industrial production, and a 100 percent jump in electric power generated.[4] This increase in consumer demands for goods and services has raised the levels of air, water, space, and noise pollution.

Another root cause of environmental problems is rising American affluence. Real income per person has about tripled in the last thirty years. As people have had more money to spend, they have bought and consumed more tangible goods, discarded them more quickly, and produced more solid waste. All of this has added to environmental degradation. With the number of urban dwellers doubling and with per capita real income quadrupling about every forty years, one wonders whether we can even meet the challenge of providing urban amenities.[5] Add to the causes our general tendency to value quantity over quality, our governmental failure to demand an accounting of the social costs of environmental pollution, and our ignorance of the interrelated nature of the global ecosystem, and a more sophisticated and accurate causal explanation of environmental decay emerges. What's more important, we're less likely to point the finger of blame at one economic sector of society and demand that it shoul-

---

3. *Davis and Blomstrom, p. 439.*

4. *Steiner, p. 235.*

5. *See Neil H. Jacoby, "The Environmental Crisis," The Center Magazine, November–December, 1970, pp. 37–48.*

der the costs of pollution control. In the last analysis the enemy in the war against environmental decadence turns out to be all of us. Any solution to the question of who should pay the costs of pollution control that ignores this runs grave risks of committing social injustices.

Those Who Would Benefit

A second popular reply to the payment problem is that those who will benefit from environmental improvement should pay the costs. In essence, this position boils down to the general public's paying the bill. Looked at another way, the public pays polluters to stop polluting.

The trouble with this argument is that it seems to make an indefensible distinction between beneficiary and nonbeneficiary. The fact is that every individual, rich or poor, and every institution, large or small, constitutes the group termed "beneficiaries," since all stand to profit from environmental improvement, albeit not to the same degree. As a result, the claim that those who will benefit should pay the costs is not satisfactory unless one means everyone; everyone stands to benefit since everyone is touched by pollution. If, on the other hand, this position means that individuals and groups should pay to the degree that they will benefit, then one must wonder how this could possibly be determined. But perhaps the most serious objection to this thesis is that it seems to leave out responsibility as a legitimate criterion of compensation.

In the last analysis, any equitable solution to the problem of who should pay the bill of environmental cleanup should take into account responsibility and benefit. The preceding analysis suggests that we all share the blame for pollution and collectively stand to benefit from environmental improvement. This doesn't mean that individual entities cannot be isolated as being chronic and flagrant polluters, or that certain individuals will not benefit more than others, as, for example, residents of the Los Angeles basin might benefit more from stringently enforced federal auto-emission-control standards than some Americans living in a remote corner of Wyoming. Rather, the point is that a fair and just program for assigning costs begins in a recognition that we all bear the responsibility for environmental problems and that we all stand to benefit from correcting them.

But even if we agree that it is only fair that everyone shares the cost of environmental improvement, we can still wonder about how the bill ought to be paid. To illustrate, suppose that you have willfully neglected to have a diseased and infirm tree removed from your property. One day it falls over, destroying your neighbor's $500 fence. Clearly the responsibility for the destruction is yours, and you should pay the costs of the repair. But what's the fairest way to pay for the damage? In one lump sum? In installments? Maybe you're handy and suggest that you will rebuild your neighbor's fence, thus saving yourself the cost of labor. The neighbor is skeptical; she wants a reputable firm to do the job. So, even though equity dictates that you should pay for the damage, the question of how you should pay for it, or be made to pay for it, raises separate and distinct questions of fairness. This same problem exists in the case of environmental improvement. Even if we assume that society, taken to mean individuals and institutions as a collective unit, ought to pay the cost of an improved environment, we can still ask how the bill should be paid. What would be the fairest distribution among those who will pay the initial costs of environmental improvement?

Cost Allocation

Most persons would probably agree that environmental pollution cannot be stopped without business and government working together. The interface between government and business in this area is especially evident in determining how the costs of environmental improvement should be met. Thus, the main proposals for revitalizing the environment conceptualize government as initiating programs that will prod business into responsible action. This does not mean that some businesses have not voluntarily undertaken programs that reflect an enlarged sense of environmental responsibility. But individual businesses by and large have not voluntarily instituted programs because doing so would put them at a competitive disadvantage; they would internalize a cost which a less responsible competitor would not. So at the outset we assume that government-business partnership is required to deal with environmental problems. The moral question that concerns us, then, is the fairest way of allocating costs for environmental revitalization.

Three proposals have gained most attention. Although similar in some respects, they carry different assumptions about the role of government and business in society, as well as about what's fair and just. The three approaches are the use of regulations, incentives, and pricing mechanisms or effluent charges. Each approach has distinct advantages and weaknesses; each raises some questions of social justice.

Regulations

The regulatory approach makes use of direct public regulation and control in determining how the pollution bill is paid. This approach can take the form of establishing environmental standards through legislation which is then applied by administrative agencies and courts. An effluent standard, for example, would prohibit industries from releasing more than a certain percentage of fly ash from a smokestack. Thus, an industry would be required to install a fly-ash control device in order to comply with the standard.

There is a clear advantage to such a regulatory approach: standards would be legally enforceable. Firms not meeting them could be fined or even shut down. Also, from the view of morality, such standards would be fair in that they would be applied to all industries in the same way. There are, however, distinct disadvantages in this approach, which carry moral overtones.

First, there's the question of compliance. If such universal standards are applied without regard for the idiosyncratic nature of each industry, serious inequities could arise about the comparative competitive positions of firms. For example, one firm might find that its costs for complying with water-pollution standards are insignificant because it has access to high quality water to begin with. In contrast, another might be forced to incur substantial costs because its water source is of low quality.

Then there's the problem of displacement costs resulting from industrial relocation or shutdown. For example, in the fall of 1977 Youngstown Sheet and Tube Company moved its corporate headquarters and some production lines to the Chicago area, thus eliminating 500 jobs and causing serious economic problems in nearby communities. One of the reasons for the transfer was the need to implement water-pollution controls, which stole vital capital. Consider also the marginal firms that would fail while attempting to meet the costs of such standards. When air-pollution regulations were applied to a sixty-year-old cement plant in San Juan Bautista, California, the plant had to close because it was too obsolete to meet the standard economically. The shutdown has seriously injured the economy of the town, which had been primarily supported by the cement plant.[6] Similarly, in one western city two paper mills announced within a period of two weeks that they were closing because they simply couldn't meet environmental standards. One mill had been in the town eighty years and had employed 750 workers with a payroll of $6 million annually. The other firm had employed over 300 workers. The closing of these plants, resulted in a loss of over 1,000 jobs with attendant human suffering.[7]

Moreover, while universal environmental standards do carry an aspect of fairness in that they apply to all in the same way, this very factor raises questions about their effectiveness. In attempting to legislate realistic and reliable standards for all, will government so dilute the standards that they become ineffectual? Consider the cases of areas whose physical environment is cleaner than government standards. In such cases, should an industry be allowed to pollute up to the maximum of the standard? The Supreme Court thinks not. In a case brought before it by the Sierra Club in 1973, the Court ruled that states with relatively clean air must prohibit industries from producing significant air pollution even though Environmental Protection Agency (EPA) standards are not violated. In this case a firm and ultimately the consumer are being forced to pay the costs of meeting an environmental standard that, in fact, is sterner than the one competitors must meet elsewhere.

Clearly, then, a regulatory approach to environmental improvement, while having advantages, also raises serious questions of both an operational and just nature. It also invites debate over precisely what constitutes an acceptable quality of environment to begin with, a subject which is bound to raise hotly debated value judgments.

Incentives

A widely supported approach to the problem of cost allocation for environmental improvement is government investment, subsidy, and general economic incentive. Pay polluters to stop polluting.

For example, the government might give a firm a tax incentive for the purchase and use of pollution equipment. Or it might offer matching grants to companies that install such devices. The advantage of such an approach is that it

6.   *Davis and Blomstrom, p. 440.*

7.   *Ibid., p. 454.*

minimizes governmental interference in business operations and encourages voluntary action rather than coercing compliance, as in the case of regulation. By allowing firms to move at their own pace, it avoids the evident unfairness to firms that cannot meet regulatory standards and must either relocate or fail. In addition, whereas regulated standards can encourage minimum legal compliance, an incentive approach provides an economic reason for going beyond minimal compliance. Firms have a financial inducement to do more than just meet EPA standards.

At the same time incentives are not without disadvantages that bear moral overtones. First, as an essentially voluntary device, an incentive program is likely to be slow. Environmental problems that cry out for a solution may continue to fester. Incentives may, in fact, postpone urgently needed action. In addition, any kind of governmental incentive program amounts to a subsidy for polluters. Polluting firms are being paid not to pollute. While this may address the economics of pollution more effectively than any other proposal, it nonetheless raises at least theoretical questions about the justice of compensating not the victims of pollution but some of the egregious polluters. This problem grows darker when one realizes that as indirect government expenditures, incentives rarely involve governmental scrutiny. Thus a firm already guilty of pollution can rather easily bury or manipulate the total costs of antipollution equipment within a nest of other business expenditures reported in tax returns. Not only is the government thereby defrauded but it is left without any realistic way of determining the cost-effectiveness payoff of its incentive program.[8] So, while incentive proposals have distinct advantages over strict regulation, they too raise practical and moral questions.

Pricing Mechanisms, or Effluent Charges

A third approach to the cost-allocation problem involves programs designed to charge firms for the amount of pollution they produce. This could take the form of pricing mechanisms, or effluent charges, which spell out the cost for a specific kind of pollution in a specific area at a specific time. The prices would vary from place to place and time to time, and be tied to the amount of damage caused. For example, during the summer months in the Los Angeles basin, a firm might pay much higher charges for fly ash emitted into the environment than it would during the winter months. Whatever the set of prices, they would apply equally to every producer of a given type of pollution at the same time and place. The more a firm pollutes, the more it pays.

One advantage in this approach is that it places the cost of pollution control on the polluters. Pricing mechanisms or effluent charges would penalize, not compensate, industrial polluters. For many persons this is inherently more fair than a program that compensates polluters.

Also, since costs are internalized, firms should be encouraged to do more than meet the minimal requirements established under a strict regulatory policy. Under this approach a firm, in theory, could be charged for any amount of

8. *See Steiner, p. 247.*

pollution and not just incur legal penalties whenever it exceeded an EPA standard. In effect, the pollution costs become production costs.

Another plus: pricing mechanisms and effluent charges, rather than treating firms collectively, consider them individually. They allow firms to have different levels of pollution depending on the peculiarities of their locations, the damage they likely cause, and the seasonal constraints they operate under.

On the other hand, these programs raise noteworthy questions such as the arbitrary nature of pollution costs. Who would determine effluent charges and a fair price? Any decisions are bound to reflect value judgments that are at least debatable. What's more, companies located in areas that require strict environmental control clearly would operate at a competitive disadvantage vis-à-vis companies in a less troubled environment. As in the case of regulations, then, a question of fair treatment arises. Similarly, some companies would relocate or fail, with serious consequences not only for the firm but for individuals and communities directly and indirectly affected. Finally, it seems reasonable at least to wonder whether such a proposal, like incentives, is actually a license to pollute. After all, if a company determines that it is cheaper for it to pollute than not to, it might feel free to do just that. Pricing mechanisms and effluent charges in theory could run counter to the objectives of a war on environmental degradation.

In sum, while each of these approaches to cost allocation has decided advantages, none is without serious weaknesses that raise moral concern. Since there appears no ideal approach, and since these or variations of these programs are the ones currently available for meeting this urgent problem, we're left expecting that a combination of regulation, incentive, and effluent charge is called for. Any such combination must consider not only the most expeditious and effectual approach to the problem, but also the fairest mix among those who will pay the bill. This likely will call for inputs from all sectors of society, a deliberate commitment on the part of all parties to work in concert, a sizable measure of good faith, and perhaps above all else a heightened and sophisticated sense of social justice. This is no mean challenge.

Ethical Theories

Unfortunately, the environmental problems we face are further compounded by intense passion, often characterized by accusations and recriminations. Usually persons who emote the most speak from what they consider to be a position of moral rectitude. They are right; others are wrong. Although this self-righteousness can take various forms, it seems most characteristic of environmentalists who insist that business is morally obliged to do everything it can to reduce pollution and restore the environment to something resembling its virgin state.

As sincere and understandable as these demands may be, they do little if anything to improve the threatening ecological conditions that confront us. They seem based on an inability or unwillingness to distinguish between the proposition that business must consider the negative side effects of its activities and the proposition that individual businesses must take whatever action is necessary to stop pollution and correct the environment. As we'll see in applying the moral theories, these propositions require separate and distinct moral justification, which may be available for the first but not for the second.

At the outset we should note that some scholars seriously question whether business even has a general responsibility to the environment. For example, some contend that environmental problems, like other social issues, are strictly "people problems" to be managed through duly constituted political apparatus. Others, like economists Milton Friedman and Henry Manne, argue that business's primary responsibility is to its stockholders, who expect the maximization of their investment. In effect, business's only responsibility is to maximize profits. Thus, when businesses start introducing extraneous considerations such as environmental improvement, they violate this fundamental stockholder trust. The first question we ask the ethical theories to address, then, is whether ethically there's any theoretical basis for claiming that business has an obligation to consider the environmental impact of its activities. If business does, must an individual firm always act in a way calculated to improve the physical environment?

Turning first to consequential theories, given the current climate, egoism could support the proposition that business must take cognizance of the side effects of its activities. We say this because sensitivity to ecological concerns would seem to advance the egoistic standard of producing more good for self than its opposite. After all, if business remains oblivious to environmental concerns, governmental regulations will eventually dictate how, when, and where production will take place, thus wresting from the private sector a significant measure of self-control. History supports this hypothesis. Consider one example, business's traditional aloofness to employee welfare in the first third of the present century. Business acknowledged little if any responsibility for conditions such as employee layoffs and general displacement. In an attempt to rectify this situation, Congress passed the Social Security Act of 1935, which compels the employer to pay the lion's share of the costs for employee protection.

Another point in egoism's support of business responsibility for the environment is that favorable social conditions generally mean a more favorable business operation. Conversely, unfavorable social conditions spell unfavorable business operations. Although the social costs of environmental improvement may, in the short run, mean a reduction of corporate profits, in the long haul they would mean a qualitatively improved society. And, in the words of Henry Ford II, "Improving the quality of society . . . is nothing more than another step in the evolutionary process of taking a more far-sighted view of return on investment."[9]

To the degree that business satisfies human needs it survives and prospers. As we've mentioned in earlier chapters, needs exist on the physical and social levels. When basic physical needs such as decent pay and job security are met, social needs such as fair and equal treatment in the marketplace and equal

9. Business Week, *November 1, 1969, p. 64.*

opportunity arise. Certainly figuring high on the list of social needs today must be the need for a healthful environment. In acknowledging environmental obligations, business takes the first step toward improving the physical quality of life and, from an egoistic view, a positive step toward self-enrichment in the long run.

In effect, then, egoism would call for a strict cost-effectiveness analysis of environmental sensitivity. Such an analysis would suggest that in the long run business serves its best interests by being aware of the negative side effects of its activities. Thus it bears a general obligation to introduce environmental concerns into its planning and decisions.

At the same time egoism would allow for an act, policy, or decision that was antienvironmental, providing it was in the best long-term interests of the firm. Thus, egoistically a firm could be morally justified, indeed obligated, to go right on emitting environmentally undesirable amounts of fly ash. The justification would be its own best long-term interests.

In a similar way, utilitarianism would generally apply a cost-effectiveness analysis to determine whether or not business should at least introduce environmental factors into production decisions. Technically, act utilitarianism would judge the morality of any business activity on the total good produced for the greatest number. But the rightness of any act with an environmental impact could not be ascertained without considering social costs. Therefore, act utilitarianism seemingly provides a theoretical basis for business sensitivity to the negative side effects of its activities. Indeed, any action with an environmental impact that's taken without regard to its social costs would be an incomplete application of act utilitarianism.

Similarly, rule utilitarianism could support environmental sensitivity from an evaluation of the rule which embodies it: "Business ought to take account of the negative side effects of its activities." It's hard to imagine today how going against this rule would produce more total good than abiding by it.

As with egoism, this doesn't mean that act and rule utilitarianism would endorse any action taken to improve the environment. For the act utilitarian, the rightness of each act depends on the total good it would produce. For the rule utilitarian the rightness of the act depends on the total good that implementing the rule under which the act falls would produce. Thus, whether or not a firm ought to limit the amount of particulates it emits into the atmosphere would depend on a calculation of the total effects of following a rule under which this act falls: "A firm ought to limit (to whatever amount) the particulates that it emits into the atmosphere." In practice, since rule utilitarianism essentially deals with the effects of a universal, while act utilitarianism deals with the effects of a particular, it is likely that rule utilitarianism would prohibit more individual pollution practices than act utilitarianism might.

Much the same may be said of Fletcher's situationalism. Again, given today's environmental conditions, it's difficult to imagine any firm's acting from agape, loving concern, without at least considering the total impact of its activities on the physical environment. As with act utilitarianism, a firm that overlooked this factor in reckoning the agape calculus of its behavior would not be conforming with the situationalist principle of calculating the greatest amount of neighbor welfare. Again, however, firms are not thereby obliged to act always in the best interests of ecological integrity or improvement. For ultimately the environmental impact of a specific act is merely one consideration to be introduced when evaluating it within a context of loving concern.

It seems safe to speculate, then, that these consequential theories are all capable of providing a theoretical basis for the proposition that ethically a firm must consider the unfavorable side effects of its behavior on the physical environment. At the same time, they provide considerable latitude in determining the proper action to take in a specific instance.

Nonconsequential theories also seem to provide the theoretical scaffolding for environmental sensitivity. Specifically, we can look at the Golden Rule as asking business people with direct influence over environment-related activities to place themselves in the position of those with less instrumental control over such actions. In that role, would they want persons with significant influence to consider the negative environmental impact of their actions? The answer would appear to be affirmative. Again, however, when it comes to making a choice between two actions, one of which is favorable to the physical environment and the other not, the Golden Rule seems to provide no clearer direction than consequential theories do. In fact, it is fraught with considerably more difficulties, because of the many private interests involved. Whereas egoism can turn to self-interest as the final standard and utilitarianism to the total good, the Golden Rule seems to enjoin a consideration of all private interests: a most formidable task. Since environmental matters by their nature pose intrinsic questions of the social good, the Golden Rule seems especially inadequate for managing them because technically it does not base decisions of rightness and wrongness, good and bad, on such considerations.

Kant's categorical imperative would decisively call for general business sensitivity to environmental concerns, for to act otherwise would appear to be inconsistent with the principal thrust of nature, which is self-preservation and survival. As for specific acts and decision, although Kant's theory doesn't provide crystal-clear moral direction, it nevertheless could not support ecological activities hostile to life and health. Such activities would appear to violate Kant's principle that humans must never be used as means to social ends. We must quickly add, however, that social institutions such as business are at the same time vital to the economic nature of human beings. As a result, serious problems can arise about the morality of imposing and implementing environmental standards which undermine these institutions or inhibit them from functioning in a way that advances the economic nature of human beings. In a word, such standards in theory could have the effect of undermining the nature of humans as much as a smokestack belching fly ash into the atmosphere obviously does.

What we seem to have with Kant, then, is a clear moral injunction for business to consider the negative side effects of its activities. As for specific environmental improvements, we must examine the logical possibility of universalizing the rule which a specific action or maxim invokes, giving special attention to the principle that humans must never be used as means to ends.

Like the preceding theories Ross's prima facie duties would obligate business to consider the environmental effects of its activities. This seems clear from a consideration of Ross's overriding noninjury principle. But again this doesn't mean that a firm wouldn't be morally justified at times in acting in a way that damages the environment. For in the last analysis, the firm's actual duty is determined by a reckoning of all the prima facie duties involved.

Rawls's natural duty of noninjury could be used to justify the claim that business must be conscious of the environmental effects of its actions. This evaluation is strengthened when we introduce the principle of paternalism, which obliges those with the power over others to introduce the interests of those who can't speak for themselves or who have limited control over the actions that affect them. Furthermore, if we asked persons in the original position to indicate whether or not they'd prefer people in a position to influence the quality of the physical environment to be cognizant of the environmental impact of their activities, they'd likely say yes.

In applying Rawls's maximin principle to a concrete business decision of whether to implement a specific activity calculated to improve the quality of the environment, the ultimate decision seems to rely on an application of Rawls's difference principle. Is the action calculated to advantage all or at least the most disadvantaged in society? Many factors must be taken into account here, including the nature of the pollution, the location of it, the damage it's likely to cause. It is conceivable, however, that at times the right thing to do would be to pollute, if not polluting would in fact worsen the plight of those already least advantaged, as it might in some communities that are surviving marginally. These firms still would have an obligation to work on ways to reduce the pollution, for that would benefit all.

Like the preceding, the proportionality theory would decisively support the proposition that ethically business must be aware of the negative side effects of its activities.[10] It must calculate the social costs of its operations. To do otherwise is to act irresponsibly and immorally.

At the same time, however, the proportionality theory seems to leave open the question of specific environment-related actions. As always, the nature of the evil, whether major or minor, must be taken into consideration. In cases where a firm is willing a major evil as a means or end, it's clearly acting immorally. But where it's allowing or risking a major evil, or willing, allowing, or risking a minor evil, a proportional reason may justify its activities.

It's important to point out here that environmental standards functioning as laws, while undoubtedly influencing the moral decision under all these theories, do not dictate what is the right thing to do or, in fact, whether business has a general environmental responsibility. The mere fact that no law forbids an industry from blighting the landscape with ugly signs and billboards does not at all relieve business of its obligation under these theories to consider the impact of such behavior. By the same token just because an environmental standard

10. Garrett, p. 187.

proscribes a firm's emitting more than a certain percentage of particulates into the atmosphere, thereby the firm is not acting morally if it simply honors this standard and does not try to reduce atmospheric pollution below this standard.

It appears that all the theories agree that business must recognize the negative side effects of its activities. At the same time they provide flexibility in determining the morality of a specific environment-related activity. Obviously, a great deal more in the way of understanding the implications of these moral theories needs be done before they can serve as comprehensive moral directives for resolving environmental problems. For this reason, we've been intentionally general in our application of them, although it's hoped not painfully so. Finally, as always, our applications bear the qualification that they are open to other interpretations, both corrective and elaborative. These are encouraged.

CASE PRESENTATION
When Compliance Isn't Enough

Rick Epstein couldn't understand the problem. After all, his metal working firm was complying with all existing pollution-control laws. And yet somehow he'd incurred the wrath of a local environmental protection group that wanted him to stop polluting a river that passed through the center of town.

Epstein had informed the group that the pollution they referred to amounted to such an insignificant amount that any reasonable person, even a federal agency, would consider it a tolerable social cost for the benefits of doing business. But the committee didn't see it that way.

"Your obligations," one member told him, "extend beyond the letter of the law."

Another member indicated that federal regulations simply served as guidelines. The goal of the environmental movement was to stop all pollution, minor as well as major. As one member put it, "You should remember that all major pollution probably began as what you call an insignificant insult to the environment." In the same vein, another member pointed out that while Epstein's effluent discharge didn't amount to much in isolation, taken together with all other so-called tolerable amounts, it was contributing to a serious water-pollution problem.

In reply, Epstein asked the group if they realized how much pollution-control equipment would cost. He would have to pay about $70,000 for installation and over $20,000 annually for operating expenses. "Such an expense," he pleaded, "won't make a dime's worth of difference in my product." Then he added, "But I can tell you one thing: I'm going to have to charge more than a dime more if I do what you're asking."

The committee deplored this economic reality but said that if that was the only way to erase pollution, then so be it.

"Easy for you to say," Epstein told them bitterly, "but I sell my product nationally. Do you have any idea of the competitive disadvantage you're imposing on me? Why, it wouldn't surprise me that, in addition to freezing salaries, your proposal would cause a production tailspin that would force me to lay off workers." Then Epstein asked them sharply: "Are you sure people would rather have cleaner water than a steady job?"

The committee remained adamant in its demands. It told Epstein that it would return in ten days to find out what Epstein intended to do to curb pollution of the river. Should he do nothing, they were prepared to take him to court.

1. *What should Epstein do?*

2. *What moral directions do the ethical theories provide?*

3. *Do you think that the environmental committee is right in making this demand of Epstein?*

4. *If Epstein complies with the committee's demands, what would be the fairest way to allocate control costs?*

CASE PRESENTATION
Sharpening the Competitive Edge

Elliott Dornan, president of Morhauser Minerals, thought that his company's environmental problems were well behind them—and with reason. Just six months earlier Morhauser had been singled out by government agencies and environmental groups alike as having taken most responsible measures to control air pollution. But now the plight of Morhauser's chief competitor, Eastern Mountain Minerals, had again ensnared Morhauser in environmental concerns.

The reason that Morhauser's policies and actions had gained such positive response was that they squarely met recently enacted state regulations for air-pollution control. These regulations were considerably more stringent than those prescribed by the Environmental Protection Agency. Indeed, a number of firms had insisted that they were too stringent, so severe in fact that they threatened to drive some firms right out of business. One of these firms was Eastern Mountain.

Being an older firm, Eastern Mountain operated with equipment that, according to the state's regulations, was environmentally obsolete. Eastern faced monumental economic problems in adapting its machinery to the new standards. No one denied this, not even the state's environmental control board. On the contrary, the control board readily admitted that Eastern probably couldn't afford the price of modernizing its equipment. And it conceded the real possibility that Eastern might have to shut down, thus displacing over 500 workers and seriously injuring the economies of several neighboring communities. The economic control board didn't want to be unfair. So, it invited the management of Eastern to submit an alternative that would have the effect of complying with regulations while preserving the integrity of the firm.

Eastern Mountain replied by requesting that the board grant it a five-year extension on the deadline for complying with the new standards. In the interim it hoped that it would be able to devise economical technology for dealing with its pollution problem. Board members, recognizing the adverse impact of the plant's failure, were inclined to grant the request, providing that no other firm that already had met the standards strenuously objected. After all, firms like Morhauser asked for and received no extensions. In fact, the board had led them to believe that the state would make no exceptions, that if a firm couldn't meet the standards by the deadline, they would have to shut down. It was on this basis that Elliott Dornan had pushed ahead with an expensive pollution-control effort that, while not crippling the firm, nonetheless had cut deeply enough into profits that Morhauser had been forced to reject labor's salary and fringe demands for the current year and even had to increase prices modestly.

As Dornan read the board's invitation to appear at a meeting scheduled to review Eastern Mountain's request, he felt righteously outraged that the board even should be entertaining an extension bid, which would preserve Eastern's competitive edge over Morhauser for at least five more years. In fact, Dornan felt that the board was passing the buck, putting him in the position of bad guy. Dornan realized that all he had to do was object on grounds of fairness and perhaps threaten to obtain injunctive relief, and Eastern would be denied its request.

But Dornan's decision wasn't easy. While clearly being faced with a golden opportunity to dislodge his chief competition, Dornan didn't like to see any business, even a competitor, succumb to essentially non-business-related factors. In fact, he had joined with Eastern two years before in vigorously resisting the implementation of environmental standards. Dornan hated to think about the numbers of people who would be thrown out of work and the economic pinch communities would suffer if Eastern were forced to shut down. Then there was the matter of potential antitrust action. If enough marginal firms like Eastern failed, Morhauser would dominate the minerals interest in the area. A pronounced industrial interest like that might be viewed as monopolistic. Finally, Dornan was philosophically adverse to any government action that had the effect of driving a wedge between common business interests. He instinctively felt that once an environmental agency succeeded in pitting one business against another, then business would begin to relinquish autonomy and self-control.

1. *What should Dornan do?*

2. *What moral directions do the ethical theories provide?*

3. *Is the board being morally remiss in entertaining Eastern's request?*

4. *If you were a board member, what action would you recommend?*

CASE PRESENTATION
Sharing the Blame

SCENE:	The office of the director of a midwestern advertising agency
CHARACTERS:	Donna Ellis, assistant director of advertising Bryan Lavelle, director
SITUATION:	Donna Ellis is vehemently protesting the agency's complicity in an ad campaign commissioned by Mid-Valley Gas and Electric, a utility firm with pronounced antienvironment tendencies. Mid-Valley has consistently propagandized for increased electrical power use. Its latest campaign solicits public support to build more power plants to provide adequate service. Some persons doubt whether such plants are needed. Vigorously promoting less power use might accomplish what additional plants would be intended to do. Ellis is particularly incensed about a leaflet her agency has worked up to accompany the bills consumers will receive in the months ahead. The content of the leaflet is captured in the bold-print headline on the first page. It reads: "Balance Ecology With Power."
Ellis:	The point is that ecology is not a thing to be balanced against anything else.
Lavelle:	What do you mean?
Ellis:	I mean this ad is tremendously misleading. It misses the whole concept of ecology, its essential meaning. *Ecology* refers to a science of the interrelatedness of everything. To speak of balancing it with anything else is just plain dumb. In fact, it's downright distorting. It gives the impression that somehow we must be just as concerned with energy as we are with the ecology.
Lavelle:	But isn't that true?
Ellis:	It's not so much a question of truth as one of emphasis and impact within an advertising gestalt.
Lavelle:	Gestalt?
Ellis:	That's right. Look, we both know that for years now Mid-Valley has been trying to get people to use more power. Now with the energy crunch on, they're obviously concerned with maintaining their mind-boggling profits while at the same time not appearing to be callously indifferent to environmental concerns. The result is this ad. Taken within the total framework

of where Mid-Valley's coming from, it amounts to a not-so-subtle pitch calculated to marshal public support for building additional power plants, which they've already begun to lobby for in Washington and in the state capitol.

Lavelle: But you can't expect them not to. I mean, calling for power conservation and a moratorium on plant construction just isn't in their best business interests.

Ellis: Obviously. But that doesn't mean we should assist them in furthering what may be of highly questionable social value.

Lavelle: But Donna, that's totally unrealistic. You're asking us to sit in judgment of the moral worth of our clients' interests.

Ellis: I'm suggesting that on matters as serious as a firm's environmental responsibilities, we must act in a socially responsible way.

Lavelle: You realize, of course, that we already devote 20 percent of our advertising time to what we consider sound social causes? Nobody can accuse this agency of being socially indifferent.

Ellis: But that's a cop-out. Remember, only a small fraction of that time is earmarked for environmental matters. What's worse, it seems to me we're undoing what little good we may be achieving when we run ads like this. It *talks* about the research necessary to deal with environmental pollution, but we both know that Mid-Valley has done no research at all.

Lavelle: But it's not our job to sit in judgment of our clients' interests. That's the job of government.

Ellis: But certainly we should sit in judgment of our own activities, shouldn't we?

Lavelle: Okay, let's do that, let's really do it. Do you think we'd be doing the right thing if we jeopardized Mid-Valley's three-million-dollar annual account with us by imposing our own environmental philosophy on their ads or telling them to peddle their propaganda elsewhere? What about our stockholders? Our own employees? Our other accounts? We've got obligations to them as well, you know.

Ellis: Sure we do, but that shouldn't blind us to our social obligations. Simply because we function in this society as information communicators, we're not relieved of the obligation to examine the likely impact of that information, the impressions it gives, the opinions it helps form, the attitudes it molds. That we ourselves don't operate belching smokestacks or discharge waste into rivers doesn't mean we have no business responsibilities to the environment. The fact is that on en-

> vironmental questions our role is a pivotal one. We control what the most obvious vested interests can say to generate public opinion. If Mid-Valley persists in behaving in an environmentally irresponsible way, we share the blame.

Lavelle: Donna, I hear what you're saying and appreciate your concerns, but this is a decision I'm going to have to mull over. I may even have to go to the board.

Ellis: I think you should.

1. *Is Donna Ellis right in speaking out?*

2. *What should Lavelle do? If he takes the matter to the board, what do you think the board should do?*

3. *What moral directions do the ethical theories provide?*

4. *With respect to the environment, do you think advertising agencies have any general responsibilities?*

5. *If the board chooses to take no action, what should Donna Ellis do?*

Pollution: Can the People Be Innocent While Their Systems Are Guilty?

David R. Frew

In the first chapter of this book, we mentioned that individuals within complex organizational structures frequently lose sight of or are oblivious to any personal responsibility they may bear for the behavior of their organizations' activities. For example, it's not uncommon for individuals to recognize that their organizations are environmental polluters; they may even deplore it while remaining content to play their organizational roles and thereby contributing to the problem. Seeing individuals behave in what he terms this "ecologically schizophrenic manner," Professor of Behavioral Sciences David R. Frew of Gannon College wonders how an organization can behave in a way that is so different from the desires and ends of its aggregate membership. In the following article, Frew answers his question through the concept of synergy, that is, that property by which a system of component parts takes on an identity and exhibits behavior different from the aggregate of the parts of the system. In effect, Professor Frew suggests that the behavior of any human organization may differ essentially from the behavior of its members. If he is right, then no matter how ecologically sensitive and morally aware any of its members are, the organizational system may continue to pollute. What's more, organizational members likely will persist in neatly divorcing themselves from the behavior of their organizations, thus leaving the destructive behavior unchallenged and ultimately unchanged. Professor Frew's prescription is a systemic morality, characterized by an understanding and acceptance of responsibility for the outcome of one's participation in any social organization.

Two very diverse events recently led to the formulation of a thesis which is presented in this paper; that thesis involves the synergistic property of organizational behavior. First, an essay by Charles Hampden-Turner entitled, "Synergy as the Optimization of Differentiation and Integration by the Human Personality (1)," very effectively dealt with the idea of synergy as an important aspect of both the physical and social systems of life. Secondly, research activity as an organization theorist occasioned a visit to a rather large corporation which is a major polluter of both air and water in

David R. Frew, "Pollution: Can the People Be Innocent While Their Systems Are Guilty?" Academy of Management Review, March 1973. Reprinted by permission.

its community.[1] A relationship, which became apparent almost immediately, served to explain the pollution in terms of the synergy. The purpose of this paper, then, is to evolve and discuss the basic relationship between these two concepts—organizational behavior and environmental pollution.

Synergy

In its purest definition, synergism[2] is energy which exists in unexplainable opposition to entropy,[3] the movement of all organisms toward death. More specifically, it is that property by which an arrangement or system of component parts takes on an identity which is essentially different from the aggregate of the parts of the system.[4] An example of this process is the human body which is a combination of water and a number of rather complex carbon molecules. If a strange being from another planet were studying the earth's water, for example, he might view a human being as simply an unusual arrangement of H_2O. But clearly, the particular arrangement, that is to say the person himself, takes on an identity which transcends his "parts list." Another and perhaps more visible example is a transistor radio. In its unassembled form the instrument consists of transistors, capacitors, resistors, diodes, wire, and a number of other parts. But the particular combination of those parts which is called a radio suddenly exhibits behavior which is unlike the behavior which might be expected of a typical electrical part. It plays music!

The Components of Human Behavior

Returning to the practical matter at hand, the task is to understand the actions of particular business firms. Essential to that problem, however, is an introduction to the notion of human behavior.

Most living organisms exhibit behavior of one sort or another, and many sciences have organized themselves around the study of this behavior. For example, zoologists study animal behavior, and botanists study the behavior of plants. The study of human behavior, however, is particularly fascinating and challenging to science because unlike most of his cohabitor organisms in the known

world, man's behavior takes place on a number of nesting levels.

First there is individual behavior, the component which mankind has in common with other organisms and which has concerned psychologists for many years. Each of us is a behavior generating device which responds to all kinds of stimuli by behaving in various ways. At a second level there is group behavior. People have persistently demonstrated a tendency to congregate into groups for the pursuit of goals which would appear to be unattainable on the basis of individual efforts alone (5, p. 5). There is some controversy surrounding the notion that this aspect of human behavior is particular only to humans. Some say that other primates also exhibit group behavior (3, p. 250), but for the moment, that shall remain an open question, since it is the third and final component, organizational behavior, which is most critical to the present discussion.

Organizations

There is very little controversy surrounding the observation that man appears to be the only species that ties together individuals and groups into the logically structured multi-goal seeking systems which have come to be called organizations. It is a fact that these systems have become, at least for western man, the core of life. Almost all of us work, play, worship, and recreate under the auspices of one or more formal organizations. From the attention which has been focused upon this 20th century phenomenon a new behavioral science has emerged calling itself Organization Theory[5] and addressing itself to the profound problems of behavior; both inter-and-intra-organizational.

One Organization in Perspective

As a caseworking theorist, the author recently was exposed to a number of persons who were working at various levels in the hierarchy of a company which is popularly considered to be a substantial polluter. From interviews with these persons, an extremely simple but at the same time profound realization emerged. Although each interviewee recognized his organization's role as a polluter, none either was acting in a way which would be interpreted (at least in a direct sense) as causing the pollution, nor was any individual in a position to end or to significantly change the process.

In a lengthy discussion with the president of the corporation, it became apparent that the man who occupied the role of president was just as concerned about the pollution as the people who were standing outside of the front gate with vindictive signs. He indicated his love for "nature" and discussed at some length his particular hobbies, which included forestry, bird watching and a number of other kinds of activities which appeared to be, at least at the surface level, incongruous with the behavior of his organization. Further interview sessions with executives, middle managers, and finally rank and file workers of the same organization confirmed this finding. Members of the organization consistently were in opposition to the pollution which their company was generating, but at the same time they were content to continue their day to day existence as contributors to the very problem which they opposed. One respondent commented that it was only a matter of time until the plant in question utterly despoiled its entire surrounding area and that it was a "real crime" since the area was at one time a beautiful natural resource. When questioned further about his personal response to the situation, he stated that he was powerless to stop the process but that he had purchased a second home (out of the immediate surrounding area) and was planning to move as the effects of the plant became ecologically overwhelming.

The Dilemma of Organizational Synergy

Seeing these relatively intelligent and thoughtful persons acting in such an ecologically schizophrenic manner was a particularly frightening revelation. How can an organization behave in a way that is so different from the desires and the ends of its aggregate membership?

Perhaps the answer to this dilemma revolves about the concept of synergy. Just as the behavior of a transistor radio is essentially different from the behavior of any individual component, the behavior of a human organization may be essentially different from the behavior of its component parts, the members of the organization.

It may be concluded, then, that organizational synergy is a product of systemic or structured relationships which are implied by the concept of organization itself. Further, this synergism, by the nature of synergistic behavior, would appear not to be closely related to the kinds of behavior which are expected of the components of the organizations—individuals and/or groups. The implied danger is that while we seem to expect that interorganizational behavior will essentially appear as, and affect society as, a multiplication or aggregate of individual behavior, the property of organizational synergy would suggest that this is not true. Using individual or group behavior, the actions of organizations have and will continue to be unpredictable.

The Implications

Given a number of random behavior generating devices, in the form of organizations within society, one might well expect to encounter some social problems in terms of behavioral manifestations. This is particularly true considering the extent to which our resources are controlled by contemporary organizations.

Thus, it might be expected, due to the random nature of inter-organizational behavior (random in the sense of human values), that some of the resulting activities of organizations would be of negative social value. Pollution is a prime example of this kind of behavior. While organizations may consist of altruistic, nature loving ecologists, the systems themselves continue to pollute.

A Prescription

We live in an organized society and in an organized world. But as yet we have not begun to evaluate the problem of organizational behavior which is in opposition to human values from an ecological viewpoint. If we are to create a new world, one which will provide an improved life style for all, it would seem that we must cease our naive practice of assuming that our organizations, by definition, must help us. To the contrary, the empirical evidence indicates the ever-present danger of organizations behaving in ways which violate basic social justice. The synergistic property of organizational behavior would appear to make this fact not just logical, but perfectly predictable.

To meet and solve this challenge we must seek increasing knowledge of organized activity and the behavior which follows. We must try to explain, by way of behavioral sciences, the previously unexpected behavior of these organizations which we have generated. We can no longer plead innocent, as individuals, to the responsibility for the behavior of our social systems. Rather, a new consciousness is called for: an understanding and acceptance of responsibility for the outcome of our participation in social organizations. It is only with this kind of a systemic morality that we will be able to work for ecological balance by utilizing both internal and external organizational pressures.

Notes

1. For obvious reasons the name of the particular firm shall remain anonymous; however, the role of that firm as polluter is almost without question. It has been and continues to be a source of controversy in its community news media and among residents. Even the people who worked for the firm recognized their own pollution problem.
2. For another definition of the term see Katz and Kahn, p. 33 (ref. 2).
3. Katz and Kahn also deal with the entropy concept. See pp. 19, 21, 23, 28 (ref. 2).
4. Much of the credit for arriving at this definition must be given to Charles Hampden-Turner's essay (ref. 1).
5. A comprehensive introduction to the field is contained in the first chapter of *Organizational Psychology* by Edgar Schein (ref. 4).

References

1. Hampden-Turner, Charles. "Synergy as the Optimization of Differentiation and Integration by the Human Personality," in J. W. Lorsch and Paul R. Lawrence (Eds.), *Studies in Organizational Design* (Homewood, Ill.: Irwin, 1970), pp. 187–196.
2. Katz, D., and R. L. Kahn. *The Social Psychology of Organizations* (New York: Wiley, 1966).
3. Pfeiffer, John. *The Emergence of Man* (New York: Harper & Row, 1969).
4. Schein, Edgar. *Organizational Psychology* (Englewood Cliffs, N.J.: Prentice-Hall, 1964).
5. Shepherd, Clovis. *Small Groups* (San Francisco: Chandler, 1964).

Ecological Responsibility and Economic Justice

Norman J. Faramelli

Cleaning up the environment is and will continue to be costly. In all likelihood, no one will end up paying the entire cost; all will end up paying some of it. Obviously, some persons are better off financially and can pay their share easier than others. Some persons will be hardpressed to pay their share of the bill, perhaps to pay anything at all. What's more, some persons will benefit more than others. Indeed, there are those who believe that most of the solutions proposed for environmental quality will have a negative impact on those least able to pay: the poor and lower-income groups. Norman J. Faramelli, associate director of the Boston Industrial Mission and author of the following article, is one of them. He argues that economic and distributive justice must become an essential part of all ecological discussions. Specifically, he contends that the ecological movement cannot be divorced from the needs of the poor, that the allocation of the costs of pollution control must be thoroughly investigated for economic fairness, and that a new distribution of income and wealth must be part of all ecological debates.

Written in 1970, this article carries references to a past that events have already made remote (for example, Earth

This article by Norman Faramelli, associate director of the Boston Industrial Mission, is reprinted with the permission of the author and the Andover Newton Quarterly *from vol. 11. pp. 81–93 (November, 1970).*

Day, April 22, 1970). But it is nonetheless timely because it rightly places environmental matters in the broader context of human need.

According to ecologists, we are threatened with extinction within 50 years if current pollution trends are allowed to continue. Despite some overstatements by a few "prophets of doom," an increasing number of reasonable people recognize that the ecological problem has reached a crisis stage. All during 1970, leading magazines, newspapers, radio, and TV announced that we are entering an "age of ecology."[1] Although its popularity reached a zenith on Earth Day (22 April, 1970), ecology is still very much before the public. But despite the widespread rhetoric, the environmental problems are becoming more critical, as summer smog along the East coast has amply illustrated.

In theory, everyone wants a clean environment. But the real questions are: "How serious is the ecology problem in light of our other pressing needs?" and "Who is going to pay for pollution control?" With regard to the latter, we must heed the cry of both the ecologist and the economist: "There are no free lunches"; someone will pay for a clean environment. It is the belief of this writer that *ecology is a profoundly serious matter, yet most of the solutions suggested for environmental quality will have, directly or indirectly, adverse effects on the poor and lower income groups.* Hence, economic or distributive justice must become an active component in all ecology debates.

The Lord has entrusted man with the created order; he is to be a responsible steward of God's creation. Although the development of an environmental ethic is essential and long overdue, it should not overlook nor underplay the special role that man (particularly the poor and the oppressed) plays in the Judeo-Christian tradition.[2] Now that an environmental ethic is being shaped, it is imperative that it be in harmony with concerns for economic justice.

As a prolegomenon to the central concerns of ecology and justice, we should first establish the seriousness of the so-called ecological crisis. For the problems of relating justice and ecology are real only if the environmental issues are truly significant. If environmental damage is not as bad as publicized, then we are suffering from grand delusions.

A Worsening Problem

One can recite a litany of woes concerning land, air, water, and noise pollution:

Timber forests in the West are fast disappearing because we refuse to reuse paper. One of the wonders of creation, the Redwoods in California, is reducing in number. On the East Coast, the valuable salt marshes are being dredged and filled in by real estate and land developers, a move which is destroying some of our most productive land and damaging chains of marine life. In Appalachia, strip mining has ravaged several states, and after the coal has been removed and the landscape destroyed, some states pass laws curbing strip mining. Add to these the cluttering of the countryside with billboards and junk. A U.N. report released in 1969 noted that each year in the U.S. we discard 26 billion bottles, 7 million automobiles, and 48 billion cans.[3] It is no surprise that rubbish disposal is a mounting problem.

That same report noted that the U.S. emits 148 million tons of pollutants into the air each year, mostly from automobiles and power generators. The air pollution that used to be limited to central cities has now spread well beyond the suburbs. For example, the trees in the Sierra Nevada mountains, 100 miles from Los Angeles, are dying from air pollutants. The same holds true for other urban areas. Emphysema and other respiratory disorders are on the increase. Also, some studies have shown the links between air pollution and cancer growth.

Water pollution worsens each day. Lake Erie is undergoing a nonreversible biological decay, and many experts believe it might soon be a sewer. The Cuyahoga River in Cleveland, rich in contaminants, actually caught on fire, but it was not the first! In certain areas in the mid-West the "nitrogen run-offs" from fertilizers are the principal causes of water pollution. The phosphates from detergents are creating magnificent algae blooms in our waterways which upset the ecological balance, and pesticides are poisoning our oceans. In addition, oil spills, such as the ones by Union Oil off Santa Barbara, Chevron off the Gulf, and oil tankers regularly, are polluting our oceans and beaches.

To this litany we can add the problems of noise pollution. Studies have shown that it influences arterial and neurological disorders. The noise near jet ports is already unbearable, yet the jets get bigger, faster, and noisier.

If the items listed above represented the worst levels of pollution to which man will be subjected, we could all breathe a sigh of relief. But conditions are getting worse, because current trends are being exacerbated. The effects of newly installed pollution control devices are more than offset by expanding the pollution base via increased production. For instance, Detroit has endowed us with 9 million new internal combustion engines per year and now anticipates that within 10 years it will be manufacturing 12–13 million automobiles per year.[4] Power consumption is slated to double every ten years, which may lead to an enormous production of pollutants. Our President and others marvel at the U.S. Gross National Product, which will reach 1 trillion dollars in 1970 and will increase to 1.5 trillion within 10 years. If a substantial amount of this growth is in the material sector, pollution will significantly increase. And, of course, all of these problems are made worse by rapid population increases. By the year 2000, the American population will increase from 200 to 300 million. Thus, one can see that the problems are serious, and necessitate a new ethic for the environment and a new look at our consumption of material resources.

The Two Revolutions

In the midst of the burgeoning interest for ecology, a few voices have warned that ecology is becoming a new cop-out, a way to refocus the enthusiasm of the young (especially college students) away from the war, urban problems, and poverty. One can rationalize that the young are frustrated over Vietnam, almost completely alienated from poverty and the ghettos, so ecology buffs are now in vogue. In many ways, ecology is a logical successor to the middle-class concerns of conservation. But that explanation is too simplistic and misses entirely the seriousness of the ecological crisis.

The ecology rage must be understood in light of the two cultural, social, and political revolutions occurring in our society today. They can be termed the "pre-affluent" and "post-affluent" revolutions. The first is dominated by the poor and the black communities. Their primary focus is on social and economic justice as well as freedom and self-determination. The quest of the powerless and the alienated is primarily for human dignity and the restructuring of power relationships. Some in this revolution, however, want to move beyond "getting a fair piece of the pie" to new life styles where "soul" or spontaneity is an essential ingredient. But most want a redistribution of power—political, economic, and social. For the alienated youth in the "post-affluent" revolution, however, the emphasis is not on power, but on new life-styles. There is a flat rejection of the values of over-consumption, technical efficiency, and economic growth that has dominated American society.[5] The ecology movement is closely linked with the "post-affluent" revolution. Only those who have been reared in affluent suburbs can rebel against over-consumption and the banality of materialism. It is no surprise that ecologists like Barry Commoner, Lamont Cole, Paul Ehrlich, and Eugene Odum receive their biggest ovations in jammed college auditoriums. The differences between the two movements were vividly expressed by a welfare rights organizer to a group of young ecology radicals. He said: "We will have some problems understanding one another for our welfare mothers want what you are rejecting."[6]

Those who have been involved with urban and poverty problems have often distrusted the "ecology fad." On the other hand, most ecology enthusiasts, and especially the old-line conservationists who are becoming attuned to ecology, almost completely ignore the problems of the ghettos and the poor. Ecology, for them, has more to do with saving a certain marine species than eradicating rats from infested ghetto apartments! To the ghetto resident, air pollution is clearly not at the top of his priority list. As one black community organizer in Chicago said recently: "The one thing I don't look forward to is living in a pollution-free, unjust and repressive society."

Distrust of the Ecology Movement: Is It Really a "Cop-Out"?

Distrust for the ecology movement is increasing on all sides. *Time* magazine (3 August, 1970) reports a burgeoning anti-ecology movement. Some critics believe that the environment cannot be as bad as many scientists say. Others sense the profound changes in the industrial system and life styles that the quest for environmental quality will demand; hence, they are "bugging out" by ignoring the issue. Others believe that the ecology movement has been characterized by too much radical pessimism and alarmism.

The anti-ecology sentiment among the poor, especially the blacks, is still prevalent. For example, one Black Panther leader in Roxbury said: "It is a sick society that can beat and murder black people on the streets, butcher thousands of children in Vietnam, spend billions in arms to destroy mankind, and then come to the conclusion that air pollution is America's number one problem."[7]

Why do the poor distrust the ecology movement? First, a clean environment is not on their priority list, at least not in terms of air and water pollution. The poor are part of a different revolution; their focus is on justice. Also, the ecology groups have almost totally ignored the needs of the poor. Most of the images of environmental quality refer to improved life styles for suburban dwellers—cleaner air, more trees, better hiking, boating, and swimming, etc. There is almost no emphasis on urban ecology.

Another reason the poor distrust ecology is related to the priorities of the nation stated in President Nixon's State of the Union Message. In a speech replete with many references to the environment, he said, "Restoring nature to its natural state is a cause beyond party and beyond factions. It has become a common cause of all the people of this country." The President also noted that Americans have to make "some very hard decisions" on priorities, which meant "rejecting pending programs which would benefit some of the people when their net effect would result in price increases for all the people."[8] In other words, urban spending, which benefits the white and black poor, is inflationary!

The lack of any references in the address to black America, the sparse references to poverty and urban blight, and the copious references to "law and order" illustrated the current concerns facing American society. It is not too surprising that many black citizens felt alienated by the President's address, saw in it the omens of repression, and from it, deduced that interest in ecology is a "cop-out." To the poor it was more than an isolated speech; it articulated a growing national mood. Hence, one can understand their charges that "ecology is a club over our heads; it's a cop-out; it's a middle-class issue."

But will funds actually be diverted from poverty to ecology? As of now, the funds spent on either ecology or poverty are pitifully small. This year the federal government approved 800 million dollars for water pollution programs, although far more is needed. Expenditures on poverty are also grossly inadequate. To choose ecology instead of poverty, or vice versa, is to make a bad choice. We should not be asked to select between schools and homes for urban dwellers, on the one hand, and a clean environment on the other, while the ABM is expanded, the supersonic transport is developed, and Vietnam continues almost untouched by sanity. Despite the deceptive Defense Department cuts, new weapons systems are still top priority items on the national agenda and devour a substantial part of the federal budget. Today over 60¢ of every federal tax dollar is used to pay off past or current wars or to plan new ones. An apt metaphor to describe the competing concerns of ecology and poverty is two people arguing over the crumbs from a loaf of bread while others run away with the slices! From the standpoint of resources expended, the issue of "ecology as a cop-out on the poor" is largely academic since both ecology and poverty are being starved. Given the pittances that are now spent on ecology, the "war on pollution" proposed by the current administration will probably be as ineffective as the "war on poverty" was in dealing with the problems of the poor.

Both ecology and poverty have to be seen in light of other national priorities. Dr. George Wiley, Executive Director of the National Welfare Rights Organization, summarized the problem of national priorities when he spoke at the Harvard Teach-In. After acknowledging the seriousness of the ecological crisis, he addressed a challenge to the environmentalists:

> It is going to be necessary to have substantial government expenditures for the programs of environmental control—that means you will be directly competing with poor people for very scarce government dollars. And if you are not in a position to mount a confrontation with the military-industrial complex, if you are not prepared to join with poor people in saying that the war in Vietnam has got to end, that we've got to stop military imperialism around the world, that we've got to cut out the wasteful military expenditures . . . quite clearly poor people will pay the cost of your ecology program.[9]

But let us suppose that ecology is taken seriously. Have we properly assessed the impact of the proposed remedies on low-income households? This is necessary from two standpoints: (a) someone has to pay for pollution control and the poor will be asked to pay disproportionately, and (b) some of the remedies proposed to halt pollution, such as curbing economic growth, will have severe repercussions on the poor.

Who Pays for Pollution Control?

The idea posted by *Life* magazine and others that "Ecology is everybody's issue" is misleading. There is a widespread illusion that at last we have found a real national issue that is non-controversial, and thus, we act as if a clean environment can be obtained without cost. If, for example, the managers of a chemical or power plant install expensive pollution control equipment, they can do one of three things to cover expenditures: (1) raise the price of the product, (2) appeal for a government subsidy, or (3) reduce corporate profits.

Capital expenditure in pollution control equipment is basically an investment in non-productive devices. Given our current accounting procedures, such a venture increases the cost of production. We have for years assumed that disposal of waste into the air or waterways is free! The ecological costs have seldom been calculated, let alone included in the costs of production. To do any of the three items will tend to slow down consumption and attack our cherished sacred cow—an increasing "standard of living." Raising the price of a product will surely reduce the amount that a family can buy. The price increase is tantamount to a sales tax—a regressive form of taxation that hurts the poor most severely when imposed on necessities. Each person will pay the same increased amount per item, but some can pay it easily and others cannot.

The federal subsidy also does not come free of charge because the tax-payer will ultimately pay it, even if by a progressive income tax. Any tax credits offered to industries for cleaner effluents are really another form of subsidy for pollution control. The third alternative—lowering the corporate profits—seems unlikely, given the power, prestige of, and lack of public controls over large corporations. If profits were somehow substantially reduced, however, industrial expansion would slow down. Of the three alternatives, the first seems to be the most likely. Yet increasing the price of the products will affect the poor most severely, unless we make special allowances or adopt new pricing mechanisms.

In order to have economic justice and ecological sanity we might have to revamp radically our pricing structure. For instance, we now pay less for additional units of electric power consumption, which means that the tenth electrical appliance is actually cheaper (per kilowatt hour) to operate than the first. We are enticed into consuming increasing amounts of electric power that result in environmental contamination. In order to preserve a sound environment with economic justice, the basic units of power should be offered at the cheapest possible rates. Then a graduated price scale might be imposed on additional amounts so that the ninth appliance (a freezer?) will be more costly to operate than the first (a refrigerator?). The inversion of the rate structure would discourage profligate use of power.

Economic Growth and Environmental Destruction

An increasing Gross National Product (GNP) has functioned in American society as a God-concept does in a religious society. In short, Americans worship economic growth. Yet increased economic growth which comes about by increased material and power consumption is always accompanied by increased pollution. Hence, many ecologists and others believe that we must begin to deal with root causes and not symptoms. And perpetually increasing consumption levels of power and material goods (compounded by the population explosion) are the root causes.

But will not more technology solve the population problem? Our perennial faith in the "technical fix" to solve all of our pollution problems is being shattered. That notion naively assumes that no matter how badly the side effects of current technology destroy the environment, new technologies will appear that will fully ameliorate the damages. Just as the drug user becomes addicted to heroin, our society has become addicted to the technical fix. Technology, of course, can be useful in developing pollution control devices, but exclusive reliance on new technologies to extricate us from our follies has not and will not work repeatedly. We produce new problems faster than we solve old ones. In many instances *initial steps that produced the pollution will have to be stopped.* In fact, sometimes the technical fix creates problems that are more dangerous than the ones it tried to remedy. For example, the detergent used to free the ocean of the oil from the Torrey Canyon did more damage to marine life than the oil spilled!

There is a growing pool of data that shows that increased production will cause increased environmental contamination, even after the best pollution control devices are installed. Our current methods, for instance, extract raw materials from the earth and turn them into products that soon become obsolete. The disposal of these products often presents serious environmental problems. A classic case is that of bauxite ore which is extracted in Latin America and converted into billions of aluminum cans per year. Their disposal presents a fantastic problem since the cans do not decompose. Hence, many of our most secluded wildernesses are strewn with beer cans!

In order to conserve our natural resources a tax on extracting raw materials needs to be imposed as well as a tax on the disposal of the product. That is, the real cost of depleting natural resources and the cost of disposing of manufactured products should be included in the costs of production. Obviously, taxing the origin and the end of the production processes would make recycling of products a more competitive operation. This would allow us to move to what the economist Kenneth Boulding has called, the "spaceship earth" society. Boulding believes that the U.S. is now wedded to a "cowboy" economy which knows no limits on natural resources and has no ecological constraints.[10] A spaceship earth concept is one where the materials are recycled, just as occurs on space flights.

But a massive recycle industry cannot be developed without power consumption and environmental deterioration. Massive recycle industries would allow us to preserve natural resources and help solve the disposal problem, but the second law of thermodynamics cannot be reversed. Any power generating operation has some heat loss, and that is always a form of pollution! So increased recycling cannot be viewed as an unlimited process. Thus, some scientists are calling for a slowdown in economic growth.

Ecologists, who challenge the notion of endless material economic growth, are being joined by a host of others. For instance, former Secretary of Interior Stewart Udall speaks freely of the madness involved in equating the GNP with national well-being. The geologist Preston Cloud, speaking in Boston to the last meeting of the American Association for the Advancement of Science, remarked that "growth is a Trojan horse, with the diplomatic privileges of a sacred cow." Even the ecology features in *Time* (2 February, 1970 and 2 March, 1970) noted that the whirling dervish doctrine of perpetual growth should be challenged. The biologist René Dubos has commented on the insanity of such a notion as: "Produce more than you consume, so that you can consume more."[11] There is a serious question whether ecological constraints will allow growth to increase indefinitely. Although the idea strikes at the heart of Keynesian economics, it is being espoused by responsible physical, biological, and social scientists, who are not ordinarily viewed as "kooks" or "alarmists."

Before proceeding, it should be first specified that not all economic growth results in pollution. Increased sales of pollution control equipment and gains in the "service" sector also increase the GNP. But growth in sectors that cause vast pollution should be restrained. Thus the issue is not growth or no growth, but what kind of growth.

Economic Growth and High Employment Levels

A cutback in material production, however, would have profound repercussions on the poor and lower income groups. Those who have doubts about this should observe the rising unemployment which is a result of our current attempt to "cool off" an inflationary economy. (Unemployment rates have already risen from 3.3 percent to over 5 percent.)[12] Also, most industrialized nations finance their poverty programs via incremental economic growth or a growth dividend.[13] More growth means more jobs for all (especially the poor and lower middle income groups) and more public funds available to finance welfare programs (i.e., without further tax increases). We are addicted to the "trickle down theory," i.e., everyone must receive more if the poor are to receive more. That this theory has not been fully effective in ending poverty is irrelevant; it has worked in part. The poor may not have been helped appreciably by economic growth, but they certainly will suffer acutely if the growth rate declines. This paradox, which can lead to a host of questions about the structural injustices in our economic system, cannot be pursued at this juncture.[14]

These effects on the poor and lower middle income families are most severe in an automated society. For years there has been a stalemate in the debate: "Does automation produce or reduce jobs?" The experts have argued on both sides of the issue. But from the maze of data some clear trends are discernible. During the Eisenhower years when economic growth was slow, unemployment rates soared (3 percent in 1953 to 5 percent in 1960). From 1962–68 (a period of economic growth) the unemployment rates dropped from 5.6 percent in 1962 to 3.5 percent in 1968. Such statistics led the "pro-automation" experts to say: "See! Automation produces more jobs, as long as economic growth is sustained." But if the ecological problems are as serious as many believe, then that provisional clause "as long as economic growth is sustained" radically alters the debate. For automation always increases productivity (i.e., units produced per man hour). If automation did not, it would be senseless to add new machinery. With a stagnant growth rate and increasing productivity, the logical result must be

higher levels of unemployment as well as a shorter work week.

As our society becomes more industrialized, there is a shift from the "goods" to the "service" sector. As productivity increases (due to automation), more jobs will be available in the service sector. However, reliance on the service sector to take up all of the economic slack is another myth. With a slow industrial growth rate, the entire economy will slow down. Hence, the problems of unemployment that will result from the slowing down of economic growth, the necessity of an adequate guaranteed annual income for all, and the need for a redistribution of national income, must be included in all serious ecology debates.

The challenges should be clear to us. Although environmental problems are becoming critical, they must be interpreted in light of other problems and priorities. If the cost of pollution control is passed directly on to the consumer on all items, low income families will be affected disproportionately. If new technologies cannot solve the environmental crisis and a slowdown in material production is demanded, the low income families will again bear the brunt of it, as more and more of them will join the ranks of the unemployed. In the first instance, new pricing schemes are necessary in order to have ecological sanity and economic justice. In the latter case, we must either radically revamp our schemes for the distribution of national wealth and income *or* use ecology as a club over the heads of the poor and lower-middle income families. There are no other alternatives unless one decides that ecology is not a real problem. The mounting scientific evidence, however, stands as a staunch testimony against those who claim that ecology is a "faddish" and "overrated" issue.

Global Ecology and Economic Justice: The Challenge to Social Ethics

The ethical implications of the above discussion are obvious—man must be a steward of God's creation at the same time he works for social and economic justice for *all*. We can sacrifice neither the God of Genesis nor the God of the prophets. We should realize, therefore, that the problems from the outset are not just national but global. As a result ecology and distributive justice have to be considered in an international context. Unfortunately, the wider global aspects of economic development of poor nations, the gap between the rich and poor nations, the ecological problems associated with full world-wide industrialization, cannot be explored in detail here.

One point, however, should be touched upon, i.e., the disproportionate consumption of the earth's resources by Americans. The U.S., with 6 percent of the world's population, now uses roughly 40–60 percent of the non-renewable resources utilized each year.[15] In order to sustain our increasing "standard of living," by 1980, with around 5 percent of the world's population, the U.S. will need roughly 55–70 percent of the non-renewable resources used each year. Can economic justice be a global reality if this trend continues? Is development of the third world precluded by our need for their raw materials?[16] After all, non-renewable resources are finite, and took billions of years of evolution to reach their current state, and hence should be used sparingly and justly.

Therefore, the current American lifestyles should be challenged. Concern for economic justice should lead an affluent American to say: "We must consume less, enjoy it more, and share our abundance with others at home and abroad." To some, that might sound naïve, soft-headed, unrealistic, and unpragmatic. Despite name calling, it may point to a central and essential ecological fact which is consonant with our theological and ethical heritage. In order to attain economic justice the gap between the rich and the poor should be closed. With modern technology, managerial skills, and capital resources largely concentrated in the hands of industrialized nations, the rich-poor gap is widening. For example, from 1967 to 1969 the per capita income in the U.S. rose from $3,270 to $3,800, an increase of $530. Even discounting for inflation, that increase was about twice that of the entire annual per capita income in Guatemala which stagnated around $250. Some African and Asian nations are even poorer.

Many believe that it was the Judeo-Christian mandate that "man should have dominion" (*Gen.* 1:26) over nature which led to the ecological crisis.[17] Thus, a reformation of a theology and ethic of nature is necessary. But this should not be done divorced from the notions of distributive justice

especially in the economic realm. And the above statistics clearly point out the need.

A responsible environmental ethic would recognize man's finitude and his place in the cosmos. He has been selected to be a custodian of God's creation and to transform the natural order for human welfare. But he must appreciate the limits of technical transformation. The side-effects of all of his actions must be carefully calculated, and appropriate plans made to offset their negative effects. He must further understand that even the positive aspects of his technical transformations affect various people differently. The costs and the benefits of each technical modification are not shared equally, so the question of *who pays the costs and who receives the benefits is essential.* A new environmental ethic would attempt to distribute the costs and benefits justly.

In order to manifest our ethical concerns, four things should be done simultaneously:

1. We should direct citizens to see the root causes of the ecological crisis. The nation must move beyond the anti-pollution fad and deal with causes not symptoms. The myth that equates increased material prosperity with the "good life" has to be challenged.

2. We should expose and oppose those who would use the current momentum of the ecology movement as the issue of the "silent majority," divorced from the needs of the poor. Rats, congested and dilapidated living spaces, and a repressive atmosphere are part of urban ecology. The rat infested apartment should not receive less ecological emphasis than bird sanctuaries!

3. We should thoroughly investigate the allocation of the costs of pollution control. Often those who receive most of the benefits pay only a small portion of the costs, and vice versa. Passing the cost to the consumer might affect the poor unfairly.

4. We should insure that the consequences of altering the economic growth rate become an integral part of all ecology discussions. A new distribution of income and wealth must be reckoned with.

Yet we should move beyond the immediate · American situation to visions of global ecology.

America offers false hopes to many poor nations that they, too, can imitate the American model of development. That model may be extremely difficult to reproduce and suicidal if it is reproduced. For instance, if the current global population (3 billion) consumed at current American levels, the carbon dioxide and carbon monoxide levels would increase by a factor of 250 and sulfur dioxide by a factor of 200. The image of 7 billion people in 2000 consuming at even higher than American levels is horrendous even with extensive pollution control and recycling industries. There are limits to technology. Presently, America's over-consumption and over-pollution are made possible and sustained because of global injustice.

Can economic justice become a global reality as long as Americans are enamoured with an ever increasing "standard of living?" But if the entire world population were able to reach the consumption level of all Americans, would there be enough natural resources to sustain them? Would the resulting global pollution destroy the planetary life support systems? The answers to these questions depend on much scientific and technical data. But science and technology alone cannot provide the entire answer. Fundamentally, these are questions of human value and the human spirit. For example, the identity of increased "standard of living" with psychic well-being and the "good life," so firmly established in the U.S. and industrialized nations, poses a spiritual as well as an economic problem. Theological and ethical reflection must link together ecology and distributive justice and move beyond national to global concerns.

In summary, we can say that the ecological crisis is grave, far more serious than the current publicity indicates. Much of the current debate still focuses on symptoms, not causes. There is still rampant the pious hope that new technologies will save us from the foibles and over-application of old technologies. New and more radical solutions are necessary. But the consequences of the solutions on all segments of society and the structural changes needed to offset the consequences must be dealt with. If economic justice for all is not an essential part of the debate, the ecology issue, despite its importance, will inadvertently be used as a club over the heads of the poor and lower-middle income groups, which includes most of black America.

Notes

1. In January—April, 1970, for example, *Look, Time, Newsweek, Life, Fortune* and many other popular and professional journals either devoted issues to or did feature stories on ecology. Since then there has been a constant bombardment via the mass media.

2. The science of ecology emphasizes the "web of life," i.e., man is just one species in a complex and interrelated biosphere. Hence, most ecologists reject the anthropocentric focus of much of traditional theology. When the ecologically minded do theology, they construct a new kind of "nature mysticism." See Fred Elder, *Crisis in Eden* (Nashville: Abingdon Press, 1970) and the works of ecological scientists—Loren Eiseley and Ian McHarg. Man's peculiar responsibility to transform as well as to protect the natural order is, unfortunately, de-emphasized. In addition, most of the writings on an ethic of ecology devote almost no space to the special environmental problems of the poor. See F. F. Darling and J. P. Milton, *The Future Environments of North America* (New York: Natural History Press, 1966).

3. United Nations report on the environment released on 22 June, 1969.

4. From a report issued by *U.S. News and World Report*, July, 1969, which was reprinted in the *Philadelphia Inquirer*, "The Spectacular 70s," 17 August, 1969.

5. See T. Roszak, *The Making of a Counter Culture* (Garden City, New York: Doubleday & Company, Inc., 1969) for a brilliant explication of the youth movement. His work stands in sharp contrast to black theologians and other black writers who emphasize political and economic justice in a racist society.

6. This comment was made at a meeting held by the Boston Industrial Mission in April 1970 between Boston Area Ecology Action and the Massachusetts Welfare Rights Organization.

7. The words are an "almost exact" quote from an address made by Eugene Jones in Trinity Lutheran Church, Roxbury, Massachusetts, during a memorial service to the late Dr. Martin Luther King, Jr., on 4 April, 1970. They were enthusiastically received by the predominantly black audience.

8. Delivered to the U.S. Congress on 22 January, 1970, and reproduced in *Vital Speeches*, 1 February, 1970, pp. 226–229.

9. Quoted in *Earth Day—The Beginning* (New York: Bantam Books, Inc., 1970), p. 216. The Boston Industrial Mission has explored with Dr. Wiley and others from the National Welfare Rights

Organization and ecology groups possible avenues of cooperation between the two movements.

10. See Kenneth Boulding's "Economics of the Coming Spaceship Earth" in G. de Bell's *The Environmental Handbook* (New York: Ballantine Books, Inc., 1970), pp. 96–101. See also the brochure *The Boston Industrial Mission at Mid-Decade,* Cambridge, BIM, May, 1970.

11. *So Human an Animal* (New York: Charles Scribner & Sons, 1968).

12. Figures are from the Bureau of Labor Statistics, Dept. of Labor, Washington, D.C.

13. Increased economic growth means a bigger pie and a bigger slice for all. Most economists argue that economic growth avoids class tensions, since everyone appears to be getting more even if the relative gaps remain unchanged. For the relationships between economic growth and employment, see "Technology and The American Economy," *Report of the National Commission on Technology, Automation and Economic Progress* (Washington, D.C.: U.S. Government Printing Office, February, 1966). See also economic textbooks, especially those by Keynesian economists. For the futility of endless economic growth, see E. Mishan, *Technology and Growth: The Price We Pay* (New York: Frederick A. Praeger, Inc., 1970).

14. For an insightful analysis and critique of income distribution, see G. Kolko, *Wealth and Power in America* (New York: Frederick A. Praeger, Inc., 1962).

15. See Lincoln Day and Alice Day, *Too Many Americans* (Boston: Houghton-Mifflin Company, 1964), p. 31.

16. See Charles Park, *Affluence in Jeopardy: Minerals and the Political Economy* (San Francisco: Freeman, Cooper & Co., 1968) and P. Jallé, *The Pillage of the Third World* (New York: Monthly Review Press, 1968).

17. See Lynn White, "The Historical Roots of the Ecologic Crisis," *Science* (10 March, 1967) . . . for an indictment of the Christian tradition. Man is the egocentric manipulator who cuts himself off from nature. White calls for a new theological vision, one which sees St. Francis of Assisi as the patron saint of ecology.

Environmental Ethic and the Attitude Revolution

Eugene P. Odum

One reason that environmental pollution has reached a critical stage is that individually and collectively we have not thought ecologically about the use of environmental resources. Speaking from the viewpoint of morality, while we have a well-developed ethic based on person-to-person relationships and person-to-society relationships, we have not extended that ethic to include an ethical relationship between people and their environment. In the following article, internationally recognized ecological expert Eugene P. Odum says that we must do just that. Specifically, Professor Odum contends that if we are going to avoid self-destruction, we must formulate an environmental ethic which will provide the necessary legal and economic incentives to effect a change of attitude. This new attitude should recognize that continued population growth, increased use of technology, and constant pollution can put such demands on the earth's finite resources that dignified human existence, perhaps human existence itself, will be seriously jeopardized. Professor Odum's remarks seem particularly relevant for business, whose role in the environmental crisis is well documented, and whose attitude toward the physical world around it seems to have led to flagrant atmospheric pollution.

As human population growth, technology, pollution, and demands on finite resources begin to tax the earth's capacity, the theory that man and environment are a whole must be put into practice if man is to avoid self-destruction. "Holism" in terms of planning and management requires a fundamental change in man's attitude toward his environment and, most important of all, an ethical basis for the necessary legal and economic incentives. The "environmental awareness movement," which began in the late 1960s is evidence that people's attitudes are changing rapidly, and so it would seem that the development of an environmental ethic is but a logical extension of general ethics.

Among recent ecologists who have considered the philosophical aspects of man and environment, the late Aldo Leopold, in his essays on the "land ethic,"[1] wrote about three ethics: (1) religion as a man-to-man ethic, (2) democracy as a man-to-society ethic, and (3) a yet undeveloped ethical relationship between man and his environment. We would agree with Leopold that these three "ethics" are stages in the development of a general ethic in which man extends his thinking in stepwise fashion from man-to-man relationships to the totality of human existence. We can also present strong scientific and technological reasons for the proposition that such a major extension of the general theory of ethics is now necessary for human survival.

First, it would be prudent to define more precisely what is meant by "an environmental ethic" before presenting the case for considering it an extension of general ethics rather than a "new" ethic. In his earliest essay in 1933 Leopold wrote:

> When god-like Odysseus returned from the wars in Troy, he hanged, all on one rope, some dozen slave girls whom he suspected of misbehavior during his absence. This hanging involved no question of propriety, much less justice. The disposal of property was then, as now, a matter of expediency, not of right and wrong. Criteria of right and wrong were not lacking from Odysseus' Greece. The ethical structure of that day covered wives, but had not been extended to human chattels.
>
> During the three thousand years which have since elapsed, ethical criteria have been extended to many fields of conduct, with corresponding shrinkages in those judged by expediency only. This extension of ethics is actually a process of ecological evolution. Its sequences may be described in biological as well as philosophical terms. An ethic, biologically, is a limitation on freedom of action in the struggle for existence. An ethic, philosophically, is a differentiation of social from anti-social conduct. These are two definitions of one thing. The thing has its origin in the tendency of independent individuals and societies to evolve modes of cooperation. The biologist calls these symbioses. Man elaborated certain advanced

symbioses called politics and economies. Like their simpler biological antecedents, they enable individuals and groups to exploit each other in an orderly way. Their first yardstick was expediency. As the complexity of the human community increased expediency-yardsticks were no longer sufficient. One by one it has evolved and superimposed upon them a set of ethical yardsticks. The first ethic dealt with the relationship between individuals. Later accretions dealt with the relationship between individuals and society. Christianity tries to integrate the individual to society, Democracy to integrate social organization to the individual. There is yet no ethic dealing with man's relationship to land and to the nonhuman animals and plants which grow upon it. Land, like Odysseus' slave-girls, is still property. The land-relation is still strictly economic, entailing privileges, but not obligations. The extension of ethics to this third element in human environment is, if we read evolution correctly, an ecological possibility. It is the third step in a sequence. The first two have already been taken. Civilized man exhibits, in his own mind, evidence that the third is needed. For example, his sense of right and wrong may be aroused quite as strongly by desecration of a nearby woodlot as by a famine in China. Individual thinkers, since the days of Ezekiel and Isaiah have asserted that the despoliation of land is not only inexpedient, but wrong. Society, however, has not yet affirmed their belief. I regard the present conservation movement as the embryo of such an affirmation.

Thus Leopold eloquently stated the case of a natural evolution of thinking about ethics, and he correctly predicted that the early "conservation movement" signaled the beginning of societal acceptance of an environmental ethic. What the conservationists of the 1930s could not have anticipated was the rapid rate of deterioration of man's environment that has accompanied the concentrated use of fuel power in cities and agriculture, the exponential growth of population that is supported and encouraged by this exploitation of fuel, and the shift from a technology based on making and using things that by and large can be recycled in nature to a technology based on the chemical conversion of natural products into poisons and nondegradable substances which can no longer be recycled by natural processes. It is the change in kind as well as the increase in amount of technology that places increasing stress on man's natural life-support system.

Just as the slaves of old eventually rose up and destroyed their masters, so will the damaged environment lead to destruction of man if he continues to treat the environment only as an expedient slave. Accordingly it matters not whether one takes the cynical viewpoint that man becomes ethical only when he has to or whether one believes that the goodness and wiseness in human behavior eventually surfaces. We can confidently expect that the decade of 1970 to 1980 will bring greater acceptance of the third ethic, because it must. In fact, we could argue with considerable logic that the progress man has made in formalizing the first two ethics will come to naught, unless the third and final component is accepted and put into legal and economic practice. Without a quality environment, there can be no organized society or quality individuals.

Cybernetics, the science of control theory, provides a convenient way to view the environmental problem as a whole. In cybernetic language a system such as a natural ecological system (ecosystem), or a human society, can exist in two general states: (1) a "transient" state in which the whole is growing or otherwise changing with time and (2) a "steady state" in which the system is maintained in an overall equilibrium. For the purposes of our analogy, we can think of the positive transient state as "youth" and the steady state as "maturity." There is, of course, the possibility of a negative transient state or "old age," which comes sooner or later to the individual, but which we assume need not come to the world ecosystem as a whole; at least, that possibility is not of immediate concern to society.

A growth or "youthful" stage is under the influence of what is called "positive feedback" in that each increase accelerates another increase, often in geometric progression (a doubling followed by doubling, etc.). For the individual, the population, or for a new business, growth and positive feedback are necessary for survival. All organisms and living systems, in general, including nations of people, have an inherent tendency to grow, borne out of the necessity for survival. We see this in the development of a "growth ethic" in pioneer countries, such as the United

States during the nineteenth and first half of the twentieth centuries. However, growth does not and cannot continue unrestricted because "negative feedback" control also comes into play, either due to some limitation imposed by the external environment or due to the action of an internal governor that brings about an orderly slowdown and establishes a set point at which growth in size stops (but this does not mean that growth in quality need stop). As systems become larger and more complex, more of the energy that it transforms must be fed back to maintain and control the quality of the intricate structure that has resulted from growth; quality maintenance replaces quantitative growth as "the strategy of survival" in the mature system. In summary then ultimate survival depends both on positive and negative feedback and on a set point control mechanism that prevents "overshoots," that is, damaging "boom-and-bust" oscillations that could cause the death of the system.

From this brief and elementary discourse on cybernetics, it can be seen that sooner or later transition from youth to maturity must be faced at all levels of life, whether they be cells, organs, teenagers, society, or the ecosystem as a whole. In the individual there is a built-in governor in the form of a genetic code (a sort of computer) that first organizes growth, then slows it down, and then maintains optimum coordinated function in a state of maturity for a relatively long time. Viewing the United States as an ecosystem, we see that environmental constraints (depletion of resources, pollution, declining quality of living space, etc.) are beginning to provide negative feedback. As writers in the popular press are beginning to stress, this nation, whether we like it or not, is beginning to mature and stratify. Many of our current problems, both domestic and international, stem from our failure to face up to this fact. Thus, what was desirable in the youthful stage becomes undesirable in the mature stage. For example, high birth rates, rapid industrial growth and exploitation of unused resources are advantageous in a pioneer society. We can be justly proud of the fact that the United States has been able to grow and develop so well. However, as saturation levels are approached, all the "good" things become "bad" and the strategy of survival requires a shift to opposite poles, as for example, birth control, recycling of resources, regulation of land use, waste treatment, and so forth. Growth beyond the optimum becomes cancer. Cancer is an everpresent threat to any mature system and must be constantly guarded against. Unfortunately society has no built-in "genetic code" that automatically monitors the transition from youth to maturity. We have not yet agreed on optimum levels of population and energy transformation.

The theme of this essay, then, is that external environmental constraints will not be adequate negative feedback for society. So strong is the economic positive feedback of technological growth that overshoots seem inevitable if only external limits are involved. There must also be internal governors if transition is to be orderly and relatively free of cancerous excursions. Leopold's

third ethic, or the extension of ethics to include man-in-environment relationships, must become an integral part of man's philosophy, if for no other reason than that such an extension provides the needed internal governor. Science can define reasonable levels and limits of growth and energy usage that are optimum for the quality of human existence, but ethics coupled with the legal and economic expediencies that derive from ethical behavior are absolutely necessary if we are to make the orderly transition to maturity.

Notes

1. "The Conservation Ethic," *Journal of Forestry* 31 (1933): 634–643; "The Land Ethic," in *A Sand County Almanac* (New York: Oxford University Press, 1949).

For Further Reading

Banfield, E. C. *The unheavenly city: The nature and future of our urban crisis.* Boston: Little, Brown, 1970.

Barkley, P. W., & Seckler, D. W. *Economic growth and the environmental decay.* New York: Harcourt Brace Jovanovich, 1972.

Carson, R. *Silent spring.* New York: Fawcett, 1967.

Chamberlain, N. *Enterprise and environment.* New York: McGraw-Hill, 1968.

Dorst, J. *Before nature dies.* Boston: Houghton Mifflin, 1970.

Edmunds, S., & Letey, J. *Environmental administration.* New York: McGraw-Hill, 1973.

Ehrlich, P. R. *The population bomb.* New York: Ballantine Books, 1968.

_____, & Ehrlich, A. H. *Population, resources, environment.* San Francisco: Miller Freeman Publications, 1970.

Falk, R. A. *This endangered planet.* New York: Random House, 1971.

Graham, F., Jr. *Since silent spring.* Boston: Houghton Mifflin, 1970.

Turner, J. S. *The chemical feast.* New York: Grossman, 1970.

Watson, T., Jr. *A business and its beliefs.* New York: McGraw-Hill, 1963.

Part IV
BUSINESS AND ITS BASIS

10
TOWARD A MORAL ATMOSPHERE

In January, 1977, the Firestone Tire and Rubber Company announced that it had discontinued making its controversial "500" steel-belted radial, which, according to a House subcommittee, had been associated with fifteen deaths and thirty-one injuries. In the spring of 1978, the subcommittee found that, in fact, Firestone had continued making the tire, despite its announcement.

Immediately after the subcommittee's finding, newspapers reported a Firestone spokesperson as denying that Firestone had misled the public. He claimed that the 1977 announcement was intended as a "rolling phase-out," not a discontinuance notification. When asked why Firestone had not then corrected the media misrepresentation of the company's intent, the spokesperson said that Firestone's policy was to ask for corrections only when it was beneficial to the company to do so. In this case, it would seem that what the company viewed as beneficial was incompatible with a commitment to accuracy and consumer safety.

It would not be difficult to find a condemnation of Firestone's conduct in each of the moral theories we've discussed in this text. But moral theories do not explain why behavior such as Firestone's continues to function as an integral part of business operations. This inquiry might seem more sociological than ethical, and, yet, it may bear directly on the issue of business morality.

Recall that in our opening chapter we made a substantial case for the need for business ethics because of increased ethical content in business decisions. We also portrayed business's current moral dilemma as arising from the absence of a clear moral standard, from its inability to define and assign rights and responsibilities, and from its underdeveloped sense of moral accountability. But while describing business's dilemma, we never ventured to surmise why business today seems so inept in dealing with the moral dimension of business decisions. Why does business lack a clear-cut moral standard? Why can't it properly define and assign rights and responsibilities? Why does it suffer from a stunted sense of moral accountability? Applying these questions in a concrete situation, we could ask why conduct like Firestone's is common. How can individuals who have a personal ethic of never intentionally deceiving or endangering someone act so unconscionably in their business enterprises? In a real sense, until business and the people in it seriously contemplate these questions, they will not make much moral headway; for even if they have the theoretical wherewithal to make moral decisions, they must first create a climate in which moral decisions can be made. And without an atmosphere conducive to moral decision making, the level of business morality is likely to remain low.

What is a business atmosphere that supports the making of moral decisions? Surely it would be an organizational climate that emphatically endorses, encourages, and expects moral behavior from all of its members. Also, it would be a climate in which morality functions as an essential component of business policy and decision and not merely as an afterthought or promotional gambit. It would also be an atmosphere in which organizational members are made as accountable for their moral achievements and failures as they are for their economic ones. The unsettling fact is that rarely do we find such a business atmosphere. No wonder we witness such frightful behavior. Who would expect a plant to grow in the absence of light and water?

In this final chapter, we wish to emphasize the crucial need for business to start cultivating an atmosphere conducive to moral decision making. We'll see that in part this involves an inventory of the conditions that presently war against ethics in business. Specifically, we'll consider some of the conceptual building blocks of capitalism in order to determine their relationship to what we'll call a proper moral atmosphere. We'll also consider the impact of standard operating procedure on the ability and willingness of business people to make moral decisions. This capstone chapter in our study of ethics in business calls upon persons both in and out of business to work together to establish a climate in which people of good will and faith can deal with the rising ethical content of business decisions and can resolve the moral dilemma that business currently faces.

Systemic Assumptions

The word *systemic* refers to system, that is, some kind of organizational form. We are concerned primarily with the economic system, which helps define the relationship between business and its primary claimants. In our society that economic system is capitalism. When we speak of systemic assumptions, then, we have in mind both the functional assumptions of capitalism and the moral implications of these assumptions. Before unravelling them, we should first attempt to define capitalism. Because the definition of something is often facilitated through the use of contrast, we'll elaborate on the nature of capitalism by distinguishing it from another influential economic system, socialism.

The Nature of Capitalism

Defining any "ism" is problematic because rarely do all interested parties agree on its essential characteristics. Moreover, an "ism" is infrequently practiced by all people in the same way. Capitalism is no exception.

In defining capitalism, some persons would emphasize its self-interest quality, others its division of labor, still others its exclusion of government interference: different emphasis, different definitions. Defining capitalism isn't made any easier by turning to "model" capitalistic nations. Which nations do we choose: the Scandinavian nations, England, the United States? The fact is that no two capitalistic nations are identical in their practice of capitalism.

For purposes of simplicity, we will define capitalism ideally as an economic system in which the major portion of production and distribution is in private hands, operating under what is often termed a profit or market system. This definition seems adequate in that it contains two generally agreed upon defining characteristics of a capitalistic economic system. First, in a capitalistic system the means of production are privately owned. Individuals own society's capital equipment and have the right to use what they own for private gain. Second, capitalism relies primarily on the market system to determine the distribution of resources and wealth. This concept needs dilatation.

The market system is a complex mode of organizing society, in which an essentially unfettered and spontaneous pursuit of private interests is thought to effect social order and efficiency. In other words, under pure capitalism (which, of course, does not exist), the economic factors operating in society are free to interplay with one another and establish an equilibrium that will provide the best use of resources in satisfying human material wants. Thus, in the United States (with the exception of government expenditures for health, education, welfare, military equipment, and highways), no central agency or commission dictates the nature of what will be produced, its quantity or its means of production. How then are these things determined? Supply and demand are supposed to provide answers. What is produced is determined by consumer wants. In an economy like ours, suppliers of goods and services keep adjusting supplies and changing prices in response to variations in consumer demand. The ultimate goal is a balance between supply and demand. In effecting this goal, the market system allocates its resources among society's various interests and thus establishes income levels for different social classes.

To better understand these dimensions of capitalism, it is helpful to contrast capitalism with its polar opposite, socialism, again keeping in mind the impossibility of presenting anything but an idealized concept of it. *In contrast with capitalism, socialism is an economic system primarily characterized by public ownership of property and a planned economy.* Under socialism a society's equipment is not owned by individuals (capitalists) but by public bodies. Equally important, socialism depends primarily on planning rather than on the market system for both its overall allocation of resources and its distribution of income. This means that crucial economic decisions are made not by individuals but by the government. In the Soviet Union, for example, government agencies decide the number of automobiles—including models, styles, and colors—to be produced each year. In effect, top levels of government formulate production and cost objectives, which are then converted to specific production quotas and budgets that individual plant managers must follow.[1]

Having some idea about what capitalism is and how it contrasts with

1. *Swindle, p. 9.*

socialism, let us turn to *some* of capitalism's basic assumptions. We will focus on three assumptions that not only include many subsidiary beliefs but also bear directly on the issue at hand: the atmosphere proper to moral decision making in business.

SELF-INTEREST.   A belief that plays a formative role in the development of classical capitalism is that individuals are creatures of self-interest. Classical capitalism also believes that individuals should pursue self-interest because by so doing, economic progress and a constantly increasing social dividend will be ensured. Generally speaking, capitalism holds that the surest way to undermine social well-being is to interfere with the pursuit of economic self-interest as practiced in a market economy.

To taste the flavor of this capitalistic stress on self-interest, one should at least place it in the context of the laissez-faire individualism formulated in the economic and social philosophy of the eighteenth and nineteenth centuries. The doctrine of laissez-faire individualism maintained that business and commerce should be free from governmental control, thus enabling the entrepreneur to pursue free enterprise. For example, Adam Smith (1723–1790), author of *Wealth of Nations* and the leading exponent of laissez-faire economics, insisted that government interference in private enterprise must be reduced, free competition must be encouraged, and enlightened self-interest made the rule of the day. Similarly, John Stuart Mill feared government interference in the economy. Mill believed that government interference was justifiable only when society itself could not find solutions to problems. Such problems should then be resolved according to the principle of utility: what produces the greatest happiness for the greatest number of people. But under no circumstances, Mill argued, should the government unnecessarily restrict individual freedom, including the individual's right to realize as much pleasure and progress for self as possible.[2]

This emphasis on self-interest and noninterference took concrete form in the capitalistic claim that individuals have the right to own and manage property and to accumulate profits. In this way, classical capitalists thought, property and profit would serve as incentives for individuals to pursue self-interest which would produce the greatest social benefit. In a word, economic and social progress was thought to be ensured when individuals pursued self-interest.

We can isolate, then, three beliefs that accompanied the emphasis on self-interest and individual freedom as it appeared in the eighteenth and nineteenth centuries.

1. Individuals should be free to pursue their own interests without interference, providing they don't impinge on the rights and interests of others.

2. Individuals should be allowed to earn as much money as they can and to spend it however they choose.

3. Individuals should not expect government to aid or inhibit their economic growth, for such interference destroys individual incentive and creates indolence.

2.   *See Vincent Barry,* Looking at Ourselves: An Introduction to Philosophy *(Belmont, Calif.: Wadsworth, 1977), pp. 304-306.*

Obviously much has happened since the foundation of classical capitalism to make such contentions at least questionable. Basically, individuals have lost control of the means of production. As Karl Marx (1818–1883) observed as early as the nineteenth century, exorbitant costs, complex machinery, increasing demands, and intense competition have all worked against individual productiveness. Furthermore, specialization in certain industries, such as textile and steel, have significantly undermined job satisfaction. Also, the earlier economy of the Industrial Revolution was characterized by relatively free and open competition, but the later economy of our own time is made up of relatively few enormous companies that can conspire to fix prices, eliminate competition, and monopolize an industry. True, antitrust actions have tried to regulate industry, as in the cases of such corporate behemoths as Standard Oil and ITT. But on the whole such actions have been largely ineffectual. In fact, corporate giants have in some cases spawned even bigger offspring in the form of multinationals, firms doing business in several countries. Moreover, it is no secret that the accumulated strength of business has placed it in the position of being a sort of corporate or industrial state, an economic colossus that can negotiate independently with governments, solicit favorable franchises and tariffs, and influence self-serving legislation. Little wonder, then, that scholars like Philip Slater contend that the doctrine of rugged individualism and pursuit of self-interest as advanced by classical capitalistic economists like Smith underlies many of our social ills.[3]

We can grasp Slater's criticism by recalling some of the issues we've raised in this text. Take, for example, the issue of private lives versus company image. When a company infringes on the private lives of its workers, it does so from an impulse of self-interest: it desires to protect the welfare of the firm. When it objects to internalizing the costs of expensive pollution-control devices, it again is motivated by self-concern: it doesn't want to discolor its profit picture by incurring nonproductive costs. Similarly, when business balks at being told whom to hire, for example, women and minorities, it does so to preserve its autonomy in the selection of the human resources to be used in the production process. The fact is that while the traditional emphasis on self-interest may not appear in as unvarnished a form as it once did, it remains nonetheless a most influential business imperative that frequently lies at the heart of moral debate. At the very least, then, it seems that if business is to effect an atmosphere of moral decision making, it must reexamine this assumption and reformulate it so that organizational self-interests can harmonize with individual and societal interests. Curiously, this seems in the best interests of business, since failure in this would invite the dismantling of the capitalistic system.

THE ECONOMIC CREATURE. The assumption that people act out of self-interest and personal advantage is intimately tied to another assumption on which capitalism is based: that people's self-interests coincide with their economic interests. In effect, capitalism views human beings—whether producer, worker, or consumer—as essentially economic creatures, individuals who recognize and are motivated by their own economic self-interests.

3. *Philip Slater*, The Pursuit of Loneliness *(Boston: Beacon Press, 1971)*.

The implications of this assumption are noteworthy. As an example, consider consumerism. In theory, capitalism assumes that consumers have full knowledge of the diverse choices available to them in the marketplace. They know the different price structures of different producers of a similar product, are aware of the differences in quality, and can make the "best choice" of quality and price. One need only recall the things we said in Chapter 7 to question these assumptions, chief among which is the complex nature of the economic choices that today's consumers must frequently make. Even with agencies and interest groups to represent them, today's consumers rarely pose an equal match for powerful organizations that can manipulate and fix prices in the marketplace. What's more, the economic theory of human nature implies that consumers who need a good or service will have the ability to buy it. But current economic facts of life belie this. Intractable inflation accompanied by high unemployment means that for many consumers wants go unmet. A similar analysis could be made of this theory when applied to producers, or workers.

But perhaps the most morally significant thing about capitalism's view of the economic creature is that it presents little in the way of an ideal that either individuals or societies may aspire to. As economist Robert Heilbroner has observed, it presents no high sense of human mission or purpose on either the personal or the collective levels, as other views of human nature have. Christianity, for example, long has aspired to the ideal of a truly religious community united in agape, selfless love. And socialism has idealized human beings as "transformed from the competitive, acquisitive beings that they are (and that they are *encouraged* to be) under all property-dominated, market-oriented systems, into the cooperative human being who finds fulfillment in unselfishness and who presumably can develop only in the benign environment of a propertyless, non-market social system."[4] Such ideals give ideologies a powerfully persuasive spiritual basis and lay the foundation for social responsibility. Apparently lacking such ideals, capitalism is hard pressed to make these provisions.

LABOR THEORY OF VALUE. Another linchpin in the capitalistic ideology is its labor theory of value. Thus, Smith contended that labor creates value. In other words, value does not emerge from nature, from the world around us. Rather than emanating from, say, agriculture, value emerges from human labor making something of the natural environment. In a word, nothing but labor has any real value. All else is for human manipulation.

This theory, which may strike us as archaic, nonetheless represents an idea that Karl Marx and others have accepted unquestioningly. Note that the labor theory of value divides humans from the natural world and reduces nature to the role of a resource of human manipulation. In effect, the wealth of nature is disregarded; the idea that it has any intrinsic value is dismissed. Although it would be naive to attribute business's role in environmental pollution exclusively to a commitment to this theory of value, no doubt it partially explains why business seems preoccupied with the balance of industry rather than with the balance of nature. The enormous problems we face today in restoring the envi-

---

4. *Robert Heilbroner,* The Economic Problem *(Englewood Cliffs, N.J.: Prentice-Hall, 1972), p. 725.*

ronment testify to the folly of such an emphasis and, by implication, the inadequacy of this assumption itself.

There are undoubtedly an array of other assumptions that underlie capitalism and involve moral issues; for example, capitalism's division of labor. Smith demonstrated that dividing the production process and labor into areas of specialization increased capital and usually strengthened economic productivity. But as we mentioned in Chapter 4, the division of labor has developed to an unbearably boring and repetitive degree. The result is that industry often produces as much worker alienation as anything else. To deal satisfactorily with the problem of job atmosphere, then, may require a fresh look at the capitalistic concept of the division of labor.

To reiterate, if business is to make any real progress in dealing with the moral issues arising out of its relations with its claimants, it must scrutinize the philosophical assumptions underlying its attitudes and operations. Nevertheless, an examination of systemic assumptions will not of itself create the atmosphere needed for moral behavior, although it is certainly a promising start. Business must also unflinchingly evaluate for deficiencies the operational procedures that arise out of the capitalistic ethos.

Operational Deficiencies

Given the systemic assumptions just discussed, it's not difficult to understand why business and industry have never been interested in determining and evaluating their social performance. In fact, business's natural indifference to social performance traditionally has been reinforced by society's expectations, which until recently amounted to little more than that business perform economically. Thus, in the past, if people couldn't or wouldn't work for long hours at little pay, they were fired; if a firm had to conserve capital, it laid off workers; if, to sell a product, business had to blatantly misrepresent it, it did so. Generally speaking, when such actions produced favorable economic results, they were considered to be in the public interest. Productivity, in effect, was business's sole social responsibility.

In the last thirty years, however, things have changed. Rising affluence, an easing of the economic strains of the first half of the twentieth century, the information explosion, increased education, a change in values, all have drawn society's attention to a variety of social problems. Equal opportunity, ecology, urban blight, poverty, the quality of work life, and consumerism share center stage. In a word, society has become aware of the interface between itself and business. More important, it has deepened its recognition of business's influence on these issues and broadened its concept of the social role business should play. As we noted in Chapter 1, business's role as part of a social system and societal expectations have contributed mightily to the increased ethical content of business decisions. But business cannot meet the demands of its broadened role and of societal expectations because, operationally, it simply isn't equipped to. It can't because business has been regulated to function strictly as an economic entity.

To illustrate, it is common knowledge that moral training plays little if any role in a person's preparation for entry into the business world. Once in business, people quickly learn what they must do to survive. True, their actions are often incompatible with their own moral codes. But nowhere is anyone encouraged to deal with this conflict in an open, mature way. In most cases, employees of a firm are expected to suppress individual moral urges and think about "the good of the firm" instead. In short, when functioning as business persons, people are expected to surrender their own moral instincts or at least not to develop or broaden them. It's little wonder, then, that the most common line of defense for questionable business behavior is the cynical retort, "But that's business."

The fact is that business nationwide has been deficient in requiring moral accountability at any level of its operations. Even where codes of conduct exist, they are often vague and general (as discussed in Chapter 2) or function as so much moral eyewash. Surely such codes have done little to reduce the numbers of shoddy products that business produces but doesn't stand behind, or lessen the promises business makes but doesn't deliver. Codes do not seem to inhibit price setting and fixing, to prevent tendencies to circumvent the law or get by with minimal compliance, or to overcome the practiced indifference with which organizations commonly treat employees and customers. Indeed, business's unwillingness and operational inability to require moral accountability of itself and its people puts it in an untenably defensive position.

Thus, when charges of business irresponsibility are made, business lacks the wherewithal to deal with them constructively. Rather, business likely as not responds with the righteous indignation of a person who is convinced that anything done in the name of commerce is thereby exempt from considerations of human decency, social responsibility, and moral accountability. And if such unshakable conviction in the rightness of its position doesn't win the day, business can always wrap itself in the red-white-and-blue of free enterprise, thus reducing legitimate inquiry to some sort of subversion. In a word, there's very little in the operations of business which is calculated to induce ethical behavior.

So, it seems that if business is to create a moral atmosphere, it must not only take a good long look at its operational assumptions but also face up to the operational deficiencies that are allowing, even encouraging, immorality. Having done that, business must fashion its operations so that moral behavior will be encouraged, supported, acknowledged, and, in a word, made possible. How can business do this? What strategy can business employ to create an atmosphere conducive to moral decision making?

Such a strategy must begin with an unequivocal, highly visible commitment to ethical behavior in business. At the very least this expression of attitude and interest would include the following actions:

1. Business should acknowledge the importance, even necessity, of conducting business morally.

2. Business should make a genuine effort to encourage organization members to take moral responsibilities seriously. This action would mean ending the

subtle and not-so-subtle punitive steps taken against persons who "buck the system."

3. Business should terminate its defensiveness in the face of criticism. It should actively solicit other views, especially those expressed by business's primary claimants. This means that business should invite outside opinions instead of waiting until outside opinions are storming the citadel. Indeed, business would be wise to enlist the services of persons trained and skilled in moral philosophy, a kind of corporate moralist.

4. Business must recognize the pluralistic nature of the social system of which it is a part. Society consists of diverse, interlocked groups all vying to maintain their autonomy and advance their best interests. These groups are so related that the actions of one inevitably affect the standing of another on a variety of levels: economic, political, educational, cultural. As part of society, business affects many groups and they affect business. When business fails to recognize this, it loses sight of the social framework that governs its relationships with the external environment.

Undoubtedly other general directives could be added to this short list. But these seem a good beginning toward effecting a climate proper to moral decision making. It's vital, however, that business take some practical measures to implement these philosophical expressions of attitudes and intentions. A good starting place would be the social audit.

Social Audit

A social audit is a systematic study and evaluation of an organization's social performance, as distinguished from a financial audit which evaluates a business's economic performance. A social audit is concerned primarily with the impact of business operations on the social quality of life. It produces a *report of social performance,* that is, an account of organizational activities that affect the general welfare of society.

In addressing the general welfare of society, a social performance report considers the total needs of the whole community or society. It tends to stress general humanistic values and places traditional economic and technical values within that framework. In essence, therefore, a social performance report, as measured through a social audit, is concerned with the human impact of business events and not with just their economic ramifications.[5] While hardly a new concept, the idea of systematically measuring a firm's social performance through a social audit has recently taken hold because of the increased ethical content of business decisions and the rising level of societal expectations of how business should behave.

What areas does a social audit evaluate? It deals with any area of business activity that has a significant social impact and can become involved with ecology, consumerism, community needs, women and other disadvantaged groups, quality of work life. Specifically, a social audit might measure whether a firm is

---

5. *Blomstrom and Davis, pp. 510–511.*

ensuring employment and advancement opportunities for minorities; whether it is providing direct financial aid in the form of scholarships and school programs; whether it is installing modern pollution-control equipment; whether it is helping to underwrite art institutions and other cultural aspects of community life. In effect, a social audit catalogs what a firm is doing in each area of major social concern where expectations of business performance run high. It reveals at a glance whether an organization is involved in improving society and the nature and extent of its commitment.

Undoubtedly, the social audit has its weaknesses and problems.

1. By nature the social audit reveals only what an organization is doing, not whether its actions are producing favorable results. At the same time, social results are difficult to quantify. How do you measure the environmental impact of a firm's decision not to advertise via billboards?

2. Another weakness relates to the difficulty in establishing a causal connection between a firm's action and some social result. How much of a reduction in ghetto crime, for example, might be attributed to a firm's program for training the unskilled? Without this information it's impossible to calculate accurately the impact of such an initiative.

3. The absence of norms is also problematic. Precisely what should be included in a social audit? How will it be measured?

4. A social audit does not determine what is acceptable social performance. Just what level of involvement ought a firm to seek?

5. Because a social audit generally addresses social problems, it can easily overlook that wide range of moral problems that arise within a firm under the all-inclusive heading of interpersonal relations.

Despite these clear and admitted drawbacks, the social audit has several strengths which recommend it as at least a tangible departure point for more ethical behavior in business.

1. By definition the social audit addresses many important social issues which include a nest of moral concerns. We've considered three concerns in this text: women and disadvantaged groups, consumerism, and ecology.

2. The audit does show the amount of effort that a business is making. At a glance one can detect what efforts a firm is making in social areas such as equal rights and opportunities or improved job atmosphere. This is important because as many moral issues are likely to arise from organizational indifference, apathy, and noninvolvement as from what a firm actually does.

3. The social audit puts the firm using it on record as being committed to more responsible social behavior at every structural level. Specifically, it has the effect of notifying employees that the firm encourages and expects responsible behavior. This alone is likely to go a long way toward raising the moral level of business people as well as treating their moral schizophrenia, a subject we discussed in Chapter 1.

4. The social audit provides management with invaluable data by which it can determine how closely the organization is approaching its goals and standards. It's one thing for an organization to be committed to clarity, accuracy, and completeness in advertising; it's quite another to deliver on these standards. The social audit can show in concrete terms what an organization is doing to effect this goal, for example by having all advertising copy read by a disinterested party.

5. The social audit enables management to protect owner interests by generating cost data on specific programs. This is important, for as the demand on business for social performance increases, the potential for wasting or misdirecting corporate/owner funds increases. The social audit can minimize this problem by providing a detailed reckoning of the organization's social performance expenditures in money, time, and quality.

6. The social audit enables organizations to deal more forthrightly and effectively with the demands of its primary claimants. Invariably today numerous interest groups seek to know what an organization is doing specifically to ease a social problem. Often the aforementioned defensive posture business strikes in such an instance is a result of its own ignorance and inability to say exactly what it is doing, trying to do, or planning to do. The social audit provides these data. When thoroughly formulated, the data allow organizations to anticipate group demands, thus equipping business to defuse potentially volatile situations.

7. While in no way telling the firm or its members what is the morally right thing to do, by nature the social audit introduces a concern for rightness, which logically precedes a moral judgment. Simply put, when individuals are concerned about doing the right thing, they're more likely to behave responsibly than when they're unconcerned about morality. A concern for rightness is a prerequisite for moral action.

Just as we noted that capitalism embraces certain systemic assumptions that affect the moral climate of business, so we can observe some operational deficiencies that have grown out of these assumptions and counter an atmosphere proper to moral decision making. Chief among these deficiencies is the reality that many businesses still lack operational apparatuses which could encourage, direct, and evaluate the firm's and the individual's social performance. Thus some sort of social audit would be helpful. Although not perfect, the social audit has enough strengths to recommend it as a sound, practical way for organizations and their members to start cultivating moral responsibility.

Conclusion

In the last analysis whether business makes substantial, token, or no moral progress in the next decade depends very much on the nature and degree of its involvement in the world around it. Numerous psychologists and sociologists have commented on and documented the American tendency—on both the individual and organizational level—to remain uninvolved in events that do not directly affect us. Perhaps the classic illustration is the Kitty Genovese case that occurred in the 1960s. A young woman, Kitty Genovese, was stabbed to death before thirty-eight eyewitnesses. During the half hour her assailant took to complete his bloody deed, thirty-eight eyewitnesses looked on, horrified and incredulous, but mute and unmoved. Fortunately business firms don't subject individuals to such atrocities, but firms surely expose employees to highly questionable behavior. And, sad to say, some business persons meet such behavior with comparable noninvolvement, summed up in a "don't rock the boat" attitude. Similarly, organizations themselves frequently react to the burning issues of the day with indifference bred from the narrowest conception of the role they serve in society.

The tendency to remain uninvolved is probably the most serious obstacle to the formulation of a useful and satisfying business code of ethics, because it betrays a lack of concern. To be concerned is to perceive the importance of something to one's own life or to the lives of others, to perceive a personal responsibility for the direction that the object of our concern takes, and to make an effort to translate these perceptions into appropriate actions.[6] Without this concern, we can't formulate a moral position on any issue. Without it, individual and organizational values are likely to remain underdeveloped.

The question, then, is whether or not business cares enough to be moral. The answer will depend to a great extent on the people in it and on the extent of their own involvement with the world around them. Ultimately business can only be as concerned, involved, and moral as are the people in it.

6.   Vincent Barry, Personal and Social Ethics, (Belmont, Calif.: Wadsworth, 1978), p. 346.

Redefining the Rights and Responsibilities of Capital

Hazel Henderson

There's little question that society today is struggling to adapt to a new order of human needs and priorities. Are the basic assumptions and enabling institutions of capitalism adequate to assist in this struggle? Can traditional concepts of free enterprise, profits, and private property adequately cope with the complex pressures of conditions such as dwindling resources, inflation, unemployment? In the following article, world-renowned futurist and co-director of The Princeton Center for Alternative Futures, Hazel Henderson, seriously doubts that the foregoing questions may be answered in the affirmative. To begin with, she views the new challenges to the rights associated with capital, property, and management as a natural outgrowth of the historical processes of human emancipation from all forms of arbitrary power. She attempts to show why and how the structure of industrial/technological economies that has evolved over two centuries has been accounted for inadequately. What's needed, Dr. Henderson suggests, is a redefinition of some basic concepts such as "success" and "profit."

(Note: To give you some idea of the provocative nature of her remarks, the editors of Management Review, *the journal in which this article first appeared, printed an "editor's note" that accompanied this article. In it the editor described Dr. Henderson's essay as "controversial" and confessed that it likely would "provoke a few readers to anger." At the same time, the editor voiced a commitment to a "responsibility" to treat "unsafe" subjects. All of which raises an*

additional tantalizing moral question for editors and readers of business periodicals: is compatibility with traditional capitalistic ideology a morally legitimate criterion for the editors of a business periodical to use in deciding whether or not to print an article? More to the point, is it moral for the editors of a business periodical to refuse to print an article that, while in every way meets its publication standards, runs against the grain of what is considered traditional capitalistic thinking?)

New challenges to the rights associated with capital, property, and management represent a natural progression of the historical processes of human emancipation from all forms of arbitrary power from the Magna Carta signed by Britain's King John in 1215 to our own Declaration of Independence, the Bill of Rights, and the United Nations Charter of Human Rights. Investors and corporate managers were naive to imagine that this drive for human emancipation and democratic participation would stop at the doors of the corporate executive suite or at the factory gate.

According to a 1975 survey conducted by the Peoples Bicentennial Commission, one out of three Americans believes that our capitalistic system is on the decline; two out of three favor basic changes in our economic system; a majority of the public favors employee ownership and control of U.S. corporations; 74 percent favor consumer representation on corporate boards; and 58 percent believe that major corporations tend to dominate and determine the actions of our public officials in Washington.

This crisis of confidence is not merely a question of legitimacy. It was inevitable that such highly visible, nondemocratic institutions as our large corporations, existing in the midst of a political democracy, would be challenged. The issue runs much deeper and involves the objective questions of incompetence, inability to address new societal needs, and concern over their very rationality in the face of competing examples in our evolving society and alternative images of the future.

Managing the Macro System: Competing Models of Reality

The politics of mixed, market-oriented, industrial societies in the upcoming decade can best be understood as a battle between two major views:

The private enterprise "Golden Goose" as the major creator of societal wealth, which is the dominant business image.

The emerging image (captured by Michael Harrington in *The Twilight of Capitalism*) of the government and the taxpayers as little more than the private sector's "milking cow," where business is seen as reaping private profits at the expense of escalating costs while using its lobbying power to compel taxpayers to underwrite the risks and investments that heretofore have been the chief justification for the profit system. Managerial ineptness is also a part of this conceptual crisis in all industrial societies as they face new constraints of global interdependence, technological complexity, population pressures, and resource confrontations.

At the global level, the crisis of industrialism in market-oriented, mixed, and socialistic economies involves an insistent paradox: Advancing levels of technological complexity systematically destroy free market conditions and render laissez-faire policies all but impossible. On the other hand, human beings clearly have not yet learned how to plan such societies. Facing this paradox and acknowledging our conceptual confusion are the first agonizing steps to finding a "Third Way."

Karl Polanyi pointed out in 1944 (in *The Great Transformation*) that the "free market," held in such awe by neoclassical economists, was not derived from any natural order or from any "human propensity to barter," as Adam Smith imagined. Markets have always existed in human societies, but we forget that until the industrial revolution in England, they were local and not interlinked, and that they had never been used as the dominant resource-allocation system. In fact, most of the world's cultures until that time had used two other major production/allocation systems—reciprocity and redistribution—and free-market *systems* are rare aberrations in human history.

Polanyi notes that this free-market system, far from being derived from God, began in England as a package of bitterly contested social legislation, over which a civil war was fought in the early 1600s. This legislative package, which created the free-market system, included two crucial planks:

the enclosure of land, so that it could be bought and sold freely as a commodity, and the driving off the land of formerly self-reliant peasants and cottagers, so that they were forced to sell their labor as a commodity.

This, and other legislation breaking down regional barriers to trading and cash-based transactions, set the stage for national markets and formed the basis of the industrial revolution, with its huge increases in production of goods and concomitant increase in social devastation and human misery.

All this happened a hundred years before Adam Smith was born. Understandably, Smith chose to examine the fascinating cybernetic panorama of small-scale economic factors that had arisen by then: buyers and sellers meeting each other in this newly interlinked system of markets with relatively equal power and information. Smith marveled that the behavior of all seemed to be regulated for the good of all by the market's "invisible hand." Even then, there were two potential trouble spots: the embarrassing number of wandering, starving paupers, over whom social theorists fretted, and the appearance of occasional "nuisances" visited on innocent bystanders, such as smells, smoke, and fumes of manufacturers—forerunners, of course, of the avalanche of "externalities" our own system visits upon us today.

This basic Adam Smith model of the free market and the elegant equilibrium of supply and demand it proposes still exercise hypnotic power over the minds of most economists and business people. In fact, in the current debate about "deregulation," many propose that we turn the clock back and return to this simpler world.

Even in 1934, when John Maynard Keynes showed in his *General Theory of Employment, Interest and Money* that this model was inadequate for understanding macroeconomic cycles and recessions, his basically disequilibrium model was swallowed, but never digested, in what economists call the "neoclassical Keynesian synthesis." Actually, no synthesis occurred and the earlier Smith equilibrium model (which lent itself so well to rewarding academic virtuosity and mathematical pseudorigor) still informs the basic paradigms of even the avowed Keynesians.

The result is that the structure of industrial/technological economies that has evolved steadily over the past 200 years has been accounted for

inadequately. Economics is still based on reversible, Newtonian models of locomotion, while, as Nicholas Georgescu-Roegen has shown (*The Entropy Law and the Economic Process*), economies are evolutionary and involve qualitative change over time, generally associated with rises in entropy, and such processes cannot be modeled by arithmetic or econometric means.

This confusion is now at the basis of most national economic policy debates. Therefore, the crisis of microeconomics over the governance of corporations and the crisis of macroeconomic management are two sides of the same conceptual crisis in the discipline of economics itself. While economists continue to fight the Great Depression, the structure of the industrial economies they seek to understand has been irreversibly transformed.

Yet business still claims that wealth is generated in the private sector and then funneled to the public sector via taxes, where it is either transferred to the "unproductive" or used to make social investments in democratically determined public goods and services. This Adam Smith model recognizes little exercise of power or infliction of social costs.

From a vantage point of 200 years ago, with a small population and an empty, resource-rich continent, this Golden Goose model was a fairly accurate view of reality. Today, however, it no longer describes our economy adequately or indicates the extent to which private-sector profits are won by incurring public costs. Indeed, the only portion of the Gross National Product that is growing may be this social costs sector, and because we add these social costs into our GNP as if they were real production, we are further deluded when the GNP goes up.

The major political debate in mixed industrial economies concerns whether inflation or unemployment is the more serious social evil. These twin scourges of mature industrial economies are still portrayed by many economists as tradeoffs: the two horns of a so-called dilemma referred to as the Phillips Curve. However, even Phillips did not postulate a Phillips Curve; in fact, his 1958 paper merely presented a tentative hypothesis of such a possible tradeoff, based on inconclusive data. But the half-life of such ideas is persistent, and the Phillips Curve is still solemnly taught to economics students and appears in most of their textbooks.

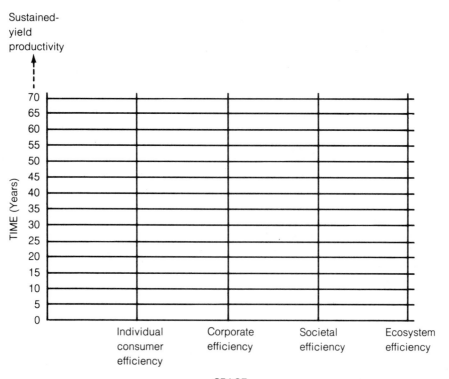

Figure 1.   Time and System Scale Coordinates for Determining "Efficiency"

Western leaders, after their 1977 spring economic summit meeting in London, at last acknowledged, however, that inflation and unemployment could no longer be portrayed as simple tradeoffs. Structural inflation and structural unemployment are both related not so much to the Phillips Curve as to the excessive resource and energy dependence and capital intensity of these economies.

Private production units continue to substitute capital for labor (subsidized by tax credits and other incentives) in order to maximize another illusory variable misnamed "labor productivity" or "output per employee-hour," ignoring other aspects of efficiency as shown in Figure 1. They disregard an inevitable result: More and more workers are shaken out of the bottom of the economy by such processes, and their productivity falls to below zero. In fact, they become part of the soaring social cost side of the national ledger as they collect unemployment and welfare benefits.

Progressive substitution of natural resources and capital for human resources also leads to increased environmental destruction and resource depletion. An environmentally sound society requires full employment and the substitution of idle human resources for natural resources.

As for the inflation phenomenon, I have suggested that its new contributory factors are best understood today from beyond the discipline of economics. Although economists recognize such additional factors as the Vietnam War, the U.S. balance of payments deficits, the role of the OPEC cartel, and increased interdependencies, they still overlook two other sources of inflation.

The first is rooted in the internal dynamics of mature industrial societies and can best be described in terms of general systems theory—that is, "inflation" can be seen from this vantage point as a multiple crisis of suboptimization, where individuals, firms, and institutions simply attempt to "externalize" costs from their own balance sheets and push them onto each other or around the system.

The meta-level tradeoff faced by most of these societies is the axiom that each order of magnitude of technological mastery and managerial scope inevitably dictates an equivalent order of magnitude of costly government coordination and regulation. This tradeoff is essentially that between increased complexity, specialization, and division of labor on the one hand and the necessary levels of communication, coordination, regulation, and transaction costs such societies incur (which leads them, at some point, to become inherently inflationary) on the other. I have termed this syndrome "the Entropy State." In this state, finally, the complexity and interdependence become so unmanageable that the unanticipated social costs incurred exceed the real productivity of the system. Since, as mentioned above, these social costs are *added* to the GNP, this wheel-spinning economic activity expresses itself in increased rates of inflation.

The second cause of inflation, best viewed from the vantage point of thermodynamics, arises from the sharp declines experienced in the productivity of capital investments because of the declining resource base of industrial societies. Since their raw materials and energy must be extracted from ever more degraded and inaccessible deposits, more and more capital must be cycled back into this process, with ever lower net yields. Thus, there are fewer real goods and services available, people work harder for a smaller net return, and money becomes less valuable.

Pollyanna rationalizations about "consuming our way back to prosperity" will not work, and bailing out wounded, obsolescent corporations in order to save jobs will make things worse.

Further evidence of the structural nature of our economic problems is that we have excessive liquidity in this obsolescent corporate sector, which still enjoys high credit ratings and the benefits of retained earnings, although its often-stagnant markets do not warrant new capital investment. In the meantime, in the innovative alternative economy and the small business sector, where the greatest potential for growth and employment lies, capital at affordable interest rates is not available to meet the needs of higher-risk innovators, co-ops, land trusts, urban and rural development corporations, and all the other very important new institutions of the alternative economy of sustained-yield productivity.

Merely lowering interest rates across the board will exact a heavy price of irrational overinvestment in the declining industrial sector for whatever trickle-down benefits accrue to the growing, innovative sector. Thus, markets can no longer be relied on at the macro level to do an adequate job of reallocating societal resources to meet new conditions, just as their inadequacies in reprogramming corporate activities have led to the reexamination of the legitimacy of private enterprise at the micro level. However, as I have tried to show, the new challenges also involve serious concerns over the inaccuracy of its dominant paradigms and its consequent incompetence and irrationality.

The Micro-level Issue: Corporate Governance and the Right to Manage

A sure sign of the growing conceptual ferment is the heightening rhetoric in our mass media. Business last year launched (with some dollars commandeered from the U.S. Commerce Department) a $2.5 million "public service" campaign prepared by the tax-exempt Advertising Council to "educate" Americans about their economic system.

An immediate howl of wrath was registered from a coalition of public-interest and corporate-accountability groups and advocate organizations for consumer and environmental protection, minority rights, and economic alternatives. Their successful challenge of the Federal Communications Commission's fairness doctrine led the way for their counter-advertising campaign, whose theme was "If you think the system is working, ask someone who isn't."

Predictably, economists of all stripes lined themselves up on both sides of the issue. Meanwhile, other skirmishes continue: Corporate-accountability forces back legislation for federal chartering of corporations; electricity consumers win minimum "lifeline" rates from utility commissions; and some of the costly burden of assessing the impacts of technological innovation is shifting back from taxpayers to the innovators.

Can We Learn a Lesson?

Great Britain, the world's oldest industrial society and the cradle of the U.S. political system, provides a useful microcosm of how the last act in the drama of industrialism might play out. In Great Britain, the obsolete and impacted production system, together with the legacies of class oppression and colonial exploitation, is generating soaring social and transaction costs. In lieu of clear policies, inflation is now managing the system. The British syndrome merits our study because it may be a forerunner of difficulties we will encounter.

At its zenith at the turn of this century, Great Britain, an island the size of Maine, controlled a worldwide empire on which, literally, the sun never set. Seventy-five years later, the pound sterling had been battered to its nadir, and the country, facing the prospect of bankruptcy, had called on its last line of credit from the International Monetary Fund.

Typically, Britain's problems have been portrayed in the world press as stemming from the laziness and intransigence of its workforce. This view does not embrace the realities of Britain's deep-seated class system and the extent to which British workers seek revenge and reparations for the past exploitation of the industrial revolution; nor does it take into account the extent of nepotism and incompetence in the ranks of British management.

When the Labor Party emerged with a majority after World War II, the workers had high expectations. These were dashed as they discovered Britain's coffers were almost bare. They had been depleted by war and the dismantling of the empire, and bills were coming due on a host of promises made by their forefathers to colonial people now seeking their fortunes as British citizens. All these social bills were over and above the more familiar social and environmental costs rising in all industrialized societies.

It is little wonder that Britain's political situation began to degenerate into an acrimonious class war over the no-longer-growing pie. The country polarized between labor and capital in an electoral tug of war that seems unable to produce a majority to end the stalemate. This situation was predicted by Joan Robinson, Karl Polanyi, and others, who foresaw that the weakness of market-oriented democracies might result in the forces of labor (votes) and the forces of capital (money) becoming deadlocked. There is the danger that any demagogue who promises to run the railroads on time could get elected, as occurred in Germany and Italy after the Great Depression.

The rhetoric of the current British class struggle is being conducted, on the side of business and management, in terms of the Golden Goose and a conflict between combating inflation and combating unemployment. On the workers' side, the rhetoric is in terms of the "social contract," state socialism, worker control, and, to a lesser extent, the ideologies of Marx, Trotsky, and Mao.

Meanwhile, consumers, unorganized taxpayers, small business people, and farmers look on in horror, while environmentalists, students, and younger trade unionists favor the rhetoric and experimentation of decentralism, alternative technology, and themes similar to those exemplified by the alternative economy in the United States.

It is now possible to prove that inflation and unemployment are not mutually exclusive. Even if British industrialists managed to force the workers to the point of slavery, Great Britain would still experience high rates of inflation. Wages constitute only a fraction of Britain's startling inflation rates. The balance comes from other factors:

1. The basic reality is that Britain's 52 million citizens occupy a land area whose carrying capacity can support only half its population. Even Britain's food import bill is crippling.

2. Fuel and raw materials imports to keep its industrial and consumer sections operating at current levels represent an almost monthly balance-of-payments crisis.

3. Its industrial base is inappropriate, excessively energy-materials intensive, and geared to saturated markets.

4. Its infrastructure—ports, cities, transportation, housing, and communications facilities—is obsolescent, and an excessive fraction of its resources must go to servicing this dead capital.

In addition, British decision making is over-centralized, nepotistic, and error-prone. It still strains to make capital investments in its declining heavy industrial base. It has also committed itself to a catastrophically costly nuclear energy program, which British analysts have pointed out may not produce any net energy for decades. The measure of governmental confusion was illustrated in the recent Labor government decision to bail out the U.S.-based Chrysler Corporation, in order to save (at an approximate prorated cost of $13,000 each) a relatively small number of jobs. Britain will continue to muddle along until the old conceptual framework changes to admit the existence of structural changes and drastically new conditions. Only then can a transition strategy emerge, out of a new consensus about the nature of reality.

We in the United States are facing a similar economic transition and are trapped in a similar conceptual cul-de-sac. But the United States has several important advantages:

1. The United States is still enormously rich; its carrying capacity has not yet been reached. We have perhaps two decades of maneuvering room and flexibility. For example, it has been conservatively estimated that we could squeeze 50 percent of the energy waste out of our economy without affecting our GNP.

2. The United States has a reservoir of flexibility in its political system. It is not yet polarized into the sterile right-left axis that is compounding Britain's problems. Our pluralistic system is best expressed as a circular spectrum (see Figure 2).

This pluralistic system still permits new ideas to emerge and allows for vigorous dialog, which will be necessary to achieve a consensus on the nature of our new conditions. Corporate critics can debate executives; labor, environmentalists, civil rights groups, and consumers can form coalitions on pragmatic concerns. In Britain, by contrast, if you come from a working-class background, you are often considered a traitor to your class for aspiring to a managerial position. Such social desperation brings forth interesting initiatives, one of which we will review briefly.

The Lucas Plan

About two years ago, workers employed by the Lucas Aerospace Company were faced with layoffs because of the loss of military contracts and British government spending cutbacks. Lucas shop stewards developed, on their own time and with their own resources and technical advisors, an alternative corporate plan to convert Lucas Aerospace Company into a producer of sophisticated and intermediate technology-based products to serve civilian markets in Great Britain and overseas.

The Lucas Plan, which would have done credit to a management consulting firm, was backed up by 800 pages of technical documenta-tion, inventorying Lucas's productive capabilities and matching them to unexploited markets that had been surveyed. The plan included a range of new products from solar electric cars, simple electric vehicles, and prosthetic devices for the handicapped to cheap, solar-powered irrigation pumps, cookers, and plowing "snails" (as developed by E. F. Schumacher's Intermediate Technology Development Group) to environmentally benign technologies for home heating and energy generation. This alternative plan for Lucas's future was made a part of the labor-management contract negotiations.

As in the unfolding of a Greek tragedy, Lucas management rejected the plan out of hand. *The Engineer*, in its May 13, 1976 issue, commented, "Management based its reply on a reaffirmation of its established business strategy serving aerospace and defense. In doing so, it paid no regard to the damage to personnel morale inflicted on the highly qualified senior engineers, technicians, and shop-floor engineering workers."

Taking the other side was an editorial in a management-oriented journal on "What Industry Can Learn From the Lucas Affair." It stated that the Lucas Plan was a forerunner of a development that would affect all of British industry and noted a surge of union recruitment of middle management, whose plant authority had been emasculated by paternalistic corporate head offices. It warned that in any atmosphere of layoffs, workers would be more likely to anticipate issues, such as the obsolescence of a company's product line, in the same way the Lucas workers had.

The editorial even conceded the "legitimacy" of the issues raised, but could not deal conceptually with the plan's espousal of less capital-intensive, intermediate technologies and products, whereby the capital cost of creating and maintaining each workplace would be reduced. Parroting management's error in factor mixing and its self-destructive dedication to capital-intensive technology under new conditions of capital shortage, the editorial summed up the dying industrial position: "What the Lucas employees should be pressing for is greater automation—at the same time ensuring that the displaced men are found other jobs."

For their part, the Lucas workers submitted the plan as a direct challenge to the Lucas management's competence and right to manage. Even

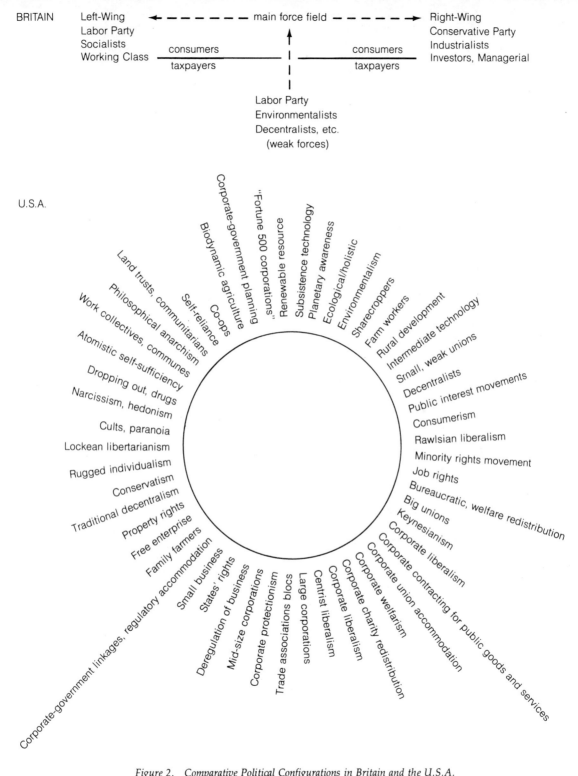

BRITAIN

Left-Wing
Labor Party
Socialists
Working Class

◄ – – – – main force field – – – – ►

consumers

taxpayers

consumers

taxpayers

Right-Wing
Conservative Party
Industrialists
Investors, Managerial

Labor Party
Environmentalists
Decentralists, etc.
(weak forces)

U.S.A.

Corporate-government planning
Biodynamic agriculture
"Fortune 500 corporations"
Renewable resource
Subsistence technology
Planetary awareness
Ecological/holistic
Environmentalism
Sharecroppers
Farm workers
Rural development
Intermediate technology
Small, weak unions
Decentralists
Public interest movements
Consumerism
Rawlsian liberalism
Minority rights movement
Job rights
Bureaucratic, welfare redistribution
Big unions
Keynesianism
Corporate liberalism
Corporate contracting for public goods and services
Corporate union accommodation
Corporate charity redistribution
Corporate welfarism
Corporate liberalism
Centrist liberalism
Large corporations
Trade associations blocs
Corporate protectionism
Mid-size corporations
Deregulation of business
States' rights
Small business
Corporate-government linkages, regulatory accommodation
Family farmers
Free enterprise
Property rights
Traditional decentralism
Conservatism
Rugged individualism
Lockean libertarianism
Cults, paranoia
Narcissism, hedonism
Dropping out, drugs
Atomistic self-sufficiency
Work collectives, communes
Philosophical anarchism
Land trusts, communitarians
Self-reliance
Co-ops

Figure 2. Comparative Political Configurations in Britain and the U.S.A.

if management had accepted the plan instantly and agreed to invest in the modest conversion, it is unlikely that the workers would have been satisfied. The bottom line for them was to demonstrate management's incompetence and embarrass their bosses publicly.

What we in the United States would consider the pragmatic solution—worker stock options, bonuses, more participation in production decisions—would have been rejected by the Lucas workers as a "co-option" and traitorous to their class solidarity. Thus, the atmosphere in Britain is one of worker confrontation of the managerial class, and only victory over the bosses is enough to assuage workers' feelings.

Yugoslavian Approach

Equally instructive and less dismal examples of the redefinition of the rights of capital are available in Europe. Most of them involve various forms of accommodation by management of the aspirations of workers for more control over their working lives, constitutionally defined rights to job security, and democratic participation in shaping industrial production and the goals it serves.

In Yugoslavia, these aspirations are well articulated and constitutionally recognized. Yugoslavian concepts of property rights and responsibilities are similar in many ways to those of our own founding fathers.

For example, Benjamin Franklin's view in 1785 was that "superfluous property is the creature of society." He said: "Simple and mild laws were sufficient to guard the property that was merely necessary. When, by virtue of the first laws, part of the society accumulated wealth and grew powerful, they enacted others more severe and would protect their property at the expense of humanity. This was abusing their power and commencing a tyranny."

In Yugoslavia, there is a similar distinction between property rights to assure personal security and autonomy (a greater percentage of Yugoslavs than Americans own their own homes) and the right endlessly to accumulate property that may then be used to oppress others.

In the Yugoslavian economy, private enterprises are legal up to a scale employing 15 workers. Any enterprise employing more than 15 must govern itself with a workers council. Potential workers

councils can also draw up a business plan and present it to one of the country's worker-managed banks; a loan committee of peers will decide whether the enterprise should be capitalized.

The key tenets of the Yugoslavs appear to be:

1. Keeping industries, and thus populations, decentralized and preventing the catastrophic urbanization that has plagued market-driven industrialism all over the planet.

2. Maximizing worker participation in their unique brand of economic democracy and limiting the arbitrary right to manage associated with capital in market economies.

3. Avoiding the equally feared pitfalls of Stalinist, bureaucratic communism and centrally planned state capitalism, which they see as characterizing much of Western Europe and the United States.

However, as a small country situated between the Soviet Union and a European economy it sees as dominated by U.S.-based multinationals, Yugoslavia is subject to attempts to bring in 50-50 joint ventures to build large, capital-intensive facilities, such as a petrochemical plant and a nuclear power station. Such dabbling with Western capital-intensive technology will significantly alter the decentralized character and modest well-being of its society, and may well lead to the centralized decision making and concomitant inequality it has so assiduously sought to avoid.

Other European Plans

Basically, the Yugoslav insistence on smaller, decentralized enterprises is spreading and focuses attention on the fact that human beings are not yet competent at national planning or at distributing surpluses. It highlights the intellectual arrogance of administrators, managers, and bureaucrats, whether planners of multinational corporations or of national governments. In this same spirit of growing humility, the 1976–1980 French regional plan includes new "Small is Beautiful" incentives to decentralize France's industries and limit their size.

European socialists and labor movements are turning away from old concepts of highly centralized socialism and nationalization of industries, and both Italian and French communists have demonstrated their freedom from Moscow. European socialism, as political scientist Norman Birnbaum has pointed out, has deep, *precapitalist* cultural roots, based on earlier notions of community, religious ideas about the value of work, and human dignity.

Human emancipation in Europe now focuses on expanding economic democracy as well; from the worker-management parity now achieved on German corporate boards to Sweden's much-discussed Meidner Plan, which would transfer 20 percent of the annual profits of all Swedish companies with 50 or more employees to workers' trust funds over a 10- or 15-year period if enacted.

Other proposals favor specifically changing corporate charters so that they are managed, not for the primary benefit of their stockholders, but to balance the interests of all "stakeholders," including stockholders, employees, customers, franchisees, and the general public.

Similar ideas are often rhetorically embraced by U.S. corporate executives, but if such existing informal power is acknowledged, these managers are surely courting its constitutional legitimation, as by Ralph Nader's proposed federal chartering.

One thing is clear. Global communications assure continued exportation to the United States of all these European initiatives in decentralizing economic power, as our own delegations visit Norway's Industrial Democracy Project and Sweden's self-managed Volvo plants, and as European delegates comprised half of those attending the Third International Conference on Self-Management held at the American University, Washington, D.C., in June 1976.

Self-management in the United States and Canada is in its infancy by European standards and is viewed as mostly timid efforts at "job enrichment," which, as one Canadian theorist stated, were "merely cosmetic efforts to co-opt workers into more efficient self-exploitation so as to increase corporate profits."

However, unions such as the United Auto Workers are taking up the cause of improving the quality of working life. The UAW is also countering inequitably shared costs and benefits of automation by calling for work spreading.

It is hardly surprising that the United States is considered backward in moving toward more industrial democracy, in spite of the fact that, as Eberts and Whitton point out in the *American Sociological Review* of December 1970, Alexis de Tocqueville's case that we might end up as a "manufacturing aristocracy" is more persuasive than that of Marx. The U.S. resource base and the rapid exploitation that free-market systems allow have produced an avalanche of goods and increased incomes that have kept workers reasonably well satisfied up to now. In many cases, they have been dealt in with stock options, pension plans, bonuses, and other incentives.

Indeed, Peter Drucker has claimed that through the growth of employee pension funds, we have unwittingly become a socialist economy. However, this case is unpersuasive, since it does not constitute socialism in the accepted sense, nor does it acknowledge that the workers do not control or vote these stock holdings. They are controlled by fiduciaries and banks, normally much more closely allied with the interests of management than of labor.

It is ironic that employee stock ownership trusts (ESOTs), designed to aid workers acquire stock or actually purchase companies from their employers, could result in workers being palmed off with unprofitable "bum steers." Legislative support of these trusts was won at the price of further corporate tax credits. Thus their costs were spread onto taxpayers rather than shared with stockholders and managers.

It is even possible that the ESOTs might slow down the economic transition to a sustainable economy by giving workers an additional stake in declining industries. Negotiating this transition will certainly require greater worker participation in order to speed the flow of innovative ideas and help create a consensus for concerted action in all sectors of our economy.

Bridging mechanisms will also be needed. A prime example is the Canadian Local Initiatives Program (LIP), which functions as a counter-cyclical fiscal program for creating public service-type jobs. But whereas U.S. job programs are centrally controlled and often abused or ineffective, the LIP jobs are created by funding community-developed projects at the local level. The result is a much closer matching of locally unemployed workers to local needs, with a minimum of central bureaucracy. Other bridging mechanisms that might serve as models include the purchase of local plants by residents of an area and their municipalities. In a recent case, the town of Herkimer, N.Y., its residents, and the plant's workers bought a library supply/furniture company from Sperry-Rand Corporation in the face of a threatened shutdown.

Other economic innovations in the pipeline include state development banks, modeled after the successful Bank of North Dakota, and community-development corporations to help launch co-ops, land trusts, and all the other organs of the new, sustainable productive system and its alternative institutions and technologies. The newly organized Massachusetts Community Development Finance Corporation is such a financial institution, empowered to buy stock in any enterprise that is owned in common by residents in a given geographical area.

All these entrepreneurial efforts are informed by an understanding of use value, rather than mere exchange value, and are developing theories of household economics that verify the efficiencies of small-scale operations and their success in meeting the needs and goals of their own participants. In the future, it is likely that most productive enterprises will begin to define their success more broadly than in the old terms of "bottom-line profits." They will move toward redefining success in terms of their own participants' varied criteria and goals. The rigid, totalitarian effects of the single "profit" yardstick will be relieved and lost pluralism will be restored to our economic life.

Lastly, a prerequisite in the ongoing transformation of concepts of the rights and responsibilities of capital, property, and management is the redefinition of profit. We need to enact legislation to invalidate the destructive and erroneous notions of speculators concerning "free lunches"

and "windfall profits," which are usually won at the expense of the environment or other people, or charged to future generations.

The longer-term, more holistic view of planetary interdependence must eventually prevail because it is scientifically accurate. Our narrow concepts of time and space must be expanded so that we see that in a large enough context, all our individual self-interests are identical as well as coterminous with community and species self-interest.

This view must modify our illusory concepts of today, whereby "profit" is becoming little more than "creative accounting" and externalizing costs to others or society. "Profit" is now too vague and unscientific a concept to program private resource allocations accurately. It should give way to specific system-defined efficiency criteria and the new accounting model by which "profit" is redefined as "success in terms of the democratically determined goals of the participants in the productive enterprise."

These enterprises must be governed with legislative checks and balances incorporating more accurate concepts of efficiencies of scale and quantification or short- and long-term social costs, as reflected in a more appropriate measure of GNP. Japan's Net National Welfare indicator, by which "wealth" sheds some of its present connotations of capital and material accumulation and gives way to a redefinition as "human enrichment," could serve as a guide. Even then, a brighter future will depend on our ability to mesh our efforts at retooling our institutions and our technological means. Still greater efforts must be expended on retooling ourselves, our concepts, and our paradigms and recycling our culture.

How to Put Corporate Responsibility Into Practice

Terry W. McAdam

In recent years pressure has mounted for corporate action on social problems. Corporate managers increasingly realize that they must allocate resources wisely to achieve worthwhile results and eliminate or minimize unproductive or counter-productive efforts. The question that faces business leaders today is not whether we should act more responsibly, but how we should do it. In the following article author Terry McAdam addresses this question by presenting an approach to social responsibility. His proposal is noteworthy not because it provides an irrefutable way for

Reprinted with permission of the publisher from Business and Society Review/Innovation, No. 6 (Summer 1973), pp. 8–16.

business to meet its responsibilities to society but because it provides a framework within which individuals and organizations may seriously begin to evaluate social responsibilities. Mr. McAdam's presentation of categories of social responsibility moves the social responsibility debate to its next logical level of moral awareness: what should business do and how should it do it?

Most early corporate ventures into the arena of social responsibility were reflex actions. Perceived social pressure and the threat of increasing legal pressure prompted management to react intuitively and subjectively to social responsibility issues. Today, such "knee jerk" responses to the wide array of problems and pressures are poorly received by just about everyone. The number of social responsibility issues has multiplied and their complexity has increased. Corporations are no longer regarded as purely economic institutions, but social ones as well. As more and more companies respond to the mounting pressures for corporate action, corporate managers are realizing that they must allocate their resources more systematically and rationally to achieve meaningful results and minimize unproductive and counterproductive efforts. The question is: How?

Here is one approach a company can take to tackle the social responsibility issues that confront it. It includes some basic steps familiar to most corporate managers—analyzing the issues, evaluating performance, setting priorities, allocating resources to those priorities, and implementing policies and programs that deal with the issues within resource constraints.

Stimulants to Action

In the past five years, more corporations than ever before have begun to grapple with the issues grouped under the rubric of "corporate social responsibility." For example, research by H. Eilbert and I. R. Parnet indicates that over 90 per cent of the largest corporations in the United States have now assigned formal responsibility for such issues to either an officer or a high-level committee. Before 1965, less than 20 per cent of these companies had such a position.

Three developments seem to be responsible for stimulating so many companies to take action:

1. *Pressures on corporations to deal with social responsibility issues have intensified.* According to Louis Harris and Associates, the proportion of the general public having "a great deal of con-

fidence" in top business leaders declined from 55 per cent to 27 per cent in 1973. This same decline in confidence shows up in answers to more detailed questions about corporate performance in *both* business and social areas. Several reasons appear to be behind this dissatisfaction: (a) irresponsible behavior by a few corporate managers; (b) widespread and growing public disenchantment with all large institutions and their leadership; and (c) the increased popularization of social responsibility issues by the press and groups such as the Council on Economic Priorities and the Corporate Accountability Research Group. In addition, the proliferation of proxy proposals and stockholder suits indicates that the public, and public advocates, are tending more and more to hold management accountable for corporate behavior. As Ralph Nader has said, "A way to get more corporate responsibility is simply to recognize the principle that people who have power and make decisions should be more accountable for the consequences of their decisions and not . . . insulated to the degree they are at the present time from the arm of the law through corporate shielding."

Government has added to the pressures by placing more consumer protection/social responsibility legislation on the books in the past ten years than in the prior one hundred. The number of proposed bills dealing with social responsibility issues and the corporation has skyrocketed. Local community pressures for corporate involvement also appear to be increasing. Executives across the country report a steady stream of requests for their active participation in local affairs and for corporate cash (and materials) contributions to new causes. Moreover, local regulations and laws have multiplied (e.g., local laws banning high-phosphate-content detergents).

Finally, some executives—particularly those whose plants and offices are in deteriorating urban areas—feel physically threatened by the hostile attitudes and behavior surfacing in their communities. They find themselves forced to deal with social issues to safeguard not only their corporate profit performance but, more important, their employees and property.

2. *Many of the arguments against some form of corporate involvement have, for the most part, been dismantled or refuted by persuasive counterarguments.* Since the subject has been discussed and debated in the literature ad nauseam, this article assumes that the reader generally agrees that some form of socially responsible corporate behavior is both appropriate and beneficial to the corporation. A first cut at how to evaluate such behavior is given later on.

3. *Corporate managers are adopting new attitudes about the kinds of activities their companies should undertake.* Many businessmen and women are taking a broader interest as individuals in the work, life styles, and social fabric that surround them. At home and with friends, they are engaging in more substantive discussions of their work and its social implications. There appears to be a greater willingness to question institutional objectives, strategies and performance. While not a new phenomenon, it seems clearly on the upswing. The net result of the expanding concerns of today's business people has been a growing interest in the issues of corporate social responsibility. As economist Robert Heilbroner puts it, in *In the Name of Profit*, "I suspect that . . . businessmen themselves recoil from the implication that they are 'only' moneymakers. One of the problems of the theology of capitalism is that capitalists do not like to act like the creatures of pure self-interest that they are supposed to be." Moreover, as these attitudes develop and spread, corporations are finding it advantageous to improve their performance records on social responsibility issues in order to attract and hold high-quality personnel, many of whom are also embracing new sentiments about the social responsibilities of business.

With this background in mind, how can a company begin to evaluate its present record on social responsibility issues? How can it reflect that concern in its corporate objectives, strategy, and programs? How can it deploy its resources to strengthen performance in the future? And, should such actions prove useful and effective, how can they be integrated into the everyday management processes?

Approaching the Problem

Though no easy solution is conveniently at hand, some helpful ideas can be distilled from corporations' past experiences and current experiments in dealing with the wide spectrum of social responsibility issues. Businessmen we have talked to in different industries say that to make any headway with social responsibility issues inside large and complex corporations, one must be positive and flexible, adhere to several ground rules, and recognize the major pitfalls. Our own modest experience to date confirms this.

1. *Be positive and flexible.* A *positive* approach shows up in management's determination to seek progress in agreed-upon areas in an agreed-upon time. Implicit here is a common understanding of the facts and the issues in the selected areas. A *flexible* approach shows up in the organization's willingness to explore a variety of "problem" definitions, performance measures, program solutions, and other actions required to achieve the progress desired. Moreover, it means not losing heart if progress is slow or if the positive intentions of the effort are not immediately recognized as such by some corporate constituencies.

2. *Adhere to several ground rules.* From corporate experience and the literature, we find several valuable rules for getting the program off to a good start:

   Make a top management commitment to appraise corporate social responsibility performance objectively and to change corporate policy, if appropriate, on the basis of the facts and information developed. This appraisal will rest on definitions and measures of social responsibility which must be developed as part of the overall evaluative process. A clear commitment and subsequent action by the chief executive officer can enormously improve social responsibility performance— perhaps more so than any other single factor.

   Get line management to participate in this performance appraisal. Line managers and members of the corporation's operation units should be encouraged to gather and evaluate facts on performance and to develop alternative proposals for changing or correcting corporate performance in their areas of responsibility. Their participation in developing new behavior patterns increases 100-fold the program's chances of success.

Control expectations throughout the organization by setting modest goals initially, and then push hard to raise them as progress is made. In addition, it is wise to create an experimental atmosphere that encourages people to try new analytic and programmatic approaches and to accept the fact that some mistakes may be made.

Concentrate early efforts on understanding company performance and on deciding what action to take, rather than on how and what to report to the corporation's various constituencies.

Install a formal follow-up procedure. Developing and implementing policies to upgrade a company's overall social responsibility performance is a long-term proposition. It requires repeated efforts with correction, follow-up, and lots of hard work.

3. *Recognize major pitfalls.* Despite good intentions, sound plans, and enthusiasm, a company can still run into pitfalls in dealing with social responsibility issues. It may find, for example, that progress and performance are difficult to measure quantitatively; the complexity of some of the issues consumes "excessive" analytical time; agreement on the parameters of analysis (and even concern) is hard to reach; and addressing social responsibility issues generates internal friction at many levels of the corporation.

If the company recognizes that these pitfalls exist and that it must take them in its stride, it can soon get down to the real work of analyzing social responsibility issues.

Analyze the Issues

The quantitative measurement of corporate performance in most social responsibility areas is still a crude science, at best. But despite this state of the art, a corporation desiring to tackle the most crucial issues can do so. The following seven steps serve as a starting point:

1. *Identify and define performance categories relevant to a social responsibility review of the company.* This step can be completed by segregating social responsibility issues into categories of corporate action, using the following types of questions as a guide: Are the action areas measured by the same kinds of performance yardsticks? Do they tend to be managed by similar organizational units? Do they affect one specific constituency? And so on. The objective is to break down the totality of the corporation's actions and their related social impact into a manageable number of categories for analysis and evaluation. Summarized in Table 1 is a set of categories recently developed by one U.S. corporation; these may serve as thought-starters.

These categories are broken down into greater detail in Table 2.

These categories are limited in number and are not mutually exclusive; they contain at least two issues that are relatively new—environmental control and minority/women hiring and advancement. Furthermore, they may not be comprehensive from some points of view (e.g., military production is not included). And no doubt other issues will emerge from the shifting social scene—but the point is to group issues and activities into a manageable number of categories and get started.

Table 1.   Categories of Social Responsibility Issues

a.	Product line (e.g. dangerous products)
b.	Marketing practices (e.g. misleading advertising)
c.	Employee education and training
d.	Corporate philanthropy
e.	Environmental control
f.	External relations (including community development, government relations, disclosure of information, and international operations)
g.	Employee relations, benefits, and satisfaction with work
h.	Minority and women employment and advancement
i.	Employee safety and health

Table 2.   Categories of Social Responsibility Issues

Product Line

Internal standards for product
  Quality, e.g., does it last?
  Safety, e.g., can it harm users or children finding it?
  Disposal, e.g., is it biodegradable?
  Design, e.g., will its use or even "easy" misuse cause
  pain, injury or death?

Average product life comparisons versus
  Competition
  Substitute products
  Internal standards of state-of-the-art
  Regular built-in obsolescence

Product performance
  Efficacy, e.g., does it do what it is supposed to do?
  Guarantees/warranties, e.g., are guarantees sufficient,
  reasonable?
  Service policy
  Service availability
  Service pricing
  Utility

Packaging
  Environmental impact (degree of disposability;
  recycleability)
  Comparisons with competition (type and extent of
  packaging)

Marketing Practices

Sales practices
  Legal standards
  "Undue" pressure (a qualitative judgment)

Credit practices against legal standards

Accuracy of advertising claims—specific government
complaints

Consumer complaints about marketing practices
  Clear explanation of credit terms
  Clear explanation of purchase price
  Complaint answering policy
  —Answered at all
  —Investigated carefully
  —Grievances redressed (and cost)
  —Remedial action to prevent future occurrences

Adequate consumer information on
  Product use, e.g., dosage, duration of use, etc.
  Product misuse

Fair pricing
  Between countries
  Between states
  Between locations
Packaging

Employee Education and Training

Policy on leaves of absence for
  Full-time schooling
  Courses given during working hours

Dollars spent on training
  Formal vocational training
  Training for disadvantaged worker
  OJT (very difficult to isolate)
  Tuition (job-related versus nonjob-related)
  Special upgrading and career development programs
  Compare versus competition

Special training program results (systematic evaluations)
  Number trained in each program per year
  Cost per trainee (less subsidy)
  Number or percent workers still with company

Plans for future programs

Career training and counseling

Failure rates

Extend personnel understanding
  Jobs
  Skills required later
  Incentive system now available
  Specific actions for promotion

Corporate Philanthropy

Contribution performance
  By category, for example:
  —Art
  —Education
  —Poverty
  —Health
  —Community development
  —Public service advertising
  Dollars (plus materials and manhours if available)
  —As a percent of pretax earnings
  —Compared to competition

Selection criteria for contributions

Procedures for performance tracking of recipient
institutions or groups

Programs for permitting and encouraging employee
involvement in social projects
  On company time
  After hours only
  Use of company facilities and equipment
  Reimbursement of operating units for replaceable
  "lost" time
  Manpower support
  —Number of people
  —Man-hours

Table 2.   Categories of Social Responsibility Issues (Continued)

Extent of employee involvement in philanthropy decision-making

Environmental Control

Measurable pollution resulting from
  Acquisition of raw materials
  Production processes
  Products
  Transportation of intermediate and finished products

Violations of government (federal, state, and local) standards

Cost estimates to correct current deficiencies

Extent to which various plants exceed current legal standards, e.g., particulate matter discharged

Resources devoted to pollution control
  Capital expenditures (absolute and percent)
  R & D investments
  Personnel involved full time; part time
  Organizational "strength" of personnel involved

Competitive company performance, e.g., capital expenditures

Effort to monitor new standards as proposed

Programs to keep employees alert to spills and other pollution-related accidents

Procedures for evaluating environmental impact of new packages or products.

External Relations

Community Development
Support of minority and community enterprises through
  Purchasing
  Subcontracting

Investment practices
  Ensuring equal opportunity before locating new facilities
  Identifying opportunities to serve community needs through business expansion (e.g., housing rehabilitation or teaching machines)
  Funds in minority banks

Government Relations
Specific input to public policy through research and analysis

Participation and development of business/government programs

Political contributions

Disclosure of Information/Communications
Extent of public disclosure of performance by activity category

Measure of employee understanding of programs such as:
  Pay and benefits
  Equal opportunity policies and programs
  Position of major economic or political issues (as appropriate)

Relations/communications with constituencies such as stockholders, fund managers, major customers, and so on

International
Comparisons of policy and performance between countries and versus local standards

Employee Relations, Benefits, and Satisfaction With Work

Comparisons with competition (and/or national averages)
  Salary and wage levels
  Retirement plans
  Turnover and retention by level
  Profit sharing
  Day care and maternity
  Transportation
  Insurance, health programs and other fringes
  Participation in ownership of business through stock purchases

Comparisons of operating units on promotions, terminations, hires against breakdowns of
  Age
  Sex
  Race
  Education level

Performance review system and procedures for communication with employees whose performance is below average

Promotion policy—equitable and understood

Transfer policy

Termination policy (i.e., how early is "notice" given)

General working environment and conditions
  Physical surroundings
  —Heat
  —Ventilation
  —Space/person
  —Lighting
  —Air conditioning
  —Noise
  Leisure, recreation, cultural opportunities

Fringe benefits as a percent of salary for various salary levels

Table 2.   Categories of Social Responsibility Issues (Continued)

Evaluation of employee benefit preferences (questions can be posed as choices)

Evaluation of employee understanding of current fringe benefits

Union/industrial relations
  Grievances
  Strikes

Confidentiality and security of personal data

Minority and Women Employment and Advancement

Current hiring policies in relation to the requirements of all affirmative action programs

Specific program of accountability for performance

Company versus local, industry and national performance
  Number and percent minority and women employees hired by various job classifications over last 5 years
  Number and percent of new minority and women employees in last 2 to 3 years by job classification
  Minority and women and nonminority turnover
  Indictments for discriminatory hiring practices

Percent minority and women employment in major facilities relative to minority labor force available locally

Number of minority group and women members in positions of high responsibility

Promotion performance of minority groups and women

Specific hiring and job upgrading goals established for minority groups and women
  Basic personnel strategy
  Nature and cost of special recruiting efforts
  Risks taken in hiring minority groups and women

Programs to ease integration of minority groups and women into company operations, e.g., awareness efforts

Specialized minority and women career counseling

Special recruiting efforts for minority groups and women

Opportunities for the physically handicapped
  Specific programs
  Numbers employed

Employee Safety and Health

Work environment measures
  OSHA requirements (and extent of compliance)
  Other measures of working conditions

Safety performance
  Accident frequency (number of hours lost per million worked)
  Accident frequency (number of lost time accidents per million hours)
  Disabling injuries
  Fatalities

Services provided (and cost of programs and manpower) for:
  Addictive treatment (alcohol, narcotics)
  Mental health

Spending for safety equipment
  Required by law/regulation
  Not required

Special safety programs (including safety instruction)

Comparisons of health and safety performance with competition and industry in general

Developments/innovations in health and safety

Employee health measures, e.g., sick days, examinations

Food facilities
  Cost/serving to employee; to company
  Nutritional evaluation

---

2. *Briefly review performance across all activity categories in order to identify areas of high vulnerability or opportunity, and to get an overview for resource allocation decisions that must be made later.* A simple way to get started is to pose, and attempt to answer, a series of questions about corporate activities. For example:

Is anyone's life, health, or safety endangered by our actions or products?

Do we comply with all laws and regulations—federal, state, and local?

What are the major in-house concerns regarding our social responsibility performance?

What will be the impact of continuing a given activity—on our employees, customers, stockholders, and the public in general?

If we change our actions will our constituencies understand why? Will they misinterpret our motives?

Is new legislation likely to be implemented which will regulate this activity?

What action has our competition taken? Industry in general?

Can we estimate the total cost of each activity area?

After attempting to answer such questions, a company should be able to assess which activity areas are most vulnerable to criticism, which are most in need of being improved either by increasing current efforts or implementing new ones, and which present opportunities to contribute to the solution of social problems while expanding the business.

3. *Select the most critical activity areas and review performance in depth.* This step can be initiated by meshing a first cut at perceived activity categories (from step 1) with the types of questions posed in step 2. It should be extended, whenever possible, by developing specific quantitative data. If quantitative measurement is not possible, either because facts are not available or reliable measures of performance have not yet been developed, one can retreat to a description of management procedures and policy to estimate qualitatively the corporation's position or performance. Table 2 illustrates potential areas to analyze in reviewing each activity category. They are by no means complete. New measures and analytical approaches can be added every day. Any company seriously evaluating its performance will no doubt add detailed measures in each category when tailoring this general approach to its own situation and data.

4. *Develop a basic strategy for each activity area.* This strategy should not dictate specific program responses, but should help to provide general guidelines for major resource allocation decisions, and integrate social responsibility thinking into everyday corporate planning, evaluating, and management. Table 3 summarizes various philosophies and the level of effort most likely to flow from them. A company can, of course, modify these general level-of-effort options for different activity categories. Admittedly, the strategic choices made will be influenced by the personal values of the top executives and the type of organization they and their associates would like the corporation to be in the future.

Having set a general level of effort, the company can define the boundaries of the major activity areas by answering questions such as, Which activities can, and must, we

Table 3

Social Responsibility Philosophy	Resulting Level of Effort
Lead the industry	Substantial experimentation and applied research; some failures should be anticipated when breaking new ground
Be progressive	Large effort to grapple with full range of issues; some breaking of new ground likely
Do only what is required	Careful investigation of all requirements, plus advance planning for likely new requirements
Fight all the way	No action other than defensive reaction to likely criticism/investigations

accept responsibility for now? In the near future? How far should our responsibility go? Should other members of the industry be involved? How?

5. *Set specific realistic objectives for new programs or for revisions in existing activities.* The discipline of setting specific objectives is worthwhile for three reasons: (a) It encourages managers to think carefully about the resources allocated to each program; (b) It makes the goals clear to everyone; and (c) Most important, this is the point at which possible trade-offs between short-term "social responsibility accomplishment" and short-term profit can begin to emerge and be evaluated.

6. *Develop, implement, and monitor the new or revised programs.* If the line units have participated in the steps so far, they will likely have many practical ideas about the programs needed to improve or change activities in their areas. In addition to them, however, analytic support from some staff or other group may be needed to ensure that the analysis is objective and that effective new programs are developed. The work done in developing, implementing, and monitoring the programs should be aimed at making sure that the projects respond to the results of a specific performance review; the objectives for proposed programs are clearly defined; resource trade-off decisions are based on a "best possible"

understanding of the costs and likely benefits of alternative programs: and programs that are implemented remain effective. Feedback on performance is vital to ensure that the organization sustains its commitment to action.

No matter how well one has laid the groundwork, however, operating units may still resist the changes. This resistance will decrease, it is to be hoped, as companies begin to reap the benefits of the new programs.

7. *Integrate this approach into the basic management processes*. Ultimately, if sustained attention is to be paid to social responsibility performance, this approach must be integrated into the basic processes of managing the business, from corporate planning and strategy to individual job descriptions and incentive programs. Without this integration, the approach is a meaningless exercise.

Organize the Effort

How a company organizes its social responsibility effort depends on many variables—the quality of personnel involved, the degree of their commitment to the social responsibility issues, their ability to secure line management input and support for policy changes, and their capacity to follow through on implementing new programs. The best organizational arrangement for one company may be quite inappropriate for another. Five possible approaches include:

1. *The Officer*. To be effective in an organization of any size, the officer must be in a reasonably high-level position, well-respected, and supported by a quality staff. If his charter embraces the full range of corporate social responsibility issues, he will have to be prepared to devote most of his time to the task. Because of the heavy time commitment, a company electing this approach generally rotates the job every two to three years to ensure that qualified managers will be receptive to such an assignment. With each change of officer, however, comes the risk that the continuity and drive of the effort will slacken. This is particularly true if the company has jumped into the task without any corporate responsibility strategy or "game plan." Thus, changeover procedures must be carefully

thought out for this approach to work effectively.

2. *The Task Force*. The task force is a commonly used approach. Since it tends, however, to be crisis-oriented (as are many corporate responses to social responsibility issues), it is not very effective for mid- to long-range planning. Another drawback of the task force is that it is less able to implement changes in operating practices because few permanent lines of communication exist between it and company operating units. Finally, task force members are nearly always part-time participants in the review and development process, and unless they have first-rate staff support, they may not acquire sufficient understanding of specific problems. On the plus side, the task force approach is a good way to get an activity started quickly. If team members are carefully selected, the task force can bring together a group knowledgeable in many key operating elements of the business. Thus, the important factors to make this option effective are good people, a focused effort, and quality staff work.

3. *The Permanent Board Committee*. A board-level committee has several arguments in its favor:

As tangible evidence of top management's commitment to deal with social responsibility issues, it is a stimulus for the effort to gain support at key operating levels.

With the muscle of individual board members behind the effort, the review procedure can be rigorous and thorough.

Since most board members have a broad perspective, their approach to social responsibility issues can be more comprehensive.

Outside board members often can bring new insights to the subject and thus can contribute significantly to the effort.

To make this approach work, however, the board committee must be supported by adequate staff and have access to objective and quantitative reviews of operating performance. Since board members are further away from daily operations, their need for good support and information is imperative if they are to fully understand the problems. With proper backup, this option can be a highly effective one. Its principal drawback is that it may be difficult to maintain a reasonable rate of progress because of the heavy time demands on board members.

4. *The Permanent Management Committee.* A permanent management committee has many of the attributes of the board committee. It has the same need for good staff work, sufficient time commitment of committee members, and specific background information for decision making. Though a management committee is more familiar with the business than a board committee, it may be hampered somewhat by a lack of objectivity.

5. *The Permanent Organization Group.* Having within the organization structure a permanent department or group continuously engaged in analyzing, resolving, and responding to corporate social responsibility issues may be the best option of all. Such a group can, over time, build up stronger communication lines than any of the other approaches. Through regular feedback, it can keep the company alert to issues and ensure continuity of analytic efforts. It also offers continuing evidence of top management's commitment to social responsibility. The only danger is that a permanent organizational unit risks drifting out of the mainstream of activity and becoming too narrowly focused on one pet issue. Although such specialization can be a positive influence on company performance in the chosen area, it prevents management from dealing systematically with the remaining issues.

Regardless of which organizational option, or combination of options, is chosen, the likelihood of positive results is enhanced if:

The organizational unit reports progress regularly to top management, reaffirming top-level interest.

Analysts working on corporate social responsibility issues have full access to company data once they have secured management's agreement to a general line of inquiry.

The unit keeps detailed performance records and formalizes analytic procedures so that subsequent efforts can build on knowledge acquired in earlier efforts.

Reviews of individual performance in social responsibility activities are integrated into the corporation's overall personnel or performance review system as confidence grows in which factors to measure.

In net, there is still a great deal to be learned about how to analyze and respond to corporate social responsibility issues. This article has proposed some analytic and organizational approaches that have emerged from the limited and occasionally mixed corporate experience to date. Though progress in strengthening management techniques for dealing with social responsibility issues may be slow, the learning process seems to have begun in earnest. In one sense, this effort is just in time. The pace of change is accelerating as new issues are raised and new pressures are brought to bear. As techniques for analyzing and responding to corporate social responsibility issues are sharpened and integrated into the ongoing practices of planning and managing the business, corporate efforts in this area should become much more effective. Should corporations take the first step? As Oliver Wendell Holmes once said, "The opportunity and challenge is there to go beyond the merely profitable and take part in the action and the passion of our time. . . ."

Buddhist Economics

E. F. Schumacher

As implied in this chapter, economics is not a science of absolute and unchanging truths. On the contrary, many fundamental presuppositions support the economic edifice which has evolved in Western society and within which we continue to operate. These, as we've seen, may underlie a great number of the moral problems evident in business today.

E.F. Schumacher, Small Is Beautiful: Economics As If People Mattered *(New York: Harper & Row; London: Blond & Briggs, 1973), pp. 50–58. Copyright ©1973 by E. F. Schumacher. Reprinted by permission of the publishers.*

But what are the alternatives? What, if any, optional assumptions do we have which may lead to alternative, and perhaps morally more desirable, courses of economic behavior?

In the following selection, exerpted from his book Small is Beautiful: Economics As If People Mattered, *E. F. Schumacher, founder-chairperson of the Intermediate Technology Development Group in London, addresses this problem. In essence, the author contrasts the views of modern Western economists with Buddhist economists on the function of work, employment, the purpose of economic activity, and the use of natural resources. Schumacher concludes that it is not a choice between one or the other of these economic philosophies, but the task of finding "the right path of development, the Middle Way between materialist heedlessness and traditionalist immobility." The great strength of this essay is that Schumacher succinctly and provocatively brings into question many of the economic axioms of modern industrial life in the West. He makes us ponder the thorny moral issues that rise in the soil of these postulates.*

"Right Livelihood" is one of the requirements of the Buddha's Noble Eightfold Path. It is clear, therefore, that there must be such a thing as Buddhist economics.

Buddhist countries have often stated that they wish to remain faithful to their heritage. So Burma: "The New Burma sees no conflict between religious values and economic progress. Spiritual health and material well-being are not enemies: they are natural allies." Or: "We can blend successfully the religious and spiritual values of our heritage with the benefits of modern technology." Or: "We Burmans have a sacred duty to conform both our dreams and our acts to our faith. This we shall ever do."[1]

All the same, such countries invariably assume that they can model their economic development plans in accordance with modern economics, and they call upon modern economists from so-called advanced countries to advise them, to formulate the policies to be pursued, and to construct the grand design for development, the Five-Year Plan or whatever it may be called. No one seems to think that a Buddhist way of life would call for Buddhist economics, just as the modern materialist way of life has brought forth modern economics.

Economists themselves, like most specialists, normally suffer from a kind of metaphysical blindness, assuming that theirs is a science of absolute and invariable truths, without any presuppositions. Some go as far as to claim that economic laws are as free from "metaphysics" or "values" as the law of gravitation. We need not, however, get involved in arguments of methodology. Instead, let us take some fundamentals and see what they look like when viewed by a modern economist and a Buddhist economist.

There is universal agreement that a fundamental source of wealth is human labor. Now, the modern economist has been brought up to consider "labor" or work as little more than a necessary evil. From the point of view of the employer, it is in any case simply an item of cost, to be reduced to a minimum if it cannot be eliminated altogether, say, by automation. From the point of view of the workman, it is a "disutility"; to work is to make a sacrifice of one's leisure and comfort, and wages are a kind of compensation for the sacrifice. Hence the ideal from the point of view of the employer is to have output without employees, and the ideal from the point of view of the employee is to have income without employment.

The consequences of these attitudes both in theory and in practice are, of course, extremely far-reaching. If the ideal with regard to work is to get rid of it, every method that "reduces the work load" is a good thing. The most potent method, short of automation, is the so-called "division of labor" and the classical example is the pin factory eulogized in Adam Smith's *Wealth of Nations*. Here it is not a matter of ordinary specialization, which mankind has practiced from time immemorial, but of dividing up every complete process of production into minute parts, so that the final product can be produced at great speed without anyone having had to contribute more than a totally insignificant and, in most cases, unskilled movement of his limbs.

The Buddhist point of view takes the function of work to be at least threefold: to give a man a chance to utilize and develop his faculties; to enable him to overcome his ego-centeredness by joining with other people in a common task; and to bring forth the goods and services needed for a becoming existence. Again, the consequences that flow from this view are endless. To organize work in such a manner that it becomes meaningless, boring, stultifying, or nerve-racking for the worker would be little short of criminal; it would indicate a greater concern with goods than with people, an evil lack of compassion and a soul-destroying degree of attachment to the most primitive side of this worldly existence. Equally, to strive for leisure as an alternative to work would be considered a complete misunderstanding of one of the basic truths of human existence, namely that work and leisure are complementary parts of the same living process and cannot be separated without destroying the joy of work and the bliss of leisure.

From the Buddhist point of view, there are therefore two types of mechanization which must be clearly distinguished: one that enhances a man's skill and power and one that turns the work of man over to a mechanical slave, leaving man in a position of having to serve the slave. How to tell the one from the other? "The craftsman himself," says Ananda Coomaraswamy, a man equally competent to talk about the modern West as the ancient East, "can always, if allowed to, draw the delicate distinction between the machine and the tool. The carpet loom is a tool, a contrivance for holding warp threads at a stretch for the pile to be woven round them by the craftsmen's fingers; but the power loom is a machine, and its significance as a destroyer of culture lies in the fact that it does the essentially human part of the work."[2] It is clear, therefore, that Buddhist economics must be very different from the economics of modern materialism, since the Buddhist sees the essence of civilization not in a multiplication of wants but in the purification of human character. Character, at the same time, is formed primarily by a man's work. And work, properly conducted in conditions of human dignity and freedom, blesses those who do it and equally their products. The Indian philosopher and economist J. C. Kumarappa sums the matter up as follows:

> If the nature of the work is properly appreciated and applied, it will stand in the same relation to the higher faculties as food is to the physical body. It nourishes and enlivens the higher man and urges him to produce the best he is capable of. It directs his free will along the proper course and disciplines the animal in him into progressive channels. It furnishes an excellent background for man to display his scale of values and develop his personality.[3]

If a man has no chance of obtaining work, he is in a desperate position, not simply because he lacks an income but because he lacks this nourishing and enlivening factor of disciplined work which nothing can replace. A modern economist may engage in highly sophisticated calculations on whether full employment "pays" or whether it might be more "economic" to run an economy at less than full employment so as to ensure a greater mobility of labor, a better stability of wages, and so forth. His fundamental criterion of success is simply the total quantity of goods produced during a given period of time. "If the marginal urgency of goods is low," says Professor Galbraith in *The Affluent Society*, "then so is the urgency of employing the last man or the last million men in the labor force." And again: "If . . . we can afford some unemployment in the interest of stability—a proposition, incidentally, of impeccably conservative antecedents—then we can afford to give those who are unemployed the goods that enable them to sustain their accustomed standard of living."

From a Buddhist point of view, this is standing the truth on its head by considering goods as more important than people and consumption as more important than creative activity. It means shifting the emphasis from the worker to the product of work, that is, from the human to the subhuman, a surrender to the forces of evil. The very start of Buddhist economic planning would be a planning for full employment, and the primary purpose of this would in fact be employment for everyone who needs an "outside" job: it would not be the maximization of employment nor the maximization of production.

While the materialist is mainly interested in goods, the Buddhist is mainly interested in liberation. But Buddhism is "The Middle Way" and therefore in no way antagonistic to physical well-being. It is not wealth that stands in the way of liberation but the attachment to wealth; not the enjoyment of pleasurable things but the craving for them. The keynote of Buddhist economics, therefore, is simplicity and nonviolence. From an economist's point of view, the marvel of the Buddhist way of life is the utter rationality of its pattern—amazingly small means leading to extraordinarily satisfactory results.

For the modern economist this is very difficult to understand. He is used to measuring the "standard of living" by the amount of annual consumption, assuming all the time that a man who consumes more is "better off" than a man who consumes less. A Buddhist economist would consider this approach excessively irrational: since consumption is merely a means to human well-being, the aim should be to obtain the maximum of well-being with the minimum of consumption. Thus, if the purpose of clothing is a certain amount of temperature comfort and an attractive appearance, the task is to attain this purpose with the smallest possible effort, that is, with the smallest annual destruction of cloth and with the help of designs that involve the smallest possible input of toil. The less toil there is, the more time and strength is left for artistic creativity. It would be highly uneconomic, for instance, to go in for complicated tailoring, like the modern west, when a much more beautiful effect can be achieved by the skillful draping of uncut material. It would be the height of folly to make material so that it should wear out quickly and the height of barbarity to make anything ugly, shabby, or mean. What has just been said about clothing applies equally to all other human requirements. The ownership and the consumption of goods is a means to an end, and Buddhist economics is the systematic study of how to attain given ends with the minimum means.

Modern economics, on the other hand, considers consumption to be the sole end and purpose of all economic activity, taking the factors of production—land, labor, and capital—as the means. The former, in short, tries to maximize human satisfactions by the optimal pattern of consumption, while the latter tries to maximize consumption by the optimal pattern of productive effort. It is easy to see that the effort needed to sustain a way of life which seeks to attain the optimal pattern of consumption is likely to be much smaller than the effort needed to sustain a drive for maximum consumption. We need not be surprised, therefore, that the pressure and strain of living is very much less in, say, Burma than it is in the United States, in spite of the fact that the amount of labor-saving machinery used in the former country is only a minute fraction of the amount used in the latter.

Simplicity and nonviolence are obviously closely related. The optimal pattern of consumption, producing a high degree of human satisfaction by means of a relatively low rate of consumption, allows people to live without great pressure and strain and to fulfill the primary injunction of Buddhist teaching: "Cease to do evil; try to do good." As physical resources are everywhere limited, people satisfying their needs by means of a modest use of resources are obviously less likely to be at each other's throats than people depending upon a high rate of use. Equally, people who live in highly self-sufficient local communities are less likely to get involved in large-scale violence than people whose existence depends on worldwide systems of trade.

From the point of view of Buddhist economics, therefore, production from local resources for local needs is the most rational way of economic life, while dependence on imports from afar and the consequent need to produce for export to unknown and distant peoples is highly uneconomic and justifiable only in exceptional cases and on a small scale. Just as the modern economist would admit that a high rate of consumption of transport services between a man's home and his place of work signifies a misfortune and not a high standard of life, so the Buddhist economist would hold that to satisfy human wants from faraway sources rather than from sources nearby signifies failure rather than success. The former tends to take statistics showing an increase in the number of ton/miles per head of the population carried by a country's transport system as proof of economic progress, while to the latter—the Buddhist economist—the same statistics would indicate a highly undesirable deterioration in the *pattern* of consumption.

Another striking difference between modern economics and Buddhist economics arises over the use of natural resources. Bertrand de Jouvenel, the eminent French political philosopher, has characterized "western man" in words which may be taken as a fair description of the modern economist:

> He tends to count nothing as an
> expenditure, other than human effort; he does
> not seem to mind how much mineral matter he
> wastes and, far worse, how much living matter
> he destroys. He does not seem to realize at all
> that human life is a dependent part of an
> ecosystem of many different forms of life. As
> the world is ruled from towns where men are

cut off from any form of life other than human, the feeling of belonging to an ecosystem is not revived. This results in a harsh and improvident treatment of things upon which we ultimately depend, such as water and trees.[4]

The teaching of the Buddha, on the other hand, enjoins a reverent and nonviolent attitude not only to all sentient beings but also, with great emphasis, to trees. Every follower of the Buddha ought to plant a tree every few years and look after it until it is safely established, and the Buddhist economist can demonstrate without difficulty that the universal observation of this rule would result in a high rate of genuine economic development independent of any foreign aid. Much of the economic decay of southeast Asia (as of many other parts of the world) is undoubtedly due to a heedless and shameful neglect of trees.

Modern economics does not distinguish between renewable and nonrenewable materials, as its very method is to equalize and quantify everything by means of a money price. Thus, taking various alternative fuels, like coal, oil, wood, or water-power: the only difference between them recognized by modern economics is relative cost per equivalent unit. The cheapest is automatically the one to be preferred, as to do otherwise would be irrational and "uneconomic." From a Buddhist point of view, of course, this will not do; the essential difference between nonrenewable fuels like coal and oil on the one hand and renewable fuels like wood and water-power on the other cannot be simply overlooked. Nonrenewable goods must be used only if they are indispensable, and then only with the greatest care and the most meticulous concern for conservation. To use them heedlessly or extravagantly is an act of violence, and while complete nonviolence may not be attainable on this earth, there is nonetheless an ineluctable duty on man to aim at the ideal of nonviolence in all he does.

Just as a modern European economist would not consider it a great economic achievement if all European art treasures were sold to America at attractive prices, so the Buddhist economist would insist that a population basing its economic life on nonrenewable fuels is living parasitically, on capital instead of income. Such a way of life could have no permanence and could therefore be justified

only as a purely temporary expedient. As the world's resources of nonrenewable fuels—coal, oil, and natural gas—are exceedingly unevenly distributed over the globe and undoubtedly limited in quantity, it is clear that their exploitation at an ever-increasing rate is an act of violence against nature which must almost inevitably lead to violence between men.

This fact alone might give food for thought even to those people in Buddhist countries who care nothing for the religious and spiritual values of their heritage and ardently desire to embrace the materialism of modern economics at the fastest possible speed. Before they dismiss Buddhist economics as nothing better than a nostalgic dream, they might wish to consider whether the path of economic development outlined by modern economics is likely to lead them to places where they really want to be. Towards the end of his courageous book *The Challenge of Man's Future*, Professor Harrison Brown of the California Institute of Technology gives the following appraisal:

> Thus we see that, just as industrial society is fundamentally unstable and subject to reversion to agrarian existence, so within it the conditions which offer individual freedom are unstable in their ability to avoid the conditions which impose rigid organization and totalitarian control. Indeed, when we examine all of the foreseeable difficulties which threaten the survival of industrial civilization, it is difficult to see how the achievement of stability and the maintenance of individual liberty can be made compatible.[5]

Even if this were dismissed as a long-term view there is the immediate question of whether "modernization," as currently practiced without regard to religious and spiritual values, is actually producing agreeable results. As far as the masses are concerned, the results appear to be disastrous—a collapse of the rural economy, a rising tide of unemployment in town and country, and the growth of a city proletariat without nourishment for either body or soul.

It is in the light of both immediate experience and long-term prospects that the study of Buddhist economics could be recommended even to those who believe that economic growth is more important than any spiritual or religious values. For it is not a question of choosing between "modern growth" and "traditional stagnation." It is a question of finding the right path of development, the Middle Way between materialist heedlessness and traditionalist immobility, in short, of finding "Right Livelihood."

Notes

1. Economic and Social Board, Government of the Union of Burma, *The New Burma* (1954).

2. Ananda K. Coomaraswamy, *Art and Swadeshi* (Madras, India: Ganesh & Co.).

3. J. C. Kumarappa, *Economy of Permanence*, 4th ed. (Sarva-Seva Sangh Publication, Rajghat, Kashi, 1958).

4. Richard B. Gregg, *A Philosophy of Indian Economic Development* (Ahmedabad, India: Navajivan Publishing House, 1958).

5. Harrison Brown, *The Challenge of Man's Future* (New York: Viking, 1954).

For Further Reading

Baier, K., & Rescher, N. (Eds.). *Values and the future.* New York: Free Press, 1969.

Bauer, R. A., & Fenn, D. H., Jr. *The corporate social audit.* New York: Russell Sage Foundation, 1972.

Center for Law and Social Policy. *A proposal in corporate responsibility.* Washington, D.C.: Author, 1969.

Farmer, R. N., & Hougue, W. D. *Corporate social responsibility.* Chicago: Science Research Associates, Inc., 1973.

Gaddis, P. O. *Corporate accountability.* New York: Harper & Row, 1964.

Heilbroner, R. L., et al. *In the name of profit.* Garden City, N.Y.: Doubleday, 1972.

Jacoby, N. H. *Corporate power and social responsibility.* New York: Macmillan, 1973.

Meadows, D., et al. *The limits to growth.* New York: Universe Books, 1970.

Monson, R. J., Jr. *Modern American capitalism: Ideologies and issues.* Boston: Houghton Mifflin, 1963.

Nowlan, S. E., & Shayon, D. R. *Profiles in involvement.* Philadelphia: Human Resources Corp., 1972.

Toffler, A. *Future shock.* New York: Random House, 1970.

Weber, M. *The protestant ethic and the spirit of capitalism.* New York: Charles Scribner's Sons, 1952.

INDEX